GUIN

SOCCER

WHO'S WHO

Jack Rollin

Cover design: Ad Vantage Studios

©Jack Rollin and Guinness Publishing Ltd, 1984, 1986, 1989, 1990, 1991, 1992, 1993, 1994

First Published in 1984
Second edition 1986
Third edition 1989
Fourth edition 1990
Fifth edition 1991
Sixth edition 1992
Seventh edition 1993

Published in Great Britain by Guinness Publishing Ltd,
33 London Road, Enfield, Middlesex

Database Typeset in Monotype Times Roman by BPC Whitefriars
Printed and bound in Great Britain by
BPC Paperbacks Ltd

'Guinness' is a registered trademark of Guinness Publishing Ltd

A catalogue record for this book is
available from the British Library

ISBN 0-85112-777-0

THE AUTHOR

Jack Rollin was born in London in 1932 and educated at King's, Harrow. There he played soccer, while later at Westcliff-on-Sea High School it was rugby. Within ten days of joining the Royal Air Force he was playing in a Welsh Cup tie for RAF Bridgnorth and in the services he learned shorthand and typing, resuming his career in journalism and covering the 1954 World Cup in Switzerland in a freelance capacity.

In 1958 an ankle injury ended his own career during which, at the age of 14, he had been offered a trial with the United States club Chicago Maroons. He wisely declined a one-off re-appearance in 1971 against the European cup finalists Panathinaikos of Greece.

For ten years Jack Rollin was Editor of the weekly magazine *Soccer Star* and its companion monthly *World Soccer* before becoming a freelance again in 1970. Since then he has researched football for BBC Television, acted as an assistant to commentators on 'Match of the Day', spoken on radio and appeared on television programmes. He has contributed to *What's on in London* and *Radio Times* and in 1975 he won the Designers and Art Directors Association Silver Award for *Radio Times World Cup Special* for the most outstanding specialist feature of the year.

In 1972 he became one of the compilers of the *Rothmans Football Yearbook* and later became its Editor. He has provided advice on the football sections of the *Encyclopaedia Britannica* and *Guinness Book of Records*. He is a football columnist for the *Sunday Telegraph*.

Jack Rollin contributed to three part-works: *The Game* (8 vols. 1970); *Book of Football* (6 vols. 1972) and *Football Handbook* (1979–80). His articles have appeared in programmes for matches at Wembley Stadium since 1963. He has produced handbooks which include *World Soccer Digest* 1961, 1962 and 1963 and *World Cup Digest* 1966.

In 1978 he carried out the international research for the BBC Television Series 'The Game of the Century' and produced the first edition of *The Guinness Book of Soccer Facts and Feats*.

Other books he has written: *England's World Cup Triumph* (1966), *A Source Book of Football* (1971), *The History of Aldershot Football Club* (1975), *World Cup Guide* (1982), *Soccer at War 1939–45* (1985), *Soccer: The Records* (1985), *Soccer: Records, Facts and Champions* (1988), *Soccer Shorts* (1988) and *More Soccer Shorts* (1991), *The Guinness Record of the World Cup 1930–1994* (1994), *The Football Fact Book* (1990 and 1993). In 1974 he contributed the South American section for John Moynihan's *Football Fever*.

The author is married to June and has a daughter Glenda.

FOREWORD

I am delighted to welcome the eighth edition of the *Guinness Soccer Who's Who* by Jack Rollin. It is certainly on a par with all the quality reference books in the Guinness library and will prove an invaluable help to all administrators, managers, soccer writers and supporters of football throughout the United Kingdom.

It is a difficult task to keep abreast of the changing face of personnel at clubs and Jack Rollin is to be congratulated on achieving this task successfully. There are precise details of professional players in England, Wales and Scotland which can be found by quick and easy alphabetical reference and it provides all the information necessary for a football fact-finder.

The book will occupy a prominent place on my desk and I do not hesitate to recommend it.

Gordon Taylor

Gordon Taylor,
Chief Executive, The Professional Footballers' Association

Front cover, from left:
Ryan Giggs (Manchester United), Andy Townsend (Aston Villa), David Robertson (Glasgow Rangers), Rob Jones (Liverpool), Kevin Donovan (West Bromwich Albion).
Photos: Allsport UK Ltd (Anton Want/David Cannon/Shaun Botterill); Action Images

INTRODUCTION

This book features the statistical League careers of all players who made FA Carling Premiership and Endsleigh Insurance League appearances during the 1993–94 season as well as those in the Scottish Premier Division and Falkirk the promoted team from the First Division.

Other players in England who did not appear last season are also included.

Club names in italics indicate temporary transfers where they have not become permanent moves in the same season. Italic figures refer to Colchester United, Lincoln City and Darlington in the GM Vauxhall Conference as well as Aldershot in 1991–92. All appearances include those as substitute.

The Editor would like to thank Alan Elliott for providing details of Scottish League players and also acknowledge the co-operation and assistance of the FA Premier League and Football League in the compilation of this book. In particular Mike Foster of the FA Premier League and Sheila Murphy and Debbie Birch of the Football League.

Bibliography: *Rothmans Football Yearbook*

Also published by Guinness:
The Guinness Book of League Football Grounds
European Soccer Who's Who
The Guinness Record of World Soccer
The Guinness Record of the FA Cup
The Guinness Record of the World Cup
The Football Fact Book
More Soccer Shorts
The Football Encyclopedia
Chelsea Player by Player
Tottenham Hotspur Player by Player
Arsenal Player by Player
Leeds United Player by Player
Everton Player by Player
Liverpool in Europe

ABBOTT, Greg
Born Coventry 14.12.63.   Ht 5 9
Wt 10 10
Midfield. From Apprentice.

1981–82	Coventry C	—	—
1982–83	Bradford C	11	—
1983–84		35	3
1984–85		42	6
1985–86		39	10
1986–87		33	7
1987–88		32	5
1988–89		28	4
1989–90		35	3
1990–91		26	—
1991–92	Halifax T	28	1
From Guiseley			
1992–93	Hull C	27	1
1993–94		40	6

ABEL, Graham
Born Runcorn 17.9.60.   Ht 6 2   Wt 13 00
Defender. From Northwich V and Runcorn.

1985–86	Chester C	23	2
1986–87		41	1
1987–88		45	2
1988–89		40	3
1989–90		41	7
1990–91		29	4
1991–92	Chester C	44	9
1992–93		33	1
1993–94	Crewe Alex	20	1

ABLETT, Gary
Born Liverpool 19.11.65.   Ht 6 0
Wt 11 04
Defender. From Apprentice. England B, Under-21.

1983–84	Liverpool	—	—
1984–85		—	—
1984–85	*Derby Co*	6	—
1985–86	Liverpool	—	—
1986–87	*Hull C*	5	—
1986–87	Liverpool	5	1
1987–88		17	—
1988–89		35	—
1989–90		15	—
1990–91		23	—

1991–92		14	—
1991–92	Everton	17	1
1992–93		40	—
1993–94		32	1

ABRAHAM, Gareth
Born Merthyr Tydfil 13.2.69.   Ht 6 4
Wt 12 11
Defender. From Trainee.

1987–88	Cardiff C	2	1
1988–89		31	2
1989–90		37	1
1990–91		2	—
1991–92		15	—
1992–93		—	—
1992–93	Hereford U	19	1
1993–94		30	1

ABRAHAMS, Paul
Born Colchester 31.10.73   Ht 5 8
Wt 10 06
Forward. From Trainee.

1991–92	Colchester U	7	—
1992–93		23	6
1993–94		4	—

ADAMCZUK, Dariusz
Born Stettin 21.10.69   Ht 5 10   Wt 12 0
Midfield. Eintracht Frankfurt.

1993–94	Dundee	11	1

ADAMS, Darren
Born Newham 12.1.74   Ht 5 7   Wt 10 07
Forward. From Danson Furnace.

1993–94	Cardiff C	14	1

ADAMS, Mick
Born Sheffield 8.11.61.   Ht 5 6   Wt 11 11
Defender. From Apprentice. England Youth.

1979–80	Gillingham	4	—
1980–81		13	—
1981–82		31	2
1982–83		44	3
1983–84	Coventry C	17	1
1984–85		31	3
1985–86		31	3
1986–87		11	2

Season	Club	App	Goals
1986–87	Leeds U	17	1
1987–88		40	—
1988–89		16	1
1988–89	Southampton	8	—
1989–90		15	—
1990–91		30	—
1991–92		34	3
1992–93		38	4
1993–94		19	—
1993–94	Stoke C	10	3

ADAMS, Neil

Born Stoke 23.11.65. Ht 5 8 Wt 10 08
Forward. From Local. England Under-21.

Season	Club	App	Goals
1985–86	Stoke C	32	4
1986–87	Everton	12	—
1987–88		8	—
1988–89		—	—
1988–89	*Oldham Ath*	9	—
1989–90	Oldham Ath	27	4
1990–91		31	6
1991–92		26	4
1992–93		32	9
1993–94		13	—
1993–94	Norwich C	14	—

ADAMS, Tony

Born London 10.10.66. Ht 6 3 Wt 13 11
Defender. From Apprentice. England
Youth, B, Under-21, 31 full caps.

Season	Club	App	Goals
1983–84	Arsenal	3	—
1984–85		16	—
1985–86		10	—
1986–87		42	6
1987–88		39	2
1988–89		36	4
1989–90		38	5
1990–91		30	1
1991–92		35	2
1992–93		35	—
1993–94		35	—

ADCOCK, Tony

Born Bethnal Green 27.2.63. Ht 5 10
Wt 11 09
Forward. From Apprentice.

Season	Club	App	Goals
1980–81	Colchester U	1	—
1981–82		40	5
1982–83		30	17

Season	Club	App	Goals
1983–84		43	26
1984–85		28	24
1985–86		33	15
1986–87		35	11
1987–88	Manchester C	15	5
1987–88	Northampton T	18	10
1988–89		46	17
1989–90		8	3
1989–90	Bradford C	28	5
1990–91		10	1
1990–91	Northampton T	21	3
1991–92		14	7
1991–92	Peterborough U	24	7
1992–93		45	16
1993–94		42	12

ADEBOLA, Dele

Born Liverpool 23.6.75 Ht 6 3 Wt 12 06
Forward. From Trainee.

Season	Club	App	Goals
1992–93	Crewe Alex	6	—
1993–94		—	—

ADEKOLA, David

Born Nigeria 18.5.68. Ht 5 11 Wt 12 02
Forward.

Season	Club	App	Goals
1992–93	Bury	16	8
1993–94		19	4
1993–94	*Exeter C*	3	1

AFFOR, Louis

Born London 29.8.72. Ht 5 4 Wt 11 07
Forward. From Southend U trainee.

Season	Club	App	Goals
1993–94	Barnet	3	—

AGANA, Tony

Born London 2.10.63. Ht 6 0 Wt 12 02
Forward. From Weymouth.

Season	Club	App	Goals
1987–88	Watford	15	1
1987–88	Sheffield U	12	2
1988–89		46	24
1989–90		31	10
1990–91		16	2
1991–92		13	4
1991–92	Notts C	13	1
1991–92	*Leeds U*	2	—
1992–93	Notts Co	29	2
1993–94		20	4

AGIADIS, Nicholas

Born Middlesbrough 18.11.75
Forward. From Trainee.

Season	Club	App	Goals
1993–94	Middlesbrough	—	—

AGNEW, Paul

Born Lisburn 15.8.65. Ht 5 9 Wt 10 07
Defender. From Cliftonville. Northern
Ireland Schools, Youth, Under-23.

Season	Club	App	Goals
1983–84	Grimsby T	1	—
1984–85		12	—
1985–86		16	—
1986–87		29	—
1987–88		38	1
1988–89		34	—
1989–90		24	2
1990–91		7	—
1991–92		24	—
1992–93		23	—
1993–94		23	—

AGNEW, Steve

Born Shipley 9.11.65. Ht 5 8 Wt 11 10
Midfield. From Apprentice.

Season	Club	App	Goals
1983–84	Barnsley	1	—
1984–85		10	1
1985–86		2	—
1986–87		33	—
1987–88		25	6
1988–89		39	6
1989–90		46	8
1990–91		38	8
1991–92	Blackburn R	2	—
1992–93		—	—
1992–93	*Portsmouth*	5	—
1992–93	Leicester C	9	1
1993–94		36	3

AINSCOUGH, Paul

Born Blackburn 22.8.75 Ht 5 11
Wt 10 08
Midfield. From Trainee.

Season	Club	App	Goals
1993–94	Blackburn R	—	—

AINSWORTH, Gareth

Born Blackburn 10.5.73. Ht 5 10
Wt 12 05
Midfield. From Blackburn R Trainee.

Season	Club	App	Goals
1991–92	Preston NE	5	—

Season	Club	App	Goals
1992–93	Cambridge U	4	1
1992–93	Preston NE	26	—
1993–94		38	11

AITKEN, Roy

Born Irvine 24.11.58. Ht 6 0 Wt 13 00
Midfield. From Celtic BC. Scotland
Schools, Under-21, 57 full caps.

Season	Club	App	Goals
1975–76	Celtic	12	—
1976–77		33	5
1977–78		33	2
1978–79		36	5
1979–80		35	3
1980–81		33	4
1981–82		33	3
1982–83		33	6
1983–84		31	5
1984–85		33	3
1985–86		36	—
1986–87		42	1
1987–88		43	1
1988–89		32	—
1989–90		18	2
1989–90	Newcastle U	22	1
1990–91		32	—
1991–92	St Mirren	34	1
1992–93	Aberdeen	26	2
1993–94		1	—

AIZLEWOOD, Mark

Born Newport 1.10.59. Ht 6 1 Wt 13 12
Defender. From Apprentice. Wales Under-
21, 38 full caps.

Season	Club	App	Goals
1975–76	Newport Co	6	—
1976–77		5	—
1977–78		27	1
1977–78	Luton T	—	—
1978–79		39	—
1979–80		10	—
1980–81		23	—
1981–82		26	3
1982–83		—	—
1982–83	Charlton Ath	22	1
1983–84		31	1
1984–85		38	3
1985–86		35	3
1986–87		26	1
1986–87	Leeds U	15	—
1987–88		17	—

3

Season	Club		Apps	Goals
1988–89	....		38	3
1989–90	Bradford C		39	1
1990–91	Bristol C		42	2
1991–92	....		34	1
1992–93	....		20	—
1993–94	....		5	—
1993–94	Cardiff C		22	2

AKINBIYI, Adeola
Born Hackney 10.10.74 Ht 6 1 Wt 12 08
Forward.

1992–93	Norwich C		—	—
1993–94	....		2	—
1993–94	*Hereford U*		4	2

ALDRIDGE, John
Born Liverpool 18.9.58. Ht 5 11
Wt 11 04
Forward. From South Liverpool. Eire 57
caps.

1978–79	Newport Co		—	—
1979–80	....		38	14
1980–81	....		27	7
1981–82	....		36	11
1982–83	....		41	17
1983–84	....		28	20
1983–84	Oxford U		8	4
1984–85	....		42	30
1985–86	....		39	23
1986–87	....		25	15
1986–87	Liverpool		10	2
1987–88	....		36	26
1988–89	....		35	21
1989–90	....		2	1
1989–90	Real Sociedad		28	16
1990–91	....		35	17
1991–92	Tranmere R		43	22
1992–93	....		30	21
1993–94	....		34	21

ALDRIDGE, Martin
Born Northampton 6.12.74.
Forward. From Trainee.

1991–92	Northampton T		5	—
1992–93	....		9	2
1993–94	....		29	8

ALEXANDER, Graham
Born Coventry 10.10.71. Ht 5 10
Wt 11 08
Defender. From Trainee.

1989–90	Scunthorpe U		—	—
1990–91	....		1	—
1991–92	....		36	5
1992–93	....		41	5
1993–94	....		41	4

ALEXANDER, Ian
Born Glasgow 26.1.63. Ht 5 8 Wt 10 07
Defender. From Leicester J.

1981–82	Rotherham U		8	—
1982–83	....		3	—
1983–84	Motherwell		16	1
1984–85	....		8	1
1984–85	Morton		7	1
From Pezoporikos				
1986–87	Bristol R		22	1
1987–88	....		45	1
1988–89	....		42	1
1989–90	....		43	1
1990–91	....		39	1
1991–92	....		41	1
1992–93	....		41	1
1993–94	....		18	—

ALEXANDER, Tim
Born Chertsey 29.3.74 Ht 6 0 Wt 12 00
Defender.

| 1992–93 | Barnet .... | | — | — |
| 1993–94 | .... | | 32 | — |

ALLAN, Derek
Born Irving 24.12.74 Ht 6 0 Wt 12 00
Defender. From Ayr United BC.

1992–93	Ayr U		5	—
1992–93	Southampton		1	—
1993–94	....		—	—

ALLEN, Bradley
Born Harold Wood 13.9.71. Ht 5 7
Wt 10 00
Forward. From Schoolboys. England
Youth, Under-21.

| 1988–89 | QPR .... | | 1 | — |
| 1989–90 | .... | | — | — |

Season	Club	Apps	Goals
1990–91		10	2
1991–92		11	5
1992–93		25	10
1993–94		21	7

ALLEN, Chris
Born Oxford 18.11.72.   Ht 5 11   Wt 12 02
Forward. From Trainee.

Season	Club	Apps	Goals
1990–91	Oxford U	—	—
1991–92		14	1
1992–93		31	3
1993–94		45	3

ALLEN, Clive
Born London 20.5.61.   Ht 5 10   Wt 12 03
Forward. From Apprentice. England
Schools, Youth, Under-21, 3 full caps.
Football League.

Season	Club	Apps	Goals
1978–79	QPR	10	4
1979–80		39	28
1980–81	Arsenal	—	—
1980–81	Crystal Palace	25	9
1981–82	QPR	37	13
1982–83		25	13
1983–84		25	14
1984–85	Tottenham H	13	7
1985–86		19	9
1986–87		39	33
1987–88		34	11
From Bordeaux			
1989–90	Manchester C	30	10
1990–91		20	4
1991–92		3	2
1991–92	Chelsea	16	7
1991–92	West Ham U	4	1
1992–93		27	14
1993–94		7	2
1993–94	Millwall	12	—

ALLEN, Leighton
Born Brighton 22.1.73   Ht 6 0   Wt 11 02
Forward.

Season	Club	Apps	Goals
1992–93	Wimbledon	—	—
1993–94		—	—

ALLEN, Malcolm
Born Dioniolen 21.3.67.   Ht 5 8   Wt 11 08
Forward. From Apprentice. Wales Youth,
B, 14 full caps.

Season	Club	Apps	Goals
1984–85	Watford	—	—
1985–86		13	2
1986–87		4	—
1987–88		22	3
1987–88	*Aston Villa*	4	—
1988–89	Norwich C	23	5
1989–90		12	3
1989–90	Millwall	8	2
1990–91		21	7
1991–92		11	5
1992–93		41	10
1993–94	Newcastle U	9	5

ALLEN, Martin
Born Reading 14.8.65.   Ht 5 10   Wt 11 00
Midfield. From school. England Youth,
Under-21 Football League.

Season	Club	Apps	Goals
1983–84	QPR	—	—
1984–85		5	—
1985–86		31	3
1986–87		32	5
1987–88		38	4
1988–89		28	4
1989–90		2	—
1989–90	West Ham U	39	9
1990–91		40	3
1991–92		19	—
1992–93		34	4
1993–94		26	6

ALLEN, Paul
Born Aveley 28.8.62.   Ht 5 7   Wt 10 10
Midfield. From Apprentice. England
Youth, Under-21.

Season	Club	Apps	Goals
1979–80	West Ham U	31	2
1980–81		3	1
1981–82		28	—
1982–83		33	—
1983–84		19	—
1984–85		38	3
1985–86	Tottenham H	33	1
1986–87		37	3
1987–88		39	3
1988–89		37	1
1989–90		32	6

Season	Club	App	Goals
1990–91		36	3
1991–92		39	3
1992–93		38	3
1993–94		1	—
1993–94	Southampton	32	1

ALLISON, Neil
Born Hull 20.10.73. Ht 6 2   Wt 11 10
Defender. From Trainee.

Season	Club	App	Goals
1990–91	Hull C	1	—
1991–92		7	—
1992–93		11	—
1993–94		28	1

ALLISON, Wayne
Born Huddersfield 16.10.68. Ht 6 1
Wt 12 06
Forward.

Season	Club	App	Goals
1986–87	Halifax T	8	4
1987–88		35	4
1988–89		41	15
1989–90	Watford	7	—
1990–91	Bristol C	37	6
1991–92		43	10
1992–93		39	4
1993–94		39	15

ALLON, Joe
Born Gateshead 12.11.66. Ht 5 11
Wt 12 02
Forward. From Trainee. England Youth.

Season	Club	App	Goals
1984–85	Newcastle U	1	—
1985–86		3	1
1986–87		5	1
1987–88	Swansea C	32	11
1988–89		2	—
1988–89	Hartlepool U	21	4
1989–90		45	18
1990–91		46	28
1991–92	Chelsea	11	2
1991–92	*Port Vale*	6	—
1992–93	Chelsea	3	—
1992–93	Brentford	24	6
1993–94		21	13
1993–94	*Southend U*	3	—
1993–94	Port Vale	4	2

ALLPRESS, Tim
Born Hitchin 27.1.71. Ht 6 0   Wt 12 00
Defender. From Trainee.

Season	Club	App	Goals
1989–90	Luton T	1	—
1990–91		—	—
1991–92		—	—
1991–92	*Preston NE*	9	—
1992–93	Luton T	—	—
From Bayer Uerdingen			
1993–94	Colchester U	23	—

ALSFORD, Julian
Born Poole 24.12.72. Ht 6 2   Wt 13 06
Defender.

Season	Club	App	Goals
1991–92	Watford	—	—
1992–93		5	—
1993–94		8	1

AMPADU, Kwame
Born Bradford 20.12.70. Ht 5 10
Wt 11 10
Forward. From Trainee. Eire Youth,
Under-21.

Season	Club	App	Goals
1988–89	Arsenal	—	—
1989–90		2	—
1990–91		—	—
1990–91	*Plymouth Arg*	6	1
1990–91	*WBA*	7	1
1991–92	WBA	21	3
1992–93		10	—
1993–94		11	—
1993–94	Swansea C	13	—

ANDERS, Jason
Born Rochdale 13.3.74. Ht 5 10
Wt 10 06
Forward. From Trainee.

Season	Club	App	Goals
1990–91	Rochdale	2	—
1991–92		—	—
1992–93		15	1
1993–94		—	—

ANDERSON, Colin
Born Newcastle 26.4.62. Ht 5 10
Wt 10 08
Midfield. From Apprentice.

Season	Club	App	Goals
1979–80	Burnley	—	—
1980–81		2	—

6

Season	Club	App	Goals
1981–82		4	—
1982–83	Torquay U	42	5
1983–84		39	4
1984–85		28	2
1984–85	*QPR*	—	—
1984–85	WBA	—	—
1985–86		11	—
1986–87		28	1
1987–88		23	1
1988–89		42	6
1989–90		13	—
1990–91		23	2
1991–92	Walsall	26	2
1992–93	Hereford U	35	—
1993–94		35	1

ANDERSON, Iain
Born Glasgow 23.7.77
Forward. Duntocher BC.

Season	Club	App	Goals
1993–94	Dundee	1	1

ANDERSON, Lee
Born Bury 4.10.73. Ht 5 8 Wt 10 08
Defender. From Trainee.

Season	Club	App	Goals
1991–92	Bury	5	—
1992–93		13	—
1993–94		11	—

ANDERSON, Viv
Born Nottingham 29.8.56. Ht 6 1
Wt 12 02
Defender. From Apprentice. England
Under-21 B, 30 full caps, Football League.

Season	Club	App	Goals
1974–75	Nottingham F	16	—
1975–76		21	—
1976–77		38	1
1977–78		37	3
1978–79		40	1
1979–80		41	3
1980–81		31	—
1981–82		39	—
1982–83		25	1
1983–84		40	6
1984–85	Arsenal	41	3
1985–86		39	2
1986–87		40	4
1987–88	Manchester U	31	2
1988–89		6	—
1989–90		16	—

Season	Club	App	Goals
1990–91		1	—
1990–91	Sheffield W	22	2
1991–92		22	3
1992–93		26	3
1993–94	Barnsley	20	3

ANDERSSON, Patrik
Born Borgeby 18.8.71
Defender. From Malmo. Sweden full caps.

Season	Club	App	Goals
1992–93	Blackburn R	11	—
1993–94		1	—

To Moenchengladbach

ANDERTON, Darren
Born Southampton 3.3.72. Ht 6 1
Wt 12 00
Forward. From Trainee. England Youth,
Under-21, 3 full caps .

Season	Club	App	Goals
1989–90	Portsmouth	—	—
1990–91		20	—
1991–92		42	7
1992–93	Tottenham H	34	6
1993–94		37	6

ANDREWS, Ian
Born Nottingham 1.12.64. Ht 6 2
Wt 13 07
Goalkeeper. From Apprentice. England
Youth.

Season	Club	App	Goals
1982–83	Leicester C	—	—
1983–84		2	—
1983–84	*Swindon T*	1	—
1984–85	Leicester C	31	—
1985–86		39	—
1986–87		42	—
1987–88		12	—
1988–89	Celtic	5	—
1988–89	*Leeds U*	1	—
1989–90	Celtic	—	—
1989–90	Southampton	3	—
1990–91		1	—
1991–92		1	—
1992–93		—	—
1993–94		5	—

ANDREWS, Philip
Born Andover 14.9.76
Midfield. From Trainee.

Season	Club	App	Goals
1993–94	Brighton	5	—

7

ANGELL, Brett
Born Marlborough 20.8.68. Ht 6 1
Wt 12 00
Forward. From Portsmouth and
Cheltenham T.

Season	Club		
1987–88	Derby Co	—	—
1988–89	Stockport Co	26	5
1989–90		44	23
1990–91	Southend U	42	15
1991–92		43	21
1992–93		13	5
1993–94		5	4
1993–94	*Everton*	1	—
1993–94	Southend U	12	2
1993–94	Everton	15	1

ANGUS, Ian
Born Glasgow 19.11.61. Ht 5 10
Wt 10 03
Midfield. From Eastercraigs.

Season	Club		
1979–80	Aberdeen	—	—
1980–81		19	1
1981–82		1	1
1982–83		5	3
1983–84		12	—
1984–85		28	2
1985–86		17	2
1986–87		2	1
1986–87	Dundee	29	4
1987–88		40	6
1988–89		15	—
1989–90		4	—
1989–90	*Plymouth Arg*	—	—
1990–91	Motherwell	20	2
1991–92		25	3
1992–93		31	3
1993–94		11	—

ANGUS, Terry
Born Coventry 14.1.66. Ht 6 0   Wt 12 00
Defender. From VS Rugby.

Season	Club		
1990–91	Northampton T	42	2
1991–92		37	2
1992–93		37	2
1993–94	Fulham	36	2

ANNAN, Richard
Born Leeds 4.12.68 Ht 5 8   Wt 10 00
Defender. From Guiseley.

Season	Club		
1991–92	Crewe Alex	—	—
1992–93		9	—
1993–94		10	1

ANNON, Darren
Born London 17.2.72
Forward. From Carshalton Ath.

Season	Club		
1993–94	Brentford	9	1

ANSAH, Andy
Born Lewisham 19.3.69. Ht 5 9
Wt 10 02
Forward. From Crystal Palace.

Season	Club		
1988–89	Brentford	7	2
1989–90		1	—
1989–90	Southend U	7	1
1990–91		40	9
1991–92		40	9
1992–93		30	7
1993–94		27	7

ANTHONY, Graham
Born Jarrow 9.8.75 Ht 5 10   Wt 10 08
Midfield. From Trainee.

Season	Club		
1993–94	Sheffield U	—	—

ANTHROBUS, Steve
Born Lewisham 10.11.68. Ht 6 0
Wt 12 02
Forward.

Season	Club		
1986–87	Millwall		
1987–88		3	—
1988–89		3	—
1989–90		15	4
1989–90	*Southend U*	—	—
1989–90	Wimbledon	10	—
1990–91		3	—
1991–92		10	—
1992–93		5	—
1993–94		—	—
1993–94	*Peterborough U*	2	—

AOUF, Tamer
Born London 7.12.74 Ht 6 1
Goalkeeper. From Trainee.

Season	Club		
1993–94	Brentford	—	—

APPIAH, Sam
Born Ghana 14.4.75 Ht 5 10 Wt 11 08
Forward. From Trainee.
1993–94 Charlton Ath ....   — —

APPLEBY, Matthew
Born Middlesbrough 16.4.72. Ht 5 10
Wt 11 02
Defender. From Trainee.
1989–90	Newcastle U	—	—
1990–91		1	—
1991–92		18	—
1992–93		—	—
1993–94		1	—
1993–94	*Darlington*	10	1

APPLEBY, Richie
Born Middlesbrough 18.9.75
Midfield. From Trainee.
1993–94 Newcastle U ....   — —

ARCHDEACON, Owen
Born Greenock 4.3.66. Ht 5 7 Wt 10 08
Midfield. From Gourock United. Scotland
Youth, Under-21.
1982–83	Celtic	—	—
1983–84		1	—
1984–85		3	1
1985–86		23	3
1986–87		29	2
1987–88		10	1
1988–89		10	—
1989–90	Barnsley	21	3
1990–91		45	2
1991–92		40	6
1992–93		38	6
1993–94		42	2

ARCHER, Lee
Born Bristol 6.11.72. Ht 5 6 Wt 9 06
Midfield. From Trainee.
1991–92	Bristol R	5	—
1992–93		2	1
1993–94		37	5

ARDLEY, Neil
Born Epsom 1.9.72. Ht 5 8 Wt 11 10
Midfield. From Trainee. England
Under-21.
1990–91	Wimbledon	1	—
1991–92		8	—
1992–93		26	4
1993–94		16	1

ARKINS, Vinny
Born Dublin 18.9.70. Ht 6 1 Wt 11 07
Forward. From Home Farm. Eire Youth,
Under-21.
1987–88	Dundee Utd	—	—
1988–89		—	—
From Shamrock R			
1991–92	St Johnstone	21	5
1992–93		26	6
1993–94		1	—

ARMSTRONG, Alun
Born Gateshead 22.2.75
Forward. From school.
1993–94 Newcastle U ....   — —

ARMSTRONG, Chris
Born Newcastle 19.6.71. Ht 6 0
Wt 11 00
Forward.
1988–89	Wrexham	—	—
1989–90		22	3
1990–91		38	10
1991–92	Millwall	25	4
1992–93		3	1
1992–93	Crystal Palace	35	15
1993–94		43	22

ARMSTRONG, Gordon
Born Newcastle 15.7.67. Ht 6 0
Wt 11 10
Midfield. From Apprentice.
1984–85	Sunderland	4	—
1985–86		14	2
1986–87		41	5
1987–88		37	5
1988–89		45	8
1989–90		46	8
1990–91		35	6

Season	Club	App	Goals
1991–92		40	10
1992–93		45	3
1993–94		26	2

ARMSTRONG, Lachlan
Born Melbourne 22.4.73 Ht 5 9 Wt 10 8
Forward. From Hamilton Th.

Season	Club	App	Goals
1990–91	Dundee	—	—
1991–92		—	—
1992–93		1	—
1993–94		1	—

ARNOLD, Ian
Born Durham City 4.7.72. Ht 5 9
Wt 11 00
Forward. From Trainee.

Season	Club	App	Goals
1989–90	Middlesbrough	—	—
1990–91		2	—
1991–92		1	—
1992–93	Carlisle U	29	6
1993–94		14	5

ARNOTT, Andy
Born Chatham 18.10.73. Ht 6 1
Wt 12 00
Forward. From Trainee.

Season	Club	App	Goals
1990–91	Gillingham	—	—
1991–92		19	2
1992–93		15	6
1992–93	*Manchester U*	—	—
1993–94	Gillingham	10	2

ARNOTT, Doug
Born Lanark 5.8.64. Ht 5 7 Wt 10 07
Forward. From Pollok Juniors.

Season	Club	App	Goals
1986–87	Motherwell	1	—
1987–88		2	—
1988–89		14	1
1989–90		30	5
1990–91		29	14
1991–92		26	8
1992–93		33	6
1993–94		29	8

ARTHUR, Gordon
Born Kirkcaldy 30.5.58 Ht 5 11 Wt 12 0
Goalkeeper. From Dundonald Bluebell.

Season	Club	App	Goals
1977–78	Stirling Albion	1	—

Season	Club	App	Goals
1978–79		2	—
1979–80		39	—
1980–81		39	—
1981–82		34	—
1982–83		35	—
1983–84		34	—
1984–85	Dumbarton	35	—
1985–86		38	—
1986–87		31	—
1987–88		40	—
1988–89	Raith R	39	—
1989–90		39	—
1990–91		34	—
1991–92		44	—
1992–93		17	—
1993–94		1	—

ASHBY, Barry
Born London 21.11.70. Ht 6 2 Wt 12 03
Defender. From Trainee.

Season	Club	App	Goals
1988–89	Watford	—	—
1989–90		18	1
1990–91		23	—
1991–92		21	—
1992–93		35	—
1993–94		17	2
1993–94	Brentford	8	1

ASHCROFT, Lee
Born Preston 7.9.72. Ht 5 10 Wt 11 00
Forward. From Trainee. England
Under-21.

Season	Club	App	Goals
1990–91	Preston NE	14	1
1991–92		38	5
1992–93		39	7
1993–94	WBA	21	3

ASHDJIAN, John
Born Hackney 13.9.72. Ht 5 10
Wt 10 07
Forward. From Northampton T Trainee.

Season	Club	App	Goals
1991–92	Scarborough	32	9
1992–93		28	5
1993–94		7	—

ASHLEY, Kevin

Born Birmingham 31.12.68.   Ht 5 7
Wt 10 04
Defender. From Apprentice.

Season	Club	App	Goals
1986–87	Birmingham C	7	—
1987–88		1	—
1988–89		15	—
1989–90		31	1
1990–91		3	—
1990–91	Wolverhampton W	16	—
1991–92		44	1
1992–93		28	—
1993–94		—	—

ASPIN, Neil

Born Gateshead 12.4.65.   Ht 6 0
Wt 12 06
Defender. From Apprentice.

Season	Club	App	Goals
1981–82	Leeds U	1	—
1982–83		15	—
1983–84		21	1
1984–85		32	1
1985–86		38	2
1986–87		41	1
1987–88		26	—
1988–89		33	—
1989–90	Port Vale	42	—
1990–91		41	1
1991–92		42	—
1992–93		35	—
1993–94		40	1

ASPINALL, Warren

Born Wigan 13.9.67.   Ht 5 8   Wt 11 00
Forward. From Apprentice. England
Youth.

Season	Club	App	Goals
1984–85	Wigan Ath	10	1
1985–86		—	—
1985–86	Everton	1	—
1985–86	*Wigan Ath*	41	21
1986–87	Everton	6	—
1986–87	Aston Villa	12	3
1987–88		32	11
1988–89	Portsmouth	40	11
1989–90		3	—
1990–91		33	4
1991–92		24	4
1992–93		27	2
1993–94		5	—

Season	Club	App	Goals
1993–94	*Swansea C*	5	—
1993–94	Bournemouth	24	5

ATHERTON, Peter

Born Orrell 6.4.70.   Ht 5 11   Wt 12 03
Defender. From Trainee. England
Under-21.

Season	Club	App	Goals
1987–88	Wigan Ath	16	—
1988–89		40	1
1989–90		46	—
1990–91		46	—
1991–92		1	—
1991–92	Coventry C	35	—
1992–93		39	—
1993–94		40	—

ATKIN, Paul

Born Nottingham 3.9.69.   Ht 6 0
Wt 12 11
Defender. From Trainee. England Youth.

Season	Club	App	Goals
1987–88	Notts Co	—	—
1988–89		—	—
1988–89	Bury	1	—
1989–90		9	1
1990–91		11	—
1991–92	York C	33	1
1992–93		31	2
1993–94		14	—

ATKINS, Ian

Born Birmingham 16.1.57.   Ht 6 0
Wt 12 03
Midfield. From Apprentice.

Season	Club	App	Goals
1974–75	Shrewsbury T	—	—
1975–76		32	4
1976–77		43	7
1977–78		41	10
1978–79		44	11
1979–80		39	3
1980–81		39	6
1981–82		40	17
1982–83	Sunderland	37	4
1983–84		40	2
1984–85		—	—
1984–85	Everton	6	1
1985–86		1	—
1985–86	Ipswich T	21	2
1986–87		40	1
1987–88		16	1

Season	Club	App	Goals
1987–88	Birmingham C	8	1
1988–89		40	3
1989–90		45	2
1990–91	Colchester U	*41*	*7*
1991–92	Birmingham C	8	—
1992–93		—	—
1992–93	Cambridge U	2	—
1993–94	Sunderland	—	—
1993–94	Doncaster R	7	—

ATKINS, Mark

Born Doncaster 14.8.68. Ht 6 1
Wt 12 00
Defender.

Season	Club	App	Goals
1986–87	Scunthorpe U	26	—
1987–88		22	2
1988–89	Blackburn R	46	6
1989–90		41	7
1990–91		42	4
1991–92		44	6
1992–93		31	5
1993–94		15	1

ATKINSON, Brian

Born Darlington 19.1.71. Ht 5 10
Wt 12 00
Midfield. From Trainee. England
Under-21.

Season	Club	App	Goals
1988–89	Sunderland	3	—
1989–90		13	—
1990–91		6	—
1991–92		30	2
1992–93		36	2
1993–94		29	—

ATKINSON, Dalian

Born Shrewsbury 21.3.68. Ht 6 0
Wt 13 10
Forward. England B.

Season	Club	App	Goals
1985–86	Ipswich T	1	—
1986–87		8	—
1987–88		17	8
1988–89		34	10
1989–90	Sheffield W	38	10
1990–91	Real Sociedad	26	12
1991–92	Aston Villa	14	1
1992–93		28	11
1993–94		29	8

ATKINSON, Graeme

Born Hull 11.11.71. Ht 5 8 Wt 10 08
Forward. From Trainee.

Season	Club	App	Goals
1989–90	Hull C	13	1
1990–91		16	—
1991–92		25	8
1992–93		46	6
1993–94		40	7

AUNGER, Geoff

Born Red Deer 4.2.68. Ht 5 8 Wt 11 10
Forward. From Ipswich T, Vancouver
86ers. Canada full caps.

Season	Club	App	Goals
1993–94	Luton T	5	1

AUSTIN, Dean

Born Hemel Hempstead 26.4.70. Ht 6 0
Wt 12 04
Defender. From St. Albans C.

Season	Club	App	Goals
1989–90	Southend U	7	—
1990–91		44	—
1991–92		45	2
1992–93	Tottenham H	34	—
1993–94		23	—

AUSTIN, Kevin

Born London 12.2.73 Ht 5 9 Wt 10 12
Defender. From Saffron Walden.

Season	Club	App	Goals
1993–94	Leyton Orient	30	—

AWFORD, Andy

Born Worcester 14.7.72. Ht 5 9
Wt 11 09
Defender. From Worcester C, Portsmouth
Trainee. England Youth, Under-21.
Football League.

Season	Club	App	Goals
1988–89	Portsmouth	4	—
1989–90		—	—
1990–91		14	—
1991–92		45	—
1992–93		44	—
1993–94		35	—

BAAH, Peter
Born Littleborough 1.5.73. Ht 5 9
Wt 10 04
Forward. From Trainee.

Season	Club	Apps	Goals
1991–92	Blackburn R	1	—
1992–93	Fulham	16	—
1993–94		33	4

BABB, Phil
Born Lambeth 30.11.70. Ht 6 0
Wt 12 03
Defender. Eire 5 full caps.

Season	Club	Apps	Goals
1988–89	Millwall	—	—
1989–90		—	—
1990–91	Bradford C	34	10
1991–92		46	4
1992–93	Coventry C	34	—
1993–94		40	3

BADDELEY, Lee
Born Cardiff 12.7.74. Ht 6 1 Wt 12 06
Defender. From Trainee.

Season	Club	Apps	Goals
1990–91	Cardiff C	2	—
1991–92		18	—
1992–93		8	—
1993–94		30	—

BAGNALL, John
Born Southport 23.11.73 Ht 6 0
Wt 12 00
Goalkeeper. From Preston NE.

Season	Club	Apps	Goals
1993–94	Chester C	—	—

BAILEY, Danny
Born Leyton 21.5.64. Ht 5 9 Wt 12 07
Midfield. From Apprentice.

Season	Club	Apps	Goals
1980–81	Bournemouth	2	—
From Local			
1983–84	Torquay U	1	—
From Wealdstone			
1989–90	Exeter C	46	1
1990–91		18	1
1990–91	Reading	26	2
1991–92		24	—
1992–93		—	—
1992–93	*Fulham*	3	—
1992–93	Exeter C	27	—
1993–94		34	—

BAILEY, Dennis
Born Lambeth 13.11.65. Ht 5 10
Wt 11 06
Forward. From Fulham, Farnborough T.

Season	Club	Apps	Goals
1987–88	Crystal Palace	5	1
1988–89		—	—
1988–89	*Bristol R*	17	9
1989–90	Birmingham C	43	18
1990–91		32	5
1990–91	*Bristol R*	6	1
1991–92	QPR	24	9
1992–93		15	1
1993–94		—	—
1993–94	*Charlton Ath*	4	—
1993–94	*Watford*	8	4

BAILEY, Neil
Born Wigan 26.9.58
Defender. From Apprentice.

Season	Club	Apps	Goals
1976–77	Burnley	—	—
1977–78		—	—
1978–79	Newport Co	21	1
1979–80		29	1
1980–81		21	1
1981–82		18	—
1982–83		40	4
1983–84		5	—
1983–84	Wigan Ath	23	1
1984–85		12	—
1985–86		6	1
1986–87	Stockport Co	17	—
1986–87	*Newport Co*	9	1
1987–88	Stockport Co	34	—
1988–89		—	—
Retired			
1992–93	Blackpool	8	—
1993–94		1	—

BAIN, Kevin
Born Kirkcaldy 19.9.72 Ht 6 0 Wt 11 9
Defender. From Abbey Star. Scotland U-16, U-21.

Season	Club	Apps	Goals
1989–90	Dundee	1	—
1990–91		—	—
1991–92		—	—
1992–93		24	—
1993–94		7	—

BAIRD, Ian
Born Rotherham 1.4.64.   Ht 6 2
Wt 12 12
Forward. From Apprentice. England Schools.

Season	Club	App	Goals
1981–82	Southampton	—	—
1982–83		11	2
1983–84		6	1
1983–84	*Cardiff C*	12	6
1984–85	Southampton	5	2
1984–85	*Newcastle U*	5	1
1984–85	Leeds U	10	6
1985–86		35	12
1986–87		40	15
1987–88	Portsmouth	20	1
1987–88	Leeds U	10	3
1988–89		43	10
1989–90		24	4
1989–90	Middlesbrough	19	5
1990–91		44	14
1991–92	Hearts	30	6
1992–93		34	9
1993–94	Bristol C	19	5

BAKER, Clive
Born North Walsham 14.3.59   Ht 5 9
Wt 11 00
Goalkeeper. From Amateur.

Season	Club	App	Goals
1977–78	Norwich C	2	—
1978–79		2	—
1979–80		—	—
1980–81		—	—
1981–82		—	—
1982–83		—	—
1983–84		—	—
1984–85	Barnsley	37	—
1985–86		42	—
1986–87		39	—
1987–88		44	—
1988–89		46	—
1989–90		37	—
1990–91		46	—
1991–92	Coventry C	—	—
1992–93	Ipswich T	31	—
1993–94		15	—

BAKER, Paul
Born Newcastle 5.1.63.   Ht 6 1   Wt 13 06

Season	Club	App	Goals
1984–85	Southampton	—	—

Season	Club	App	Goals
1985–86	Carlisle U	35	2
1986–87		36	9
1987–88	Hartlepool U	39	19
1988–89		40	7
1989–90		43	16
1990–91		46	12
1991–92		29	13
1992–93	Motherwell	9	1
1992–93	Gillingham	21	6
1993–94		33	8

BALDRY, Simon
Born Huddersfield 12.2.76   Ht 5 10
Forward. From Trainee.

Season	Club	App	Goals
1993–94	Huddersfield T	10	2

BALL, Kevin
Born Hastings 12.11.64.   Ht 5 9   Wt 12 00
Defender. From Apprentice.

Season	Club	App	Goals
1983–84	Portsmouth	1	—
1984–85		—	—
1985–86		9	—
1986–87		16	—
1987–88		29	1
1988–89		14	1
1989–90		36	2
1990–91	Sunderland	33	3
1991–92		33	1
1992–93		43	3
1993–94		36	—

BALL, Steve
Born Colchester 2.9.69.   Ht 6 0   Wt 12 01
Midfield. From Trainee.

Season	Club	App	Goals
1987–88	Arsenal	—	—
1988–89		—	—
1989–90	Colchester U	4	—
1990–91	Norwich C	—	—
1991–92		2	—
1992–93	Colchester U	24	4
1993–94		32	2

BALL, Steve
Born Leeds 22.11.73   Ht 5 6   Wt 10 10
Defender. From Leeds U trainee.

Season	Club	App	Goals
1992–93	Darlington	22	2
1993–94		20	1

BALMER, Stuart

Born Falkirk 20.6.69. Ht 6 1 Wt 13 00
Defender. From Celtic BC.

Season	Club	Apps	Goals
1987–88	Celtic	—	—
1988–89		—	—
1989–90		—	—
1990–91	Charlton Ath	24	—
1991–92		18	—
1992–93		45	2
1993–94		31	1

BAMBER, Dave

Born St. Helens 1.2.59. Ht 6 3 Wt 13 10
Forward. From Manchester Univ.

Season	Club	Apps	Goals
1979–80	Blackpool	7	1
1980–81		15	3
1981–82		38	15
1982–83		26	10
1983–84	Coventry C	19	3
1983–84	Walsall	10	3
1984–85		10	4
1984–85	Portsmouth	4	1
1985–86		—	—
1985–86	Swindon T	23	9
1986–87		42	9
1987–88		41	13
1988–89	Watford	18	3
1988–89	Stoke C	23	6
1989–90		20	2
1989–90	Hull C	19	3
1990–91		9	2
1990–91	Blackpool	23	17
1991–92		42	26
1992–93		24	13
1993–94		22	4

BAMBER, Lee

Born Burnley 31.10.68
Goalkeeper. From Gt Harwood, Bamber
Bridge, Chorley.

Season	Club	Apps	Goals
1993–94	Preston NE	1	—

BANGER, Nicky

Born Southampton 25.2.71. Ht 5 9
Wt 11 07
Forward. From Trainee.

Season	Club	Apps	Goals
1988–89	Southampton	—	—
1989–90		—	—

Season	Club	Apps	Goals
1990–91		6	—
1991–92		4	—
1992–93		27	6
1993–94		14	—

BANKS, Ian

Born Mexborough 9.1.61. Ht 5 10
Wt 13 05
Midfield. From Apprentice.

Season	Club	Apps	Goals
1978–79	Barnsley	2	—
1979–80		38	3
1980–81		45	14
1981–82		42	15
1982–83		37	5
1983–84	Leicester C	26	3
1984–85		33	9
1985–86		31	2
1986–87		3	—
1986–87	Huddersfield T	37	8
1987–88		41	9
1988–89	Bradford C	30	3
1988–89	WBA	4	—
1989–90	Barnsley	37	3
1990–91		33	2
1991–92		26	2
1992–93	Rotherham U	45	5
1993–94		31	3

BANKS, Steven

Born Hillingdon 9.2.72. Ht 6 0 Wt 13 02
Goalkeeper. From Trainee.

Season	Club	Apps	Goals
1991–92	West Ham U	—	—
1993–94		—	—
1993–94	Gillingham	29	—

BANNISTER, Gary

Born Warrington 22.7.60. Ht 5 8
Wt 11 10
Forward. From Apprentice. England
Under-21.

Season	Club	Apps	Goals
1978–79	Coventry C	4	1
1979–80		7	—
1980–81		11	2
1981–82	Sheffield W	42	21
1982–83		39	20
1983–84		37	14
1984–85	QPR	42	17
1985–86		36	16
1986–87		34	15

Season	Club	Apps	Goals
1987–88	....	24	8
1987–88	Coventry C	8	1
1988–89	....	24	8
1989–90	....	11	2
1989–90	WBA	13	2
1990–91	....	44	13
1991–92	....	15	3
1991–92	*Oxford U*	10	2
1992–93	Nottingham F	31	8
1993–94	Stoke C	15	2

BANNON, Eamonn

Born Edinburgh 18.4.58.   Ht 5 9
Wt 11 11
Midfield. From Links BC. Scotland
Schools, Under-21, 9 full caps.

Season	Club	Apps	Goals
1976–77	Hearts	13	1
1977–78	....	39	12
1978–79	....	19	5
1978–79	Chelsea	19	1
1979–80	....	6	—
1979–80	Dundee U	24	4
1980–81	....	34	8
1981–82	....	36	12
1982–83	....	32	10
1983–84	....	33	7
1984–85	....	35	10
1985–86	....	31	11
1986–87	....	39	9
1987–88	....	26	1
1988–89	Hearts	30	2
1989–90	....	33	2
1990–91	....	19	2
1991–92	....	13	2
1992–93	....	19	1
1993–94	Hibernian	1	—

BARACLOUGH, Ian

Born Leicester 4.12.70.   Ht 6 1   Wt 12 00
Midfield. From Trainee.

Season	Club	Apps	Goals
1988–89	Leicester C	—	—
1989–90	....	—	—
1989–90	*Wigan Ath*	9	2
1990–91	Leicester C	—	—
1990–91	*Grimsby T*	4	—
1991–92	Grimsby T	—	—
1992–93	....	1	—
1992–93	Lincoln C	36	5
1993–94	....	37	5

BARADA, Taylor

Born Charlottesville 14.8.72
Goalkeeper.

Season	Club	Apps	Goals
1993–94	Notts Co	—	—
1993–94	*Colchester U*	1	—

BARBER, Fred

Born Ferryhill 26.8.63.   Ht 5 10   Wt 12 00
Goalkeeper. From Apprentice.

Season	Club	Apps	Goals
1981–82	Darlington	—	—
1982–83	....	12	—
1983–84	....	46	—
1984–85	....	45	—
1985–86	....	32	—
1985–86	Everton	—	—
1986–87	....	—	—
1986–87	Walsall	36	—
1987–88	....	46	—
1988–89	....	44	—
1989–90	....	25	—
1989–90	*Peterborough U*	6	—
1990–91	Walsall	2	—
1990–91	*Chester*	8	—
1990–91	*Blackpool*	2	—
1991–92	Peterborough U	39	—
1992–93	....	—	—
1992–93	*Colchester U*	10	—
1992–93	*Chesterfield*	—	—
1993–94	Peterborough U	24	—

BARBER, Phil

Born Tring 10.6.65.   Ht 5 11   Wt 12 06
Forward. From Aylesbury.

Season	Club	Apps	Goals
1983–84	Crystal Palace	9	2
1984–85	....	23	4
1985–86	....	39	9
1986–87	....	31	5
1987–88	....	37	7
1988–89	....	46	6
1989–90	....	30	1
1990–91	....	19	1
1991–92	Millwall	29	4
1992–93	....	46	8
1993–94	....	35	—

BARCLAY, Dominic

Born Bristol 5.9.76
Forward. From Trainee.

Season	Club	Apps	Goals
1993–94	Bristol C	2	—

BARDSLEY, David

Born Manchester 11.9.64. Ht 5 10
Wt 11 00
Defender. From Apprentice. England
Youth, 2 full caps.

1981–82	Blackpool	1	—
1982–83		28	—
1983–84		16	—
1983–84	Watford	25	—
1984–85		17	—
1985–86		13	2
1986–87		41	5
1987–88		4	—
1987–88	Oxford U	34	1
1988–89		37	6
1989–90		3	—
1989–90	QPR	31	1
1990–91		38	—
1991–92		41	—
1992–93		40	3
1993–94		32	—

BARKER, Richard

Born Sheffield 30.5.75 Ht 6 0 Wt 11 08
Forward. From Trainee.

| 1993–94 | Sheffield W | — | — |

BARKER, Simon

Born Farnworth 4.11.64. Ht 5 9
Wt 11 00
Midfield. From Apprentice. England
Under-21.

1982–83	Blackburn R	—	—
1983–84		28	3
1984–85		38	2
1985–86		41	10
1986–87		42	11
1987–88		33	9
1988–89	QPR	25	1
1989–90		28	3
1990–91		35	1
1991–92		34	6
1992–93		25	1
1993–94		37	5

BARKUS, Lea

Born Reading 7.12.74. Ht 5 7 Wt 10 02
Forward. From Trainee.

| 1991–92 | Reading | 6 | 1 |

| 1992–93 | | 9 | — |
| 1993–94 | | — | — |

BARLOW, Andy

Born Oldham 24.11.65. Ht 5 9 Wt 11 01
Defender.

1984–85	Oldham Ath	33	—
1985–86		26	—
1986–87		29	2
1987–88		26	—
1988–89		15	—
1989–90		44	1
1990–91		46	—
1991–92		28	2
1992–93		6	—
1993–94		6	—
1993–94	*Bradford C*	2	—

BARLOW, Martin

Born Barnstable 25.6.71. Ht 5 7
Wt 10 03
Midfield. From Trainee.

1988–89	Plymouth Arg	1	—
1989–90		1	—
1990–91		30	1
1991–92		28	3
1992–93		24	1
1993–94		26	2

BARLOW, Stuart

Born Liverpool 16.7.68. Ht 5 10
Wt 11 02
Forward.

1990–91	Everton	2	—
1991–92		7	—
1991–92	*Rotherham U*	—	—
1992–93	Everton	26	5
1993–94		22	3

BARMBY, Nick

Born Hull 11.2.74 Ht 5 6 Wt 11 04
Forward. From Trainee. England Youth,
Under-21.

1991–92	Tottenham H	—	—
1992–93		22	6
1993–94		27	5

BARNARD, Darren
Born Rinteln 30.11.71.   Ht 5 10   Wt 12 00
Defender. From Wokingham.

Season	Club	Apps	Goals
1990–91	Chelsea	—	—
1991–92		4	—
1992–93		13	1
1993–94		12	1

BARNES, Andy
Born Croydon 31.3.67.   Ht 5 11
Wt 12 06
Forward. From Sutton U.

Season	Club	Apps	Goals
1991–92	Crystal Palace	1	—
1992–93		—	—
1993–94		—	—
1993–94	Carlisle U	2	—

BARNES, Bobby
Born Kingston 17.12.62.   Ht 5 7
Wt 10 09
Forward. From Apprentice.

Season	Club	Apps	Goals
1980–81	West Ham	6	1
1981–82		3	—
1982–83		—	—
1983–84		13	2
1984–85		20	2
1985–86		1	—
1985–86	Scunthorpe U	6	—
1985–86	Aldershot	14	8
1986–87		25	11
1987–88		10	7
1987–88	Swindon T	28	10
1988–89		17	3
1988–89	Bournemouth	10	—
1989–90		4	—
1989–90	Northampton T	37	18
1990–91		43	13
1991–92		18	6
1991–92	Peterborough U	15	5
1992–93		26	3
1993–94		8	1
1993–94	Partick T	7	—

BARNES, David
Born London 16.11.61.   Ht 5 10
Wt 11 01
Defender. From Apprentice. England
Youth.

Season	Club	Apps	Goals
1979–80	Coventry C	3	—
1980–81		—	—
1981–82		6	—
1981–82	Ipswich T	—	—
1982–83		6	—
1983–84		11	—
1984–85		—	—
1984–85	Wolves	23	1
1985–86		38	1
1986–87		26	2
1987–88		1	—
1987–88	Aldershot	30	—
1988–89		39	1
1989–90	Sheffield U	24	—
1990–91		28	1
1991–92		15	—
1992–93		13	—
1993–94		2	—
1993–94	Watford	5	—

BARNES, John
Born Jamaica 7.11.63.   Ht 5 11   Wt 12 07
Forward. From Sudbury Court. England
Under-21, 73 full caps.

Season	Club	Apps	Goals
1981–82	Watford	36	13
1982–83		42	10
1983–84		39	11
1984–85		40	12
1985–86		39	9
1986–87		37	10
1987–88	Liverpool	38	15
1988–89		33	8
1989–90		34	22
1990–91		35	16
1991–92		12	1
1992–93		27	5
1993–94		26	3

BARNES, Paul
Born Leicester 16.11.67.   Ht 5 10
Wt 12 09
Forward. From Apprentice.

Season	Club	Apps	Goals
1985–86	Notts Co	14	4
1986–87		—	—
1987–88		11	2
1988–89		15	7
1989–90		13	1
1989–90	Stoke C	5	—
1990–91		6	—
1990–91	Chesterfield	1	—

18

Season	Club	Appearances	Goals
1991–92	Stoke C	13	3
1992–93	York C	40	21
1993–94		42	24

BARNESS, Anthony
Born London 25.3.72.   Ht 5 10   Wt 13 01
Defender. From Trainee.

Season	Club	Appearances	Goals
1990–91	Charlton Ath	—	—
1991–92		22	1
1992–93		5	—
1992–93	Chelsea	2	—
1993–94		—	—
1993–94	*Middlesbrough*	—	—

BARNETT, Ben
Born London 18.12.69
Forward. From Heybridge Swifts.

Season	Club	Appearances	Goals
1993–94	Barnet	2	—

BARNETT, Dave
Born London 16.4.67.   Ht 6 0   Wt 12 08
Defender. From Windsor & Eton.

Season	Club	Appearances	Goals
1988–89	Colchester U	20	—
1989–90	WBA	—	—
1990–91	Walsall	5	—
From Kidderminster H			
1991–92	Barnet	4	—
1992–93		36	2
1993–94		19	1
1993–94	Birmingham C	9	—

BARNETT, Gary
Born Stratford 11.3.63.   Ht 5 6   Wt 9 13
Forward. From Apprentice.

Season	Club	Appearances	Goals
1980–81	Coventry C	—	—
1990–91	Huddersfield T	22	1
1981–82		—	—
1982–83	Oxford U	22	2
1982–83	*Wimbledon*	5	1
1983–84	Oxford U	19	7
1984–85		2	—
1984–85	*Fulham*	2	1
1985–86	Oxford U	2	—
1985–86	Fulham	36	6
1986–87		42	9
1987–88		42	9
1988–89		28	5
1989–90		32	1

Season	Club	Appearances	Goals
1990–91	Huddersfield T	22	1
1991–92		31	3
1992–93		46	7
1993–94		1	—
1993–94	Leyton Orient	36	7

BARNHOUSE, David
Born Swansea 19.3.75.   Ht 5 8   Wt 11 09
Defender. From Trainee.

Season	Club	Appearances	Goals
1991–92	Swansea C	1	—
1992–93		—	—
1993–94		3	—

BARRAS, Tony
Born Teesside 29.3.71.   Ht 6 0   Wt 12 03
Forward. From Trainee.

Season	Club	Appearances	Goals
1988–89	Hartlepool U	3	—
1989–90		9	—
1990–91	Stockport Co	40	—
1991–92		42	5
1992–93		14	—
1993–94		3	—
1993–94	*Rotherham U*	5	1

BARRATT, Tony
Born Salford 18.10.65.   Ht 5 8   Wt 11 01
Defender. From Billingham T.

Season	Club	Appearances	Goals
1985–86	Grimsby T	22	—
From Billingham T			
1986–87	Hartlepool U	23	—
1987–88		43	3
1988–89		32	1
1988–89	York C	12	—
1989–90		46	4
1990–91		29	1
1991–92		21	3
1992–93		10	—
1993–94		19	2

BARRETT, Earl
Born Rochdale 28.4.67.   Ht 5 11
Wt 11 00
Defender. From Apprentice. England B,
Under-21, 3 full caps.

Season	Club	Appearances	Goals
1984–85	Manchester C	—	—
1985–86		1	—
1985–86	*Chester C*	12	—
1986–87	Manchester C	2	—

Season	Club	App	Goals
1987–88	....	—	—
1987–88	Oldham Ath................	18	—
1988–89	....	44	—
1989–90	....	46	2
1990–91	....	46	3
1991–92	....	29	2
1991–92	Aston Villa.................	13	—
1992–93	....	42	1
1993–94	....	39	—

BARRETT, Scott
Born Derby 2.4.63   Ht 5 11   Wt 13 08
Goalkeeper. From Ilkeston T.

Season	Club	App	Goals
1984–85	Wolverhampton W.....	4	—
1985–86	....	21	—
1986–87	....	5	—
1987–88	Stoke C.....................	27	—
1988–89	....	17	—
1989–90	....	7	—
1989–90	*Colchester U*..............	13	—
1989–90	*Stockport Co*.............	10	—
1990–91	Colchester U..............	*42*	—
1991–92	....	*42*	*1*
1992–93	Gillingham.................	34	—
1993–94	....	13	—

BARRICK, Dean
Born Hemsworth 30.9.69.   Ht 5 9
Wt 12 00
Midfield. From Trainee.

Season	Club	App	Goals
1987–88	Sheffield W................	—	—
1988–89	....	8	2
1989–90	....	3	—
1990–91	....	—	—
1990–91	Rotherham U	19	2
1991–92	....	34	1
1992–93	....	46	4
1993–94	Cambridge U..............	44	1

BARRON, Michael
Born Chester le Street 22.12.74   Ht 5 10
Wt 11 03
Defender. From trainee.

Season	Club	App	Goals
1992–93	Middlesbrough............	—	—
1993–94	....	2	—

BARROW, Graham
Born Chorley 13.6.54.   Ht 6 2   Wt 13 07
Midfield. From Altrincham.

Season	Club	App	Goals
1981–82	Wigan Ath	41	12
1982–83	....	28	3
1983–84	....	42	5
1984–85	....	38	9
1985–86	....	30	7
1986–87	Chester C...................	41	5
1987–88	....	38	4
1988–89	....	35	3
1989–90	....	28	1
1990–91	....	20	—
1991–92	....	40	2
1992–93	....	33	2
1993–94	....	13	—

BARROW, Lee
Born Belper 1.5.73   Ht 5 11   Wt 13 00
Defender. From Trainee.

Season	Club	App	Goals
1991–92	Notts Co....................	—	—
1992–93	Scarborough...............	11	—
1992–93	Torquay U	15	2
1993–94	....	20	—

BARTLETT, Neal
Born Southampton 7.4.75   Ht 5 10
Wt 11 12
Midfield. From Trainee.

Season	Club	App	Goals
1992–93	Southampton	1	—
1993–94	....	7	—

BARTON, Warren
Born London 19.3.69.   Ht 5 10   Wt 11 00
Defender. From Leytonstone/Ilford.
England B.

Season	Club	App	Goals
1989–90	Maidstone U...............	42	—
1990–91	Wimbledon	37	3
1991–92	....	42	1
1992–93	....	23	2
1993–94	....	39	2

BARTRAM, Vince
Born Birmingham 7.8.68.   Ht 6 2
Wt 13 04
Goalkeeper. From Local.

Season	Club	App	Goals
1985–86	Wolverhampton W.....	—	—
1986–87	....	1	—

Season	Club	App	Goals
1987–88		—	—
1988–89		—	—
1989–90		—	—
1989–90	*Blackpool*	9	—
1990–91	Wolverhampton W	4	—
1990–91	*WBA*	—	—
1991–92	Bournemouth	46	—
1992–93		45	—
1993–94		41	—

BART-WILLIAMS, Chris

Born Freetown 16.6.74. Ht 5 11
Wt 11 00
Midfield. From Trainee. England Youth,
Under-21.

Season	Club	App	Goals
1990–91	Leyton Orient	21	2
1991–92		15	—
1991–92	Sheffield W	15	—
1992–93		34	6
1993–94		37	8

BASHAM, Mike

Born Barking 27.9.73 Ht 6 2 Wt 12 08
Midfield. From Trainee.

Season	Club	App	Goals
1992–93	West Ham U	—	—
1993–94		—	—
1993–94	*Colchester U*	1	—
1993–94	Swansea C	5	—

BASS, David

Born Frimley 29.11.74. Ht 5 11
Wt 12 07
Forward. From Trainee.

Season	Club	App	Goals
1991–92	Reading	3	—
1992–93		5	—
1993–94		1	—

BATES, Jamie

Born London 24.2.68. Ht 6 1 Wt 12 12
Defender. From Trainee.

Season	Club	App	Goals
1986–87	Brentford	24	1
1987–88		23	1
1988–89		36	1
1989–90		15	—
1990–91		32	2
1991–92		42	1
1992–93		24	—
1993–94		45	2

BATTERSBY, Tony

Born Doncaster 30.8.75 Ht 5 10
Wt 11 08
Forward. From Trainee.

Season	Club	App	Goals
1993–94	Sheffield U	—	—

BATTY, David

Born Leeds 2.12.68. Ht 5 7 Wt 10 07
Midfield. From Trainee. England B,
Under-21, 15 full caps.

Season	Club	App	Goals
1987–88	Leeds U	23	1
1988–89		30	—
1989–90		42	—
1990–91		37	—
1991–92		40	2
1992–93		30	1
1993–94		9	—
1993–94	Blackburn R	26	—

BAYES, Ashley

Born Lincoln 19.4.72. Ht 6 1 Wt 13 05
Goalkeeper. From Trainee.

Season	Club	App	Goals
1989–90	Brentford	1	—
1990–91		—	—
1991–92		1	—
1992–93		2	—
1993–94	Torquay U	32	—

BAZELEY, Darren

Born Northampton 5.10.72. Ht 5 10
Wt 11 02
Forward. From Trainee. England
Under-21.

Season	Club	App	Goals
1989–90	Watford	1	—
1990–91		7	—
1991–92		34	6
1992–93		22	1
1993–94		10	1

BEADLE, Peter

Born London 13.5.72. Ht 6 0 Wt 11 12
Forward. From Trainee.

Season	Club	App	Goals
1988–89	Gillingham	2	—
1989–90		10	2
1990–91		22	7
1991–92		33	5
1992–93	Tottenham H	—	—
1992–93	*Bournemouth*	9	2

Season	Club	Apps	Goals
1993–94	Tottenham H	—	—
1993–94	*Southend U*	8	1

BEAGRIE, Peter

Born Middlesbrough 28.11.65.   Ht 5 8
Wt 9 10
Midfield. From Local. England B,
Under-21.

Season	Club	Apps	Goals
1983–84	Middlesbrough	—	—
1984–85		7	1
1985–86		26	1
1986–87	Sheffield U	41	9
1987–88		43	2
1988–89	Stoke C	41	7
1989–90		13	—
1989–90	Everton	19	—
1990–91		17	2
1991–92		27	3
1991–92	*Sunderland*	5	1
1992–93	Everton	22	3
1993–94		29	3
1993–94	Manchester C	9	1

BEARD, Mark

Born Roehampton 8.10.74   Ht 5 10
Wt 10 12
Defender. From Trainee.

Season	Club	Apps	Goals
1992–93	Millwall	—	—
1993–94		14	1

BEARDSLEY, Peter

Born Newcastle 18.1.61.   Ht 5 8
Wt 11 07
Forward. From Wallsend BC. England B,
52 full caps. Football League.

Season	Club	Apps	Goals
1979–80	Carlisle U	37	8
1980–81		43	10
1981–82		22	4
From Vancouver Whitecaps			
1982–83	Manchester U	—	—
From Vancouver Whitecaps			
1983–84	Newcastle U	35	20
1984–85		38	17
1985–86		42	19
1986–87		32	5
1987–88	Liverpool	38	15
1988–89		37	10
1989–90		29	10
1990–91		27	11

Season	Club	Apps	Goals
1991–92	Everton	42	15
1992–93		39	10
1993–94	Newcastle U	35	21

BEARDSMORE, Russell

Born Wigan 28.9.68.   Ht 5 6   Wt 8 10
Midfield. From Apprentice. England
Under-21.

Season	Club	Apps	Goals
1986–87	Manchester U	—	—
1987–88		—	—
1988–89		23	2
1989–90		21	2
1990–91		12	—
1991–92		—	—
1991–92	*Blackburn R*	2	—
1992–93	Manchester U	—	—
1993–94	Bournemouth	24	—

BEASANT, Dave

Born Willesden 20.3.59.   Ht 6 4   Wt 14 01
Goalkeeper. From Edgware T. England B,
2 full caps.

Season	Club	Apps	Goals
1979–80	Wimbledon	2	—
1980–81		34	—
1981–82		46	—
1982–83		46	—
1983–84		46	—
1984–85		42	—
1985–86		42	—
1986–87		42	—
1987–88		40	—
1988–89	Newcastle U	20	—
1988–89	Chelsea	22	—
1989–90		38	—
1990–91		35	—
1991–92		21	—
1992–93		17	—
1992–93	*Grimsby T*	6	—
1992–93	*Wolverhampton W*	4	—
1993–94	Chelsea	—	—
1993–94	Southampton	25	—

BEASLEY, Andy

Born Sedgley 5.2.64.   Ht 6 2   Wt 13 06
Goalkeeper. From Apprentice.

Season	Club	Apps	Goals
1981–82	Luton T.	—	—
1982–83		—	—
1983–84		—	—
1983–84	*Mansfield T*	—	—

Season	Club	App	Goals
1983–84	*Gillingham*	—	—
1984–85	Mansfield T	3	—
1985–86		—	—
1986–87		—	—
1986–87	*Peterborough U*	7	—
1987–88	Mansfield T	8	—
1987–88	*Scarborough*	4	—
1988–89	Mansfield T	6	—
1989–90		26	—
1990–91		42	—
1991–92		9	—
1992–93		—	—
1992–93	*Bristol R*	1	—
1993–94	Doncaster R	37	—

BEAUCHAMP, Joe

Born Oxford 13.3.71. Ht 5 10 Wt 11 10
Forward. From Trainee.

Season	Club	App	Goals
1988–89	Oxford U	1	—
1989–90		3	—
1990–91		4	—
1991–92		27	7
1991–92	*Swansea C*	5	2
1992–93	Oxford U	44	7
1993–94		45	6

BEAUMONT, Chris

Born Sheffield 5.12.65. Ht 5 11 Wt 11 07
Forward. From Denaby.

Season	Club	App	Goals
1988–89	Rochdale	34	7
1989–90	Stockport Co	22	5
1990–91		45	15
1991–92		34	2
1992–93		44	14
1993–94		32	1

BEAUMONT, David

Born Edinburgh 10.12.63. Ht 5 10
Wt 11 05
Midfield. 'S' Form. Scotland Youth,
Under-21.

Season	Club	App	Goals
1980–81	Dundee U	—	—
1981–82		—	—
1982–83		—	—
1983–84		2	—
1984–85		18	1
1985–86		13	—
1986–87		28	—
1987–88		10	1

Season	Club	App	Goals
1988–89		18	1
1988–89	Luton T	15	—
1989–90		19	—
1990–91		33	—
1991–92		9	—
1991–92	Hibernian	21	—
1992–93		16	—
1993–94		26	2

BECKETT, Nathan

Born Hertford 31.5.75 Ht 6 2 Wt 13 00
Defender. From Trainee.

Season	Club	App	Goals
1993–94	Leyton Orient	—	—

BECKFORD, Darren

Born Manchester 12.5.67. Ht 6 1
Wt 11 01
Forward. From Apprentice. England
Youth.

Season	Club	App	Goals
1984–85	Manchester C	4	—
1985–86		3	—
1985–86	*Bury*	12	5
1986–87	Manchester C	4	—
1986–87	*Port Vale*	11	4
1987–88	Port Vale	40	9
1988–89		42	20
1989–90		42	17
1990–91		43	22
1991–92	Norwich C	30	7
1992–93		8	1
1992–93	Oldham Ath	7	3
1993–94		22	6

BECKFORD, Jason

Born Manchester 14.2.70. Ht 5 9
Wt 12 04
Forward. From Trainee. England Youth.

Season	Club	App	Goals
1987–88	Manchester C	5	—
1988–89		8	1
1989–90		5	—
1990–91		2	—
1990–91	*Blackburn R*	4	—
1991–92	Manchester C	—	—
1991–92	*Port Vale*	5	1
1991–92	Birmingham C	4	1
1992–93		3	1
1993–94		—	—
1993–94	*Bury*	3	—

BECKHAM, David
Born Leytonstone 2.5.75   Ht 5 11
Wt 10 09
Midfield. From Trainee.

1992–93 Manchester U	—	—
1993–94	—	—

BEDROSSIAN, Ara
Born Cyprus 2.6.67   Ht 5 9   Wt 10 00
Midfield.

1992–93 Fulham	9	—
1993–94	30	1

BEECH, Chris
Born Blackpool 16.9.74
Forward. From Trainee.

1992–93 Blackpool	1	—
1993–94	35	2

BEECH, Chris
Born Congleton 5.11.75
Forward. From Trainee.

1992–93 Manchester C	—	—
1993–94	—	—

BEENEY, Mark
Born Pembury 30.12.67.   Ht 6 4
Wt 14 07
Goalkeeper.

1986–87 Gillingham	2	—
1987–88 Maidstone U	—	—
1988–89	—	—
1989–90	33	—
1989–90 *Aldershot*	7	—
1990–91 Maidstone U	17	—
1990–91 Brighton & HA	2	—
1991–92	25	—
1992–93	42	—
1992–93 Leeds U	1	—
1993–94	22	—

BEESLEY, Paul
Born Wigan 21.7.65.   Ht 6 1   Wt 11 11
Defender. From Marine.

1984–85 Wigan Ath	2	—
1985–86	17	—
1986–87	39	—
1987–88	42	1
1988–89	44	2
1989–90	11	—
1989–90 Leyton Orient	32	1
1990–91 Sheffield U	37	1
1991–92	40	2
1992–93	39	2
1993–94	25	—

BEESTON, Carl
Born Stoke 30.6.67.   Ht 5 9   Wt 12 04
Midfield. From Apprentice. England
Under-21.

1984–85 Stoke C	1	—
1985–86	5	—
1986–87	—	—
1987–88	12	—
1988–89	23	2
1989–90	38	2
1990–91	37	2
1991–92	43	3
1992–93	27	3
1993–94	—	—

BEEVER, Anthony
Born Huddersfield 18.9.74   Ht 6 0
Wt 12 05
Forward. From Trainee.

1992–93 Rochdale	1	—
1993–94	—	—

BEINLICH, Stefan
Born Berlin 13.1.72.   Ht 5 11   Wt 11 02
Forward. From Bergmann Borsig.

1991–92 Aston Villa	2	—
1992–93	7	—
1993–94	7	1

BELL, Michael
Born Newcastle 15.11.71.   Ht 5 8
Wt 10 04
Midfield. From Trainee.

1989–90 Northampton T	6	—
1990–91	28	—
1991–92	30	4
1992–93	39	5
1993–94	38	—

BELLAMY, Gary

Born Worksop 4.7.62.   Ht 6 2   Wt 11 05
Defender. From Apprentice.

Season	Club	Apps	Goals
1980–81	Chesterfield	3	—
1981–82		25	—
1982–83		42	—
1983–84		38	1
1984–85		22	2
1985–86		12	2
1986–87		42	2
1987–88	Wolverhampton W	24	2
1988–89		43	1
1989–90		39	3
1990–91		26	3
1991–92		4	—
1991–92	*Cardiff C*	9	—
1992–93	Wolverhampton W	—	—
1992–93	Leyton Orient	39	4
1993–94		29	1

BENALI, Francis

Born Southampton 30.12.68.   Ht 5 10
Wt 11 00
Forward. From Apprentice.

Season	Club	Apps	Goals
1986–87	Southampton	—	—
1987–88		—	—
1988–89		7	—
1989–90		27	—
1990–91		12	—
1991–92		22	—
1992–93		33	—
1993–94		37	—

BENJAMIN, Ian

Born Nottingham 11.12.61.   Ht 5 11
Wt 13 01
Forward. From Apprentice. England
Youth.

Season	Club	Apps	Goals
1978–79	Sheffield U	2	2
1979–80		3	1
1979–80	WBA	—	—
1980–81		2	—
1981–82	Notts Co	—	—
1982–83	Peterborough U	46	6
1983–84		34	8
1984–85	Northampton T	44	18
1985–86		46	22
1986–87		46	18
1987–88		14	1

Season	Club	Apps	Goals
1987–88	· Cambridge U	25	2
1988–89	Chester C	22	2
1988–89	Exeter C	20	3
1989–90		12	1
1989–90	Southend U	15	4
1990–91		46	13
1991–92		45	9
1992–93		16	7
1992–93	Luton T	10	1
1993–94		3	1
1993–94	Brentford	14	2

BENN, Wayne

Born Pontefract 7.8.76.   Ht 5 10   Wt 11 00
Defender. From Trainee.

Season	Club	Apps	Goals
1993–94	Bradford C	—	—

BENNETT, Craig

Born Doncaster 29.8.73.   Ht 6 0
Wt 12 00
Forward. From Trainee.

Season	Club	Apps	Goals
1990–91	Doncaster R	2	—
1991–92		5	—
1992–93		1	—
1993–94		—	—

BENNETT, Frankie

Born Birmingham 3.1.69   Ht 5 8
Wt 11 11
Forward.

Season	Club	Apps	Goals
1992–93	Southampton	—	—
1993–94		8	1

BENNETT, Gary

Born Liverpool 20.9.63.   Ht 5 11
Wt 12 00
Forward. From Local.

Season	Club	Apps	Goals
1984–85	Wigan Ath	20	3
1985–86	Chester C	43	13
1986–87		33	13
1987–88		43	10
1988–89		7	—
1988–89	Southend U	17	2
1989–90		25	4
1989–90	Chester C	8	1
1990–91		30	3
1991–92		42	11
1992–93	Wrexham	35	16

Season	Club	League Appearances/Goals	
1993–94		41	32

BENNETT, Gary
Born Manchester 4.12.61. Ht 6 1
Wt 12 01
Defender. From Amateur.

Season	Club	League Appearances/Goals	
1979–80	Manchester C	—	—
1980–81		—	—
1981–82	Cardiff C	19	1
1982–83		36	8
1983–84		32	2
1984–85	Sunderland	37	3
1985–86		28	3
1986–87		41	4
1987–88		38	2
1988–89		40	3
1989–90		36	3
1990–91		37	2
1991–92		39	3
1992–93		15	—
1993–94		38	—

BENNETT, Gary
Born Enfield 2.9.69 Ht 5 7   Wt 10 06
Midfield. From Trainee.

Season	Club	League Appearances/Goals	
1988–89	Colchester U	9	1
1989–90		36	4
1990–91		*36*	*9*
1991–92		*39*	*16*
1992–93		38	8
1993–94		4	—

BENNETT, Ian
Born Worksop 10.10.71. Ht 6 0
Wt 12 00
Goalkeeper. From Newcastle U Trainee.

Season	Club	League Appearances/Goals	
1991–92	Peterborough U	7	—
1992–93		46	—
1993–94		19	—
1993–94	Birmingham C	22	—

BENNETT, Mickey
Born London 27.7.69. Ht 5 10 Wt 11 11
Midfield. From Apprentice. England
Youth.

Season	Club	League Appearances/Goals	
1986–87	Charlton Ath	2	—
1987–88		16	1
1988–89		11	—

Season	Club	League Appearances/Goals	
1989–90		6	1
1989–90	Wimbledon	7	1
1990–91		6	—
1991–92		5	1
1992–93	Brentford	38	4
1993–94		8	—
1993–94	Charlton Ath	10	1

BENNETT, Tom
Born Falkirk 12.12.69. Ht 5 11   Wt 11 08
Defender. From Trainee.

Season	Club	League Appearances/Goals	
1987–88	Aston Villa	—	—
1988–89	Wolverhampton W	2	—
1989–90		30	—
1990–91		26	—
1991–92		38	2
1992–93		1	—
1993–94		10	—

BENNETT, Troy
Born Barnsley 25.12.75
Midfield. From Trainee.

Season	Club	League Appearances/Goals	
1992–93	Barnsley	2	—
1993–94		—	—

BENSTEAD, Graham
Born Aldershot 20.8.63. Ht 6 2 Wt 12 04
Goalkeeper. From Apprentice. England
Youth.

Season	Club	League Appearances/Goals	
1981–82	QPR	—	—
1982–83		—	—
1983–84		—	—
1984–85		—	—
1984–85	*Norwich C*	1	—
1985–86	Norwich C	—	—
1986–87		13	—
1987–88		2	—
1987–88	*Colchester U*	18	—
1987–88	*Sheffield U*	8	—
1988–89	Sheffield U	39	—
1989–90		—	—
1990–91	Brentford	45	—
1991–92		37	—
1992–93		25	—
1993–94		5	—

BENSTOCK, Danny
Born London 10.7.70
Defender. From Barking.

Season	Club	Apps	Goals
1992–93	Leyton Orient	9	—
1993–94		12	—

BENT, Junior
Born Huddersfield 1.3.70. Ht 5 5
Wt 10 06
Forward. From Trainee.

Season	Club	Apps	Goals
1987–88	Huddersfield T	7	—
1988–89		22	5
1989–90		7	1
1989–90	*Burnley*	9	3
1989–90	Bristol C	1	—
1990–91		20	2
1991–92		17	2
1991–92	*Stoke C*	1	—
1992–93	Bristol C	20	3
1993–94		20	2

BENTLEY, Jim
Born Liverpool 11.6.76. Ht 6 1 Wt 13 00
Defender. From Trainee.

Season	Club	Apps	Goals
1993–94	Manchester C	—	—

BERESFORD, David
Born Middlesbrough 11.11.76
Midfield. From Trainee.

Season	Club	Apps	Goals
1993–94	Oldham Ath	1	—

BERESFORD, John
Born Sheffield 4.9.66. Ht 5 5 Wt 10 04
Midfield. From Apprentice. England
Schools, Youth.

Season	Club	Apps	Goals
1983–84	Manchester C	—	—
1984–85		—	—
1985–86		—	—
1986–87	Barnsley	27	1
1987–88		34	3
1988–89		27	1
1988–89	Portsmouth	2	—
1989–90		28	—
1990–91		42	2
1991–92		35	6
1992–93	Newcastle U	42	1
1993–94		34	—

BERESFORD, Marlon
Born Lincoln 2.9.69. Ht 6 1 Wt 12 06
Goalkeeper. From Trainee.

Season	Club	Apps	Goals
61987–88	Sheffield W	—	—
1988–89		—	—
1989–90		—	—
1989–90	*Bury*	1	—
1989–90	*Ipswich T*	—	—
1990–91	Sheffield W	—	—
1990–91	*Northampton T*	13	—
1990–91	*Crewe Alex*	3	—
1991–92	Sheffield W	—	—
1991–92	*Northampton T*	15	—
1992–93	Burnley	44	—
1993–94		46	—

BERG, Henning
Born Eidsvell 1.9.69
Defender. From Lillestrom. Norway full
caps.

Season	Club	Apps	Goals
1992–93	Blackburn R	4	—
1993–94		41	1

BERGSSON, Gudni
Born Iceland 21.7.65. Ht 6 1 Wt 12 03
Defender. From Valur. Iceland Youth,
Under-21, full caps.

Season	Club	Apps	Goals
1988–89	Tottenham H	8	—
1989–90		18	—
1990–91		12	1
1991–92		28	1
1992–93		5	—
1993–94		—	—

BERKLEY, Austin
Born Dartford 28.1.73. Ht 5 9 Wt 10 10
Midfield. From Trainee.

Season	Club	Apps	Goals
1990–91	Gillingham	—	—
1991–92		3	—
1992–93	Swindon T	—	—
1993–94		—	—

BERNARD, Paul
Born Edinburgh 30.12.72. Ht 5 11
Wt 11 08
Midfield. From Trainee. Scotland
Under-21.

Season	Club	Apps	Goals
1990–91	Oldham Ath	2	1
1991–92		21	5

Season	Club	Apps	Goals
1992–93		33	4
1993–94		32	5

BERRY, Greg
Born Essex 5.3.71. Ht 5 10 Wt 12 00
Forward. From East Thurrock.

Season	Club	Apps	Goals
1989–90	Leyton Orient	9	1
1990–91		35	5
1991–92		36	8
1992–93	Wimbledon	3	—
1993–94		4	1
1993–94	Millwall	10	1

BERRY, Neil
Born Edinburgh 6.4.63 Ht 6 0 Wt 12 0
Defender. From Apprentice. Scotland Youth.

Season	Club	Apps	Goals
1980–81	Bolton W	—	—
1981–82		3	—
1982–83		9	—
1983–84		14	—
1984–85		6	—
1984–85	Hearts	3	—
1985–86		32	2
1986–87		30	3
1987–88		35	—
1988–89		32	1
1989–90		10	1
1990–91		19	1
1991–92		—	—
1992–93		17	1
1993–94		30	—

BERRY, Trevor
Born Surrey 1.8.74. Ht 5 07 Wt 10 08
Forward. From Bournemouth.

Season	Club	Apps	Goals
1991–92	Aston Villa	—	—
1992–93		—	—
1993–94		—	—

BERRYMAN, Stephen
Born Blackburn 26.12.66.
Goalkeeper.

Season	Club	Apps	Goals
1989–90	Hartlepool U	1	—
1990–91	Exeter C	—	—
1990–91	Cambridge U	1	—
1991–92	Barnet	—	—
1992–93		—	—

BETT, Jim
Born Hamilton 25.11.59. Ht 5 11
Wt 12 03
Midfield. From school. Scotland Schools, Under-21, 25 full caps.

Season	Club	Apps	Goals
1976–77	Airdrieonians	1	—
1977–78		7	—
From Iceland and Lokeren			
1980–81	Rangers	34	4
1981–82		35	11
1982–83		35	6
From Lokeren			
1985–86	Aberdeen	24	3
1986–87		38	4
1987–88		38	10
1988–89		31	5
1989–90		30	3
1990–91		36	7
1991–92		38	1
1992–93		17	—
1993–94		6	—

BETTS, Simon
Born Middlesbrough 3.3.73 Ht 5 8
Wt 10 07
Defender. From Trainee.

Season	Club	Apps	Goals
1991–92	Ipswich T	—	—
1992–93	Scarborough	—	—
1992–93	Colchester U	23	—
1993–94		33	1

BIBBO, Sal
Born Basingstoke 24.8.74 Ht 6 2
Wt 13 00
Goalkeeper. From Bournemouth.

Season	Club	Apps	Goals
1993–94	Sheffield U	—	—

BIGGINS, Wayne
Born Sheffield 20.11.61. Ht 5 10
Wt 11 00
Forward. From Apprentice.

Season	Club	Apps	Goals
1979–80	Lincoln C	—	—
1980–81		8	1
From Matlock Town and King's Lynn			
1983–84	Burnley	20	8
1984–85		46	18

Season	Club	League Appearances/Goals	
1985–86	....	12	3
1985–86	Norwich C	28	7
1986–87	....	31	4
1987–88	....	20	5
1988–89	Manchester C	32	9
1989–90	Stoke C	35	10
1990–91	....	38	12
1991–92	....	41	22
1992–93	....	8	2
1992–93	Barnsley	34	14
1993–94	....	13	2
1993–94	Celtic	9	—
1993–94	Stoke C	10	4

BILLING, Peter
Born Liverpool 24.10.64.   Ht 6 2
Wt 13 00
Defender. From South Liverpool.

Season	Club	League Appearances/Goals	
1985–86	Everton	1	—
1986–87	....	—	—
1986–87	Crewe Alex	19	—
1987–88	....	32	—
1988–89	....	37	1
1989–90	Coventry C	18	—
1990–91	....	15	—
1991–92	....	22	1
1992–93	....	3	—
1992–93	*Port Vale*	12	—
1993–94	Port Vale	8	—

BILLY, Chris
Born Huddersfield 2.1.73.   Ht 5 11
Wt 11 08
Forward. From Trainee.

Season	Club	League Appearances/Goals	
1991–92	Huddersfield T	10	2
1992–93	....	13	—
1993–94	....	34	—

BIRCH, Paul
Born West Bromwich 20.11.62.   Ht 5 6
Wt 10 04
Midfield. From Apprentice.

Season	Club	League Appearances/Goals	
1980–81	Aston Villa	—	—
1981–82	....	—	—
1982–83	....	—	—
1983–84	....	22	2
1984–85	....	25	3
1985–86	....	27	2
1986–87	....	29	3

Season	Club	League Appearances/Goals	
1987–88	....	38	6
1988–89	....	12	—
1989–90	....	12	—
1990–91	....	8	—
1990–91	Wolverhampton W	20	2
1991–92	....	45	8
1992–93	....	28	3
1993–94	....	32	1

BIRD, Anthony
Born Cardiff 1.9.74   Ht 5 10   Wt 11 09
Forward. From Trainee. Wales Under-21.

Season	Club	League Appearances/Goals	
1991–92	Cardiff C	—	—
1992–93	....	9	1
1993–94	....	35	5

BISHOP, Charlie
Born Nottingham 16.2.68.   Ht 6 0
Wt 12 01
Defender. From Stoke C Apprentice.

Season	Club	League Appearances/Goals	
1986–87	Watford	—	—
1987–88	Bury	17	—
1988–89	....	38	3
1989–90	....	30	1
1990–91	....	29	2
1991–92	Barnsley	28	—
1992–93	....	43	—
1993–94	....	38	1

BISHOP, Eddie
Born Liverpool 28.11.62.   Ht 5 8
Wt 11 07
Midfield. From Winsford U, Northwich
Vic, Altrincham, Runcorn.

Season	Club	League Appearances/Goals	
1987–88	Tranmere R	5	1
1988–89	....	35	8
1989–90	....	28	7
1990–91	....	8	3
1990–91	Chester C	19	7
1991–92	....	21	4
1991–92	*Crewe Alex*	3	—
1992–93	Chester C	29	6
1993–94	....	18	2

BISHOP, Ian
Born Liverpool 29.5.65.   Ht 5 9   Wt 10 12
Midfield. From Apprentice. England B.

Season	Club	League Appearances/Goals	
1983–84	Everton	1	—

1983–84	*Crewe Alex*..................	4	—
1984–85	Everton	—	—
1984–85	Carlisle U....................	30	2
1985–86	....	36	6
1986–87	....	42	3
1987–88	....	24	3
1988–89	Bournemouth..............	44	2
1989–90	Manchester C	19	2
1989–90	West Ham U	17	2
1990–91	....	40	4
1991–92	....	41	1
1992–93	....	22	1
1993–94	....	36	1

BISSETT, Nicky

Born Fulham 5.4.64. Ht 6 2 Wt 12 10
Defender. From Barnet.

1988–89	Brighton......................	16	—
1989–90	....	29	6
1990–91	....	3	—
1991–92	....	13	1
1992–93	....	12	—
1993–94	....	12	1

BJORNEBYE, Stig Inge

Born Norway 11.12.69 Ht 5 10 Wt 11 09
Defender. From Rosenborg. Norway full
caps.

| 1992–93 | Liverpool .... | 11 | — |
| 1993–94 | .... | 9 | — |

BLACK, Kingsley

Born Luton 22.6.68. Ht 5 8 Wt 10 11
Midfield. From school. Northern Ireland,
30 full caps.

1986–87	Luton T	—	—
1987–88	....	13	—
1988–89	....	37	8
1989–90	....	36	11
1990–91	....	37	7
1991–92	....	4	—
1991–92	Nottingham F.............	25	4
1992–93	....	24	5
1993–94	....	37	3

BLACK, Simon

Born Marston Green 9.11.75
Midfield. From Trainee.

| 1993–94 | Birmingham C............ | 2 | — |

BLACK, Tom

Born Lanark 11.10.62. Ht 5 8 Wt 10 12
Defender. From Bellshill YM.

1980–81	Airdrieonians	—	—
1981–82	....	—	—
1982–83	....	5	—
1983–84	....	32	4
1984–85	....	37	1
1985–86	....	12	—
1986–87	....	24	1
1987–88	....	29	1
1988–89	....	37	4
1989–90	St Mirren	31	1
1990–91	....	34	2
1991–92	....	9	1
1992–93	Kilmarnock.................	10	1
1993–94	....	44	4

BLACKMORE, Clayton

Born Neath 23.9.64. Ht 5 9 Wt 11 06
Midfield. From Apprentice. Wales Schools,
Youth, Under-21, 38 full caps.

1982–83	Manchester U.............	—	—
1983–84	....	1	—
1984–85	....	1	—
1985–86	....	12	3
1986–87	....	12	1
1987–88	....	22	3
1988–89	....	28	3
1989–90	....	28	2
1990–91	....	35	4
1991–92	....	33	3
1992–93	....	14	—
1993–94	....	—	—

BLACKSTONE, Ian

Born Harrogate 7.8.64. Ht 6 0 Wt 13 00
Forward. From Harrogate T.

1990–91	York C........................	28	6
1991–92	....	30	8
1992–93	....	39	16
1993–94	....	32	7

BLACKWELL, Dean

Born London 5.12.69. Ht 6 1 Wt 12 10
Defender. From Trainee. England
Under-21.

| 1988–89 | Wimbledon .... | — | — |

Season	Club	League App	Goals
1989–90	....	3	—
1989–90	*Plymouth Arg*..............	7	—
1990–91	Wimbledon	35	—
1991–92	....	4	1
1992–93	....	24	—
1993–94	....	18	—

BLACKWELL, Kevin
Born Luton 21.12.58   Ht 5 11   Wt 12 10
Goalkeeper. From Boston U, Barnet.

Season	Club	App	Goals
1987–88	Scarborough................	21	—
1988–89	....	15	—
1989–90	....	8	—
1989–90	Notts Co	—	—
1990–91	....	—	—
1991–92	....	—	—
1992–93	....	—	—
1992–93	Torquay U	18	—
1993–94	Huddersfield T...........	1	—

BLADES, Paul
Born Peterborough 5.1.65.   Ht 6 0
Wt 10 12
Defender. From Apprentice. England
Youth.

Season	Club	App	Goals
1982–83	Derby Co	6	—
1983–84	....	4	—
1984–85	....	22	—
1985–86	....	30	—
1986–87	....	16	—
1987–88	....	31	—
1988–89	....	38	1
1989–90	....	19	—
1990–91	Norwich C	21	—
1991–92	....	26	—
1992–93	Wolverhampton W	40	1
1993–94	....	35	1

BLAKE, Mark
Born Portsmouth 19.12.67.   Ht 6 1
Wt 12 08
Defender. From Apprentice. England
Youth.

Season	Club	App	Goals
1985–86	Southampton	1	—
1986–87	....	8	1
1987–88	....	6	1
1988–89	....	3	—
1989–90	....	—	—
1989–90	*Colchester U*................	4	1

Season	Club	App	Goals
1989–90	*Shrewsbury T*..............	10	—
1990–91	Shrewsbury T..............	46	2
1991–92	....	39	—
1992–93	....	32	1
1993–94	....	15	—

BLAKE, Mark
Born Nottingham 16.12.70.   Ht 5 11
Wt 12 07
Midfield. From Trainee. England Schools,
Youth, Under-21.

Season	Club	App	Goals
1989–90	Aston Villa.................	9	—
1990–91	....	7	—
1990–91	*Wolverhampton W*.......	2	—
1991–92	Aston Villa.................	14	2
1992–93	....	1	—
1993–94	Portsmouth	15	—
1993–94	Leicester C................	11	1

BLAKE, Nathan
Born Cardiff 27.1.72.   Ht 5 10   Wt 12 00
Defender. From Chelsea Trainee and
Cardiff C Trainee. Wales B, Under-21, 2
full caps.

Season	Club	App	Goals
1989–90	Cardiff C.................	6	—
1990–91	....	40	4
1991–92	....	31	6
1992–93	....	34	11
1993–94	....	20	14
1993–94	Sheffield U	12	5

BLAKE, Noel
Born Jamaica 12.1.62.   Ht 6 0   Wt 13 11
Defender. From Walsall Amateur and
Sutton Coldfield T.

Season	Club	App	Goals
1979–80	Aston Villa.................	3	—
1980–81	....	—	—
1981–82	....	1	—
1981–82	*Shrewsbury T*	6	—
1982–83	Aston Villa.................	—	—
1982–83	Birmingham C	37	3
1983–84	....	39	2
1984–85	Portsmouth	42	3
1985–86	....	42	4
1986–87	....	41	3
1987–88	....	19	—
1988–89	Leeds U	44	4
1989–90	....	7	—
1989–90	Stoke C....................	18	—

Season	Club	Apps	Goals
1990–91	....	44	3
1991–92	....	13	—
1991–92	*Bradford C*	6	—
1992–93	Bradford C	32	3
1993–94	....	7	—
1993–94	Dundee...........................	23	2

BLATHERWICK, Steve
Born Nottingham 20.9.73 Ht 6 1
Wt 12 12
Defender. From Notts Co.

Season	Club	Apps	Goals
1992–93	Nottingham F..............	—	—
1993–94	....	3	—
1993–94	*Wycombe W*.................	2	—

BLISSETT, Gary
Born Manchester 29.6.64. Ht 6 1
Wt 11 13
Forward. From Manchester C, Manchester U. Amateur and Altrincham.

Season	Club	Apps	Goals
1983–84	Crewe Alex	22	3
1984–85	....	29	9
1985–86	....	38	11
1986–87	....	33	16
1986–87	Brentford	10	5
1987–88	....	41	9
1988–89	....	36	6
1989–90	....	37	11
1990–91	....	26	10
1991–92	....	37	17
1992–93	....	46	21
1993–94	Wimbledon	18	3

BLISSETT, Luther
Born W. Indies 1.2.58. Ht 5 10 Wt 12 03
Forward. From Juniors. England Under-21, B, 14 full caps.

Season	Club	Apps	Goals
1975–76	Watford	3	1
1976–77	....	4	—
1977–78	....	33	6
1978–79	....	41	21
1979–80	....	42	10
1980–81	....	42	11
1981–82	....	40	19
1982–83	....	41	27
1983–84	AC Milan.....................	30	5
1984–85	Watford	41	21
1985–86	....	23	7
1986–87	....	35	11

Season	Club	Apps	Goals
1987–88	....	25	4
1988–89	....	3	1
1988–89	Bournemouth..............	30	19
1989–90	....	46	18
1990–91	....	45	19
1991–92	Watford	42	10
1992–93	....	—	—
1992–93	*WBA*	3	1
1993–94	Bury	10	1
1993–94	*Mansfield T*.................	5	1

BLOUNT, Mark
Born Derby 5.1.74 Ht 5 10 Wt 12 00
Midfield. From Gresley R.

Season	Club	Apps	Goals
1993–94	Sheffield U	—	—

BLYTH, Ian
Born Coventry 21.10.74.
Defender. From Trainee.

Season	Club	Apps	Goals
1991–92	Leicester C.................	—	—
1992–93	....	—	—
1993–94	....	—	—

BOARDMAN, Craig
Born Barnsley 30.11.70. Ht 6 0 Wt 11 08
Defender. From Trainee.

Season	Club	Apps	Goals
1991–92	Nottingham F..............	—	—
1992–93	....	—	—
1993–94	Peterborough U..........	—	—

BOARDMAN, Paul
Born Tottenham 6.11.67 Ht 6 0
Wt 11 02
Forward.

Season	Club	Apps	Goals
1992–93	Plymouth Arg..............	2	1
1993–94	....	1	—

BODEN, Chris
Born Wolverhampton 13.10.73. Ht 5 09
Wt 11 00
Defender. From Trainee.

Season	Club	Apps	Goals
1991–92	Aston Villa..................	—	—
1992–93	....	—	—
1993–94	....	—	—
1993–94	*Barnsley*	4	—

BODIN, Paul

Born Cardiff 13.9.64. Ht 6 0 Wt 13 01
Midfield. From Chelsea Amateur. Wales
Youth, Under-21, 22 full caps.

Season	Club	App	Goals
1981–82	Newport Co	—	—
1982–83	Cardiff C	31	—
1983–84		26	3

From Bath C

Season	Club	App	Goals
1987–88	Newport Co	6	1
1987–88	Swindon T	5	1
1988–89		16	1
1989–90		41	5
1990–91		31	2
1990–91	Crystal Palace	5	—
1991–92		4	—
1991–92	*Newcastle U*	6	—
1991–92	Swindon T	21	2
1992–93		35	11
1993–94		32	7

BODLEY, Mick

Born Hayes 14.9.67. Ht 5 11 Wt 12 00
Defender. From Apprentice.

Season	Club	App	Goals
1985–86	Chelsea	—	—
1986–87		—	—
1987–88		6	1
1988–89		—	—
1988–89	Northampton T	20	—
1989–90		—	—
1990–91	Barnet	—	—
1991–92		36	1
1992–93		33	2
1993–94	Southend U	16	1

BOERE, Jeroen

Born Arnheim 18.11.67. Ht 6 3 Wt 13 05
Forward. From Go Ahead Eagles.

Season	Club	App	Goals
1993–94	West Ham U	4	—
1993–94	*Portsmouth*	5	—

BOGIE, Ian

Born Newcastle 6.12.67. Ht 5 7
Wt 12 00
Midfield. From Apprentice. England
Schools.

Season	Club	App	Goals
1985–86	Newcastle U	—	—
1986–87		1	—
1987–88		7	—

Season	Club	App	Goals
1988–89		6	—
1988–89	Preston NE	13	1
1989–90		35	3
1990–91		31	8
1991–92	Millwall	25	—
1992–93		22	—
1993–94		4	1
1993–94	Leyton Orient	34	3

BOHINEN, Lars

Born Vadso 8.9.66. Ht 5 11 Wt 12 02
Midfield. From Young Boys Berne.

Season	Club	App	Goals
1993–94	Nottingham F	23	1

BOLAND, Willie

Born Ennis 6.8.75. Ht 5 9 Wt 11 02
Midfield. From Trainee.

Season	Club	App	Goals
1992–93	Coventry C	1	—
1993–94		27	—

BOLDER, Bob

Born Dover 2.10.58. Ht 6 3 Wt 14 06
Goalkeeper. From Dover.

Season	Club	App	Goals
1976–77	Sheffield W	—	—
1977–78		23	—
1978–79		19	—
1979–80		31	—
1980–81		39	—
1981–82		42	—
1982–83		42	—
1983–84	Liverpool	—	—
1984–85		—	—
1985–86		—	—
1985–86	Sunderland	22	—
1985–86	*Luton T*	—	—
1986–87	Charlton Ath	26	—
1987–88		35	—
1988–89		38	—
1989–90		38	—
1990–91		39	—
1991–92		46	—
1992–93		27	—
1993–94		—	—

BOLLAN, Gary

Born Dundee 24.3.73. Ht 5 11 Wt 12 4
Midfield. From Celtic BC. Scotland
Under-21.

Season	Club	App	Goals
1987–88	Celtic	—	—

33

Season	Club	Apps	Goals
1988–89		—	—
1989–90		—	—
1990–91	Dundee U	2	—
1991–92		10	1
1992–93		15	3
1993–94		12	—

BOND, Kevin
Born London 22.6.57. Ht 6 2 Wt 13 10
Defender. From Bournemouth Apprentice.
England B.

Season	Club	Apps	Goals
1974–75	Norwich C	—	—
1975–76		1	—
1976–77		3	—
1977–78		28	—
1978–79		42	2
1979–80		40	9
1980–81		28	1
From Seattle S			
1981–82	Manchester C	33	3
1982–83		40	3
1983–84		34	4
1984–85		3	1
1984–85	Southampton	33	1
1985–86		34	1
1986–87		34	1
1987–88		39	3
1988–89	Bournemouth	27	1
1989–90		31	—
1990–91		30	2
1991–92		38	1
1992–93	Exeter C	18	—
1993–94		1	—

BOND, Richie
Born Blyth 27.10.65 Ht 5 11 Wt 11 06
Forward. From Blyth Spartans.

Season	Club	Apps	Goals
1991–92	Blackpool	—	—
1992–93		1	—
1993–94	Carlisle U	—	—

BONNER, Mark
Born Ormskirk 7.6.74. Ht 5 10 Wt 11 00
Midfield. From Trainee.

Season	Club	Apps	Goals
1991–92	Blackpool	3	—
1992–93		15	—
1993–94		40	7

BONNER, Pat
Born Donegal 25.5.60. Ht 6 2 Wt 13 01
Goalkeeper. From Keadie Rovers. Eire
Youth, Under-21, 73 full caps.

Season	Club	Apps	Goals
1978–79	Celtic	2	—
1979–80		—	—
1980–81		36	—
1981–82		36	—
1982–83		36	—
1983–84		33	—
1984–85		34	—
1985–86		30	—
1986–87		43	—
1987–88		32	—
1988–89		26	—
1989–90		36	—
1990–91		36	—
1991–92		19	—
1992–93		33	—
1993–94		31	—

BOOTH, Andrew
Born Huddersfield 17.3.73. Ht 5 10
Wt 10 03
Forward. From Trainee.

Season	Club	Apps	Goals
1991–92	Huddersfield T	3	—
1992–93		5	2
1993–94		26	10

BOOTH, Scott
Born Aberdeen 16.12.71. Ht 5 7
Wt 10 03
Forward. From Schools. Scotland Under-
21, 5 full caps.

Season	Club	Apps	Goals
1988–89	Aberdeen	—	—
1989–90		2	—
1990–91		19	6
1991–92		33	5
1992–93		29	13
1993–94		25	4

BOOTHROYD, Adrian
Born Bradford 8.2.71. Ht 5 8 Wt 10 12
Defender. From Trainee.

Season	Club	Apps	Goals
1989–90	Huddersfield T	10	—
1990–91	Bristol R	3	—
1991–92		13	—
1992–93	Hearts	4	—

1993–94	....	—	—
1993–94	Mansfield T...............	23	1

BOOTY, Justin

Born Colchester 2.6.76
Forward. From Trainee.

1993–94	Colchester U..............	1	—

BOOTY, Martyn

Born Kirby Muxloe 30.5.71.   Ht 5 8
Wt 12 01
Defender. From Trainee.

1991–92	Coventry C................	3	—
1992–93	....	—	—
1993–94	....	2	—
1993–94	Crewe Alex	31	1

BORROWS, Brian

Born Liverpool 20.12.60.   Ht 5 10
Wt 10 12
Defender. From Amateur. England B.

1979–80	Everton	—	—
1980–81	....	—	—
1981–82	....	15	—
1982–83	....	12	—
1982–83	Bolton W	9	—
1983–84	....	44	—
1984–85	....	42	—
1985–86	Coventry C	41	—
1986–87	....	41	1
1987–88	....	33	—
1988–89	....	38	1
1989–90	....	37	1
1990–91	....	38	6
1991–92	....	35	—
1992–93	....	38	2
1993–94	....	29	—
1993–94	*Bristol C*....................	6	—

BOSNICH, Mark

Born Fairfield 13.1.72.   Ht 6 1   Wt 13 07
Goalkeeper. From Croatia Sydney.
Australia full caps.

1989–90	Manchester U	1	—
1990–91	....	2	—
1991–92	Aston Villa.................	1	—
1992–93	....	17	—
1993–94	....	28	—

BOTTOMLEY, Paul

Born Harrogate 11.9.65
Defender. From Guiseley, Bridlington T.

1993–94	*Doncaster R*	10	1

BOULD, Steve

Born Stoke 16.11.62.   Ht 6 4   Wt 14 02
Defender. From Apprentice. England 2
full caps.

1980–81	Stoke C	—	—
1981–82	....	2	—
1982–83	....	14	—
1982–83	*Torquay U*....................	9	—
1983–84	Stoke C	38	2
1984–85	....	38	3
1985–86	....	33	—
1986–87	....	28	1
1987–88	....	30	—
1988–89	Arsenal....................	30	2
1989–90	....	19	—
1990–91	....	38	—
1991–92	....	25	1
1992–93	....	24	1
1993–94	....	25	1

BOUND, Matthew

Born Trowbridge 9.11.72.   Ht 6 2
Wt 13 12
Defender. From Trainee.

1990–91	Southampton	1	—
1991–92	....	—	—
1992–93	....	3	—
1993–94	....	1	—
1993–94	*Hull C*....................	7	1

BOWDEN, Jon

Born Stockport 21.1.63.   Ht 6 10
Wt 11 07
Midfield. From Local.

1979–80	Oldham Ath................	—	—
1980–81	....	—	—
1981–82	....	5	2
1982–83	....	31	2
1983–84	....	31	1
1984–85	....	15	—
1985–86	....	—	—
1985–86	Port Vale....................	36	3
1986–87	....	34	4

1987–88	Wrexham	26	1
1988–89		42	10
1989–90		33	1
1990–91		40	5
1991–92		6	3
1991–92	Rochdale	31	6
1992–93		35	8
1993–94		29	3

BOWEN, Jason
Born Merthyr 24.8.72. Ht 5 6   Wt 10 07
Midfield. From Trainee. Wales Under-21.

1990–91	Swansea C	3	—
1991–92		11	—
1992–93		38	10
1993–94		41	11

BOWEN, Mark
Born Neath 7.12.63. Ht 5 8   Wt 11 13
Defender. From Apprentice. Wales
Schools, Youth, Under-21, 27 full caps.

1981–82	Tottenham H	—	—
1982–83		—	—
1983–84		7	—
1984–85		6	—
1985–86		2	1
1986–87		2	1
1987–88	Norwich C	24	1
1988–89		35	2
1989–90		38	7
1990–91		37	1
1991–92		36	3
1992–93		42	1
1993–94		41	5

BOWLING, Ian
Born Sheffield 27.7.65. Ht 6 3   Wt 14 08
Goalkeeper. From Gainsborough T.

1988–89	Lincoln C	8	—
1989–90		—	—
1989–90	*Hartlepool U*	1	—
1990–91	Lincoln C	16	—
1991–92		20	—
1992–93		15	—
1992–93	*Bradford C*	7	—
1993–94	Bradford C	23	—

BOWMAN, David
Born Tunbridge Wells 10.3.64.   Ht 5 10
Wt 11 02
Midfield. From Salvesen BC. Scotland
Under-21, 6 full caps.

1980–81	Hearts	17	1
1981–82		16	1
1982–83		39	5
1983–84		33	—
1984–85		11	1
1984–85	Coventry C	10	—
1985–86		30	2
1986–87	Dundee U	29	—
1987–88		39	1
1988–89		29	1
1989–90		24	1
1990–91		20	1
1991–92		41	3
1992–93		24	—
1993–94		35	2

BOWMAN, Robert
Born Durham 21.11.75.
Defender. From Trainee.

1992–93	Leeds U	4	—
1993–94		—	—

BOWRY, Bobby
Born Croydon 19.5.71   Ht 5 8   Wt 10 00
Midfield.

1991–92	Crystal Palace	—	—
1992–93		11	1
1993–94		21	—

BOWYER, Gary
Born Manchester 26.6.71.   Ht 6 0
Wt 12 13
Defender.

1989–90	Hereford U	14	2
1990–91	Nottingham F	—	—
1991–92		—	—
1992–93		—	—
1993–94		—	—

BOWYER, Lee
Born London 3.1.77   Ht 5 9   Wt 9 11
Midfield. From Trainee.

1993–94	Charlton Ath	—	—

BOYD, Tom
Born Glasgow 24.11.65.   Ht 5 11
Wt 11 04
Defender. 'S' Form. Scotland Youth, B,
Under-21, 21 full caps.

Season	Club		
1983–84	Motherwell	13	—
1984–85		36	—
1985–86		31	—
1986–87		31	—
1987–88		42	2
1988–89		36	1
1989–90		33	1
1990–91		30	2
1991–92	Chelsea	23	—
1991–92	Celtic	13	1
1992–93		42	—
1993–94		38	—

BOZINOSKI, Vlado
Born Macedonia 30.3.64   Ht 5 10
Wt 11 03
Midfield. From Hellas, FC Brugge, Beira
Mar, Sporting Lisbon.

Season	Club		
1992–93	Ipswich T	9	—
1993–94		—	—

BRACE, Deryn
Born Haverfordwest 15.3.75   Ht 5 9
Wt 10 03
Defender. From Trainee.

Season	Club		
1993–94	Norwich C	—	—
1993–94	Wrexham	1	—

BRACEWELL, Paul
Born Stoke 19.7.62.   Ht 5 8   Wt 10 09
Midfield. From Apprentice. England
Under-21, 3 full caps.

Season	Club		
1979–80	Stoke C	6	—
1980–81		40	2
1981–82		42	1
1982–83		41	2
1983–84	Sunderland	38	4
1984–85	Everton	37	2
1985–86		38	3
1986–87		—	—
1987–88		—	—
1988–89		20	2
1989–90		—	—

Season	Club		
1989–90	Sunderland	37	2
1990–91		37	—
1991–92		39	—
1992–93	Newcastle U	25	2
1993–94		32	1

BRACEY, Lee
Born Ashford 11.9.68.   Ht 6 1   Wt 12 08
Goalkeeper. From Trainee.

Season	Club		
1987–88	West Ham U	—	—
1988–89	Swansea C	30	—
1989–90		31	—
1990–91		35	—
1991–92		3	—
1991–92	Halifax T	32	—
1992–93		41	—
1993–94	Bury	40	—

BRADBURY, Shaun
Born Birmingham 11.2.74   Ht 5 10
Wt 11 00
Forward. From Trainee.

Season	Club		
1992–93	Wolverhampton W	2	2
1993–94		—	—

BRADLEY, Darren
Born Birmingham 24.11.65.   Ht 5 7
Wt 11 12
Defender. From Apprentice. England
Youth.

Season	Club		
1983–84	Aston Villa	—	—
1984–85		2	—
1985–86		18	—
1985–86	WBA	10	—
1986–87		14	1
1987–88		19	—
1988–89		26	—
1989–90		27	2
1990–91		39	1
1991–92		37	2
1992–93		42	1
1993–94		24	2

BRADLEY, Russell
Born Birmingham 28.3.66.   Ht 6 0
Wt 12 05
Midfield. From Dudley T.

Season	Club		
1987–88	Nottingham F	—	—

Season	Club		
1988–89		—	—
1988–89	*Hereford U*	12	1
1989–90	Hereford U	33	1
1990–91		41	2
1991–92		3	—
1991–92	Halifax T	26	2
1992–93		30	1
1993–94	Scunthorpe U	34	1

BRADSHAW, Carl

Born Sheffield 2.10.68. Ht 6 0 Wt 11 00
Forward. From Apprentice. England
Youth.

Season	Club		
1986–87	Sheffield W	9	2
1986–87	*Barnsley*	6	1
1987–88	Sheffield W	20	2
1988–89		3	—
1988–89	Manchester C	5	—
1989–90		—	—
1989–90	Sheffield U	30	3
1990–91		27	1
1991–92		18	2
1992–93		32	1
1993–94		40	1

BRADSHAW, Darren

Born Sheffield 19.3.67. Ht 5 11 Wt 11 04
Midfield. From Matlock T.

Season	Club		
1987–88	Chesterfield	18	—
1987–88	York C	25	1
1988–89		34	2
1989–90		—	—
1989–90	Newcastle U	12	—
1990–91		7	—
1991–92		19	—
1992–93	Peterborough U	34	—
1993–94		39	1

BRADY, Gary

Born Glasgow 7.9.76 Ht 5 7
Midfield. From Trainee.

Season	Club		
1993–94	Tottenham H	—	—

BRADY, Jon

Born Newcastle (Aus) 14.1.75 Ht 5 10
Wt 10 06
Forward. From Adamstown Rosebuds.

Season	Club		
1993–94	Swansea C	—	—

BRADY, Kieron

Born Glasgow 17.9.71. Ht 5 9 Wt 11 13
Midfield. From Trainee. Eire Youth,
Under-21.

Season	Club		
1989–90	Sunderland	11	2
1990–91		14	2
1991–92		8	3
1992–93		—	—
1992–93	*Doncaster R*	4	3
1993–94	Doncaster R	—	—

BRAIN, Simon

Born Evesham 31.3.66. Ht 5 6 Wt 10 08
Forward. From Cheltenham T.

Season	Club		
1990–91	Hereford U	22	8
1991–92		41	10
1992–93		21	2
1993–94		3	—

BRAMMER, David

Born Bromborough 28.2.75 . Ht 5 9
Wt 10 05
Midfield. From Trainee.

Season	Club		
1992–93	Wrexham	2	—
1993–94		22	2

BRANAGAN, Keith

Born Fulham 10.7.66. Ht 6 1 Wt 13 00
Goalkeeper.

Season	Club		
1983–84	Cambridge U	1	—
1984–85		19	—
1985–86		9	—
1986–87		46	—
1987–88		35	—
1987–88	Millwall	—	—
1988–89		—	—
1989–90		16	—
1989–90	*Brentford*	2	—
1990–91	Millwall	18	—
1991–92		12	—
1991–92	*Gillingham*	1	—
1991–92	*Fulham*	—	—
1992–93	Bolton W	46	—
1993–94		10	—

BRANCH, Graham

Born Heswall 12.2.72. Ht 6 2 Wt 13 00
Forward. From Heswall Ath.

Season	Club		
1991–92	Tranmere R	4	—

Season	Club		App	Goals
1992–93			3	—
1992–93	*Bury*		4	1
1993–94	Tranmere R		13	—

BRANNAN, Ged
Born Liverpool 15.1.72. Ht 6 0 Wt 13 03
Defender. From Trainee.

Season	Club		App	Goals
1990–91	Tranmere R		18	1
1991–92			18	1
1992–93			38	1
1993–94			45	9

BRASS, Chris
Born Easington 24.7.75 Ht 5 9 Wt 11 03
Defender. From Trainee.

Season	Club		App	Goals
1993–94	Burnley		—	—

BRAZIL, Derek
Born Dublin 14.12.68. Ht 5 11 Wt 10 05
Defender. From Rivermount BC. Eire
Youth, B, Under-21, Under-23.

Season	Club		App	Goals
1985–86	Manchester U		—	—
1986–87			—	—
1987–88			—	—
1988–89			1	—
1989–90			1	—
1990–91			—	—
1990–91	*Oldham Ath*		1	—
1991–92	Manchester U		—	—
1991–92	*Swansea C*		12	1
1992–93	Cardiff C		34	—
1993–94			31	—

BRAZIL, Gary
Born Tunbridge Wells 19.9.62. Ht 5 11
Wt 10 02
Forward. From Crystal Palace Apprentice.

Season	Club		App	Goals
1980–81	Sheffield U		3	—
1981–82			1	—
1982–83			33	5
1983–84			19	2
1984–85			6	2
1984–85	*Port Vale*		6	3
1984–85	Preston NE		17	3
1985–86			43	14
1986–87			45	18
1987–88			36	14
1988–89			25	9

Season	Club		App	Goals
1988–89	Newcastle U		7	—
1989–90			16	2
1990–91	Fulham		41	4
1991–92			46	14
1992–93			30	7
1993–94			46	14

BREACKER, Tim
Born Bicester 2.7.65. Ht 5 11 Wt 13 00
Defender. England Under-21.

Season	Club		App	Goals
1983–84	Luton T		2	—
1984–85			35	—
1985–86			36	—
1986–87			29	1
1987–88			40	1
1988–89			22	—
1989–90			38	1
1990–91			8	—
1990–91	West Ham U		24	1
1991–92			34	2
1992–93			39	2
1993–94			40	3

BRECKIN, Ian
Born Rotherham 24.2.75 Ht 6 1
Wt 12 09
Defender. From Trainee.

Season	Club		App	Goals
1993–94	Rotherham U		10	—

BREEN, Gary
Born London 12.12.73. Ht 6 1 Wt 12 07
Defender. From Charlton Ath.

Season	Club		App	Goals
1991–92	Maidstone U		19	—
1992–93	Gillingham		29	—
1993–94			22	—

BREITKREUTZ, Matthias
Born Crivitz 12.5.71. Ht 5 9 Wt 11 03
Midfield. From Bergmann Borsig.

Season	Club		App	Goals
1991–92	Aston Villa		8	—
1992–93			3	—
1993–94			2	—

BRENNAN, Mark
Born Rossendale 4.10.65. Ht 5 10
Wt 10 13
Midfield. From Apprentice. England
Youth, Under-21.

Season	Club		App	Goals
1982–83	Ipswich T		—	—

Season	Club	Apps	Goals
1983–84	....	19	1
1984–85	....	36	2
1985–86	....	40	3
1986–87	....	37	7
1987–88	....	36	6
1988–89	Middlesbrough...........	25	3
1989–90	....	40	3
1990–91	Manchester C	16	3
1991–92	....	13	3
1992–93	....	—	—
1992–93	Oldham Ath...............	14	3
1993–94	....	11	—

BRENTANO, Steve
Born Hull 9.11.61
Defender. From North Ferriby U.

Season	Club	Apps	Goals
1984–85	Hull C..........................	2	—
1985–86	....	8	—
1986–87	....	2	—
From Bridlington T			
1993–94	Doncaster R...............	1	—

BRESSINGTON, Graham
Born Eton 8.7.66. Ht 6 0 Wt 12 00
Defender. From Wycombe W.

Season	Club	Apps	Goals
1987–88	Lincoln C...................	12	—
1988–89	....	30	1
1989–90	....	43	2
1990–91	....	37	—
1991–92	....	3	—
1992–93	....	28	4
1993–94	Southend U...............	28	3

BREVETT, Rufus
Born Derby 24.9.69. Ht 5 8 Wt 11 00
Defender. From Trainee.

Season	Club	Apps	Goals
1987–88	Doncaster R...............	17	—
1988–89	....	23	—
1989–90	....	42	—
1990–91	....	27	3
1990–91	QPR...................	10	—
1991–92	....	7	—
1992–93	....	15	—
1993–94	....	7	—

BREWSTER, Craig
Born Dundee 13.12.66. Ht 5 11 Wt 10 7
Midfield. From Stobwell J.

Season	Club	Apps	Goals
1985–86	Forfar Ath.................	16	2

Season	Club	Apps	Goals
1986–87	....	32	3
1987–88	....	39	2
1988–89	....	37	9
1989–90	....	38	8
1990–91	....	29	11
1991–92	Raith R...............	42	12
1992–93	....	44	22
1993–94	Dundee U...................	33	16

BRIEN, Tony
Born Dublin 10.2.69. Ht 5 11 Wt 11 09
Defender. From Apprentice.

Season	Club	Apps	Goals
1986–87	Leicester C...................	—	—
1987–88	....	15	1
1988–89	....	1	—
1988–89	Chesterfield................	29	1
1989–90	....	43	3
1990–91	....	43	3
1991–92	....	41	—
1992–93	....	39	1
1993–94	....	9	—
1993–94	Rotherham U	26	2

BRIGGS, Gary
Born Leeds 8.5.58. Ht 6 3 Wt 12 10
Defender. From Apprentice.

Season	Club	Apps	Goals
1977–78	Middlesbrough............	—	—
1977–78	Oxford U...................	20	2
1978–79	....	39	—
1979–80	....	46	1
1980–81	....	42	1
1981–82	....	45	1
1982–83	....	37	1
1983–84	....	38	3
1984–85	....	42	4
1985–86	....	38	—
1986–87	....	40	3
1987–88	....	18	1
1988–89	....	15	1
1989–90	Blackpool	17	2
1990–91	....	30	—
1991–92	....	24	—
1992–93	....	33	1
1993–94	....	32	1

BRIGHT, Mark
Born Stoke 6.6.62. Ht 6 0 Wt 13 00
Forward. From Leek T.

Season	Club	Apps	Goals
1981–82	Port Vale......................	2	—

Season	Club	Apps	Goals
1982–83		1	1
1983–84		26	9
1984–85	Leicester C	16	—
1985–86		24	6
1986–87		2	—
1986–87	Crystal Palace	28	8
1987–88		38	25
1988–89		46	20
1989–90		36	12
1990–91		32	9
1991–92		42	17
1992–93		5	1
1992–93	Sheffield W	30	11
1993–94		40	19

BRIGHTWELL, David
Born Lutterworth 7.1.71. Ht 6 1
Wt 13 05
Midfield. From Trainee.

Season	Club	Apps	Goals
1987–88	Manchester C	—	—
1988–89		—	—
1989–90		—	—
1990–91		—	—
1990–91	*Chester C*	6	—
1991–92	Manchester C	4	—
1992–93		8	—
1993–94		22	1

BRIGHTWELL, Ian
Born Lutterworth 9.4.68. Ht 5 10
Wt 11 07
Midfield. From Congleton T. England
Schools, Youth, Under-21.

Season	Club	Apps	Goals
1986–87	Manchester C	16	1
1987–88		33	5
1988–89		26	6
1989–90		28	2
1990–91		33	—
1991–92		40	1
1992–93		21	1
1993–94		7	—

BRISCOE, Lee
Born Pontefract 30.9.75. Ht 5 7   Wt 10 09
Forward. From Trainee.

Season	Club	Apps	Goals
1993–94	Sheffield W	1	—

BRISSETT, Jason
Born Redbridge 7.9.74
Forward. From Arsenal trainee.

Season	Club	Apps	Goals
1993–94	Peterborough U	30	—

BRITTON, Gerard
Born Glasgow 20.10.70. Ht 6 1   Wt 11 0
Forward. From Celtic BC.

Season	Club	Apps	Goals
1987–88	Celtic	—	—
1988–89		—	—
1989–90		—	—
1990–91		2	—
1991–92		—	—
1991–92	*Reading*	2	—
1992–93	Partick T	40	12
1993–94		22	3
1993–94	Dundee	17	1

BROCK, Kevin
Born Middleton Stoney 9.9.62. Ht 5 9
Wt 10 12
Midfield. From Apprentice. England
Schools, Under-21.

Season	Club	Apps	Goals
1979–80	Oxford U	19	2
1980–81		26	5
1981–82		28	5
1982–83		37	4
1983–84		45	3
1984–85		37	6
1985–86		23	—
1986–87		31	1
1987–88	QPR	26	2
1988–89		14	—
1988–89	Newcastle U	21	2
1989–90		44	2
1990–91		38	5
1991–92		35	4
1992–93		7	2
1993–94		—	—
1993–94	*Cardiff C*	14	2

BROCKLEHURST, David
Born Chesterfield 7.3.74 Ht 5 10
Wt 10 08
Forward. From Trainee.

Season	Club	Apps	Goals
1992–93	Sheffield U	—	—
1993–94		—	—

BRODDLE, Julian
Born Laughton 1.11.64. Ht 5 9 Wt 11 07
Midfield. From Apprentice.

Season	Club		
1981–82	Sheffield U	1	—
1982–83		—	—
1983–84	Scunthorpe U	13	1
1984–85		45	14
1985–86		41	7
1986–87		38	10
1987–88		7	—
1987–88	Barnsley	19	1
1988–89		38	3
1989–90		20	—
1989–90	Plymouth Arg	9	—
1990–91		—	—
1990–91	*Bradford C*	—	—
1990–91	St Mirren	10	—
1991–92		35	2
1992–93	Partick T	6	—
1992–93	*Scunthorpe U*	5	—
1993–94	Raith R	18	—

BRODIE, Stephen
Born Sunderland 14.1.73. Ht 5 10
Wt 11 00
Forward. From Trainee.

Season	Club		
1991–92	Sunderland	—	—
1992–93		—	—
1993–94		4	—

BROOKE, David
Born Barnsley 23.11.75. Ht 5 11
Wt 11 03
Midfield. From Trainee.

Season	Club		
1993–94	Barnsley	—	—

BROOKS, Shaun
Born London 9.10.62. Ht 5 7 Wt 11 00
Midfield. From Apprentice. England
Schools, Youth.

Season	Club		
1979–80	Crystal Palace	1	—
1980–81		17	—
1981–82		25	2
1982–83		7	2
1983–84		4	—
1983–84	Orient	36	9
1984–85		29	5
1985–86		38	7

Season	Club		
1986–87		45	5
1987–88	Bournemouth	37	6
1988–89		36	3
1989–90		35	4
1990–91		13	—
1991–92		7	—
1992–93		—	—
1992–93	*Stockport Co*	—	—
1993–94	Crewe Alex	—	—

BROUGH, John
Born Heanor 8.1.73 Ht 6 1 Wt 12 07
Forward. From Trainee.

Season	Club		
1991–92	Notts Co	—	—
1992–93	Shrewsbury T	14	1
1993–94		2	—

BROWN, Grant
Born Sunderland 19.11.69. Ht 6 0
Wt 11 12
Defender. From Trainee.

Season	Club		
1987–88	Leicester C	2	—
1988–89		12	—
1989–90	Lincoln C	34	2
1990–91		32	1
1991–92		37	1
1992–93		40	1
1993–94		38	3

BROWN, Ian
Born Ipswich 11.9.65 Ht 5 10 Wt 11 05
Forward. From Chelmsford C.

Season	Club		
1992–93	Bristol C	—	—
1993–94		11	1
1993–94	*Colchester U*	4	1

BROWN, John
Born Stirling 26.1.62. Ht 5 11 Wt 10 02
Defender. From Blantyre Welfare.

Season	Club		
1979–80	Hamilton A	19	—
1980–81		38	6
1981–82		28	5
1982–83		9	—
1983–84		39	—
1984–85	Dundee	34	7
1985–86		29	11
1986–87		31	10
1987–88		20	3

Season	Club		App	Goals
1987–88	Rangers		9	2
1988–89			29	1
1989–90			27	1
1990–91			27	1
1991–92			25	4
1992–93			39	4
1993–94			24	—

BROWN, Jon

Born Barnsley 8.9.66.   Ht 5 10   Wt 11 03
Defender. From Denaby U.

Season	Club	App	Goals
1990–91	Exeter C	29	—
1991–92		35	—
1992–93		40	1
1993–94		23	—

BROWN, Karl

Born Unsworth 7.2.75   Ht 5 5   Wt 9 09
Midfield. From Trainee.

Season	Club	App	Goals
1993–94	Manchester U	—	—

BROWN, Kenny

Born Barking 11.7.67.   Ht 5 8   Wt 11 06
Defender. From Apprentice.

Season	Club	App	Goals
1984–85	Norwich C	—	—
1985–86		—	—
1986–87		18	—
1987–88		7	—
1988–89	Plymouth Arg	39	1
1989–90		44	—
1990–91		43	3
1991–92	West Ham U	27	3
1992–93		15	2
1993–94		9	—

BROWN, Linton

Born Driffield 12.4.68   Ht 5 9   Wt 11 00
Midfield. From Guiseley.

Season	Club	App	Goals
1992–93	Halifax T	3	—
1992–93	Hull C	23	1
1993–94		42	9

BROWN, Mark

Born Jersey 8.7.75
Midfield. From Trainee.

Season	Club	App	Goals
1993–94	Exeter C	—	—

BROWN, Mike

Born Birmingham 8.2.68.   Ht 5 9
Wt 10 12
Forward. From Apprentice.

Season	Club	App	Goals
1985–86	Shrewsbury T	—	—
1986–87		22	2
1987–88		41	5
1988–89		41	—
1989–90		43	1
1990–91		43	1
1991–92	Bolton W	27	3
1992–93		6	—
1992–93	Shrewsbury T	17	1
1993–94		41	7

BROWN, Phil

Born South Shields 30.5.59.   Ht 5 11
Wt 11 06
Defender. From Local.

Season	Club	App	Goals
1978–79	Hartlepool U	—	—
1979–80		10	—
1980–81		46	1
1981–82		44	4
1982–83		44	2
1983–84		31	—
1984–85		42	1
1985–86	Halifax T	45	2
1986–87		46	12
1987–88		44	5
1988–89	Bolton W	46	4
1989–90		46	1
1990–91		45	—
1991–92		37	2
1992–93		40	5
1993–94		42	2

BROWN, Richard

Born Nottingham 13.1.67.   Ht 5 10
Wt 11 02
Defender. From Derby Co, Ilkeston T.

Season	Club	App	Goals
1984–85	Sheffield W	—	—
1985–86		—	—
From Kettering T			
1990–91	Blackburn R	—	—
1990–91	*Maidstone U*	3	—
1991–92	Blackburn R	26	—
1992–93		2	—
1993–94		—	—

BROWN, Steve
Born Northampton 6.7.66. Ht 5 9
Wt 10 12
Forward.

Season	Club		
1985–86	Northampton T	—	—
From Irthlingborough D			
1989–90	Northampton T	21	1
1990–91		40	2
1991–92		35	3
1992–93		38	9
1993–94		24	4
1993–94	Wycombe W	9	2

BROWN, Steve
Born Brighton 13.5.72. Ht 6 1 Wt 12 08
Defender. From Trainee.

Season	Club		
1990–91	Charlton Ath	—	—
1991–92		1	—
1992–93		—	—
1993–94		19	—

BROWN, Steve
Born Southend 6.12.73 Ht 5 11
Wt 11 10
Forward. From Trainee.

Season	Club		
1992–93	Southend U	10	2
1993–94	Scunthorpe U	—	—
1993–94	Colchester U	34	11

BROWN, Steven
Born Sheffield 15.10.74 Ht 5 9 Wt 10 05
Midfield. From Trainee.

Season	Club		
1993–94	Sheffield W	—	—

BROWN, Tom
Born Glasgow 1.4.68 Ht 5 7 Wt 10 0
Midfield. Glenafton Ath.

Season	Club		
1993–94	Kilmarnock	31	5

BROWN, Wayne
Born Southampton 14.1.77
Goalkeeper. From Trainee.

Season	Club		
1993–94	Bristol C	1	—

BROWNE, Paul
Born Glasgow 17.2.75 Ht 6 1 Wt 12 00
Defender. From Trainee.

Season	Club		
1993–94	Aston Villa	—	—

BROWNING, Marcus
Born Bristol 22.4.71. Ht 5 11 Wt 12 00
Forward. From Trainee.

Season	Club		
1989–90	Bristol R	1	—
1990–91		—	—
1991–92		11	—
1992–93		19	1
1992–93	*Hereford U*	7	5
1993–94	Bristol R	31	4

BRUCE, Steve
Born Newcastle 31.12.60. Ht 6 0
Wt 12 6
Defender. From Apprentice. England
Youth.

Season	Club		
1978–79	Gillingham	—	—
1979–80		40	6
1980–81		41	4
1981–82		45	6
1982–83		39	7
1983–84		40	6
1984–85	Norwich C	39	1
1985–86		42	8
1986–87		41	3
1987–88		19	2
1987–88	Manchester U	21	2
1988–89		38	2
1989–90		34	3
1990–91		31	13
1991–92		37	5
1992–93		42	5
1993–94		41	3

BRUNSKILL, Iain
Born Ormskirk 5.11.76 Ht 5 10
Wt 12 05
Defender. From Trainee.

Season	Club		
1993–94	Liverpool	—	—

BRYAN, Marvin
Born Paddington 2.8.75 Ht 6 0 Wt 12 02
Forward. From Trainee.

Season	Club		
1992–93	QPR	—	—
1993–94		—	—

BRYANT, Matthew
Born Bristol 21.9.70. Ht 6 1 Wt 12 11
Defender. From Trainee.

Season	Club		
1989–90	Bristol C	—	—

1990–91	....	22	1
1990–91	*Walsall*	13	—
1991–92	Bristol C	43	2
1992–93	....	41	1
1993–94	....	28	—

BRYDEN, Lee
Born Stockton 15.11.74 Ht 5 11
Wt 11 00
Defender. From Trainee.

1992–93	Liverpool	—	—
1993–94	....	—	—

BRYSON, Ian
Born Kilmarnock 26.11.62. Ht 5 11
Wt 11 11
Midfield.

1981–82	Kilmarnock	14	3
1982–83	....	28	1
1983–84	....	25	4
1984–85	....	36	3
1985–86	....	38	14
1986–87	....	32	10
1987–88	....	42	5
1988–89	Sheffield U	37	8
1989–90	....	39	9
1990–91	....	29	7
1991–92	....	34	9
1992–93	....	16	3
1993–94	Barnsley	16	3
1993–94	Preston NE	25	2

BUCKLE, Paul
Born Hatfield 16.12.70. Ht 5 8 Wt 10 08
Midfield. From Trainee.

1987–88	Brentford	1	—
1988–89	....	—	—
1989–90	....	10	—
1990–91	....	26	—
1991–92	....	15	1
1992–93	....	5	—
1993–94	....	—	—
1993–94	Torquay U	16	2

BUDDEN, John
Born Croydon 17.7.71 Ht 6 0 Wt 12 2
Defender. Crystal Palace trainee.

1993–94	St Johnstone	2	—

BUGLIONE, Martin
Born London 19.6.68. Ht 6 1 Wt 11 9
Forward. From Margate.

1992–93	St Johnstone	7	2
1993–94	....	10	—

BULL, Gary
Born West Bromwich 12.6.66. Ht 5 9
Wt 11 07
Forward.

1986–87	Southampton	—	—
1987–88	....	—	—
1987–88	Cambridge U	9	3
1988–89	....	10	1
To Barnet			
1991–92	Barnet	42	20
1992–93	....	41	17
1993–94	Nottingham F	11	—

BULL, Steve
Born Tipton 28.3.65. Ht 5 11 Wt 11 04
Forward. From Apprentice. England
Under-21, B, 13 full caps.

1985–86	WBA	1	—
1986–87	....	3	2
1986–87	Wolverhampton W	30	14
1987–88	....	44	34
1988–89	....	45	37
1989–90	....	42	24
1990–91	....	43	26
1991–92	....	43	20
1992–93	....	36	16
1993–94	....	27	14

BULLIMORE, Wayne
Born Sutton-in-Ashfield 12.9.70. Ht 5 9
Wt 10 06
Midfield. From Trainee. FA Schools.

1988–89	Manchester U	—	—
1989–90	....	—	—
1990–91	....	—	—
1990–91	Barnsley	—	—
1991–92	....	18	1
1992–93	....	17	—
1993–94	....	—	—
1993–94	Stockport Co	—	—
1993–94	Scunthorpe U	18	3

BULLOCK, Darren
Born Worcester 12.2.69   Ht 5 8   Wt 12 04
Midfield. From Nuneaton.

| 1993–94 | Huddersfield T | 20 | 3 |

BULLOCK, Martin
Born Derby 5.3.75   Ht 5 5   Wt 10 07
Forward. From Eastwood T.

| 1993–94 | Barnsley | — | — |

BUNBURY, Alex
Born British Guyana 18.6.67   Ht 5 10
Wt 11 00
Forward. From Montreal Supra. Canada
full caps.

| 1992–93 | West Ham U | 4 | — |
| 1993–94 | | — | — |

To Maritimo

BURCHELL, Lee
Born Birmingham 12.11.76   Ht 5 7
Wt 10 06
Midfield. From Trainee.

| 1993–94 | Aston Villa | — | — |

BURGESS, Daryl
Born Birmingham 20.4.71.   Ht 5 11
Wt 12 03
Defender. From Trainee.

1989–90	WBA	34	—
1990–91		25	—
1991–92		36	2
1992–93		18	1
1993–94		43	2

BURGESS, Dave
Born Liverpool. 20.1.60.   Ht 5 10
Wt 11 04
Defender. From Local.

1981–82	Tranmere R	46	1
1982–83		46	—
1983–84		44	—
1984–85		41	—
1985–86		41	—
1986–87	Grimsby T	31	—
1987–88		38	—
1988–89	Blackpool	46	—

1989–90		19	1
1990–91		—	—
1991–92		16	—
1992–93		20	—
1992–93	*Carlisle U*	6	—
1993–94	Carlisle U	40	1

BURKE, David
Born Liverpool 6.8.60.   Ht 5 10   Wt 11 00
Defender. From Apprentice. England
Youth.

1977–78	Bolton W	—	—
1978–79		20	1
1979–80		27	—
1980–81		22	—
1981–82	Huddersfield T	41	1
1982–83		44	1
1983–84		42	—
1984–85		31	1
1985–86		—	—
1986–87		21	—
1987–88		10	—
1987–88	Crystal Palace	31	—
1988–89		39	—
1989–90		11	—
1990–91	Bolton W	14	—
1991–92		37	—
1992–93		43	—
1993–94		12	—

BURKE, Mark
Born Solihull 12.2.69.   Ht 5 10   Wt 11 08
Forward. From Apprentice. England
Youth.

1986–87	Aston Villa	1	—
1987–88		6	—
1987–88	Middlesbrough	16	—
1988–89		29	5
1989–90		12	1
1990–91		—	—
1990–91	*Darlington*	5	1
1990–91	*Ipswich T*	—	—
1990–91	Wolverhampton W	6	—
1991–92		18	2
1992–93		32	8
1993–94		12	1
1993–94	*Luton T*	3	—

BURKE, Raphael
Born Bristol 3.7.74   Ht 5 8   Wt 10 07
Forward. From Trainee.

Season	Club		
1992–93	Manchester U	—	—
1993–94	Bristol C	—	—

BURLEY, Craig
Born Ayr 24.9.71.   Ht 6 1   Wt 11 07
Midfield. From Trainee. Scotland
Under-21.

Season	Club		
1989–90	Chelsea	—	—
1990–91		1	—
1991–92		8	—
1992–93		3	—
1993–94		23	3

BURLEY, George
Born Cumnock 3.6.56   Ht 5 10   Wt 11 0
Defender. Apprentice. Scotland Schools,
Youth, Under-21, Under-23, 11 full caps.

Season	Club		
1973–74	Ipswich T	20	—
1974–75		31	—
1975–76		42	—
1976–77		40	2
1977–78		31	1
1978–79		38	1
1979–80		38	—
1980–81		23	—
1981–82		29	—
1982–83		31	1
1983–84		28	—
1984–85		37	—
1985–86		6	—
1985–86	Sunderland	27	—
1986–87		27	—
1987–88		—	—
1988–89	Gillingham	46	2
1989–90	Motherwell	34	—
1990–91		20	—
1990–91	Ayr U	12	—
1991–92		9	—
1992–93		33	—
1993–94		13	—
1993–94	Falkirk	1	—
1993–94	Motherwell	5	—

BURNETT, Wayne
Born London 4.9.71.   Ht 5 9   Wt 10 11
Midfield. From Trainee.

Season	Club		
1989–90	Leyton Orient	3	—
1990–91		1	—
1991–92		36	—
1992–93	Blackburn R	—	—
1993–94	Plymouth Arg	32	2

BURNHAM, Jason
Born Mansfield 8.5.73.   Ht 5 10   Wt 11 07
Defender. From Notts County Trainee,
Northampton T Trainee.

Season	Club		
1991–92	Northampton T	40	2
1992–93		31	—
1993–94		17	—

BURNS, Alex
Born Bellshill 4.8.73   Ht 5 8   Wt 10 0
Midfield. Shotts Bon-Accord.

Season	Club		
1992–93	Motherwell	—	—
1993–94		4	1

BURNS, Chris
Born Manchester 9.11.67.   Ht 6 0
Wt 12 00
Midfield. From Cheltenham T.

Season	Club		
1990–91	Portsmouth	—	—
1991–92		46	8
1992–93		32	1
1993–94		12	—
1993–94	*Swansea C*	4	—
1993–94	*Bournemouth*	14	1

BURNS, Tommy
Born Glasgow 16.2.56   Ht 5 11   Wt 11 3
Midfield. From Maryhill J. Scotland U-21,
8 full caps.

Season	Club		
1974–75	Celtic	1	—
1975–76		5	—
1976–77		22	1
1977–78		23	3
1978–79		29	3
1979–80		15	—
1980–81		33	4
1981–82		33	9
1982–83		17	7
1983–84		33	9

Season	Club	League Appearances/Goals	
1984–85	....	27	7
1985–86	....	34	5
1986–87	....	17	—
1987–88	....	27	2
1988–89	....	32	2
1989–90	....	9	—
1989–90	Kilmarnock	22	3
1990–91	....	37	8
1991–92	....	41	3
1992–93	....	39	2
1993–94	....	12	—

BURRIDGE, John
Born Workington 3.12.51.   Ht 5 11
Wt 13 03
Goalkeeper. From Apprentice.

Season	Club		
1968–69	Workington	1	—
1969–70	....	—	—
1970–71	....	26	—
1970–71	Blackpool	3	—
1971–72	....	34	—
1972–73	....	22	—
1973–74	....	30	—
1974–75	....	38	—
1975–76	....	7	—
1975–76	Aston Villa	30	—
1976–77	....	35	—
1977–78	....	—	—
1977–78	*Southend U*	6	—
1977–78	Crystal Palace	10	—
1978–79	....	42	—
1979–80	....	36	—
1980–81	....	—	—
1980–81	QPR	19	—
1981–82	....	20	—
1982–83	Wolverhampton W	42	—
1983–84	....	32	—
1984–85	....	—	—
1984–85	*Derby Co*	6	—
1984–85	Sheffield U	30	—
1985–86	....	42	—
1986–87	....	37	—
1987–88	Southampton	31	—
1988–89	....	31	—
1989–90	....	—	—
1989–90	Newcastle U	28	—
1990–91	....	39	—
1991–92	Hibernian	35	—
1992–93	....	30	—

Season	Club		
1993–94	Newcastle U	—	—
1993–94	Scarborough	3	—
1993–94	Lincoln C	4	—
1993–94	Aberdeen	3	—

BURROWS, Adrian
Born Sutton 16.1.59.   Ht 5 11   Wt 11 12
Defender. From Local.

Season	Club		
1979–80	Mansfield T	17	—
1980–81	....	20	3
1981–82	....	41	2
1982–83	Northampton T	43	4
1983–84	....	45	—
1984–85	Plymouth Arg	39	—
1985–86	....	7	2
1986–87	....	17	1
1987–88	....	23	1
1987–88	*Southend U*	6	—
1988–89	Plymouth Arg	43	1
1989–90	....	46	1
1990–91	....	45	4
1991–92	....	15	3
1992–93	....	20	1
1993–94	....	22	—

BURROWS, David
Born Dudley 25.10.68.   Ht 5 10   Wt 11 08
Defender. From Apprentice. England B,
Under-21.

Season	Club		
1985–86	WBA	1	—
1986–87	....	15	1
1987–88	....	21	—
1988–89	....	9	—
1988–89	Liverpool	21	—
1989–90	....	26	—
1990–91	....	35	—
1991–92	....	30	1
1992–93	....	30	2
1993–94	....	4	—
1993–94	West Ham U	25	1

BURTON, Deon
Born Ashford 25.10.76
Forward. From Trainee.

Season	Club		
1993–94	Portsmouth	2	—

BURTON, Mark
Born Barnsley 7.5.73 Ht 5 8 Wt 11 07
Midfield. From Trainee.

Season	Club		
1991–92	Barnsley	—	—
1992–93		5	—
1993–94		—	—

BURTON, Nick
Born Bury St Edmunds 2.10.75 Ht 5 11
Wt 11 12
Defender. From Portsmouth trainee.

Season	Club		
1993–94	Torquay U	8	2

BURTON, Simon
Born Bolton 29.12.73 Ht 5 10 Wt 10 04
Forward. From Trainee.

Season	Club		
1992–93	Preston NE	21	3
1993–94		3	—

BUSHELL, Steve
Born Manchester 28.12.72. Ht 5 9
Wt 11 00
Midfield. From Trainee.

Season	Club		
1990–91	York C	15	—
1991–92		16	—
1992–93		8	—
1993–94		31	4

BUSST, Dave
Born Birmingham 30.6.67 Ht 6 1
Wt 12 10
Defender. From Moor Green.

Season	Club		
1991–92	Coventry C	—	—
1992–93		10	—
1993–94		3	—

BUTLER, John
Born Liverpool 7.2.62. Ht 5 11 Wt 11 07
Defender. From Prescot Cables.

Season	Club		
1981–82	Wigan Ath	1	—
1982–83		40	5
1983–84		41	3
1984–85		45	3
1985–86		36	—
1986–87		36	—
1987–88		26	1
1988–89		20	3

Season	Club		
1988–89	Stoke C	25	1
1989–90		44	—
1990–91		31	2
1991–92		42	3
1992–93		44	1
1993–94		35	—

BUTLER, Lee
Born Sheffield 30.5.66. Ht 6 2 Wt 14 02
Goalkeeper. From Haworth Colliery.

Season	Club		
1986–87	Lincoln C	30	—
1987–88	Aston Villa	—	—
1988–89		4	—
1989–90		—	—
1990–91		4	—
1990–91	*Hull C*	4	—
1991–92	Barnsley	43	—
1992–93		28	—
1993–94		37	—

BUTLER, Martin
Born Wordsley 15.9.74 Ht 5 10
Wt 10 12
Forward. From Trainee.

Season	Club		
1993–94	Walsall	15	3

BUTLER, Neal
Born Newport Pagnall 11.9.75
Midfield. From Luton T trainee.

Season	Club		
1993–94	Colchester U	—	—

BUTLER, Paul
Born Bradford 2.11.72. Ht 6 2 Wt 13 00
Defender. From Trainee.

Season	Club		
1990–91	Rochdale	2	—
1991–92		25	—
1992–93		16	2
1993–94		38	2

BUTLER, Peter
Born Halifax 27.8.66. Ht 5 9 Wt 11 02
Midfield. From Apprentice.

Season	Club		
1984–85	Huddersfield T	4	—
1985–86		1	—
1985–86	*Cambridge U*	14	1
1986–87	Bury	11	—
1986–87	Cambridge U	29	4
1987–88		26	5

Season	Club		App	Goals
1987–88	Southend U		15	3
1988–89			35	2
1989–90			41	2
1990–91			42	2
1991–92			9	—
1991–92	*Huddersfield T*		7	—
1992–93	West Ham U		39	2
1993–94			26	1

BUTLER, Steve

Born Birmingham 27.1.62.   Ht 6 2
Wt 13 00
Forward. From Windsor and Eton,
Wokingham.

1984–85	Brentford		3	1
1985–86			18	2
To Maidstone U (1986)				
1989–90			44	21
1990–91			32	20
1990–91	Watford		10	1
1991–92			43	8
1992–93			9	—
1992–93	*Bournemouth*		1	—
1992–93	Cambridge U		23	6
1993–94			33	21

BUTLER, Tony

Born Stockport 28.9.72.   Ht 6 2   Wt 11 12
Defender. From Trainee.

1990–91	Gillingham		6	—
1991–92			5	—
1992–93			41	—
1993–94			27	1

BUTT, Nicky

Born Manchester 21.1.75   Ht 5 10
Wt 11 00
Midfield. From Trainee. England Youth.

1992–93	Manchester U		1	—
1993–94			1	—

BUTTERFIELD, Tim

Born Sheffield 18.10.74   Ht 5 11
Midfield. From Trainee.

1993–94	Sheffield U		—	—

BUTTERS, Guy

Born Hillingdon 30.10.69.   Ht 6 3
Wt 13 00
Defender. From Trainee. England
Under-21.

1988–89	Tottenham H		28	1
1989–90			7	—
1989–90	*Southend U*		16	3
1990–91	Portsmouth		23	—
1991–92			33	2
1992–93			15	1
1993–94			15	1

BUTTERWORTH, Ian

Born Crewe 25.1.65.   Ht 6 1   Wt 12 10
Defender. From Apprentice. England
Under-21.

1981–82	Coventry C		14	—
1982–83			30	—
1983–84			24	—
1984–85			22	—
1985–86	Nottingham F		23	—
1986–87			4	—
1986–87	Norwich C		28	—
1987–88			35	—
1988–89			37	2
1989–90			22	—
1990–91			31	—
1991–92			31	1
1992–93			26	1
1993–94			25	—

BYFIELD, Darren

Born Birmingham 29.9.76   Ht 5 10
Wt 11 00
Forward. From Trainee.

1993–94	Aston Villa		—	—

BYNG, David

Born Coventry 9.7.77
Forward. From Trainee.

1993–94	Torquay U		3	2

BYRNE, Chris

Born Manchester 9.2.75   Ht 5 9   Wt 10 08
Midfield. From Trainee.

1993–94	Crewe Alex		—	—

BYRNE, David

Born London 5.3.61.   Ht 5 8   Wt 10 09
Forward. From Kingstonian.

Season	Club		
1985–86	Gillingham	23	3
1986–87	Millwall	40	4
1987–88		23	2
1988–89		—	—
1988–89	*Cambridge U*	4	—
1988–89	*Blackburn R*	4	—
1988–89	Plymouth Arg	13	1
1989–90		32	1
1989–90	*Bristol R*	2	—
1990–91	Plymouth Arg	14	—
1990–91	Watford	17	2
1991–92		—	—
1991–92	*Reading*	7	2
1991–92	*Fulham*	5	—
1992–93	St Johnstone	12	—
1993–94	Partick T	23	—
1993–94	*Walsall*	5	—

BYRNE, John

Born Manchester 1.2.61.   Ht 5 11
Wt 13 01
Forward. From Apprentice. Eire 23 full
caps.

Season	Club		
1978–79	York C	—	—
1979–80		9	2
1980–81		38	6
1981–82		29	6
1982–83		43	12
1983–84		46	27
1984–85		10	2
1984–85	QPR	23	3
1985–86		36	12
1986–87		40	11
1987–88		27	4
From Le Havre			
1990–91	Brighton	38	9
1991–92		13	5
1991–92	Sunderland	27	7
1992–93		6	1
1992–93	Millwall	13	1
1992–93	*Brighton*	7	2
1993–94	Millwall	4	—
1993–94	Oxford U	30	7

BYRNE, Paul

Born Dublin 30.6.72   Ht 5 11   Wt 13 0
Midfield. From Trainee. Eire Youth.

Season	Club		
1989–90	Oxford U	3	—
1990–91		2	—
1991–92		1	—
From Bangor			
1993–94	Celtic	22	2

BYRNE, Ray

Born Newry 4.7.72.   Ht 6 1   Wt 11 02
Defender. From Newry.

Season	Club		
1991–92	Nottingham F	—	—
1992–93		—	—
1993–94		—	—

BYRNE, Wesley

Born Dublin 9.2.77
Defender. From Trainee.

Season	Club		
1993–94	Middlesbrough	—	—

CABLE, Marc

Born Dartford 18.9.74   Ht 5 11   Wt 11 02
Defender. From Trainee.

Season	Club	Apps	Goals
1993–94	Wimbledon	—	—

CADETTE, Richard

Born Hammersmith 21.3.65.   Ht 5 8
Wt 11 07
Forward. From Wembley.

Season	Club	Apps	Goals
1984–85	Orient	21	4
1985–86	Southend U	44	24
1986–87		46	24
1987–88	Sheffield U	28	7
1988–89	Brentford	32	12
1989–90		16	1
1989–90	*Bournemouth*	8	1
1990–91	Brentford	28	6
1991–92		11	1
1991–92	Falkirk	14	3
1992–93		31	8
1993–94		39	18

CAIG, Anthony

Born Whitehaven 11.4.74   Ht 6 1
Wt 13 05
Goalkeeper. From Trainee.

Season	Club	Apps	Goals
1992–93	Carlisle U	1	—
1993–94		20	—

CAIRNS, Darren

Born Glasgow 1.9.74   Ht 5 10   Wt 11 02
Midfield. From Trainee.

Season	Club	Apps	Goals
1992–93	Hull C	—	—
1993–94		—	—

CALDERWOOD, Colin

Born Stranraer 20.1.65.   Ht 6 0   Wt 12 00
Defender. From Amateur. Football
League.

Season	Club	Apps	Goals
1981–82	Mansfield T	1	—
1982–83		28	—
1983–84		30	1
1984–85		41	—
1985–86	Swindon T	46	2
1986–87		46	1
1987–88		34	1
1988–89		43	4
1989–90		46	3
1990–91		23	2
1991–92		46	5
1992–93		46	2
1993–94	Tottenham H	26	—

CALDWELL, Peter

Born Dorchester 5.6.72.   Ht 6 1   Wt 13 00
Goalkeeper. From Trainee.

Season	Club	Apps	Goals
1991–92	QPR	—	—
1992–93		—	—
1993–94		—	—

CALLAGHAN, Aaron

Born Dublin 8.10.66.   Ht 5 11   Wt 11 02
Defender. From Apprentice. Eire Youth,
Under-21.

Season	Club	Apps	Goals
1984–85	Stoke C	5	—
1985–86		—	—
1985–86	*Crewe Alex*	8	—
1986–87	Stoke C	2	—
1986–87	Oldham Ath	5	—
1987–88		11	2
1988–89	Crewe Alex	41	4
1989–90		41	2
1990–91		39	—
1991–92		37	—
1992–93	Preston NE	35	2
1993–94		1	—

CALVERT, Mark

Born Consett 11.9.70.   Ht 5 9   Wt 11 05
Forward. From Trainee.

Season	Club	Apps	Goals
1988–89	Hull C	5	—
1989–90		—	—
1990–91		7	—
1991–92		11	1
1992–93		7	—
1993–94	Scarborough	42	3

CAME, Mark

Born Exeter 14.9.61.   Ht 6 0   Wt 12 13
Defender. From Winsford U.

Season	Club	Apps	Goals
1983–84	Bolton W	—	—
1984–85		23	1
1985–86		35	1
1986–87		43	—
1987–88		43	5
1988–89		2	—
1989–90		19	—

Season	Club	Apps	Goals
1990–91		8	—
1991–92		18	—
1992–93		4	—
1992–93	Chester C	17	—
1993–94		30	1

CAMERON, Colin

Born Kirkcaldy 23.10.72 Ht 5 6 Wt 9 6
Forward. From Lochore Welfare.

Season	Club	Apps	Goals
1990–91	Raith R	—	—
1991–92	*Sligo R*	—	—
1992–93	Raith R	16	1
1993–94		41	6

CAMERON, Ian

Born Glasgow 24.8.66. Ht 5 9 Wt 10 04
Midfield. 'S' Form. Scotland Schools,
Youth.

Season	Club	Apps	Goals
1983–84	St Mirren	8	—
1984–85		9	1
1985–86		12	—
1986–87		31	6
1987–88		41	8
1988–89		26	2
1989–90	Aberdeen	11	—
1990–91		10	1
1991–92		6	—
1992–93	Partick T	41	5
1993–94		41	1

CAMPBELL, Calum

Born Erskine 7.11.65 Ht 6 1 Wt 12 0
Forward. From Kilbirnie Ladeside.

Season	Club	Apps	Goals
1987–88	Airdrieonians	42	15
1988–89		36	14
1989–90	Partick T	34	18
1990–91		26	4
1990–91	Kilmarnock	7	4
1991–92		38	10
1992–93		24	4
1993–94		1	—

CAMPBELL, Dave

Born Eglinton 2.6.65 Ht 5 10 Wt 11 02
Midfield. From Oxford BC (Northern
Ireland). Northern Ireland 10 caps.

Season	Club	Apps	Goals
1983–84	Nottingham F	—	—
1984–85		1	—

Season	Club	Apps	Goals
1985–86		18	3
1986–87		14	—
1986–87	*Notts Co*	18	2
1987–88	Nottingham F	8	—
1987–88	Charlton Ath	21	1
1988–89		9	—
1988–89	*Plymouth Arg*	1	—
1988–89	Bradford C	12	1
1989–90		23	3
1990–91		—	—
1990–91	*Shamrock R*	9	3
1991–92		22	2
1991–92	Bradford C	—	—
1992–93	WBA	—	—
1992–93	Rotherham U	1	—
1992–93	Burnley	8	—
1993–94		—	—
1993–94	*Lincoln C*	4	1

CAMPBELL, Jamie

Born Birmingham 21.10.72. Ht 6 1
Wt 11 03
Forward. From Trainee.

Season	Club	Apps	Goals
1991–92	Luton T	11	—
1992–93		9	1
1993–94		16	—

CAMPBELL, Kevin

Born Lambeth 4.2.70. Ht 6 1 Wt 13 08
Forward. From Trainee. England Under-
21, B.

Season	Club	Apps	Goals
1987–88	Arsenal	1	—
1988–89		—	—
1988–89	*Leyton Orient*	16	9
1989–90	Arsenal	15	2
1989–90	*Leicester C*	11	5
1990–91	Arsenal	22	9
1991–92		31	13
1992–93		37	4
1993–94		37	14

CAMPBELL, Sean

Born Bristol 31.12.74
Forward. From Trainee.

Season	Club	Apps	Goals
1993–94	Colchester U	4	—

CAMPBELL, Sol
Born Newham 18.9.74 Ht 6 0 Wt 12 00
Defender. From Trainee. England Youth,
Under-21.

Season	Club	Apps	Goals
1992–93	Tottenham H	1	1
1993–94		34	—

CAMPBELL, Stuart
Born Bexley 2.1.75 Ht 5 9 Wt 10 07
Defender. From Trainee.

Season	Club	Apps	Goals
1993–94	Arsenal	—	—

CANHAM, Scott
Born London 5.11.74 Ht 5 7 Wt 11 07
Midfield. From Trainee.

Season	Club	Apps	Goals
1993–94	West Ham U	—	—

CANHAM, Tony
Born Leeds 8.6.60. Ht 5 8 Wt 11 05
Midfield. From Harrogate Railway.

Season	Club	Apps	Goals
1984–85	York C	3	1
1985–86		41	13
1986–87		38	9
1987–88		18	2
1988–89		41	9
1989–90		34	4
1990–91		41	5
1991–92		31	5
1992–93		29	4
1993–94		36	3

CANTONA, Eric
Born Paris 24.5.66 Ht 6 1 Wt 12 10
Forward. France full caps.

Season	Club	Apps	Goals
1983–84	Auxerre	2	—
1984–85		4	2
1985–86		7	—
1985–86	Martigues	—	—
1986–87	Auxerre	36	13
1987–88		32	8
1988–89	Marseille	22	5
1988–89	Bordeaux	11	6
1989–90	Montpellier	33	10
1990–91	Marseille	18	8
1991–92	Nimes	17	2
1991–92	Leeds U	15	3
1992–93		13	6
1992–93	Manchester U	22	9

Season	Club	Apps	Goals
1993–94		34	18

CANTONA, Joel
Born Paris 26.10.67 Ht 5 10
Midfield. From Ujpest Dozsa.

Season	Club	Apps	Goals
1993–94	Stockport Co	3	—

CAPLETON, Mel
Born London 24.10.73 Ht 5 11 Wt 12 00
Goalkeeper.

Season	Club	Apps	Goals
1992–93	Southend U	—	—
1993–94	Blackpool	—	—

CARBON, Matthew
Born Nottingham 8.6.75 Ht 6 2
Wt 11 13
Defender. From Trainee.

Season	Club	Apps	Goals
1992–93	Lincoln C	1	—
1993–94		9	—

CARBONE, Anthony
Born Perth 13.10.74 Ht 5 10 Wt 11 06
Midfield. From Perth Italia.

Season	Club	Apps	Goals
1993–94	Nottingham F	—	—

CAREY, Alan
Born Greenwich 21.8.75
Defender. From Trainee.

Season	Club	Apps	Goals
1993–94	Reading	1	—

CAREY, Brian
Born Cork 31.5.68. Ht 6 3 Wt 11 13
Defender. From Cork C. Eire 3 full caps.

Season	Club	Apps	Goals
1989–90	Manchester U	—	—
1990–91		—	—
1990–91	*Wrexham*	3	—
1991–92	Manchester U	—	—
1991–92	*Wrexham*	13	1
1992–93	Manchester U	—	—
1993–94	Leicester C	27	—

CARMICHAEL, David
Born Immingham 5.3.75
Forward. From Trainee.

Season	Club	Apps	Goals
1993–94	Coventry C	—	—

CARMICHAEL, Matt

Born Singapore 13.5.64. Ht 6 2
Wt 11 07
Forward. From Army.

Season	Club		
1989–90	Lincoln C	26	5
1990–91		26	2
1991–92		40	7
1992–93		41	4
1993–94	Scunthorpe U	42	18

CARPENTER, Richard

Born Sheppey 30.9.72. Ht 5 10 Wt 13 00
Midfield. From Trainee.

Season	Club		
1990–91	Gillingham	9	1
1991–92		3	—
1992–93		28	—
1993–94		40	3

CARR, Cliff

Born London 19.6.64. Ht 5 8 Wt 10 12
Midfield. From Apprentice. England
Under-21.

Season	Club		
1982–83	Fulham	6	1
1983–84		41	4
1984–85		38	4
1985–86		35	4
1986–87		25	1
1987–88	Stoke C	41	—
1988–89		41	1
1989–90		22	—
1990–91		20	—
1991–92	Shrewsbury T	1	1
1991–92	Mansfield T	20	—
1992–93	Chesterfield	42	1
1993–94		23	—

CARR, Darren

Born Bristol 4.9.68. Ht 6 2 Wt 13 00
Defender.

Season	Club		
1985–86	Bristol R	1	—
1986–87		20	—
1987–88		9	—
1987–88	Newport Co	9	—
1987–88	Sheffield U	3	—
1988–89		10	1
1989–90		—	—
1990–91		—	—
1990–91	Crewe Alex	36	—

1991–92		36	3
1992–93		32	2
1993–94	Chesterfield	28	1

CARR, Franz

Born Preston 24.9.66. Ht 5 7 Wt 10 12
Midfield. From Apprentice. England
Schools, Youth, Under-21.

Season	Club		
1984–85	Blackburn R	—	—
1985–86	Nottingham F	23	3
1986–87		36	4
1987–88		22	4
1988–89		23	3
1989–90		14	1
1989–90	*Sheffield W*	12	—
1990–91	Nottingham F	13	2
1990–91	*West Ham U*	3	—
1991–92	Newcastle U	15	2
1992–93		10	1
1992–93	Sheffield U	8	3
1993–94		10	1

CARR, Stephen

Born Dublin 29.8.76 Ht 5 9
Defender. From Trainee.

Season	Club		
1993–94	Tottenham H	1	—

CARRAGHER, Matthew

Born Liverpool 14.1.76 Ht 5 9 Wt 10 07
Defender. From Trainee.

Season	Club		
1993–94	Wigan Ath	32	—

CARROLL, Dave

Born Paisley 20.9.66 Ht 6 0 Wt 12 00
Midfield. From Ruislip Manor.

Season	Club		
1993–94	Wycombe W	41	6

CARRUTHERS, Martin

Born Nottingham 7.8.72. Ht 5 11
Wt 11 07
Forward. From Trainee.

Season	Club		
1990–91	Aston Villa	—	—
1991–92		3	—
1992–93		1	—
1992–93	*Hull C*	13	6

1993–94	Stoke C	34	5

CARSLEY, Lee
Born Birmingham 28.2.74   Ht 5 10
Wt 11 11
Defender.

1992–93	Derby Co	—	—
1993–94		—	—

CARSON, Tom
Born Alexandria 26.3.59   Ht 6 0   Wt 12 0
Goalkeeper. From Vale of Leven.

1978–79	Dumbarton	—	—
1979–80		3	—
1980–81		33	—
1981–82		39	—
1982–83		37	—
1983–84		37	—
1984–85	Dundee	20	—
1985–86		—	—
1986–87	*Hibernian*	2	—
1987–88	*Partick T*	6	—
1987–88	*Queen of the S*	7	—
1987–88	*Dunfermline Ath*	5	—
1987–88	*Ipswich T*	1	—
1987–88	Dundee	6	—
1988–89		2	—
1989–90		16	—
1990–91		33	—
1991–92		—	—
1991–92	*Dumbarton*	6	—
1992–93	Raith R	27	—
1993–94		8	—

CARSTAIRS, Jim
Born St. Andrews 29.1.71.   Ht 6 0
Wt 12 05
Defender. From Trainee.

1988–89	Arsenal	—	—
1989–90		—	—
1990–91		—	—
1990–91	*Brentford*	8	—
1991–92	Cambridge U	—	—
1991–92	Stockport C	20	—
1992–93		14	1
1993–94		—	—

CARTER, Danny
Born Hackney 29.6.69.   Ht 5 11
Wt 11 12
Midfield. From Billericay.

1988–89	Leyton Orient	1	—
1989–90		31	5
1990–91		42	5
1991–92		20	2
1992–93		29	3
1993–94		36	7

CARTER, Ian
Born Birmingham 20.9.67
Defender. Canada full caps.

1993–94	Peterborough U	11	—

CARTER, Jimmy
Born London 9.11.65.   Ht 5 10   Wt 11 01
Midfield. From Apprentice.

1983–84	Crystal Palace	—	—
1984–85		—	—
1985–86	QPR	—	—
1986–87	Millwall	12	1
1987–88		26	—
1988–89		20	5
1989–90		28	2
1990–91		24	2
1990–91	Liverpool	5	—
1991–92		—	—
1991–92	Arsenal	6	—
1992–93		16	2
1993–94		—	—
1993–94	*Oxford U*	5	—

CARTER, Mark
Born Liverpool 17.12.60.   Ht 5 9
Wt 11 06
Forward. From S. Liverpool, Bangor C, Runcorn.

1991–92	Barnet	36	19
1992–93		41	11
1993–94		5	—
1993–94	Bury	36	20

CARTER, Tim

Born Bristol 5.10.67. Ht 6 2 Wt 13 11
Goalkeeper. From Apprentice. England
Youth.

Season	Club	App	Goals
1985–86	Bristol R	2	—
1986–87		38	—
1987–88		7	—
1987–88	*Newport Co*	1	—
1987–88	*Carlisle U*	4	—
1987–88	Sunderland	1	—
1988–89		2	—
1988–89	*Bristol C*	3	—
1989–90	Sunderland	18	—
1990–91		1	—
1991–92		2	—
1991–92	*Birmingham C*	2	—
1992–93	Sunderland	13	—
1993–94	Hartlepool U	18	—
1993–94	Millwall	2	—

CARTWRIGHT, Lee

Born Rawtenstall 19.9.72. Ht 5 8
Wt 10 06
Midfield. From Trainee.

Season	Club	App	Goals
1990–91	Preston NE	14	1
1991–92		33	4
1992–93		34	3
1993–94		39	1

CASCARINO, Tony

Born St Paul's Cray 1.9.62. Ht 6 2
Wt 13 12
Forward. From Crockenhill. Eire 50 full
caps.

Season	Club	App	Goals
1981–82	Gillingham	24	5
1982–83		38	15
1983–84		37	12
1984–85		43	16
1985–86		34	14
1986–87		43	16
1987–88	Millwall	39	20
1988–89		38	13
1989–90		28	9
1989–90	Aston Villa	10	2
1990–91		36	9
1991–92	Celtic	24	4
1991–92	Chelsea	11	2
1992–93		9	2
1993–94		20	4

CASE, Jimmy

Born Liverpool 18.5.54. Ht 5 9 Wt 12 08
Midfield. From Sth Liverpool. England
Under-23.

Season	Club	App	Goals
1973–74	Liverpool	—	—
1974–75		1	—
1975–76		27	6
1976–77		27	1
1977–78		33	5
1978–79		37	7
1979–80		37	3
1980–81		24	1
1981–82	Brighton	33	3
1982–83		35	3
1983–84		35	4
1984–85		24	—
1984–85	Southampton	10	1
1985–86		36	2
1986–87		39	3
1987–88		38	—
1988–89		34	—
1989–90		33	3
1990–91		25	1
1991–92	Bournemouth	40	1
1992–93	Halifax T	21	2
1992–93	Wrexham	4	—
1993–94	Darlington	1	—
From Sittingbourne			
1993–94	Brighton	21	—

CASH, Stuart

Born Tipton 5.9.65. Ht 5 10 Wt 11 11
Defender. From Halesowen.

Season	Club	App	Goals
1989–90	Nottingham F	—	—
1989–90	*Rotherham U*	8	1
1990–91	Nottingham F	—	—
1990–91	*Brentford*	11	—
1991–92	Nottingham F	—	—
1991–92	*Shrewsbury T*	8	1
1992–93	Chesterfield	23	—
1993–94		6	—

CASKEY, Darren

Born Basildon 21.8.74. Ht 5 8 Wt 11 09
Midfield. From Trainee.

Season	Club	App	Goals
1991–92	Tottenham H	—	—
1992–93		—	—
1993–94		25	4

CASPER, Chris
Born Burnley 28.4.75 Ht 5 11 Wt 10 09
Defender. From Trainee.

Season	Club		
1992–93	Manchester U	—	—
1993–94		—	—

CASTLE, Steve
Born Barkingside 17.5.66. Ht 5 11
Wt 12 05
Midfield. From Apprentice.

Season	Club		
1984–85	Orient	21	1
1985–86		23	4
1986–87		24	5
1987–88		42	10
1988–89		24	6
1989–90		27	7
1990–91		45	12
1991–92		37	10
1992–93	Plymouth Arg	31	11
1993–94		44	21

CASTLEDINE, Gary
Born Dumfries 27.3.70. Ht 5 8 Wt 11 04
Forward.

Season	Club		
1990–91	Mansfield T	—	—
1991–92		7	—
1992–93		28	3
1993–94		21	—

CASTLEDINE, Stewart
Born London 22.1.73. Ht 6 0 Wt 12 00
Midfield. From Trainee.

Season	Club		
1991–92	Wimbledon	2	—
1992–93		—	—
1993–94		3	1

CATLIN, Bob
Born London 22.6.65 Ht 6 2 Wt 14 00
Goalkeeper. From Marconi.

Season	Club		
1992–93	Notts Co	2	—
1992–93	*Birmingham C*	8	—
1993–94	Notts Co	1	—

CAWLEY, Peter
Born London 15.9.65. Ht 6 4 Wt 13 00
Defender. From Chertsey.

Season	Club		
1986–87	Wimbledon	—	—

Season	Club		
1986–87	*Bristol R*	10	—
1987–88	Wimbledon	—	—
1988–89		1	—
1988–89	*Fulham*	5	—
1989–90	Bristol R	3	—
1990–91	Southend U	7	1
1990–91	Exeter C	7	—
1991–92	Barnet	3	—
1992–93		—	—
1992–93	Colchester U	24	3
1993–94		36	1

CAWTHORN, Paul
Born Pontefract 26.5.75 Ht 5 6 Wt 10 00
Midfield. From Trainee.

Season	Club		
1992–93	Scarborough	3	—
1993–94		8	1

CECERE, Michele
Born Chester 4.1.68. Ht 6 0 Wt 11 04
Forward. From Apprentice.

Season	Club		
1985–86	Oldham Ath	—	—
1986–87		14	4
1987–88		25	2
1988–89		13	2
1988–89	Huddersfield T	31	4
1989–90		23	4
1989–90	*Stockport Co*	1	—
1990–91	Huddersfield T	—	—
1990–91	Walsall	32	6
1991–92		35	8
1992–93		39	16
1993–94		6	2
1993–94	Exeter C	2	—

CHALK, Martyn
Born Louth 30.8.69. Ht 5 6 Wt 10 00
Forward. From Louth U.

Season	Club		
1990–91	Derby Co	—	—
1991–92		7	1
1992–93		—	—
1993–94		—	—

CHALLENDER, Greg
Born Rochdale 5.2.73 Ht 6 0 Wt 12 08
Defender. From Mossley.

Season	Club		
1993–94	Preston NE	10	2

CHALMERS, Grant

Born Guernsey 12.9.69   Ht 5 10
Wt 11 10
Midfield. From Northerners.

1992–93	Brentford	11	1
1993–94		—	—
1993–94	Doncaster R	—	—

CHAMBERLAIN, Alec

Born March 20.6.64.   Ht 6 2   Wt 13 01
Goalkeeper. From Ramsey T.

1981–82	Ipswich T	—	—
1982–83	Colchester U	—	—
1983–84		46	—
1984–85		46	—
1985–86		46	—
1986–87		46	—
1987–88	Everton	—	—
1987–88	*Tranmere R*	15	—
1988–89	Luton T	6	—
1989–90		38	—
1990–91		38	—
1991–92		24	—
1992–93		32	—
1992–93	*Chelsea*	—	—
1993–94	Sunderland	43	—

CHAMBERLAIN, Mark

Born Stoke 19.11.61.   Ht 5 9   Wt 10 07
Forward. From Apprentice. England
Schools, Under-21, 8 full caps.

1978–79	Port Vale	8	—
1979–80		11	—
1980–81		31	9
1981–82		46	8
1982–83	Stoke C	37	6
1983–84		40	7
1984–85		28	1
1985–86		7	3
1985–86	Sheffield W	21	2
1986–87		24	5
1987–88		21	1
1988–89	Portsmouth	28	6
1989–90		38	6
1990–91		25	2
1991–92		16	1
1992–93		41	4
1993–94		19	1

CHANDLER, Dean

Born London 6.5.76   Ht 6 0   Wt 11 05
Defender. From Trainee.

| 1993–94 | Charlton Ath | — | — |

CHANNING, Justin

Born Reading 19.11.68.   Ht 5 11
Wt 11 07
Defender. From Apprentice. England
Youth.

1986–87	QPR	2	—
1987–88		14	1
1988–89		9	1
1989–90		23	2
1990–91		5	—
1991–92		—	—
1992–93		2	1
1992–93	Bristol R	25	3
1993–94		29	5

CHAPMAN, Daniel

Born Deptford 21.11.74
Midfield. From Trainee.

| 1992–93 | Millwall | — | — |
| 1993–94 | | — | — |

CHAPMAN, Gary

Born Bradford 1.5.64.   Ht 5 8   Wt 11 07
Forward. From Local.

1988–89	Bradford C	2	—
1989–90		3	—
1989–90	Notts Co	19	4
1990–91		6	—
1990–91	*Mansfield T*	6	—
1991–92	Notts Co	—	—
1991–92	Exeter C	20	4
1992–93		4	1
1992–93	Torquay U	8	—
1993–94	Darlington	41	7

CHAPMAN, Ian

Born Brighton 31.5.70.   Ht 5 9   Wt 12 05
Defender. FA Schools.

1986–87	Brighton	5	—
1987–88		—	—
1988–89		19	—
1989–90		42	1
1990–91		23	—

1991–92		37	2
1992–93		34	1
1993–94		45	3

CHAPMAN, Lee
Born Lincoln 5.12.59. Ht 6 2 Wt 13 00
Forward. From Amateur. England B, Under-21.

1978–79	Stoke C	—	—
1978–79	*Plymouth Arg*	4	—
1979–80	Stoke C	17	3
1980–81		41	15
1981–82		41	16
1982–83	Arsenal	19	3
1983–84		4	1
1983–84	Sunderland	15	3
1984–85	Sheffield W	40	15
1985–86		31	10
1986–87		41	19
1987–88		37	19
From Niort			
1988–89	Nottingham F	30	8
1989–90		18	7
1989–90	Leeds U	21	12
1990–91		38	21
1991–92		38	16
1992–93		40	13
1993–94	Portsmouth	5	2
1993–94	West Ham U	30	7

CHAPPLE, Phil
Born Norwich 26.11.66. Ht 6 2 Wt 12 07
Defender. From Apprentice.

1984–85	Norwich C	—	—
1985–86		—	—
1986–87		—	—
1987–88		—	—
1987–88	Cambridge U	6	1
1988–89		46	3
1989–90		45	5
1990–91		43	5
1991–92		29	3
1992–93		18	2
1993–94	Charlton Ath	44	5

CHAPPLE, Shaun
Born Swansea 14.2.73. Ht 5 11 Wt 12 03
Midfield. From Trainee. Wales Under-21.

| 1991–92 | Swansea C | 21 | 2 |

| 1992–93 | | 4 | — |
| 1993–94 | | 29 | 3 |

CHARD, Phil
Born Corby 16.10.60. Ht 5 8 Wt 11 03
Midfield. From Nottingham F. Amateur.

1978–79	Peterborough U	6	1
1979–80		20	2
1980–81		—	—
1981–82		39	3
1982–83		44	4
1983–84		38	7
1984–85		25	1
1985–86	Northampton T	41	7
1986–87		40	12
1987–88		34	8
1987–88	Wolverhampton W	9	2
1988–89		19	3
1989–90		6	—
1989–90	Northampton T	29	2
1990–91		43	7
1991–92		29	3
1992–93		34	6
1993–94		28	1

CHARLERY, Ken
Born Stepney 28.11.64. Ht 6 1 Wt 12 07
Forward. From Fisher Ath, Basildon U, Beckton U (1989).

1989–90	Maidstone U	30	2
1990–91		29	9
1990–91	Peterborough U	4	—
1991–92		37	16
1992–93		10	3
1992–93	Watford	32	11
1993–94		16	2
1993–94	Peterborough U	26	8

CHARLES, Gary
Born London 13.4.70. Ht 5 9 Wt 10 13
Defender. England Under-21, 2 full caps.

1987–88	Nottingham F	—	—
1988–89		1	—
1988–89	*Leicester C*	8	—
1989–90	Nottingham F	1	—
1990–91		10	—
1991–92		30	1
1992–93		14	—
1993–94	Derby Co	43	1

CHARLES, Steve

Born Sheffield 10.5.60. Ht 5 9 Wt 10 07
Midfield. From Sheffield University.
England Schools.

Season	Club		
1979–80	Sheffield U	14	1
1980–81		31	6
1981–82		30	1
1982–83		35	—
1983–84		11	1
1984–85		2	1
1984–85	Wrexham	32	7
1985–86		40	20
1986–87		41	10
1987–88	Mansfield T	46	12
1988–89		46	7
1989–90		43	7
1990–91		39	4
1991–92		40	6
1992–93		23	3
1992–93	*Scunthorpe U*	4	—
1992–93	Scarborough	16	3
1993–94		37	7

CHARLTON, Simon

Born Huddersfield 25.10.71. Ht 5 7
Wt 10 11
Defender. From Trainee. FA Schools.

Season	Club		
1989–90	Huddersfield T	3	—
1990–91		30	—
1991–92		45	—
1992–93		46	1
1993–94	Southampton	33	1

CHARNLEY, Chic

Born Glasgow 11.6.63 Ht 5 9 Wt 11 12
Midfield. Pollok Juniors.

Season	Club		
1987–88	Clydebank	28	10
1988–89		3	1
1988–89	Hamilton A	14	—
1988–89	Partick T	14	4
1989–90		29	11
1990–91		30	7
1991–92	St Mirren	26	4
1991–92	*Bolton W*	3	—
From Djurgaarden			
1993–94	Partick T	26	1

CHARNOCK, Phil

Born Southport 14.2.75 Ht 5 11
Wt 11 02
Midfield. From Trainee.

Season	Club		
1992–93	Liverpool	—	—
1993–94		—	—

CHEESEWRIGHT, John

Born Hornchurch 12.1.73. Ht 6 0
Wt 11 05
Goalkeeper. From Tottenham H. Trainee.

Season	Club		
1990–91	Southend U	—	—
1991–92	Birmingham C	1	—
From Braintree T			
1993–94	Colchester U	17	—

CHEETHAM, Michael

Born Amsterdam 30.6.67. Ht 5 11
Wt 11 05
Midfield. From Army.

Season	Club		
1988–89	Ipswich T	3	—
1989–90		1	—
1989–90	Cambridge U	36	10
1990–91		44	7
1991–92		22	3
1992–93		17	—
1993–94		13	2

CHERRILL, Matthew

Born Sheffield 10.10.73 Ht 5 10
Wt 11 12
Midfield. From Trainee.

Season	Club		
1992–93	Sheffield U	—	—
1993–94		—	—

CHERRY, Paul

Born Derby 14.10.64. Ht 6 0 Wt 11 07
Midfield. From Salvesen BC.

Season	Club		
1984–85	Hearts	3	—
1985–86		5	—
1986–87	Cowdenbeath	35	5
1987–88		35	8
1988–89	St Johnstone	39	2
1989–90		39	4
1990–91		20	—
1991–92		24	1
1992–93		16	1
1993–94		33	—

CHERRY, Steve
Born Nottingham 5.8.60. Ht 6 1
Wt 13 00
Goalkeeper. From Apprentice. England
Youth.

Season	Club	Apps	Goals
1977–78	Derby Co	—	—
1978–79		—	—
1979–80		4	—
1980–81	*Port Vale*	4	—
1981–82	Derby Co	4	—
1982–83		31	—
1983–84		38	—
1984–85	Walsall	41	—
1985–86		30	—
1986–87		—	—
1986–87	Plymouth Arg	21	—
1987–88		37	—
1988–89		15	—
1988–89	*Chesterfield*	10	—
1988–89	Notts Co	18	—
1989–90		46	—
1990–91		46	—
1991–92		42	—
1992–93		44	—
1993–94		45	—

CHETTLE, Steve
Born Nottingham 27.9.68. Ht 6 1
Wt 12 00
Defender. From Apprentice. England
Under-21.

Season	Club	Apps	Goals
1986–87	Nottingham F	—	—
1987–88		30	—
1988–89		28	2
1989–90		22	1
1990–91		37	2
1991–92		22	1
1992–93		30	—
1993–94		46	1

CHILDS, Gary
Born Birmingham 19.4.64. Ht 5 7
Wt 10 08
Midfield. From Apprentice. England
Youth.

Season	Club	Apps	Goals
1981–82	WBA	2	—
1982–83		—	—
1983–84		1	—
1983–84	Walsall	30	2

Season	Club	Apps	Goals
1984–85		40	2
1985–86		33	5
1986–87		28	8
1987–88	Birmingham C	32	1
1988–89		23	1
1989–90	Grimsby T	44	5
1990–91		25	4
1991–92		29	3
1992–93		17	—
1993–94		31	6

CHIVERS, Gary
Born Stockwell 15.5.60. Ht 5 11
Wt 11 05
Defender. From Apprentice.

Season	Club	Apps	Goals
1978–79	Chelsea	5	—
1979–80		29	2
1980–81		40	2
1981–82		29	—
1982–83		30	—
1983–84	Swansea C	10	—
1983–84	QPR	—	—
1984–85		23	—
1985–86		14	—
1986–87		23	—
1987–88	Watford	14	—
1987–88	Brighton	10	—
1988–89		46	6
1989–90		41	3
1990–91		39	3
1991–92		38	1
1992–93		43	—
1993–94	Bournemouth	26	2

CHRISTIE, David
Born Salford 26.2.73. Ht 6 1 Wt 12 00
Forward. From Trainee.

Season	Club	Apps	Goals
1991–92	Preston NE	2	—
1992–93		2	—
1992–93	Halifax T	9	—
1993–94	Bury	—	—

CHRISTIE, Max
Born Edinburgh 7.11.71. Ht 5 5
Wt 10 04
Midfield. From Hutcheson V. Scotland
Under-21.

Season	Club	Apps	Goals
1988–89	Hearts	—	—
1989–90		—	—

Season	Club	Apps	Goals
1990–91	....	—	—
1991–92	Meadowbank T	34	1
1991–92	Dundee....................	1	—
1992–93	....	3	—
1993–94	....	1	—

CLARIDGE, Steve
Born Portsmouth 10.4.66. Ht 5 11
Wt 11 08
Forward. From Portsmouth, Fareham.

Season	Club	Apps	Goals
1984–85	Bournemouth..............	6	1
1985–86	....	1	—
From Weymouth			
1988–89	Crystal Palace.............	—	—
1988–89	Aldershot	37	9
1989–90	....	25	10
1989–90	Cambridge U	20	4
1990–91	....	30	12
1991–92	....	29	12
1992–93	Luton T	16	2
1992–93	Cambridge U	29	7
1993–94	....	24	11
1993–94	Birmingham C............	18	7

CLARK, Billy
Born Christchurch 19.5.67. Ht 6 0
Wt 12 03
Defender. From Local.

Season	Club	Apps	Goals
1984–85	Bournemouth..............	1	—
1985–86	....	1	—
1986–87	....	—	—
1987–88	....	2	—
1987–88	Bristol R	31	1
1988–89	....	11	—
1989–90	....	—	—
1990–91	....	14	1
1991–92	....	24	1
1992–93	....	24	1
1993–94	....	36	1

CLARK, Howard
Born Coventry 19.9.68. Ht 5 11
Wt 11 01
Defender. From Apprentice.

Season	Club	Apps	Goals
1986–87	Coventry C	—	—
1987–88	....	—	—
1988–89	....	9	1
1989–90	....	9	—
1990–91	....	2	—

Season	Club	Apps	Goals
1991–92	....	—	—
1991–92	*Darlington*	5	—
1991–92	Shrewsbury T..............	23	—
1992–93	....	33	—
1993–94	Hereford U	37	6

CLARK, John
Born Edinburgh 22.9.64. Ht 6 0
Wt 13 01
Defender. 'S' Form. Scotland Youth.

Season	Club	Apps	Goals
1981–82	Dundee U	—	—
1982–83	....	1	—
1983–84	....	9	1
1984–85	....	10	3
1985–86	....	11	1
1986–87	....	30	3
1987–88	....	28	3
1988–89	....	20	2
1989–90	....	29	1
1990–91	....	18	2
1991–92	....	35	1
1992–93	....	37	2
1993–94	....	14	—
1993–94	Stoke C	12	—

CLARK, Lee
Born Wallsend 27.10.72. Ht 5 7
Wt 11 07
Midfield. From Trainee. England Youth,
Under-21.

Season	Club	Apps	Goals
1989–90	Newcastle U................	—	—
1990–91	....	19	2
1991–92	....	29	5
1992–93	....	46	9
1993–94	....	29	2

CLARK, Martin
Born Uddington 13.10.68. Ht 5 9
Wt 10 11
Defender. From Hamilton A.

Season	Club	Apps	Goals
1987–88	Clyde..........................	26	—
1988–89	....	25	2
1988–89	Nottingham F..............	—	—
1989–90	....	—	—
1989–90	*Falkirk*	3	1
1989–90	*Mansfield T*	14	1
1990–91	Mansfield T.................	24	—
1991–92	....	9	—
1992–93	Partick T.....................	8	—

1993–94 .... 11 —

CLARK, Martin
Born Accrington 12.9.70   Ht 5 10
Wt 10 06
Defender. From Accrington S.
1992–93 Crewe Alex .... — —
1993–94 .... — —

CLARK, Paul
Born Benfleet 14.9.58.   Ht 5 9   Wt 13 07
Midfield. From Apprentice. England
Schools, Youth.

1976–77	Southend U	25	—
1977–78		8	1
1977–78	Brighton	26	3
1978–79		33	4
1979–80		11	2
1980–81		9	—
1981–82	*Reading*	2	—
1982–83	Southend U	31	1
1983–84		20	—
1984–85		29	1
1985–86		39	1
1986–87		46	—
1987–88		30	—
1988–89		16	—
1989–90		25	—
1990–91		40	—
1991–92	Gillingham	42	—
1992–93		35	1
1993–94		13	—

CLARK, Richard
Born Nuneaton 6.4.77   Ht 5 11   Wt 12 04
Goalkeeper. From Trainee.
1993–94 Nottingham F .... — —

CLARK, Simon
Born Boston 12.3.67
Defender. From Boston U, Holbeach,
King's Lynn, Hendon, Stevenage Borough.
1993–94 Peterborough U .... 1 —

CLARK, Tim
Born Croydon 30.1.75
Midfield. From Trainee.
1993–94 Crystal Palace .... — —

CLARKE, Adrian
Born Suffolk 28.9.74   Ht 5 10   Wt 11 00
Forward. From Trainee.
1993–94 Arsenal .... — —

CLARKE, Andy
Born London 22.7.67.   Ht 5 10   Wt 11 07
Forward. From Barnet.

1990–91	Wimbledon	12	3
1991–92		34	3
1992–93		33	5
1993–94		23	2

CLARKE, Chris
Born Barnsley 1.5.74
Goalkeeper. From Trainee.
1992–93 Bolton W .... — —
1993–94 .... — —

CLARKE, David
Born Nottingham 3.12.64.   Ht 5 10
Wt 11 00
Midfield. From Apprentice. England
Youth.

1982–83	Notts Co	16	—
1983–84		20	—
1984–85		22	—
1985–86		42	1
1986–87		23	6
1987–88	Lincoln C	*30*	*5*
1988–89		36	4
1989–90		30	2
1990–91		15	—
1991–92		28	—
1992–93		31	2
1993–94		7	1
1993–94	Doncaster R	16	—

CLARKE, Dean
Born Hereford 28.7.77
Forward. From Trainee.
1993–94 Hereford U .... 1 —

CLARKE, Matthew
Born Sheffield 3.11.73   Ht 6 3   Wt 11 07
Goalkeeper. From Trainee.
1992–93 Rotherham U .... 9 —

64

Season	Club	Apps	Goals
1993–94		30	—

CLARKE, Nicky
Born Walsall 20.8.67.   Ht 5 11   Wt 13 11
Defender. From Apprentice.

Season	Club	Apps	Goals
1984–85	Wolverhampton W	—	—
1985–86		23	1
1986–87		24	—
1987–88		8	—
1988–89		8	—
1989–90		3	—
1990–91		14	—
1991–92		1	—
1991–92	Mansfield T	16	1
1992–93		12	1
1992–93	*Chesterfield*	7	—
1993–94	Mansfield T	15	3
1993–94	*Doncaster R*	5	—
From Bromsgrove R			
1993–94	*Preston NE*	—	—

CLARKE, Stephen
Born Saltcoats 29.8.63.   Ht 5 10
Wt 10 02
Defender. From Beith Juniors. Scotland
Youth, Under-21, B, 6 full caps. Football
League.

Season	Club	Apps	Goals
1981–82	St Mirren	—	—
1982–83		31	—
1983–84		33	2
1984–85		33	—
1985–86		31	3
1986–87		23	1
1986–87	Chelsea	16	—
1987–88		38	1
1988–89		36	—
1989–90		24	3
1990–91		18	1
1991–92		31	1
1992–93		20	—
1993–94		39	—

CLARKE, Tim
Born Stourbridge 19.9.68.   Ht 6 3
Wt 13 07
Goalkeeper. From Halesowen.

Season	Club	Apps	Goals
1990–91	Coventry C	—	—
1991–92	Huddersfield T	39	—
1992–93		31	—

Season	Club	Apps	Goals
1992–93	*Rochdale*	2	—
From Halesowen			
1993–94	Shrewsbury T	—	—

CLARKE, Wayne
Born Wolverhampton 28.2.61.   Ht 6 0
Wt 11 08
Forward. From Apprentice. England
Schools, Youth.

Season	Club	Apps	Goals
1977–78	Wolverhampton W	1	—
1978–79		8	1
1979–80		16	2
1980–81		24	3
1981–82		29	6
1982–83		39	12
1983–84		31	6
1984–85	Birmingham C	40	17
1985–86		28	5
1986–87		24	16
1986–87	Everton	10	5
1987–88		27	10
1988–89		20	3
1989–90	Leicester C	11	1
1989–90	Manchester C	9	—
1990–91		7	1
1990–91	*Shrewsbury T*	7	6
1990–91	*Stoke C*	9	3
1991–92	Manchester C	5	1
1991–92	*Wolverhampton W*	1	—
1992–93	Walsall	39	21
1993–94	Shrewsbury T	28	11

CLARKSON, Ian
Born Birmingham 4.12.70.   Ht 5 11
Wt 12 00
Defender. From Trainee.

Season	Club	Apps	Goals
1988–89	Birmingham C	9	—
1989–90		20	—
1990–91		37	—
1991–92		42	—
1992–93		28	—
1993–94		—	—
1993–94	Stoke C	14	—

CLARKSON, Phil
Born Hambleton 13.11.68.   Ht 5 10
Wt 10 08
Midfield. From Fleetwood.

Season	Club	Apps	Goals
1991–92	Crewe Alex	28	6

Season	Club	Apps	Goals
1992–93		35	13
1993–94		7	2

CLAYTON, Gary
Born Sheffield 2.2.63. Ht 5 11 Wt 12 08
Midfield. From Rotherham U Apprentice, Burton Alb.

Season	Club	Apps	Goals
1986–87	Doncaster R	35	5
1987–88	Cambridge U	45	5
1988–89		46	1
1989–90		10	1
1990–91		6	—
1990–91	*Peterborough U*	4	—
1991–92	Cambridge U	11	3
1992–93		36	3
1993–94		25	4
1993–94	Huddersfield T	17	1

CLELAND, Alec
Born Glasgow 10.12.70. Ht 5 8 Wt 10 00
Defender. From S Form. Scotland Under-21.

Season	Club	Apps	Goals
1987–88	Dundee U	1	—
1988–89		9	—
1989–90		15	—
1990–91		20	2
1991–92		31	4
1992–93		24	—
1993–94		33	1

CLEMENTS, Steve
Born Slough 26.9.72. Ht 5 10 Wt 11 10
Midfield. From Trainee.

Season	Club	Apps	Goals
1991–92	Arsenal	—	—
1992–93		—	—
1993–94	Hereford U	7	—

CLODE, Mark
Born Plymouth 24.2.73. Ht 5 6 Wt 9 06
Midfield. From Trainee.

Season	Club	Apps	Goals
1991–92	Plymouth Arg	—	—
1992–93		—	—
1993–94	Swansea C	28	1

CLOSE, Shaun
Born Islington 8.9.66. Ht 5 8 Wt 10 01
Forward. From Trainee.

Season	Club	Apps	Goals
1984–85	Tottenham H	—	—
1985–86		—	—
1986–87		2	—
1987–88		7	—
1987–88	Bournemouth	16	6
1988–89		23	2
1989–90		—	—
1989–90	Swindon T	11	—
1990–91		14	—
1991–92		12	1
1992–93		7	—
1993–94	Barnet	27	2

CLOUGH, Nigel
Born Sunderland 19.3.66. Ht 5 9
Wt 11 04
Forward. From AC Hunters England B, Under-21, 14 full caps.

Season	Club	Apps	Goals
1984–85	Nottingham F	9	1
1985–86		39	15
1986–87		42	14
1987–88		34	19
1988–89		36	14
1989–90		38	9
1990–91		37	14
1991–92		34	5
1992–93		42	10
1993–94	Liverpool	27	7

COATES, Jonathan
Born Swansea 27.6.75 Ht 5 8 Wt 10 04
Forward. From Trainee.

Season	Club	Apps	Goals
1993–94	Swansea C	4	1

COATSWORTH, Gary
Born Sunderland 7.10.68. Ht 6 0
Wt 13 02
Defender.

Season	Club	Apps	Goals
1986–87	Barnsley	—	—
1987–88		6	—
1988–89		—	—
1989–90	Darlington	*3*	*1*
1990–91		12	1
1991–92		10	1
1991–92	Leicester C	3	—
1992–93		10	2
1993–94		19	2

COCKERILL, Glenn
Born Grimsby 25.8.59. Ht 5 10 Wt 12 03
Midfield. From Louth U.

Season	Club		
1976–77	Lincoln C	4	—
1977–78		13	1
1978–79		35	6
1979–80		19	3
1979–80	Swindon T	10	1
1980–81		16	—
1981–82	Lincoln C	44	11
1982–83		38	8
1983–84		33	6
1983–84	Sheffield U	10	1
1984–85		40	7
1985–86		12	2
1985–86	Southampton	30	7
1986–87		42	7
1987–88		39	2
1988–89		34	6
1989–90		36	4
1990–91		32	2
1991–92		37	4
1992–93		23	—
1993–94		14	—
1993–94	Leyton Orient	19	2

CODNER, Robert
Born Walthamstow 23.1.65. Ht 5 11
Wt 11 08
Midfield. From Leicester C, Barnet.

Season	Club		
1988–89	Brighton	28	1
1989–90		45	9
1990–91		42	8
1991–92		45	6
1992–93		43	3
1993–94		40	8

COLCOMBE, Scott
Born West Bromwich 15.12.71. Ht 5 6
Wt 10 00
Midfield. From Trainee.

Season	Club		
1989–90	WBA	—	—
1990–91		—	—
1991–92	Torquay U	28	—
1992–93		24	1
1993–94		27	—

COLDICOTT, Stacy
Born Worcester 29.4.74 Ht 5 11
Wt 11 02
Defender. From Trainee.

Season	Club		
1991–92	WBA	—	—
1992–93		14	—
1993–94		5	—

COLE, Andy
Born Nottingham 15.10.71. Ht 5 11
Wt 11 02
Forward. From Trainee. England Youth,
Under-21. Football League.

Season	Club		
1989–90	Arsenal	—	—
1990–91		1	—
1991–92		—	—
1991–92	*Fulham*	13	3
1991–92	*Bristol C*	12	8
1992–93	Bristol C	29	12
1992–93	Newcastle U	12	12
1993–94		40	34

COLE, Anthony
Born Gateshead 18.9.72 Ht 6 1 Wt 12 13
Defender. From Middlesbrough trainee.

Season	Club		
1992–93	St Johnstone	7	—
1993–94		1	—

COLEMAN, Chris
Born Swansea 10.6.70. Ht 6 2 Wt 12 10
Defender. From Apprentice. Wales Under-
21, 4 full caps.

Season	Club		
1987–88	Swansea C	30	—
1988–89		43	—
1989–90		46	2
1990–91		41	—
1991–92	Crystal Palace	18	4
1992–93		38	5
1993–94		46	3

COLEMAN, Simon
Born Worksop 13.3.68. Ht 6 0 Wt 10 08
Midfield.

Season	Club		
1985–86	Mansfield T	—	—
1986–87		2	—
1987–88		44	2
1988–89		45	5
1989–90		5	—

Season	Club		Apps	Goals
1989–90	Middlesbrough		36	1
1990–91			19	1
1991–92	Derby Co		43	2
1992–93			25	—
1993–94			2	—
1993–94	Sheffield W		15	1

COLGAN, Nick

Born Eire 19.9.73 Ht 6 1 Wt 12 00
Goalkeeper. From Drogheda.

1992–93	Chelsea		—	—
1993–94			—	—
1993–94	*Crewe Alex*		—	—

COLKIN, Lee

Born Nuneaton 15.7.74. Ht 5 11
Wt 12 00
Defender. From Trainee.

1991–92	Northampton T		3	—
1992–93			13	—
1993–94			20	1

COLLETT, Andy

Born Middlesbrough 28.10.73 Ht 5 11
Wt 12 00
Goalkeeper. From Trainee.

1991–92	Middlesbrough		—	—
1992–93			2	—
1993–94			—	—

COLLIER, Danny

Born Eccles 15.1.74 Ht 6 3 Wt 12 08
Defender. From Trainee.

1992–93	Wolverhampton W		—	—
1993–94			—	—

COLLIER, Darren

Born Stockton 1.12.67. Ht 5 11
Wt 11 09
Goalkeeper. From Middlesbrough.

1988–89	Blackburn R		1	—
1989–90			16	—
1990–91			10	—
1991–92			—	—
1992–93			—	—
1993–94	Darlington		42	—

COLLINGS, Paul

Born Liverpool 30.9.68 Ht 6 2 Wt 12 00
Goalkeeper.

1988–89	Tranmere R		1	—
1989–90			—	—
1990–91			3	—
1991–92	Bury		—	—
1992–93			—	—
1993–94			1	—

COLLINS, David

Born Dublin 30.10.71. Ht 6 1 Wt 12 10
Defender. From Trainee. Eire Youth,
Under-21.

1989–90	Liverpool		—	—
1990–91			—	—
1991–92			—	—
1991–92	*Wigan Ath*		9	—
1992–93	Oxford U		13	—
1993–94			26	—

COLLINS, John

Born Galashiels 31.1.68. Ht 5 7 Wt 9 10
Midfield. From Hutchison Vale BC.
Scotland Youth, Under-21, 18 full caps.

1984–85	Hibernian		—	—
1985–86			19	1
1986–87			30	1
1987–88			44	6
1988–89			35	2
1989–90			35	6
1990–91	Celtic		35	1
1991–92			38	11
1992–93			43	8
1993–94			38	8

COLLINS, Simon

Born Pontefract 16.12.73 Ht 6 0
Wt 11 02
Midfield. From Trainee.

1992–93	Huddersfield T		1	—
1993–94			1	—

COLLINS, Wayne

Born Manchester 4.3.69 Ht 6 0 Wt 12 00
Midfield. From Winsford U.

1993–94	Crewe Alex		35	2

COLLYMORE, Stan

Born Stone 22.1.71. Ht 6 2 Wt 14 00
Forward. From Stafford R.

Season	Club	App	Goals
1990–91	Crystal Palace	6	—
1991–92		12	1
1992–93		2	—
1992–93	Southend U	30	15
1993–94	Nottingham F	28	19

COLQUHOUN, John

Born Stirling 14.7.63. Ht 5 7 Wt 11 00
Forward. From Grangemouth Inter.

Season	Club	App	Goals
1980–81	Stirling Albion	13	—
1981–82		37	13
1982–83		39	21
1983–84		15	11
1983–84	Celtic	12	2
1984–85		20	2
1985–86	Hearts	36	8
1986–87		43	13
1987–88		44	15
1988–89		36	5
1989–90		36	6
1990–91		36	7
1991–92	Millwall	27	3
1992–93	Sunderland	20	—
1993–94	Hearts	41	4

COMYN, Andy

Born Manchester 2.6.68. Ht 6 1 Wt 12 00
Defender. From Alvechurch.

Season	Club	App	Goals
1989–90	Aston Villa	4	—
1990–91		11	—
1991–92	Derby Co	46	1
1992–93		17	—
1993–94	Plymouth Arg	46	5

CONNELL, Graham

Born Glasgow 31.10.74 Ht 5 10 Wt 11 05
Midfield. From Trainee.

Season	Club	App	Goals
1993–94	Ipswich T	—	—

CONNELLY, Dino

Born Glasgow 6.1.70. Ht 5 9 Wt 10 08
Midfield. From Celtic BC, Arsenal
Trainee. Scotland Schools, Youth.

Season	Club	App	Goals
1987–88	Arsenal	—	—
1988–89		—	—
1989–90		—	—
1990–91	Barnsley	9	—
1991–92		3	—
1991–92	*Wigan Ath*	12	2
1992–93	Barnsley	1	—
1992–93	*Carlisle U*	3	—
1992–93	Wigan Ath	7	—
1993–94		13	1

CONNELLY, Sean

Born Sheffield 26.6.70 Ht 5 10 Wt 11 10
Defender. From Hallam.

Season	Club	App	Goals
1991–92	Stockport Co	—	—
1992–93		7	—
1993–94		32	—

CONNOLLY, Karl

Born Prescot 9.2.70. Ht 5 11 Wt 11 02
Midfield. From Napoli (Liverpool Sunday
League).

Season	Club	App	Goals
1990–91	Wrexham	—	—
1991–92		36	8
1992–93		42	9
1993–94		39	2

CONNOLLY, Patrick

Born Glasgow 25.6.70. Ht 5 8 Wt 9 04
Forward. From S Form. Scotland
Under-21.

Season	Club	App	Goals
1986–87	Dundee U	—	—
1987–88		—	—
1988–89		2	—
1989–90		15	5
1990–91		10	2
1991–92		5	—
1992–93		42	16
1993–94		28	5

CONNOLLY, Tony

Born Cork 17.6.75 Ht 5 8 Wt 11 07
Forward. From Trainee.

Season	Club	App	Goals
1993–94	Arsenal	—	—

CONNOR, James

Born Middlesbrough 22.8.74
Midfield.

Season	Club	App	Goals
1992–93	Millwall	—	—

1993–94 .... — —

CONNOR, Robert

Born Kilmarnock 4.8.60.   Ht 5 11
Wt 11 04
Midfield. From Ayr U BC. Scotland
Youth, B, Under-21, 4 full caps.

Season	Club	Apps	Goals
1977–78	Ayr U	9	—
1978–79		29	—
1979–80		38	9
1980–81		39	8
1981–82		30	—
1982–83		39	4
1983–84		39	7
1984–85	Dundee	34	7
1985–86		35	2
1986–87		2	—
1986–87	Aberdeen	32	4
1987–88		34	1
1988–89		36	4
1989–90		34	1
1990–91		29	6
1991–92		11	—
1992–93		6	—
1993–94		25	1

CONROY, Mike

Born Glasgow 31.12.65.   Ht 6 0   Wt 11 00
Forward. From Apprentice.

Season	Club	Apps	Goals
1983–84	Coventry C	—	—
1983–84	Clydebank	2	—
1984–85		26	11
1985–86		28	7
1986–87		36	9
1987–88		22	11
1987–88	St Mirren	10	1
1988–89	Reading	13	4
1989–90		34	2
1990–91		33	1
1991–92	Burnley	38	24
1992–93		39	6
1993–94	Preston NE	32	12

CONWAY, Paul

Born London 17.4.70
Forward. From Oldham Ath.

Season	Club	Apps	Goals
1993–94	Carlisle U	18	4

COOK, Andy

Born Romsey 10.8.69.   Ht 5 9   Wt 10 12
Defender. From Apprentice.

Season	Club	Apps	Goals
1987–88	Southampton	2	—
1988–89		3	—
1989–90		4	1
1990–91		7	—
1991–92		—	—
1991–92	Exeter C	38	—
1992–93		32	1
1993–94	Swansea C	28	—

COOK, Anthony

Born Hemel Hempstead 17.9.76
Midfield. From Trainee.

Season	Club	Apps	Goals
1993–94	Colchester U	2	—

COOK, Jason

Born Edmonton 29.12.69   Ht 5 7
Wt 10 06
Midfield. From Trainee.

Season	Club	Apps	Goals
1988–89	Tottenham H	—	—
1989–90	Southend U	29	1
1990–91		1	—
1991–92	Colchester U	*32*	*2*
1992–93		34	1
1993–94		1	—

COOK, Mitch

Born Scarborough 15.10.61.   Ht 6 0
Wt 12 0
Midfield. From Scarborough.

Season	Club	Apps	Goals
1984–85	Darlington	31	3
1985–86		3	1
1985–86	Middlesbrough	6	—
1986–87	Scarborough	—	—
1987–88		38	5
1988–89		43	5
1989–90	Halifax T	37	2
1990–91		17	—
1990–91	*Scarborough*	9	1
1990–91	*Darlington*	9	—
1991–92	Darlington	27	3
1991–92	Blackpool	8	—
1992–93		9	—
1993–94		45	—

COOK, Paul
Born Liverpool 22.2.67.   Ht 5 11
Wt 10 10
Midfield.

Season	Club		
1984–85	Wigan Ath	2	—
1985–86		13	2
1986–87		27	4
1987–88		41	8
1988–89	Norwich C	4	—
1989–90		2	—
1989–90	Wolverhampton W	28	2
1990–91		42	6
1991–92		43	8
1992–93		44	1
1993–94		36	2

COOKSEY, Scott
Born Birmingham 24.6.72   Ht 6 0
Goalkeeper. From Derby Co, Shrewsbury
T, Bromsgrove R.

1993–94	Peterborough U	3	—

COOPER, Colin
Born Durham 28.2.67.   Ht 5 11   Wt 11 05
Defender. England Under-21.

1984–85	Middlesbrough	—	—
1985–86		11	—
1986–87		46	—
1987–88		43	2
1988–89		35	2
1989–90		21	2
1990–91		32	—
1991–92	Millwall	36	2
1992–93		41	4
1993–94	Nottingham F	37	7

COOPER, David
Born Welwyn 7.3.73.   Ht 6 0   Wt 12 00
Defender. From Luton T Trainee.

1991–92	Exeter C	13	—
1992–93		20	—
1993–94		1	—

COOPER, Davie
Born Hamilton 25.2.56.   Ht 5 8   Wt 12 05
Forward. From Hamilton Avondale.
Scotland Under-21. 22 full caps.

1974–75	Clydebank	26	4

1975–76		26	13
1976–77		38	11
1977–78	Rangers	35	6
1978–79		30	5
1979–80		30	2
1980–81		25	3
1981–82		30	3
1982–83		31	5
1983–84		34	6
1984–85		32	5
1985–86		32	4
1986–87		42	8
1987–88		33	1
1988–89		23	1
1989–90	Motherwell	31	6
1990–91		34	6
1991–92		39	3
1992–93		43	2
1993–94		10	—

COOPER, Gary
Born Edgware 20.11.65.   Ht 5 8   Wt 11 03
Defender. From Brentford, QPR and
Fisher Ath (1989).

1989–90	Maidstone U	33	4
1990–91		27	3
1990–91	Peterborough U	6	1
1991–92		33	4
1992–93		35	3
1993–94		14	2
1993–94	Birmingham C	18	1

COOPER, Geoff
Born Kingston 27.12.60.   Ht 5 10
Wt 11 00
Midfield. From Bognor Regis.

1987–88	Brighton	2	—
1988–89		5	—
To Barnet			
1991–92	Barnet	14	1
1992–93		17	—
1993–94	Wycombe W	—	—
1993–94	Barnet	36	3

COOPER, Kevin
Born Derby 8.2.75   Ht 5 6   Wt 9 10
Midfield. From Trainee.

1993–94	Derby Co	—	—

COOPER, Mark

Born Wakefield 18.12.68.   Ht 5 8
Wt 11 04
Midfield. From Trainee.

Season	Club		
1987–88	Bristol C	—	—
1988–89		—	—
1989–90	Exeter C	5	—
1989–90	Southend U	5	—
1990–91	Exeter C	42	11
1991–92		3	1
1991–92	Birmingham C	33	4
1992–93		6	—
1992–93	Fulham	9	—
1992–93	Huddersfield T	10	4
1993–94	Fulham	5	—
1993–94	Wycombe W	2	1
1993–94	Exeter C	21	8

COOPER, Mark

Born Cambridge 5.4.67.   Ht 6 2   Wt 13 04
Forward. From Apprentice.

Season	Club		
1983–84	Cambridge U	2	—
1984–85		18	3
1985–86		19	1
1986–87		32	13
1986–87	Tottenham H	—	—
1987–88		—	—
1987–88	Shrewsbury T	6	2
1987–88	Gillingham	31	8
1988–89		18	3
1988–89	Leyton Orient	14	4
1989–90		39	11
1990–91		22	9
1991–92		18	6
1992–93		28	7
1993–94		29	8

COOPER, Paul

Born Darlington 24.12.75
Forward. From Trainee.

Season	Club		
1993–94	Darlington	1	—

COOPER, Steve

Born Birmingham 22.6.64.   Ht 5 11
Wt 10 12
Forward.

Season	Club		
1983–84	Birmingham C	—	—
1983–84	Halifax T	7	1

Season	Club		
1984–85	Mansfield T	—	—
1984–85	Newport Co	38	11
1985–86	Plymouth Arg	38	8
1986–87		12	4
1987–88		23	3
1988–89	Barnsley	35	6
1989–90		30	5
1990–91		12	2
1990–91	Tranmere R	17	2
1991–92		9	1
1991–92	Peterborough U	9	—
1992–93	Tranmere R	6	—
1992–93	Wigan Ath	4	—
1993–94	York C	29	5

CORAZZIN, Carlo

Born Canada 25.12.71   Ht 5 9   Wt 12 05
Forward. From Vancouver 86ers.

Season	Club		
1993–94	Cambridge U	28	10

CORK, Alan

Born Derby 4.3.59.   Ht 6 0   Wt 12 00
Forward. From Amateur.

Season	Club		
1977–78	Derby C	—	—
1977–78	Lincoln C	5	—
1977–78	Wimbledon	17	4
1978–79		45	22
1979–80		42	12
1980–81		41	23
1981–82		6	—
1982–83		7	5
1983–84		42	29
1984–85		28	11
1985–86		38	11
1986–87		30	5
1987–88		34	9
1988–89		25	2
1989–90		31	5
1990–91		25	5
1991–92		19	2
1991–92	Sheffield U	8	2
1992–93		27	2
1993–94		19	3

CORMACK, Peter

Born Liverpool 8.6.74   Ht 6 0   Wt 11 05
Defender.

Season	Club		
1990–91	Meadowbank T	1	—
1991–92		1	—

Season	Club	App	Goals
1992–93	Newcastle U	—	—
1993–94		—	—

CORNFORTH, John

Born Whitley Bay 7.10.67.   Ht 6 1
Wt 12 08
Midfield. From Apprentice.

Season	Club	App	Goals
1984–85	Sunderland	1	—
1985–86		—	—
1986–87		—	—
1986–87	*Doncaster R*	7	3
1987–88	Sunderland	12	2
1988–89		15	—
1989–90		2	—
1989–90	*Shrewsbury T*	3	—
1989–90	*Lincoln C*	9	1
1990–91	Sunderland	2	—
1991–92	Swansea C	17	—
1992–93		44	5
1993–94		38	6

CORNWELL, John

Born Bethnal Green 13.10.64.   Ht 6 4
Wt 13 00
Midfield. From Apprentice.

Season	Club	App	Goals
1981–82	Orient	3	—
1982–83		31	3
1983–84		42	7
1984–85		36	10
1985–86		44	8
1986–87		46	7
1987–88	Newcastle U	24	1
1988–89		9	—
1988–89	Swindon T	6	—
1989–90		19	—
1990–91	Southend U	19	2
1991–92		43	—
1992–93		39	3
1993–94		—	—
1993–94	*Cardiff C*	5	2
1993–94	*Brentford*	4	—
1993–94	*Northampton T*	13	1

COSTELLO, Lorcan

Born Dublin 11.11.76   Ht 5 9   Wt 11 02
Defender. From Trainee.

Season	Club	App	Goals
1993–94	Coventry C	—	—

COSTELLO, Peter

Born Halifax 31.10.69.   Ht 6 0   Wt 12 00
Forward. From Trainee.

Season	Club	App	Goals
1988–89	Bradford C	8	2
1989–90		12	—
1990–91	Rochdale	34	10
1990–91	Peterborough U	5	—
1991–92		1	—
1991–92	*Lincoln C*	3	—
1992–93	Peterborough U	2	—
1992–93	Lincoln C	27	7
1993–94		11	—

COTON, Tony

Born Tamworth 19.5.61.   Ht 6 2
Wt 13 07
Goalkeeper. From Mile Oak. England B.

Season	Club	App	Goals
1978–79	Birmingham C	—	—
1979–80		—	—
1979–80	*Hereford U*	—	—
1980–81	Birmingham C	3	—
1981–82		15	—
1982–83		28	—
1983–84		41	—
1984–85		7	—
1984–85	Watford	33	—
1985–86		40	—
1986–87		31	—
1987–88		37	—
1988–89		46	—
1989–90		46	—
1990–91	Manchester C	33	—
1991–92		37	—
1992–93		40	—
1993–94		31	—

COTTEE, Tony

Born West Ham 11.7.65.   Ht 5 7
Wt 11 03
Forward. From Apprentice. England
Youth, Under-21, 7 full caps.

Season	Club	App	Goals
1982–83	West Ham U	8	5
1983–84		39	15
1984–85		41	17
1985–86		42	20
1986–87		42	22
1987–88		40	13
1988–89	Everton	36	13
1989–90		27	13

Season	Club	Apps	Goals
1990–91	....	29	10
1991–92	....	24	8
1992–93	....	26	12
1993–94	....	39	16

COTTERELL, Leo
Born Cambridge 2.9.74   Ht 5 9   Wt 10 00
Defender. From Trainee.

Season	Club	Apps	Goals
1993–94	Ipswich T..................	—	—

COTTERILL, Steve
Born Cheltenham 20.7.64.   Ht 6 1
Wt 12 05
Forward. From Burton A.

Season	Club	Apps	Goals
1988–89	Wimbledon	4	1
1989–90	....	2	1
1990–91	....	4	1
1991–92	....	—	—
1992–93	....	7	3
1992–93	*Brighton*	11	4
1993–94	Bournemouth..............	37	14

COUGHLIN, Russell
Born Swansea 15.2.60.   Ht 5 8   Wt 11 12
Midfield. From Apprentice.

Season	Club	Apps	Goals
1977–78	Manchester C	—	—
1978–79	....	—	—
1978–79	Blackburn R	11	—
1979–80	....	10	—
1980–81	....	3	—
1980–81	Carlisle U..................	25	3
1981–82	....	37	5
1982–83	....	38	2
1983–84	....	30	3
1984–85	Plymouth Arg.............	38	3
1985–86	....	45	10
1986–87	....	40	5
1987–88	....	8	—
1987–88	Blackpool..................	24	2
1988–89	....	43	5
1989–90	....	35	1
1990–91	....	—	—
1990–91	*Shrewsbury T*	5	—
1990–91	Swansea C..................	29	—
1991–92	....	33	1
1992–93	....	39	1
1993–94	Exeter C..................	35	—

COUSIN, Scott
Born Leeds 31.1.75.
Goalkeeper. From Trainee.

Season	Club	Apps	Goals
1991–92	Leeds U	—	—
1992–93	....	—	—
1993–94	....	—	—

COUSINS, Jason
Born Hayes 4.10.70.   Ht 5 11   Wt 12 00
Defender. From Trainee.

Season	Club	Apps	Goals
1989–90	Brentford	13	—
1990–91	....	8	—
To Wycombe W			
1993–94	Wycombe W	37	1

COUZENS, Andrew
Born Shipley 4.6.75   Ht 5 9   Wt 11 07
Defender. From Trainee.

Season	Club	Apps	Goals
1992–93	Leeds U	—	—
1993–94	....	—	—

COWAN, Tom
Born Bellshill 28.8.69.   Ht 5 8   Wt 10 08
Defender. From Netherdale BC.

Season	Club	Apps	Goals
1988–89	Clyde............	16	2
1988–89	Rangers..................	4	—
1989–90	....	3	—
1990–91	....	5	—
1991–92	Sheffield U	20	—
1992–93	....	21	—
1993–94	....	4	—
1993–94	*Stoke C*	14	—
1993–94	*Huddersfield T*.............	10	—

COWANS, Gordon
Born Durham 27.10.58.   Ht 5 7   Wt 9 8
Midfield. From Apprentice. England
Youth, Under-21, B, 10 full caps.

Season	Club	Apps	Goals
1975–76	Aston Villa..................	1	—
1976–77	....	18	3
1977–78	....	35	7
1978–79	....	34	4
1979–80	....	42	6
1980–81	....	42	5
1981–82	....	42	6
1982–83	....	42	10
1983–84	....	—	—
1984–85	....	30	1

Season	Club	Apps	Goals
1985–86	Bari	20	—
1986–87		38	3
1987–88		36	—
1988–89	Aston Villa	33	2
1989–90		34	4
1990–91		38	1
1991–92		12	—
1991–92	Blackburn R	26	1
1992–93		24	1
1993–94	Aston Villa	11	—
1993–94	Derby Co	19	—

COWE, Steven
Born Gloucester 29.9.74   Ht 5 7
Wt 10 02
Midfield. From Trainee.

Season	Club	Apps	Goals
1993–94	Aston Villa	—	—

COX, Ian
Born Croydon 25.3.71   Ht 6 0   Wt 12 02
Midfield. From Carshalton Ath.

Season	Club	Apps	Goals
1993–94	Crystal Palace	—	—

COX, Neil
Born Scunthorpe 8.10.71.   Ht 6 00
Wt 12 10
Midfield. From Trainee. England
Under-21.

Season	Club	Apps	Goals
1989–90	Scunthorpe U	—	—
1990–91		17	1
1990–91	Aston Villa	—	—
1991–92		7	—
1992–93		15	1
1993–94		20	2

COX, Paul
Born Nottingham 1.1.72.   Ht 5 11
Wt 11 12
Defender. From Trainee.

Season	Club	Apps	Goals
1990–91	Notts Co	—	—
1991–92		1	—
1992–93		21	1
1993–94		19	—

COYLE, Owen
Born Glasgow 14.7.66.   Ht 5 11   Wt 10 5
Forward. From Renfrew YM. Eire Under-21, B, 1 full cap.

Season	Club	Apps	Goals
1984–85	Dumbarton	—	—

Season	Club	Apps	Goals
1985–86		16	5
1986–87		43	17
1987–88		41	14
1988–89		3	—
1988–89	Clydebank	36	16
1989–90		27	17
1989–90	Airdrieonians	10	10
1990–91		28	20
1991–92		43	11
1992–93		42	9
1993–94	Bolton W	30	7

COYLE, Ronald
Born Glasgow 4.8.64   Ht 5 11   Wt 12 9
Midfield. From Celtic BC.

Season	Club	Apps	Goals
1983–84	Celtic	—	—
1984–85		1	—
1985–86		1	—
1986–87	Middlesbrough	3	—
1987–88	Rochdale	24	1
1987–88	Raith R	16	3
1988–89		36	1
1989–90		28	2
1990–91		35	1
1991–92		29	—
1992–93		35	1
1993–94		41	1

COYNE, Danny
Born St Asaph 27.8.73   Ht 6 0   Wt 13 00
Goalkeeper. From Trainee. Wales
Under-21.

Season	Club	Apps	Goals
1991–92	Tranmere R	—	—
1992–93		1	—
1993–94		5	—

COYNE, Tommy
Born Glasgow 14.11.62.   Ht 5 11
Wt 12 00
Forward. From Hillwood BC. Eire 13 full
caps.

Season	Club	Apps	Goals
1981–82	Clydebank	31	9
1982–83		38	18
1983–84		11	10
1983–84	Dundee U	18	3
1984–85		21	3
1985–86		13	2
1986–87	Dundee	20	9
1987–88		43	33

Season	Club		Apps	Goals
1988–89			26	9
1988–89	Celtic		7	—
1989–90			23	7
1990–91			26	18
1991–92			39	15
1992–93			10	3
1992–93	Tranmere R		12	1
1993–94	Motherwell		26	12

CRABBE, Scott

Born Edinburgh 12.8.68.   Ht 5 7
Wt 10 00
Midfield. From Tynecastle BC. Scotland
Under-21.

Season	Club		Apps	Goals
1986–87	Hearts		5	—
1987–88			5	—
1988–89			1	—
1989–90			35	12
1990–91			21	3
1991–92			41	15
1992–93			8	1
1992–93	Dundee U		27	4
1993–94			21	2

CRADDOCK, Jody

Born Redditch 25.7.75   Ht 6 0   Wt 11 10
Defender. From Christchurch.

Season	Club		Apps	Goals
1993–94	Cambridge U		20	—

CRAIG, Albert

Born Glasgow 3.1.62.   Ht 5 8   Wt 11 03
Midfield. From Yoker Ath.

Season	Club		Apps	Goals
1981–82	Dumbarton		13	2
1982–83			32	7
1983–84			26	4
1984–85			35	4
1985–86			32	6
1986–87	Hamilton A		16	5
1986–87	Newcastle U		6	—
1987–88			3	—
1987–88	*Hamilton A*		6	1
1988–89	Newcastle U		1	—
1988–89	Northampton T		2	1
1988–89	Dundee		6	2
1989–90			20	2
1990–91			12	3
1991–92			25	7
1992–93	Partick T		29	1
1993–94			38	14

CRAINIE, Danny

Born Kilsyth 24.5.62.   Ht 5 8   Wt 10 11
Forward. From Celtic BC.

Season	Club		Apps	Goals
1979–80	Celtic		—	—
1980–81			—	—
1981–82			16	7
1982–83			7	—
1983–84			1	—
1983–84	Wolverhampton W		28	3
1984–85			13	—
1984–85	*Blackpool*		6	—
1985–86	Wolverhampton W		23	1
1985–86	Dundee		3	—
From Cork C, Wollongong C				
1990–91	Airdrieonians		28	1
1991–92			3	—
1992–93	Kilmarnock		9	1
1993–94			14	1

CRAMB, Colin

Born Lanark 23.6.74   Ht 6 0   Wt 11 09
Forward. From Hamilton Accies BC.

Season	Club		Apps	Goals
1990–91	Hamilton Acad		3	2
1991–92			12	1
1992–93			33	7
1993–94	Southampton		1	—

CRANE, Adrian

Born Leicester 6.9.74   Ht 5 9   Wt 11 00
Midfield. From Trainee.

Season	Club		Apps	Goals
1993–94	Leicester C		—	—

CRANE, Steve

Born Essex 3.6.72   Ht 5 9   Wt 12 00
Forward. From USA.

Season	Club		Apps	Goals
1992–93	Gillingham		7	1
1993–94			6	—

CRANSON, Ian

Born Easington 2.7.64.   Ht 6 0   Wt 13 04
Defender. From Apprentice. England
Under-21.

Season	Club		Apps	Goals
1982–83	Ipswich T		—	—
1983–84			8	—
1984–85			20	1
1985–86			42	1
1986–87			32	2
1987–88			29	1

Season	Club	App	Goals
1987–88	Sheffield W	4	—
1988–89		26	—
1989–90	Stoke C	17	2
1990–91		9	—
1991–92		41	2
1992–93		45	3
1993–94		44	—

CRAVEN, Peter
Born Hanover 30.6.68
Midfield. From Park Avenue.

Season	Club	App	Goals
1991–92	Bury	—	—
1992–93	Halifax T	7	—
1993–94	Preston NE	—	—

CRAWFORD, Stephen
Born Dunfermline 9.1.74   Ht 5 10
Wt 10 7
Midfield. From Rosyth Recreation.
Scotland Under-21.

Season	Club	App	Goals
1992–93	Raith R	20	3
1993–94		36	5

CREANEY, Gerry
Born Coatbridge 13.4.70.   Ht 5 10
Wt 10 07
Forward. From Celtic BC. Scotland
Under-21.

Season	Club	App	Goals
1987–88	Celtic	—	—
1988–89		—	—
1989–90		6	1
1990–91		31	7
1991–92		32	14
1992–93		26	9
1993–94		18	5
1993–94	Portsmouth	18	11

CREASER, Glyn
Born London 1.9.59   Ht 6 4   Wt 15 06
Defender. From Barnet.

Season	Club	App	Goals
1993–94	Wycombe W	15	2

CRICHTON, Paul
Born Pontefract 3.10.68.   Ht 6 1
Wt 12 05
Goalkeeper. From Apprentice.

Season	Club	App	Goals
1986–87	Nottingham F	—	—
1986–87	Notts Co	5	—

Season	Club	App	Goals
1986–87	Darlington	5	—
1986–87	Peterborough U	4	—
1987–88	Nottingham F	—	—
1987–88	Darlington	3	—
1987–88	Swindon T	4	—
1987–88	Rotherham U	6	—
1988–89	Nottingham F	—	—
1988–89	Torquay U	13	—
1988–89	Peterborough U	31	—
1989–90		16	—
1990–91	Doncaster R	20	—
1991–92		16	—
1992–93		41	—
1993–94	Grimsby T	46	—

CRISP, Richard
Born Wordsley 23.5.72   Ht 5 7   Wt 10 05
Midfield. From Trainee.

Season	Club	App	Goals
1991–92	Aston Villa	—	—
1992–93		—	—
1992–93	Scunthorpe U	8	—
1993–94	Aston Villa	—	—

CROCKER, Marcus
Born Plymouth 8.10.74   Ht 5 10
Wt 11 05
Forward. From Trainee.

Season	Club	App	Goals
1992–93	Plymouth Arg	4	—
1993–94		1	—

CROFT, Brian
Born Chester 27.9.67.   Ht 5 9   Wt 10 10
Midfield.

Season	Club	App	Goals
1984–85	Chester C	—	—
1985–86		1	—
1986–87		21	1
1987–88		37	2
1988–89	Cambridge U	17	2
1989–90	Chester C	44	3
1990–91		38	—
1991–92		32	—
1992–93	QPR	—	—
1993–94		—	—
1993–94	Shrewsbury T	4	—

CROFT, Gary
Born Burton-on-Trent 17.2.74.   Ht 5 9
Wt 10 08
Defender. From Trainee.

Season	Club	App	Goals
1990–91	Grimsby T	1	—

Season	Club	Apps	Goals
1991–92		—	—
1992–93		32	—
1993–94		36	1

CRONIN, Gareth
Born Cork 18.2.75
Defender. From Trainee.

Season	Club	Apps	Goals
1992–93	Sunderland	—	—
1993–94		—	—
1993–94	*Bradford C*	—	—

CROOK, Ian
Born Romford 18.1.63.   Ht 5 8   Wt 10 06
Midfield. From Apprentice. England B.

Season	Club	Apps	Goals
1980–81	Tottenham H	—	—
1981–82		4	—
1982–83		4	—
1983–84		3	—
1984–85		5	1
1985–86		4	—
1986–87	Norwich C	33	5
1987–88		23	1
1988–89		26	1
1989–90		35	—
1990–91		32	3
1991–92		21	1
1992–93		34	3
1993–94		38	—

CROSBY, Andy
Born Rotherham 3.3.73.   Ht 6 2
Wt 13 00
Defender. From Leeds U Trainee.

Season	Club	Apps	Goals
1991–92	Doncaster R	22	—
1992–93		29	—
1993–94		—	—
1993–94	Darlington	25	—

CROSBY, Gary
Born Sleaford 8.5.64.   Ht 5 7   Wt 9 11
Midfield. From Lincoln U.

Season	Club	Apps	Goals
1986–87	Lincoln C	7	—
From Grantham			
1987–88	Nottingham F	14	1
1988–89		13	—
1989–90		34	5
1990–91		29	2
1991–92		33	3

Season	Club	Apps	Goals
1992–93		23	1
1993–94		6	—
1993–94	*Grimsby T*	3	—

CROSS, Jonathan
Born Wallasey 2.3.75.   Ht 5 10   Wt 11 04
Midfield. From Trainee.

Season	Club	Apps	Goals
1991–92	Wrexham	6	—
1992–93		37	7
1993–94		25	2

CROSS, Mark
Born Abergavenny 6.5.76
Forward. From Trainee.

Season	Club	Apps	Goals
1992–93	Hereford U	1	—
1993–94		—	—

CROSS, Nicky
Born Birmingham 7.2.61.   Ht 5 9
Wt 11 12
Forward. From Apprentice.

Season	Club	Apps	Goals
1978–79	WBA	—	—
1979–80		—	—
1980–81		2	1
1981–82		22	2
1982–83		32	4
1983–84		25	3
1984–85		24	5
1985–86	Walsall	44	21
1986–87		39	16
1987–88		26	8
1987–88	Leicester C	17	6
1988–89		41	9
1989–90	Port Vale	42	13
1990–91		19	2
1991–92		8	—
1992–93		38	12
1993–94		37	12

CROSS, Paul
Born Barnsley 31.10.65.   Ht 5 7   Wt 9 06
Midfield. From Apprentice.

Season	Club	Apps	Goals
1983–84	Barnsley	—	—
1984–85		1	—
1985–86		20	—
1986–87		18	—
1987–88		38	—
1988–89		—	—

Season	Club	Apps	Goals
1989–90	....	36	—
1990–91	....	2	—
1991–92	....	3	—
1991–92	*Preston NE*	5	—
1991–92	Hartlepool U	21	—
1992–93	....	37	1
1993–94	....	16	—
1993–94	Darlington	26	2

CROSS, Ryan
Born Plymouth 11.10.72. Ht 6 1
Wt 13 06
Defender. From Trainee.

Season	Club	Apps	Goals
1990–91	Plymouth Arg	7	—
1991–92	....	12	—
1992–93	Hartlepool U	33	2
1993–94	....	17	—
1993–94	Bury	17	—

CROSS, Steve
Born Wolverhampton 22.12.59. Ht 5 10
Wt 11 05
Defender. From Apprentice.

Season	Club	Apps	Goals
1976–77	Shrewsbury T	5	—
1977–78	....	1	—
1978–79	....	19	2
1979–80	....	19	—
1980–81	....	35	2
1981–82	....	34	3
1982–83	....	33	5
1983–84	....	41	9
1984–85	....	40	5
1985–86	....	35	8
1986–87	Derby Co	6	—
1987–88	....	15	3
1988–89	....	19	—
1989–90	....	8	—
1990–91	....	21	—
1991–92	....	4	—
1991–92	Bristol R	32	2
1992–93	....	11	—
1993–94	....	—	—

CROSSEY, Scott
Born Somerset 18.2.75. Ht 5 6 Wt 9 07
Midfield. From Trainee.

Season	Club	Apps	Goals
1993–94	Bristol R	—	—

CROSSLEY, Mark
Born Barnsley 16.6.69. Ht 6 0 Wt 13 09
Goalkeeper. England Under-21.

Season	Club	Apps	Goals
1987–88	Nottingham F	—	—
1988–89	....	2	—
1989–90	....	8	—
1989–90	*Manchester U*	—	—
1990–91	Nottingham F	38	—
1991–92	....	36	—
1992–93	....	37	—
1993–94	....	37	—

CROSSLEY, Matt
Born Basingstoke 18.3.68. Ht 6 2
Wt 13 07
Defender. From Overton U.

Season	Club	Apps	Goals
1993–94	Wycombe W	39	2

CRUMPLIN, John
Born Bath 26.5.67. Ht 5 8 Wt 11 10
Midfield. From Bognor Regis.

Season	Club	Apps	Goals
1986–87	Brighton	5	—
1987–88	....	26	2
1988–89	....	12	—
1989–90	....	25	2
1990–91	....	46	—
1991–92	....	29	—
1992–93	....	32	1
1993–94	....	32	2

CULLEN, Jon
Born Durham 10.1.73.
Defender. From Trainee.

Season	Club	Apps	Goals
1990–91	Doncaster R	1	—
1991–92	....	8	—
1992–93	....	—	—
1993–94	....	—	—

CULLEN, Tony
Born Newcastle 30.9.69. Ht 5 6
Wt 11 07
Forward. From Local.

Season	Club	Apps	Goals
1988–89	Sunderland	7	—
1989–90	....	16	—
1989–90	*Carlisle U*	2	1
1990–91	Sunderland	5	—
1990–91	*Rotherham U*	3	1
1991–92	Sunderland	1	—

1991–92	*Bury*	4	—
1992–93	Swansea C	27	3
1993–94	Doncaster R	—	—

CULVERHOUSE, David
Born Harlow 9.9.73. Ht 6 0 Wt 11 06
Defender. From Trainee.

1991–92	Tottenham H	—	—
1992–93		—	—
1993–94		—	—

CULVERHOUSE, Ian
Born Bishop's Stortford 22.9.64.
Ht 5 10 Wt 11 02
Defender. From Apprentice. England
Youth.

1982–83	Tottenham H	—	—
1983–84		2	—
1984–85		—	—
1985–86		—	—
1985–86	Norwich C	30	—
1986–87		25	—
1987–88		33	—
1988–89		38	—
1989–90		32	—
1990–91		34	—
1991–92		21	—
1992–93		41	—
1993–94		42	1

CUNDY, Jason
Born Wimbledon 12.11.69. Ht 6 1
Wt 13 07
Defender. From Trainee. England
Under-21.

1988–89	Chelsea	—	—
1989–90		—	—
1990–91		29	—
1991–92		12	1
1991–92	*Tottenham H*	10	—
1992–93	Tottenham H	15	1
1993–94		—	—

CUNNINGHAM, Aaron
Born New Jersey 11.11.73
Forward. From Trainee.

| 1993–94 | Portsmouth | — | — |

CUNNINGHAM, Ken
Born Dublin 28.6.71. Ht 6 0 Wt 11 08
Defender. Eire Under-21, B.

1989–90	Millwall	5	—
1990–91		23	—
1991–92		17	—
1992–93		37	—
1993–94		39	1

CUNNINGHAM, Tony
Born Jamaica 12.11.57. Ht 6 1 Wt 13 13
Forward. From Stourbridge.

1979–80	Lincoln C	38	12
1980–81		34	6
1981–82		46	11
1982–83		5	3
1982–83	Barnsley	29	7
1983–84		13	4
1983–84	Sheffield W	28	5
1984–85	Manchester C	18	1
1984–85	Newcastle U	13	1
1985–86		17	1
1986–87		17	2
1987–88	Blackpool	40	10
1988–89		31	7
1989–90	Bury	25	8
1990–91		33	9
1990–91	Bolton W	9	4
1991–92	Rotherham U	36	18
1992–93		33	6
1993–94	Doncaster R	25	1
1993–94	Wycombe W	5	—

CUNNINGTON, Shaun
Born Bourne 4.1.66. Ht 5 10 Wt 11 07
Defender. From Bourne T.

1982–83	Wrexham	4	—
1983–84		42	—
1984–85		41	6
1985–86		42	2
1986–87		46	1
1987–88		24	3
1987–88	Grimsby T	15	2
1988–89		44	1
1989–90		44	3
1990–91		46	2
1991–92		33	5
1992–93	Sunderland	39	7
1993–94		11	1

CURBISHLEY, Alan

Born Forest Gate 8.11.57. Ht 5 11
Wt 11 10
Midfield. From Apprentice. England
Schools, Youth, Under-21.

Season	Club	App	Goals
1974–75	West Ham U	2	—
1975–76		14	2
1976–77		10	1
1977–78		32	1
1978–79		27	1
1979–80	Birmingham C	42	3
1980–81		29	6
1981–82		29	1
1982–83		30	1
1982–83	Aston Villa	7	—
1983–84		26	1
1984–85		3	—
1984–85	Charlton Ath	23	2
1985–86		30	4
1986–87		10	—
1987–88	Brighton	34	6
1988–89		37	6
1989–90		45	1
1990–91	Charlton Ath	25	—
1991–92		1	—
1992–93		1	—
1993–94		1	—

CURETON, Jamie

Born Bristol 28.8.75 Ht 5 8 Wt 10 05
Forward. From Trainee.

Season	Club	App	Goals
1992–93	Norwich C	—	—
1993–94		—	—

CURLE, Keith

Born Bristol 14.11.63. Ht 6 0 Wt 12 07
Defender. From Apprentice. England B, 3
full caps.

Season	Club	App	Goals
1981–82	Bristol R	20	2
1982–83		12	2
1983–84	Bristol R	—	—
1983–84	Torquay U	16	5
1983–84	Bristol C	6	—
1984–85		40	—
1985–86		44	1
1986–87		28	—
1987–88		3	—
1987–88	Reading	30	—
1988–89		10	—

Season	Club	App	Goals
1988–89	Wimbledon	18	—
1989–90		38	2
1990–91		37	1
1991–92	Manchester C	40	5
1992–93		39	4
1993–94		29	1

CURRAN, Chris

Born Manchester 6.1.71. Ht 6 1
Wt 12 06
Forward. From Trainee.

Season	Club	App	Goals
1989–90	Crewe Alex	1	—
1990–91		4	—
1991–92		—	—
1991–92	Scarborough	8	2
1992–93		32	2
1993–94	Carlisle U	6	1

CURRAN, Chris

Born Birmingham 17.9.71. Ht 5 11
Wt 11 09
Defender. From Trainee.

Season	Club	App	Goals
1989–90	Torquay U	1	—
1990–91		13	—
1991–92		17	—
1992–93		34	—
1993–94		41	1

CURRAN, Henry

Born Glasgow 9.10.66. Ht 5 8 Wt 11 04
Midfield. From Eastercraigs.

Season	Club	App	Goals
1984–85	Dumbarton	2	—
1985–86		6	—
1986–87		8	—
1986–87	Dundee U	3	—
1987–88		6	—
1988–89		6	—
1989–90	St Johnstone	31	3
1990–91		35	9
1991–92		39	8
1992–93		34	8
1993–94		39	3

CURRIE, Darren

Born Hampstead 29.11.74 Ht 5 9
Wt 11 07
Midfield. From Trainee.

Season	Club	App	Goals
1993–94	West Ham U	—	—

CURRIE, David

Born Stockton 27.11.62.   Ht 5 11
Wt 12 09
Forward. From Local.

Season	Club	Apps	Goals
1981–82	Middlesbrough	1	—
1982–83		8	—
1983–84		39	15
1984–85		39	12
1985–86		26	4
1986–87	Darlington	45	12
1987–88		31	21
1987–88	Barnsley	15	7
1988–89		41	16
1989–90		24	7
1989–90	Nottingham F	8	1
1990–91	Oldham Ath	27	2
1991–92		4	1
1991–92	Barnsley	37	7
1992–93		35	4
1992–93	*Rotherham U*	5	2
1993–94	Barnsley	3	1
1993–94	*Huddersfield T*	7	1

CURTIS, Andy

Born Doncaster 2.12.72.   Ht 5 10
Wt 11 07
Midfield. From Trainee.

Season	Club	Apps	Goals
1990–91	York C	5	—
1991–92		7	—
1992–93	Peterborough U	11	1
1993–94		—	—

CURTIS, Len

Born Dublin 2.1.73   Ht 5 11   Wt 13 00
Defender. From Leeds U.

Season	Club	Apps	Goals
1992–93	Rotherham U	—	—
1993–94		—	—

CURTIS, Tommy

Born Exeter 1.3.73.   Ht 5 8   Wt 11 04
Midfield. From School.

Season	Club	Apps	Goals
1991–92	Derby Co	—	—
1992–93		—	—
1993–94	Chesterfield	36	3

CUSACK, Nick

Born Rotherham 24.12.65.   Ht 6 0
Wt 11 13
Forward. From Alvechurch.

Season	Club	Apps	Goals
1987–88	Leicester C	16	1
1988–89	Peterborough U	44	10
1989–90	Motherwell	31	11
1990–91		29	4
1991–92		17	2
1991–92	Darlington	21	6
1992–93	Oxford U	39	4
1993–94		20	6
1993–94	*Wycombe W*	4	—

CZACHOWSKI, Pietr

Born Warsaw 7.11.66   Ht 5 10   Wt 11 9
Forward. Legia Warsaw.

Season	Club	Apps	Goals
1993–94	Dundee	18	1

DAILLY, Christian
Born Dundee 23.10.73.   Ht 5 10
Wt 10 11
Forward. S Form. Scotland B, Under-21.

Season	Club	Apps	Goals
1990–91	Dundee U	18	5
1991–92		8	—
1992–93		14	4
1993–94		38	4

DAIR, Jason
Born Dunfermline 15.6.74   Ht 5 11
Wt 10 8
Forward. From Castlebridge. Scotland
Under-21.

Season	Club	Apps	Goals
1991–92	Raith R	4	—
1992–93		15	1
1993–94		38	6

DAISH, Liam
Born Portsmouth 23.9.68.   Ht 6 2
Wt 13 05
Defender. From Apprentice. Eire Under-
21, 1 full cap.

Season	Club	Apps	Goals
1986–87	Portsmouth	1	—
1987–88		—	—
1988–89	Cambridge U	28	—
1989–90		42	1
1990–91		13	1
1991–92		22	—
1992–93		16	—
1993–94		18	2
1993–94	Birmingham C	19	—

DAKIN, Simon
Born Nottingham 30.11.74   Ht 5 11
Wt 11 07
Defender. From Derby Co.

Season	Club	Apps	Goals
1993–94	Hull C	9	—

DALE, Carl
Born Colwyn Bay 29.4.66.   Ht 6 0
Wt 12 00
Forward. From Bangor C.

Season	Club	Apps	Goals
1987–88	Chester C	—	—
1988–89		41	22
1989–90		31	9
1990–91		44	10
1991–92	Cardiff C	41	22

Season	Club	Apps	Goals
1992–93		20	8
1993–94		15	3

DALEY, Philip
Born Walton 12.4.67.   Ht 6 2   Wt 12 09
Forward. From Newton.

Season	Club	Apps	Goals
1989–90	Wigan Ath	33	6
1990–91		41	10
1991–92		38	14
1992–93		31	6
1993–94		18	3

DALEY, Tony
Born Birmingham 18.10.67.   Ht 5 8
Wt 10 08
Forward. From Apprentice. England
Youth, 7 full caps.

Season	Club	Apps	Goals
1984–85	Aston Villa	5	—
1985–86		23	2
1986–87		33	3
1987–88		14	3
1988–89		29	5
1989–90		32	6
1990–91		23	2
1991–92		34	7
1992–93		13	2
1993–94		27	1

DALTON, Paul
Born Middlesbrough 25.4.67.   Ht 5 11
Wt 11 07
Midfield. From Brandon.

Season	Club	Apps	Goals
1987–88	Manchester U	—	—
1988–89		—	—
1988–89	Hartlepool U	17	2
1989–90		45	11
1990–91		46	11
1991–92		43	13
1992–93	Plymouth Arg	32	9
1993–94		40	12

DALY, Sean
Born Lambeth 18.11.74
Defender. From Trainee.

Season	Club	Apps	Goals
1993–94	Crystal Palace	—	—

DALZIEL, Gordon

Born Motherwell 16.3.62   Ht 5 10
Wt 10 13
Forward. From Bonkle YC.

Season	Club	Apps	Goals
1978–79	Rangers	—	—
1979–80		1	—
1980–81		—	—
1981–82		17	6
1982–83		15	3
1983–84	Manchester C	5	—
1984–85	Partick T	25	6
1985–86		18	—
1986–87	East Stirling	10	2
1986–87	Raith R	11	7
1987–88		42	25
1988–89		36	11
1989–90		39	20
1990–91		39	25
1991–92		39	26
1992–93		44	32
1993–94		27	8

DANIEL, Ray

Born Luton 10.12.64.   Ht 5 8   Wt 11 09
Midfield. From Apprentice.

Season	Club	Apps	Goals
1982–83	Luton T	3	—
1983–84		7	2
1983–84	*Gillingham*	5	—
1984–85	Luton T	7	1
1985–86		5	1
1986–87	Hull C	9	—
1987–88		26	2
1988–89		23	1
1989–90	Cardiff C	43	1
1990–91		13	—
1990–91	Portsmouth	14	—
1991–92		8	—
1992–93		40	4
1993–94		16	—

DANIELS, Scott

Born Benfleet 22.11.69.   Ht 6 1   Wt 11 09
Defender. From Trainee.

Season	Club	Apps	Goals
1987–88	Colchester U	1	—
1988–89		26	—
1989–90		46	—
1990–91		*40*	*1*
1991–92	Exeter C	43	3
1992–93		26	2

1993–94		41	2

DANZEY, Michael

Born Widnes 8.2.71   Ht 6 1   Wt 12 00
Forward. From Trainee.

Season	Club	Apps	Goals
1988–89	Nottingham F	—	—
1989–90		—	—
1989–90	*Chester C*	2	—
1990–91	Peterborough U	1	—
From St Albans			
1992–93	Cambridge U	2	—
1993–94		14	3
1993–94	*Scunthorpe U*	3	1

DARBY, Duane

Born West Midlands 17.10.73.   Ht 5 11
Wt 12 06
Forward. From Trainee.

Season	Club	Apps	Goals
1991–92	Torquay U	14	2
1992–93		34	12
1993–94		36	8

DARBY, Julian

Born Bolton 3.10.67.   Ht 6 0   Wt 11 04
Defender. England Schools.

Season	Club	Apps	Goals
1984–85	Bolton W	—	—
1985–86		2	—
1986–87		28	—
1987–88		35	2
1988–89		44	5
1989–90		46	10
1990–91		45	9
1991–92		44	6
1992–93		21	4
1993–94		5	—
1993–94	Coventry C	26	5

DARTON, Scott

Born Ipswich 27.3.75
Defender. From Trainee.

Season	Club	Apps	Goals
1992–93	WBA	2	—
1993–94		6	—

DAUGHTRY, Paul

Born Oldham 14.2.73   Ht 5 8
Forward. From Winsford.

Season	Club	Apps	Goals
1993–94	Stockport Co	—	—

84

DAVEY, Simon

Born Swansea 1.10.70. Ht 5 10 Wt 11 02
Midfield. From Trainee.

1986–87	Swansea C	1	—
1987–88		4	—
1988–89		3	—
1989–90		18	2
1990–91		18	2
1991–92		5	—
1992–93	Carlisle U	38	5
1993–94		42	9

DAVID, Lionel

Born Nantes 28.9.66. Ht 6 1 Wt 12 7
Midfield. From La Roche sur Yon.

| 1992–93 | Dundee | 8 | — |
| 1993–94 | | 1 | — |

DAVIDSON, Craig

Born Harold Wood 2.5.74 Ht 5 11
Wt 11 08
Defender. From Trainee.

| 1993–94 | Southend U | — | — |

DAVIDSON, Ross

Born Chertsey 13.11.73. Ht 5 8 Wt 11 04
Defender. From Walton & Hersham.

| 1993–94 | Sheffield U | — | — |

DAVIES, Billy

Born Glasgow 31.5.64. Ht 5 6 Wt 10 9
Midfield. School.

1980–81	Rangers	—	—
1981–82		4	—
1982–83		4	—
1983–84		3	1
1984–85		—	—
1985–86		—	—
1986–87	IF Elfsborg		
1987–88	St Mirren	18	—
1988–89		27	4
1989–90		29	1
1990–91	Lincoln C	6	—
1990–91	Dunfermline Ath	26	—
1991–92		33	—
1992–93		41	10
1993–94		4	—
1993–94	Motherwell	10	—

DAVIES, Gareth

Born Hereford 11.12.73.
Defender. From Trainee. Wales Under-21.

1991–92	Hereford U	4	—
1992–93		32	1
1993–94		31	—

DAVIES, John

Born Glasgow 25.9.66. Ht 5 7 Wt 10 0
Midfield. From Anniesland U.

1985–86	Clydebank	3	—
1986–87		14	—
From Jonkoping			
1987–88	Clydebank	22	3
1988–89		38	3
1989–90		31	5
1990–91		14	1
1990–91	St Johnstone	21	1
1991–92		40	—
1992–93		38	4
1993–94		32	5

DAVIES, Kevin

Born Sheffield 26.3.77 Ht 6 0 Wt 12 12
Forward. From Trainee.

| 1993–94 | Chesterfield | 24 | 4 |

DAVIES, Martin

Born Swansea 28.6.74 Ht 6 2 Wt 13 07
Goalkeeper. From Trainee.

| 1992–93 | Coventry C | — | — |
| 1993–94 | | — | — |

DAVIES, Michael

Born Stretford 19.1.66. Ht 5 8 Wt 10 07
Defender. From Apprentice.

1983–84	Blackpool	3	—
1984–85		17	—
1985–86		36	5
1986–87		42	6
1987–88		38	—
1988–89		30	2
1989–90		23	—
1990–91		37	1
1991–92		29	1
1992–93		30	1
1993–94		24	—

DAVIES, Simon
Born Winsford 23.4.74 Ht 5 11 Wt 10 02
Midfield. From Trainee.

Season	Club	Apps	Goals
1992–93	Manchester U	—	—
1993–94		—	—
1993–94	*Exeter C*	6	1

DAVIES, Stephen
Born Crewe 7.9.74 Ht 5 11
Defender. From Trainee.

Season	Club	Apps	Goals
1993–94	Stoke C	—	—

DAVIS, Darren
Born Sutton-in-Ashfield 5.2.67. Ht 6 0
Wt 11 00
Defender. From Apprentice. England
Youth.

Season	Club	Apps	Goals
1983–84	Notts Co	1	—
1984–85		4	—
1985–86		22	1
1986–87		45	—
1987–88		20	—
1988–89	Lincoln C	38	2
1989–90		34	—
1990–91		30	2
1990–91	Maidstone U	11	—
1991–92		20	2
From Frickley Ath			
1993–94	Scarborough	25	1

DAVIS, Kelvin
Born Bedford 29.9.76 Ht 6 1 Wt 13 06
Goalkeeper. From Trainee.

Season	Club	Apps	Goals
1993–94	Luton T	1	—

DAVIS, Mike
Born Bristol 19.10.74 Ht 6 0 Wt 12 00
Forward. From Yate T.

Season	Club	Apps	Goals
1992–93	Bristol R	1	1
1993–94		10	—

DAVIS, Neil
Born Bloxwich 15.8.73. Ht 5 8 Wt 11 00
Forward. From Redditch U.

Season	Club	Apps	Goals
1991–92	Aston Villa	—	—
1992–93		—	—
1993–94		—	—

DAVIS, Paul
Born London 9.12.61. Ht 5 10 Wt 10 13
Midfield. From Apprentice. England B,
Under-21.

Season	Club	Apps	Goals
1979–80	Arsenal	2	—
1980–81		10	1
1981–82		38	4
1982–83		41	4
1983–84		35	1
1984–85		24	1
1985–86		29	4
1986–87		39	4
1987–88		29	5
1988–89		12	1
1989–90		11	1
1990–91		37	3
1991–92		12	—
1992–93		6	—
1993–94		22	—

DAVIS, Steve
Born Birmingham 26.7.65. Ht 6 0
Wt 12 07
Defender. From Stoke C. Apprentice.
England Youth.

Season	Club	Apps	Goals
1983–84	Crewe Alex	24	—
1984–85		40	—
1985–86		45	1
1986–87		33	—
1987–88		3	—
1987–88	Burnley	33	5
1988–89		37	—
1989–90		31	1
1990–91		46	5
1991–92	Barnsley	9	—
1992–93		11	—
1993–94		—	—

DAVIS, Steve
Born Hexham 30.10.68. Ht 6 2 Wt 12 08
Defender. From Trainee.

Season	Club	Apps	Goals
1987–88	Southampton	—	—
1988–89		—	—
1989–90		4	—
1989–90	*Burnley*	9	—
1990–91	Southampton	3	—
1990–91	*Notts Co*	2	—
1991–92	Burnley	40	6
1992–93		37	2

Season	Club	Apps	Goals
1993–94	....	42	7

DAVISON, Aidan
Born Sedgefield 11.5.68.   Ht 6 2
Wt 13 11
Goalkeeper. From Billingham Syn.

Season	Club	Apps	Goals
1987–88	Notts Co	—	—
1988–89	....	1	—
1989–90	....	—	—
1989–90	*Leyton Orient*	—	—
1989–90	Bury	—	—
1989–90	*Chester C*	—	—
1990–91	Bury	—	—
1990–91	*Blackpool*	—	—
1991–92	Millwall	33	—
1992–93	....	1	—
1993–94	Bolton W	31	—

DAVISON, Bobby
Born South Shields 17.7.59.   Ht 5 9
Wt 11 09
Forward. From Seaham C.W.

Season	Club	Apps	Goals
1980–81	Huddersfield T	2	—
1981–82	Halifax T	46	20
1982–83	....	17	9
1982–83	Derby Co	26	8
1983–84	....	40	14
1984–85	....	46	24
1985–86	....	41	17
1986–87	....	40	19
1987–88	....	13	1
1987–88	Leeds U	16	5
1988–89	....	39	14
1989–90	....	29	11
1990–91	....	5	1
1991–92	....	2	—
1991–92	*Derby Co*	10	8
1991–92	*Sheffield U*	11	4
1992–93	Leicester C	25	6
1993–94	....	—	—
1993–94	Sheffield U	9	—

DAWES, Ian
Born Croydon 22.2.63.   Ht 5 10
Wt 11 10
Defender. From Apprentice. England
Schools.

Season	Club	Apps	Goals
1980–81	QPR	—	—

Season	Club	Apps	Goals
1981–82	....	5	—
1982–83	....	42	—
1983–84	....	42	2
1984–85	....	42	—
1985–86	....	42	1
1986–87	....	23	—
1987–88	....	33	—
1988–89	Millwall	30	1
1989–90	....	38	4
1990–91	....	40	—
1991–92	....	36	—
1992–93	....	46	—
1993–94	....	21	—

DAWS, Nick
Born Manchester 15.3.70   Ht 5 11
Wt 13 02
Midfield. From Altrincham.

Season	Club	Apps	Goals
1992–93	Bury	36	1
1993–94	....	37	1

DAWS, Tony
Born Sheffield 10.9.66.   Ht 5 8   Wt 11 10
Forward. From Apprentice. England
Youth.

Season	Club	Apps	Goals
1984–85	Notts Co	7	1
1985–86	....	1	—
1986–87	Sheffield U	11	3
1987–88	Scunthorpe U	10	3
1988–89	....	46	24
1989–90	....	33	11
1990–91	....	34	14
1991–92	....	36	7
1992–93	....	24	4
1992–93	Grimsby T	6	1
1993–94	....	10	—
1993–94	Lincoln C	14	3

DAY, Chris
Born Whipps Cross 28.7.74   Ht 6 0
Wt 12 00
Goalkeeper. From Trainee.

Season	Club	Apps	Goals
1992–93	Tottenham H	—	—
1993–94	....	—	—

DAY, Mervyn

Born Chelmsford 26.6.55.   Ht 6 2
Wt 15 01
Goalkeeper. From Apprentice. England
Youth, Under-23.

Season	Club	Apps	Goals
1972–73	West Ham U	—	—
1973–74		33	—
1974–75		42	—
1975–76		41	—
1976–77		42	—
1977–78		23	—
1978–79		13	—
1979–80	Orient	42	—
1980–81		40	—
1981–82		42	—
1982–83		46	—
1983–84	Aston Villa	14	—
1984–85		16	—
1984–85	Leeds U	18	—
1985–86		40	—
1986–87		34	—
1987–88		44	—
1988–89		45	—
1989–90		44	—
1990–91		—	—
1990–91	Coventry C	—	—
1991–92	Leeds U	—	—
1991–92	Luton T	4	—
1991–92	Sheffield U	1	—
1992–93	Leeds U	2	—
1993–94	Carlisle U	16	—

DE SOUZA, Juan

Born Newham 11.2.70   Ht 6 1
Forward. From Dagenham & Redbridge.

Season	Club	Apps	Goals
1993–94	Birmingham C	7	—

DEAN, Craig

Born Nuneaton 1.7.75   Ht 5 10   Wt 11 07
Midfield. From Trainee.

Season	Club	Apps	Goals
1993–94	Manchester U	—	—

DEANE, Brian

Born Leeds 7.2.68.   Ht 6 3   Wt 12 07
Forward. From Apprentice. England B, 3
full caps.

Season	Club	Apps	Goals
1985–86	Doncaster R	3	—
1986–87		20	2
1987–88		43	10
1988–89	Sheffield U	43	22
1989–90		45	21
1990–91		38	13
1991–92		30	12
1992–93		41	14
1993–94	Leeds U	41	11

DEARDEN, Kevin

Born Luton 8.3.70.   Ht 5 11   Wt 12 08
Goalkeeper. From Trainee.

Season	Club	Apps	Goals
1988–89	Tottenham H	—	—
1988–89	Cambridge U	15	—
1989–90	Tottenham H	—	—
1989–90	Hartlepool U	10	—
1989–90	Oxford U	—	—
1989–90	Swindon T	1	—
1990–91	Tottenham H	—	—
1990–91	Peterborough U	7	—
1990–91	Hull C	3	—
1991–92	Tottenham H	—	—
1991–92	Rochdale	2	—
1991–92	Birmingham C	12	—
1992–93	Tottenham H	1	—
1992–93	Portsmouth	—	—
1993–94	Tottenham H	—	—
1993–94	Brentford	35	—

DEARY, John

Born Ormskirk 18.10.62.   Ht 5 10
Wt 12 04
Midfield. From Apprentice.

Season	Club	Apps	Goals
1979–80	Blackpool	—	—
1980–81		10	—
1981–82		27	—
1982–83		45	6
1983–84		31	6
1984–85		32	13
1985–86		40	7
1986–87		44	3
1987–88		37	3
1988–89		37	5
1989–90	Burnley	41	2
1990–91		43	7
1991–92		40	6
1992–93		32	3
1993–94		43	4

DEAS, Paul

Born Perth 22.2.72.   Ht 5 11   Wt 11 00
Midfield. From Kinnoull J. Scotland
Under-21.

Season	Club		
1990–91	St Johnstone	1	—
1991–92		18	—
1992–93		25	1
1993–94		36	—

DEBONT, Andy

Born Wolverhampton 7.2.74   Ht 6 2
Wt 15 06
Goalkeeper. From Trainee.

Season	Club		
1992–93	Wolverhampton W	—	—
1993–94		—	—

DELAP, Rory

Born Coldfield 6.7.76
Midfield. From Trainee.

Season	Club		
1992–93	Carlisle U	1	—
1993–94		1	—

DEMPSEY, Mark

Born Dublin 10.12.72.   Ht 5 8   Wt 11 02
Midfield. From Trainee. Eire Under-21.

Season	Club		
1990–91	Gillingham	2	—
1991–92		30	2
1992–93		16	—
1993–94		—	—

DENNIS, Shaun

Born Kirkcaldy 20.12.69   Ht 6 1   Wt 13 7
Defender. From Lochgelly Albert.
Scotland U-21.

Season	Club		
1988–89	Raith R	10	—
1989–90		18	—
1990–91		35	1
1991–92		42	—
1992–93		31	1
1993–94		43	3

DENNIS, Tony

Born Eton 1.12.63.   Ht 5 7   Wt 10 02
Midfield. From Plymouth Arg, Bideford,
Taunton, Slough.

Season	Club		
1988–89	Cambridge U	18	3
1989–90		17	2

Season	Club		
1990–91		20	2
1991–92		40	2
1992–93		16	1
1993–94	Chesterfield	10	—

DENNISON, Robert

Born Banbridge 30.4.63.   Ht 5 7
Wt 11 00
Forward. From Glenavon. Northern
Ireland 17 full caps.

Season	Club		
1985–86	WBA	12	1
1986–87		4	—
1986–87	Wolverhampton W	10	3
1987–88		43	3
1988–89		43	8
1989–90		46	8
1990–91		42	5
1991–92		22	1
1992–93		37	5
1993–94		14	2

DESBOROUGH, Mickey

Born London 28.11.69
Goalkeeper. From Chelmsford C.

Season	Club		
1993–94	Colchester U	1	—

DEVLIN, Mark

Born Irvine 18.1.73.   Ht 5 10   Wt 11 04
Midfield. From Trainee.

Season	Club		
1990–91	Stoke C	21	2
1991–92		—	—
1992–93		3	—
1993–94		—	—

DEVLIN, Paul

Born Birmingham 14.4.72.   Ht 5 8
Wt 10 05
Forward. From Stafford R.

Season	Club		
1991–92	Notts Co	2	—
1992–93		32	3
1993–94		41	7

DEWHURST, Robert

Born Keighley 10.9.71.   Ht 6 3   Wt 13 01
Defender. From Trainee.

Season	Club		
1990–91	Blackburn R	13	—
1991–92		—	—
1991–92	*Darlington R*	11	1

Season	Club	Apps	Goals
1992–93	Blackburn R	—	—
1992–93	*Huddersfield T*	7	—
1993–94	Blackburn R	—	—
1993–94	Hull C	27	2

DIBBLE, Andy

Born Cwmbran 8.5.65.   Ht 6 2   Wt 13 07
Goalkeeper. From Apprentice. Wales
Schools, Youth, Under-21, 3 full caps.

Season	Club	Apps	Goals
1981–82	Cardiff C	1	—
1982–83		20	—
1983–84		41	—
1984–85	Luton T	13	—
1985–86		7	—
1985–86	*Sunderland*	12	—
1986–87	Luton T	1	—
1986–87	*Huddersfield T*	5	—
1987–88	Luton T	9	—
1988–89	Manchester C	38	—
1989–90		31	—
1990–91		3	—
1990–91	*Aberdeen*	5	—
1990–91	*Middlesbrough*	19	—
1991–92	Manchester C	2	—
1991–92	*Bolton W*	13	—
1991–92	*WBA*	9	—
1992–93	Manchester C	2	—
1992–93	*Oldham Ath*	—	—
1993–94	Manchester C	11	—

DICHIO, Daniele

Born London 19.10.74.   Ht 6 3   Wt 11 00
Forward. From Trainee.

Season	Club	Apps	Goals
1993–94	QPR	—	—
1993–94	*Barnet*	9	2

DICKENS, Alan

Born Plaistow 3.9.64.   Ht 5 11   Wt 12 05
Midfield. From Apprentice. England
Youth, Under-21.

Season	Club	Apps	Goals
1982–83	West Ham U	15	6
1983–84		10	—
1984–85		25	2
1985–86		41	4
1986–87		36	3
1987–88		28	3
1988–89		37	5
1989–90	Chelsea	22	1
1990–91		16	—

Season	Club	Apps	Goals
1991–92		10	—
1992–93		—	—
1992–93	*WBA*	3	1
1992–93	Brentford	15	1
1993–94	Colchester U	32	3

DICKINS, Matt

Born Sheffield 3.9.70.   Ht 6 4   Wt 14 00
Goalkeeper. From Trainee.

Season	Club	Apps	Goals
1989–90	Sheffield U	—	—
1989–90	*Leyton Orient*	—	—
1990–91	Lincoln C	7	—
1991–92		20	—
1991–92	Blackburn R	1	—
1992–93		—	—
1992–93	*Blackpool*	19	—
1993–94	Blackburn R	—	—
1993–94	*Lincoln C*	—	—

DICKOV, Paul

Born Glasgow 1.11.72.   Ht 5 5   Wt 11 05
Forward. From Trainee. Scotland
Under-21.

Season	Club	Apps	Goals
1992–93	Arsenal	3	2
1993–94		1	—
1993–94	*Luton T*	15	1
1993–94	*Brighton*	8	5

DICKS, Julian

Born Bristol 8.8.68.   Ht 5 10   Wt 13 00
Defender. From Apprentice. England
Under-21, B.

Season	Club	Apps	Goals
1985–86	Birmingham C	23	—
1986–87		34	—
1987–88		32	1
1987–88	West Ham U	8	—
1988–89		34	2
1989–90		40	9
1990–91		13	4
1991–92		23	3
1992–93		34	11
1993–94		7	—
1993–94	Liverpool	24	3

DIGBY, Fraser

Born Sheffield 23.4.67.   Ht 6 1   Wt 12 12
Goalkeeper. From Apprentice. England
Youth, Under-21.

Season	Club	Apps	Goals
1984–85	Manchester U	—	—

Season	Club	Apps	Goals
1985–86		—	—
1985–86	*Oldham Ath*	—	—
1985–86	*Swindon T*	—	—
1986–87	Manchester U	—	—
1986–87	Swindon T	39	—
1987–88		31	—
1988–89		46	—
1989–90		45	—
1990–91		41	—
1991–92		21	—
1992–93		33	—
1992–93	*Manchester U*	—	—
1993–94	Swindon T	28	—

DIGWEED, Perry
Born London 26.10.59.   Ht 6 0   Wt 11 04
Goalkeeper. From Apprentice.

Season	Club	Apps	Goals
1976–77	Fulham	1	—
1977–78		—	—
1978–79		2	—
1979–80		11	—
1980–81		1	—
1980–81	Brighton	15	—
1981–82		12	—
1982–83		15	—
1983–84		4	—
1983–84	*WBA*	—	—
1984–85	Brighton	—	—
1984–85	*Charlton Ath*	—	—
1985–86	Brighton	33	—
1986–87		22	—
1987–88	*Newcastle U*	—	—
1987–88	*Chelsea*	3	—
1988–89	Brighton	1	—
1989–90		11	—
1990–91		42	—
1991–92		20	—
1992–93		4	—
1992–93	*Wimbledon*	—	—
1993–94	Wimbledon	—	—
1993–94	Watford	26	—

DIJKSTRA, Meindert
Born Eindhoven 28.2.67   Ht 5 11
Wt 12 00
Defender. From Willem II.

Season	Club	Apps	Goals
1992–93	Notts Co	11	—
1993–94		18	1

DILLON, Kevin
Born Sunderland 18.12.59.   Ht 6 0
Wt 12 07
Midfield. From Apprentice. England
Youth, Under-21.

Season	Club	Apps	Goals
1977–78	Birmingham C	17	1
1978–79		36	2
1979–80		31	6
1980–81		39	2
1981–82		36	1
1982–83		27	3
1982–83	Portsmouth	11	5
1983–84		36	9
1984–85		37	9
1985–86		31	5
1986–87		39	8
1987–88		32	9
1988–89		29	—
1989–90	Newcastle U	43	—
1990–91		19	—
1991–92	Reading	29	3
1992–93		40	1
1993–94		32	—

DINEEN, Jack
Born Brighton 29.9.70   Ht 5 7   Wt 10 10
Midfield. From Brighton, Torsby.

Season	Club	Apps	Goals
1993–94	Scarborough	2	—

DINNIE, Alan
Born Glasgow 14.5.63.   Ht 5 10   Wt 11 00
Defender. From Baillieston J.

Season	Club	Apps	Goals
1987–88	Partick T	37	1
1988–89		31	1
1989–90		14	2
1989–90	Dundee	22	—
1990–91		25	3
1991–92		29	—
1992–93		26	1
1993–94		7	—

DINNING, Tony
Born Wallsend 12.4.75
Defender.

Season	Club	Apps	Goals
1993–94	Newcastle U	—	—

DIXON, Ben
Born Lincoln 16.9.74.   Ht 6 1   Wt 11 00
Forward. From Trainee.

Season	Club		
1991–92	Lincoln C	3	—
1992–93		2	—
1993–94		8	—

DIXON, Kerry
Born Luton 24.7.61.   Ht 6 0   Wt 14 01
Forward. From Tottenham H Apprentice
and Dunstable. England Under-21, 8 full
caps.

Season	Club		
1980–81	Reading	39	13
1981–82		42	12
1982–83		35	26
1983–84	Chelsea	42	28
1984–85		41	24
1985–86		38	14
1986–87		36	10
1987–88		33	11
1988–89		39	25
1989–90		38	20
1990–91		33	10
1991–92		35	5
1992–93	Southampton	9	2
1992–93	*Luton T*	17	3
1993–94	Luton T	29	9

DIXON, Lee
Born Manchester 17.3.64.   Ht 5 8
Wt 11 08
Defender. From Local. England B, 21 full
caps.

Season	Club		
1982–83	Burnley	3	—
1983–84		1	—
1983–84	Chester	16	1
1984–85		41	—
1985–86	Bury	45	5
1986–87	Stoke C	42	3
1987–88		29	2
1987–88	Arsenal	6	—
1988–89		33	1
1989–90		38	5
1990–91		38	5
1991–92		38	4
1992–93		29	—
1993–94		33	—

DOBBIN, Jim
Born Dunfermline 17.9.63.   Ht 5 9
Wt 10 07
Midfield. From Whitburn BC. Scotland
Youth.

Season	Club		
1980–81	Celtic	—	—
1981–82		—	—
1982–83		—	—
1983–84		2	—
1983–84	*Motherwell*	2	—
1983–84	Doncaster R	11	2
1984–85		17	1
1985–86		31	6
1986–87		5	4
1986–87	Barnsley	30	4
1987–88		16	2
1988–89		41	5
1989–90		28	1
1990–91		14	—
1991–92	Grimsby T	32	6
1992–93		39	6
1993–94		29	4

DOBBS, Gerald
Born London 24.1.71.   Ht 5 8   Wt 11 07
Defender. From Trainee.

Season	Club		
1990–91	Wimbledon	—	—
1991–92		4	—
1992–93		19	1
1993–94		10	—

DOBIE, Mark
Born Carlisle 8.11.63.   Ht 5 11   Wt 11 07
Forward. From Gretna.

Season	Club		
1990–91	Cambridge U	—	—
1991–92	Torquay U	20	2
1992–93	Darlington	36	8
1993–94		—	—

DOBSON, Tony
Born Coventry 5.2.69.   Ht 6 1   Wt 12 10
Defender. From Apprentice. England
Under-21.

Season	Club		
1986–87	Coventry C	1	—
1987–88		1	—
1988–89		16	—
1989–90		30	—
1990–91		6	1

Season	Club	League Appearances/Goals
1990–91	Blackburn R	17 —
1991–92		5 —
1992–93		19 —
1993–94		— —
1993–94	Portsmouth	24 2

DODD, Jason
Born Bath 2.11.70. Ht 5 10   Wt 11 13
Defender. England Under-21.

1988–89	Southampton	— —
1989–90		22 —
1990–91		19 —
1991–92		28 —
1992–93		30 1
1993–94		10 —

DODDS, Billy
Born New Cumnock 5.2.69. Ht 5 8
Wt 10 10
Forward. From Apprentice.

1986–87	Chelsea	1 —
1987–88		— —
1987–88	*Partick T*	30 9
1988–89	Chelsea	2 —
1989–90	Dundee	30 13
1990–91		37 15
1991–92		42 19
1992–93		41 16
1993–94		24 5
1993–94	St Johnstone	20 6

DOHERTY, Kevin
Born Londonderry 2.9.75 Ht 5 9
Wt 11 00
Forward. From Trainee.

1993–94	Southampton	— —

DOHERTY, Neil
Born Barrow 21.2.69 Ht 5 9
Midfield. From Trainee.

1987–88	Watford	— —
From Barrow		
1993–94	Birmingham C	13 1

DOLAN, Jim
Born Salsburgh 22.2.69. Ht 5 10
Wt 10 07
Forward. From Motherwell BC.

1987–88	Motherwell	— —

Season	Club	League Appearances/Goals
1988–89		5 —
1989–90		12 —
1990–91		8 1
1991–92		32 2
1992–93		25 2
1993–94		36 —

DOLBY, Chris
Born Dewsbury 4.9.74 Ht 5 8   Wt 9 12
Forward. From Trainee.

1993–94	Rotherham U	1 —

DOLBY, Tony
Born Greenwich 16.4.74   Ht 5 10
Wt 12 02
Forward. From Trainee.

1991–92	Millwall	— —
1992–93		18 1
1993–94		17 —
1993–94	*Barnet*	16 2

DOLING, Stuart
Born Newport, IOW 28.10.72. Ht 5 6
Wt 10 06
Midfield. From Trainee.

1990–91	Portsmouth	— —
1991–92		13 2
1992–93		6 —
1993–94		13 1

DOMINGUEZ, Jose
Born Lisbon 16.2.74   Ht 5 3
Forward. From Benfica.

1993–94	Birmingham C	5 —

DONAGHY, Mal
Born Belfast 13.9.57.   Ht 5 9   Wt 10 00
Defender. From Larne. Northern Ireland
Under-21, 91 full caps.

1978–79	Luton T	40 —
1979–80		42 1
1980–81		42 —
1981–82		42 9
1982–83		40 3
1983–84		40 1
1984–85		42 1
1985–86		42 —
1986–87		42 —

Season	Club	Apps	Goals
1987–88	....	32	1
1988–89	....	6	—
1988–89	Manchester U	30	—
1989–90	....	14	—
1989–90	*Luton T*	5	—
1990–91	Manchester U	25	—
1991–92	....	20	—
1992–93	Chelsea......................	40	2
1993–94	....	28	1

DONALD, Graeme

Born Stirling 14.4.74. Ht 6 0 Wt 11 04
Forward. From Gairdoch U. Scotland
Under-21.

Season	Club	Apps	Goals
1991–92	Hibernian..................	5	3
1992–93	....	4	—
1993–94	....	6	—

DONALDSON, O'Neill

Born Birmingham 24.11.69. Ht 6 0
Wt 11 04
Forward. From Hinckley.

Season	Club	Apps	Goals
1991–92	Shrewsbury T..............	19	2
1992–93	....	—	—
1993–94	....	9	2

DONNELLY, Darren

Born Liverpool 28.12.71. Ht 5 10
Wt 11 06
Forward. From Trainee.

Season	Club	Apps	Goals
1990–91	Blackburn R	2	—
1991–92	....	—	—
1992–93	....	—	—
1993–94	Chester C....................	9	—

DONNELLY, Simon

Born Glasgow 1.12.74. Ht 5 9 Wt 10 12
Forward. Celtic BC. Scotland Under-21.

Season	Club	Apps	Goals
1993–94	Celtic..........................	12	5

DONOVAN, Kevin

Born Halifax 17.12.71. Ht 5 7 Wt 10 10
Forward. From Trainee.

Season	Club	Apps	Goals
1989–90	Huddersfield T............	1	—
1990–91	....	6	1
1991–92	....	10	—
1991–92	*Halifax T*	6	—
1992–93	Huddersfield T............	3	—

Season	Club	Apps	Goals
1992–93	WBA..........................	32	6
1993–94	....	37	8

DONOWA, Lou

Born Ipswich 24.9.64. Ht 5 9 Wt 11 00
Forward. From Apprentice. England
Under-21.

Season	Club	Apps	Goals
1982–83	Norwich C	1	—
1983–84	....	25	4
1984–85	....	34	7
1985–86	....	2	—
1985–86	*Stoke C*	4	1
From Coruna, Willem II Tilburg			
1989–90	Ipswich T	23	1
1990–91	Bristol C	24	3
1991–92	Birmingham C	26	2
1992–93	....	21	2
1992–93	*Crystal Palace*.............	—	—
1992–93	*Burnley*......................	4	—
1993–94	Birmingham C	21	5
1993–94	*Shrewsbury T*	4	—

DOOLAN, John

Born South Liverpool 10.11.68. Ht 5 10
Wt 10 12
Midfield. From Knowsley U.

Season	Club	Apps	Goals
1991–92	Wigan Ath	2	—
1992–93	....	17	—
1993–94	....	—	—

DORIGO, Tony

Born Australia 31.12.65. Ht 5 10
Wt 10 09
Defender. From Apprentice. England B,
Under-21, 15 full caps.

Season	Club	Apps	Goals
1983–84	Aston Villa.................	1	—
1984–85	....	31	—
1985–86	....	38	1
1986–87	....	41	—
1987–88	Chelsea......................	40	—
1988–89	....	40	6
1989–90	....	35	3
1990–91	....	31	2
1991–92	Leeds U	38	3
1992–93	....	33	1
1993–94	....	37	—

DOW, Andrew

Born Dundee 7.2.73. Ht 5 9 Wt 10 07
Midfield. From Sporting Club 85. Scotland Under-21.

1990–91	Dundee	—	—
1991–92		4	—
1992–93		14	1
1993–94	Chelsea	14	—

DOWE, Julian

Born Manchester 9.9.75 Ht 6 1 Wt 12 04
Forward. From Trainee.

1992–93	Wigan Ath	—	—
1993–94		—	—

DOWELL, Wayne

Born Co Durham 28.12.73 Ht 5 10 Wt 11 02
Defender. From Trainee.

1992–93	Burnley	—	—
1993–94		—	—

DOWIE, Iain

Born Hatfield 9.1.65. Ht 6 1 Wt 13 07
Forward. From Hendon. Northern Ireland Under-23, 25 full caps.

1988–89	Luton T	8	—
1989–90		29	9
1989–90	*Fulham*	5	1
1990–91	Luton T	29	7
1990–91	West Ham U	12	4
1991–92		—	—
1991–92	Southampton	30	9
1992–93		36	11
1993–94		39	5

DOWNING, Keith

Born Oldbury 23.7.65. Ht 5 8 Wt 11 00
Midfield. From Mile Oak R.

1984–85	Notts Co	12	—
1985–86		3	—
1986–87		8	1
1987–88	Wolverhampton W	34	1
1988–89		32	1
1989–90		31	3
1990–91		31	1
1991–92		32	—
1992–93		31	2
1993–94	Birmingham C	1	—

DOWNS, Greg

Born Carlton 13.12.58. Ht 5 9 Wt 10 07
Defender. From Apprentice.

1976–77	Norwich C	—	—
1977–78		1	—
1977–78	*Torquay U*	1	1
1978–79	Norwich C	3	—
1979–80		18	—
1980–81		29	2
1981–82		28	1
1982–83		28	—
1983–84		42	4
1984–85		20	—
1985–86	Coventry C	41	—
1986–87		39	2
1987–88		27	2
1988–89		22	—
1989–90		17	—
1990–91	Birmingham C	17	—
1991–92	Hereford U	40	2
1992–93		38	—
1993–94		27	—

DOYLE, Maurice

Born Ellesmere Port 17.10.69. Ht 5 8 Wt 10 07
Forward. From Trainee.

1987–88	Crewe Alex	4	—
1988–89		4	2
1989–90	QPR	—	—
1990–91	*Crewe Alex*	7	2
1990–91	*Wolverhampton W*	—	—
1991–92	QPR	—	—
1992–93		5	—
1993–94		1	—

DOYLE, Steve

Born Neath 2.6.58. Ht 5 9 Wt 11 01
Midfield. From Apprentice. Wales Under-21.

1974–75	Preston NE	13	—
1975–76		24	1
1976–77		22	—
1977–78		32	1
1978–79		29	2
1979–80		14	—
1980–81		27	1

Season	Club	Apps	Goals
1981–82	....	36	3
1982–83	Huddersfield T...........	42	2
1983–84	....	36	2
1984–85	....	36	2
1985–86	....	42	—
1986–87	....	5	—
1986–87	Sunderland................	33	—
1987–88	....	32	1
1988–89	....	35	1
1989–90	Hull C	36	2
1990–91	....	11	—
1990–91	Rochdale................	31	—
1991–92	....	27	—
1992–93	....	18	—
1993–94	....	34	1

DOZZELL, Jason

Born Ipswich 9.12.67.   Ht 6 1   Wt 12 13
Forward. From school. England Youth,
Under-21.

Season	Club	Apps	Goals
1983–84	Ipswich T	5	1
1984–85	....	14	2
1985–86	....	41	3
1986–87	....	42	2
1987–88	....	39	1
1988–89	....	29	11
1989–90	....	46	8
1990–91	....	30	6
1991–92	....	45	11
1992–93	....	41	7
1993–94	Tottenham H	32	8

DRAPER, Mark

Born Derby 11.11.70.   Ht 5 10   Wt 11 00
Midfield. From Trainee. England
Under-21.

Season	Club	Apps	Goals
1988–89	Notts Co	20	3
1989–90	....	34	3
1990–91	....	45	9
1991–92	....	35	1
1992–93	....	44	11
1993–94	....	44	13

DREYER, John

Born Alnwick 11.6.63.   Ht 6 1   Wt 11 06
Defender. From Wallingford T.

Season	Club	Apps	Goals
1984–85	Oxford U	—	—
1985–86	....	—	—
1985–86	*Torquay U*	5	—

Season	Club	Apps	Goals
1985–86	*Fulham*	12	2
1986–87	Oxford U	25	2
1987–88	....	35	—
1988–89	Luton T	18	1
1989–90	....	38	2
1990–91	....	38	3
1991–92	....	42	2
1992–93	....	38	2
1993–94	....	40	3

DRINKELL, Kevin

Born Grimsby 18.6.60.   Ht 5 11   Wt 12 06
Forward. From Apprentice.

Season	Club	Apps	Goals
1976–77	Grimsby T	4	2
1977–78	....	26	5
1978–79	....	28	7
1979–80	....	33	16
1980–81	....	41	7
1981–82	....	28	6
1982–83	....	39	17
1983–84	....	36	15
1984–85	....	35	14
1985–86	Norwich C	41	22
1986–87	....	42	16
1987–88	....	38	12
1988–89	Rangers	32	12
1989–90	....	4	—
1989–90	Coventry C	22	5
1990–91	....	15	—
1991–92	....	4	—
1991–92	*Birmingham C*	5	2
1992–93	Falkirk	35	7
1993–94	....	20	6

DRUCE, Mark

Born Oxford 3.3.74.   Ht 5 11   Wt 11 11
Forward. From Trainee.

Season	Club	Apps	Goals
1991–92	Oxford U	2	—
1992–93	....	4	1
1993–94	....	19	—

DRURY, Nathan

Born Leeds 15.1.76   Ht 6 0   Wt 11 02
Defender. From Trainee.

Season	Club	Apps	Goals
1992–93	Nottingham F	—	—
1993–94	....	—	—

DRYDEN, Richard

Born Stroud 14.6.69.   Ht 6 0   Wt 11 02
Defender.

Season	Club		
1986–87	Bristol R	6	—
1987–88		6	—
1988–89		1	—
1988–89	Exeter C	21	—
1989–90		30	7
1990–91	*Manchester C*	—	—
1991–92	Notts Co	29	1
1992–93		2	—
1992–93	*Plymouth Arg*	5	—
1992–93	Birmingham C	11	—
1993–94		34	—

DRYSDALE, Jason

Born Bristol 17.11.70.   Ht 5 10   Wt 12 00
Defender. From Trainee. England Youth.
Football League.

Season	Club		
1988–89	Watford	—	—
1989–90		20	—
1990–91		30	—
1991–92		37	5
1992–93		39	6
1993–94		19	—

DUBERRY, Michael

Born Enfield 14.10.75   Ht 6 1   Wt 12 13
Defender. From Trainee.

Season	Club		
1993–94	Chelsea	1	—

DUBLIN, Dion

Born Leicester 22.4.69.   Ht 6 0   Wt 12 04
Forward.

Season	Club		
1987–88	Norwich C	—	—
1988–89	Cambridge U	21	6
1989–90		46	15
1990–91		46	16
1991–92		43	15
1992–93	Manchester U	7	1
1993–94		5	1

DUBLIN, Keith

Born Wycombe 29.1.66.   Ht 6 0
Wt 12 10
Defender. From Apprentice. England
Youth.

Season	Club		
1983–84	Chelsea	1	—

Season	Club		
1984–85		11	—
1985–86		11	—
1986–87		28	—
1987–88	Brighton	46	5
1988–89		43	—
1989–90		43	—
1990–91	Watford	43	—
1991–92		46	—
1992–93		46	1
1993–94		33	1

DUDLEY, Derek

Born Birmingham 2.2.70.
Goalkeeper. From VS Rugby.

Season	Club		
1993–94	WBA	—	—

DUFFIELD, Peter

Born Middlesbrough 4.2.69.   Ht 5 6
Wt 10 07
Forward.

Season	Club		
1986–87	Middlesbrough	—	—
1987–88	Sheffield U	11	1
1987–88	*Halifax T*	12	6
1988–89	Sheffield U	38	11
1989–90		5	2
1990–91		2	—
1990–91	*Rotherham U*	17	4
1991–92	Sheffield U	2	—
1992–93		—	—
1992–93	*Blackpool*	5	1
1992–93	*Bournemouth*	—	—
1992–93	*Stockport Co*	7	4
1992–93	*Crewe Alex*	2	—
1993–94	Sheffield U	—	—
1993–94	Hamilton A	36	19

DUFFIN, Stuart

Born Glasgow 27.6.75   Ht 5 9   Wt 11 07
Forward.

Season	Club		
1993–94	Bristol C	—	—

DUFFY, Chris

Born Manchester 31.10.73   Ht 5 10
Wt 11 11
Midfield. From Trainee.

Season	Club		
1992–93	Crewe Alex	—	—
1993–94	Wigan Ath	27	1

DUFFY, Jim

Born Glasgow 27.4.59. Ht 5 10   Wt 11 04
Defender. From Maryhill Jun.

Season	Club	Apps	Goals
1978–79	Celtic	—	—
1979–80		—	—
1980–81		—	—
1981–82	Morton	20	—
1982–83		27	—
1983–84		38	2
1984–85		34	1
1985–86	Dundee	36	—
1986–87		42	2
1987–88		5	—
1988–89	Falkirk manager		
1989–90	Dundee	8	—
1990–91	Partick T	34	2
1991–92		38	2
1992–93	Dundee	39	—
1993–94		35	—

DUFFY, Neil (Cornelius)

Born Glasgow 5.6.67.   Ht 6 1   Wt 11 13
Defender. From Shamrock (SA).

Season	Club	Apps	Goals
1989–90	Dundee U	—	—
1990–91	Falkirk	25	2
1991–92		39	2
1992–93		34	5
1993–94		23	9
1993–94	Dundee	9	2

DUNLOP, Simon

Born Grimsby 24.11.74   Ht 5 11
Wt 12 00
Midfield. From Trainee.

Season	Club	Apps	Goals
1993–94	Grimsby T	—	—

DUNN, Iain

Born Derwent 1.4.72.   Ht 5 11   Wt 10 10
Forward. From School. England Youth.

Season	Club	Apps	Goals
1988–89	York C	26	6
1989–90		18	2
1990–91		33	3
1991–92	Chesterfield	13	1
From Goole T			
1992–93	Huddersfield T	28	3
1993–94		34	6

DUNNE, Joe

Born Dublin 25.5.73.   Ht 5 8   Wt 11 06
Midfield. From Trainee. Eire Youth,
Under-21.

Season	Club	Apps	Goals
1990–91	Gillingham	26	—
1991–92		11	—
1992–93		4	—
1993–94		37	—

DUNPHY, Sean

Born Rotherham 5.11.70.   Ht 6 3
Wt 13 05
Defender. From Trainee.

Season	Club	Apps	Goals
1989–90	Barnsley	6	—
1990–91	Lincoln C	—	—
1991–92		5	1
1992–93		31	1
1993–94		17	—
1993–94	*Doncaster R*	1	—

DURBIN, Gary

Born Bristol 16.12.74   Ht 5 9   Wt 12 04
Midfield. From Trainee.

Season	Club	Apps	Goals
1993–94	Bristol C	—	—

DURIE, Gordon

Born Paisley 6.12.65.   Ht 6 0   Wt 12 00
Forward. From Hill of Beath Hawthorn.
Scotland B, Under-21, 27 full caps.

Season	Club	Apps	Goals
1981–82	East Fife	13	1
1982–83		25	2
1983–84		34	16
1984–85		9	7
1984–85	Hibernian	22	8
1985–86		25	6
1985–86	Chelsea	1	—
1986–87		25	5
1987–88		26	12
1988–89		32	17
1989–90		15	5
1990–91		24	12
1991–92	Tottenham H	31	7
1992–93		17	3
1993–94		10	1
1993–94	Rangers	24	12

DURKAN, Kieron

Born Chester 1.12.73. Ht 5 10 Wt 11 05
Midfield. From Trainee.

Season	Club	App	Goals
1991–92	Wrexham	1	—
1992–93		1	—
1993–94		10	1

DURNIN, John

Born Bootle 18.8.65. Ht 5 10 Wt 11 04
Forward. From Waterloo Dock.

Season	Club	App	Goals
1985–86	Liverpool	—	—
1986–87		—	—
1987–88		—	—
1988–89		—	—
1988–89	*WBA*	5	2
1988–89	Oxford U	19	3
1989–90		42	13
1990–91		26	9
1991–92		37	8
1992–93		37	11
1993–94	Portsmouth	28	6

DURRANT, Iain

Born Glasgow 29.10.66. Ht 5 8 Wt 9 07
Midfield. From Glasgow United. Scotland
Youth, Under-21, 11 full caps.

Season	Club	App	Goals
1984–85	Rangers	5	—
1985–86		30	2
1986–87		39	4
1987–88		40	10
1988–89		8	2
1989–90		—	—
1990–91		4	1
1991–92		13	—
1992–93		30	3
1993–94		23	—

DURRANT, Lee

Born Gt Yarmouth 18.12.73 Ht 5 10
Wt 11 07
Midfield. From Trainee.

Season	Club	App	Goals
1992–93	Ipswich T	—	—
1993–94		7	—

DUXBURY, Lee

Born Skipton 7.10.69. Ht 5 10 Wt 11 07
Midfield. From Trainee.

Season	Club	App	Goals
1988–89	Bradford C	1	—

Season	Club	App	Goals
1989–90		12	1
1989–90	*Rochdale*	10	—
1990–91	Bradford C	45	5
1991–92		46	5
1992–93		42	5
1993–94		43	9

DUXBURY, Mike

Born Accrington 1.9.59. Ht 5 9
Wt 11 02
Defender. From Apprentice. England
Under-21, 10 full caps.

Season	Club	App	Goals
1976–77	Manchester U	—	—
1977–78		—	—
1978–79		—	—
1979–80		—	—
1980–81		33	2
1981–82		24	—
1982–83		42	1
1983–84		39	—
1984–85		30	1
1985–86		23	1
1986–87		32	1
1987–88		39	—
1988–89		18	—
1989–90		19	—
1990–91	Blackburn R	22	—
1991–92		5	—
1991–92	Bradford C	16	—
1992–93		36	—
1993–94		13	—

DYCHE, Sean

Born Kettering 28.6.71. Ht 6 0 Wt 11 07
Midfield. From Trainee.

Season	Club	App	Goals
1988–89	Nottingham F	—	—
1989–90		—	—
1989–90	Chesterfield	22	2
1990–91		28	2
1991–92		42	3
1992–93		20	1
1993–94		20	—

DYER, Alex

Born West Ham 14.11.65. Ht 5 11
Wt 11 12
Midfield. From Watford Apprentice.

Season	Club	App	Goals
1983–84	Blackpool	9	—
1984–85		36	8

Season	Club		Apps	Goals
1985–86	....		39	8
1986–87	....		24	3
1986–87	Hull C........................		17	4
1987–88	....		28	8
1988–89	....		15	2
1988–89	Crystal Palace		7	2
1989–90	....		10	—
1990–91	Charlton Ath		35	7
1991–92	....		13	—
1992–93	....		30	6
1993–94	Oxford U		38	5

DYER, Bruce
Born Ilford 13.4.75 Ht 5 10 Wt 11 02
Forward. From Trainee. England
Under-21.

Season	Club		Apps	Goals
1992–93	Watford		2	—
1993–94	....		29	6
1993–94	Crystal Palace		11	—

DYKSTRA, Sieb
Born Kerkrade 20.10.66. Ht 6 5
Wt 14 07
Goalkeeper. From Roda JC.

Season	Club		Apps	Goals
1991–92	Motherwell..................		1	—
1992–93	....		35	—
1993–94	....		44	—

DYSON, Jon
Born Mirfield 18.12.71 Ht 6 1 Wt 12 00
Defender. From school.

Season	Club		Apps	Goals
1991–92	Huddersfield T............		—	—
1992–93	....		15	—
1993–94	....		22	—

EADEN, Nicky
Born Sheffield 12.12.72 Ht 6 0 Wt 12 00
Defender. From Trainee.

Season	Club		Apps	Goals
1991–92	Barnsley		—	—
1992–93	....		2	—
1993–94	....		37	2

EADIE, Darren
Born Chippenham 10.6.75 Ht 5 7
Wt 10 00
Forward. From Trainee. England
Under-21.

Season	Club		Apps	Goals
1992–93	Norwich C..................		—	—
1993–94	....		15	3

EARLE, Robbie
Born Newcastle, Staffs. 27.1.65. Ht 5 9
Wt 10 10
Forward. From Stoke C.

Season	Club		Apps	Goals
1981–82	Port Vale....................		—	—
1982–83	....		8	1
1983–84	....		12	—
1984–85	....		46	15
1985–86	....		46	15
1986–87	....		35	6
1987–88	....		25	4
1988–89	....		44	13
1989–90	....		43	12
1990–91	....		35	11
1991–92	Wimbledon		40	14
1992–93	....		42	7
1993–94	....		42	9

EBBRELL, John
Born Bromborough 1.10.69. Ht 5 7
Wt 9 12
Midfield. FA Schools, England Youth, B,
Under-21.

Season	Club		Apps	Goals
1986–87	Everton		—	—
1987–88	....		—	—
1988–89	....		4	—
1989–90	....		17	—
1990–91	....		36	3
1991–92	....		39	1
1992–93	....		24	1
1993–94	....		39	4

EBDON, Marcus

Born Pontypool 17.10.70. Ht 5 9
Wt 11 00
Midfield. From Trainee. Wales Under-21.

Season	Club	Apps	Goals
1988–89	Everton	—	—
1989–90		—	—
1990–91		—	—
1991–92	Peterborough U	15	2
1992–93		28	4
1993–94		10	—

ECKHARDT, Jeff

Born Sheffield 7.10.65. Ht 6 0 Wt 11 07
Defender.

Season	Club	Apps	Goals
1984–85	Sheffield U	7	—
1985–86		33	2
1986–87		22	—
1987–88		12	—
1987–88	Fulham	29	1
1988–89		43	2
1989–90		40	2
1990–91		29	2
1991–92		43	7
1992–93		30	6
1993–94		35	5

EDESON, Matthew

Born Beverley 11.8.76 Ht 5 10 Wt 11 00
Forward. From Trainee.

Season	Club	Apps	Goals
1992–93	Hull C	2	—
1993–94		—	—

EDGHILL, Richard

Born Oldham 23.9.74 Ht 5 9 Wt 10 01
Defender. From Trainee. England
Under-21.

Season	Club	Apps	Goals
1992–93	Manchester C	—	—
1993–94		22	—

EDINBURGH, Justin

Born Brentwood 18.12.69. Ht 5 10
Wt 11 08
Defender. From Trainee.

Season	Club	Apps	Goals
1988–89	Southend U	15	—
1989–90		22	—
1989–90	*Tottenham H*	—	—
1990–91	Tottenham H	16	1
1991–92		23	—

Season	Club	Apps	Goals
1992–93		32	—
1993–94		25	—

EDMONDSON, Darren

Born Coniston 4.11.71. Ht 6 0 Wt 12 02
Defender. From Trainee.

Season	Club	Apps	Goals
1990–91	Carlisle U	31	—
1991–92		27	2
1992–93		34	—
1993–94		22	3

EDWARDS, Andy

Born Epping 17.9.71. Ht 6 2 Wt 13 06
Midfield. From Trainee.

Season	Club	Apps	Goals
1988–89	Southend U	1	—
1989–90		8	—
1990–91		2	1
1991–92		9	—
1992–93		41	—
1993–94		42	1

EDWARDS, David

Born Bridgnorth 13.1.74. Ht 5 10
Wt 10 08
Midfield. From Trainee.

Season	Club	Apps	Goals
1991–92	Walsall	22	1
1992–93		5	—
1993–94		—	—

EDWARDS, Matthew

Born Hammersmith 15.6.71 Ht 5 10
Wt 11 00
Midfield. From Trainee.

Season	Club	Apps	Goals
1989–90	Tottenham H	—	—
1990–91		—	—
1990–91	*Reading*	8	—
1991–92	Tottenham H	—	—
1992–93	Brighton	33	2
1993–94		27	4

EDWARDS, Mike

Born Bebbington 10.9.74 Ht 5 11
Wt 11 05
Midfield. From Trainee.

Season	Club	Apps	Goals
1993–94	Tranmere R	—	—

EDWARDS, Neil

Born Aberdare 5.12.70. Ht 5 8 Wt 11 02
Goalkeeper. From Trainee.

Season	Club	Apps	Goals
1988–89	Leeds U	—	—

Season	Club	App	Goals
1989–90		—	—
1990–91		—	—
1990–91	*Huddersfield T*	—	—
1991–92	Stockport Co	39	—
1992–93		35	—
1993–94		26	—

EDWARDS, Paul

Born Liverpool 22.2.65. Ht 5 11
Wt 11 05
Goalkeeper. From St. Helens T.

Season	Club	App	Goals
1988–89	Crewe Alex	10	—
1989–90		8	—
1990–91		9	—
1991–92		2	—
1992–93	Shrewsbury T	42	—
1993–94		42	—

EDWARDS, Paul R

Born Birkenhead 25.12.63. Ht 5 11
Wt 11 00
Defender. From Altrincham.

Season	Club	App	Goals
1987–88	Crewe Alex	13	1
1988–89		45	4
1989–90		28	1
1989–90	Coventry C	8	—
1990–91		23	—
1991–92		5	—
1992–93		—	—
1992–93	Wolverhampton W	35	—
1993–94		11	—
1993–94	WBA	15	—

EDWARDS, Robert

Born Manchester 23.2.70. Ht 5 8
Wt 11 07
Forward. From Trainee.

Season	Club	App	Goals
1987–88	Crewe Alex	6	1
1988–89		4	—
1989–90		4	—
1990–91		29	11
1991–92		28	6
1992–93		23	7
1993–94		12	2

EDWARDS, Robert

Born Kendal 1.7.73. Ht 6 0   Wt 11 06
Defender. Wales Under-21.

Season	Club	App	Goals
1989–90	Carlisle U	12	—

Season	Club	App	Goals
1990–91		36	5
1990–91	Bristol C	—	—
1991–92		20	1
1992–93		18	—
1993–94		38	2

EDWARDS, Russell

Born Beckenham 21.12.73. Ht 6 2
Wt 12 07
Defender. From Local.

Season	Club	App	Goals
1992–93	Crystal Palace	—	—
1993–94		—	—
1993–94	Barnet	5	1

EDWORTHY, Mark

Born Barnstaple 24.12.72. Ht 5 7
Wt 9 08
Midfield. From Trainee.

Season	Club	App	Goals
1990–91	Plymouth Arg	—	—
1991–92		15	—
1992–93		15	—
1993–94		12	—

EELES, Tony

Born Chatham 15.11.70. Ht 5 6
Wt 10 08
Midfield. From Trainee.

Season	Club	App	Goals
1988–89	Gillingham	3	—
1989–90		33	2
1990–91		6	—
1991–92		17	1
1992–93		14	2
1993–94		—	—

EHIOGU, Ugo

Born London 3.11.72. Ht 6 2   Wt 13 03
Defender. From Trainee. England
Under-21.

Season	Club	App	Goals
1990–91	WBA	2	—
1991–92	Aston Villa	8	—
1992–93		4	—
1993–94		17	—

EKOKU, Efan

Born Manchester 8.6.67. Ht 6 1
Wt 12 00
Forward. From Sutton U. Nigeria full
caps.

Season	Club	App	Goals
1990–91	Bournemouth	20	3

Season	Club	Apps	Goals
1991–92		28	11
1992–93		14	7
1992–93	Norwich C	4	3
1993–94		27	12

ELAD, Efon
Born Hillingdon 5.9.70   Ht 5 10
Wt 12 00
Forward. From Cologne.

Season	Club	Apps	Goals
1993–94	Northampton T	10	—

ELI, Roger
Born Bradford 11.9.65.   Ht 5 11
Wt 11 03
Defender. From Apprentice.

Season	Club	Apps	Goals
1983–84	Leeds U	—	—
1984–85		1	—
1985–86		1	—
1985–86	Wolverhampton W	14	—
1986–87		4	—
1987–88	Cambridge U	—	—
1987–88	Crewe Alex	27	1
1988–89	York C	4	1
1988–89	Bury	2	—
From Northwich Vic			
1989–90	Burnley	29	—
1990–91		26	1
1991–92		33	10
1992–93		11	—
1993–94		—	—

ELKINS, Gary
Born Wallingford 4.5.66.   Ht 5 09
Wt 11 12
Midfield. From Apprentice. England
Youth.

Season	Club	Apps	Goals
1983–84	Fulham	—	—
1984–85		21	—
1985–86		13	—
1986–87		9	—
1987–88		29	—
1988–89		22	1
1989–90		10	1
1989–90	*Exeter C*	5	—
1990–91	Wimbledon	10	—
1991–92		18	1
1992–93		18	—
1993–94		18	1

ELLIOTT, Matthew
Born Surrey 1.11.68.   Ht 6 3   Wt 14 05
Defender. From Epsom & Ewell.

Season	Club	Apps	Goals
1988–89	Charlton Ath	—	—
1988–89	Torquay U	13	2
1989–90		33	2
1990–91		45	6
1991–92		33	5
1991–92	*Scunthorpe U*	8	1
1992–93	Scunthorpe U	39	6
1993–94		14	1
1993–94	Oxford U	32	5

ELLIOTT, Robbie
Born Newcastle 25.12.73.   Ht 5 10
Wt 10 13
Defender. From Trainee.

Season	Club	Apps	Goals
1990–91	Newcastle U	6	—
1991–92		9	—
1992–93		—	—
1993–94		15	—

ELLIOTT, Tony
Born Nuneaton 30.11.69.   Ht 6 0
Wt 12 12
Goalkeeper. England Youth.

Season	Club	Apps	Goals
1986–87	Birmingham C	—	—
1987–88		—	—
1988–89		—	—
1988–89	Hereford U	23	—
1989–90		29	—
1990–91		5	—
1991–92		18	—
1992–93	Huddersfield T	15	—
1993–94	Carlisle U	6	—

ELLIS, Tony
Born Salford 20.10.64.   Ht 5 11   Wt 11 00
Forward. From Horwich RMI, Northwich
Vic.

Season	Club	Apps	Goals
1986–87	Oldham Ath	5	—
1987–88		3	—
1987–88	Preston NE	24	4
1988–89		45	19
1989–90		17	3
1989–90	Stoke C	24	6
1990–91		38	9
1991–92		15	4

1992–93	Preston NE	35	22
1993–94		37	26

ELLISON, Tony
Born Bishop Auckland 13.1.73. Ht 6 0
Wt 12 00
Forward. From Trainee.

1990–91	Darlington	13	3
1991–92		27	10
1992–93		3	—
1992–93	*Hartlepool U*	4	1
1993–94	Darlington	29	4

EMBERSON, Carl
Born Epsom 13.7.73 Ht 6 1 Wt 13 11
Goalkeeper. From Trainee.

1991–92	Millwall	—	—
1992–93		—	—
1992–93	*Colchester U*	13	—
1993–94	Millwall	—	—

EMBLEN, Neil
Born Bromley 19.6.71
Defender. From Sittingbourne.

1993–94	Millwall	12	—

EMBLETON, Daniel
Born Liverpool 27.3.75 Ht 5 11
Wt 11 04
Goalkeeper. From Trainee.

1992–93	Liverpool	—	—
1993–94		—	—

EMERSON, Dean
Born Salford 27.12.62. Ht 5 9 Wt 12 11
Midfield. From Local.

1981–82	Stockport Co	23	1
1982–83		45	3
1983–84		44	1
1984–85		44	2
1985–86	Rotherham U	45	7
1986–87		10	1
1986–87	Coventry C	19	—
1987–88		20	—
1988–89		18	—
1989–90		12	—
1990–91		24	—
1991–92		21	—

1992–93	Hartlepool U	32	1
1993–94		13	—
1993–94	Stockport Co	8	—

ENGLISH, Isaac
Born Paisley 12.11.71. Ht 5 8 Wt 10 00
Forward. From Gleniffer Th.

1989–90	St Mirren	—	—
1989–90	Partick T	6	2
1990–91		13	2
1991–92		26	5
1992–93		13	—
1993–94		36	4

ENGLISH, Tony
Born Luton 19.10.66 Ht 6 0 Wt 12 04
Defender. From Coventry C apprentice.
England Youth.

1984–85	Colchester U	22	3
1985–86		45	13
1986–87		32	7
1987–88		43	2
1988–89		36	8
1989–90		44	2
1990–91		*40*	*7*
1991–92		*38*	*6*
1992–93		33	1
1993–94		42	4

ESDAILLE, David
Born Manchester 22.7.63 Ht 5 8
Wt 11 00
Midfield.

1992–93	Wrexham	4	—
1992–93	Bury	6	—
1993–94		—	—

EUSTACE, Scott
Born Leicester 13.6.75 Ht 6 0 Wt 12 04
Forward. From Trainee.

1993–94	Leicester C	1	—

EVANS, Ceri
Born Christchurch 2.10.63. Ht 6 1
Wt 14 02
Defender. From Otago Univ, Worcester
Coll. (Oxford). New Zealand full caps.

1988–89	Oxford U	4	—

1989–90	....	24 2
1990–91	....	18 1
1991–92	....	29 —
1992–93	....	41 —
1993–94	....	— —

EVANS, Darren
Born Wolverhampton 30.9.74   Ht 5 10
Wt 11 00
Defender. From Trainee.

1993–94	Aston Villa.................	— —

EVANS, David A
Born 25.11.75
Forward. From Trainee.

1993–94	Cardiff C.....................	1 —

EVANS, Gareth
Born Coventry 14.1.67.   Ht 5 8   Wt 10 06
Forward. From Apprentice.

1984–85	Coventry C..................	— —
1985–86		6 —
1986–87		1 —
1986–87	Rotherham U	34 9
1987–88		29 4
1987–88	Hibernian....................	12 2
1988–89		35 5
1989–90		28 3
1990–91	*Northampton T*............	2 —
1990–91	*Stoke C*......................	5 1
1991–92	Hibernian....................	41 6
1992–93		39 6
1993–94		40 4

EVANS, John
Born Liverpool 8.9.74   Ht 5 10   Wt 11 00
Midfield. From Trainee.

1993–94	Tranmere R	— —

EVANS, Mark
Born Leeds 24.8.70.   Ht 6 0   Wt 11 08
Goalkeeper. From Trainee.

1988–89	Bradford C	3 —
1989–90		5 —
1990–91		3 —
1991–92		1 —
1992–93	Scarborough................	20 —
1993–94		26 —

EVANS, Mike
Born Plymouth 1.1.73.   Ht 6 0   Wt 11 02
Forward. From Trainee.

1990–91	Plymouth Arg.............	4 —
1991–92		13 —
1992–93		23 1
1992–93	*Blackburn R*	— —
1993–94	Plymouth Arg.............	22 9

EVANS, Nicky
Born Bedford 6.7.58.   Ht 6 0   Wt 11 10
Midfield. From Kettering T, QPR,
Peterborough U, Wycombe W.

1991–92	Barnet	9 1
1992–93		18 4
1993–94		12 3

EVANS, Paul
Born Oswestry 1.9.74.   Ht 5 6   Wt 10 08
Midfield. From Trainee.

1991–92	Shrewsbury T...............	2 —
1992–93		4 —
1993–94		13 —

EVANS, Richard
Born Ebbw Vale 12.4.68.   Ht 5 11
Wt 11 07
Midfield. From Weymouth.

1991–92	Bristol R	2 1
1992–93		11 —
1992–93	*Exeter C*.....................	5 2
1993–94	Bristol R	2 —

EVANS, Stewart
Born Maltby 15.11.60.   Ht 6 4   Wt 11 05
Forward. From Apprentice.

1978–79	Rotherham U	— —
1979–80		— —
From Gainsborough T		
1980–81	Sheffield U	— —
1981–82	Wimbledon	18 4
1982–83		42 14
1983–84		45 12
1984–85		40 14
1985–86		30 6
1986–87	WBA	14 1
1986–87	Plymouth Arg.............	5 —
1987–88		37 10

Season	Club		League Appearances/Goals	
1988–89		3	—
1988–89	Rotherham U	25	6
1989–90		20	4
1990–91		20	4
1990–91	*Torquay U*	15	5
1991–92	Crewe Alex	17	4
1992–93		26	1
1993–94		40	7

Season	Club		
1990–91		36	6
1991–92		41	9
1992–93		46	16
1993–94	Burnley	45	19

EVANS, Terry
Born London 12.4.65. Ht 6 5 Wt 15 01
Defender. From Hillingdon B.

Season	Club		
1985–86	Brentford	19	1
1986–87		1	—
1987–88		29	4
1988–89		45	5
1989–90		44	3
1990–91		36	2
1991–92		44	8
1992–93		11	—
1993–94		—	—
1993–94	Wycombe W	22	6

EVANS, Terry
Born Pontypridd 8.1.76
Defender. From Trainee.

Season	Club		
1993–94	Cardiff C	5	—

EVANS, Wayne
Born Welshpool 25.8.71 Ht 5 10
Wt 12 05
Defender. From Welshpool.

Season	Club		
1993–94	Walsall	41	—

EVERSHAM, Paul
Born Hereford 28.1.75 Ht 5 9 Wt 11 07
Midfield. From Trainee.

Season	Club		
1993–94	Hereford U	8	1

EYRE, John
Born Humberside 9.10.74
Forward. From Trainee.

Season	Club		
1993–94	Oldham Ath	2	—

EYRES, David
Born Liverpool 26.2.64. Ht 5 10
Wt 11 00
Forward. From Rhyl.

Season	Club		
1989–90	Blackpool	35	7

FAIRBAIRN, Neil
Born Ashington 4.10.74   Ht 5 11
Wt 11 00
Goalkeeper. From Trainee.

Season	Club	Apps	Goals
1993–94	Wimbledon	—	—

FAIRCLOUGH, Chris
Born Nottingham 12.4.64.   Ht 5 11
Wt 11 02
Defender. From Apprentice. England
Under-21.

Season	Club	Apps	Goals
1981–82	Nottingham F	—	—
1982–83		15	—
1983–84		31	—
1984–85		35	—
1985–86		—	—
1986–87		26	1
1987–88	Tottenham H	40	4
1988–89		20	1
1988–89	Leeds U	11	—
1989–90		42	8
1990–91		34	4
1991–92		31	2
1992–93		30	3
1993–94		40	4

FAIRCLOUGH, Wayne
Born Nottingham 27.4.68.   Ht 5 10
Wt 12 02
Defender. From Apprentice.

Season	Club	Apps	Goals
1985–86	Notts Co	5	—
1986–87		9	—
1987–88		29	—
1988–89		20	—
1989–90		8	—
1989–90	Mansfield T	13	—
1990–91		41	6
1991–92		25	3
1992–93		33	1
1993–94		29	2

FAIRWEATHER, Carlton
Born London 22.9.61.   Ht 5 11   Wt 11 00
Forward. From Tooting & Mitcham.

Season	Club	Apps	Goals
1984–85	Wimbledon	13	2
1985–86		20	7
1986–87		26	8
1987–88		21	4

Season	Club	Apps	Goals
1988–89		26	3
1989–90		21	1
1990–91		5	1
1991–92		6	—
1992–93		—	—
1993–94	Carlisle U	12	1

FALCONER, Willie
Born Aberdeen 5.4.66.   Ht 6 1   Wt 11 09
Midfield. From Lewis United. Scotland
Schools, Youth.

Season	Club	Apps	Goals
1982–83	Aberdeen	1	—
1983–84		8	1
1984–85		16	4
1985–86		8	—
1986–87		8	—
1987–88		36	8
1988–89	Watford	33	5
1989–90		30	3
1990–91		35	4
1991–92	Middlesbrough	25	5
1992–93		28	5
1993–94	Sheffield U	23	3
1993–94	Celtic	14	1

FALLON, Sean
Born New Zealand 11.5.76   Ht 6 0
Wt 12 08
Forward. From Trainee.

Season	Club	Apps	Goals
1993–94	Liverpool	—	—

FARNINGHAM, Ray
Born Dundee 10.4.61.   Ht 5 8   Wt 10 07
Forward. From Celtic BC.

Season	Club	Apps	Goals
1978–79	Forfar Ath	1	—
1979–80		38	5
1980–81		34	4
1981–82		39	5
1982–83		21	3
1983–84		37	6
1984–85		31	4
1985–86		37	2
1986–87		2	—
1986–87	Motherwell	29	3
1987–88		29	6
1988–89		18	3
1989–90	Dunfermline Ath	17	—
1990–91		10	—
1991–92		4	1

1991–92	Partick T	33	7
1992–93		37	8
1993–94		2	—
1993–94	Dundee	24	2

FARNWORTH, Simon
Born Chorley 28.10.63.   Ht 6 0   Wt 11 13
Goalkeeper. From Apprentice. England
Schools.

1981–82	Bolton W	—	—
1982–83		—	—
1983–84		36	—
1984–85		46	—
1985–86		31	—
1986–87		—	—
1986–87	*Stockport Co*	10	—
1986–87	*Tranmere R*	7	—
1986–87	Bury	14	—
1987–88		39	—
1988–89		45	—
1989–90		7	—
1990–91	Preston NE	23	—
1991–92		23	—
1992–93		35	—
1993–94	Wigan Ath	42	—

FARQUHAR, Alistair
Born Aberfeldy 15.8.76   Ht 5 8   Wt 10 12
Forward. From Trainee.

1993–94	Coventry C	—	—

FARRELL, Andy
Born Colchester 7.10.65.   Ht 6 0
Wt 11 00
Defender. From School.

1983–84	Colchester U	15	—
1984–85		38	—
1985–86		24	1
1986–87		28	4
1987–88	Burnley	45	3
1988–89		36	4
1989–90		36	2
1990–91		37	2
1991–92		39	3
1992–93		42	3
1993–94		22	2

FARRELL, David
Born Glasgow 29.10.69.   Ht 5 9   Wt 10 12
Midfield. From Oxford U Apprentice.

1988–89	Hibernian	—	—
1989–90		—	—
1990–91		2	—
1991–92		6	—
1992–93		12	—
1993–94		35	2

FARRELL, David
Born Birmingham 11.11.71   Ht 5 11
Wt 11 02
Forward. From Redditch U.

1992–93	Aston Villa	2	—
1992–93	*Scunthorpe U*	5	1
1993–94	Aston Villa	4	—

FARRELL, Sean
Born Watford 28.2.69.   Ht 6 1   Wt 12 08
Midfield. From Apprentice.

1986–87	Luton T	—	—
1987–88		—	—
1987–88	*Colchester U*	9	1
1988–89	Luton T	—	—
1989–90		1	—
1990–91		20	1
1991–92		4	—
1991–92	*Northampton T*	4	1
1991–92	Fulham	25	10
1992–93		35	12
1993–94		34	9

FARRELLY, Gareth
Born Dublin 28.8.75   Ht 6 0   Wt 12 07
Midfield. From Home Farm.

1992–93	Aston Villa	—	—
1993–94		—	—

FARRINGTON, Mark
Born Liverpool 15.6.65.   Ht 5 10
Wt 11 12
Forward. From Everton Apprentice.

1983–84	Norwich C	2	—
1984–85		12	2
1984–85	Cambridge U	10	1
1985–86	Cardiff C	31	3
From Feyenoord			
1991–92	Brighton	14	1

| 1992–93 | ... | 8 | 2 |
| 1993–94 | | 6 | 1 |

FASHANU, John
Born Kensington 18.9.63.   Ht 6 1
Wt 11 12
Forward. From Cambridge U. Amateur.
England 2 full caps.

1979–80	Norwich C	—	—
1980–81		—	—
1981–82		5	1
1982–83		2	—
1983–84		—	—
1983–84	*Crystal Palace*	1	—
1983–84	Lincoln C	26	6
1984–85		10	4
1984–85	Millwall	25	4
1985–86		25	8
1985–86	Wimbledon	9	4
1986–87		37	11
1987–88		38	14
1988–89		30	12
1989–90		24	11
1990–91		35	20
1991–92		38	18
1992–93		29	6
1993–94		36	11

FASHANU, Justin
Born Kensington 19.2.61.   Ht 6 1
Wt 13 01
Forward. From Apprentice. England
Youth, Under-21, B.

1978–79	Norwich C	16	5
1979–80		34	11
1980–81		40	19
1981–82	Nottingham F	32	3
1982–83	Southampton	9	3
1982–83	Nottingham F	—	—
1982–83	Notts Co	15	7
1983–84		17	5
1884–85		32	8
1985–86	Brighton	16	2
1986–87		—	—
From Edmonton
1989–90	Manchester C	2	—
1989–90	West Ham U	2	—
1989–90	Leyton Orient	5	—

From Toronto B
1991–92	Newcastle U	—	—
1991–92	Torquay U	21	10
1992–93		20	5
1992–93	Airdrieonians	16	5
1993–94	Hearts	11	1

FAULKNER, David
Born Sheffield 8.10.75
Defender. From Trainee.
| 1992–93 | Sheffield W | — | — |
| 1993–94 | | — | — |

FEAR, Peter
Born London 10.9.73   Ht 5 10   Wt 11 05
Defender. From Trainee. England
Under-21.
| 1992–93 | Wimbledon | 4 | — |
| 1993–94 | | 23 | 1 |

FEARON, Ron
Born Romford 19.11.60   Ht 6 0   Wt 11 12
Goalkeeper. From QPR Apprentice.
1979–80	Reading	—	—
1980–81		6	—
1981–82		42	—
1982–83		13	—
From Sutton
1987–88	Ipswich T	10	—
1988–89		18	—
1988–89	*Brighton*	7	—
1989–90		—	—
1990–91	Leyton Orient	—	—
1991–92	Ipswich T	—	—
1992–93		—	—
1992–93	*Walsall*	1	—
1993–94	Southend U	—	—

FEENEY, Mark
Born Derry 26.7.74   Ht 5 7
Midfield. From Trainee.
| 1992–93 | Barnsley | 2 | — |
| 1993–94 | | — | — |

FELGATE, David

Born Blaenau Ffestiniog 4.3.60.   Ht 6 2
Wt 13 06
Goalkeeper. From Blaenau Ffestiniog.
Wales Schools, Under-21, 1 full cap.

Season	Club	App	Goals
1978–79	Bolton W	—	—
1978–79	*Rochdale*	35	—
1979–80	Bolton W	—	—
1979–80	*Bradford C*	—	—
1979–80	Crewe Alex	14	—
1979–80	*Rochdale*	12	—
1980–81	Bolton W	—	—
1980–81	Lincoln C	42	—
1981–82		43	—
1982–83		46	—
1983–84		46	—
1984–85		21	—
1984–85	*Cardiff C*	4	—
1984–85	*Grimsby T*	12	—
1985–86	Grimsby T	12	—
1985–86	Bolton W	15	—
1986–87		20	—
1986–87	*Rotherham U*	—	—
1987–88	Bolton W	46	—
1988–89		46	—
1989–90		40	—
1990–91		46	—
1991–92		25	—
1992–93		—	—
1993–94	Bury	—	—
1993–94	Wolverhampton W	—	—
1993–94	Chester C	34	—

FENSOME, Andy

Born Northampton 18.2.69.   Ht 5 8
Wt 11 02
Midfield. From Trainee.

Season	Club	App	Goals
1986–87	Norwich C	—	—
1987–88		—	—
1988–89		—	—
1988–89	*Newcastle U*	—	—
1989–90	Cambridge U	24	—
1990–91		36	—
1991–92		34	1
1992–93		30	—
1993–94		2	—
1993–94	Preston NE	31	1

FENTON, Graham

Born Wallsend 22.5.74.   Ht 5 10
Wt 11 03
Forward. From Trainee.

Season	Club	App	Goals
1991–92	Aston Villa	—	—
1992–93		—	—
1993–94		12	1
1993–94	*WBA*	7	3

FENWICK, Paul

Born London 25.8.69   Ht 6 1   Wt 12 01
Defender. From Winnipeg Fury.

Season	Club	App	Goals
1992–93	Birmingham C	10	—
1993–94		9	—

FENWICK, Terry

Born Camden, Co. Durham 17.11.59.
Ht 5 10   Wt 11 12
Defender. From Apprentice. England
Youth, Under-21, 20 full caps.

Season	Club	App	Goals
1976–77	Crystal Palace	—	—
1977–78		10	—
1978–79		24	—
1979–80		15	—
1980–81		21	—
1980–81	QPR	19	2
1981–82		36	5
1982–83		39	3
1983–84		41	10
1984–85		41	2
1985–86		37	7
1986–87		21	1
1987–88		22	3
1987–88	Tottenham H	17	—
1988–89		34	8
1989–90		10	—
1990–91		4	—
1990–91	*Leicester C*	8	1
1991–92	Tottenham H	23	—
1992–93		5	—
1993–94	Swindon T	26	—

FERDINAND, Les

Born London 18.12.66.   Ht 5 11
Wt 13 05
Forward. From Hayes. England 6 full
caps.

Season	Club	App	Goals
1986–87	QPR	2	—

Season	Club	Appearances	Goals
1987–88		1	—
1987–88	*Brentford*	3	—
1988–89	QPR	—	—
1988–89	*Besiktas*	—	—
1989–90	QPR	9	2
1990–91		18	8
1991–92		23	10
1992–93		37	20
1993–94		36	16

FEREDAY, Wayne

Born Warley 16.6.63. Ht 5 9 Wt 11 08
Midfield. From Apprentice. England Under-21.

Season	Club	Appearances	Goals
1980–81	QPR	6	2
1981–82		4	—
1982–83		5	—
1983–84		17	4
1984–85		26	7
1985–86		34	2
1986–87		37	2
1987–88		37	4
1988–89		31	—
1989–90	Newcastle U	25	—
1990–91		8	—
1990–91	Bournemouth	18	—
1991–92		5	—
1991–92	WBA	22	2
1992–93		16	1
1993–94		10	—
1993–94	Cardiff C	17	1

FERGUSON, Darren

Born Glasgow 9.2.72. Ht 5 10 Wt 10 04
Midfield. From Trainee. Scotland Under-21.

Season	Club	Appearances	Goals
1990–91	Manchester U	5	—
1991–92		4	—
1992–93		15	—
1993–94		3	—
1993–94	Wolverhampton W	14	—

FERGUSON, Derek

Born Glasgow 31.7.67. Ht 5 8 Wt 10 11
Midfield. From Gartcosh United. Scotland Schools, Youth, Under-21, 2 full caps.

Season	Club	Appearances	Goals
1983–84	Rangers	1	—
1984–85		8	—
1985–86		19	—
1986–87		30	1
1987–88		32	4
1988–89		16	2
1989–90		5	—
1989–90	*Dundee*	4	—
1990–91	Hearts	28	2
1991–92		38	1
1992–93		37	1
1993–94	Sunderland	41	—

FERGUSON, Duncan

Born Stirling 27.12.71. Ht 6 3 Wt 13 05
Forward. From Carse Thistle. Scotland Under-21, 4 full caps.

Season	Club	Appearances	Goals
1990–91	Dundee U	9	1
1991–92		38	15
1992–93		30	12
1993–94	Rangers	10	1

FERGUSON, Iain

Born Newarthill 4.8.62. Ht 5 7 Wt 10 07
Forward. From Fir Park BC. Scotland Youth, Under-21.

Season	Club	Appearances	Goals
1979–80	Dundee	13	5
1980–81		11	1
1981–82		34	12
1982–83		29	9
1983–84		33	12
1984–85	Rangers	28	6
1985–86		4	—
1986–87	*Dundee*	3	2
1986–87	Dundee U	36	16
1987–88		39	11
1988–89	Hearts	29	5
1989–90		11	1
1989–90	*Charlton Ath*	1	—
1989–90	*Bristol C*	11	2
1990–91	Hearts	12	2
1990–91	Motherwell	15	8
1991–92		20	—
1992–93		15	2
1993–94		1	—

FERGUSON, Ian

Born Glasgow 15.3.67. Ht 5 10 Wt 10 11
Midfield. From Clyde BC. Scotland B, Under-21, 8 full caps.

Season	Club	Appearances	Goals
1984–85	Clyde	2	—
1985–86		19	4

Season	Club	League Appearances/Goals	
1986–87		5	—
1986–87	St Mirren	35	4
1987–88		22	6
1987–88	Rangers	8	1
1988–89		30	6
1989–90		24	—
1990–91		11	1
1991–92		16	1
1992–93		30	4
1993–94		35	5

FERGUSON, Ian
Born Dunfermline 5.8.68. Ht 6 1
Wt 12 00
Forward. From Lochgelly Albert.

Season	Club	League Appearances/Goals	
1987–88	Raith R	9	4
1988–89		28	4
1989–90		32	6
1990–91		33	8
1991–92		9	1
1991–92	Hearts	30	4
1992–93		24	4
1993–94		6	1
1993–94	St Johnstone	22	3

FERNANDES, Tamer
Born London 7.12.74 Ht 6 3 Wt 13 07
Goalkeeper. From Trainee.

Season	Club	League Appearances/Goals	
1993–94	Brentford	1	—

FERNEY, Martin
Born Lambeth 8.11.71. Ht 5 11
Wt 12 04
Defender. From Trainee.

Season	Club	League Appearances/Goals	
1990–91	Fulham	14	—
1991–92		—	—
1992–93		16	1
1993–94		23	—

FETTIS, Alan
Born Newtonards 1.2.71. Ht 6 1
Wt 11 04
Goalkeeper. From Ards. Northern Ireland
4 full caps.

Season	Club	League Appearances/Goals	
1991–92	Hull C	43	—
1992–93		20	—
1993–94		37	—

FEUER, Tony
Born Las Vegas 20.5.71 Ht 6 7
Goalkeeper.

Season	Club	League Appearances/Goals	
1993–94	West Ham U	—	—

FICKLING, Ashley
Born Sheffield 15.11.72 Ht 5 10
Wt 11 08
Defender. From Trainee.

Season	Club	League Appearances/Goals	
1991–92	Sheffield U	—	—
1992–93		—	—
1992–93	*Darlington*	14	—
1993–94	Darlington	1	—

FILAN, John
Born Sydney 8.2.70 Ht 5 11 Wt 12 10
Goalkeeper. From Budapest St George.

Season	Club	League Appearances/Goals	
1992–93	Cambridge U	6	—
1993–94		46	—

FINDLAY, William
Born Kilmarnock 29.8.70. Ht 5 10
Wt 10 13
Midfield. From Kilmarnock BC. Scotland
Under-21.

Season	Club	League Appearances/Goals	
1987–88	Hibernian	—	—
1988–89		3	1
1989–90		10	—
1990–91		26	2
1991–92		9	—
1992–93		7	—
1993–94		20	3

FINLAY, Darren
Born Belfast 19.12.73. Ht 5 4 Wt 10 00
Defender. From Trainee.

Season	Club	League Appearances/Goals	
1991–92	QPR	—	—
1992–93		—	—
1993–94		—	—

FINLEY, Alan
Born Liverpool 10.12.67. Ht 6 3
Wt 14 03
Defender. From Marine.

Season	Club	League Appearances/Goals	
1988–89	Shrewsbury T	34	1
1989–90		29	1
1990–91	Stockport Co	19	3

1991–92	....	18	1
1992–93	....	22	1
1992–93	*Carlisle U*....................	1	—
1993–94	Stockport Co	7	—
1993–94	*Rochdale*.....................	1	—

FINNEY, Stephen
Born Hexham 31.10.73. Ht 5 10
Wt 12 00
Forward. From Trainee.

1991–92	Preston NE.................	2	1
1992–93	....	4	—
1992–93	Manchester C	—	—
1993–94	....	—	—

FINNIGAN, John
Born Wakefield 29.3.76 Ht 5 8 Wt 10 05
Midfield. From Trainee.

| 1992–93 | Nottingham F............. | — | — |
| 1993–94 | .... | — | — |

FINNIGAN, Tony
Born Wimbledon 17.10.62. Ht 5 10
Wt 11 09
Defender. From Crystal Palace
Apprentice.

1980–81	Fulham	—	—
1981–82	....	—	—
1982–83	....	—	—
1983–84	....	—	—
1984–85	Crystal Palace.............	11	1
1985–86	....	36	3
1986–87	....	41	6
1987–88	....	17	—
1988–89	Blackburn R	17	—
1989–90	....	19	—
1990–91	Hull C........................	18	1
1990–91	Swindon T	3	—
1991–92	Brentford	3	—
1992–93	....	—	—
1993–94	Barnet........................	6	1

FISHER, Neil
Born St Helens 7.11.70. Ht 5 8 Wt 11 00
Midfield. From Trainee.

1990–91	Bolton W	—	—
1991–92	....	7	1
1992–93	....	4	—

| 1993–94 | .... | 2 | — |

FITZGERALD, Scott
Born London 13.8.69. Ht 6 0 Wt 12 02
Defender. From Trainee. Eire Under-21,
B.

1988–89	Wimbledon	—	—
1989–90	....	1	—
1990–91	....	—	—
1991–92	....	36	1
1992–93	....	20	—
1993–94	....	28	—

FITZPATRICK, Paul
Born Liverpool 5.10.65. Ht 6 4 Wt 12 00
Midfield.

1984–85	Tranmere R	—	—
1985–86	Liverpool	—	—
1984–85	Preston NE	—	—
1984–85	Bolton W	3	—
1985–86	....	11	—
1986–87	Bristol C	19	2
1987–88	....	24	5
1988–89	....	1	—
1988–89	Carlisle U...................	32	—
1988–89	*Preston NE*	2	—
1989–90	Carlisle U...................	45	4
1990–91	....	32	—
1991–92	Leicester C	26	4
1992–93	....	1	—
1992–93	Birmingham C	7	—
1992–93	*Bury*	9	—
1993–94	Hamilton A.................	18	1
1993–94	Northampton T	2	1

FJORTOFT, Jan-Aage
Born Aalesund 10.1.67 Ht 6 3 Wt 13 04
Forward. From Rapid Vienna.

| 1993–94 | Swindon T .... | 36 | 12 |

FLAHAVAN, Aaron
Born Southampton 15.12.75 Ht 6 1
Wt 12 10
Goalkeeper. From Trainee.

| 1993–94 | Portsmouth .... | — | — |

FLATTS, Mark

Born Haringay 14.10.72 Ht 5 06 Wt 9 08
Midfield. From Trainee.

Season	Club	Apps	Goals
1992–93	Arsenal	10	—
1993–94		3	—
1993–94	*Cambridge U*	5	1
1993–94	*Brighton*	10	1

FLECK, Robert

Born Glasgow 11.8.65. Ht 5 10 Wt 10 03
Forward. From Possil YM. Scotland
Youth, Under-21, 4 full caps.

Season	Club	Apps	Goals
1983–84	Partick T	2	1
1983–84	Rangers	1	—
1984–85		8	—
1985–86		15	3
1986–87		40	19
1987–88		21	7
1987–88	Norwich C	18	7
1988–89		33	10
1989–90		27	7
1990–91		29	5
1991–92		36	11
1992–93	Chelsea	31	2
1993–94		9	1
1993–94	*Bolton W*	7	1

FLEMING, Craig

Born Calder 6.10.71. Ht 6 0 Wt 11 07
Defender. From Trainee.

Season	Club	Apps	Goals
1988–89	Halifax T	1	—
1989–90		10	—
1990–91		46	—
1991–92	Oldham Ath	32	1
1992–93		24	—
1993–94		37	—

FLEMING, Curtis

Born Manchester 8.10.68. Ht 5 8
Wt 11 04
Defender. From St Patrick's Ath. Eire
Youth, Under-21, B.

Season	Club	Apps	Goals
1988–89	Swindon T	—	—
From St Patrick's Ath			
1991–92	Middlesbrough	28	—
1992–93		24	—
1993–94		40	—

FLEMING, Gary

Born Londonderry 17.2.67. Ht 5 9
Wt 11 03
Defender. From Apprentice. Northern
Ireland 28 full caps.

Season	Club	Apps	Goals
1984–85	Nottingham F	2	—
1985–86		16	—
1986–87		34	—
1987–88		22	—
1988–89		—	—
1989–90	Manchester C	14	—
1989–90	*Notts Co*	3	—
1989–90	Barnsley	12	—
1990–91		44	—
1991–92		42	—
1992–93		46	—
1993–94		46	—

FLEMING, Paul

Born Halifax 6.9.67. Ht 5 7 Wt 11 08
Defender.

Season	Club	Apps	Goals
1985–86	Halifax T	13	—
1986–87		15	—
1987–88		9	—
1988–89		23	—
1989–90		40	1
1990–91		39	—
1991–92	Mansfield T	38	—
1992–93		—	—
1993–94		28	—

FLEMING, Terry

Born Marston Green 5.1.73. Ht 5 9
Wt 11 00
Forward. From Trainee.

Season	Club	Apps	Goals
1990–91	Coventry C	2	—
1991–92		—	—
1992–93		11	—
1993–94	Northampton T	31	1

FLETCHER, Andrew

Born Saltburn 12.8.71. Ht 6 0 Wt 13 00
Forward. From Trainee.

Season	Club	Apps	Goals
1989–90	Middlesbrough	—	—
1990–91	Scarborough	6	1
1991–92		21	5
1992–93		21	5
From Billingham			
1993–94	Hartlepool U	—	—

FLETCHER, Steve
Born Hartlepool 26.6.72. Ht 6 2
Wt 14 00
Forward. From Trainee.

Season	Club	Apps	Goals
1990–91	Hartlepool U	14	2
1991–92		18	2
1992–93	Bournemouth	31	4
1993–94		36	6

FLIES, Brian
Born Denmark 29.8.69
Goalkeeper. From Naestved.

Season	Club	Apps	Goals
1993–94	Dundee U	1	—

FLITCROFT, David
Born Bolton 14.1.74. Ht 6 0 Wt 13 09
Forward. From Trainee.

Season	Club	Apps	Goals
1991–92	Preston NE	—	—
1992–93		8	2
1993–94		—	—
1993–94	*Lincoln C*	2	—
1993–94	Chester C	8	1

FLITCROFT, Gary
Born Bolton 6.11.72. Ht 5 11 Wt 11 08
Defender. From Trainee. England
Under-21.

Season	Club	Apps	Goals
1991–92	Manchester C	—	—
1991–92	*Bury*	12	—
1992–93	Manchester C	32	5
1993–94		21	3

FLO, Jostein
Born Norway 3.10.64. Ht 6 4 Wt 14 00
Forward. From Sogndal. Norway full
caps.

Season	Club	Apps	Goals
1993–94	Sheffield U	33	9

FLOUNDERS, Andy
Born Hull 13.12.63. Ht 5 11 Wt 11 06
Forward. From Apprentice.

Season	Club	Apps	Goals
1980–81	Hull C	5	—
1981–82		13	5
1982–83		23	13
1983–84		30	9
1984–85		39	14
1985–86		25	10
1986–87		24	3
1986–87	Scunthorpe U	15	6
1987–88		45	24
1988–89		46	16
1989–90		44	18
1990–91		46	23
1991–92	Rochdale	42	17
1992–93		32	14
1992–93	*Rotherham U*	6	2
1993–94	Rochdale	11	—
1993–94	*Carlisle U*	8	1

FLOWERS, Paul
Born London 7.9.74. Ht 5 11 Wt 12 06
Defender. From Trainee.

Season	Club	Apps	Goals
1992–93	Colchester U	3	—
1993–94		—	—

FLOWERS, Tim
Born Kenilworth 3.2.67. Ht 6 2
Wt 14 01
Goalkeeper. From Apprentice. England
Youth, Under-21, 2 full caps.

Season	Club	Apps	Goals
1984–85	Wolverhampton W	38	—
1985–86		25	—
1985–86	*Southampton*	—	—
1986–87	Southampton	9	—
1986–87	*Swindon T*	2	—
1987–88	Southampton	9	—
1987–88	*Swindon T*	5	—
1988–89	Southampton	7	—
1989–90		35	—
1990–91		37	—
1991–92		41	—
1992–93		42	—
1993–94		12	—
1993–94	Blackburn R	29	—

FLYNN, Mike
Born Oldham 23.2.69. Ht 6 0 Wt 11 00
Defender. From Trainee.

Season	Club	Apps	Goals
1986–87	Oldham Ath	—	—
1987–88		31	1
1988–89		9	—
1988–89	Norwich C	—	—
1989–90		—	—
1989–90	Preston NE	23	1
1990–91		35	1
1991–92		43	3

1992–93	....	35	2
1992–93	Stockport Co	10	—
1993–94	....	46	1

FLYNN, Sean

Born Birmingham 13.3.68. Ht 5 8
Wt 11 08
Midfield. From Halesowen T.

1991–92	Coventry C	22	2
1992–93	....	7	—
1993–94	....	36	3

FOLEY, Steve

Born Liverpool 4.10.62. Ht 5 7   Wt 11 03
Midfield. From Apprentice.

1980–81	Liverpool	—	—
1981–82	....	—	—
1982–83	....	—	—
1983–84	....	—	—
1983–84	*Fulham*	3	—
1984–85	Grimsby T	31	2
1985–86	Sheffield U	28	5
1986–87	....	38	9
1987–88	Swindon T	35	4
1988–89	....	40	8
1989–90	....	23	4
1990–91	....	44	7
1991–92	....	9	—
1991–92	Stoke C	20	1
1992–93	....	44	7
1993–94	....	43	2

FORAN, Mark

Born Aldershot 30.10.73. Ht 6 4
Wt 13 12
Defender. From Trainee.

1991–92	Millwall	—	—
1992–93	....	—	—
1993–94	....	—	—
1993–94	Sheffield U	—	—

FORD, Bobby

Born Oxford 22.9.74 Ht 5 8 Wt 10 06
Midfield. From Trainee.

| 1992–93 | Oxford U .... | — | — |
| 1993–94 | .... | 14 | — |

FORD, John

Born Birmingham 12.4.68. Ht 6 1
Wt 13 01
Midfield. From Cradley T.

1991–92	Swansea C	44	—
1992–93	....	43	3
1993–94	....	27	1

FORD, Mark

Born Pontefract 10.10.75 Ht 5 7
Wt 10 03
Midfield. From Trainee.

| 1992–93 | Leeds U .... | — | — |
| 1993–94 | .... | 1 | — |

FORD, Mike

Born Bristol 9.2.66. Ht 6 0   Wt 11 02
Defender. From Apprentice.

| 1983–84 | Leicester C .... | — | — |
| From Devizes |
1984–85	Cardiff C	20	1
1985–86	....	44	4
1986–87	....	36	1
1987–88	....	45	7
1988–89	Oxford U	10	1
1989–90	....	31	2
1990–91	....	28	1
1991–92	....	9	1
1992–93	....	44	4
1993–94	....	41	1

FORD, Stuart

Born Sheffield 20.7.71. Ht 5 11   Wt 11 13
Goalkeeper. From Trainee.

1989–90	Rotherham U	1	—
1990–91	....	—	—
1991–92	....	4	—
1991–92	*Scarborough*	6	—
1992–93	Scarborough................	22	—
1993–94	Bury	—	—
1993–94	Doncaster R................	6	—

FORD, Tony

Born Grimsby 14.5.59. Ht 5 9 Wt 12 02
Forward. From Apprentice. England B.

1975–76	Grimsby T	14	—
1976–77	....	6	—
1977–78	....	34	2

Season	Club	Apps	Goals
1978–79		45	15
1979–80		37	5
1980–81		28	4
1981–82		35	7
1982–83		37	4
1983–84		42	8
1984–85		42	6
1985–86		34	3
1985–86	*Sunderland*	9	1
1986–87	Stoke C	41	6
1987–88		44	7
1988–89		27	—
1988–89	WBA	11	1
1989–90		42	8
1990–91		46	5
1991–92		15	—
1991–92	Grimsby T	22	1
1992–93		17	2
1993–94		29	—
1993–94	*Bradford C*	5	—

FOREMAN, Darren

Born Southampton 12.2.68.   Ht 5 10
Wt 10 08
Forward. England Schools.

Season	Club	Apps	Goals
1986–87	Barnsley	16	1
1987–88		9	4
1988–89		5	—
1989–90		17	3
1989–90	Crewe Alex	14	3
1990–91		9	1
1990–91	Scarborough	14	5
1991–92		24	2
1992–93		42	27
1993–94		3	—

FOREMAN, Matthew

Born Gateshead 15.2.75   Ht 6 0
Defender. From Trainee.

Season	Club	Apps	Goals
1993–94	Sheffield U	—	—

FORMBY, Kevin

Born Ormskirk 22.7.71   Ht 5 11
Wt 12 00
Forward. From Burscough.

Season	Club	Apps	Goals
1993–94	Rochdale	5	—

FORREST, Craig

Born Vancouver 20.9.67.   Ht 6 5
Wt 14 00
Goalkeeper. From Apprentice. Canada full caps.

Season	Club	Apps	Goals
1985–86	Ipswich T	—	—
1986–87		—	—
1987–88		—	—
1987–88	*Colchester U*	11	—
1988–89	Ipswich T	28	—
1989–90		45	—
1990–91		43	—
1991–92		46	—
1992–93		11	—
1993–94		27	—

FORRESTER, Jamie

Born Bradford 1.11.74   Ht 5 7   Wt 10 00
Forward. From Auxerre. England Youth.

Season	Club	Apps	Goals
1992–93	Leeds U	6	—
1993–94		3	—

FORRESTER, Paul

Born Edinburgh 3.11.72   Ht 5 8
Wt 12 00
Forward.

Season	Club	Apps	Goals
1992–93	Middlesbrough	—	—
1993–94		1	—

FORSTER, Nick

Born Oxted 8.9.73   Ht 5 9   Wt 11 05
Forward. From Horley T.

Season	Club	Apps	Goals
1992–93	Gillingham	26	6
1993–94		41	18

FORSYTH, Mike

Born Liverpool 20.3.66.   Ht 5 11
Wt 12 02
Defender. From Apprentice. England Youth, B, Under-21.

Season	Club	Apps	Goals
1983–84	WBA	8	—
1984–85		10	—
1985–86		11	—
1985–86	*Northampton T*	—	—
1985–86	Derby Co	—	—
1986–87		41	1
1987–88		39	3
1988–89		38	—

Season	Club	App	Goals
1989–90		38	—
1990–91		35	—
1991–92		43	1
1992–93		41	1
1993–94		28	2

FOSTER, Adrian
Born Kidderminster 20.7.71.   Ht 5 9
Wt 11 00
Forward. From Trainee.

Season	Club	App	Goals
1989–90	WBA	14	1
1990–91		5	—
1991–92		8	1
1992–93	Torquay U	36	9
1993–94		39	15

FOSTER, Colin
Born Chislehurst 16.7.64.   Ht 6 4
Wt 14 01
Defender. From Apprentice.

Season	Club	App	Goals
1981–82	Orient	23	2
1982–83		43	2
1983–84		11	1
1984–85		42	1
1985–86		36	2
1986–87		19	2
1986–87	Nottingham F	9	1
1987–88		39	2
1988–89		18	2
1989–90		6	—
1989–90	West Ham U	22	1
1990–91		36	3
1991–92		24	—
1992–93		6	1
1993–94		5	—
1993–94	Notts Co	9	—
1993–94	Watford	6	1

FOSTER, John
Born Manchester 19.9.73   Ht 5 10
Wt 11 01
Defender. From Trainee.

Season	Club	App	Goals
1992–93	Manchester C	—	—
1993–94		1	—

FOSTER, Stephen
Born Mansfield 3.12.74
Defender. From Trainee.

Season	Club	App	Goals
1993–94	Mansfield T	5	—

FOSTER, Steve
Born Portsmouth 24.9.57.   Ht 6 1
Wt 14 00
Defender. From Apprentice. England
Under-21, 3 full caps.

Season	Club	App	Goals
1975–76	Portsmouth	11	—
1976–77		31	1
1977–78		31	3
1978–79		36	2
1979–80	Brighton	38	1
1980–81		42	1
1981–82		40	2
1982–83		36	1
1983–84		16	1
1983–84	Aston Villa	7	1
1984–85		8	2
1984–85	Luton T	25	1
1985–86		35	3
1986–87		28	2
1987–88		39	2
1988–89		36	3
1989–90	Oxford U	35	4
1990–91		38	3
1991–92		22	2
1992–93	Brighton	35	4
1993–94		34	2

FOSTER, Wayne
Born Leigh 11.9.63.   Ht 5 8   Wt 11 00
Forward. From Apprentice. England
Youth.

Season	Club	App	Goals
1981–82	Bolton W	23	2
1982–83		24	4
1983–84		30	3
1984–85		28	4
1985–86	Preston NE	31	3
1986–87	Hearts	31	4
1987–88		39	4
1988–89		9	1
1989–90		17	1
1990–91		28	1
1991–92		7	—
1992–93		11	—
1993–94		17	1

FOWLER, Jason
Born Bristol 20.8.74   Ht 6 1   Wt 11 06
Midfield. From Trainee.

Season	Club	App	Goals
1992–93	Bristol C	1	—

1993–94		1	—

FOWLER, John
Born Preston 27.10.74. Ht 5 10 Wt 11 10
Midfield. From Trainee.

1991–92	Cambridge U	—	—
1992–93		3	—
1992–93	*Preston NE*	6	—
1993–94	Cambridge U	20	—

FOWLER, Lee
Born Nottingham 26.1.69. Ht 5 8
Wt 11 07
Forward. From Trainee.

1987–88	Stoke C	1	—
1988–89		—	—
1989–90		15	—
1990–91		17	—
1991–92		16	—
1992–93	Preston NE	32	2
1993–94		—	—
1993–94	Doncaster R	11	—

FOWLER, Robbie
Born Liverpool 9.4.75. Ht 5 9 Wt 11 08
Forward. From Trainee. England
Under-21.

1991–92	Liverpool	—	—
1992–93		—	—
1993–94		28	12

FOX, Mark
Born Basingstoke 17.11.75.
Midfield. From Trainee.

1993–94	Brighton	12	—

FOX, Peter
Born Scunthorpe 5.7.57. Ht 5 10
Wt 12 04
Goalkeeper. From Apprentice.

1972–73	Sheffield W	1	—
1973–74		—	—
1974–75		20	—
1975–76		27	—
1976–77		1	—
1976–77	*West Ham U*	—	—
1977–78	Sheffield W	—	—
1977–78	*Barnsley*	1	—

1977–78	Stoke C	—	—
1978–79		1	—
1979–80		23	—
1980–81		42	—
1981–82		38	—
1982–83		35	—
1983–84		42	—
1984–85		14	—
1985–86		37	—
1986–87		39	—
1987–88		17	—
1988–89		29	—
1989–90		38	—
1990–91		44	—
1991–92		—	—
1992–93		10	—
1992–93	*Wrexham*	—	—
1993–94	Exeter C	26	—

FOX, Ruel
Born Ipswich 14.1.68. Ht 5 6 Wt 10 00
Midfield. From Apprentice.

1985–86	Norwich C	—	—
1986–87		3	—
1987–88		34	2
1988–89		4	—
1989–90		7	3
1990–91		28	4
1991–92		37	2
1992–93		34	4
1993–94		25	7
1993–94	Newcastle U	14	2

FOX, Simon
Born Basingstoke 28.8.77.
Forward. From Trainee.

1993–94	Brighton	1	—

FOYLE, Martin
Born Salisbury 2.5.63. Ht 5 10 Wt 11 02
Forward. From Amateur.

1980–81	Southampton	—	—
1981–82		—	—
1982–83		7	1
1983–84		5	—
1983–84	*Blackburn R*	—	—
1984–85	Aldershot	44	15
1985–86		20	9
1986–87		34	11

Season	Club		App	Goals
1986–87	Oxford U		4	—
1987–88			33	10
1988–89			40	14
1989–90			13	2
1990–91			36	10
1991–92	Port Vale		43	11
1992–93			16	4
1993–94			37	18

FRAIL, Stephen

Born Glasgow 10.8.69. Ht 5 9 Wt 10.09
Midfield. From Possilpark YM.

Season	Club	App	Goals
1985–86	Dundee	—	—
1986–87		—	—
1987–88		4	—
1988–89		23	1
1989–90		6	—
1990–91		26	—
1991–92		3	—
1992–93		7	—
1993–94		32	—
1993–94	Hearts	9	2

FRAIN, David

Born Sheffield 11.10.62. Ht 5 8 Wt 10 05
Forward. From Rowlinson YC.

Season	Club	App	Goals
1985–86	Sheffield U	7	1
1986–87		19	3
1987–88		18	1
1988–89	Rochdale	42	12
1989–90	Stockport Co	29	2
1990–91		43	3
1991–92		39	4
1992–93		41	—
1993–94		33	3

FRAIN, John

Born Birmingham 8.10.68. Ht 5 7
Wt 11 10
Midfield. From Apprentice.

Season	Club	App	Goals
1985–86	Birmingham C	3	—
1986–87		3	1
1987–88		14	2
1988–89		28	3
1989–90		38	1
1990–91		42	3
1991–92		44	5
1992–93		45	6
1993–94		26	2

FRANCE, Darren

Born Hull 8.8.67. Ht 6 0 Wt 14 02
Forward. From North Ferriby.

Season	Club	App	Goals
1991–92	Hull C	17	4
1992–93		26	3
1993–94	Doncaster R	1	—

FRANCIS, John

Born Dewsbury 21.11.63. Ht 5 8
Wt 11 02
Forward. From Emley.
1987–

Season	Club	App	Goals
1988	Halifax T	4	—
1988–89	Sheffield U	22	1
1989–90		20	5
1989–90	Burnley	19	4
1990–91		45	14
1991–92		37	8
1992–93	Cambridge U	29	3
1992–93	Burnley	9	1
1993–94		43	7

FRANCIS, Kevin

Born Moseley 6.12.67. Ht 6 7 Wt 15 08
Forward. From Mile Oak R.

Season	Club	App	Goals
1988–89	Derby Co	—	—
1989–90		8	—
1990–91		2	—
1990–91	Stockport Co	13	5
1991–92		35	15
1992–93		42	28
1993–94		45	28

FRANCIS, Sean

Born Birmingham 1.8.72. Ht 5 10
Wt 11 09
Forward. From Trainee.

Season	Club	App	Goals
1989–90	Birmingham C	—	—
1990–91		3	—
1991–92		3	—
1992–93		—	—
1993–94	Northampton T	1	—

FRANCIS, Steve

Born Billericay 29.5.64. Ht 5 11
Wt 11 05
Goalkeeper. From Apprentice. England
Youth.

Season	Club	App	Goals
1981–82	Chelsea	29	—

Season	Club	App	Goals
1982–83	....	37	—
1983–84	....	—	—
1984–85	....	2	—
1985–86	....	3	—
1986–87	....	—	—
1986–87	Reading................	14	—
1987–88	....	34	—
1988–89	....	22	—
1989–90	....	46	—
1990–91	....	34	—
1991–92	....	32	—
1992–93	....	34	—
1993–94	Huddersfield T............	46	—

FRANCIS, Trevor

Born Plymouth 19.4.54. Ht 5 10
Wt 11 07
Forward. From Apprentice. England
Youth, Under-23, 52 full caps.

Season	Club	App	Goals
1970–71	Birmingham C............	22	15
1971–72	....	39	12
1972–73	....	31	6
1973–74	....	37	6
1974–75	....	23	13
1975–76	....	35	17
1976–77	....	42	21
1977–78	....	42	25
From Detroit E			
1978–79	Birmingham C............	9	3
1978–79	Nottingham F..............	20	6
From Detroit E			
1979–80	Nottingham F..............	30	14
1980–81	....	18	6
1981–82	....	2	2
1981–82	Manchester C	26	12
1982–83	Sampdoria..................	14	7
1983–84	....	15	3
1984–85	....	24	6
1985–86	....	15	1
1986–87	Atalanta................	21	1
1987–88	Rangers................	18	—
1987–88	QPR......................	9	—
1988–89	....	19	7
1989–90	....	4	5
1989–90	Sheffield W..................	12	—
1990–91	....	38	4
1991–92	....	20	1
1992–93	....	5	—
1993–94	....	1	—

FREEDMAN, Doug

Born Glasgow 21.1.74 Ht 5 9 Wt 11 00
Forward. From Trainee.

Season	Club	App	Goals
1991–92	QPR......................	—	—
1992–93	....	—	—
1993–94	....	—	—

FREEMAN, Clive

Born Leeds 12.9.62 Ht 5 8 Wt 12 08
Defender. From Altrincham.

Season	Club	App	Goals
1987–88	Doncaster R..............	—	—
From Bridlington T			
1990–91	Swansea C..................	2	—
1991–92	....	12	—
1991–92	*Carlisle U*......................	4	—
From Altrincham			
1993–94	Doncaster R................	25	2

FREESTONE, Roger

Born Newport 19.8.68. Ht 6 2 Wt 12 03
Goalkeeper. Wales Under-21.

Season	Club	App	Goals
1986–87	Newport Co................	13	—
1986–87	Chelsea....................	6	—
1987–88	....	15	—
1988–89	....	21	—
1989–90	....	—	—
1989–90	*Swansea C*..................	14	—
1989–90	*Hereford U*..................	8	—
1990–91	Chelsea....................	—	—
1991–92	Swansea C..................	42	—
1992–93	....	46	—
1993–94	....	46	—

FRODSHAM, Ian

Born Liverpool 22.12.75 Ht 5 09
Wt 11 00
Midfield. From Trainee.

Season	Club	App	Goals
1992–93	Liverpool	—	—
1993–94	....	—	—

FROGGATT, Steve

Born Lincoln 9.3.73. Ht 5 10 Wt 11 00
Midfield. From Trainee. England
Under-21.

Season	Club	App	Goals
1990–91	Aston Villa................	—	—
1991–92	....	9	—
1992–93	....	17	1
1993–94	....	9	1

FRY, Chris

Born Cardiff 23.10.69. Ht 5 9   Wt 9 06
Forward. From Trainee.

1988–89	Cardiff C	9	—
1989–90		23	1
1990–91		23	—
1991–92	Hereford U	37	3
1992–93		37	4
1993–94		16	3
1993–94	Colchester U	17	—

FULTON, Stephen

Born Greenock 10.8.70.   Ht 5 10
Wt 11 00
Midfield. From Celtic BC. Scotland
Under-21.

1986–87	Celtic	—	—
1987–88		—	—
1988–89		3	—
1989–90		16	—
1990–91		21	—
1991–92		30	2
1992–93		6	—
1993–94	Bolton W	4	—
1993–94	*Peterborough U*	3	—

FUNNELL, Simon

Born Brighton 8.8.74.   Ht 6 0   Wt 12 08
Forward. From Trainee.

1991–92	Brighton	1	—
1992–93		2	—
1993–94		24	2

FURLONG, Carl

Born Liverpool 18.10.76   Ht 5 11
Wt 12 06
Forward. From Trainee.

| 1993–94 | Wigan Ath | 2 | 1 |

FURLONG, Paul

Born London 1.10.68.   Ht 6 0   Wt 12 11
Forward. From Enfield.

1991–92	Coventry C	37	4
1992–93	Watford	41	19
1993–94		38	18

FURNELL, Andy

Born Peterborough 13.2.77
Forward. From Trainee.

| 1993–94 | Peterborough U | 10 | 1 |

FUTCHER, Paul

Born Chester 25.9.56.   Ht 6 0   Wt 12 03
Defender. From Apprentice. England
Under-21. Football League.

1972–73	Chester	2	—
1973–74		18	—
1974–75	Luton T	19	—
1975–76		41	—
1976–77		40	1
1977–78		31	—
1978–79	Manchester C	24	—
1979–80		13	—
1980–81	Oldham Ath	36	1
1981–82		37	—
1982–83		25	—
1982–83	Derby Co	17	—
1983–84		18	—
1983–84	Barnsley	10	—
1984–85		36	—
1985–86		37	—
1986–87		36	—
1987–88		41	—
1988–89		41	—
1989–90		29	—
1990–91	Halifax T	15	—
1990–91	Grimsby T	22	—
1991–92		29	—
1992–93		35	—
1993–94		39	—

GABBIADINI, Marco

Born Nottingham 20.1.68.   Ht 5 10
Wt 12 04
Forward. From Apprentice. England B,
Under-21.

Season	Club	App	Goals
1984–85	York C	1	—
1985–86		22	4
1986–87		29	9
1987–88		8	1
1987–88	Sunderland	35	21
1988–89		36	18
1989–90		46	21
1990–91		31	9
1991–92		9	5
1991–92	Crystal Palace	15	5
1991–92	Derby Co	20	6
1992–93		44	9
1993–94		39	13

GABBIADINI, Ricardo

Born Newport 11.3.70.   Ht 5 11
Wt 13 06
Forward. From Trainee.

Season	Club	App	Goals
1987–88	York C	1	—
1988–89	Sunderland	—	—
1989–90		1	—
1989–90	*Blackpool*	5	3
1989–90	*Brighton*	1	—
1989–90	*Grimsby T*	3	1
1990–91	Sunderland	—	—
1990–91	*Crewe Alex*	2	—
1990–91	Hartlepool U	5	—
1991–92		9	2
1991–92	Scarborough	7	1
1992–93	Carlisle U	24	3
1993–94	Chesterfield	—	—

GAGE, Kevin

Born Chiswick 21.4.64.   Ht 5 9   Wt 11 02
Defender. From Apprentice. England
Youth.

Season	Club	App	Goals
1980–81	Wimbledon	1	—
1981–82		21	1
1982–83		26	4
1983–84		24	4
1984–85		37	2
1985–86		29	1
1986–87		30	3
1987–88	Aston Villa	44	2

Season	Club	App	Goals
1988–89		28	3
1989–90		22	3
1990–91		21	—
1991–92		—	—
1991–92	Sheffield U	22	2
1992–93		27	—
1993–94		21	—

GALE, Shaun

Born Reading 8.10.69.   Ht 6 0   Wt 11 06
Defender. From Trainee.

Season	Club	App	Goals
1989–90	Portsmouth	—	—
1990–91		3	—
1991–92		—	—
1992–93		—	—
1993–94		—	—

GALE, Tony

Born London 19.11.59.   Ht 6 1   Wt 13 07
Defender. From Apprentice. England
Youth, Under-21.

Season	Club	App	Goals
1977–78	Fulham	38	8
1978–79		36	2
1979–80		42	4
1980–81		40	1
1981–82		44	1
1982–83		42	2
1983–84		35	1
1984–85	West Ham U	37	—
1985–86		42	—
1986–87		32	2
1987–88		18	—
1988–89		31	—
1989–90		36	1
1990–91		24	1
1991–92		25	—
1992–93		23	1
1993–94		32	—

GALLACHER, Bernard

Born Johnstone 22.3.67.   Ht 5 9
Wt 11 00
Defender. From Apprentice.

Season	Club	App	Goals
1984–85	Aston Villa	—	—
1985–86		—	—
1986–87		1	—
1987–88		43	—
1988–89		4	—
1989–90		7	—

Season	Club	League Appearances/Goals
1990–91	....	2 —
1990–91	*Blackburn R*	4 —
1991–92	Doncaster R	2 —
1991–92	Brighton	31 1
1992–93	....	14 —
1993–94	Northampton T	5 —

GALLACHER, John

Born Glasgow 26.1.69   Ht 5 10   Wt 10 08
Forward.

Season	Club	League Appearances/Goals
1987–88	Falkirk	2 —
1988–89	....	16 5
1989–90	Newcastle U	28 6
1990–91	....	1 —
1291–92	....	— —
1992–93	Hartlepool U	21 1
1993–94	....	2 1
1993–94	Falkirk	6 —

GALLACHER, Kevin

Born Clydebank 23.11.66.   Ht 5 7
Wt 9 11
Forward. From Duntocher BC. Scotland
Youth, B, Under-21, 19 full caps.

Season	Club	League Appearances/Goals
1983–84	Dundee U	— —
1984–85	....	— —
1985–86	....	20 3
1986–87	....	37 10
1987–88	....	26 4
1988–89	....	31 9
1989–90	....	17 1
1989–90	Coventry C	15 3
1990–91	....	32 11
1991–92	....	33 8
1992–93	....	20 6
1992–93	Blackburn R	9 5
1993–94	....	30 7

GALLAGHER, Tommy

Born Nottingham 25.8.74   Ht 5 10
Wt 10 08
Defender. From Trainee.

Season	Club	League Appearances/Goals
1992–93	Notts Co	— —
1993–94	....	13 —

GALLEN, Joe

Born Hammersmith 2.9.72   Ht 5 11
Wt 11 08
Forward. From Trainee.

Season	Club	League Appearances/Goals
1991–92	Watford	— —
1992–93	....	— —
1992–93	*Exeter C*	6 —
1993–94	Shrewsbury T	6 1

GALLEN, Kevin

Born Hammersmith 21.9.75   Ht 5 11
Wt 12 03
Forward. From Trainee.

Season	Club	League Appearances/Goals
1992–93	QPR	— —
1993–94	....	— —

GALLEN, Stephen

Born London 21.11.73.   Ht 6 00
Wt 12 00
Defender. From Trainee.

Season	Club	League Appearances/Goals
1991–92	QPR	— —
1992–93	....	— —
1993–94	....	— —

GALLIMORE, Tony

Born Crewe 21.2.72.   Ht 5 10   Wt 11 10
Midfield. From Trainee.

Season	Club	League Appearances/Goals
1989–90	Stoke C	1 —
1990–91	....	7 —
1991–92	....	3 —
1991–92	*Carlisle U*	16 —
1992–93	Stoke C	— —
1992–93	*Carlisle U*	8 1
1993–94	Carlisle U	40 1

GALLOWAY, Michael

Born Nottingham 13.10.74
Midfield. From Trainee.

Season	Club	League Appearances/Goals
1993–94	Notts Co	— —

GALLOWAY, Mick

Born Oswestry 30.5 65.   Ht 5 11
Wt 11 07
Defender. From Amateur. Scotland
Youth, Under-21, 1 full cap.

Season	Club	League Appearances/Goals
1983–84	Mansfield T	17 —
1984–85	....	31 3

Season	Club	Apps	Goals
1985–86	....	6	—
1985–86	Halifax T	19	—
1986–87	....	43	3
1987–88	....	17	2
1987–88	Hearts	25	6
1988–89	....	31	2
1989–90	Celtic...................	33	2
1990–91	....	6	1
1991–92	....	34	2
1992–93	....	30	3
1993–94	....	22	—

GAMBLE, Bradley
Born London 4.2.75   Ht 5 7   Wt 9 12
Midfield. From Trainee.

Season	Club	Apps	Goals
1993–94	Leyton Orient	1	—

GANNON, Jim
Born London 7.9.68.   Ht 6 2   Wt 13 00
Defender. From Dundalk.

Season	Club	Apps	Goals
1988–89	Sheffield U...................	—	—
1989–90	....	—	—
1989–90	*Halifax T*	2	—
1989–90	Stockport Co	7	1
1990–91	....	41	6
1991–92	....	43	16
1992–93	....	46	12
1993–94	....	35	4
1993–94	*Notts Co*...................	2	—

GANNON, John
Born Wimbledon 18.12.66.   Ht 5 8
Wt 10 10
Midfield. From Apprentice.

Season	Club	Apps	Goals
1984–85	Wimbledon	—	—
1985–86	....	1	1
1986–87	....	2	—
1986–87	*Crewe Alex*...................	15	—
1987–88	Wimbledon	13	1
1988–89	....	—	—
1988–89	*Sheffield U*...................	16	1
1989–90	Sheffield U...................	39	3
1990–91	....	22	—
1991–92	....	32	1
1992–93	....	27	1
1993–94	....	14	—
1993–94	*Middlesbrough*.............	7	—

GARDINER, Mark
Born Cirencester 25.12.66.   Ht 5 10
Wt 10 07
Forward. From Apprentice.

Season	Club	Apps	Goals
1983–84	Swindon T	1	—
1984–85	....	4	—
1985–86	....	1	—
1986–87	....	4	—
1986–87	Torquay U	22	3
1987–88	....	27	1
1988–89	Crewe Alex	38	10
1989–90	....	26	6
1990–91	....	33	10
1991–92	....	38	5
1992–93	....	13	1
1993–94	....	34	1

GARDINER, Matthew
Born Birmingham 28.3.74   Ht 5 4
Wt 10 10
Defender. From Trainee.

Season	Club	Apps	Goals
1992–93	Torquay U	7	—
1993–94	....	—	—

GARLAND, Peter
Born Croydon 20.1.71.   Ht 5 9   Wt 12 00
Midfield. From Trainee. England Youth.

Season	Club	Apps	Goals
1989–90	Tottenham H	—	—
1990–91	....	1	—
1991–92	....	—	—
1991–92	Newcastle U...................	2	—
1992–93	....	—	—
1992–93	Charlton Ath	13	1
1993–94	....	27	1

GARNER, Darren
Born Plymouth 10.12.71.   Ht 5 6
Wt 10 01
Midfield. From Trainee.

Season	Club	Apps	Goals
1988–89	Plymouth Arg	1	—
1989–90	....	1	—
1990–91	....	5	1
1991–92	....	10	—
1992–93	....	10	—
1993–94	....	—	—

GARNER, Simon
Born Boston 23.11.59.   Ht 5 9   Wt 11 12
Forward. From Apprentice.

Season	Club	App	Goals
1978–79	Blackburn R	25	8
1979–80		28	6
1980–81		33	7
1981–82		36	14
1982–83		41	22
1983–84		42	19
1984–85		37	12
1985–86		38	12
1986–87		40	10
1987–88		40	14
1988–89		44	20
1989–90		43	18
1990–91		12	1
1991–92		25	5
1992–93	WBA	25	8
1993–94		8	—
1993–94	Wycombe W	12	3

GARNETT, Shaun
Born Wallasey 22.11.69.   Ht 6 2
Wt 11 00
Midfield. From Trainee.

Season	Club	App	Goals
1987–88	Tranmere R	1	—
1988–89		—	—
1989–90		4	—
1990–91		16	1
1991–92		8	—
1992–93		5	1
1992–93	*Chester C*	9	—
1992–93	*Preston NE*	10	2
1992–93	*Wigan Ath*	13	1
1993–94	Tranmere R	26	2

GARRETT, Scott
Born Gateshead 9.1.74.
Defender.

Season	Club	App	Goals
1991–92	Hartlepool U	—	—
1992–93		—	—
1993–94		14	—

GARVEY, Steve
Born Tameside 22.11.73.   Ht 5 9
Wt 11 01
Forward. From Trainee.

Season	Club	App	Goals
1990–91	Crewe Alex	1	—

Season	Club	App	Goals
1991–92		11	—
1992–93		10	1
1993–94		—	—

GASCOIGNE, Paul
Born Gateshead 27.5.67.   Ht 5 10
Wt 11 07
Midfield. From Apprentice. England B,
Under-21, 29 full caps.

Season	Club	App	Goals
1984–85	Newcastle U	2	—
1985–86		31	9
1986–87		24	5
1987–88		35	7
1988–89	Tottenham H	32	6
1989–90		34	6
1990–91		26	7
1991–92		—	—
1992–93	Lazio	22	4
1993–94		17	2

GAUGHAN, Steve
Born Doncaster 14.4.70.   Ht 5 11
Wt 11 02
Midfield.

Season	Club	App	Goals
1987–88	Doncaster R	4	—
1988–89		34	2
1989–90		29	1
1990–91	Sunderland	—	—
1991–92		—	—
1991–92	Darlington	20	—
1992–93		37	1
1993–94		32	3

GAVIN, Mark
Born Bailleston 10.12.63.   Ht 5 8
Wt 10 07
Midfield. From Apprentice.

Season	Club	App	Goals
1981–82	Leeds U	—	—
1982–83		7	1
1983–84		12	1
1984–85		11	1
1984–85	*Hartlepool U*	7	—
1985–86	Carlisle U	13	1
1985–86	Bolton W	8	1
1986–87		41	2
1987–88	Rochdale	23	6
1987–88	Hearts	7	—
1988–89		2	—
1988–89	Bristol C	29	3

Season	Club	League Appearances/Goals
1989–90	....	40 3
1990–91	Watford	13 —
1991–92	....	— —
1991–92	Bristol C	14 1
1992–93	....	19 1
1993–94	....	8 —
1993–94	Exeter C	12 —

GAVIN, Pat

Born Hammersmith 5.6.67.   Ht 6 0
Wt 12 00
Forward. From Hanwell T.

Season	Club	League Appearances/Goals
1988–89	Gillingham	13 7
1989–90	Leicester C	— —
1989–90	*Gillingham*	34 1
1990–91	Leicester C	3 —
1990–91	Peterborough U	11 5
1991–92	....	11 —
1992–93	....	1 —
1992–93	Barnet	— —
1992–93	Northampton T	14 4
1993–94	Wigan Ath	30 6

GAYLE, Brian

Born London 6.3.65.   Ht 6 1   Wt 12 07
Defender.

Season	Club	League Appearances/Goals
19°4–85	Wimbledon	12 1
1985–86	....	13 —
1986–87	....	32 1
1987–88	....	26 1
1988–89	Manchester C	41 3
1989–90	....	14 —
1989–90	Ipswich T	20 —
1990–91	....	33 4
1991–92	....	5 —
1991–92	Sheffield U	33 3
1992–93	....	31 2
1993–94	....	13 3

GAYLE, John

Born Birmingham 30.7.64.   Ht 6 4
Wt 13 01
Forward. From Burton Alb.

Season	Club	League Appearances/Goals
1988–89	Wimbledon	2 —
1989–90	....	11 1
1990–91	....	7 1
1990–91	Birmingham C	22 6
1991–92	....	3 1
1992–93	....	19 3

Season	Club	League Appearances/Goals
1993–94	....	— —
1993–94	*Walsall*	4 1
1993–94	Coventry C	3 —

GAYLE, Marcus

Born Hammersmith 27.9.70.   Ht 6 2
Wt 12 13
Midfield. From Trainee. England Youth.

Season	Club	League Appearances/Goals
1988–89	Brentford	3 —
1989–90	....	9 —
1990–91	....	33 6
1991–92	....	38 6
1992–93	....	38 4
1993–94	....	35 6
1993–94	Wimbledon	10 —

GAYLE, Mark

Born Bromsgrove 21.10.69.   Ht 6 0
Wt 12 00
Goalkeeper. From Trainee.

Season	Club	League Appearances/Goals
1988–89	Leicester C	— —
1989–90	Blackpool	— —
From Worcester C		
1991–92	Walsall	24 —
1992–93	....	41 —
1993–94	....	10 —
1993–94	Crewe Alex	8 —
1993–94	*Liverpool*	— —

GEDDES, Bobby

Born Inverness 12.8.60   Ht 6 0   Wt 11 4
Goalkeeper. From Ross County. Scotland U-21.

Season	Club	League Appearances/Goals
1977–78	Dundee	— —
1978–79	....	— —
1979–80	....	— —
1980–81	....	20 —
1981–82	....	28 —
1982–83	....	1 —
1983–84	....	24 —
1984–85	....	16 —
1985–86	....	36 —
1986–87	....	44 —
1987–88	....	38 —
1988–89	....	34 —
1989–90	....	12 —
1990–91	Kilmarnock	38 —
1991–92	....	33 —
1992–93	....	44 —

1993–94		44	—

GEDDES, Gavin
Born Brighton 7.10.72   Ht 5 10   Wt 11 08
Midfield.

1993–94	Brighton	12	1

GEE, Phil
Born Pelsall 19.12.64.   Ht 6 0   Wt 12 01
Forward. From Riley Sports and Gresley R.

1985–86	Derby Co	4	2
1986–87		41	15
1987–88		38	6
1988–89		12	1
1989–90		8	1
1990–91		2	—
1991–92		19	1
1991–92	Leicester C	14	2
1992–93		18	4
1993–94		12	1

GEMMILL, Scot
Born Paisley 2.1.71.   Ht 5 10   Wt 10 01
Midfield. From School. Scotland Under-21.

1989–90	Nottingham F	—	—
1990–91		4	—
1991–92		39	8
1992–93		33	1
1993–94		31	8

GENTLE, Justin
Born Enfield 6.6.74   Ht 5 7   Wt 10 09
Forward. From Trainee.

1993–94	Luton T	—	—
1993–94	Colchester U	2	—

GERRARD, Paul
Born Heywood 22.1.73   Ht 6 1   Wt 12 06
Goalkeeper. From Trainee. England Under-21.

1991–92	Oldham Ath	—	—
1992–93		25	—
1993–94		16	—

GIBBS, Nigel
Born St Albans 20.11.65.   Ht 5 7
Wt 11 01
Defender. From Apprentice. England Youth, Under-21.

1983–84	Watford	3	—
1984–85		12	—
1985–86		40	1
1986–87		15	—
1987–88		30	—
1988–89		46	1
1989–90		41	—
1990–91		34	—
1991–92		43	1
1992–93		7	—
1993–94		—	—

GIBSON, Andrew
Born Dechmont 2.2.69.   Ht 5 8   Wt 11 04
Midfield. From Gairdoch U.

1987–88	Stirling Albion	5	—
1988–89		12	1
1988–89	Aberdeen	—	—
1989–90		—	—
1990–91		—	—
1991–92		5	—
1992–93		1	1
1993–94		2	—
1993–94	Partick T	11	—
1993–94	*Stockport*	—	—

GIBSON, Colin
Born Bridport 6.4.60.   Ht 5 8   Wt 11 01
Defender. From Apprentice. England Under-21, B.

1977–78	Aston Villa	—	—
1978–79		12	—
1979–80		31	2
1980–81		21	—
1981–82		23	—
1982–83		23	1
1983–84		28	1
1984–85		40	4
1985–86		7	2
1985–86	Manchester U	18	5
1986–87		24	1
1987–88		29	2
1988–89		2	—
1989–90		6	1

Season	Club	Apps	Goals
1990–91		—	—
1990–91	*Port Vale*	6	2
1990–91	Leicester C	18	1
1991–92		17	3
1992–93		9	—
1993–94		15	—

GIBSON, Terry
Born Walthamstow 23.12.62. Ht 5 5
Wt 10 00
Forward. From Apprentice. England
Schools, Youth.

Season	Club	Apps	Goals
1979–80	Tottenham H	1	—
1980–81		—	—
1981–82		1	—
1982–83		16	4
1983–84	Coventry C	36	17
1984–85		38	15
1985–86		24	11
1985–86	Manchester U	7	—
1986–87		16	1
1987–88		—	—
1987–88	Wimbledon	17	6
1988–89		17	5
1989–90		18	5
1990–91		19	5
1991–92		7	—
1991–92	*Swindon T*	9	1
1992–93	Wimbledon	8	1
1993–94	Peterborough U	1	—
1993–94	Barnet	20	4

GIGGS, Ryan
Born Cardiff 29.11.73. Ht 5 11 Wt 10 10
Forward. From School. Wales Youth,
Under-21, 11 full caps.

Season	Club	Apps	Goals
1990–91	Manchester U	2	1
1991–92		38	4
1992–93		41	9
1993–94		38	13

GILBERT, David
Born Lincoln 22.6.63. Ht 5 4 Wt 10 04
Midfield. From Apprentice.

Season	Club	Apps	Goals
1980–81	Lincoln C	1	—
1981–82		29	1
1982–83	Scunthorpe U	1	—
From Boston U			
1986–87	Northampton T	45	8

Season	Club	Apps	Goals
1987–88		41	6
1988–89		34	7
1988–89	Grimsby T	11	3
1989–90		45	10
1990–91		44	12
1991–92		41	2
1992–93		41	4
1993–94		37	4

GILCHRIST, Philip
Born Stockton 25.8.73. Ht 6 0 Wt 11 12
Defender. From Trainee.

Season	Club	Apps	Goals
1990–91	Nottingham F	—	—
1991–92	Middlesbrough	—	—
1992–93	Hartlepool U	24	—
1993–94		35	—

GILKES, Michael
Born Hackney 20.7.65. Ht 5 8 Wt 10 02
Forward.

Season	Club	Apps	Goals
1984–85	Reading	16	2
1985–86		9	2
1986–87		7	—
1987–88		39	4
1988–89		46	9
1989–90		42	2
1990–91		21	1
1991–92		20	—
1991–92	*Chelsea*	1	—
1991–92	*Southampton*	6	—
1992–93	Reading	38	12
1993–94		39	2

GILL, Martin
Born Sunderland 7.9.73
Midfield. From Hartlepool U.

Season	Club	Apps	Goals
1992–93	Scarborough	—	—
1993–94		—	—

GILLARD, Ken
Born Dublin 30.4.72. Ht 5 9 Wt 11 08
Defender. From Trainee.

Season	Club	Apps	Goals
1991–92	Luton T	—	—
1992–93		—	—
1992–93	Northampton T	9	—
1993–94		14	—

GILLESPIE, Gary

Born Stirling 5.7.60. Ht 6 2 Wt 12 07
Defender. From school. Scotland Under-
21, 13 full caps.

Season	Club	Apps	Goals
1977–78	Falkirk	22	—
1978–79	Coventry C	15	—
1979–80		38	1
1980–81		37	1
1981–82		40	2
1982–83		42	2
1983–84	Liverpool	—	—
1984–85		12	1
1985–86		14	3
1986–87		37	—
1987–88		35	4
1988–89		15	1
1989–90		13	4
1990–91		30	1
1991–92	Celtic	24	2
1992–93		18	—
1993–94		27	—

GILLESPIE, Keith

Born Larne 18.2.75 Ht 5 9 Wt 11 00
Forward. From Trainee.

Season	Club	Apps	Goals
1992–93	Manchester U	—	—
1993–94		—	—
1993–94	*Wigan Ath*	8	4

GILMORE, Craig

Born Leeds 8.12.76 Ht 5 10 Wt 11 00
Defender. From Trainee.

Season	Club	Apps	Goals
1993–94	Nottingham F	—	—

GILZEAN, Ian

Born London 10.12.69 Ht 6 1 Wt 12 10
Forward. From Trainee.

Season	Club	Apps	Goals
1991–92	Tottenham H	—	—
1992–93	Dundee	24	5
1992–93	*Doncaster R*	3	—
1993–94	Northampton T	33	10

GINTER, Tony

Born Plymouth 6.11.74
Midfield. From Trainee.

Season	Club	Apps	Goals
1992–93	Torquay U	1	—
1993–94		—	—

GITTENS, Jon

Born Moseley 22.1.64. Ht 6 0 Wt 12 06
Defender. From Paget R.

Season	Club	Apps	Goals
1985–86	Southampton	4	—
1986–87		14	—
1987–88	Swindon T	29	—
1988–89		29	1
1989–90		40	4
1990–91		28	1
1990–91	Southampton	8	—
1991–92		11	—
1991–92	*Middlesbrough*	12	1
1992–93	Middlesbrough	13	—
1993–94	Portsmouth	30	1

GLASS, James

Born Epsom 1.8.73. Ht 6 1 Wt 11 10
Goalkeeper. From Trainee.

Season	Club	Apps	Goals
1991–92	Crystal Palace	—	—
1992–93		—	—
1993–94		—	—

GLASSER, Neil

Born Johannesbury 17.10.74. Ht 5 9
Wt 11 03
Midfield. From Trainee.

Season	Club	Apps	Goals
1991–92	Nottingham F	—	—
1992–93		—	—
1993–94	Notts Co	—	—

GLEGHORN, Nigel

Born Seaham 12.8.62. Ht 6 0 Wt 13 04
Midfield. From Seaham Red Star.

Season	Club	Apps	Goals
1985–86	Ipswich T	21	2
1986–87		29	7
1987–88		16	2
1988–89	Manchester C	32	6
1989–90		2	1
1989–90	Birmingham C	43	9
1990–91		42	6
1991–92		46	17
1992–93		11	1
1992–93	Stoke C	34	7
1993–94		40	3

GLOVER, Dean

Born West Bromwich 29.12.63. Ht 5 10
Wt 11 13
Defender. From Apprentice.

Season	Club		
1981–82	Aston Villa	—	—
1982–83		—	—
1983–84		—	—
1984–85		5	—
1985–86		18	—
1986–87		—	—
1986–87	*Sheffield U*	5	—
1987–88		5	—
1987–88	Middlesbrough	38	4
1988–89		12	1
1988–89	Port Vale	22	—
1989–90		44	4
1990–91		41	1
1991–92		46	1
1992–93		39	3
1993–94		46	3

GLOVER, Lee

Born Kettering 24.4.70. Ht 5 10
Wt 12 01
Forward. From Trainee. Scotland
Under-21.

Season	Club		
1986–87	Nottingham F	—	—
1987–88		20	3
1988–89		—	—
1989–90		—	—
1989–90	*Leicester C*	5	1
1989–90	*Barnsley*	8	—
1990–91	Nottingham F	8	1
1991–92		16	—
1991–92	*Luton T*	1	—
1992–93	Nottingham F	14	—
1993–94		18	5

GOATER, Shaun

Born Bermuda 25.2.70. Ht 6 1 Wt 12 00
Forward. Bermuda full caps.

Season	Club		
1988–89	Manchester U	—	—
1989–90		—	—
1989–90	Rotherham U	12	2
1990–91		22	2
1991–92		24	9
1992–93		23	7
1993–94		39	13
1993–94	*Notts Co*	1	—

GODDARD, Paul

Born Harlington 12.10.59. Ht 5 7
Wt 12 00
Forward. From Apprentice. England
Under-21, 1 full cap.

Season	Club		
1977–78	QPR	7	1
1978–79		23	6
1979–80		40	16
1980–81	West Ham U	37	17
1981–82		39	15
1982–83		39	10
1983–84		5	1
1984–85		40	9
1985–86		6	1
1986–87		4	1
1986–87	Newcastle U	26	11
1987–88		35	8
1988–89	Derby Co	31	7
1989–90		18	8
1989–90	Millwall	14	1
1990–91		6	—
1990–91	Ipswich T	19	6
1991–92		24	4
1992–93		25	3
1993–94		4	—

GONZAQUE, Michael

Born Canning Town 27.3.75 Ht 6 1
Wt 12 03
Defender. From Trainee.

Season	Club		
1993–94	Southend U	—	—

GOODACRE, Sam

Born Sheffield 1.12.70 Ht 5 7 Wt 10 12
Forward. From school.

Season	Club		
1989–90	Sheffield W	—	—
1990–91		—	—
1991–92	Scunthorpe U	—	—
1992–93		21	9
1993–94		18	3

GOODEN, Ty

Born Canvey Island 23.10.72 Ht 5 8
Wt 12 06
Midfield. From Arsenal, Wycombe W.

Season	Club		
1993–94	Swindon T	4	—

GOODING, Mick
Born Newcastle 12.4.59.   Ht 5 7
Wt 10 13
Forward. From Bishop Auckland.

Season	Club		
1979–80	Rotherham U	34	3
1980–81		37	4
1981–82		22	2
1982–83		9	1
1982–83	Chesterfield	12	—
1983–84		—	—
1983–84	Rotherham U	26	7
1984–85		44	10
1985–86		40	8
1986–87		46	8
1987–88	Peterborough U	44	18
1988–89		3	3
1988–89	Wolverhampton W	31	4
1989–90		13	—
1989–90	Reading	27	3
1990–91		44	7
1991–92		40	3
1992–93		40	3
1993–94		41	7

GOODMAN, Don
Born Leeds 9.5.66.   Ht 5 10   Wt 11 10
Forward. From School.

Season	Club		
1983–84	Bradford C	2	—
1984–85		25	5
1985–86		20	4
1986–87		23	5
1986–87	WBA	10	2
1987–88		40	7
1988–89		36	15
1989–90		39	21
1990–91		22	8
1991–92		11	7
1991–92	Sunderland	22	11
1992–93		41	16
1993–94		35	10

GOODMAN, Jon
Born Walthamstow 2.6.71.   Ht 5 11
Wt 12 11
Forward. From Bromley. Football League.

Season	Club		
1990–91	Millwall	23	5
1991–92		17	3
1992–93		35	12
1993–94		19	7

GOODRIDGE, Gregory
Born Barbados 10.7.71   Ht 5 6   Wt 10 00
Forward. From Lambada.

Season	Club		
1993–94	Torquay U	8	1

GOODWIN, Shaun
Born Rotherham 14.6.69.   Ht 5 8
Wt 10 11
Midfield. From Trainee.

Season	Club		
1987–88	Rotherham U	3	—
1988–89		41	4
1989–90		38	6
1990–91		34	3
1991–92		39	5
1992–93		30	1
1993–94		38	8

GORAM, Andy
Born Bury 13.4.64.   Ht 5 11   Wt 11 06
Goalkeeper. From West Bromwich
Apprentice. Scotland Under-21, 29 full
caps.

Season	Club		
1981–82	Oldham Ath	3	—
1982–83		38	—
1983–84		22	—
1984–85		41	—
1985–86		41	—
1986–87		41	—
1987–88		9	—
1987–88	Hibernian	33	1
1988–89		36	—
1989–90		34	—
1990–91		35	—
1991–92	Rangers	44	—
1992–93		34	—
1993–94		8	—

GORDON, Dale
Born Gt Yarmouth 9.1.67.   Ht 5 10
Wt 11 08
Forward. From Apprentice. England
Schools, Youth B, Under-21.

Season	Club		
1983–84	Norwich C	—	—
1984–85		23	3
1985–86		6	1
1986–87		41	5
1987–88		21	3
1988–89		38	5

Season	Club	App	Goals
1989–90	....	26	3
1990–91	....	36	7
1991–92	....	15	4
1991–92	Rangers........................	23	5
1992–93	....	22	1
1993–94	West Ham U	8	1

GORDON, Dean
Born Croydon 10.2.73. Ht 6 0 Wt 11 05
Defender. From Trainee. England Under-21.

Season	Club	App	Goals
1991–92	Crystal Palace..............	4	—
1992–93	....	10	—
1993–94	....	45	5

GORE, Ian
Born Liverpool 10.1.68. Ht 5 11
Wt 12 04
Midfield.

Season	Club	App	Goals
1986–87	Birmingham C	—	—
From Southport			
1987–88	Blackpool......................	—	—
1988–89	....	21	—
1989–90	....	34	—
1990–91	....	41	—
1991–92	....	41	—
1992–93	....	30	—
1993–94	....	29	—

GORMAN, Paul
Born Macclesfield 18.9.68. Ht 5 9
Wt 12 02
Forward.

Season	Club	App	Goals
1987–88	Doncaster R................	7	1
1988–89	....	9	1
From Fisher Ath			
1990–91	Charlton Ath	8	2
1991–92	....	8	3
1992–93	....	10	2
1993–94	....	14	1

GORMLEY, Eddie
Born Dublin 23.10.68. Ht 5 7 Wt 10 07
Midfield. From Bray W. Eire Youth, Under-21.

Season	Club	App	Goals
1987–88	Tottenham H	—	—
1988–89	....	—	—
1988–89	*Chesterfield*	4	—

Season	Club	App	Goals
1988–89	*Motherwell*	—	—
1989–90	Tottenham H	—	—
1989–90	*Shrewsbury T*	—	—
1990–91	Doncaster R................	40	5
1991–92	....	37	5
1992–93	....	41	6
1993–94	....	—	—

GOSLING, Mike
Born Ipswich 6.7.75 Ht 5 6 Wt 11 05
Midfield. From Trainee.

Season	Club	App	Goals
1993–94	York C........................	—	—

GOSNEY, Andy
Born Southampton 8.11.63. Ht 6 4
Wt 13 02
Goalkeeper. From Apprentice. England Youth.

Season	Club	App	Goals
1981–82	Portsmouth	1	—
1982–83	....	—	—
1983–84	....	—	—
1984–85	....	—	—
1985–86	....	4	—
1986–87	....	—	—
1987–88	....	4	—
1988–89	....	14	—
1989–90	....	—	—
1990–91	....	24	—
1991–92	....	1	—
1991–92	*York C*	5	—
1992–93	Birmingham C	21	—
1993–94	Exeter C......................	1	—

GOSS, Jeremy
Born Cyprus 11.5.65. Ht 5 9 Wt 10 09
Midfield. Amateur. England Youth, Wales 6 full caps.

Season	Club	App	Goals
1982–83	Norwich C	—	—
1983–84	....	1	—
1984–85	....	5	—
1985–86	....	—	—
1986–87	....	1	—
1987–88	....	22	2
1988–89	....	—	—
1989–90	....	7	—
1990–91	....	19	1
1991–92	....	33	1
1992–93	....	25	1
1993–94	....	34	6

GOUCK, Andy
Born Blackpool 8.6.72. Ht 5 9   Wt 11 02
Midfield. From Trainee.

Season	Club		
1989–90	Blackpool	8	1
1990–91		5	—
1991–92		24	2
1992–93		29	4
1993–94		27	2

GOUGH, Richard
Born Stockholm 5.4.62. Ht 6 0   Wt 12 00
Defender. From Witz University. Scotland
Under-21, 61 full caps.

Season	Club		
1980–81	Dundee U	4	—
1981–82		30	1
1982–83		34	8
1983–84		33	3
1984–85		33	6
1985–86		31	5
1986–87	Tottenham H	40	2
1987–88		9	—
1987–88	Rangers	31	5
1988–89		35	4
1989–90		26	—
1990–91		26	—
1991–92		33	2
1992–93		25	2
1993–94		37	3

GOULD, Jonathan
Born Paddington 18.7.68. Ht 6 1
Wt 12 07
Goalkeeper.

Season	Club		
1990–91	Halifax T	23	—
1991–92		9	—
1991–92	WBA	—	—
1992–93	Coventry C	9	—
1993–94		9	—

GOULOOZE, Richard
Born Holland 16.11.67   Ht 5 11   Wt 13 06
Defender. From SC Heerenveen.

Season	Club		
1992–93	Derby Co	12	—
1993–94		—	—

GOWSHALL, Joby
Born Louth 7.8.75.
Defender. From Trainee.

Season	Club		
1993–94	Grimsby T	—	—

GRAHAM, Alastair
Born Glasgow 11.8.66   Ht 6 3   Wt 12 7
Forward. From Anniesland U.

Season	Club		
1984–85	Clydebank	1	—
1985–86		2	—
1986–87		—	—
1987–88	Albion R	28	10
1988–89		39	15
1989–90		31	7
1990–91	Ayr U	38	8
1991–92		40	14
1992–93		30	9
1992–93	Motherwell	4	1
1993–94		5	—
1993–94	Raith R	36	5

GRAHAM, Benjamin
Born Pontypool 23.9.75
Defender. From Trainee.

Season	Club		
1993–94	Cardiff C	1	—

GRAHAM, Deniol
Born Cannock 4.10.69. Ht 5 10
Wt 10 05
Forward. From Trainee. Wales Under-21.

Season	Club		
1987–88	Manchester U	1	—
1988–89		—	—
1989–90		1	—
1990–91		—	—
1991–92	Barnsley	21	1
1992–93		15	1
1992–93	*Preston NE*	8	—
1993–94	Barnsley	2	—
1993–94	*Carlisle U*	2	1

GRAHAM, Jimmy
Born Glasgow 15.11.69. Ht 5 11
Wt 11 00
Defender. From Trainee.

Season	Club		
1988–89	Bradford C	1	—
1989–90		6	—
1989–90	*Rochdale*	11	—
1990–91	Rochdale	28	1
1991–92		31	—
1992–93		38	—
1993–94		29	—

GRAHAM, Mark
Born Newry 24.10.74   Ht 5 6   Wt 10 00
Forward. From Trainee.
1993–94 QPR .... — —

GRAHAM, Richard
Born Dewsbury 28.11.74
Midfield. From Trainee.
1993–94 Oldham Ath .... 5 —

GRAINGER, Martin
Born Enfield 23.8.72   Ht 5 11   Wt 12 00
Defender. From Trainee.
1989–90 Colchester U 7 2
1990–91 .... 5 —
1991–92 .... 18 —
1992–93 .... 31 3
1993–94 .... 8 2
1993–94 Brentford 31 2

GRANT, Brian
Born Bannockburn 19.6.64.   Ht 5 9
Wt 10 07
Midfield. From Fallin Violet.
1981–82 Stirling Alb .... 1 —
1982–83 .... 1 —
1983–84 .... 24 3
1984–85 Aberdeen .... — —
1985–86 .... — —
1986–87 .... 15 4
1987–88 .... 7 1
1988–89 .... 26 1
1989–90 .... 31 6
1990–91 .... 32 2
1991–92 .... 33 6
1992–93 .... 29 3
1993–94 .... 30 2

GRANT, Kim
Born Ghana 25.9.72.   Ht 5 10   Wt 10 12
Forward. From Trainee.
1990–91 Charlton Ath 12 2
1991–92 .... 4 —
1992–93 .... 21 2
1993–94 .... 30 1

GRANT, Peter
Born Bellshill 30.8.65.   Ht 5 9   Wt 10 03
Midfield. From Celtic BC. Scotland
Schools, Youth, B, Under-21, 2 full caps.
1982–83 Celtic .... — —
1983–84 .... 3 —
1984–85 .... 20 4
1985–86 .... 30 1
1986–87 .... 37 1
1987–88 .... 37 2
1988–89 .... 21 —
1989–90 .... 26 —
1990–91 .... 27 —
1991–92 .... 22 —
1992–93 .... 31 2
1993–94 .... 28 —

GRANT, Roderick
Born Gloucester 16.9.66   Ht 5 11
Wt 11 0
Forward. Strathbrock Juniors.
1986–87 Cowdenbeath 24 14
1987–88 .... 32 11
1988–89 .... 8 2
1988–89 St Johnstone 28 5
1989–90 .... 37 19
1990–91 .... 30 7
1991–92 .... 25 2
1992–93 Dunfermline Ath 32 4
1993–94 Partick T 37 13

GRANT, Tony
Born Liverpool 14.11.74   Ht 5 7   Wt 9 06
Midfield. From Trainee.
1993–94 Everton .... — —

GRANVILLE, Danny
Born Islington 19.1.75   Ht 5 11   Wt 12 05
Midfield. From Trainee.
1993–94 Cambridge U 11 5

GRAY, Andy
Born Lambeth 22.2.64.   Ht 5 11
Wt 13 03
Midfield. From Corinthian C. and
Dulwich H. England Under-21, 1 full cap.
1984–85 Crystal Palace 21 5
1985–86 .... 30 10

135

1986–87	....	30	6
1987–88	....	17	6
1987–88	Aston Villa..........	19	1
1988–89	....	18	3
1988–89	QPR	11	2
1989–90	Crystal Palace	35	6
1990–91	....	30	4
1991–92	....	25	2
1991–92	*Tottenham H*........	14	1
1992–93	Tottenham H	17	1
1992–93	*Swindon T*..........	3	—
1993–94	Tottenham H	2	1

GRAY, Andy
Born Southampton 25.10.73. Ht 5 6
Wt 10 10
Forward. From Trainee.

1991–92	Reading.............	1	—
1992–93	....	11	3
1993–94	....	5	—

GRAY, Andy
Born Essex 22.11.74 Ht 5 9 Wt 10 00
Defender. From Trainee.

| 1993–94 | Charlton Ath .... | — | — |

GRAY, Kevin
Born Sheffield 7.1.72. Ht 6 0 Wt 13 08
Midfield. From Trainee.

1988–89	Mansfield T.........	1	—
1989–90	....	16	—
1990–91	....	31	1
1991–92	....	18	—
1992–93	....	33	—
1993–94	....	42	2

GRAY, Martin
Born Stockton 17.8.71. Ht 5 9 Wt 10 11
Midfield. From Trainee.

1989–90	Sunderland..........	—	—
1990–91	....	—	—
1990–91	*Aldershot*..........	5	—
1991–92	Sunderland	1	—
1992–93	....	12	1
1993–94	....	22	—

GRAY, Michael
Born Sunderland 3.8.74
Defender. From Trainee.

| 1992–93 | Sunderland.......... | 27 | 2 |
| 1993–94 | .... | 22 | 1 |

GRAY, Philip
Born Belfast 2.10.68. Ht 5 10 Wt 12 03
Forward. From Apprentice. Northern
Ireland Schools, Youth, Under-23, 9 full
caps.

1986–87	Tottenham H	1	—
1987–88	....	1	—
1988–89	....	1	—
1989–90	....	—	—
1989–90	*Barnsley*	3	—
1990–91	Tottenham H	6	—
1990–91	*Fulham*	3	—
1991–92	Luton T	14	3
1992–93	....	45	19
1993–94	Sunderland..........	41	14

GRAYSON, Simon
Born Ripon 16.12.69. Ht 5 11 Wt 12 13
Defender. From Trainee.

1987–88	Leeds U	2	—
1988–89	....	—	—
1989–90	....	—	—
1990–91	....	—	—
1991–92	....	—	—
1991–92	Leicester C	13	—
1992–93	....	24	1
1993–94	....	40	1

GRAYSTON, Neil
Born Keighley 25.11.75 Ht 5 8 Wt 10 09
Defender. From Trainee.

| 1993–94 | Bradford C .... | 2 | — |

GREEN, Richard
Born Wolverhampton 22.11.67. Ht 6 1
Wt 13 11
Defender.

1986–87	Shrewsbury T........	15	—
1987–88	....	31	2
1988–89	....	39	3
1989–90	....	40	—
1990–91	....	—	—

Season	Club	App	Goals
1990–91	Swindon T	—	—
1991–92		—	—
1991–92	Gillingham	12	4
1992–93		39	3
1993–94		39	4

GREEN, Scott
Born Walsall 15.1.70. Ht 6 0 Wt 11 12
Forward. From Trainee.

Season	Club	App	Goals
1988–89	Derby Co	—	—
1989–90		—	—
1989–90	Bolton W	5	2
1990–91		41	6
1991–92		37	2
1992–93		41	6
1993–94		22	4

GREENALL, Colin
Born Billinge 30.12.63. Ht 5 10 Wt 11 06
Defender. From Apprentice.

Season	Club	App	Goals
1980–81	Blackpool	12	—
1981–82		18	—
1982–83		24	1
1983–84		39	4
1984–85		44	3
1985–86		43	1
1986–87		3	—
1986–87	Gillingham	37	2
1987–88		25	2
1987–88	Oxford U	12	—
1988–89		40	2
1989–90		15	—
1989–90	*Bury*	3	—
1990–91	Bury	31	—
1991–92		37	5
1991–92	Preston NE	9	1
1992–93		20	—
1993–94	Chester C	42	1

GREENE, David
Born Luton 26.10.73. Ht 6 2 Wt 13 05
Defender. From Trainee.

Season	Club	App	Goals
1991–92	Luton T	—	—
1992–93		1	—
1993–94		10	—

GREENMAN, Chris
Born Bristol 22.12.68. Ht 5 10 Wt 11 06
Defender. From School.

Season	Club	App	Goals
1988–89	Coventry C	—	—
1989–90		—	—
1990–91		—	—
1991–92		4	—
1992–93		2	—
1992–93	Peterborough U	9	—
1993–94		25	—

GREGAN, Sean
Born Cleveland 29.3.74. Ht 6 2 Wt 13 7
Defender. From Trainee.

Season	Club	App	Goals
1991–92	Darlington	17	—
1992–93		17	1
1993–94		23	1

GREGG, John
Born Manchester 26.3.75 Ht 5 9
Wt 11 00
Midfield. From Trainee.

Season	Club	App	Goals
1993–94	Barnsley	—	—

GREGORY, David
Born Sudbury 23.1.70. Ht 5 11 Wt 11 10
Midfield. From Trainee.

Season	Club	App	Goals
1987–88	Ipswich T	—	—
1988–89		2	—
1989–90		4	—
1990–91		21	1
1991–92		1	—
1992–93		3	1
1993–94		—	—

GREGORY, Neil
Born Zambia 7.10.72 Ht 5 11 Wt 11 10
Forward. From Trainee.

Season	Club	App	Goals
1992–93	Ipswich T	—	—
1993–94		—	—
1993–94	*Chesterfield*	3	1

GREW, Mark
Born Bilston 15.2.58. Ht 5 11 Wt 12 08
Goalkeeper. From Amateur.

Season	Club	App	Goals
1976–77	WBA	—	—
1977–78		—	—

137

Season	Club	App	Goals
1978–79		—	—
1978–79	*Wigan Ath*	4	—
1978–79	*Notts Co.*	—	—
1979–80	WBA	—	—
1980–81		—	—
1981–82		23	—
1982–83		10	—
1983–84	Leicester C	5	—
1983–84	*Oldham Ath*	5	—
1983–84	Ipswich T	—	—
1984–85		6	—
1985–86		—	—
1985–86	*Fulham*	4	—
1985–86	*WBA*	1	—
1985–86	*Derby Co.*	—	—
1986–87	Port Vale	3	—
1987–88		41	—
1988–89		37	—
1989–90		43	—
1990–91		14	—
1990–91	*Blackburn R*	13	—
1991–92	Port Vale	46	—
1992–93	Cardiff C	10	—
1993–94		11	—

GREYGOOSE, Dean

Born Thetford 18.12.64. Ht 5 11
Wt 11 05
Goalkeeper. From Apprentice. England
Youth.

Season	Club	App	Goals
1982–83	Cambridge U	—	—
1983–84		16	—
1984–85		10	—
1984–85	*Orient*	—	—
1985–86	Cambridge U	—	—
1985–86	*Lincoln C*	6	—
1985–86	Orient	1	—
1986–87		—	—
1986–87	C Palace	—	—
1987–88		—	—
1987–88	Crewe Alex	43	—
1988–89		36	—
1989–90		32	—
1990–91		31	—
1991–92		33	—
1992–93		30	—
From Northwich V			
1993–94	Walsall	—	—

GRIDELET, Phil

Born Edgware 30.4.67. Ht 5 11 Wt 12 00
Midfield. From Watford, Hendon, Barnet.

Season	Club	App	Goals
1990–91	Barnsley	4	—
1991–92		—	—
1992–93		2	—
1992–93	*Rotherham U*	9	—
1993–94	Barnsley	—	—
1993–94	Southend U	29	—

GRIFFIN, James

Born Hamilton 1.1.67. Ht 5 8 Wt 11 04
Defender. From Fir Park BC.

Season	Club	App	Goals
1985–86	Motherwell	1	—
1986–87		—	—
1987–88		6	—
1988–89		1	—
1989–90		11	—
1990–91		23	4
1991–92		22	1
1992–93		25	1
1993–94		3	—

GRIFFITH, Cohen

Born Georgetown 26.12.62. Ht 5 10
Wt 11 07
Forward. From Kettering T.

Season	Club	App	Goals
1989–90	Cardiff C	38	9
1990–91		45	9
1991–92		37	1
1992–93		34	10
1993–94		42	6

GRIFFITHS, Brian

Born Prescot 26.1.65. Ht 5 9 Wt 11 00
Forward. From St Helens T.

Season	Club	App	Goals
1988–89	Wigan Ath	29	8
1989–90		45	7
1990–91		43	12
1991–92		28	4
1992–93		44	13
1993–94	Blackpool	43	16

GRIFFITHS, Carl

Born Coventry 15.7.71. Ht 5 9 Wt 10 06
Forward. From Trainee. Wales Youth,
Under-21.

Season	Club	App	Goals
1988–89	Shrewsbury T	28	6

Season	Club	Apps	Goals
1989–90		18	4
1990–91		19	4
1991–92		27	8
1992–93		42	27
1993–94		9	5
1993–94	Manchester C	16	4

GRIFFITHS, Gareth
Born Winsford 10.4.70   Ht 6 4   Wt 14 00
Defender. From Rhyl.

Season	Club	Apps	Goals
1992–93	Port Vale	—	—
1993–94		4	2

GRITT, Steve
Born Bournemouth 31.10.57.   Ht 5 9
Wt 10 10
Midfield. From Apprentice.

Season	Club	Apps	Goals
1976–77	Bournemouth	6	3
1977–78	Charlton Ath	34	3
1978–79		39	3
1979–80		31	7
1980–81		40	—
1981–82		34	3
1982–83		27	1
1983–84		33	1
1984–85		35	1
1985–86		11	2
1986–87		14	1
1987–88		27	—
1988–89		22	2
1989–90	Walsall	20	1
1989–90	Charlton Ath	2	—
1990–91		10	—
1991–92		14	1
1992–93		7	—
1993–94		—	—

GROBBELAAR, Bruce
Born Durban 6.10.57.   Ht 6 1   Wt 13 00
Goalkeeper. From Vancouver Whitecaps.
Zimbabwe full caps.

Season	Club	Apps	Goals
1979–80	Crewe Alex	24	1
From Vancouver Whitecaps			
1980–81	Liverpool	—	—
1981–82		42	—
1982–83		42	—
1983–84		42	—
1984–85		42	—
1985–86		42	—

Season	Club	Apps	Goals
1986–87		31	—
1987–88		38	—
1988–89		21	—
1989–90		38	—
1990–91		31	—
1991–92		37	—
1992–93		5	—
1992–93	*Stoke C*	4	—
1993–94	Liverpool	29	—

GROENENDIJK, Alphonse
Born Leiden 17.5.64   Ht 6 1   Wt 12 11
Midfield. From Ajax.

Season	Club	Apps	Goals
1993–94	Manchester C	9	—

GROGAN, Darren
Born Dublin 16.12.74   Ht 5 7   Wt 10 00
Midfield. From Trainee.

Season	Club	Apps	Goals
1993–94	Tottenham H	—	—

GROVES, Paul
Born Derby 28.2.66.   Ht 5 11   Wt 11 05
Midfield. From Burton Alb.

Season	Club	Apps	Goals
1987–88	Leicester C	1	1
1988–89		15	—
1989–90		—	—
1989–90	*Lincoln C*	8	1
1989–90	Blackpool	19	1
1990–91		46	11
1991–92		42	9
1992–93	Grimsby T	46	12
1993–94		46	11

GROVES, Perry
Born London 19.4.65.   Ht 5 10   Wt 12 08
Forward. From Apprentice.

Season	Club	Apps	Goals
1981–82	Colchester U	9	—
1982–83		17	2
1983–84		42	2
1984–85		44	10
1985–86		43	12
1986–87		1	—
1986–87	Arsenal	25	3
1987–88		34	6
1988–89		21	4
1989–90		30	4
1990–91		32	3

Season	Club	League Appearances/Goals	
1991–92	....	13	1
1992–93	....	1	—
1992–93	Southampton	15	2
1993–94	....	—	—

GRUGEL, Mark
Born Liverpool 9.3.76 Ht 5 8 Wt 10 01
Midfield. From Local.

| 1993–94 | Everton .... | — | — |

GRUNSHAW, Steven
Born Blackburn 7.1.75 Ht 5 9 Wt 12 01
Forward. From Trainee.

| 1993–94 | Blackburn R .... | — | — |

GUENTCHEV, Bontcho
Born Bulgaria 7.7.64 Ht 5 10 Wt 11 07
Forward. From Etar, Locomotiv, Sporting
Lisbon. Bulgaria full caps.

| 1992–93 | Ipswich T .... | 21 | 3 |
| 1993–94 | .... | 24 | 2 |

GUINAN, Stephen
Born Birmingham 24.12.75 Ht 6 1
Wt 12 12
Forward. From Trainee.

| 1992–93 | Nottingham F.............. | — | — |
| 1993–94 | .... | — | — |

GUNN, Bryan
Born Thurso 22.12.63. Ht 6 2 Wt 13 13
Goalkeeper. From Invergordon BC.
Scotland Schools, Youth, Under-21, B, 6
full caps.

1980–81	Aberdeen......................	—	—
1981–82	....	—	—
1982–83	....	1	—
1983–84	....	—	—
1984–85	....	2	—
1985–86	....	10	—
1986–87	....	2	—
1986–87	Norwich C	29	—
1987–88	....	38	—
1988–89	....	37	—
1989–90	....	37	—
1990–91	....	34	—
1991–92	....	25	—
1992–93	....	42	—

| 1993–94 | .... | 41 | — |

GUPPY, Steve
Born Winchester 29.3.69 Ht 5 11
Wt 12 00
Midfield. From Southampton.

| 1993–94 | Wycombe W .... | 41 | 8 |

GURNEY, Andrew
Born Bristol 25.1.74 Ht 5 7 Wt 10 08
Defender. From Trainee.

| 1992–93 | Bristol R .... | — | — |
| 1993–94 | .... | 3 | — |

GYNN, Mick
Born Peterborough 19.8.61. Ht 5 5
Wt 10 10
Midfield. From Apprentice.

1978–79	Peterborough U	11	2
1979–80	....	27	1
1980–81	....	29	7
1981–82	....	46	6
1982–83	....	43	17
1983–84	Coventry C	23	2
1984–85	....	39	4
1985–86	....	12	1
1986–87	....	22	5
1987–88	....	25	3
1988–89	....	8	1
1989–90	....	34	3
1990–91	....	35	8
1991–92	....	23	3
1992–93	....	20	2
1993–94	Stoke C	21	—

HAAG, Kelly
Born Enfield 6.10.70. Ht 6 0   Wt 12 03
Forward. From Trainee.

Season	Club	App	Goals
1989–90	Brentford	5	—
1990–91	Fulham	23	3
1991–92		34	6
1992–93		10	—
1993–94	Barnet	38	8

HAALAND, Alf-Inge
Born Stavanger 23.11.72. Ht 5 10
Wt 12 12
Midfield. From Bryne.

Season	Club	App	Goals
1993–94	Nottingham F	3	—

HACKETT, Gary
Born Stourbridge 11.10.62. Ht 5 7
Wt 11 03
Forward. From Bromsgrove R.

Season	Club	App	Goals
1983–84	Shrewsbury T	31	3
1984–85		38	5
1985–86		42	6
1986–87		39	3
1987–88	Aberdeen	15	—
1987–88	Stoke C	1	—
1988–89		46	5
1989–90		26	2
1989–90	WBA	14	2
1990–91		5	—
1991–92		15	—
1992–93		10	1
1993–94		—	—
1993–94	Peterborough U	22	1

HACKETT, Warren
Born Newham 16.12.71. Ht 5 9
Wt 11 12
Defender. From Tottenham H Trainee.

Season	Club	App	Goals
1990–91	Leyton Orient	—	—
1991–92		22	—
1992–93		17	—
1993–94		33	3

HADLEY, Stewart
Born Dudley 30.12.73 Ht 6 0 Wt 13 02
Forward. From Halesowen.

Season	Club	App	Goals
1992–93	Derby Co	—	—
1993–94		—	—

Season	Club	App	Goals
1993–94	Mansfield T	14	5

HAGEN, David
Born Edinburgh 5.5.73 Ht 5 11   Wt 13 0
Midfield. From Grahamston BC. Scotland
Under-21.

Season	Club	App	Goals
1989–90	Rangers	—	—
1990–91		—	—
1991–92		—	—
1992–93		8	2
1993–94		6	1

HAGUE, Paul
Born Durham 16.9.72.   Ht 6 2   Wt 12 06
Defender. From Trainee.

Season	Club	App	Goals
1990–91	Gillingham	7	—
1991–92		—	—
1992–93		1	—
1993–94		1	—

HAILS, Julian
Born Lincoln 20.11.67.   Ht 5 10
Wt 11 01
Forward.

Season	Club	App	Goals
1989–90	Fulham	—	—
1990–91		—	—
1991–92		18	1
1992–93		46	6
1993–94		37	4

HALL, David
Born Manchester 19.10.73
Defender. From Trainee.

Season	Club	App	Goals
1992–93	Oldham Ath	—	—
1993–94		—	—

HALL, Derek
Born Manchester 5.1.65.   Ht 5 8
Wt 12 03
Midfield. From Apprentice.

Season	Club	App	Goals
1982–83	Coventry C	1	—
1983–84		—	—
1983–84	*Torquay U*	10	2
1984–85	Torquay U	45	4
1985–86	Swindon T	10	—
1986–87	Southend U	43	9
1987–88		40	3
1988–89		40	3

1989–90	Halifax T	41	4
1990–91		8	—
1991–92	Hereford U	20	—
1992–93		41	9
1993–94		42	9

HALL, Gareth
Born Croydon 20.3.69.   Ht 5 8   Wt 10 07
Defender. Wales Under-21, 9 full caps.

1986–87	Chelsea	1	—
1987–88		13	—
1988–89		22	—
1989–90		13	1
1990–91		24	—
1991–92		10	—
1992–93		37	2
1993–94		7	—

HALL, Mark
Born London 13.1.73.   Ht 5 6   Wt 10 12
Midfield. From Tottenham H Trainee.

1991–92	Southend U	3	—
1992–93		9	—
1993–94		—	—
1993–94	*Barnet*	3	—

HALL, Paul
Born Manchester 3.7.72.   Ht 5 9
Wt 10 02
Forward. From Trainee.

1989–90	Torquay U	10	—
1990–91		17	—
1991–92		38	1
1992–93		28	—
1992–93	Portsmouth	—	—
1993–94		28	4

HALL, Richard
Born Ipswich 14.3.72.   Ht 6 2   Wt 13 01
Defender. From Trainee. England
Under-21.

1989–90	Scunthorpe U	1	—
1990–91		21	3
1990–91	Southampton	1	—
1991–92		26	3
1992–93		28	4
1993–94		4	—

HALL, Wayne
Born Rotherham 25.10.68   Ht 5 9
Wt 10 04
Midfield. From Darlington.

1988–89	York C	2	—
1989–90		27	3
1990–91		46	1
1991–92		37	3
1992–93		42	1
1993–94		45	—

HALLE, Gunnar
Born Oslo 11.8.65.   Ht 5 11   Wt 11 02
Defender. From Lillestrom. Norway full
caps.

1990–91	Oldham Ath	17	—
1991–92		10	—
1992–93		41	5
1993–94		23	1

HALLIDAY, Stephen
Born Sunderland 3.5.76   Ht 5 10
Wt 11 02
Forward. From Charlton Ath.

| 1993–94 | Hartlepool U | 11 | — |

HALLWORTH, Jon
Born Stockport 26.10.65.   Ht 6 1
Wt 14 03
Goalkeeper. From School.

1983–84	Ipswich T	—	—
1984–85		—	—
1984–85	*Swindon T*	—	—
1984–85	*Fulham*	—	—
1984–85	*Bristol R*	2	—
1985–86	Ipswich T	6	—
1986–87		6	—
1987–88		33	—
1988–89		—	—
1988–89	Oldham Ath	16	—
1989–90		15	—
1990–91		46	—
1991–92		41	—
1992–93		16	—
1993–94		19	—

HALSALL, Mick
Born Bootle 21.7.61. Ht 5 10 Wt 11 04
Midfield. From Apprentice.

Season	Club	App	Goals
1979–80	Liverpool	—	—
1980–81		—	—
1981–82		—	—
1982–83		—	—
1982–83	Birmingham C	12	1
1983–84		21	2
1984–85		3	—
1984–85	Carlisle U	26	5
1985–86		41	4
1986–87		25	2
1986–87	Grimsby T	12	—
1987–88	Peterborough U	45	4
1988–89		42	1
1989–90		46	10
1990–91		45	6
1991–92		45	5
1992–93		25	2
1993–94		1	—

HAMILTON, Brian
Born Paisley 5.8.67. Ht 6 0 Wt 11 07
Midfield. From Pollok United BC.
Scotland Schools, Under-21.

Season	Club	App	Goals
1985–86	St Mirren	8	—
1986–87		28	3
1987–88		27	—
1988–89		23	1
1989–90	Hibernian	28	1
1990–91		26	2
1991–92		40	3
1992–93		41	1
1993–94		42	2

HAMILTON, Derrick
Born Bradford 15.8.76. Ht 5 11 Wt 11 10
Midfield. From Trainee.

Season	Club	App	Goals
1993–94	Bradford C	2	1

HAMILTON, Graeme
Born Stirling 22.1.74. Ht 5 10 Wt 10 10
Defender. From Gairdoch U.

Season	Club	App	Goals
1991–92	Falkirk	3	—
1992–93		—	—
1993–94		7	—

HAMILTON, Ian
Born Stevenage 14.12.67. Ht 5 9
Wt 11 03
Forward. From Apprentice.

Season	Club	App	Goals
1985–86	Southampton	—	—
1986–87		—	—
1987–88		—	—
1987–88	Cambridge U	9	1
1988–89		15	—
1988–89	Scunthorpe U	27	1
1989–90		43	6
1990–91		34	2
1991–92		41	9
1992–93	WBA	46	7
1993–94		42	3

HAMILTON, John
Born Aberdeen 9.2.76 Ht 6 0 Wt 10 10
Midfield. Keith.

Season	Club	App	Goals
1993–94	Dundee	1	—

HAMMOND, Nicky
Born Hornchurch 7.9.67. Ht 6 0
Wt 11 13
Goalkeeper. From Apprentice.

Season	Club	App	Goals
1985–86	Arsenal	—	—
1986–87		—	—
1986–87	*Bristol R*	3	—
1986–87	*Peterborough U*	—	—
1986–87	*Aberdeen*	—	—
1987–88	Swindon T	4	—
1988–89		—	—
1989–90		—	—
1990–91		5	—
1991–92		25	—
1992–93		13	—
1993–94		13	—

HAMON, Chris
Born Jersey 27.4.70. Ht 6 1 Wt 13 07
Forward. From St Peter.

Season	Club	App	Goals
1992–93	Swindon T	2	—
1993–94		1	—

HANBY, Robert
Born Pontefract 24.12.74 Ht 5 10
Wt 11 10
Defender. From Trainee.

Season	Club	App	Goals
1993–94	Barnsley	—	—

HANCOX, Richard

Born Stourbridge 14.10.70   Ht 5 10
Wt 13 00
Forward. From Stourbridge Swifts.

1992–93	Torquay U	7	—
1993–94		3	—

HANDYSIDE, Peter

Born Dumfries 31.7.74   Ht 6 1   Wt 12 03
Defender. From Trainee. Scotland
Under-21.

1992–93	Grimsby T	11	—
1993–94		13	—

HANNAH, David

Born Coatbridge 4.8.74   Ht 5 11   Wt 11 1
Midfield. From Hamilton Th. Scotland
Under-21.

1991–92	Dundee U	—	—
1992–93		5	—
1993–94		10	2

HANSON, Dave

Born Huddersfield 19.11.68
Forward. From Farsley Celtic.

1993–94	Bury	1	—

HARBEY, Graham

Born Chesterfield 29.8.64.   Ht 5 8
Wt 11 08
Defender. From Apprentice.

1982–83	Derby Co	—	—
1983–84		19	—
1984–85		4	1
1985–86		3	—
1986–87		14	—
1987–88	Ipswich T	35	1
1988–89		23	—
1989–90		1	—
1989–90	WBA	30	—
1990–91		21	1
1991–92		46	1
1992–93	Stoke C	17	—
1993–94		2	—

HARDING, Alan

Born Lincoln 20.5.75   Ht 5 8
Midfield. From Trainee.

1993–94	Sunderland	—	—

HARDING, Paul

Born Mitcham 6.3.64.   Ht 5 9   Wt 12 05
Midfield. From Barnet.

1990–91	Notts Co	24	—
1991–92		29	1
1992–93		1	—
1993–94		—	—
1993–94	*Southend U*	5	—
1993–94	*Watford*	2	—
1993–94	Birmingham C	16	—

HARDWICK, Matthew

Born Rotherham 12.9.74   Ht 5 10
Wt 11 5
Forward. From school.

1993–94	Sheffield W	—	—

HARDY, Paul

Born Plymouth 29.8.75   Ht 5 8   Wt 10 05
Midfield. From Trainee.

1993–94	Torquay U	1	—

HARDY, Phil

Born Chester 9.4.73.   Ht 5 8   Wt 11 00
Defender.

1989–90	Wrexham	1	—
1990–91		32	—
1991–92		42	—
1992–93		32	—
1993–94		25	—

HARDYMAN, Paul

Born Portsmouth 11.3.64.   Ht 5 8
Wt 11 07
Defender. From Local. England Under-21.

1983–84	Portsmouth	3	—
1984–85		15	—
1985–86		21	1
1986–87		33	—
1987–88		20	1
1988–89		25	1
1989–90	Sunderland	42	7
1990–91		32	—
1991–92		32	2
1992–93	Bristol R	37	4
1993–94		25	1

HARFORD, Mick
Born Sunderland 12.2.59. Ht 6 3
Wt 14 05
Forward. From Lambton St BC. England
B, 2 full caps.

Season	Club	App	Goals
1977–78	Lincoln C	27	9
1978–79		31	6
1979–80		36	16
1980–81		21	10
1980–81	Newcastle U	19	4
1981–82	Bristol C	30	11
1981–82	Birmingham C	12	9
1982–83		29	6
1983–84		39	8
1984–85		12	2
1984–85	Luton T	22	15
1985–86		37	22
1986–87		18	4
1987–88		25	9
1988–89		33	7
1989–90		4	—
1989–90	Derby Co	16	4
1990–91		36	8
1991–92		6	3
1991–92	Luton T	29	12
1992–93	Chelsea	28	9
1992–93	Sunderland	11	2
1993–94	Coventry C	1	1

HARFORD, Paul
Born Kent 21.10.74 Ht 6 4 Wt 13 12
Midfield. From Trainee.

Season	Club	App	Goals
1993–94	Blackburn R	—	—

HARGREAVES, Christian
Born Cleethorpes 12.5.72. Ht 5 11
Wt 11 00
Forward. From Trainee.

Season	Club	App	Goals
1989–90	Grimsby T	19	2
1990–91		18	3
1991–92		10	—
1992–93		4	—
1992–93	*Scarborough*	3	—
1993–94	Grimsby T	—	—
1993–94	Hull C	28	—

HARKES, John
Born New Jersey 8.3.67. Ht 5 10
Wt 11 10
Midfield. From United States Soccer
Federation. USA full caps.

Season	Club	App	Goals
1990–91	Sheffield W	23	2
1991–92		29	3
1992–93		29	2
1993–94	Derby Co	33	2

HARKIN, Joe
Born Derry 9.12.75 Ht 5 10 Wt 11 04
Defender. From Trainee.

Season	Club	App	Goals
1992–93	Manchester C	—	—
1993–94		—	—

HARKNESS, Steve
Born Carlisle 27.8.71. Ht 5 10 Wt 11 02
Midfield. From Trainee. England Youth.

Season	Club	App	Goals
1988–89	Carlisle U	13	—
1989–90	Liverpool	—	—
1990–91		—	—
1991–92		11	—
1992–93		10	—
1993–94		11	—
1993–94	*Huddersfield T*	5	—

HARLE, Mike
Born Lewisham 31.10.72
Defender. From Sittingbourne.

Season	Club	App	Goals
1993–94	Millwall	—	—

HARMON, Darren
Born Northampton 30.1.73. Ht 5 5
Wt 9 12
Midfield. From Trainee.

Season	Club	App	Goals
1991–92	Notts Co	—	—
1991–92	Shrewsbury T	5	2
1992–93		1	—
1992–93	Northampton T	25	1
1993–94		31	7

HARPER, Alan
Born Liverpool 1.11.60. Ht 5 8 Wt 10 09
Defender. From Apprentice. England
Youth.

Season	Club	App	Goals
1977–78	Liverpool	—	—

Season	Club	Appearances	Goals
1978–79		—	—
1979–80		—	—
1980–81		—	—
1981–82		—	—
1982–83		—	—
1983–84	Everton	29	1
1984–85		13	—
1985–86		21	—
1986–87		36	3
1987–88		28	—
1988–89	Sheffield W	24	—
1989–90		11	—
1989–90	Manchester C	21	—
1990–91		29	1
1991–92	Everton	33	—
1992–93		18	—
1993–94	Luton T	41	1

HARPER, Kevin
Born Oldham 15.1.76. Ht 5 6 Wt 10 9
Midfield. Hutcheson Vale BC.

1993–94	Hibernian	2	—

HARPER, Lee
Born Bridlington 24.3.75 Ht 5 11
Wt 12 05
Defender. From York C trainee.

1993–94	Scarborough	2	—

HARPER, Steve
Born Stoke 3.2.69. Ht 5 10 Wt 11 05
Forward. From Trainee.

1987–88	Port Vale	21	2
1988–89		7	—
1988–89	Preston NE	5	—
1989–90		36	10
1990–91		36	—
1991–92	Burnley	35	3
1992–93		34	5
1993–94		—	—
1993–94	Doncaster R	31	2

HARPER, Steve
Born Easington 3.2.70
Goalkeeper.

1993–94	Newcastle U	—	—

HARRIOTT, Marvin
Born Dulwich 20.4.74
Defender. From West Ham U trainee.
England Youth.

1991–92	Oldham Ath	—	—
1992–93		—	—
1992–93	Barnsley	—	—
1993–94		—	—
1993–94	*Leyton Orient*	8	—
1993–94	Bristol C	17	—

HARRIS, Andrew
Born Springs 26.2.77
Defender. From Trainee.

1993–94	Liverpool	—	—

HARRIS, Andy
Born Birmingham 17.11.70. Ht 5 10
Wt 12 02
Midfield. From Trainee.

1989–90	Birmingham C	1	—
1990–91		—	—
1991–92		—	—
1991–92	*Oxford U*	1	—
1991–92	Exeter C	6	—
1992–93		28	1
1993–94		4	—

HARRIS, Mark
Born Reading 15.7.63. Ht 6 1 Wt 12 05
Defender. From Wokingham.

1987–88	Crystal Palace	—	—
1988–89		2	—
1989–90		—	—
1989–90	*Burnley*	4	—
1989–90	Swansea C	41	2
1990–91		41	1
1991–92		44	3
1992–93		42	5
1993–94		46	3

HARRISON, Gary
Born Northampton 12.3.75 Ht 5 9
Wt 11 05
Forward. From Aston Villa trainee.

1993–94	Northampton T	2	—

HARRISON, Gerry

Born Lambeth 15.4.72. Ht 5 10
Wt 12 12
Midfield. From Trainee.

Season	Club		
1989–90	Watford	3	—
1990–91		6	—
1991–92	Bristol C	4	—
1991–92	*Cardiff C*	10	1
1992–93	Bristol C	33	1
1993–94		1	—
1993–94	*Hereford U*	6	—
1993–94	Huddersfield T	—	—

HARRISON, Lee

Born Billericay 12.9.71. Ht 6 2 Wt 12 02
Goalkeeper. From Trainee.

1990–91	Charlton Ath	—	—
1991–92		—	—
1991–92	*Fulham*	—	—
1991–92	*Gillingham*	2	—
1992–93	Charlton Ath	—	—
1992–93	*Fulham*	—	—
1993–94	Fulham	—	—

HARRISON, Michael

Born Cannock 19.1.73. Ht 6 1 Wt 12 02
Forward. From Trainee.

1991–92	Port Vale	—	—
1992–93		—	—
1993–94		—	—

HARRISON, Tom

Born Edinburgh 22.1.74 Ht 5 9 Wt 10 7
Midfield. From Salvesen BC.

1990–91	Hearts	3	—
1991–92		1	—
1992–93		4	1
1993–94			

HARTENBERGER, Uwe

Born Lauterecken 1.2.68
Forward. From Bayer Uerdingen.

1993–94	Reading	9	2

HARTFIELD, Charles

Born London 4.9.71. Ht 6 0 Wt 12 02
Defender. From Trainee.

1989–90	Arsenal	—	—

1990–91		—	—
1991–92	Sheffield U	7	—
1992–93		17	—
1993–94		5	—

HARTSON, John

Born Swansea 5.4.75 Ht 5 11 Wt 11 13
Forward. From Trainee. Wales Under-21.

1992–93	Luton T	—	—
1993–94		34	6

HARVEY, Jimmy

Born Lurgan 2.5.58. Ht 5 9 Wt 11 04
Midfield. From Glenavon. Northern
Ireland, Under-23.

1977–78	Arsenal	1	—
1978–79		2	—
1979–80		—	—
1979–80	*Hereford U*	11	—
1980–81	Hereford U	30	1
1981–82		42	5
1982–83		41	5
1983–84		44	9
1984–85		34	5
1985–86		42	9
1986–87		34	5
1986–87	Bristol C	2	—
1987–88		1	—
1987–88	*Wrexham*	6	—
1987–88	Tranmere R	33	3
1988–89		42	4
1989–90		46	7
1990–91		39	3
1991–92		24	1
1992–93	Crewe Alex	17	—
1993–94	Chester C	—	—

HARVEY, Lee

Born Harlow 21.12.66. Ht 5 11 Wt 11 07
Forward. From Local. England Youth.

1983–84	Leyton Orient	4	—
1984–85		4	—
1985–86		12	2
1986–87		15	1
1987–88		23	1
1988–89		29	6
1989–90		37	6
1990–91		26	3
1991–92		13	—

1992–93	................................Nottingham F	21	4
1993–94	Nottingham F.............	2	—
1993–94	Brentford	26	4

HARVEY, Richard
Born Letchworth 17.4.69. Ht 5 10
Wt 11 10
Defender. From Apprentice. England
Schools, Youth.

1986–87	Luton T	5	—
1987–88	....	—	—
1988–89	....	12	—
1989–90	....	26	—
1990–91	....	29	—
1991–92	....	32	2
1992–93	....	1	—
1992–93	*Blackpool*	5	—
1993–94	Luton T	—	—

HATELEY, Mark
Born Liverpool 7.11.61. Ht 6 1   Wt 11 07
Forward. From Apprentice. England
Youth, Under-21, 32 full caps.

1978–79	Coventry C	1	—
1979–80	....	4	—
1980–81	....	19	3
1981–82	....	34	13
1982–83	....	35	9
1983–84	Portsmouth	38	22
1984–85	AC Milan....................	21	7
1985–86	....	22	8
1986–87	....	23	2
From Monaco			
1990–91	Rangers.......................	33	10
1991–92	....	30	21
1992–93	....	37	19
1993–94	....	42	22

HATHAWAY, Ian
Born Worsley 22.8.68 Ht 5 6   Wt 11 04
Forward. From WBA Apprentice,
Bedworth U.

1988–89	Mansfield T.................	12	1
1989–90	....	22	1
1990–91	....	10	—
1990–91	Rotherham U	5	1
1991–92	....	8	—
1992–93	....	—	—
1993–94	Torquay U..................	41	7

HAUGHTON, Warren
Born Birmingham 13.9.73 Ht 5 7
Wt 10 02
Midfield. From Trainee.

1992–93	Leicester C.................	—	—
1993–94	....	—	—

HAWKE, Warren
Born Durham 20.9.70. Ht 5 10   Wt 10 11
Midfield. From Trainee.

1988–89	Sunderland..................	4	—
1989–90	....	8	1
1990–91	....	7	—
1991–92	....	4	—
1991–92	*Chesterfield*	7	1
1992–93	Sunderland..................	2	—
1992–93	*Carlisle U*...................	8	2
1992–93	*Northampton T*............	7	1
1993–94	Raith R.......................	2	—
1993–94	Scarborough................	1	—
1993–94	Berwick R	20	12

HAWORTH, Robert
Born Edgware 21.11.75 Ht 6 2   Wt 12 12
Forward. From Trainee.

1993–94	Fulham	11	1

HAY, Christopher
Born Glasgow 28.8.74 Ht 5 11   Wt 11 7
Midfield. Giffnock N.

1993–94	Celtic..........................	2	—

HAY, Darran
Born Hitchin 12.12.69
Forward.

1993–94	Cambridge U	3	—

HAYES, Martin
Born Walthamstow 21.3.66. Ht 5 10
Wt 11 12
Forward. From Apprentice. England B,
Under-21.

1983–84	Arsenal........................	—	—
1984–85	....	—	—
1985–86	....	11	2
1986–87	....	35	19
1987–88	....	27	1

Season	Club	Apps	Goals
1988–89		17	1
1989–90		12	3
1990–91	Celtic	7	—
1991–92		—	—
1991–92	*Wimbledon*	2	—
1992–93	Swansea C	15	—
1993–94		22	4

HAYLOCK, Paul
Born Lowestoft 24.3.63. Ht 5 9
Wt 11 10
Defender. From Apprentice.

Season	Club	Apps	Goals
1980–81	Norwich C	—	—
1981–82		21	—
1982–83		42	1
1983–84		39	—
1984–85		41	1
1985–86		12	1
1986–87	Gillingham	45	—
1987–88		32	—
1988–89		31	—
1989–90		44	—
1990–91		—	—
1990–91	Maidstone U	16	—
1991–92		32	1
1992–93	Shrewsbury T	18	1
1993–94	Barnet	20	—

HAYRETTIN, Hakan
Born London 4.2.70. Ht 5 9 Wt 11 02
Midfield. From Trainee.

Season	Club	Apps	Goals
1988–89	Leyton Orient	—	—
To Barnet			
1991–92	Barnet	4	—
1992–93		2	—
1992–93	*Torquay U*	4	—
1993–94	Wycombe W	19	1

HAYWARD, Steve
Born Walsall 8.9.71. Ht 5 10 Wt 11 07
Midfield. From Trainee. England Youth.

Season	Club	Apps	Goals
1988–89	Derby Co	—	—
1989–90		3	—
1990–91		1	—
1991–92		7	—
1992–93		7	1
1993–94		5	—

HAYWOOD, Paul
Born Barnsley 4.10.75 Ht 5 11 Wt 10 02
Defender. From Trainee.

Season	Club	Apps	Goals
1992–93	Nottingham F	—	—
1993–94		—	—

HAZARD, Mike
Born Sunderland 5.2.60. Ht 5 7
Wt 10 05
Midfield. From Apprentice.

Season	Club	Apps	Goals
1977–78	Tottenham H	—	—
1978–79		—	—
1979–80		3	—
1980–81		4	—
1981–82		28	5
1982–83		18	1
1983–84		11	2
1984–85		23	4
1985–86		4	1
1985–86	Chelsea	18	1
1986–87		18	6
1987–88		28	2
1988–89		4	—
1989–90		13	—
1989–90	Portsmouth	8	1
1990–91		—	—
1990–91	Swindon T	34	8
1991–92		44	6
1992–93		32	3
1993–94		9	—
1993–94	Tottenham H	17	2

HAZEL, Des
Born Bradford 15.7.67. Ht 5 11
Wt 10 13
Midfield. From Apprentice.

Season	Club	Apps	Goals
1985–86	Sheffield W	—	—
1986–87		—	—
1986–87	*Grimsby T*	9	2
1987–88	Sheffield W	6	—
1988–89	Rotherham U	42	6
1989–90		33	2
1990–91		39	3
1991–92		38	8
1992–93		36	7
1993–94		29	3

HEALD, Oliver
Born Vancouver 13.3.75
Forward.

Season	Club	App	Goals
1993–94	Port Vale	—	—

HEALD, Paul
Born Wath-on-Dearne 20.8.68. Ht 6 2
Wt 12 05
Goalkeeper. From Trainee.

Season	Club	App	Goals
1987–88	Sheffield U	—	—
1988–89		—	—
1988–89	Leyton Orient	28	—
1989–90		37	—
1990–91		38	—
1991–92		2	—
1991–92	*Coventry C*	2	—
1992–93	Leyton Orient	26	—
1992–93	*Crystal Palace*	—	—
1993–94	Leyton Orient	—	—
1993–94	*Swindon T*	2	—

HEANEY, Neil
Born Middlesbrough 3.11.71. Ht 5 9
Wt 11 09
Forward. From Trainee. England Youth,
Under-21.

Season	Club	App	Goals
1989–90	Arsenal	—	—
1990–91		—	—
1990–91	*Hartlepool U*	3	—
1991–92	Arsenal	1	—
1991–92	*Cambridge U*	13	2
1992–93	Arsenal	5	—
1993–94		1	—
1993–94	Southampton	2	—

HEATH, Adrian
Born Stoke 11.1.61. Ht 5 6 Wt 10 01
Forward. From Apprentice. England
Under-21, B.

Season	Club	App	Goals
1978–79	Stoke C	2	—
1979–80		38	5
1980–81		38	6
1981–82		17	5
1981–82	Everton	22	6
1982–83		38	10
1983–84		36	12
1984–85		17	11
1985–86		36	10

Season	Club	App	Goals
1986–87		41	11
1987–88		29	9
1988–89		7	2
From Espanol			
1989–90	Aston Villa	9	—
1989–90	Manchester C	12	2
1990–91		35	1
1991–92		28	1
1991–92	Stoke C	6	—
1992–93	Burnley	43	20
1993–94		41	9

HEATH, Michael
Born Hull 7.2.74. Ht 5 9 Wt 11 00
Goalkeeper. From Trainee.

Season	Club	App	Goals
1992–93	Tottenham H	—	—
1993–94	Scunthorpe U	2	—

HEATHCOTE, Mike
Born Durham 10.9.65. Ht 6 2 Wt 12 05
Defender. From Middlesbrough,
Spennymoor U.

Season	Club	App	Goals
1987–88	Sunderland	1	—
1987–88	*Halifax T*	7	1
1988–89	Sunderland	—	—
1989–90		8	—
1989–90	*York C*	3	—
1990–91	Shrewsbury T	39	6
1991–92		5	—
1991–92	Cambridge U	22	5
1992–93		42	2
1993–94		40	5

HEAVEY, Paul
Born Billinge 24.11.74. Ht 6 0 Wt 11 09
Forward. From Trainee.

Season	Club	App	Goals
1993–94	Preston NE	—	—

HEBBERD, Trevor
Born Winchester 19.6.58. Ht 6 0
Wt 11 04
Midfield. From Apprentice.

Season	Club	App	Goals
1976–77	Southampton	12	2
1977–78		12	1
1978–79		22	2
1979–80		36	2
1980–81		11	—
1981–82		4	—

Season	Club	League Appearances/Goals
1981–82	*Bolton W*	6 —
1981–82	*Leicester C*	4 1
1981–82	Oxford U	15 2
1982–83		39 10
1983–84		46 11
1984–85		42 6
1985–86		41 3
1986–87		38 2
1987–88		39 3
1988–89	Derby Co	37 5
1989–90		23 4
1990–91		21 1
1991–92		— —
1991–92	Portsmouth	4 —
1991–92	Chesterfield	24 —
1992–93		32 1
1993–94		18 —

HEGGS, Carl
Born Leicester 11.10.70. Ht 6 0
Wt 11 08
Forward. From Doncaster R Trainee,
Paget R.

Season	Club	League Appearances/Goals
1991–92	WBA	3 —
1992–93		17 2
1993–94		6 —

HELGASON, Gudni
Born Iceland 16.7.76
Forward. From Volsungur.

Season	Club	League Appearances/Goals
1993–94	Sunderland	— —

HELLEWELL, Craig
Born Doncaster 9.7.75
Midfield.

Season	Club	League Appearances/Goals
1993–94	Sheffield U	— —

HELLIWELL, Ian
Born Rotherham 7.11.62. Ht 6 3
Wt 14 02
Forward. From Matlock T.

Season	Club	League Appearances/Goals
1987–88	York C	32 8
1988–89		41 11
1989–90		46 14
1990–91		41 7
1991–92	Scunthorpe U	39 9
1992–93		41 13
1993–94	Rotherham U	40 3

HEMMINGS, Tony
Born Burton 21.9.67   Ht 5 10   Wt 12 10
Forward. From Northwich Vic.

Season	Club	League Appearances/Goals
1993–94	Wycombe W	26 7

HENDERSON, Damian
Born Leeds 12.5.73.   Ht 6 2   Wt 13 07
Forward. From Trainee.

Season	Club	League Appearances/Goals
1991–92	Leeds U	— —
1992–93		— —
1993–94	Scarborough	17 5
1993–94	Scunthorpe U	20 1

HENDERSON, Nicholas
Born Edinburgh 8.2.69   Ht 5 10   Wt 11 1
Forward. Broxburn.

Season	Club	League Appearances/Goals
1990–91	Raith R	1 —
1991–92		— —
1992–93		— —
1992–93	Cowdenbeath	32 5
1993–94		22 9
1993–94	Falkirk	10 2

HENDON, Ian
Born Ilford 5.12.71.   Ht 6 0   Wt 12 10
Defender. From Trainee. England Youth,
Under-21.

Season	Club	League Appearances/Goals
1989–90	Tottenham H	— —
1990–91		2 —
1991–92		2 —
1991–92	*Portsmouth*	4 —
1991–92	*Leyton Orient*	6 —
1992–93	Tottenham H	— —
1992–93	*Barnsley*	6 —
1993–94	Leyton Orient	36 2

HENDRIE, John
Born Lennoxtown 24.10.63.   Ht 5 7
Wt 11 07
Forward. From Apprentice. Scotland
Youth.

Season	Club	League Appearances/Goals
1981–82	Coventry C	6 —
1982–83		12 2
1983–84		3 —
1983–84	*Hereford U*	6 —
1984–85	Bradford C	46 9
1985–86		42 10
1986–87		42 14

Season	Club	Appearances	Goals
1987–88	....	43	13
1988–89	Newcastle U................	34	4
1989–90	Leeds U	27	5
1990–91	Middlesbrough............	41	3
1991–92	....	38	3
1992–93	....	32	9
1993–94	....	29	13

HENDRIE, Lee
Born Birmingham 18.5.77
Midfield. From Trainee.

Season	Club	Appearances	Goals
1993–94	Aston Villa.................	—	—

HENDRY, Colin
Born Keith 7.12.65.   Ht 6 1   Wt 12 00
Defender. From Islavale. Scotland B, 6 full caps.

Season	Club	Appearances	Goals
1983–84	Dundee......................	4	—
1984–85	....	4	—
1985–86	....	20	—
1986–87	....	13	2
1986–87	Blackburn R	13	3
1987–88	....	44	12
1988–89	....	38	7
1989–90	....	7	—
1989–90	Manchester C	25	3
1990–91	....	32	1
1991–92	....	6	1
1991–92	Blackburn R	30	4
1992–93	....	41	1
1993–94	....	23	—

HENDRY, John
Born Glasgow 6.1.70.   Ht 5 11   Wt 10 06
Forward. From Hillington YC. Scotland Under-21.

Season	Club	Appearances	Goals
1988–89	Dundee......................	2	—
1989–90	....	—	—
1989–90	Forfar Ath	10	6
1990–91	Tottenham H	4	2
1991–92	....	5	1
1991–92	Charlton Ath	5	1
1992–93	Tottenham H	5	2
1993–94	....	3	—

HENRY, Liburd
Born Dominica 29.8.67.   Ht 5 11   Wt 12 09
Forward. From Colchester U, Rainham T, Millwall, Leytonstone/Ilford.

Season	Club	Appearances	Goals
1987–88	Watford	—	—
1988–89	....	1	—
1988–89	Halifax T	5	—
1989–90	Watford	9	1
1990–91	Maidstone U...............	30	2
1991–92	....	37	7
1992–93	Gillingham	28	1
1993–94	....	14	1

HENRY, Nick
Born Liverpool 21.2.69.   Ht 5 6   Wt 9 08
Midfield. From Trainee.

Season	Club	Appearances	Goals
1987–88	Oldham Ath................	5	—
1988–89	....	18	—
1989–90	....	41	—
1990–91	....	43	4
1991–92	....	42	6
1992–93	....	32	6
1993–94	....	22	—

HERRERA, Roberto
Born Torbay 12.6.70.   Ht 5 7   Wt 10 06
Defender. From Trainee.

Season	Club	Appearances	Goals
1987–88	QPR	—	—
1988–89	....	2	—
1989–90	....	1	—
1990–91	....	3	—
1991–92	....	—	—
1991–92	Torquay U...................	11	—
1992–93	QPR	—	—
1992–93	Torquay U...................	5	—
1993–94	QPR	—	—
1993–94	Fulham	23	1

HESELTINE, Wayne
Born Bradford 3.12.69   Ht 5 9   Wt 11 06
Defender. From Trainee.

Season	Club	Appearances	Goals
1987–88	Manchester U.............	—	—
1988–89	....	—	—
1989–90	....	—	—
1989–90	Oldham Ath................	1	—
1990–91	....	—	—
1991–92	....	—	—

| 1992–93 | Bradford C | 42 | 1 |
| 1993–94 | | 12 | — |

HESSENTHALER, Andy
Born Gravesend 17.8.65.   Ht 5 7
Wt 11 00
Midfield. From Redbridge Forest.

1991–92	Watford	35	1
1992–93		45	3
1993–94		42	5

HETHERSTON, Peter
Born Bellshill 6.11.64 Ht 5 9 Wt 10 7
Midfield. From Bargeddie Ams.

1984–85	Falkirk	12	2
1985–86		22	2
1986–87		36	3
1987–88	Watford	5	—
1987–88	Sheffield U	11	—
1988–89	Falkirk	31	3
1989–90		22	2
1990–91		26	4
1991–92	Raith R	31	1
1992–93		44	4
1993–94		34	5

HEWITT, Jamie
Born Chesterfield 17.5.68.   Ht 5 11
Wt 11 07
Defender. From School.

1984–85	Chesterfield	—	—
1985–86		17	—
1986–87		42	2
1987–88		28	2
1988–89		40	1
1989–90		42	6
1990–91		43	—
1991–92		37	3
1992–93	Doncaster R	27	—
1993–94		6	—
1993–94	Chesterfield	29	3

HEWLETT, Matthew
Born Bristol 25.2.76   Ht 6 2   Wt 10 11
Midfield. From Trainee.

| 1993–94 | Bristol C | 12 | — |

HICKS, Nathan
Born Plymouth 23.9.74   Ht 6 2
Defender. From Trainee.

| 1993–94 | Bristol C | — | — |

HICKS, Stuart
Born Peterborough 30.5.67.   Ht 6 1
Wt 13 00
Defender. From Peterborough U
Apprentice, Wisbech.

1987–88	Colchester U	7	—
1988–89		37	—
1989–90		20	—
1990–91	Scunthorpe U	46	1
1991–92		21	—
1992–93	Doncaster R	36	—
1993–94		—	—
1993–94	Huddersfield T	22	1
1993–94	Preston NE	4	—

HIGGINS, Dave
Born Liverpool 19.8.61.   Ht 6 0   Wt 11 00
Defender. From Eagle.

1983–84	Tranmere R	20	—
1984–85		8	—
From S. Liverpool, Caernarfon			
1987–88	Tranmere R	33	1
1988–89		43	1
1989–90		45	1
1990–91		33	2
1991–92		33	1
1992–93		40	4
1993–94		37	—

HIGNETT, Craig
Born Whiston 12.1.70.   Ht 5 10   Wt 11 00
Midfield.

1987–88	Crewe Alex	—	—
1988–89		1	—
1989–90		35	8
1990–91		38	13
1991–92		33	13
1992–93		14	8
1992–93	Middlesbrough	21	4
1993–94		29	5

HILEY, Scott
Born Plymouth 27.9.68.   Ht 5 9   Wt 10 07
Midfield. From Trainee.

Season	Club		
1986–87	Exeter C	—	—
1987–88		15	1
1988–89		37	5
1989–90		46	—
1990–91		46	2
1991–92		33	1
1992–93		33	3
1992–93	Birmingham C	7	—
1993–94		28	—

HILL, Andy
Born Maltby 20.1.65.   Ht 5 10   Wt 12 00
Defender. From Apprentice. England
Youth.

Season	Club		
1982–83	Manchester U	—	—
1983–84		—	—
1984–85	Bury	43	3
1985–86		35	2
1986–87		42	1
1987–88		43	2
1988–89		43	—
1989–90		46	2
1990–91		12	—
1990–91	Manchester C	8	1
1991–92		36	4
1992–93		24	1
1993–94		17	—

HILL, Colin
Born Hillingdon 12.11.63.   Ht 5 11
Wt 12 08
Defender. From Apprentice. Northern
Ireland 6 full caps.

Season	Club		
1981–82	Arsenal	—	—
1982–83		7	—
1983–84		37	1
1984–85		2	—
1985–86		—	—
1985–86	*Brighton*	—	—
From Maritimo			
1987–88	Colchester U	25	—
1988–89		44	—
1989–90	Sheffield U	43	—
1990–91		24	—
1991–92		15	1
1991–92	*Leicester C*	10	—

Season	Club		
1992–93	Leicester C	46	—
1993–94		31	—

HILL, Danny
Born Edmonton 1.10.74   Ht 5 9
Wt 11 00
Midfield. From Trainee.

Season	Club		
1992–93	Tottenham H	4	—
1993–94		3	—

HILL, David
Born Nottingham 6.6.66.   Ht 5 11
Wt 12 04
Midfield. From Local.

Season	Club		
1983–84	Scunthorpe U	2	—
1984–85		29	2
1985–86		42	2
1986–87		41	3
1987–88		26	3
1988–89	Ipswich T	36	—
1989–90		2	—
1990–91		23	—
1990–91	Scunthorpe U	9	1
1991–92		37	5
1992–93		19	—
1993–94	Lincoln C	32	3

HILL, Keith
Born Bolton 17.5.69.   Ht 6 0   Wt 11 03
Defender. From Apprentice.

Season	Club		
1986–87	Blackburn R	—	—
1987–88		1	—
1988–89		15	1
1989–90		25	—
1990–91		22	2
1991–92		32	—
1992–93		1	—
1992–93	Plymouth Arg	36	—
1993–94		29	1

HILL, Philip
Born Scarborough 14.6.74   Ht 5 8
Wt 11 00
Forward. From Trainee.

Season	Club		
1992–93	Notts Co	—	—
1993–94		—	—

HILLIER, David
Born Blackheath 19.12.69.   Ht 5 10
Wt 12 05
Midfield. From Trainee. England
Under-21.

Season	Club		
1987–88	Arsenal	—	—
1988–89		—	—
1989–90		—	—
1990–91		16	—
1991–92		27	1
1992–93		30	1
1993–94		15	—

HIMSWORTH, Gary
Born Appleton 19.12.69.   Ht 5 7   Wt 9 08
Forward. From Trainee.

Season	Club		
1987–88	York C	31	2
1988–89		32	2
1989–90		23	4
1990–91		2	—
1990–91	Scarborough	23	1
1991–92		36	4
1992–93		33	1
1993–94	Darlington	28	3

HINCHCLIFFE, Andy
Born Manchester 5.2.69.   Ht 5 10
Wt 12 10
Defender. From Apprentice. England
Youth, Under-21.

Season	Club		
1986–87	Manchester C	—	—
1987–88		42	1
1988–89		39	5
1989–90		31	2
1990–91	Everton	21	1
1991–92		18	—
1992–93		25	1
1993–94		26	—

HINDMARCH, Rob
Born Stannington 27.4.61.   Ht 6 1
Wt 13 04
Defender. From Apprentice. England
Youth.

Season	Club		
1977–78	Sunderland	2	—
1978–79		—	—
1979–80		21	—
1980–81		29	—

Season	Club		
1981–82		36	2
1982–83		14	—
1983–84		13	—
1983–84	*Portsmouth*	2	—
1984–85	Derby Co	22	1
1985–86		39	6
1986–87		33	2
1987–88		19	—
1988–89		25	—
1989–90		26	—
1990–91	Wolverhampton W	40	2
1991–92		—	—
1992–93		—	—
1993–94	Gillingham	—	—

HINSHELWOOD, Danny
Born Bromley 4.12.75   Ht 5 9   Wt 10 11
Defender. From Trainee.

Season	Club		
1992–93	Nottingham F	—	—
1993–94		—	—

HIRST, David
Born Barnsley 7.12.67.   Ht 5 11   Wt 13 01
Forward. From Apprentice. England
Youth, B, Under-21, 3 full caps.

Season	Club		
1985–86	Barnsley	28	9
1986–87	Sheffield W	21	6
1987–88		24	3
1988–89		32	7
1989–90		38	14
1990–91		41	24
1991–92		33	18
1992–93		22	11
1993–94		7	1

HIRST, Lee
Born Sheffield 26.1.69.   Ht 6 2   Wt 12 07
Defender.

Season	Club		
1989–90	Scarborough	10	—
1990–91		32	2
1991–92		30	2
1992–93		36	2
1993–94	Coventry C	—	—
1993–94	*Lincoln C*	7	—

HISLOP, Neil
Born London 22.2.69   Ht 6 6   Wt 12 02
Goalkeeper. From USA.

Season	Club		
1992–93	Reading	12	—

1993–94		46	—

HITCHCOCK, Kevin

Born Custom House 5.10.62. Ht 6 1
Wt 12 02
Goalkeeper. From Barking.

1983–84	Nottingham F	—	—
1983–84	*Mansfield T*	14	—
1984–85	Mansfield T	43	—
1985–86		46	—
1986–87		46	—
1987–88		33	—
1987–88	Chelsea	8	—
1988–89		3	—
1989–90		—	—
1990–91		3	—
1990–91	*Northampton T*	17	—
1991–92	Chelsea	21	—
1992–93		20	—
1992–93	*West Ham U*	—	—
1993–94	Chelsea	2	—

HOBSON, Gary

Born North Ferriby 12.11.72. Ht 6 2
Wt 12 10
Defender. From Trainee.

1990–91	Hull C	4	—
1991–92		16	—
1992–93		21	—
1993–94		36	—

HOCKADAY, David

Born Billingham 9.11.57. Ht 5 9
Wt 11 02
Defender. From Amateur.

1975–76	Blackpool	—	—
1976–77		5	—
1977–78		—	—
1978–79		18	4
1979–80		7	1
1980–81		36	4
1981–82		41	7
1982–83		40	8
1983–84	Swindon T	36	3
1984–85		22	1
1985–86		37	1
1986–87		40	1
1987–88		43	—
1988–89		44	—

1989–90		20	—
1990–91		3	—
1990–91	Hull C	35	1
1991–92		12	—
1992–93		25	1
1992–93	*Stoke C*	7	—
1993–94	Shrewsbury T	32	—

HODDLE, Carl

Born Harlow 8.3.67. Ht 6 4 Wt 11 00
Midfield. From Bishop's Stortford.

1989–90	Leyton Orient	26	2
1990–91		2	—
1991–92	Barnet	13	—
1992–93		5	2
1993–94		44	1

HODDLE, Glenn

Born Hayes 27.10.57. Ht 6 0 Wt 11 06
Midfield. From Apprentice. England
Youth, Under-21, B, 53 full caps.

1974–75	Tottenham	—	—
1975–76		7	1
1976–77		39	4
1977–78		41	12
1978–79		35	7
1979–80		41	19
1980–81		38	12
1981–82		34	10
1982–83		24	1
1983–84		24	4
1884–85		28	8
1985–86		31	7
1986–87		35	3
From Monaco			
1990–91	Chelsea	—	—
1991–92	Swindon T	22	—
1992–93		42	1
1993–94	Chelsea	19	1

HODGE, John

Born Ormskirk 1.4.69. Ht 5 6 Wt 10 00
Forward. From Exmouth.

1991–92	Exeter C	23	1
1992–93		42	9

1993–94 Swansea C.................... 27 2

HODGE, Martin
Born Southport 4.2.59.   Ht 6 1   Wt 14 06
Goalkeeper. From Apprentice.

Season	Club	App	Goals
1976–77	Plymouth Arg.............	—	—
1977–78	....	5	—
1978–79	....	38	—
1979–80	Everton	23	—
1980–81	....	2	—
1981–82	*Preston NE*	28	—
1982–83	*Oldham Ath*...............	4	—
1982–83	*Gillingham*.................	4	—
1982–83	*Preston NE*	16	—
1983–84	Sheffield W...............	42	—
1984–85	....	42	—
1985–86	....	42	—
1986–87	....	42	—
1987–88	....	29	—
1988–89	Leicester C................	19	—
1989–90	....	46	—
1990–91	....	10	—
1991–92	Hartlepool U	40	—
1992–93	....	29	—
1993–94	Rochdale....................	42	—

HODGE, Steve
Born Nottingham 25.10.62.   Ht 5 8
Wt 9 11
Midfield. From Apprentice. England
Under-21, B, 24 full caps.

Season	Club	App	Goals
1980–81	Nottingham F.............	—	—
1981–82	....	1	—
1982–83	....	39	8
1983–84	....	39	10
1984–85	....	42	12
1985–86	....	2	—
1985–86	Aston Villa.................	36	8
1986–87	....	17	4
1986–87	Tottenham H	19	4
1987–88	....	26	3
1988–89	Nottingham F.............	34	7
1989–90	....	34	10
1990–91	....	14	3
1991–92	Leeds U	23	7
1992–93	....	23	2
1993–94	....	8	1

HODGES, Glyn
Born Streatham 30.4.63.   Ht 6 0
Wt 12 03
Forward. From Apprentice. Wales Youth,
B, Under-21, 16 full caps.

Season	Club	App	Goals
1980–81	Wimbledon	30	5
1981–82	....	34	2
1982–83	....	37	9
1983–84	....	42	15
1984–85	....	22	3
1985–86	....	30	6
1986–87	....	37	9
1987–88	Newcastle U...............	7	—
1987–88	Watford	24	3
1988–89	....	27	5
1989–90	....	35	7
1990–91	Crystal Palace............	7	—
1990–91	Sheffield U	12	4
1991–92	....	26	2
1992–93	....	31	4
1993–94	....	31	2

HODGES, Kevin
Born Bridport 12.6.60.   Ht 5 8   Wt 10 08
Midfield. From Apprentice.

Season	Club	App	Goals
1977–78	Plymouth Arg.............	—	—
1978–79	....	12	—
1979–80	....	44	5
1980–81	....	41	5
1981–82	....	46	11
1982–83	....	46	11
1983–84	....	43	4
1984–85	....	45	10
1985–86	....	46	16
1986–87	....	35	5
1987–88	....	37	6
1988–89	....	31	1
1989–90	....	44	4
1990–91	....	42	3
1991–92	....	14	—
1991–92	*Torquay U*.................	3	—
1992–93	Plymouth Arg.............	4	—
1992–93	Torquay U.................	8	1
1993–94	....	29	2

HODGES, Lee
Born Epping 4.9.73   Ht 5 9   Wt 11 06
Forward. From Trainee.

Season	Club	App	Goals
1991–92	Tottenham H..............	—	—

Season	Club	Apps	Goals
1992–93	....	4	—
1992–93	*Plymouth Arg*	7	2
1993–94	Tottenham H	—	—
1993–94	*Wycombe W*	4	—

HOGG, Graeme
Born Aberdeen 17.6.64. Ht 6 1   Wt 13 01
Defender. From Apprentice. Scotland Under-21.

Season	Club	Apps	Goals
1982–83	Manchester U	—	—
1983–84	....	16	1
1984–85	....	29	—
1985–86	....	17	—
1986–87	....	11	—
1987–88	....	10	—
1987–88	*WBA*	7	—
1988–89	Portsmouth	41	1
1989–90	....	39	1
1990–91	....	20	—
1991–92	Hearts	18	1
1992–93	....	22	2
1993–94	....	17	—

HOLDEN, Rick
Born Skipton 9.9.64. Ht 5 11   Wt 12 07
Midfield.

Season	Club	Apps	Goals
1985–86	Burnley	1	—
1986–87	Halifax T	32	2
1987–88	....	35	10
1987–88	Watford	10	2
1988–89	....	32	6
1989–90	Oldham Ath	45	9
1990–91	....	42	5
1991–92	....	42	5
1992–93	Manchester C	41	3
1993–94	....	9	—
1993–94	Oldham Ath	29	6

HOLDEN, Steve
Born Luton 4.9.72. Ht 6 0   Wt 11 13
Forward. From Trainee.

Season	Club	Apps	Goals
1990–91	Leicester C	—	—
1991–92	....	1	—
1992–93	Carlisle U	21	1
1993–94	....	1	—

HOLDSWORTH, David
Born London 8.11.68. Ht 6 1   Wt 12 04
Defender. From Trainee. England Youth, Under-21.

Season	Club	Apps	Goals
1986–87	Watford	—	—
1987–88	....	—	—
1988–89	....	33	1
1989–90	....	44	3
1990–91	....	15	2
1991–92	....	33	2
1992–93	....	39	—
1993–94	....	28	—

HOLDSWORTH, Dean
Born London 8.11.68. Ht 5 11   Wt 11 13
Forward. From Trainee.

Season	Club	Apps	Goals
1986–87	Watford	2	—
1987–88	*Carlisle U*	4	1
1987–88	*Port Vale*	6	2
1988–89	Watford	10	2
1988–89	*Swansea C*	5	1
1988–89	*Brentford*	7	1
1989–90	Watford	4	1
1989–90	Brentford	39	24
1990–91	....	30	5
1991–92	....	41	24
1992–93	Wimbledon	36	19
1993–94	....	42	17

HOLLAND, Chris
Born Whalley 11.9.75. Ht 5 9   Wt 11 05
Midfield. From Trainee.

Season	Club	Apps	Goals
1993–94	Preston NE	1	—
1993–94	Newcastle U	3	—

HOLLAND, Matthew
Born Bury 11.4.74   Ht 5 9   Wt 11 00
Midfield. From Trainee.

Season	Club	Apps	Goals
1992–93	West Ham U	—	—
1993–94	....	—	—

HOLLAND, Paul
Born Lincoln 8.7.73. Ht 5 11   Wt 12 05
Midfield. From School.

Season	Club	Apps	Goals
1990–91	Mansfield T	1	—
1991–92	....	38	6
1992–93	....	39	3
1993–94	....	38	7

HOLLIS, Steve

Born Liverpool 22.8.72   Ht 6 0   Wt 11 00
Defender. From Liverpool trainee.

| 1993–94 | Wigan Ath | 1 | — |

HOLLOWAY, Ian

Born Kingswood 12.3.63.   Ht 5 8
Wt 10 10
Midfield. From Apprentice.

1980–81	Bristol R	1	—
1981–82		1	—
1982–83		31	7
1983–84		36	1
1984–85		42	6
1985–86	Wimbledon	19	2
1985–86	*Brentford*	13	2
1986–87	Brentford	16	—
1986–87	*Torquay U*	5	—
1987–88		1	—
1987–88	Bristol R	43	5
1988–89		44	6
1989–90		46	8
1990–91		46	7
1991–92	QPR	40	—
1992–93		24	2
1993–94		25	—

HOLMES, Darren

Born Sheffield 30.1.75   Ht 5 8   Wt 11 03
Midfield. From Trainee.

| 1993–94 | Sheffield W | — | — |

HOLMES, Keith

Born Oxford 4.3.74   Ht 5 10   Wt 10 10
Forward. From Trainee.

| 1992–93 | Oxford U | — | — |
| 1993–94 | | — | — |

HOLMES, Matt

Born Luton 1.8.69.   Ht 5 7   Wt 10 07
Forward. From Trainee.

1988–89	Bournemouth	4	1
1988–89	*Cardiff C*	1	—
1989–90	Bournemouth	22	2
1990–91		42	2
1991–92		46	3
1992–93	West Ham U	18	—
1993–94		34	3

HOLMES, Paul

Born Wortley 18.2.68.   Ht 5 10   Wt 11 03
Defender. From Apprentice.

1985–86	Doncaster R	5	1
1986–87		16	—
1987–88		26	—
1988–89	Torquay U	25	—
1989–90		44	2
1990–91		33	1
1991–92		36	1
1992–93	Birmingham C	12	—
1992–93	Everton	4	—
1993–94		15	—

HOLMES, Steve

Born Middlesbrough 13.1.72   Ht 6 2
Wt 13 00
Defender. From Guisborough T.

| 1993–94 | Preston NE | — | — |

HOLSGROVE, Paul

Born Wellington 26.8.69.   Ht 6 2
Wt 12 11
Midfield. From Trainee.

1986–87	Aldershot	—	—
1987–88		2	—
1988–89		1	—
1988–89	*Wimbledon*	—	—
1989–90	Aldershot	—	—
1989–90	*WBA*	—	—
From Wokingham			
1990–91	Luton T	1	—
1991–92		1	—
From Heracles			
1992–93	Millwall	11	—
1993–94		—	—

HOLZMAN, Mark

Born Bracknell 22.2.73.   Ht 5 7   Wt 10 07
Defender. From Trainee.

1991–92	Reading	16	1
1992–93		16	—
1993–94		—	—

HONEYWOOD, Lee

Born Chelmsford 3.8.71.   Ht 5 8
Wt 10 10
Defender. From Trainee.

| 1991–92 | Ipswich T | — | — |

1992–93 .... — —
1993–94 .... — —

HONOUR, Brian
Born Horden 16.2.64.   Ht 5 7   Wt 12 05
Midfield. From Apprentice.

Season	Club	App	Goals
1981–82	Darlington	1	—
1982–83		32	3
1983–84		41	1
From Peterlee			
1984–85	Hartlepool U	17	—
1985–86		46	8
1986–87		32	2
1987–88		44	—
1988–89		34	1
1989–90		9	—
1990–91		42	4
1991–92		40	4
1992–93		37	3
1993–94		17	3

HOOPER, Lyndon
Born Guyana 30.5.66   Ht 5 4
Midfield. From Toronto Blizzard. Canada
full caps.

1993–94	Birmingham C	5	—

HOOPER, Michael
Born Bristol 10.2.64.   Ht 6 2   Wt 13 05
Goalkeeper.

Season	Club	App	Goals
1983–84	Bristol C	—	—
1984–85		1	—
1984–85	*Wrexham*	20	—
1985–86	Wrexham	14	—
1985–86	Liverpool	—	—
1986–87		11	—
1987–88		2	—
1988–89		17	—
1989–90		—	—
1990–91		7	—
1990–91	*Leicester C*	14	—
1991–92	Liverpool	5	—
1992–93		9	—
1993–94		—	—
1993–94	Newcastle U	19	—

HOPE, Chris
Born Sheffield 14.11.72.   Ht 6 0   Wt 11 01
Defender. From Darlington.

Season	Club	App	Goals
1991–92	Nottingham F	—	—
1992–93		—	—
1993–94	Scunthorpe U	41	—

HOPKIN, David
Born Greenock 21.8.70   Ht 5 9   Wt 10 03
Midfield. From Pt Glasgow R BC.

Season	Club	App	Goals
1989–90	Morton	8	—
1990–91		10	—
1991–92		—	—
1992–93	Chelsea	4	—
1993–94		21	—

HOPKIN, Matthew
Born Hull 17.10.74   Ht 5 10   Wt 11 00
Midfield. From Trainee.

1993–94	Hull C	—	—

HOPKINS, Jeff
Born Swansea 14.4.64.   Ht 6 0   Wt 12 12
Defender. From Apprentice. Wales Youth,
Under-21, 16 full caps.

Season	Club	App	Goals
1980–81	Fulham	1	—
1981–82		35	—
1982–83		41	1
1983–84		33	—
1984–85		40	2
1985–86		23	—
1986–87		20	1
1987–88		26	—
1988–89	Crystal Palace	43	—
1989–90		27	2
1990–91		—	—
1991–92		—	—
1991–92	*Plymouth Arg*	8	—
1991–92	Bristol R	6	—
1992–93	Reading	36	1
1993–94		42	2

HOPPER, Tony
Born Carlisle 31.5.76
Defender. From Trainee.

1992–93	Carlisle U	1	—
1993–94		—	—

HORLOCK, Kevin
Born Bexley 1.11.72 Ht 6 0 Wt 12 00
Defender. From Trainee.

Season	Club	Apps	Goals
1991–92	West Ham U	—	—
1992–93		—	—
1992–93	Swindon T	14	1
1993–94		38	—

HORNE, Barry
Born St Asaph 18.5.62. Ht 5 10
Wt 12 02
Midfield. From Rhyl. Wales 44 full caps.

Season	Club	Apps	Goals
1984–85	Wrexham	44	6
1985–86		46	3
1986–87		46	8
1987–88	Portsmouth	39	3
1988–89		31	4
1988–89	Southampton	11	—
1989–90		29	4
1990–91		38	1
1991–92		34	1
1992–93	Everton	34	1
1993–94		32	1

HORNE, Brian
Born Billericay 5.10.67. Ht 5 11
Wt 13 13
Goalkeeper. From Apprentice. England Youth, Under-21.

Season	Club	Apps	Goals
1985–86	Millwall	—	—
1986–87		32	—
1987–88		43	—
1988–89		38	—
1989–90		22	—
1990–91		28	—
1991–92		—	—
1991–92	*Watford*	—	—
1992–93	Millwall	—	—
1992–93	*Middlesbrough*	4	—
1992–93	*Stoke C*	1	—
1992–93	Portsmouth	—	—
1993–94		3	—

HORNER, Philip
Born Leeds 10.11.66. Ht 6 1 Wt 12 07
Forward. From Lincoln C Schoolboy.

Season	Club	Apps	Goals
1984–85	Leicester C	—	—
1985–86		—	—

Season	Club	Apps	Goals
1985–86	*Rotherham U*	4	—
1986–87	Leicester C	3	—
1987–88		7	—
1988–89	Halifax T	38	3
1989–90		34	1
1990–91	Blackpool	39	7
1991–92		27	4
1992–93		46	7
1993–94		41	2

HORSEMAN, Brian
Born Cleveland 16.10.74
Defender. From Trainee.

Season	Club	Apps	Goals
1993–94	Notts Co	—	—

HORSFIELD, Geoff
Born Barnsley 1.11.73 Ht 5 10 Wt 10 07
Midfield.

Season	Club	Apps	Goals
1992–93	Scarborough	6	1
1993–94		6	—

HORTON, Duncan
Born Maidstone 18.2.67. Ht 5 10
Wt 11 12
Midfield. From Maidstone U, Charlton Ath, Welling U.

Season	Club	Apps	Goals
1991–92	Barnet	29	3
1992–93		28	—
1993–94	Wycombe W	15	—

HOUCHEN, Keith
Born Middlesbrough 25.7.60. Ht 6 2
Wt 12 08
Forward. From Chesterfield Amateur.

Season	Club	Apps	Goals
1977–78	Hartlepool U	13	4
1978–79		39	12
1979–80		41	14
1980–81		45	17
1981–82		32	18
1981–82	Orient	14	1
1982–83		32	10
1983–84		30	9
1983–84	York C	7	1
1984–85		35	12
1985–86		25	6
1985–86	Scunthorpe U	9	3
1986–87	Coventry C	20	2
1987–88		21	3

Season	Club	Apps	Goals
1988–89	....	13	2
1988–89	Hibernian....................	7	2
1989–90	....	29	8
1990–91	....	21	1
1991–92	Port Vale....................	21	4
1992–93	....	28	6
1993–94	Hartlepool U	34	8

HOUGHTON, Ray

Born Glasgow 9.1.62. Ht 5 7 Wt 10 10
Midfield. Amateur. Eire 58 full caps.

Season	Club	Apps	Goals
1979–80	West Ham U	—	—
1980–81	....	—	—
1981–82	....	1	—
1982–83	Fulham	42	5
1983–84	....	40	3
1984–85	....	42	8
1985–86	....	5	—
1985–86	Oxford U	35	4
1986–87	....	37	5
1987–88	....	11	1
1987–88	Liverpool	28	5
1988–89	....	38	7
1989–90	....	19	1
1990–91	....	32	7
1991–92	....	36	8
1992–93	Aston Villa....................	39	3
1993–94	....	30	2

HOUGHTON, Scott

Born Hitchin 22.10.71. Ht 5 5 Wt 11 06
Midfield. From Trainee. England Schools, Youth.

Season	Club	Apps	Goals
1990–91	Tottenham H	—	—
1990–91	*Ipswich T*	8	1
1991–92	Tottenham H	10	2
1992–93	....	—	—
1992–93	*Cambridge U*	—	—
1992–93	Gillingham....................	3	—
1992–93	*Charlton Ath*	6	—
1993–94	Luton T	15	1

HOULT, Russell

Born Leicester 22.11.72. Ht 6 3 Wt 14 01
Goalkeeper. From Trainee.

Season	Club	Apps	Goals
1990–91	Leicester C	—	—
1991–92	....	—	—
1991–92	*Lincoln C*	2	—

Season	Club	Apps	Goals
1991–92	*Blackpool*	—	—
1992–93	Leicester C....................	10	—
1993–94	....	—	—
1993–94	*Bolton W*	4	—

HOUSHAM, Steven

Born Gainsborough T 24.2.76
Midfield. From Trainee.

Season	Club	Apps	Goals
1993–94	Scunthorpe U	—	—

HOWARD, Andy

Born Southport 15.3.72. Ht 5 6 Wt 10 02
Midfield. From Liverpool trainee.

Season	Club	Apps	Goals
1991–92	Blackpool....................	—	—
From Fleetwood			
1992–93	Rochdale....................	15	2
1993–94	....	5	1

HOWARD, John

Born Stafford 2.4.74. Ht 6 2 Wt 13 02
Defender. From Trainee.

Season	Club	Apps	Goals
1992–93	Wolverhampton W	—	—
1993–94	....	—	—

HOWARD, Jonathan

Born Sheffield 7.10.71. Ht 6 0 Wt 12 02
Forward. From Trainee.

Season	Club	Apps	Goals
1990–91	Rotherham U	1	—
1991–92	....	10	3
1992–93	....	17	2
1993–94	....	8	—

HOWARD, Terry

Born Stepney 26.2.66. Ht 6 1 Wt 11 07
Defender. From Apprentice. England Youth.

Season	Club	Apps	Goals
1983–84	Chelsea....................	—	—
1984–85	....	4	—
1985–86	....	1	—
1985–86	*C Palace*....................	4	—
1986–87	Chelsea....................	1	—
1986–87	*Chester C*	2	—
1986–87	Leyton Orient	12	2
1987–88	....	41	2
1988–89	....	46	5
1989–90	....	45	7
1990–91	....	46	3
1991–92	....	45	4

1992–93 .... 41 5
1993–94 .... 25 2

HOWARTH, Lee
Born Bolton 3.1.68.   Ht 6 1   Wt 12 06
Defender. From Chorley.
1991–92 Peterborough U .... 7 —
1992–93 .... 30 —
1993–94 .... 25 —

HOWE, Stephen
Born Annitsford 6.11.73.   Ht 5 7
Wt 10 04
Midfield. From Trainee.
1991–92 Nottingham F .... — —
1992–93 .... — —
1993–94 .... 4 —

HOWELL, David
Born London 10.10.58.   Ht 6 0   Wt 12 00
Defender. From Fulham, Hillingdon Bor,
Hounslow, Harrow Bor, Enfield.
1991–92 Barnet 34 3
1992–93 .... 23 —
1993–94 Southend U .... 6 —

HOWELLS, David
Born Guildford 15.12.67.   Ht 5 11
Wt 11 10
Forward. From Trainee. England Youth.
1984–85 Tottenham H .... — —
1985–86 .... 1 1
1986–87 .... 1 —
1987–88 .... 11 —
1988–89 .... 27 3
1989–90 .... 34 5
1990–91 .... 29 4
1991–92 .... 31 1
1992–93 .... 18 1
1993–94 .... 18 1

HOWEY, Lee
Born Sunderland 1.4.69   Ht 6 2   Wt 13 09
Forward. From AC Hemptinne Eghezee.
1992–93 Sunderland .... 1 —
1993–94 .... 14 3

HOWEY, Steve
Born Sunderland 26.10.71.   Ht 6 1
Wt 10 05
Midfield. From Trainee.
1988–89 Newcastle U .... 1 —
1989–90 .... — —
1990–91 .... 11 —
1991–92 .... 21 1
1992–93 .... 41 2
1993–94 .... 14 —

HOWIE, Scott
Born Glasgow 4.1.72   Ht 6 2   Wt 13 07
Goalkeeper. From Ferguslie U. Scotland
Under-21.
1991–92 Clyde .... 15 —
1992–93 .... 39 —
1993–94 .... 1 —
1993–94 Norwich C .... 2 —

HOYLAND, Jamie
Born Sheffield 23.1.66.   Ht 6 0   Wt 12 08
Midfield. From Apprentice. England
Youth.
1983–84 Manchester C .... 1 —
1984–85 .... 1 —
1985–86 .... — —
1986–87 Bury 36 2
1987–88 .... 44 8
1988–89 .... 46 9
1989–90 .... 46 16
1990–91 Sheffield U .... 21 —
1991–92 .... 26 4
1992–93 .... 22 2
1993–94 .... 18 —
1993–94 *Bristol C* .... 6 —

HOYLE, Colin
Born Derby 15.1.72.   Ht 5 11   Wt 12 03
Forward. From Trainee.
1989–90 Arsenal .... — —
1989–90 *Chesterfield* .... 3 —
1990–91 Barnsley .... — —
1991–92 .... — —
1992–93 .... — —
1992–93 Bradford C 33 1
1993–94 .... 29 —

HUCKERBY, Darren
Born Nottingham 23.4.76
Midfield. From Trainee.
1993–94 Lincoln C.................. 6   1

HUGHES, Anthony
Born Liverpool 3.10.73   Ht 6 0   Wt 12 05
Defender. From Trainee. England Youth.
1992–93 Crewe Alex 17   1
1993–94 6   —

HUGHES, Bryan
Born Liverpool 19.6.76
Forward. From Trainee.
1993–94 Wrexham 11   —

HUGHES, Ceri
Born Pontypridd 26.2.71.   Ht 5 10
Wt 11 05
Midfield. From Trainee. Wales Youth,
Under-21, 4 full caps.
1989–90 Luton T 1   —
1990–91 17   1
1991–92 18   —
1992–93 29   2
1993–94 42   7

HUGHES, David
Born St Albans 30.12.72.   Ht 5 9
Wt 10 10
Midfield. From Trainee.
1991–92 Southampton .... —   —
1992–93 .... —   —
1993–94 2   —

HUGHES, Ian
Born Bangor 2.8.74.   Ht 5 11   Wt 12 00
Defender. From Trainee. Wales Under-21.
1991–92 Bury........................... 17   —
1992–93 15   —
1992–93 15   —
1993–94 38   —

HUGHES, John
Born Edinburgh 9.9.64.   Ht 6 0   Wt 13 07
Defender. From Newtongrange Star.
1988–89 Berwick R 27   10

1989–90 14   4
1989–90 Swansea C.................. 24   4
1990–91 Falkirk 32   2
1991–92 38   2
1992–93 15   —
1993–94 29   3

HUGHES, Luke
Born Sunderland 17.9.75   Ht 5 10
Wt 10 04
Forward. From Trainee.
1992–93 Nottingham F............. —   —
1993–94 .... —   —

HUGHES, Mark
Born Port Talbot 3.2.62.   Ht 6 0
Wt 12 08
Defender. From Apprentice. Wales Youth.
1979–80 Bristol R 1   —
1980–81 38   1
1981–82 22   2
1982–83 4   —
1982–83 *Torquay U*.................. 9   1
1983–84 Bristol R 9   —
1984–85 Swansea C.................. 12   —
1984–85 Bristol C 20   —
1985–86 2   —
1985–86 Tranmere R 32   —
1986–87 38   1
1987–88 20   —
1988–89 37   1
1989–90 45   4
1990–91 42   2
1991–92 33   1
1992–93 11   —
1993–94 8   —

HUGHES, Mark
Born Wrexham 1.11.63.   Ht 5 9   Wt 11 12
Forward. From Apprentice. Wales Youth,
Under-21, 53 full caps.
1980–81 Manchester U............. —   —
1981–82 .... —   —
1982–83 .... —   —
1983–84 11   4
1984–85 38   16
1985–86 40   17
From Barcelona, *Bayern Munich*
1988–89 Manchester U............. 38   14

Season	Club	League Appearances/Goals	
1989–90		37	13
1990–91		31	10
1991–92		39	11
1992–93		41	15
1993–94		36	11

HUGHES, Michael
Born Larne 2.8.71. Ht 5 6 Wt 10 08
Forward. From Carrick R. Northern
Ireland Under-23, 18 full caps.

Season	Club		
1988–89	Manchester C	1	—
1989–90		—	—
1990–91		1	—
1991–92		24	1
To Strasbourg

HUISTRA, Pieter
Born Goenga 18.1.67. Ht 5 7 Wt 11 4
Forward. From FC Twente.

Season	Club		
1990–91	Rangers	27	4
1991–92		32	5
1992–93		30	4
1993–94		21	6

HULME, Kevin
Born Farnworth 2.12.67. Ht 5 10
Wt 11 09
Forward. From Radcliffe Borough.

Season	Club		
1988–89	Bury	5	—
1989–90		19	1
1989–90	Chester C	4	—
1990–91	Bury	24	7
1991–92		30	4
1992–93		32	9
1993–94	Doncaster R	34	8

HUMES, Tony
Born Blyth 19.3.66. Ht 5 11 Wt 11 00
Defender. From Apprentice.

Season	Club		
1983–84	Ipswich T	—	—
1984–85		—	—
1985–86		—	—
1986–87		22	2
1987–88		27	—
1988–89		26	3
1989–90		24	3
1990–91		16	2
1991–92		5	—

Season	Club		
1991–92	Wrexham	8	—
1992–93		38	—
1993–94		27	1

HUMPHREY, John
Born Paddington 31.1.61. Ht 5 10
Wt 11 03
Defender. From Apprentice.

Season	Club		
1978–79	Wolverhampton W	—	—
1979–80		2	—
1980–81		12	—
1981–82		23	—
1982–83		42	3
1983–84		28	—
1984–85		42	—
1985–86	Charlton Ath	39	2
1986–87		39	—
1987–88		40	—
1988–89		38	1
1989–90		38	—
1990–91	Crystal Palace	38	1
1991–92		37	—
1992–93		32	—
1993–94		32	1
1993–94	Reading	8	—

HUMPHRIES, Mark
Born Glasgow 23.12.71 Ht 5 10
Wt 12 12
Defender. From Cove R.

Season	Club		
1990–91	Aberdeen	—	—
1991–92		2	—
1992–93		—	—
1993–94	Leeds U	—	—

HUNT, Andy
Born Thurrock 9.6.70. Ht 6 0 Wt 11 07
Forward. From Kettering T.

Season	Club		
1990–91	Newcastle U	16	2
1991–92		27	9
1992–93		—	—
1992–93	WBA	10	9
1993–94	WBA	35	12

HUNT, Jonathan
Born London 2.11.71. Ht 5 10 Wt 11 00
Forward.

Season	Club		
1991–92	Barnet	14	—

1992–93	....	19	—
1993–94	Southend U.................	42	6

HUNTER, Barry
Born Coleraine 18.11.68   Ht 6 3
Wt 12 00
Defender. From Crusaders.

1993–94	Wrexham	23	1

HUNTER, Gordon
Born Wallyford 3.5.67.   Ht 5 10
Wt 10 05
Defender. From Musselburgh Windsor.
Scotland Youth, Under-21.

1983–84	Hibernian....................	1	—
1984–85	....	6	—
1985–86	....	25	—
1986–87	....	29	—
1987–88	....	35	—
1988–89	....	33	1
1989–90	....	34	—
1990–91	....	20	1
1991–92	....	37	2
1992–93	....	23	—
1993–94	....	29	1

HUNTER, Junior
Born Lambeth 1.2.75   Ht 5 7   Wt 11 00
Forward. From Trainee.

1993–94	Cambridge U	14	—

HUNTER, Roy
Born Cleveland 29.10.73.   Ht 5 9
Wt 11 00
Midfield. From Trainee.

1991–92	WBA..........................	6	1
1992–93	....	1	—
1993–94	....	2	—

HURLOCK, Terry
Born Hackney 22.9.58.   Ht 5 9   Wt 13 03
Midfield. From Leytonstone/Ilford.
England B.

1980–81	Brentford	42	4
1981–82	....	40	2
1982–83	....	39	3
1983–84	....	32	4
1984–85	....	40	3

1985–86	....	27	2
1985–86	Reading......................	16	—
1986–87	....	13	—
1986–87	Millwall.....................	13	1
1987–88	....	28	4
1988–89	....	34	3
1989–90	....	29	—
1990–91	Rangers......................	29	2
1991–92	....	—	—
1991–92	Southampton	29	—
1992–93	....	30	—
1993–94	....	2	—
1993–94	Millwall....................	13	—

HURST, Lee
Born Nuneaton 21.9.70.   Ht 6 0
Wt 11 09
Midfield. From Trainee.

1989–90	Coventry C	—	—
1990–91	....	4	—
1991–92	....	10	—
1992–93	....	35	2
1993–94	....	—	—

HURST, Paul
Born Sheffield 25.9.74   Ht 5 7   Wt 10 04
Defender. From Trainee.

1993–94	Rotherham U	4	—

HUTCHINGS, Carl
Born London 24.9.74   Ht 5 11   Wt 11 00
Midfield. From Trainee.

1993–94	Brentford	29	—

HUTCHINGS, Chris
Born Winchester 5.7.57.   Ht 5 10
Wt 11 06
Defender. From Harrow Bor.

1980–81	Chelsea......................	12	1
1981–82	....	35	1
1982–83	....	36	—
1983–84	....	4	1
1983–84	Brighton......................	26	1
1984–85	....	42	1
1985–86	....	29	1
1986–87	....	36	—
1987–88	....	20	1
1987–88	Huddersfield T............	23	—

1988–89	....	41 5
1989–90	....	46 5
1990–91	Walsall	40 —
1991–92	Rotherham U	41 4
1992–93	....	30 —
1993–94	....	7 —

HUTCHINSON, Simon
Born Sheffield 24.9.69   Ht 5 10   Wt 13 00
Midfield. From Eastwood T.

1993–94	Wycombe W	8 —

HUTCHISON, Don
Born Gateshead 9.5.71.   Ht 6 ?   Wt 11 08
Forward. From Trainee.

1989–90	Hartlepool U	13 2
1990–91	....	11 —
1990–91	Liverpool	— —
1991–92	....	3 —
1992–93	....	31 7
1993–94	....	11 —

HUXFORD, Richard
Born Scunthorpe 25.7.69   Ht 5 10
Wt 11 06
Defender. From Kettering T.

1992–93	Barnet	33 1
1993–94	Millwall......................	31 —
1993–94	*Birmingham C*............	5 —

HYDE, Graham
Born Doncaster 10.11.70.   Ht 5 7
Wt 11 07
Midfield. From Trainee.

1988–89	Sheffield W..................	— —
1989–90	....	— —
1990–91	....	— —
1991–92	....	13 —
1992–93	....	20 1
1993–94	....	36 1

HYDE, Micah
Born Newham 10.11.74   Ht 5 9   Wt 10 05
Midfield. From Trainee.

1993–94	Cambridge U	18 2

HYDE, Paul
Born Hayes 7.4.63   Ht 6 1   Wt 15 08
Goalkeeper. From Hayes.

1993–94	Wycombe W	42 —

HYSLOP, Christian
Born Watford 14.6.72.   Ht 5 11   Wt 11 07
Defender. From Trainee.

1989–90	Southend U.................	— —
1990–91	....	11 —
1991–92	....	2 —
1992–93	....	6 —
1993–94	....	— —
1993–94	*Northampton T*............	8 —
1993–94	Colchester U..............	8 —

IGOE, Samuel
Born Spelthorne 30.9.75
Midfield. From Trainee.
1993–94 Portsmouth .... — —

ILLMAN, Neil
Born Doncaster 29.4.75 Ht 5 7 Wt 11 05
Forward. From Trainee.
1992–93 Middlesbrough .... — —
1993–94 .... 1 —

IMPEY, Andrew
Born Hammersmith 13.9.71. Ht 5 8
Wt 10 06
Forward. From Yeading. England
Under-21.
1990–91 QPR .... — —
1991–92 .... 13 —
1992–93 .... 40 2
1993–94 .... 33 3

INCE, Paul
Born Ilford 21.10.67. Ht 5 10 Wt 11 07
Midfield. From Trainee. England Youth,
Under-21, B, 14 full caps.
1985–86 West Ham U .... — —
1986–87 .... 10 1
1987–88 .... 28 3
1988–89 .... 33 3
1989–90 .... 1 —
1989–90 Manchester U .... 26 —
1990–91 .... 31 3
1991–92 .... 33 3
1992–93 .... 41 5
1993–94 .... 39 8

INGEBRIGTSEN, Kare
Born Rosenborg 11.11.65 Ht 5 7
Wt 10 03
Defender. From Rosenborg. Norway full
caps.
1992–93 Manchester C .... 7 —
1993–94 .... 8 —

INGHAM, Gary
Born Rotherham 9.10.64
Goalkeeper. From Gainsborough T,
Rotherham U.
1993–94 Doncaster R................ 1 —

INGLETHORPE, Alex
Born Epsom 14.11.71. Ht 5 10 Wt 11 07
Forward. From School.
1990–91 Watford .... 1 —
1991–92 .... 2 —
1992–93 .... — —
1993–94 .... 9 2

INGLIS, John
Born Edinburgh 16.10.66. Ht 6 0
Wt 13 0
Defender. From Hutchison Vale.
1983–84 East Fife 4 1
1984–85 .... 9 —
1985–86 .... 30 —
1986–87 .... 13 —
1986–87 Brechin C...................... 15 —
1987–88 .... 26 3
1988–89 .... 12 1
1988–89 Meadowbank T 12 1
1989–90 .... 38 3
1990–91 St Johnstone 31 1
1991–92 .... 40 —
1992–93 .... 39 1
1993–94 .... 25 1

INGRAM, Denny
Born Sunderland 27.6.76 Ht 5 10
Wt 11 08
Defender. From Trainee.
1993–94 Hartlepool U .... 13 —

INGRAM, Rae
Born Manchester 6.12.74 Ht 5 11
Wt 12 02
Defender. From Trainee.
1993–94 Manchester C .... — —

IORFA, Dominic
Born Lagos 1.10.68. Ht 6 1 Wt 12 12
Forward. From Antwerp. Nigeria full
caps.
1989–90 QPR............................ 1 —
1990–91 .... 6 —
1991–92 .... 1 —
1992–93 .... — —
1992–93 Peterborough U 26 1
1993–94 .... 34 8

IRELAND, Simon
Born Barnstaple 23.11.71. Ht 5 11
Wt 11 12
Forward. From School.

Season	Club	App	Goals
1990–91	Huddersfield T	6	—
1991–92		9	—
1991–92	*Wrexham*	5	—
1992–93	Huddersfield T	4	—
1992–93	Blackburn R	1	—
1993–94		—	—
1993–94	*Mansfield T*	9	1

IRONS, David
Born Glasgow 18.7.61. Ht 6 0 Wt 11 04
Midfield. From Kello Rovers.

Season	Club	App	Goals
1984–85	Ayr U	34	6
1985–86		37	6
1986–87		4	1
1986–87	Clydebank	23	1
1987–88		31	6
1987–88	Dunfermline Ath	11	1
1988–89		36	2
1989–90		23	2
1990–91		34	4
1991–92		2	—
1991–92	Partick T	41	8
1992–93		43	2
1993–94	St Johnstone	1	—

IRONS, Kenny
Born Liverpool 4.11.70. Ht 5 9 Wt 11 00
Forward. From Trainee.

Season	Club	App	Goals
1989–90	Tranmere R	3	—
1990–91		32	6
1991–92		43	7
1992–93		42	7
1993–94		34	3

IRONSIDE, Ian
Born Sheffield 8.3.64. Ht 6 2 Wt 13 00
Goalkeeper. From Barnsley Apprentice, N.
Ferriby U.

Season	Club	App	Goals
1987–88	Scarborough	6	—
1988–89		28	—
1989–90		14	—
1990–91		40	—
1991–92	Middlesbrough	1	—
1991–92	*Scarborough*	7	—

Season	Club	App	Goals
1992–93	Middlesbrough	12	—
1993–94		—	—
1993–94	Stockport Co	11	—

IRVINE, Brian
Born Bellshill 24.5.65. Ht 6 2 Wt 13 0
Defender. From Victoria Park. Scotland 9
full caps.

Season	Club	App	Goals
1983–84	Falkirk	3	—
1984–85		35	—
1985–86	Aberdeen	1	—
1986–87		20	1
1987–88		16	1
1988–89		27	2
1989–90		31	1
1990–91		29	2
1991–92		41	4
1992–93		39	5
1993–94		42	7

IRVINE, Jonathan
Born Burnley 18.11.74. Ht 6 0 Wt 11 12
Forward. From Trainee.

Season	Club	App	Goals
1993–94	Blackpool	—	—

IRVING, Richard
Born Halifax 10.9.75. Ht 5 8 Wt 10 07
Forward. From Trainee.

Season	Club	App	Goals
1992–93	Manchester U	—	—
1993–94		—	—

IRWIN, Denis
Born Cork 31.70.65. Ht 5 8 Wt 11 00
Defender. From Apprentice. Eire Schools,
Youth, B, Under-21, 26 full caps.

Season	Club	App	Goals
1983–84	Leeds U	12	—
1984–85		41	1
1985–86		19	—
1986–87	Oldham Ath	41	1
1987–88		43	—
1988–89		41	2
1989–90		42	1
1990–91	Manchester U	34	—
1991–92		38	4
1992–93		40	5
1993–94		42	2

ISAACS, Anthony
Born Middlesbrough 8.4.73. Ht 5 8
Wt 10 07
Midfield.

Season	Club	App	Goals
1991–92	Darlington	9	—
1992–93		22	1
1993–94		20	1

IZZET, Mustafa
Born Mile End 31.10.74 Ht 5 10
Wt 10 03
Midfield. From Trainee.

Season	Club	App	Goals
1993–94	Chelsea	—	—

JACKSON, Chris
Born Barnsley 16.1.76 Ht 6 0 Wt 12 00
Forward. From Trainee.

Season	Club	App	Goals
1992–93	Barnsley	3	—
1993–94		4	1

JACKSON, Christopher
Born Edinburgh 29.10.73 Ht 5 7
Wt 10 3
Midfield. From Salvesen BC.

Season	Club	App	Goals
1992–93	Hibernian	1	—
1993–94		11	—

JACKSON, Darren
Born Edinburgh 25.7.66. Ht 5 10
Wt 10 10
Forward. From Broxburn Am.

Season	Club	App	Goals
1985–86	Meadowbank T	39	17
1986–87		9	5
1986–87	Newcastle U	23	3
1987–88		31	2
1988–89		15	2
1988–89	Dundee U	1	—
1989–90		25	7
1990–91		33	12
1991–92		28	11
1992–93	Hibernian	36	13
1993–94		40	7

JACKSON, Darren
Born Bristol 24.9.71. Ht 6 1 Wt 12 08
Defender. From Trainee.

Season	Club	App	Goals
1989–90	Oxford U	1	—
1990–91		5	—
1991–92		5	—
1992–93		1	—
1992–93	*Reading*	5	—
1993–94	Oxford U	2	—

JACKSON, Matthew
Born Leeds 19.10.71. Ht 6 1 Wt 12 12
Defender. From School. England Schools,
Under-21.

Season	Club	App	Goals
1990–91	Luton T	—	—
1990–91	*Preston NE*	4	—
1991–92	Luton T	9	—
1991–92	Everton	30	1
1992–93		27	3

Season	Club	League Appearances/Goals
1993–94	....	38 —

JACKSON, Michael
Born West Cheshire 4.12.73.   Ht 5 11
Wt 11 10
Defender. From Trainee.

Season	Club	League Appearances/Goals
1991–92	Crewe Alex	1 —
1992–93	....	4 —
1993–94	Bury	39 —

JACKSON, Peter
Born Bradford 6.4.61.   Ht 6 0   Wt 12 07
Defender. From Apprentice.

Season	Club	League Appearances/Goals
1978–79	Bradford C	9	1
1979–80	....	12 —
1980–81	....	45	1
1981–82	....	32	8
1982–83	....	41	3
1983–84	....	42	3
1984–85	....	45	8
1985–86	....	42 —
1986–87	....	10 —
1986–87	Newcastle U	31	1
1987–88	....	28	2
1988–89	....	1 —
1988–89	Bradford C	32	3
1989–90	....	26	2
1990–91	Huddersfield T	38	1
1991–92	....	45	1
1992–93	....	39	1
1993–94	....	33 —

JACOBS, Wayne
Born Sheffield 3.2.69.   Ht 5 9   Wt 10 02
Defender. From Apprentice.

Season	Club	League Appearances/Goals
1986–87	Sheffield W	— —
1987–88	....	6 —
1987–88	Hull C	6 —
1988–89	....	33 —
1989–90	....	46	3
1990–91	....	19	1
1991–92	....	25 —
1992–93	....	— —
1993–94	Rotherham U	42	2

JAKUB, Joe
Born Falkirk 7.12.56.   Ht 5 6   Wt 9 06
Midfield. From Apprentice.

Season	Club	League Appearances/Goals
1973–74	Burnley	— —

Season	Club	League Appearances/Goals
1974–75	....	— —
1975–76	....	1 —
1976–77	....	5 —
1977–78	....	— —
1978–79	....	13 —
1979–80	....	23 —
1980–81	....	— —
1981–82	Bury	33	1
1982–83	....	46	2
1983–84	....	46	3
1984–85	....	46	11
1985–86	....	40	3
1986–87	....	44	6
1987–88	....	10	1
From AZ Alkmaar		
1988–89	Chester C	42	1
1989–90	Burnley	46	5
1990–91	....	46	3
1991–92	....	39 —
1992–93	....	32 —
1993–94	Chester C	36 —

JAMES, David
Born Welwyn 1.8.70.   Ht 6 4   Wt 14 13
Goalkeeper. From Trainee. England
Youth, Under-21.

Season	Club	League Appearances/Goals
1988–89	Watford	— —
1989–90	....	— —
1990–91	....	46 —
1991–92	....	43 —
1992–93	Liverpool	29 —
1993–94	....	14 —

JAMES, Julian
Born Tring 22.3.70.   Ht 5 10   Wt 11 10
Midfield. From Trainee. England
Under-21.

Season	Club	League Appearances/Goals
1987–88	Luton T	3 —
1988–89	....	1 —
1989–90	....	20	1
1990–91	....	17	1
1991–92	....	28	2
1991–92	*Preston NE*	6 —
1992–93	Luton T	43	2
1993–94	....	33	3

JAMES, Martin

Born Formby 18.5.71. Ht 5 10   Wt 11 07
Midfield. From Trainee.

Season	Club	App	Goals
1989–90	Preston NE	—	—
1990–91		37	2
1991–92		36	4
1992–93		25	5
1992–93	Stockport Co	8	—
1993–94		24	—

JAMES, Robbie

Born Swansea 23.3.57. Ht 5 11   Wt 13 0
Forward. From Apprentice. Wales Under-21, 47 full caps.

Season	Club	App	Goals
1972–73	Swansea C	1	—
1973–74		29	2
1974–75		42	8
1975–76		45	8
1976–77		46	14
1977–78		42	16
1978–79		43	14
1979–80		29	6
1980–81		35	8
1981–82		42	14
1982–83		40	9
1983–84	Stoke C	40	6
1984–85		8	—
1984–85	QPR	20	2
1985–86		28	1
1986–87		39	1
1987–88	Leicester C	23	—
1987–88	Swansea C	19	3
1988–89		41	9
1989–90		30	4
1990–91	Bradford C	46	3
1991–92		43	3
1992–93	Cardiff C	42	2
1993–94		9	—

JAMES, Tony

Born Sheffield 27.6.67. Ht 6 3   Wt 14 02
Defender. From Gainsborough T.

Season	Club	App	Goals
1988–89	Lincoln C	28	—
1989–90		1	—
1989–90	Leicester C	31	2
1990–91		38	8
1991–92		13	—
1992–93		16	—
1993–94		9	1

JAMIESON, Willie

Born Barnsley 27.4.63. Ht 5 11   Wt 12 00
Defender. From Tynecastle BC.

Season	Club	App	Goals
1980–81	Hibernian	28	12
1981–82		12	5
1982–83		19	2
1983–84		33	4
1984–85		25	2
1985–86	Hamilton A	39	2
1986–87		15	—
1987–88		41	4
1988–89		34	1
1989–90	Dundee	14	—
1990–91		38	2
1991–92		38	4
1992–93	Partick T	28	3
1993–94		43	1

JEFFERS, John

Born Liverpool 5.10.68. Ht 5 10
Wt 11 10
Forward. From Trainee. England Schools.

Season	Club	App	Goals
1986–87	Liverpool	—	—
1987–88		—	—
1988–89		—	—
1988–89	Port Vale	15	—
1989–90		40	1
1990–91		31	2
1991–92		33	3
1992–93		26	2
1993–94		25	1

JEFFREY, Andrew

Born Bellshill 15.1.72. Ht 5 10   Wt 12 02
Defender. From Cambridge C.

Season	Club	App	Goals
1993–94	Cambridge U	40	—

JEFFREY, Mike

Born Liverpool 11.8.71. Ht 5 11
Wt 11 06
Forward. From Trainee.

Season	Club	App	Goals
1988–89	Bolton W	9	—
1989–90		4	—
1990–91		—	—
1991–92		2	—
1991–92	*Doncaster R*	11	6
1992–93	Doncaster R	30	12
1993–94		8	1

1993–94	Newcastle U	2 —

JEMSON, Nigel
Born Preston 10.8.69. Ht 5 10   Wt 12 10
Forward. From Trainee. England Under-21.

Season	Club	App	Goals
1985–86	Preston NE	1	—
1986–87		4	3
1987–88		27	5
1987–88	Nottingham F	—	—
1988–89		—	—
1988–89	*Bolton W*	5	—
1988–89	*Preston NE*	9	2
1989–90	Nottingham F	18	4
1990–91		23	8
1991–92		6	1
1991–92	Sheffield W	20	4
1992–93		13	—
1993–94		18	5
1993–94	*Grimsby T*	6	2

JENKINS, Iain
Born Prescot 24.11.72. Ht 5 11   Wt 11 07
Defender. From Trainee.

Season	Club	App	Goals
1990–91	Everton	1	—
1991–92		3	—
1992–93		1	—
1992–93	*Bradford C*	6	—
1993–94	Chester C	34	—

JENKINS, Steve
Born Merthyr 16.7.72. Ht 5 10   Wt 11 02
Defender. From Trainee. Wales Under-21.

Season	Club	App	Goals
1990–91	Swansea C	1	—
1991–92		34	—
1992–93		33	—
1993–94		40	1

JENKINSON, Leigh
Born Thorne 9.7.69. Ht 6 0   Wt 12 02
Forward. From Trainee.

Season	Club	App	Goals
1987–88	Hull C	3	1
1988–89		11	—
1989–90		22	—
1990–91		26	—
1990–91	*Rotherham U*	7	—
1991–92	Hull C	42	8
1992–93		26	4

1992–93	Coventry C	5 —
1993–94		16 —
1993–94	*Birmingham C*	3 —

JENSEN, John
Born Denmark 3.5.65   Ht 5 10   Wt 12 06
Midfield. From Brondby. Denmark full caps.

Season	Club	App	Goals
1992–93	Arsenal	32	—
1993–94		27	—

JEPSON, Ron
Born Stoke 12.5.63. Ht 6 1   Wt 13 02
Forward. From Nantwich.

Season	Club	App	Goals
1988–89	Port Vale	2	—
1989–90		5	—
1989–90	*Peterborough U*	18	5
1990–91	Port Vale	15	—
1990–91	Preston NE	14	3
1991–92		24	5
1992–93	Exeter C	38	8
1993–94		16	13
1993–94	Huddersfield T	23	5

JESS, Eoin
Born Aberdeen 13.12.70. Ht 5 7   Wt 10 10
Forward. From Rangers S Form. Scotland Under-21, 7 full caps.

Season	Club	App	Goals
1987–88	Aberdeen	—	—
1988–89		2	—
1989–90		11	3
1990–91		27	13
1991–92		39	12
1992–93		31	12
1993–94		41	6

JEWELL, Paul
Born Liverpool 28.9.64. Ht 5 8   Wt 11 10
Forward. From Apprentice.

Season	Club	App	Goals
1982–83	Liverpool	—	—
1983–84		—	—
1984–85	Wigan Ath	26	9
1985–86		29	6
1986–87		39	9
1987–88		43	11
1988–89	Bradford C	39	4
1989–90		30	4

Season	Club	Apps	Goals
1990–91	......	38	4
1991–92	......	30	6
1992–93	......	46	16
1993–94	......	30	5

JOACHIM, Julian
Born Peterborough 20.9.74 Ht 5 6
Wt 11 10
Forward. From Trainee. England Youth,
Under-21.

Season	Club	Apps	Goals
1992–93	Leicester C	26	10
1993–94	......	36	11

JOBLING, Kevin
Born Sunderland 1.1.68. Ht 5 9
Wt 10 11
Midfield. From Apprentice.

Season	Club	Apps	Goals
1985–86	Leicester C	—	—
1986–87	......	3	—
1987–88	......	6	—
1987–88	Grimsby T	15	1
1988–89	......	32	4
1989–90	......	33	1
1990–91	......	45	—
1991–92	......	36	2
1992–93	......	14	—
1993–94	......	11	—
1993–94	Scunthorpe U	—	—

JOBSON, Richard
Born Hull 9.5.63. Ht 6 1 Wt 13 05
Defender. From Burton Alb. England B.

Season	Club	Apps	Goals
1982–83	Watford	13	1
1983–84	......	13	2
1984–85	......	2	1
1984–85	Hull C	8	—
1985–86	......	36	7
1986–87	......	40	5
1987–88	......	44	2
1988–89	......	46	1
1989–90	......	45	2
1990–91	......	2	—
1990–91	Oldham Ath	44	1
1991–92	......	36	2
1992–93	......	40	2
1993–94	......	37	5

JOHNROSE, Lenny
Born Preston 29.11.69. Ht 5 11 Wt 12 00
Forward. From Trainee.

Season	Club	Apps	Goals
1987–88	Blackburn R	1	—
1988–89	......	—	—
1989–90	......	8	3
1990–91	......	26	7
1991–92	......	7	1
1991–92	Preston NE	3	1
1991–92	Hartlepool U	15	2
1992–93	......	38	6
1993–94	......	13	3
1993–94	Bury	14	—

JOHNSEN, Erland
Born Fredrikstad (Norway) 5.4.67.
Ht 6 0 Wt 12 10
Defender. From Bayern Munich. Norway
full caps.

Season	Club	Apps	Goals
1989–90	Chelsea	18	—
1990–91	......	6	—
1991–92	......	7	—
1992–93	......	13	—
1993–94	......	28	1

JOHNSON, Alan
Born Ince 19.2.71. Ht 5 11 Wt 11 12
Defender. From Trainee.

Season	Club	Apps	Goals
1988–89	Wigan Ath	8	1
1989–90	......	33	1
1990–91	......	43	5
1991–92	......	44	4
1992–93	......	36	1
1993–94	......	16	1
1993–94	Lincoln C	16	—

JOHNSON, Andrew
Born Bath 2.5.74. Ht 5 11 Wt 11 06
Midfield. From Trainee.

Season	Club	Apps	Goals
1991–92	Norwich C	2	—
1992–93	......	2	1
1993–94	......	2	—

JOHNSON, David
Born Rother Valley 29.10.70. Ht 6 2
Wt 14 03
Forward. From Trainee.

Season	Club	Apps	Goals
1989–90	Sheffield W	—	—

Season	Club	App	Goals
1990–91	....	—	—
1991–92	....	6	—
1991–92	*Hartlepool U*	7	2
1992–93	Sheffield W..................	—	—
1992–93	*Hartlepool U*	3	—
1993–94	Lincoln C...................	41	8

JOHNSON, Gavin

Born Eye 10.10.70 Ht 5 11 Wt 11 12
Defender. From Trainee.

Season	Club	App	Goals
1988–89	Ipswich T	4	—
1989–90	....	6	—
1990–91	....	7	—
1991–92	....	42	5
1992–93	....	40	5
1993–94	....	16	1

JOHNSON, Grant

Born Dundee 24.3.72. Ht 5 11 Wt 10 00
Midfield. From Broughty Ferry. Scotland Under-21.

Season	Club	App	Goals
1990–91	Dundee U	—	—
1991–92	....	10	1
1992–93	....	17	1
1993–94	....	10	—

JOHNSON, Ian

Born Sunderland 1.9.75
Forward. From Trainee.

Season	Club	App	Goals
1993–94	Middlesbrough.............	2	—

JOHNSON, Marvin

Born Wembley 29.10.68. Ht 6 0
Wt 12 03
Defender. From Apprentice.

Season	Club	App	Goals
1986–87	Luton T	—	—
1987–88	....	9	—
1988–89	....	16	—
1989–90	....	12	—
1990–91	....	26	—
1991–92	....	—	—
1992–93	....	40	3
1993–94	....	17	—

JOHNSON, Michael

Born Nottingham 4.7.73. Ht 5 11
Wt 11 00
Defender. From Trainee.

Season	Club	App	Goals
1991–92	Notts Co	5	—

Season	Club	App	Goals
1992–93	....	37	—
1993–94	....	34	—

JOHNSON, Nigel

Born Rotherham 23.6.64. Ht 6 2
Wt 13 13
Defender. From Apprentice.

Season	Club	App	Goals
1982–83	Rotherham U	11	—
1983–84	....	43	1
1983–84	*Nottingham F*.............	—	—
1984–85	Rotherham U	35	—
1985–86	Manchester C	4	—
1986–87	....	—	—
1987–88	Rotherham U	23	—
1988–89	....	26	2
1989–90	....	43	2
1990–91	....	17	1
1991–92	....	35	2
1992–93	....	31	2
1993–94	....	—	—

JOHNSON, Richard

Born Kurri, Kurri 27.4.74. Ht 5 10
Wt 11 13
Midfield. From Trainee.

Season	Club	App	Goals
1991–92	Watford	2	—
1992–93	....	1	—
1993–94	....	27	—

JOHNSON, Ross

Born Brighton 1.2.76
Defender. From Trainee.

Season	Club	App	Goals
1993–94	Brighton......................	2	—

JOHNSON, Tommy

Born Newcastle 15.1.71. Ht 5 10
Wt 11 02
Forward. From Trainee. England Under-21.

Season	Club	App	Goals
1988–89	Notts Co	10	4
1989–90	....	40	18
1990–91	....	37	16
1991–92	....	31	9
1991–92	Derby Co....................	12	2
1992–93	....	35	8
1993–94	....	37	13

JOHNSTON, Alan

Born Glasgow 14.12.73 Ht 5 7 Wt 9 7
Forward. From Tynecastle BC. Scotland
Under-21.

Season	Club	App	Goals
1991–92	Hearts	—	—
1992–93		2	1
1993–94		28	1

JOHNSTON, Forbes

Born Aberdeen 3.8.71. Ht 5 10 Wt 9 12
Defender. From Musselburgh Ath.
Scotland Under-21.

Season	Club	App	Goals
1990–91	Falkirk	—	—
1991–92		12	—
1992–93		22	1
1993–94		15	1

JOHNSTON, Mo

Born Glasgow 30.4.63. Ht 5 9 Wt 10 06
Forward. From Milton Battlefield.
Scotland Under-21, 38 full caps.

Season	Club	App	Goals
1980–81	Partick T	—	—
1981–82		32	9
1982–83		39	22
1983–84		14	10
1983–84	Watford	29	20
1984–85		9	3
1984–85	Celtic	27	14
1985–86		32	15
1986–87		40	23
1987–88	Nantes	32	13
1988–89		34	9
1989–90	Rangers	36	15
1990–91		29	11
1991–92		11	5
1991–92	Everton	21	7
1992–93		13	3
1993–94		—	—
1993–94	Hearts	31	4

JONES, Alex

Born Blackburn 27.11.64. Ht 6 2
Wt 12 08
Defender. From Apprentice.

Season	Club	App	Goals
1982–83	Oldham Ath	2	—
1983–84		2	—
1984–85		5	—
1984–85	Stockport Co	3	—

Season	Club	App	Goals
1985–86	Oldham Ath	—	—
1986–87	Preston NE	46	1
1987–88		22	2
1988–89		30	—
1989–90		3	—
1989–90	Carlisle U	36	4
1990–91		26	—
1991–92	Rochdale	13	—
1991–92	Motherwell	12	1
1992–93		—	—
1992–93	Rochdale	29	2
1993–94		4	—

JONES, Barry

Born Prescot 20.6.70 Ht 5 10 Wt 11 02
Defender. From Prescot T.

Season	Club	App	Goals
1988–89	Liverpool	—	—
1989–90		—	—
1990–91		—	—
1991–92		—	—
1992–93	Wrexham	42	2
1993–94		33	2

JONES, David

Born Harrow 3.7.64 Ht 6 4 Wt 13 10
Forward.

Season	Club	App	Goals
1987–88	Chelsea	—	—
1988–89	Bury	1	—
1988–89	Leyton Orient	2	—
1988–89	Burnley	4	—
1989–90	Ipswich T	—	—
1989–90	Doncaster R	27	12
1990–91		13	2
1991–92	Bury	9	—
1992–93	Hull C	12	1
1993–94		—	—

JONES, Gary

Born Huddersfield 6.4.69 Ht 6 0
Wt 12 08
Forward. From Rossington Main.

Season	Club	App	Goals
1988–89	Doncaster R	17	2
1989–90		3	—
From Boston U			
1993–94	Southend U	22	3
1993–94	Lincoln C	4	2

JONES, Gary
Born Chester 10.5.75 Ht 6 3 Wt 14 00
Forward. From Trainee.

Season	Club	App	Goals
1993–94	Tranmere R	6	2

JONES, Graeme
Born Gateshead 13.3.70 Ht 6 0 Wt 12 12
Forward. From Bridlington T.

Season	Club	App	Goals
1993–94	Doncaster R	28	4

JONES, Ian
Born Germany 26.8.76
Defender. From Trainee.

Season	Club	App	Goals
1993–94	Cardiff C	2	—

JONES, Keith
Born Dulwich 14.10.64. Ht 5 9 Wt 11 02
Midfield. From Apprentice. England
Schools, Youth.

Season	Club	App	Goals
1982–83	Chelsea	2	—
1983–84		—	—
1984–85		19	2
1985–86		14	2
1986–87		17	3
1987–88		—	—
1987–88	Brentford	36	1
1988–89		40	3
1989–90		42	2
1990–91		45	6
1991–92		6	1
1991–92	Southend U	34	5
1992–93		29	1
1993–94		20	5

JONES, Kevin
Born Wrexham 16.2.74. Ht 5 10
Wt 11 00
Defender. From Trainee.

Season	Club	App	Goals
1991–92	Wrexham	1	—
1992–93		3	—
1993–94		5	—

JONES, Lee
Born Wrexham 29.5.73. Ht 5 8 Wt 10 08
Forward. From Trainee. Wales Under-21.

Season	Club	App	Goals
1990–91	Wrexham	18	5
1991–92		21	5

JONES, Lee
Born Pontypridd 9.8.70 Ht 6 3 Wt 14 04
Goalkeeper. From AFC Porth.

Season	Club	App	Goals
1991–92	Liverpool	—	—
1992–93		—	—
1993–94		—	—
1993–94	Crewe Alex	8	1

JONES, Lee
Born Pontypridd 9.8.70 Ht 6 3 Wt 14 04
Goalkeeper. From AFC Porth.

Season	Club	App	Goals
1993–94	Swansea C	—	—

JONES, Martin
Born Liverpool 27.3.75 Ht 6 1 Wt 12 00
Goalkeeper. From Trainee.

Season	Club	App	Goals
1993–94	Tranmere R	—	—

JONES, Paul
Born Chirk 18.4.67 Ht 6 3 Wt 14 00
Goalkeeper. From Kidderminster H.

Season	Club	App	Goals
1991–92	Wolverhampton W	—	—
1992–93		16	—
1993–94		—	—

JONES, Phil
Born Liverpool 1.12.69. Ht 5 8 Wt 10 09
Defender. From Trainee.

Season	Club	App	Goals
1987–88	Everton	1	—
1988–89		—	—
1989–90		—	—
1989–90	Blackpool	6	—
1990–91	Everton	—	—
1990–91	Wigan Ath	20	1
1991–92		41	1
1992–93		27	—
1993–94	Bury	4	—

JONES, Richard
Born Pontypool 26.4.69. Ht 5 11
Wt 11 01
Defender.

Season	Club	App	Goals
1986–87	Newport Co	10	—
1987–88		31	1
1988–89	Hereford U	38	1
1989–90		19	3
1990–91		40	1
1991–92		16	1
1992–93		35	3
1993–94	Swansea C	7	—

JONES, Rob

Born Wrexham 5.11.71. Ht 5 8   Wt 11 00
Defender. From Schoolboy, Trainee.
England Under-21 4 full caps.

Season	Club	App	Goals
1987–88	Crewe Alex	5	—
1988–89		19	1
1989–90		11	—
1990–91		32	1
1991–92		8	—
1991–92	Liverpool	28	—
1992–93		30	—
1993–94		38	—

JONES, Ryan

Born Sheffield 23.7.73   Ht 6 1   Wt 13 10
Midfield. From Trainee. Wales Under-21,
1 full cap.

Season	Club	App	Goals
1991–92	Sheffield W	—	—
1992–93		9	—
1993–94		27	6

JONES, Scott

Born Sheffield 1.5.75   Ht 5 10   Wt 11 08
Defender. From Trainee.

Season	Club	App	Goals
1993–94	Barnsley	—	—

JONES, Steve

Born Cambridge 17.3.70   Ht 5 11
Wt 12 00
Forward. From Billericay.

Season	Club	App	Goals
1992–93	West Ham U	6	2
1993–94		8	2

JONES, Steven

Born Teeside 31.1.74.   Ht 5 11   Wt 12 03
Goalkeeper. From Trainee.

Season	Club	App	Goals
1991–92	Hartlepool U	6	—
1992–93		3	—
1993–94		28	—

JONES, Terry

Born Liverpool 3.12.74   Ht 5 7   Wt 9 12
Midfield. From Trainee.

Season	Club	App	Goals
1993–94	Everton	—	—

JONES, Tommy

Born Aldershot 7.10.64.   Ht 5 10
Wt 11 07
Midfield. From Chelsea apprentice,
Farnborough, Weymouth.

Season	Club	App	Goals
1987–88	Aberdeen	28	3
1988–89		—	—
1988–89	Swindon T	40	6
1989–90		44	2
1990–91		43	—
1991–92		41	4
1992–93	Reading	21	1
1993–94		17	—

JONES, Vinny

Born Watford 5.1.65.   Ht 5 11   Wt 11 10
Midfield. From Wealdstone.

Season	Club	App	Goals
1986–87	Wimbledon	22	4
1987–88		24	2
1988–89		31	3
1989–90	Leeds U	45	5
1990–91		1	—
1990–91	Sheffield U	31	2
1991–92		4	—
1991–92	Chelsea	35	3
1992–93		7	1
1992–93	Wimbledon	27	1
1993–94		33	2

JORDAN, Scott

Born Newcastle 19.7.75   Ht 5 10
Wt 11 02
Midfield. From Trainee.

Season	Club	App	Goals
1992–93	York C	1	—
1993–94		—	—

JOSEPH, Matthew

Born Bethnal Green 30.9.72.   Ht 5 7
Wt 10 02
Defender. From Trainee.

Season	Club	App	Goals
1991–92	Arsenal	—	—
1992–93	Gillingham	—	—
1993–94	Cambridge U	27	2

JOSEPH, Roger

Born Paddington 24.12.65.   Ht 5 11
Wt 11 10
Defender. From Juniors. England B.

Season	Club	App	Goals
1984–85	Brentford	1	—

Season	Club	Apps	Goals
1985–86		28	1
1986–87		32	1
1987–88		43	—
1988–89	Wimbledon	31	—
1989–90		19	—
1990–91		38	—
1991–92		26	—
1992–93		32	—
1993–94		13	—

JOYCE, Joe
Born Consett 18.3.61.   Ht 5 10   Wt 11 07
Defender. From School.

Season	Club	Apps	Goals
1979–80	Barnsley	8	—
1980–81		33	—
1981–82		20	—
1982–83		32	1
1983–84		40	1
1984–85		41	—
1985–86		40	—
1986–87		34	—
1987–88		38	2
1988–89		45	—
1989–90		—	—
1990–91		3	—
1990–91	Scunthorpe U	21	—
1991–92		40	2
1992–93		30	—
1993–94	Carlisle U	29	—
1993–94	*Darlington*	4	—

JOYCE, Warren
Born Oldham 20.1.65.   Ht 5 9   Wt 11 11
Midfield. Local.

Season	Club	Apps	Goals
1982–83	Bolton W	8	—
1983–84		45	3
1984–85		45	5
1985–86		31	4
1986–87		44	5
1987–88		11	—
1987–88	Preston NE	22	—
1988–89		40	9
1989–90		44	11
1990–91		42	9
1991–92		29	5
1992–93	Plymouth Arg	30	3
1993–94	Burnley	22	4

JUDGE, Alan
Born Kingsbury 14.5.60.   Ht 5 11
Wt 11 06
Goalkeeper. From Amateur.

Season	Club	Apps	Goals
1977–78	Luton T	—	—
1978–79		—	—
1979–80		1	—
1980–81		2	—
1981–82		4	—
1982–83		4	—
1982–83	*Reading*	33	—
1983–84	Reading	41	—
1984–85		3	—
1984–85	Oxford U	—	—
1985–86		19	—
1985–86	*Lincoln C*	2	—
1986–87	Oxford U	9	—
1987–88		9	—
1987–88	*Cardiff C*	8	—
1988–89	Oxford U	20	—
1989–90		17	—
1990–91		6	—
1991–92	Hereford U	24	—
1992–93		42	—
1993–94		39	—

JULES, Mark
Born Bradford 5.9.71.   Ht 5 10   Wt 11 01
Forward. From Trainee.

Season	Club	Apps	Goals
1990–91	Bradford C	—	—
1991–92	Scarborough	41	8
1992–93		36	8
1993–94	Chesterfield	33	1

JUPP, Duncan
Born Guildford 25.1.75.   Ht 6 0   Wt 12 02
Defender. From Trainee.

Season	Club	Apps	Goals
1992–93	Fulham	3	—
1993–94		30	—

JURYEFF, Ian
Born Gosport 24.11.62.   Ht 5 11   Wt 12 0
Forward. From Apprentice.

Season	Club	Apps	Goals
1980–81	Southampton	—	—
1981–82		—	—
1982–83		—	—
From Sweden			
1983–84	Southampton	2	—

Season	Club	League Appearances/Goals	
1983–84	*Mansfield T*	12	5
1984–85	Southampton	—	—
1984–85	*Reading*	7	1
1984–85	Orient	19	7
1985–86		27	10
1986–87		13	2
1987–88		23	16
1988–89		29	9
1988–89	*Ipswich T*	2	—
1989–90	Halifax T	17	7
1989–90	Hereford U	25	3
1990–91		3	1
1990–91	Halifax T	34	9
1991–92		37	4
1992–93		1	—
1992–93	Darlington	33	6
1993–94		1	—
1993–94	Scunthorpe U	23	5

KABIA, Jason
Born Sutton in Ashfield 28.5.69.
Ht 5 11 Wt 12 00
Forward. From Oakham United.

Season	Club		
1991–92	Lincoln C	15	3
1992–93		13	1
1992–93	*Doncaster R*	5	—
1993–94	Lincoln C	—	—

KALOGERACOS, Vasili
Born Perth 21.3.75 Ht 5 7
Forward. From Floreat Athena.

Season	Club		
1993–94	Birmingham C	—	—

KAMARA, Abdul
Born Southampton 10.2.74 Ht 5 9
Wt 11 00
Midfield. From Southampton.

Season	Club		
1992–93	Bristol C	—	—
1993–94		1	—

KAMARA, Chris
Born Middlesbrough 25.12.57. Ht 6 1
Wt 12 00
Midfield. From Apprentice.

Season	Club		
1975–76	Portsmouth	24	4
1976–77		39	3
1977–78	Swindon T	40	10
1978–79		28	2
1979–80		34	5
1980–81		45	4
1981–82	Portsmouth	11	—
1981–82	Brentford	31	5
1982–83		44	11
1983–84		38	6
1984–85		39	6
1985–86	Swindon T	20	1
1986–87		42	3
1987–88		25	2
1988–89	Stoke C	38	4
1989–90		22	1
1989–90	Leeds U	11	1
1990–91		7	—
1991–92		2	—
1991–92	Luton T	28	—
1992–93		21	—
1992–93	*Sheffield U*	8	—
1992–93	*Middlesbrough*	5	—

1993–94	Sheffield U	16	—

KANCHELSKIS, Andrei
Born Kirowgrad 23.1.69.   Ht 5 10
Wt 12 04
Midfield. From Dynamo Kiev, Donezts.
USSR full caps.

1990–91	Manchester U	1	—
1991–92		34	5
1992–93		27	3
1993–94		31	6

KANE, Paul
Born Edinburgh 20.6.65.   Ht 5 8   Wt 9 09
Midfield. From Salvesen BC. Scotland
Youth.

1982–83	Hibernian	—	—
1983–84		13	1
1984–85		34	8
1985–86		32	5
1986–87		37	1
1987–88		44	10
1988–89		35	5
1989–90		31	3
1990–91		21	—
1990–91	Oldham Ath	17	—
1991–92		4	—
1991–92	Aberdeen	25	2
1992–93		27	4
1993–94		39	3

KARL, Stefan
Born Hohenm-Oelsen 3.2.70
Midfield. From Chemie, Borussia
Dortmund.

1993–94	Manchester C	6	1

KAVANAGH, Graham
Born Dublin 3.12.73   Ht 5 10   Wt 11 00
Midfield. From Home Farm.

1991–92	Middlesbrough	—	—
1992–93		10	—
1993–94		11	2
1993–94	*Darlington*	5	—

KAVANAGH, Jason
Born Birmingham 23.11.71.   Ht 5 9
Wt 11 00
Midfield. From Birmingham C schoolboys.
FA Schools. England Youth.

1988–89	Derby Co	—	—
1989–90		—	—
1990–91		11	—
1991–92		25	—
1992–93		10	—
1993–94		19	—

KAY, John
Born Sunderland 29.1.64.   Ht 5 10
Wt 11 06
Defender. From Apprentice.

1981–82	Arsenal	—	—
1982–83		7	—
1983–84		7	—
1984–85	Wimbledon	21	1
1984–85	*Middlesbrough*	8	—
1985–86	Wimbledon	26	1
1986–87		16	—
1987–88	Sunderland	46	—
1988–89		11	—
1989–90		32	—
1990–91		30	—
1991–92		41	—
1992–93		36	—
1993–94		3	—

KEANE, Roy
Born Cork 10.8.71.   Ht 5 10   Wt 11 03
Midfield. From Cobh Ramblers. Eire
Youth, Under-21, 22 full caps.

1990–91	Nottingham F	35	8
1991–92		39	8
1992–93		40	6
1993–94	Manchester U	37	5

KEARNEY, Mark
Born Ormskirk 12.6.62.   Ht 5 10
Wt 11 00
Midfield. From Marine.

1981–82	Everton	—	—
1982–83		—	—
1982–83	Mansfield T	11	1
1983–84		17	2

Season	Club		A	G
1984–85			38	4
1985–86			31	7
1986–87			43	10
1987–88			4	—
1988–89			45	2
1989–90			41	3
1990–91			20	—
1990–91	*Bury*		13	1
1990–91	Bury		9	—
1991–92			43	1
1992–93			39	2
1993–94			9	1

KEARTON, Jason

Born Ipswich (Australia) 9.7.69. Ht 6 1
Wt 11 10
Goalkeeper. From Brisbane Lions.

Season	Club		A	G
1988–89	Everton		—	—
1989–90			—	—
1990–91			—	—
1991–92			—	—
1991–92	*Stoke C*		16	—
1991–92	*Blackpool*		14	—
1992–93	Everton		5	—
1993–94			—	—

KEE, Paul

Born Belfast 8.11.69. Ht 6 3 Wt 12 05
Goalkeeper. From Ards. Northern Ireland
7 full caps.

Season	Club		A	G
1988–89	Oxford U		—	—
1989–90			21	—
1990–91			13	—
1991–92			8	—
1992–93			11	—
1993–94			3	—
1993–94	*Reading*		—	—

KEEBLE, Matthew

Born Chipping Norton 8.9.72 Ht 5 9
Wt 10 00
Forward.

Season	Club		A	G
1992–93	Oxford U		1	—
1993–94			1	—

KEELEY, John

Born Plaistow 27.7.61. Ht 6 1 Wt 14 02
Goalkeeper. From Apprentice.

Season	Club		A	G
1979–80	Southend U		4	—

Season	Club		A	G
1980–81			—	—
1981–82			27	—
1982–83			7	—
1983–84			16	—
From Chelmsford C				
1986–87	Brighton		20	—
1987–88			46	—
1988–89			37	—
1989–90			35	—
1990–91	Oldham Ath		—	—
1991–92			1	—
1991–92	*Oxford U*		6	—
1991–92	*Reading*		6	—
1992–93	Oldham Ath		1	—
1992–93	*Chester C*		4	—
1993–94	Colchester U		15	—
1993–94	Stockport Co		10	—

KEEN, Kevin

Born Amersham 25.2.67. Ht 5 8
Wt 11 00
Midfield. From Wycombe W and
Apprentice. England Schools, Youth.

Season	Club		A	G
1983–84	West Ham U		—	—
1984–85			—	—
1985–86			—	—
1986–87			13	—
1987–88			23	1
1988–89			24	3
1989–90			44	10
1990–91			40	—
1991–92			29	—
1992–93			46	7
1993–94	Wolverhampton W		41	7

KEISTER, John

Born Manchester 11.11.70 Ht 5 8
Wt 11 00
Midfield. From Faweh FC.

Season	Club		A	G
1993–94	Walsall		22	1

KELLER, Kasey

Born Washington 27.11.69. Ht 6 1
Wt 13 07
Goalkeeper. From Portland University.
USA full caps.

Season	Club		A	G
1991–92	Millwall		1	—
1992–93			45	—
1993–94			44	—

KELLY, Alan

Born Preston 11.8.68.   Ht 6 2   Wt 12 05
Goalkeeper. Eire Youth, Under-21, Under-
23, 3 full caps.

Season	Club		
1985–86	Preston NE	13	—
1986–87		22	—
1987–88		19	—
1988–89		—	—
1989–90		42	—
1990–91		23	—
1991–92		23	—
1992–93	Sheffield U	33	—
1993–94		30	—

KELLY, David

Born Birmingham 25.11.65.   Ht 5 11
Wt 11 03
Forward. From Alvechurch. Eire B,
Under-21, Under-23, 16 full caps.

Season	Club		
1983–84	Walsall	6	3
1984–85		32	7
1985–86		28	10
1986–87		42	23
1987–88		39	20
1988–89	West Ham U	25	6
1989–90		16	1
1989–90	Leicester C	10	7
1990–91		44	14
1991–92		12	1
1991–92	Newcastle U	25	11
1992–93		45	24
1993–94	Wolverhampton W	36	11

KELLY, Gary

Born Drogheda 9.7.74.   Ht 5 8   Wt 10 12
Defender. From Home Farm. Eire Youth,
5 full caps.

Season	Club		
1991–92	Leeds U	2	—
1992–93		—	—
1993–94		42	—

KELLY, Gary

Born Fulwood 3.8.66.   Ht 5 11   Wt 12 03
Goalkeeper. From Apprentice. Eire B,
Under-21.

Season	Club		
1984–85	Newcastle U	—	—
1985–86		—	—
1986–87		3	—

Season	Club		
1987–88		37	—
1988–89		9	—
1988–89	*Blackpool*	5	—
1989–90	Newcastle U	4	—
1989–90	Bury	38	—
1990–91		46	—
1991–92		46	—
1992–93		42	—
1993–94		1	—
1993–94	*West Ham U*	—	—

KELLY, Gavin

Born Beverley 29.9.68.   Ht 6 0   Wt 12 13
Goalkeeper.

Season	Club		
1987–88	Hull C	—	—
1988–89		3	—
1989–90		8	—
1989–90	*Bristol R.*	—	—
1990–91	Bristol R	7	—
1991–92		3	—
1992–93		19	—
1993–94		1	—

KELLY, Jimmy

Born Liverpool 14.2.73.   Ht 5 7   Wt 11 10
Midfield. From Trainee.

Season	Club		
1990–91	Wrexham	12	—
1991–92		9	—
1991–92	Wolverhampton W	3	—
1992–93		—	—
1992–93	*Walsall*	10	2
1993–94	Wolverhampton W	4	—
1993–94	*Wrexham*	9	—

KELLY, Mark

Born Sutton 27.11.69.   Ht 5 8   Wt 9 10
Forward. England Youth, Eire, B, Under-
21, Under-23, 4 full caps.

Season	Club		
1986–87	Portsmouth	—	—
1987–88		3	—
1988–89		28	1
1989–90		13	—
1990–91		5	1
1990–91	*Tottenham H*	—	—
1991–92	Portsmouth	—	—
1992–93		—	—
1993–94		—	—

KELLY, Mark
Born Blackpool 7.10.66. Ht 5 9
Wt 10 05
Midfield.

Season	Club	Apps	Goals
1985–86	Shrewsbury T	—	—
1986–87		—	—
1987–88	Cardiff C	36	1
1988–89		28	—
1989–90		41	1
1990–91	Fulham	18	—
1991–92		21	1
1992–93		25	1
1993–94	Blackpool	—	—

KELLY, Norman
Born Belfast 10.10.70. Ht 5 8   Wt 11 00
Midfield. From Trainee. Northern Ireland
Youth.

Season	Club	Apps	Goals
1987–88	Oldham	1	—
1988–89		1	—
1989–90		—	—
1989–90	*Wigan Ath*	4	—
1990–91	Oldham Ath	—	—
1990–91	Dunfermline Ath	2	—
1991–92		8	—
From Glenavon			
1993–94	Raith R	4	—

KELLY, Paul
Born Hillingdon 24.2.74. Ht 5 7
Wt 10 13
Midfield. From Trainee.

Season	Club	Apps	Goals
1991–92	Fulham	3	—
1992–93		—	—
1993–94		3	—

KELLY, Tom
Born Bellshill 28.3.64. Ht 5 9   Wt 12 05
Defender. From Hibs.

Season	Club	Apps	Goals
1985–86	Hartlepool U	15	—
1986–87	Torquay U	38	—
1987–88		38	—
1988–89		44	—
1989–90	York C	35	2
1989–90	Exeter C	12	2
1990–91		22	1
1991–92		32	5
1992–93		22	1

| 1992–93 | Torquay U | 18 | 3 |
| 1993–94 | | 35 | 2 |

KELLY, Tony
Born Meridan 14.2.66. Ht 5 9   Wt 11 06
Forward.

Season	Club	Apps	Goals
1982–83	Bristol C	6	1
From St Albans C			
1989–90	Stoke C	9	—
1990–91		29	3
1991–92		13	2
1991–92	*Hull C*	6	1
1992–93	Stoke C	7	—
1992–93	*Cardiff C*	5	1
1993–94	Stoke C	—	—
1993–94	Bury	35	7

KELLY, Tony
Born Prescot 1.10.64. Ht 5 10   Wt 11 09
Midfield. From Liverpool Apprentice.

Season	Club	Apps	Goals
1983–84	Derby Co	—	—
1983–84	Wigan Ath	29	2
1984–85		40	4
1985–86		32	9
1985–86	Stoke C	1	—
1986–87		35	4
1987–88	WBA	26	1
1988–89		—	—
1988–89	*Chester C*	5	—
1988–89	*Colchester U*	13	2
1988–89	Shrewsbury T	20	5
1989–90		43	5
1990–91		38	5
1991–92	Bolton W	31	2
1992–93		36	2
1993–94		35	1

KENNA, Jeff
Born Dublin 27.8.70. Ht 5 11   Wt 11 09
Defender. From Trainee. Eire Youth,
Under-21.

Season	Club	Apps	Goals
1988–89	Southampton	—	—
1989–90		—	—
1990–91		2	—
1991–92		14	—
1992–93		29	2
1993–94		41	2

KENNEDY, Andy

Born Stirling 8.10.64. Ht 6 2 Wt 13 00
Forward. From Sauchie Ath.

Season	Club		
1983–84	Rangers	13	3
1984–85		2	—
1984–85	Birmingham C	7	4
1985–86		32	6
1986–87		9	1
1986–87	*Sheffield U*	9	1
1987–88	Birmingham C	28	7
1988–89	Blackburn R	25	10
1989–90		34	13
1990–91	Watford	18	3
1991–92		7	1
1991–92	*Bolton W*	1	—
1992–93	Watford	—	—
1992–93	Brighton	30	8
1993–94		12	2

KENNEDY, Mark

Born Dublin 15.5.76 Ht 5 11 Wt 11 09
Forward. From Trainee.

Season	Club		
1992–93	Millwall	1	—
1993–94		12	4

KENNEDY, Mick

Born Salford 9.4.61. Ht 5 9 Wt 12 00
Midfield. From Apprentice. Eire Under-21,
2 caps.

Season	Club		
1978–79	Halifax T	30	—
1979–80		46	4
1980–81	Huddersfield T	42	2
1981–82		39	7
1982–83	Middlesbrough	38	5
1983–84		30	—
1984–85	Portsmouth	37	—
1985–86		39	2
1986–87		35	2
1987–88		18	—
1987–88	Bradford C	15	1
1988–89		30	1
1988–89	Leicester C	9	—
1989–90	Luton T	32	—
1990–91	Stoke C	32	3
1991–92		20	—
1992–93	Chesterfield	27	1
1993–94	Wigan Ath	17	1

KENNY, Billy

Born Liverpool 19.9.73 Ht 5 07
Wt 10 10
Midfield. From Trainee. England
Under-21.

Season	Club		
1992–93	Everton	17	1
1993–94		—	—

KENT, Kevin

Born Stoke 19.3.65. Ht 5 11 Wt 11 00
Forward. From Apprentice.

Season	Club		
1982–83	WBA	—	—
1983–84		2	—
1984–85	Newport Co	33	1
1985–86	Mansfield T	34	8
1986–87		46	6
1987–88		45	10
1988–89		39	5
1989–90		38	3
1990–91		27	4
1990–91	Port Vale	11	—
1991–92		23	—
1992–93		27	1
1993–94		30	4

KENWORTHY, Jon

Born St Asaph 18.8.74 Ht 5 7 Wt 10 06
Forward. From Trainee.

Season	Club		
1993–94	Tranmere R	16	2

KEOWN, Martin

Born Oxford 24.7.66. Ht 6 1 Wt 12 04
Defender. From Apprentice. England
Youth, Under-21 B, 11 full caps.

Season	Club		
1983–84	Arsenal	—	—
1984–85		—	—
1984–85	*Brighton*	16	—
1985–86	Arsenal	22	—
1985–86	*Brighton*	7	1
1986–87	Aston Villa	36	—
1987–88		42	3
1988–89		34	—
1989–90	Everton	20	—
1990–91		24	—
1991–92		39	—
1992–93		13	—
1992–93	Arsenal	16	—
1993–94		33	—

KERNAGHAN, Alan

Born Otley 25.4.67. Ht 6 2 Wt 13 00
Defender. From Apprentice. Eire 11 full
caps.

Season	Club	App	Goals
1984–85	Middlesbrough	8	1
1985–86		6	—
1986–87		13	—
1987–88		35	6
1988–89		23	—
1989–90		37	4
1990–91		24	—
1990–91	*Charlton Ath*	13	—
1991–92	Middlesbrough	38	2
1992–93		22	2
1993–94		6	1
1993–94	Manchester C	24	—

KERR, Andy

Born West Bromwich 7.4.66 Ht 6 0
Wt 12 07
Defender. From Telford U.

Season	Club	App	Goals
1993–94	Wycombe W	14	3

KERR, David

Born Dumfries 6.9.74 Ht 5 11 Wt 11 00
Midfield. From Trainee.

Season	Club	App	Goals
1991–92	Manchester C	—	—
1992–93		1	—
1993–94		2	—

KERR, Dylan

Born Valetta 14.1.67. Ht 5 11 Wt 12 05
Defender. From Arcadia Shepherds.

Season	Club	App	Goals
1988–89	Leeds U	3	—
1989–90		5	—
1990–91		—	—
1991–92		—	—
1991–92	*Doncaster R*	7	1
1991–92	*Blackpool*	12	1
1992–93	Leeds U	5	—
1993–94	Reading	45	2

KERR, John

Born Toronto 6.3.65 Ht 5 8 Wt 11 05
Forward. From Harrow Borough.

Season	Club	App	Goals
1987–88	Portsmouth	4	—
1987–88	*Peterborough U*	10	1
From San Diego Sockers			
1992–93	Millwall	6	1

Season	Club	App	Goals
1993–94		23	4

KERR, Paul

Born Portsmouth 9.6.64. Ht 5 8
Wt 11 03
Forward. From Apprentice.

Season	Club	App	Goals
1982–83	Aston Villa	—	—
1983–84		2	—
1984–85		10	—
1985–86		6	1
1986–87		6	2
1986–87	Middlesbrough	20	—
1987–88		44	5
1988–89		20	1
1989–90		17	1
1990–91		24	6
1990–91	Millwall	10	2
1991–92		34	12
1992–93	Port Vale	38	11
1993–94		25	4
1993–94	*Leicester C*	7	2

KERR, Stuart

Born Bournemouth 3.10.74 Ht 6 0
Wt 12 00
Forward. From Trainee.

Season	Club	App	Goals
1993–94	Bournemouth	—	—

KERRY, Chris

Born Chesterfield 15.4.76
Forward. From Trainee.

Season	Club	App	Goals
1993–94	Mansfield T	2	—

KERSLAKE, David

Born London 19.6.66. Ht 5 8 Wt 11 00
Midfield. From Apprentice. England
Schools, Youth, Under-21. Football
League.

Season	Club	App	Goals
1983–84	QPR	—	—
1984–85		1	—
1985–86		14	1
1986–87		3	—
1987–88		18	5
1988–89		21	—
1989–90		1	—
1989–90	Swindon T	28	—
1990–91		37	—
1991–92		39	1

1992–93	....	31 —
1992–93	Leeds U	8 —
1993–94	Tottenham H	17 —

KEVAN, David
Born Wigtown 31.8.68. Ht 5 8 Wt 10 12
Midfield. From Apprentice.

1985–86	Notts Co	3 —
1986–87	....	33 1
1987–88	....	32 —
1988–89	....	18 2
1989–90	....	3 —
1989–90	*Cardiff C*	7 —
1989–90	Stoke C	17 —
1990–91	....	5 —
1990–91	*Maidstone U*	3 —
1991–92	Stoke C	43 1
1992–93	....	15 1
1993–94	....	1 —
1993–94	Bournemouth	1 —

KEY, Lance
Born Kettering 13.5.68. Ht 6 2 Wt 14 13
Goalkeeper. From Histon.

1991–92	Sheffield W	— —
1991–92	*York C*	— —
1992–93	Sheffield W	— —
1993–94	....	— —
1993–94	*Oldham Ath*	2 —
1993–94	*Portsmouth*	— —

KHARINE, Dmitri
Born Moscow 16.8.68. Ht 6 2 Wt 12 04
Goalkeeper. From Moscow Torpedo,
Moscow Dynamo, CSKA Moscow. CIS
full caps.

1992–93	Chelsea	5 —
1993–94	....	40 —

KIDD, Ryan
Born Heywood 6.10.71. Ht 6 0 Wt 11 07
Defender. From Trainee.

1990–91	Port Vale	— —
1991–92	....	1 —
1992–93	Preston NE	15 —
1993–94	....	36 1

KIELY, Dean
Born Manchester 10.10.70. Ht 6 0
Wt 12 08
Goalkeeper. From WBA schoolboy. FA
Schools. England Youth.

1987–88	Coventry C	— —
1988–89	....	— —
1989–90	....	— —
1989–90	*Ipswich T*	— —
1989–90	*York C*	— —
1990–91	York C	17 —
1991–92	....	21 —
1992–93	....	40 —
1993–94	....	46 —

KILBANE, Farrell
Born Preston 21.10.74 Ht 6 0 Wt 13 00
Defender. From Cambridge U trainee.

1993–94	Preston NE	1 —

KILCLINE, Brian
Born Nottingham 7.5.62. Ht 6 2
Wt 12 00
Defender. From Apprentice. England
Under-21.

1979–80	Notts Co	16 1
1980–81	....	42 1
1981–82	....	36 3
1982–83	....	40 3
1983–84	....	24 1
1984–85	Coventry C	26 2
1985–86	....	32 7
1986–87	....	29 3
1987–88	....	28 8
1988–89	....	33 4
1989–90	....	11 1
1990–91	....	14 3
1991–92	Oldham Ath	8 —
1991–92	Newcastle U	12 —
1992–93	....	19 —
1993–94	....	1 —
1993–94	Swindon T	10 —

KILFORD, Ian
Born Bristol 6.10.73. Ht 5 10 Wt 10 05
Defender. From Trainee.

1991–92	Nottingham F	— —
1992–93	....	— —

1993–94	....	1	—
1993–94	*Wigan Ath*..................	8	3

KIMBLE, Alan

Born Poole 6.8.66. Ht 5 8 Wt 11 00
Defender.

1984–85	Charlton Ath	6	—
1985–86		—	—
1985–86	*Exeter C*	1	—
1986–87	Cambridge U	35	—
1987–88	....	41	2
1988–89	....	45	6
1989–90	....	44	8
1990–91	....	43	4
1991–92	....	45	—
1992–93	....	46	4
1993–94	Wimbledon	14	—

KING, Phil

Born Bristol 28.12.67. Ht 5 8 Wt 13 00
Defender. From Apprentice. England B.

1984–85	Exeter C......................	16	—
1985–86	....	11	—
1986–87	Torquay U	24	3
1986–87	Swindon T	21	—
1987–88	....	44	1
1988–89	....	37	2
1989–90	....	14	1
1989–90	Sheffield W.................	25	—
1990–91	....	43	—
1991–92	....	39	1
1992–93	....	12	1
1993–94	....	10	—
1993–94	*Notts Co*.....................	6	—

KINNAIRD, Paul

Born Glasgow 11.11.66. Ht 5 8 Wt 10 10
Forward. From Apprentice.

1984–85	Norwich C	—	—
1985–86	Dundee U	—	—
1986–87	....	7	—
1987–88	....	11	—
1987–88	Motherwell..................	10	—
1988–89	....	24	—
1988–89	St Mirren	6	—
1989–90	....	25	—
1990–91	....	23	4
1991–92	....	3	—
1991–92	Partick T.....................	13	2

1992–93	....	20	1
1992–93	Shrewsbury T..............	4	1
1992–93	St Johnstone	8	—
1993–94	Partick T....................	3	—

KINSELLA, Mark

Born Dublin 12.8.72 Ht 5 9 Wt 11 00
Midfield. From Home Farm.

1989–90	Colchester U...............	6	—
1990–91	....	*11*	—
1991–92	....	*42*	*3*
1992–93	....	38	6
1993–94	....	42	8

KIRBY, Ryan

Born Chingford 6.9.74 Ht 5 11 Wt 12 00
Defender. From Trainee.

1993–94	Arsenal.......................	—	—

KIRK, Steve

Born Kirkcaldy 3.1.63. Ht 5 11
Wt 11 04
Midfield. From Buckhaven Hibs.

1979–80	East Fife	25	2
1980–81	Stoke C	—	—
1981–82	....	12	—
1982–83	Partick T.....................	—	—
1982–83	East Fife	25	8
1983–84	....	33	5
1984–85	....	38	8
1985–86	....	39	14
1986–87	Motherwell..................	35	10
1987–88	....	38	4
1988–89	....	33	14
1989–90	....	34	8
1990–91	....	29	2
1991–92	....	38	6
1992–93	....	40	10
1993–94	....	36	7

KIRKHAM, Peter

Born Newcastle 28.10.74 Ht 6 0
Wt 11 04
Midfield. From Newcastle U trainee.

1993–94	Darlington	9	—

KITCHEN, Sam

Born Germany 11.6.67   Ht 5 9   Wt 11 00
Defender. From Frickley Ath.

1992–93	Leyton Orient	32	1
1993–94		11	—
1993–94	Doncaster R	14	1

KITE, Phil

Born Bristol 26.10.62.   Ht 6 1   Wt 14 07
Goalkeeper. From Apprentice. England Youth.

1980–81	Bristol R	4	—
1981–82		27	—
1982–83		46	—
1983–84		19	—
1983–84	*Tottenham H*	—	—
1984–85	Southampton	1	—
1985–86		3	—
1985–86	*Middlesbrough*	2	—
1986–87	Gillingham	17	—
1987–88		26	—
1988–89		27	—
1989–90	Bournemouth	7	—
1990–91	Sheffield U	7	—
1991–92		4	—
1991–92	*Mansfield T*	11	—
1992–93	Sheffield U	—	—
1992–93	*Plymouth Arg*	2	—
1992–93	*Rotherham U*	1	—
1992–93	*Crewe Alex*	5	—
1992–93	*Stockport Co*	5	—
1993–94	Cardiff C	18	—

KITSON, Paul

Born Co Durham 9.1.71.   Ht 5 11   Wt 10 12
Forward. From Trainee. England Under-21.

1988–89	Leicester C	—	—
1989–90		13	—
1990–91		7	—
1991–92		30	6
1991–92	Derby Co	12	4
1992–93		44	17
1993–94		41	13

KIWOMYA, Andrew

Born Huddersfield 1.10.67   Ht 5 9   Wt 10 10
Forward. From Trainee. England Youth.

1985–86	Barnsley	1	—
1986–87	Sheffield W	—	—
1987–88		—	—
1988–89		—	—
Retired injury			
1992–93	Dundee	21	1
1993–94	Rotherham U	7	—

KIWOMYA, Chris

Born Huddersfield 2.12.69.   Ht 5 10   Wt 10 12
Forward.

1986–87	Ipswich T	—	—
1987–88		—	—
1988–89		26	2
1989–90		29	5
1990–91		37	10
1991–92		43	16
1992–93		38	10
1993–94		37	5

KJELDBJERG, Jakob

Born Denmark 21.10.69   Ht 6 2   Wt 13 08
Defender. From Silkeborg.

1993–94	Chelsea	29	1

KNIGHT, Alan

Born Balham 3.6.61.   Ht 6 0   Wt 13 00
Goalkeeper. From Apprentice. England Youth, Under-21.

1977–78	Portsmouth	1	—
1978–79		—	—
1979–80		8	—
1980–81		1	—
1981–82		45	—
1982–83		46	—
1983–84		42	—
1984–85		42	—
1985–86		38	—
1986–87		42	—
1987–88		36	—
1988–89		32	—
1989–90		46	—

189

1990–91	....	22	—
1991–92	....	45	—
1992–93	....	46	—
1993–94	....	43	—

KNIGHT, Craig
Born Wrexham 24.10.73. Ht 6 1
Wt 12 00
Defender. From Trainee.

1991–92	Wrexham	1	—
1992–93	....	—	—
1993–94	....	—	—

KNIGHT, Richard
Born Burton 31.8.74 Ht 5 9 Wt 10 13
Defender. From Trainee.

1991–92	Walsall	—	—
1992–93	....	27	1
1993–94	....	2	—

KNILL, Alan
Born Slough 8.10.64. Ht 6 2 Wt 11 07
Defender. From Apprentice. Wales Youth,
1 full cap.

1982–83	Southampton	—	—
1983–84	....	—	—
1984–85	Halifax T	44	1
1985–86	....	33	2
1986–87	....	41	3
1987–88	Swansea C	46	1
1988–89	....	43	2
1989–90	Bury	43	1
1990–91	....	20	1
1991–92	....	35	1
1992–93	....	38	5
1993–94	....	8	—
1993–94	*Cardiff C*	4	—
1993–94	Scunthorpe U	25	1

KNOWLES, Cameron
Born Ripon 19.9.69
Midfield.

1993–94	Chesterfield	1	—

KNOWLES, Darren
Born Sheffield 8.10.70. Ht 5 6 Wt 10 01
Midfield. From Trainee.

1989–90	Sheffield U	—	—

1989–90	Stockport Co	9	—
1990–91	....	12	—
1991–92	....	31	—
1992–93	....	11	—
1993–94	Scarborough	42	1

KOZMA, Istvan
Born Paszto, Hungary 3.12.64. Ht 5 9
Wt 12 00
Midfield. From Ujpest Dozsa, Bordeaux.
Hungary full caps.

1989–90	Dunfermline Ath	33	6
1990–91	....	34	2
1991–92	....	23	—
1991–92	Liverpool	5	—
1992–93	....	1	—

To Ujpest Dozsa

KRISTENSEN, Bjorn
Born Malling 10.10.63. Ht 6 1 Wt 12 05
Defender. From Aarhus. Denmark full
caps.

1988–89	Newcastle U	5	—
1989–90	....	33	3
1990–91	....	40	1
1991–92	....	2	—
1992–93	....	—	—
1992–93	*Bristol C*	4	—
1992–93	Portsmouth	10	1
1993–94	....	36	—

KRIVOKAPIC, Miodrag
Born Niksic 6.9.59 Ht 6 1 Wt 12 12
Defender. From Red Star Belgrade.
Yugoslavia full caps.

1988–89	Dundee U	24	1
1989–90	....	26	—
1990–91	....	24	—
1991–92	....	—	—
1992–93	....	8	—
1993–94	Motherwell	42	1

KRUSZYNSKI, Detsi
Born Divschav 14.10.61. Ht 6 0
Wt 12 12
Midfield. From Homburg.

1988–89	Wimbledon	16	—
1989–90	....	27	2

Season	Club	App	Goals
1990–91		27	2
1991–92		1	—
1991–92	*Brentford*	8	—
1992–93	Wimbledon	—	—
1992–93	Brentford	6	—

From Saarbrucken, Homburg

Season	Club	App	Goals
1993–94	Peterborough U	3	—
1993–94	Coventry C	2	—

KUBICKI, Dariusz
Born Warsaw 6.6.63.   Ht 5 10   Wt 11 07
Defender. From Legia Warsaw.

Season	Club	App	Goals
1991–92	Aston Villa	23	—
1992–93		—	—
1993–94		2	—
1993–94	*Sunderland*	15	—

KUHL, Martin
Born Frimley 10.1.65.   Ht 5 11   Wt 11 13
Midfield. From Apprentice.

Season	Club	App	Goals
1982–83	Birmingham C	2	—
1983–84		22	1
1984–85		27	2
1985–86		37	1
1986–87		23	1
1986–87	Sheffield U	10	1
1987–88		28	3
1987–88	Watford	4	—
1988–89		—	—
1988–89	Portsmouth	32	1
1989–90		40	9
1990–91		41	13
1991–92		41	3
1992–93		3	1
1992–93	Derby Co	32	1
1993–94		27	—

KUZNETSOV, Oleg
Born Kiev 2.3.63   Ht 6 2   Wt 12 08
Defender. From Dynamo Kiev. CIS full caps.

Season	Club	App	Goals
1990–91	Rangers	2	—
1991–92		18	—
1992–93		9	—
1993–94		6	1

LAIGHT, Ellis
Born Birmingham 30.6.76   Ht 5 10
Wt 11 02
Forward. From Trainee.

Season	Club	App	Goals
1993–94	Torquay U	1	—

LAKE, Michael
Born Manchester 6.11.66.   Ht 6 1
Wt 12 11
Midfield. From Macclesfield T.

Season	Club	App	Goals
1989–90	Sheffield U	4	—
1990–91		7	—
1991–92		18	4
1992–93		6	—
1992–93	Wrexham	26	5
1993–94		30	1

LAKE, Paul
Born Manchester 28.10.68.   Ht 6 0
Wt 12 02
Midfield. From Trainee. England Under-21.

Season	Club	App	Goals
1986–87	Manchester C	3	1
1987–88		33	3
1988–89		38	3
1989–90		31	—
1990–91		3	—
1991–92		—	—
1992–93		2	—
1993–94		—	—

LAKIN, Barry
Born Dartford 19.9.73
Midfield. From Trainee.

Season	Club	App	Goals
1992–93	Leyton Orient	9	2
1993–94		15	—

LAMB, Paul
Born Plumstead 12.9.74
Midfield. From Trainee.

Season	Club	App	Goals
1992–93	Northampton T	3	—
1993–94		—	—

LAMBERT, James
Born Henley 14.9.73   Ht 5 7   Wt 10 04
Forward. From School.

Season	Club	App	Goals
1992–93	Reading	27	3
1993–94		6	—

LAMBERT, Paul

Born Glasgow 7.8.69   Ht 5 11   Wt 9—10
Midfield. Linwood Rangers BC. Scotland
Under-21.

Season	Club	App	Goals
1985–86	St Mirren	1	—
1986–87		36	2
1987–88		36	2
1988–89		16	2
1989–90		25	3
1990–91		31	2
1991–92		40	2
1992–93		39	1
1993–94		3	—
1993–94	Motherwell	32	3

LAMPKIN, Kevin

Born Liverpool 20.12.72   Ht 5 10
Wt 11 08
Midfield. From Trainee.

Season	Club	App	Goals
1991–92	Liverpool	—	—
1992–93	Huddersfield T	13	—
1993–94		—	—
1993–94	Mansfield T	13	1

LANCASHIRE, Graham

Born Blackpool 19.10.72   Ht 5 10
Wt 11 12
Forward. From Trainee.

Season	Club	App	Goals
1990–91	Burnley	1	—
1991–92		25	8
1992–93		3	—
1992–93	*Halifax T*	2	—
1993–94	Burnley	1	—
1993–94	*Chester C*	11	7

LANCASTER, Dave

Born Preston 8.9.61.   Ht 6 3   Wt 14 00
Forward. From Colne Dynamoes.

Season	Club	App	Goals
1990–91	Blackpool	8	1
1990–91	*Chesterfield*	12	4
1991–92	Chesterfield	29	7
1992–93		40	9
1993–94	Rochdale	40	14

LANDON, Chris

Born Epsom 20.10.74   Ht 5 9
Defender. From Trainee.

Season	Club	App	Goals
1993–94	Tottenham H	—	—

LANDON, Richard

Born Barnsley 22.3.70   Ht 6 3
Forward. From Bedworth U.

Season	Club	App	Goals
1993–94	Plymouth Arg	6	5

LANGE, Tony

Born London 10.12.64.   Ht 6 0   Wt 12 09
Goalkeeper. From Apprentice.

Season	Club	App	Goals
1982–83	Charlton Ath	—	—
1983–84		6	—
1984–85		2	—
1985–86		4	—
1985–86	*Aldershot*	7	—
1986–87	Aldershot	45	—
1987–88		35	—
1988–89		45	—
1989–90	Wolverhampton W	5	—
1990–91		3	—
1990–91	*Aldershot*	2	—
1991–92	Wolverhampton W	—	—
1991–92	*Torquay U*	1	—
1991–92	*Portsmouth*	—	—
1992–93	WBA	14	—
1993–94		29	—

LANGFORD, Craig

Born Solihull 12.3.75   Ht 6 1
Defender. From Trainee.

Season	Club	App	Goals
1992–93	Hereford U	1	—
1993–94		4	—

LANGFORD, Tim

Born Kingswinford 12.9.65   Ht 5 6
Wt 11 10
Forward. From Telford U.

Season	Club	App	Goals
1993–94	Wycombe W	29	8

LANGLEY, Kevin

Born St. Helens 24.5.64.   Ht 6 1
Wt 10 03
Midfield. From Apprentice.

Season	Club	App	Goals
1981–82	Wigan Ath	2	—
1982–83		28	2
1983–84		44	1
1984–85		43	1
1985–86		43	2
1986–87	Everton	16	2
1986–87	*Manchester C*	9	—

Season	Club	App	Goals
1987–88	Manchester C	—	—
1987–88	*Chester C*	9	—
1987–88	Birmingham C	7	—
1988–89		36	2
1989–90		33	—
1990–91		—	—
1990–91	Wigan Ath	39	2
1991–92		45	2
1992–93		40	—
1993–94		33	2

LAUCHLAN, James
Born Glasgow 2.2.77
Midfield. Highbury BC.

Season	Club	App	Goals
1993–94	Kilmarnock	1	—

LAUNDERS, Brian
Born Dublin 8.6.76   Ht 5 10   Wt 11 12
Forward. From Trainee.

Season	Club	App	Goals
1993–94	Crystal Palace	—	—

LAVIN, Gerard
Born Corby 5.2.74.   Ht 5 9   Wt 10 07
Midfield. From Trainee. Scotland Under-21.

Season	Club	App	Goals
1991–92	Watford	1	—
1992–93		28	—
1993–94		46	3

LAW, Bobby
Born Bellshill 24.12.65.   Ht 5 9   Wt 11 00
Midfield. From Stonehouse Violet.

Season	Club	App	Goals
1984–85	Partick T	1	—
1985–86		16	3
1986–87		31	2
1987–88		21	1
1988–89		33	—
1989–90		28	1
1990–91		27	—
1991–92		31	2
1992–93		34	—
1993–94		25	—

LAW, Nicky
Born London 8.9.61.   Ht 6 1   Wt 12 07
Defender. From Apprentice.

Season	Club	App	Goals
1979–80	Arsenal	—	—
1980–81		—	—

Season	Club	App	Goals
1981–82	Barnsley	19	—
1982–83		28	—
1983–84		31	1
1984–85		35	—
1985–86		1	—
1985–86	Blackpool	39	1
1986–87		27	—
1986–87	Plymouth Arg	12	2
1987–88		26	3
1988–89	Notts Co	44	4
1989–90		3	—
1989–90	*Scarborough*	12	—
1990–91	Rotherham U	32	2
1991–92		42	—
1992–93		44	2
1993–94		10	—
1993–94	Chesterfield	31	2

LAWFORD, Craig
Born Dewsbury 25.11.72.   Ht 5 10   Wt 11 10
Defender. From Trainee.

Season	Club	App	Goals
1989–90	Bradford C	1	—
1990–91		—	—
1991–92		—	—
1992–93		8	1
1993–94		11	—

LAWRENCE, Jamie
Born Balham 8.3.70   Ht 5 10   Wt 12 03
Forward. From Cowes.

Season	Club	App	Goals
1993–94	Sunderland	4	—
1993–94	Doncaster R	9	1

LAWS, Brian
Born Wallsend 14.10.61.   Ht 5 10   Wt 11 05
Defender. From Apprentice. England B.

Season	Club	App	Goals
1979–80	Burnley	1	—
1980–81		42	2
1981–82		44	6
1982–83		38	4
1983–84	Huddersfield T	31	—
1984–85		25	1
1984–85	Middlesbrough	11	1
1985–86		42	2
1986–87		26	8
1987–88		28	1
1988–89	Nottingham F	22	1

Season	Club	League Appearances/Goals		Season	Club	League Appearances/Goals	
1989–90		38	3	1989–90		13	—
1990–91		32	—	1989–90	*Northampton T*	9	—
1991–92		15	—	1990–91	Charlton Ath	20	1
1992–93		33	—	1991–92		39	11
1993–94		7	—	1992–93		39	5
				1993–94		39	10

LAWTON, Craig
Born Mancot 5.1.72 Ht 5 7 Wt 10 03
Midfield. From Trainee.

1991–92	Manchester U	—	—
1992–93		—	—
1993–94		—	—

LE SAUX, Graeme
Born Jersey 17.10.68. Ht 5 9 Wt 12 00
Defender. From England B, Under-21, 3 full caps.

1987–88	Chelsea	—	—
1988–89		1	—
1989–90		7	1
1990–91		28	4
1991–92		40	3
1992–93		14	—
1992–93	Blackburn R	9	—
1993–94		41	2

LE TISSIER, Matthew
Born Guernsey 14.10.68. Ht 6 1 Wt 12 10
Forward. From Vale Recreation, Trainee.
England Youth, B, 3 full caps.

1986–87	Southampton	24	6
1987–88		19	—
1988–89		28	9
1989–90		35	20
1990–91		35	19
1991–92		32	6
1992–93		40	15
1993–94		38	25

LEABURN, Carl
Born Lewisham 30.3.69. Ht 6 3 Wt 11 03
Forward. From Apprentice. England Youth.

1986–87	Charlton Ath	3	1
1987–88		12	—
1988–89		32	2

LEADBITTER, Chris
Born Middlesbrough 17.10.67. Ht 5 9 Wt 10 07
Forward. From Apprentice.

1985–86	Grimsby T	—	—
1986–87	Hereford U	6	—
1987–88		30	1
1988–89	Cambridge U	31	6
1989–90		43	4
1990–91		39	1
1991–92		25	1
1992–93		38	6
1993–94	Bournemouth	27	—

LEANING, Andy
Born York 18.5.63. Ht 6 1 Wt 14 07
Goalkeeper. From Rowntree Mackintosh.

1984–85	York C	—	—
1985–86		30	—
1986–87		39	—
1987–88	Sheffield U	21	—
1988–89		—	—
1988–89	Bristol C	6	—
1989–90		19	—
1990–91		29	—
1991–92		20	—
1992–93		1	—
1993–94		—	—
1993–94	Lincoln C	8	—

LEE, Chris
Born Halifax 18.6.71. Ht 5 10 Wt 11 07
Midfield. From Trainee.

1989–90	Bradford C	—	—
1990–91	Rochdale	26	2
1990–91	Scarborough	9	—
1991–92		41	2
1992–93		28	1
1993–94	Hull C	43	3

LEE, Dave

Born Manchester 5.11.67.   Ht 5 8
Wt 10 02
Midfield. From Blackburn Schools.

Season	Club		
1984–85	Bury	—	—
1985–86		1	—
1986–87		30	4
1987–88		40	3
1988–89		45	4
1989–90		45	8
1990–91		45	15
1991–92		2	1
1991–92	Southampton	19	—
1992–93		1	—
1992–93	Bolton W	32	5
1993–94		41	5

LEE, David

Born Kingswood 26.11.69.   Ht 6 3
Wt 13 12
Defender. From Trainee. England Youth,
Under-21.

Season	Club		
1988–89	Chelsea	20	4
1989–90		30	1
1990–91		21	1
1991–92		1	—
1991–92	*Reading*	5	5
1991–92	*Plymouth Arg*	9	1
1992–93	Chelsea	25	2
1993–94		7	1

LEE, Jason

Born Newham 9.5.71.   Ht 6 3   Wt 13 08
Forward. From Trainee.

Season	Club		
1989–90	Charlton Ath	1	—
1990–91		—	—
1990–91	*Stockport Co*	2	—
1990–91	Lincoln C	17	3
1991–92		35	6
1992–93		41	12
1993–94	Southend U	24	3
1993–94	Nottingham F	13	2

LEE, Robert

Born West Ham 1.2.66.   Ht 5 10
Wt 11 13
Forward. From Hornchurch. England
Under-21.

Season	Club		
1983–84	Charlton Ath	11	4
1984–85		39	10
1985–86		35	8
1986–87		33	3
1987–88		23	2
1988–89		31	5
1989–90		37	1
1990–91		43	13
1991–92		39	12
1992–93		7	1
1992–93	Newcastle U	36	10
1993–94		41	7

LEGG, Andy

Born Neath 28.7.66.   Ht 5 8   Wt 10 07
Midfield. From Briton Ferry.

Season	Club		
1988–89	Swansea C	6	—
1989–90		26	3
1990–91		39	5
1991–92		46	9
1992–93		46	12
1993–94	Notts Co	30	2

LEIGHTON, Jim

Born Johnstone 24.7.58.   Ht 6 1
Wt 12 09
Goalkeeper. From Dalry Thistle. Scotland
Under-21, 61 full caps.

Season	Club		
1978–79	Aberdeen	11	—
1979–80		1	—
1980–81		35	—
1981–82		36	—
1982–83		35	—
1983–84		36	—
1984–85		34	—
1985–86		26	—
1986–87		42	—
1987–88		44	—
1988–89	Manchester U	38	—
1989–90		35	—
1990–91		—	—
1990–91	*Arsenal*	—	—
1991–92	Manchester U	—	—
1991–92	*Reading*	8	—
1991–92	*Dundee*	13	—
1992–93		8	—
1992–93	*Sheffield U*	—	—
1993–94	Hibernian	44	—

LEITCH, Grant
Born South Africa 31.10.72. Ht 6 1
Wt 12 05
Forward.

1991–92	Blackpool	6	—
1992–93		17	1
1993–94		2	—

LEITCH, Scott
Born Motherwell 6.10.69 Ht 5 9 Wt 11 4
Forward. Shettleston Juniors.

1990–91	Dunfermline Ath	14	3
1991–92		33	4
1992–93		42	9
1993–94	Hearts	28	2

LENNON, Daniel
Born Whitburn 6.4.69 Ht 5 5 Wt 9 05
Midfield. From Hutchison Vale BC.

1987–88	Hibernian	1	—
1988–89		1	—
1989–90		—	—
1990–91		6	—
1991–92		11	1
1992–93		13	—
1993–94		5	1
1993–94	Raith R	7	—

LENNON, Neil
Born Lurgan 25.6.71. Ht 5 9 Wt 11 06
Defender. From Trainee. Northern Ireland Under-23, 1 full cap.

1987–88	Manchester C	1	—
1988–89		—	—
1989–90		—	—
1990–91	Crewe Alex	34	3
1991–92		—	—
1992–93		24	—
1993–94		33	4

LEONARD, Mark
Born St Helens 27.9.62. Ht 5 11
Wt 11 10
Forward. From Witton Albion.

1981–82	Everton	—	—
1982–83		—	—
1982–83	*Tranmere R*	7	—
1983–84	Crewe Alex	38	10

1984–85		16	5
1984–85	Stockport Co	23	4
1985–86		44	20
1986–87		6	—
1986–87	Bradford C	24	3
1987–88		28	10
1988–89		44	7
1989–90		24	5
1990–91		18	4
1991–92		19	—
1991–92	Rochdale	9	1
1992–93	Preston NE	22	1
1993–94	Chester C	32	8

LEONARD, Mick
Born Carshalton 9.5.59. Ht 5 11
Wt 11 00
Goalkeeper. From Epsom & Ewell.

1976–77	Halifax T	19	—
1977–78		20	—
1978–79		25	—
1979–80		5	—
1979–80	Notts Co	9	—
1980–81		4	—
1981–82		—	—
1982–83		6	—
1983–84		18	—
1984–85		31	—
1985–86		23	—
1986–87		41	—
1987–88		45	—
1988–89		27	—
1988–89	Chesterfield	16	—
1989–90		46	—
1990–91		30	—
1990–91	*Halifax T*	3	—
1991–92	Chesterfield	35	—
1992–93		17	—
1993–94		32	—

LESLIE, Steven
Born Dumfries 6.2.76
Forward.

| 1992–93 | Stoke C | — | — |
| 1993–94 | | — | — |

LEVEIN, Craig
Born Dunfermline 22.10.64.   Ht 6 0
Wt 11 04
Defender. From Lochore Welfare.
Scotland Youth, Under-21, 13 full caps.

Season	Club	App	Goals
1981–82	Cowdenbeath	15	—
1982–83		30	—
1983–84		15	—
1983–84	Hearts	22	—
1984–85		36	1
1985–86		33	2
1986–87		12	—
1987–88		21	—
1988–89		9	—
1989–90		35	—
1990–91		33	4
1991–92		36	2
1992–93		37	3
1993–94		30	3

LEVER, Mark
Born Beverley 29.3.70.   Ht 6 3   Wt 12 08
Defender. From Trainee.

Season	Club	App	Goals
1987–88	Grimsby T	1	—
1988–89		37	2
1989–90		38	2
1990–91		40	2
1991–92		36	—
1992–93		14	1
1993–94		22	—

LEWIS, Mickey
Born Birmingham 15.2.65.   Ht 5 6
Wt 10 10
Midfield. From school. England Youth.

Season	Club	App	Goals
1981–82	WBA	4	—
1982–83		5	—
1983–84		14	—
1984–85		1	—
1984–85	Derby Co	22	—
1985–86		5	1
1986–87		—	—
1987–88		16	—
1988–89	Oxford U	36	—
1989–90		45	1
1990–91		34	1
1991–92		40	4
1992–93		41	—
1993–94		46	—

LEWIS, Neil
Born Wolverhampton 28.6.74   Ht 5 7
Wt 10 09
Defender. From Trainee.

Season	Club	App	Goals
1992–93	Leicester C	7	—
1993–94		24	—

LIBURD, Richard
Born Nottingham 26.9.73   Ht 5 9
Wt 11 01
Defender. Forest Athletic.

Season	Club	App	Goals
1992–93	Middlesbrough	—	—
1993–94		41	1

LIDDELL, Andrew
Born Leeds 28.6.73.   Ht 5 8   Wt 10.05
Midfield. From Trainee. Scotland
Under-21.

Season	Club	App	Goals
1990–91	Barnsley	—	—
1991–92		1	—
1992–93		21	2
1993–94		22	1

LIGHTBOURNE, Kyle
Born Bermuda 29.9.68   Ht 6 2   Wt 11 00
Forward.

Season	Club	App	Goals
1992–93	Scarborough	19	3
1993–94		—	—
1993–94	Walsall	35	7

LIGHTFOOT, Chris
Born Wimwick 1.4.70.   Ht 6 1   Wt 12 00
Midfield. From Trainee.

Season	Club	App	Goals
1987–88	Chester C	16	1
1988–89		36	7
1989–90		40	1
1990–91		37	2
1991–92		44	5
1992–93		39	2
1993–94		37	11

LILWALL, Steve
Born Solihull 5.2.70.   Ht 5 11   Wt 12 00
Defender. From Kidderminster H.

Season	Club	App	Goals
1992–93	WBA	44	—
1993–94		13	—

LIMBER, Nicholas

Born Doncaster 23.1.74.   Ht 5 9
Wt 11 01
Midfield. From Trainee.

Season	Club	App	Goals
1990–91	Doncaster R	1	—
1991–92		12	1
1991–92	Manchester C	—	—
1992–93		—	—
1992–93	*Peterborough U*	2	—
1993–94	Manchester C	—	—
1993–94	Doncaster R	4	—

LIMPAR, Anders

Born Solna 24.9.65.   Ht 5 8   Wt 11 07
Forward. From Brommapojkarna,
Orgryte, Young Boys, Cremonese. Sweden
full caps.

Season	Club	App	Goals
1990–91	Arsenal	34	11
1991–92		29	4
1992–93		23	2
1993–94		10	—
1993–94	Everton	9	—

LINEKER, Gary

Born Leicester 30.11.60.   Ht 5 9
Wt 11 10
Forward. From Apprentice. B, England 80
full caps.

Season	Club	App	Goals
1978–79	Leicester C	7	1
1979–80		19	3
1980–81		9	2
1981–82		39	17
1982–83		40	26
1983–84		39	22
1984–85		41	24
1985–86	Everton	41	30
1986–87	Barcelona	37	22
1987–88		36	16
1988–89		26	6
1989–90	Tottenham H	38	24
1990–91		32	15
1991–92		35	28

To Grampus 8

LING, Martin

Born West Ham 15.7.66.   Ht 5 7   Wt 9 12
Forward. From Apprentice.

Season	Club	App	Goals
1983–84	Exeter C	29	—

Season	Club	App	Goals
1984–85		42	6
1985–86		45	8
1986–87	Swindon T	2	—
1986–87	Southend U	24	8
1987–88		42	7
1988–89		44	6
1989–90		25	10
1990–91		3	—
1990–91	*Mansfield T*	3	—
1990–91	*Swindon T*	1	—
1991–92	Swindon T	21	3
1992–93		43	3
1993–94		33	1

LINGER, Paul

Born Tower Hamlets 20.12.74   Ht 5 8
Wt 10 01
Midfield. From Trainee.

Season	Club	App	Goals
1992–93	Charlton Ath	2	—
1993–94		5	—

LINIGHAN, Andy

Born Hartlepool 18.6.62.   Ht 6 4
Wt 13 10
Defender. From Smiths BC. England B.

Season	Club	App	Goals
1980–81	Hartlepool U	6	—
1981–82		17	—
1982–83		45	3
1983–84		42	1
1984–85	Leeds U	42	2
1985–86		24	1
1985–86	Oldham Ath	15	1
1986–87		40	3
1987–88		32	2
1987–88	Norwich C	12	2
1988–89		37	4
1989–90		37	2
1990–91	Arsenal	10	—
1991–92		17	—
1992–93		21	2
1993–94		21	—

LINIGHAN, Brian

Born Hartlepool 2.11.73
Defender. From Trainee.

Season	Club	App	Goals
1992–93	Sheffield W	—	—
1993–94		1	—

LINIGHAN, David

Born Hartlepool 9.1.65. Ht 6 2 Wt 13 00
Defender. From Local.

Season	Club	App	Goals
1981–82	Hartlepool U	6	—
1982–83		6	1
1983–84		23	1
1984–85		17	2
1984–85	*Leeds* U	—	—
1985–86	Hartlepool U	39	1
1986–87	Derby Co	—	—
1986–87	Shrewsbury T	24	—
1987–88		41	1
1988–89	Ipswich T	41	2
1989–90		41	—
1990–91		45	3
1991–92		36	3
1992–93		42	1
1993–94		38	3

LINIGHAN, John

Born Hartlepool 2.11.73
Defender. From Trainee.

Season	Club	App	Goals
1992–93	Sheffield W	—	—
1993–94		—	—

LINTON, Des

Born Birmingham 5.9.71. Ht 6 1
Wt 13 02
Defender. From Trainee.

Season	Club	App	Goals
1989–90	Leicester C	2	—
1990–91		8	—
1991–92		1	—
1991–92	Luton T	3	—
1992–93		20	1
1993–94		33	—

LINYARD, Paul

Born Keighley 18.7.77 Ht 6 1 Wt 12 00
Goalkeeper. From Trainee.

Season	Club	App	Goals
1993–94	Hartlepool U	—	—

LITTLEJOHN, Adrian

Born Wolverhampton 26.9.70. Ht 5 10
Wt 10 04
Forward. From WBA Trainee.

Season	Club	App	Goals
1989–90	Walsall	11	—
1990–91		33	1
1991–92	Sheffield U	7	—

Season	Club	App	Goals
1992–93		27	8
1993–94		19	3

LIVETT, Simon

Born Newham 8.1.69 Ht 5 10 Wt 12 02
Midfield. From Trainee.

Season	Club	App	Goals
1986–87	West Ham U	—	—
1987–88		—	—
1988–89		—	—
1989–90		—	—
1990–91		1	—
1991–92		—	—
1992–93		—	—
1992–93	Leyton Orient	23	—
1993–94		1	—
1993–94	Cambridge U	10	—

LIVINGSTONE, Glen

Born Birmingham 13.10.72. Ht 6 2
Wt 14 01
Goalkeeper. From Trainee.

Season	Club	App	Goals
1991–92	Aston Villa	—	—
1992–93	York C	—	—
1993–94		—	—
1993–94	Walsall	3	—

LIVINGSTONE, Steve

Born Middlesbrough 8.9.69. Ht 6 1
Wt 11 04
Forward. From Trainee.

Season	Club	App	Goals
1986–87	Coventry C	3	—
1987–88		4	—
1988–89		1	—
1989–90		13	3
1990–91		10	2
1990–91	Blackburn R	18	9
1991–92		10	1
1992–93		2	—
1992–93	Chelsea	1	—
1993–94		—	—
1993–94	*Port Vale*	5	—
1993–94	Grimsby T	27	3

LLEWELLYN, Andy

Born Bristol 26.2.66. Ht 5 7 Wt 11 00
Defender. From Apprentice. England
Youth.

Season	Club	App	Goals
1983–84	Bristol C	—	—

Season	Club	League Appearances/Goals	
1984–85		22	—
1985–86		38	1
1986–87		31	—
1987–88		42	1
1988–89		16	1
1989–90		46	—
1990–91		42	—
1991–92		37	—
1992–93		12	—
1993–94		15	—
1993–94	*Exeter C*	15	—

LOCKE, Adam
Born Croydon 20.8.70.   Ht 5 10
Wt 12 02
Midfield. From Trainee.

Season	Club	League Appearances/Goals	
1988–89	Crystal Palace	—	—
1989–90		—	—
1990–91	Southend U	28	4
1991–92		10	—
1992–93		27	—
1993–94		8	—
1993–94	*Colchester U*	4	—

LOCKE, Gary
Born Edinburgh 16.6.75   Ht 5 8   Wt 10 7
Midfield. From Whitehill Welfare.
Scotland Under-21.

Season	Club	League Appearances/Goals	
1992–93	Hearts	1	—
1993–94		33	—

LOGAN, Richard
Born Barnsley 24.5.69   Ht 6 0   Wt 13 03
Defender. From Gainsborough T.

Season	Club	League Appearances/Goals	
1993–94	Huddersfield T	16	—

LOMAS, Steve
Born Hanover 18.1.74   Ht 6 0   Wt 12 08
Midfield. From Trainee. Northern Ireland
4 caps.

Season	Club	League Appearances/Goals	
1991–92	Manchester C	—	—
1992–93		—	—
1993–94		23	—

LONGDEN, Paul
Born Wakefield 28.9.62.   Ht 5 7
Wt 11 00
Defender. From Apprentice.

Season	Club	League Appearances/Goals	
1981–82	Barnsley	4	—
1982–83		1	—
1983–84	Scunthorpe U	43	—
1984–85		14	—
1985–86		31	—
1986–87		42	—
1987–88		44	—
1988–89		41	—
1989–90		46	—
1990–91		46	—
1991–92		41	—
1992–93		20	—
1993–94		—	—

LORAM, Mark
Born Brixham 13.8.67.   Ht 6 0   Wt 12 00
Forward. From Brixham.

Season	Club	League Appearances/Goals	
1984–85	Torquay U	14	2
1985–86		38	6
1985–86	*QPR*	—	—
1986–87	QPR	—	—
1986–87	*Torquay U*	13	4
1987–88	Torquay U	45	8
1988–89		37	4
1989–90		42	12
1990–91		41	7
1991–92		31	5
1991–92	*Stockport Co*	4	—
1992–93	Torquay U	—	—
1992–93	*Exeter C*	3	—
1993–94	Torquay U	1	—

LORMOR, Tony
Born Ashington 29.10.70.   Ht 6 1
Wt 12 03
Forward. From Trainee.

Season	Club	League Appearances/Goals	
1987–88	Newcastle U	5	2
1988–89		3	1
1988–89	*Norwich C*	—	—
1989–90	Newcastle U	—	—
1989–90	Lincoln C	21	8
1990–91		34	12
1991–92		35	9
1992–93		—	—
1993–94		10	1

LOSS, Colin
Born Brentwood 15.8.73.   Ht 5 11
Wt 11 04
Midfield. From Trainee.

Season	Club		
1991–92	Norwich C	—	—
1992–93	Derby Co	—	—
1993–94		—	—
From Gresley R			
1993–94	Bristol C	—	—

LOUGHLAN, Tony
Born Croydon 19.1.70
Forward. From Leicester U.

Season	Club		
1989–90	Nottingham F	2	1
1990–91		—	—
1992–93		—	—
1993–94	Lincoln C	12	2

LOVE, Graeme
Born Bathgate 7.12.73.   Ht 5 10
Wt 11 08
Midfield. From Salvesen BC.

Season	Club		
1991–92	Hibernian	1	—
1992–93		1	—
1993–94		4	—

LOVELL, Stuart
Born Sydney 9.1.72.   Ht 5 10   Wt 10 06
Midfield. From Trainee.

Season	Club		
1990–91	Reading	30	2
1991–92		24	4
1992–93		22	8
1993–94		45	20

LOVELOCK, Andrew
Born Swindon 20.12.76   Ht 5 9   Wt 10 12
Forward. From Trainee.

Season	Club		
1993–94	Coventry C	—	—

LOVELOCK, Owen
Born Swindon 21.1.75   Ht 5 8
Midfield. From Trainee.

Season	Club		
1993–94	Stoke C	—	—

LOWE, David
Born Liverpool 30.8.65.   Ht 5 10
Wt 11 10
Forward. From Apprentice. England
Youth, Under-21.

Season	Club		
1982–83	Wigan Ath	28	6
1983–84		40	8
1984–85		29	5
1985–86		46	5
1986–87		45	16
1987–88	Ipswich T	41	17
1988–89		32	6
1989–90		34	13
1990–91		13	—
1991–92		14	1
1991–92	*Port Vale*	9	2
1992–93	Leicester C	32	11
1993–94		5	—
1993–94	Port Vale	19	5

LOWE, Kenny
Born Sedgefield 6.11.64.   Ht 6 1
Wt 11 04
Midfield. From Apprentice.

Season	Club		
1981–82	Hartlepool U	4	—
1982–83		22	1
1983–84		28	2
From Barrow			
1987–88	Scarborough	4	—
1988–89		—	—
From Barrow			
1991–92	Barnet	36	3
1992–93		36	2
1993–94	Stoke C	9	—
1993–94	Birmingham C	12	1

LOWE, Matthew
Born Birmingham 25.2.74.   Ht 6 0
Wt 12 10
Goalkeeper. From Trainee.

Season	Club		
1991–92	Torquay U	7	—
1992–93		13	—
1993–94		10	—

LOWTHORPE, Adam
Born Hull 7.8.75   Ht 5 10   Wt 11 00
Defender. From Trainee.

Season	Club		
1993–94	Hull C	3	—

LUCAS, Richard
Born Sheffield 22.9.70.   Ht 5 10   Wt 11 04
Midfield. From Trainee.

Season	Club	Apps	Goals
1989–90	Sheffield U	—	—
1990–91		9	—
1991–92		1	—
1992–93		—	—
1992–93	Preston NE	26	—
1993–94		24	—

LUCKETTI, Chris
Born Littleborough 28.9.71.   Ht 6 0
Wt 12 10
Defender. From Trainee.

Season	Club	Apps	Goals
1988–89	Rochdale	1	—
1989–90		—	—
1990–91	Stockport Co	—	—
1991–92	Halifax T	36	—
1992–93		42	2
1993–94	Bury	27	1

LUDDEN, Dominic
Born Basildon 30.3.74   Ht 5 7   Wt 10 09
Midfield. From Trainee.

Season	Club	Apps	Goals
1992–93	Leyton Orient	24	1
1993–94		34	—

LUKIC, John
Born Chesterfield 11.12.60.   Ht 6 4
Wt 13 13
Goalkeeper. From Apprentice. England
Youth, B, Under-21.

Season	Club	Apps	Goals
1978–79	Leeds U	—	—
1979–80		33	—
1980–81		42	—
1981–82		42	—
1982–83		29	—
1983–84	Arsenal	4	—
1984–85		27	—
1985–86		40	—
1986–87		36	—
1987–88		40	—
1988–89		38	—
1989–90		38	—
1990–91	Leeds U	38	—
1991–92		42	—
1992–93		39	—
1993–94		20	—

LUND, Gary
Born Grimsby 13.9.64.   Ht 6 0   Wt 11 00
Forward. From school. England Youth.
Under-21.

Season	Club	Apps	Goals
1983–84	Grimsby T	7	4
1984–85		24	12
1985–86		29	8
1986–87	Lincoln C	44	13
1987–88	Notts Co	40	20
1988–89		42	8
1989–90		40	9
1990–91		16	3
1991–92		13	2
1992–93		28	4
1992–93	*Hull C*	11	3
1993–94	Notts Co	46	11

LUSCOMBE, Lee
Born Guernsey 16.7.71.   Ht 6 0   Wt 12 04
Forward. From Trainee.

Season	Club	Apps	Goals
1990–91	Southampton	—	—
1991–92		—	—
1991–92	Brentford	13	3
1992–93		29	3
1993–94	Millwall	2	—
1993–94	Doncaster R	8	—

LYDIATE, Jason
Born Manchester 29.10.71.   Ht 5 11
Wt 12 07
Defender. From Trainee.

Season	Club	Apps	Goals
1989–90	Manchester U	—	—
1990–91		—	—
1991–92		—	—
1991–92	Bolton W	1	—
1992–93		6	—
1993–94		5	—

LYNCH, Chris
Born Middlesbrough 18.11.74.   Ht 6 0
Wt 11 00
Forward. From Halifax T trainee.

Season	Club	Apps	Goals
1992–93	Hartlepool U	1	—
1993–94		19	—

LYNCH, Tommy

Born Limerick 10.10.64. Ht 6 0
Wt 12 06
Midfield. From Limerick.

Season	Club	App	Goals
1988–89	Sunderland	4	—
1989–90		—	—
1989–90	Shrewsbury T	22	—
1990–91		39	2
1991–92		40	2
1992–93		39	2
1993–94		35	4

LYNCH, Tony

Born Paddington 20.1.66. Ht 5 8
Wt 10 08
Forward. From Maidstone U.

Season	Club	App	Goals
1983–84	Brentford	2	—
1984–85		10	—
1985–86		33	6
From Wealdstone			
1991–92	Barnet	6	—
1992–93		8	1
1993–94		22	3

LYNE, Neil

Born Leicester 4.4.70. Ht 6 1 Wt 12 04
Forward. From Leicester U.

Season	Club	App	Goals
1989–90	Nottingham F	—	—
1989–90	*Walsall*	7	—
1990–91	Nottingham F	—	—
1990–91	*Shrewsbury T*	16	6
1991–92	Shrewsbury T	44	8
1992–93		20	3
1992–93	Cambridge U	14	—
1993–94		3	—
1993–94	Chesterfield	6	1

LYONS, Andy

Born Blackpool 19.10.66 Ht 5 10
Wt 11 00
Forward. From Fleetwood.

Season	Club	App	Goals
1992–93	Crewe Alex	9	2
1993–94		2	—
1993–94	Wigan Ath	33	11

LYTTLE, Des

Born Wolverhampton 24.9.71 Ht 5 9
Wt 12 00
Defender. From Worcester C.

Season	Club	App	Goals
1992–93	Swansea C	46	1
1993–94	Nottingham F	37	1

LILLIS, Jason

Born Chatham 1.10.69. Ht 5 11
Wt 11 10
Midfield. From Trainee.

Season	Club	App	Goals
1987–88	Gillingham	7	—
1988–89		22	3
1989–90	Maidstone U	33	14
1990–91		19	—
1990–91	*Carlisle U*	4	1
1991–92	Maidstone U	23	4
From Sittingbourne			
1993–94	Walsall	24	6

MABBUTT, Gary
Born Bristol 23.8.61. Ht 5 9 Wt 12 09
Defender. From Apprentice. England
Youth, Under-21, B, 16 full caps.

Season	Club	App	Goals
1978–79	Bristol R	11	—
1979–80		33	—
1980–81		42	5
1981–82		45	5
1982–83	Tottenham H	38	10
1983–84		21	2
1984–85		25	2
1985–86		32	3
1986–87		37	1
1987–88		37	2
1988–89		38	1
1989–90		36	—
1990–91		35	2
1991–92		40	2
1992–93		29	2
1993–94		29	—

McALLISTER, Brian
Born Glasgow 30.11.70. Ht 5 11
Wt 12 05
Defender. From Trainee.

Season	Club	App	Goals
1988–89	Wimbledon	—	—
1989–90		3	—
1990–91		—	—
1990–91	*Plymouth Arg*	8	—
1991–92	Wimbledon	10	—
1992–93		27	—
1993–94		13	—

McALLISTER, Gary
Born Motherwell 25.12.64. Ht 6 1
Wt 10 11
Midfield. From Fir Park BC. Scotland B,
Under-21, 28 full caps.

Season	Club	App	Goals
1981–82	Motherwell	1	—
1982–83		1	—
1983–84		21	—
1984–85		35	6
1985–86		1	—
1985–86	Leicester C	31	7
1986–87		39	10
1987–88		42	9
1988–89		46	11
1989–90		43	10

Season	Club	App	Goals
1990–91	Leeds U	38	2
1991–92		42	5
1992–93		32	5
1993–94		42	8

McALLISTER, Kevin
Born Falkirk 8.11.62. Ht 5 5 Wt 11 0
Forward.

Season	Club	App	Goals
1983–84	Falkirk	35	11
1984–85		29	7
1985–86	Chelsea	20	—
1986–87		8	—
1987–88		5	—
1987–88	*Falkirk*	6	3
1988–89	Chelsea	36	6
1989–90		24	1
1990–91		13	—
1991–92	Falkirk	42	9
1992–93		41	3
1993–94	Hibernian	36	6

McANESPIE, Stephen
Born Kilmarnock 1.2.72 Ht 5 9 Wt 10 7
Defender. Vasterhauringe.

Season	Club	App	Goals
1993–94	Raith R	3	—

McAREE, Rodney
Born Dungannon 19.8.74. Ht 5 7
Wt 10 02
Defender. From Trainee.

Season	Club	App	Goals
1991–92	Liverpool	—	—
1992–93		—	—
1993–94		—	—

McATEER, Jason
Born Liverpool 18.6.71 Ht 5 10
Wt 10 05
Midfield. From Marine. Eire 5 full caps.

Season	Club	App	Goals
1991–92	Bolton W	—	—
1992–93		21	—
1993–94		46	3

McAULEY, Sean
Born Sheffield 23.6.72 Ht 6 0 Wt 11 9
Defender. From trainee. Scotland
Under-21.

Season	Club	App	Goals
1991–92	Manchester U	—	—
1992–93	St Johnstone	26	—
1993–94		28	—

MACAULEY, Steve

Born Lytham 4.3.69. Ht 6 1   Wt 12 00
Defender. From Fleetwood.

1991–92	Crewe Alex	9	1
1992–93		25	3
1993–94		17	3

McAVENNIE, Frank

Born Glasgow 22.11.59. Ht 5 9   Wt 11 0
Forward. From Johnstone Borough and
Partick T trialist. Scotland Under-21, 5
full caps.

1981–82	St Mirren	31	13
1982–83		36	9
1983–84		34	12
1984–85		34	16
1985–86	West Ham U	41	26
1986–87		36	7
1987–88		8	—
1987–88	Celtic	32	15
1988–89		23	12
1988–89	West Ham U	9	—
1989–90		5	—
1990–91		34	10
1991–92		20	6
1992–93	Aston Villa	3	—
1992–93	Celtic	19	9
1993–94		11	1
1993–94	Swindon T	7	—

McBAIN, Roy

Born Aberdeen 7.11.74. Ht 5 10   Wt 11 1
Midfield. Dyce BC.

1992–93	Dundee U	—	—
1993–94		1	—

McCALL, Ian

Born Dumfries 13.9.64. Ht 5 10
Wt 11 07
Midfield. From Motherwell Tech.

1983–84	Queen's Park	3	1
1984–85		28	—
1985–86		35	8
1986–87	Dunfermline Ath	43	8
1987–88		4	—
1987–88	Rangers	12	1
1988–89		5	1
1989–90		4	—
1989–90	Bradford C	12	1

1990–91	Dunfermline Ath	29	4
1991–92		9	1
1991–92	Dundee	27	9
1992–93	Falkirk	35	6
1993–94		35	2

McCALL, Steve

Born Carlisle 15.10.60. Ht 5 11   Wt 12 06
Midfield. From Apprentice. England
Youth, Under-21, B.

1978–79	Ipswich T	—	—
1979–80		10	—
1980–81		31	1
1981–82		42	1
1982–83		42	4
1983–84		42	1
1984–85		31	—
1985–86		33	—
1986–87		26	—
1987–88	Sheffield W	5	—
1988–89		2	—
1989–90		3	—
1989–90	*Carlisle U*	6	—
1990–91	Sheffield W	19	2
1991–92		—	—
1991–92	Plymouth Arg	9	1
1992–93		35	1
1993–94		45	2

McCALL, Stuart

Born Leeds 10.6.64. Ht 5 6   Wt 10 01
Midfield. From Apprentice. Scotland
Under-21, 27 full caps.

1982–83	Bradford C	28	4
1983–84		46	5
1984–85		46	8
1985–86		38	4
1986–87		36	7
1987–88		44	9
1988–89	Everton	33	—
1989–90		37	3
1990–91		33	3
1991–92	Rangers	36	1
1992–93		36	5
1993–94		34	3

McCANCE, Daren

Born Consett 13.9.73. Ht 6 0   Wt 10 12
Defender. From Trainee.

1992–93	Reading	1	—

1993–94	....	—	—

McCANN, Neil
Born Greenock 11.8.74 Ht 5 10 Wt 10 0
Midfield. From Port Glasgow BC.
Scotland Under-21.

1992–93	Dundee........................	3	—
1993–94	....	22	1

McCART, Chris
Born Motherwell 17.4.67. Ht 5 9
Wt 10 05
Midfield. From Fir Park BC.

1984–85	Motherwell...................	—	—
1985–86	....	13	—
1986–87	....	—	—
1987–88	....	1	—
1988–89	....	26	—
1989–90	....	34	1
1990–91	....	36	—
1991–92	....	22	2
1992–93	....	29	3
1993–94	....	36	—

McCARTHY, Alan
Born London 11.1.72. Ht 5 11 Wt 12 10
Defender. From Trainee.

1989–90	QPR..............................	—	—
1990–91	....	2	—
1991–92	....	3	—
1992–93	....	—	—
1993–94	....	4	—
1993–94	*Watford*........................	9	—
1993–94	*Plymouth Arg*...............	2	—

McCARTHY, Jamie
Born London 14.8.73. Ht 5 10 Wt 11 07
Midfield. From Trainee.

1991–92	Wimbledon	—	—
1992–93	....	—	—
1993–94	....	—	—

McCARTHY, Jon
Born Middlesbrough 18.8.70. Ht 5 10
Wt 11 01
Forward.

1987–88	Hartlepool U	1	—
From Shepshed			
1990–91	York C........................	27	2

1991–92	....	42	6
1992–93	....	42	7
1993–94	....	44	7

McCARTHY, Paul
Born Cork 4.8.71. Ht 6 0 Wt 13 06
Defender. From Trainee. Eire Youth
Under-21.

1989–90	Brighton.......................	3	—
1990–91	....	21	—
1991–92	....	20	—
1992–93	....	30	—
1993–94	....	37	3

McCARTHY, Sean
Born Bridgend 12.9.67. Ht 6 0 Wt 12 05
Forward. From Bridgend. Wales B.

1985–86	Swansea C...................	22	3
1986–87	....	44	14
1987–88	....	25	8
1988–89	Plymouth Arg..............	38	8
1989–90	....	32	11
1990–91	Bradford C	42	13
1991–92	....	29	16
1992–93	....	42	17
1993–94	....	18	14
1993–94	Oldham Ath.................	20	4

McCARTHY, Tony
Born Dublin 9.11.69 Ht 6 1 Wt 12 03
Defender. From Shelbourne.

1992–93	Millwall........................	7	1
1993–94	....	2	—

McCLAIR, Brian
Born Bellshill 8.12.63. Ht 5 9 Wt 12 00
Forward. From Apprentice. Scotland
Youth, B, Under-21, 30 full caps.

1980–81	Aston Villa..................	—	—
1981–82	Motherwell...................	11	4
1982–83	....	28	11
1983–84	Celtic...........................	35	23
1984–85	....	32	19
1985–86	....	34	22
1986–87	....	44	35
1987–88	Manchester U	40	24
1988–89	....	38	10
1989–90	....	37	5
1990–91	....	36	13

Season	Club	Apps	Goals
1991–92	....	42	18
1992–93	....	42	9
1993–94	....	26	1

McCLELLAND, John
Born Belfast 7.12.55. Ht 6 2 Wt 13 02
Defender. From Portadown. Northern
Ireland 53 full caps. Football League.

Season	Club	Apps	Goals
1973–74	Cardiff C......................	—	—
1974–75	....	4	1
From Bangor			
1978–79	Mansfield T.................	36	1
1979–80	....	43	1
1980–81	....	46	6
1981–82	Rangers......................	14	—
1982–83	....	35	2
1983–84	....	36	2
1984–85	....	11	—
1984–85	Watford	29	1
1985–86	....	31	1
1986–87	....	41	1
1987–88	....	40	—
1988–89	....	43	—
1989–90	Leeds U	3	—
1989–90	*Watford*......................	1	—
1990–91	Leeds U	3	—
1991–92	....	18	—
1991–92	*Notts Co.*...................	6	—
1992–93	St Johnstone	26	—
1993–94	....	1	—
1993–94	Wycombe W	—	—

McCLOY, Steven
Born Girvan 28.4.75 Ht 5 9 Wt 11 9
Midfield. Craigmark Juniors.

Season	Club	Apps	Goals
1993–94	Kilmarnock.................	6	1

McCLUSKEY, George
Born Hamilton 19.9.57 Ht 5 10 Wt 12 6
Forward. From Celtic BC. Scotland U-21.

Season	Club	Apps	Goals
1975–76	Celtic...........................	4	—
1976–77	....	—	—
1977–78	....	15	6
1978–79	....	21	5
1979–80	....	23	10
1980–81	....	22	10
1981–82	....	35	21

Season	Club	Apps	Goals
1982–83	....	10	2
1983–84	Leeds U	32	8
1984–85	....	19	5
1985–86	....	22	3
1986–87	Hibernian...................	35	9
1987–88	....	31	4
1988–89	....	16	3
1989–90	Hamilton A.................	28	8
1990–91	....	35	14
1991–92	....	32	12
1992–93	Kilmarnock.................	31	11
1993–94	....	23	2

McCOIST, Ally
Born Bellshill 24.9.62. Ht 5 10 Wt 12 00
Forward. From Fir Park BC. Scotland
Youth, Under-21, 46 full caps.

Season	Club	Apps	Goals
1978–79	St Johnstone	4	—
1979–80	....	15	—
1980–81	....	38	22
1981–82	Sunderland..................	28	2
1982–83	....	28	6
1983–84	Rangers......................	30	9
1984–85	....	25	12
1985–86	....	33	24
1986–87	....	44	33
1987–88	....	40	31
1988–89	....	19	9
1989–90	....	34	14
1990–91	....	26	11
1991–92	....	38	34
1992–93	....	34	34
1993–94	....	21	7

McCORD, Brian
Born Derby 24.8.68. Ht 5 10 Wt 11 06
Midfield. From Apprentice.

Season	Club	Apps	Goals
1987–88	Derby Co....................	1	—
1988–89	....	—	—
1989–90	....	4	—
1989–90	Barnsley	16	1
1990–91	....	24	1
1991–92	....	3	—
1992–93	....	—	—
1992–93	*Mansfield T*.................	11	1
1992–93	Stockport Co	8	—

1993–94 .... — —

McCREERY, David

Born Belfast 16.9.57. Ht 5 6 Wt 10 07
Midfield. From Apprentice. Northern
Ireland Schools. Youth Under-21, 67 full
caps.

Season	Club	App	Goals
1974–75	Manchester U	2	—
1975–76		28	4
1976–77		25	2
1977–78		17	1
1978–79		15	—
1979–80	QPR	42	4
1980–81		15	—

From Tulsa R

Season	Club	App	Goals
1982–83	Newcastle U	26	—
1983–84		40	—
1984–85		35	1
1985–86		41	—
1986–87		30	—
1987–88		35	1
1988–89		36	—
1989–90	Hearts	22	—
1990–91		7	—
1991–92	Hartlepool U	30	—
1992–93	Carlisle U	22	—
1993–94		13	—

McCUE, James

Born Glasgow 29.6.75
Forward. From Trainee.

Season	Club	App	Goals
1992–93	WBA	—	—
1993–94		—	—

McDERMOTT, John

Born Middlesbrough 3.2.69. Ht 5 7
Wt 10 00
Defender.

Season	Club	App	Goals
1986–87	Grimsby T	13	—
1987–88		28	—
1988–89		38	1
1989–90		39	—
1990–91		43	—
1991–92		39	1
1992–93		38	2
1993–94		26	—

McDONALD, Alan

Born Belfast 12.10.63. Ht 6 2 Wt 12 07
Defender. From Apprentice. Northern
Ireland Youth, 43 full caps.

Season	Club	App	Goals
1981–82	QPR	—	—
1982–83		—	—
1982–83	*Charlton Ath*	9	—
1983–84	QPR	5	—
1984–85		16	1
1985–86		42	—
1986–87		39	4
1987–88		36	3
1988–89		30	—
1989–90		34	—
1990–91		17	—
1991–92		28	—
1992–93		39	—
1993–94		12	1

McDONALD, Chris

Born Edinburgh 14.10.75
Midfield. From Trainee.

Season	Club	App	Goals
1993–94	Arsenal	—	—

McDONALD, Colin

Born Edinburgh 10.4.74 Ht 5 7 Wt 10 8
Midfield.

Season	Club	App	Goals
1991–92	Hibernian	—	—
1992–93		—	—
1993–94	Falkirk	16	1

McDONALD, David

Born Dublin 2.1.71. Ht 5 11 Wt 11 07
Defender. From Trainee. Eire Youth,
Under-21, B.

Season	Club	App	Goals
1989–90	Tottenham H	—	—
1990–91		—	—
1990–91	*Gillingham*	10	—
1991–92	Tottenham H	—	—
1992–93		2	—
1992–93	*Bradford C*	7	—
1992–93	*Reading*	11	—
1993–94	Peterborough U	29	—
1993–94	Barnet	10	—

McDONALD, Neil

Born Wallsend 2.11.65.   Ht 5 11
Wt 11 04
Midfield. From Wallsend BC. England
Schools, Youth, Under-21.

Season	Club	Apps	Goals
1982–83	Newcastle U	24	4
1983–84		12	—
1984–85		36	6
1985–86		28	4
1986–87		40	7
1987–88		40	3
1988–89	Everton	25	1
1989–90		31	1
1990–91		29	2
1991–92		5	—
1991–92	Oldham Ath	17	1
1992–93		4	—
1993–94		3	—

McDONALD, Paul

Born Motherwell 20.4.68.   Ht 5 6   Wt 9 07
Forward. From Merry Street BC.

Season	Club	Apps	Goals
1986–87	Hamilton Acad	5	—
1987–88		18	—
1988–89		34	—
1989–90		38	3
1990–91		38	7
1991–92		38	5
1992–93		44	11
1993–94	Southampton	—	—

McDONALD, Rod

Born London 20.3.67.   Ht 5 10   Wt 12 07
Forward. From South Liverpool, Colne
Dynamoes.

Season	Club	Apps	Goals
1990–91	Walsall	36	5
1991–92		39	18
1992–93		39	12
1993–94		35	6

McDONOUGH, Roy

Born Solihull 16.10.58   Ht 6 1   Wt 13 07
Forward. From Apprentice.

Season	Club	Apps	Goals
1976–77	Birmingham C	2	1
1977–78		—	—
1978–79		—	—
1978–79	Walsall	34	7
1979–80		42	7
1980–81		6	1

Season	Club	Apps	Goals
1980–81	Chelsea	—	—
1980–81	Colchester U	12	2
1981–82		40	14
1982–83		41	8
1983–84	Southend U	22	4
1983–84	Exeter C	16	—
1984–85		4	1
1984–85	Cambridge U	32	5
1985–86	Southend U	38	7
1986–87		33	4
1987–88		42	9
1988–89		40	5
1989–90		33	5
1990–91	Colchester U	*24*	*8*
1991–92		*40*	*26*
1992–93		25	9
1993–94		38	7

McDOUGALD, Junior

Born Big Spring 12.1.75   Ht 5 11
Wt 10 12
Forward. From Trainee.

Season	Club	Apps	Goals
1993–94	Tottenham H	—	—

McELHATTON, Michael

Born Co.Kerry 16.4.75   Ht 6 0   Wt 12 08
Defender. From Trainee.

Season	Club	Apps	Goals
1992–93	Bournemouth	1	—
1993–94		10	—

McFARLANE, Andy

Born Wolverhampton 30.11.66.   Ht 6 3
Wt 12 06
Forward. From Cradley T.

Season	Club	Apps	Goals
1990–91	Portsmouth	—	—
1991–92		2	—
1992–93	Swansea C	24	5
1993–94		28	3

McGARGLE, Stephen

Born Gateshead 24.10.75.
Midfield. From Trainee.

Season	Club	Apps	Goals
1993–94	Middlesbrough	—	—

McGAVIN, Steve

Born North Walsham 24.1.69   Ht 5 8
Wt 11 00
Forward. From Sudbury.

Season	Club	Apps	Goals
1990–91	Colchester U	*8*	—

Season	Club	League Appearances/Goals	
1991–92	....	*39*	*20*
1992–93	....	37	9
1993–94	....	21	8
1993–94	Birmingham C	8	1

McGEACHIE, George

Born Bothkennar 5.2.59 Ht 5 11
Wt 11 12
Defender. From Bo'ness U.

1977–78	Dundee	15	2
1978–79	....	5	—
1979–80	....	28	1
1980–81	....	30	2
1981–82	....	29	3
1982–83	....	22	—
1983–84	....	23	—
1984–85	....	35	1
1985–86	....	2	—
1986–87	....	28	—
1987–88	....	14	1
1988–89	....	6	—
1989–90	....	2	—
1989–90	Raith R	14	—
1990–91	....	31	—
1991–92	....	18	—
1992–93	....	30	—
1993–94	....	20	—

McGEE, Owen

Born Teesside 29.4.70. Ht 5 5 Wt 10 08
Defender. From Trainee.

1988–89	Middlesbrough	—	—
1989–90	....	13	—
1990–91	....	8	1
1991–92	....	—	—
1991–92	Scarborough	8	—
1992–93	....	16	—
1993–94	....	—	—

McGEE, Paul

Born Dublin 17.5.68. Ht 5 6 Wt 9 10
Forward. From Bohemians. Eire
Under-21.

1988–89	Colchester U	3	—
1988–89	Wimbledon	1	1
1989–90	....	13	—
1990–91	....	27	6
1991–92	....	16	2
1992–93	....	3	—

1993–94	....	—	—
1993–94	*Peterborough U*	6	—

McGIBBON, Patrick

Born Lurgan 6.9.73 Ht 6 0 Wt 11 07
Defender. From Portadown.

1992–93	Manchester U	—	—
1993–94	....	—	—

McGINLAY, John

Born Inverness 8.4.64. Ht 5 9 Wt 11 06
Forward. From Elgin C. Scotland 2 full
caps.

1988–89	Shrewsbury T	16	5
1989–90	....	44	22
1990–91	Bury	25	9
1990–91	Millwall	2	—
1991–92	....	25	8
1992–93	....	7	2
1992–93	Bolton W	34	16
1993–94	....	39	25

McGINLAY, Pat

Born Glasgow 30.5.67. Ht 5 10 Wt 10 10
Midfield. From Scottish Junior.

1985–86	Blackpool	—	—
1986–87	....	12	1
1987–88	Hibernian	—	—
1988–89	....	2	—
1989–90	....	28	3
1990–91	....	32	1
1991–92	....	43	9
1992–93	....	40	10
1993–94	Celtic	41	10

McGINNIS, Gary

Born Dundee 21.10.63. Ht 5 11
Wt 10 03
Defender. From Dundee BC. Scotland
Schools, Youth, Under-21.

1981–82	Dundee U	—	—
1982–83	....	—	—
1983–84	....	4	—
1984–85	....	10	—
1985–86	....	4	—
1986–87	....	20	—
1987–88	....	11	—
1988–89	....	11	—
1989–90	....	7	—

Season	Club	App	Goals
1989–90	St Johnstone	11	—
1990–91		32	—
1991–92		29	—
1992–93		27	—
1993–94		28	1

McGLASHAN, Colin
Born Perth 17.3.64.   Ht 5 7   Wt 10 04
Forward. From Celtic BC.

Season	Club	App	Goals
1980–81	Dundee	—	—
1981–82		—	—
1982–83		2	—
1983–84		9	1
1984–85		—	—
1984–85	Dunfermline Ath	16	1
1984–85	Cowdenbeath	11	5
1985–86		34	15
1986–87		15	7
1986–87	Clyde	21	5
1987–88		43	16
1988–89		37	16
1989–90		39	11
1990–91	Partick T	36	10
1991–92		44	18
1992–93		22	2
1993–94		1	—

McGLASHAN, John
Born Dundee 3.6.67.   Ht 6 1   Wt 12 00
Forward. From Dundee Violet.

Season	Club	App	Goals
1988–89	Montrose	35	2
1989–90		33	9
1990–91	Millwall	8	—
1991–92		8	—
1992–93		—	—
1992–93	*Cambridge U*	1	—
1992–93	*Fulham*	5	1
1992–93	Peterborough U	18	—
1993–94		28	3

McGOLDRICK, Eddie
Born London 30.4.65.   Ht 5 10   Wt 12 00
Midfield. From Nuneaton, Kettering T.
Eire 12 full caps.

Season	Club	App	Goals
1986–87	Northampton T	39	5
1987–88		46	2
1988–89		22	2
1988–89	Crystal Palace	21	—
1989–90		22	—

Season	Club	App	Goals
1990–91		26	—
1991–92		36	3
1992–93		42	8
1993–94	Arsenal	26	—

McGORRY, Brian
Born Liverpool 16.4.70.   Ht 5 10
Wt 11 00
Midfield. From Weymouth.

Season	Club	App	Goals
1991–92	Bournemouth	8	—
1992–93		37	8
1993–94		16	3
1993–94	Peterborough U	18	3

McGOWAN, Gavin
Born Blackheath 16.1.76   Ht 5 11
Wt 12 03
Midfield. From Trainee.

Season	Club	App	Goals
1992–93	Arsenal	2	—
1993–94		—	—

McGOWAN, Jamie
Born Morecambe 5.12.70   Ht 6 0
Wt 11 1
Defender. From Morecambe.

Season	Club	App	Goals
1992–93	Dundee	21	1
1993–94		14	—
1993–94	Falkirk	9	2

McGOWNE, Kevin
Born Kilmarnock 16.12.69.   Ht 6 0
Wt 11 04
Defender. From Hurlford U.

Season	Club	App	Goals
1989–90	St Mirren	2	—
1990–91		10	—
1991–92		36	1
1992–93	St Johnstone	26	1
1993–94		40	—

McGRATH, Lloyd
Born Birmingham 24.2.65.   Ht 5 5
Wt 11 06
Midfield. From Apprentice. England
Youth, Under-21.

Season	Club	App	Goals
1982–83	Coventry C	—	—
1983–84		1	—
1984–85		23	—
1985–86		32	—

Season	Club	App	Goals
1986–87		30	3
1987–88		17	—
1988–89		8	—
1989–90		13	—
1990–91		14	—
1991–92		40	1
1992–93		25	—
1993–94		11	—

McGRATH, Paul
Born Greenford 4.12.59. Ht 6 2
Wt 14 00
Defender. From St Patrick's Ath. Eire 65
full caps. Football League.

Season	Club	App	Goals
1981–82	Manchester U	—	—
1982–83		14	3
1983–84		9	1
1984–85		23	—
1985–86		40	3
1986–87		35	2
1987–88		22	2
1988–89		20	1
1989–90	Aston Villa	35	1
1990–91		35	—
1991–92		41	1
1992–93		42	4
1993–94		30	1

McGRAW, Mark
Born Rutherglen 5.1.71 Ht 5 11
Wt 10 07
Forward. From Port Glasgow R.

Season	Club	App	Goals
1988–89	Morton	1	—
1989–90		11	3
1990–91	Hibernian	13	—
1991–92		24	1
1992–93		2	—
1993–94		2	—

McGREAL, John
Born Birkenhead 2.6.72. Ht 5 11
Wt 10 08
Defender. From Trainee.

Season	Club	App	Goals
1990–91	Tranmere R	3	—
1991–92		—	—
1992–93		—	—
1993–94		15	1

McGREGOR, Paul
Born Liverpool 17.12.74. Ht 5 10
Wt 10 04
Forward. From Trainee.

Season	Club	App	Goals
1991–92	Nottingham F	—	—
1992–93		—	—
1993–94		—	—

McGRILLEN, Paul
Born Glasgow 19.8.71 Ht 5 8 Wt 10 05
Forward. From Motherwell BC. Scotland
Under-21.

Season	Club	App	Goals
1990–91	Motherwell	2	—
1991–92		16	—
1992–93		22	6
1993–94		40	5

McGUCKIN, Thomas
Born Middlesbrough 24.4.73. Ht 6 2
Wt 12 02
Defender. From Trainee.

Season	Club	App	Goals
1991–92	Hartlepool U	7	—
1992–93		14	1
1993–94		35	2

McGUGAN, Paul
Born Glasgow 17.7.64. Ht 6 2 Wt 12 00
Defender. From Eastercraigs.

Season	Club	App	Goals
1980–81	Celtic	—	—
1981–82		—	—
1982–83		—	—
1983–84		1	—
1984–85		3	—
1985–86		21	2
1986–87		22	—
1987–88		2	—
1987–88	Barnsley	29	1
1988–89		20	1
1989–90		—	—
1990–91		—	—
1990–91	Chesterfield	22	1
1991–92		37	3
1992–93		13	2
1993–94		5	—

McHUGH, Michael
Born Donegal 3.4.71. Ht 5 11 Wt 11 00
Forward.

Season	Club	App	Goals
1989–90	Bradford C	—	—

Season	Club	Apps	Goals
1990–91	....	1	—
1991–92	....	9	—
1992–93	....	16	4
1993–94	....	5	—
1993–94	Scarborough..............	3	—

McILHARGEY, Steve
Born Ferryhill 28.8.63.   Ht 6 0   Wt 11 07
Goalkeeper. From Blantyre Celtic.
Scotland Schools.

Season	Club	Apps	Goals
1987–88	Walsall	—	—
1988–89	....	—	—
1989–90	Blackpool....................	22	—
1990–91	....	44	—
1991–92	....	28	—
1992–93	....	3	—
1993–94	....	4	—
1993–94	*Chester C*	1	—

McINALLY, Alan
Born Ayr 10.2.63.   Ht 6 1   Wt 13 03
Forward. From Ayr U BC. Scotland 8 full
caps.

Season	Club	Apps	Goals
1980–81	Ayr U	6	—
1981–82	....	17	9
1982–83	....	35	7
1983–84	....	35	16
1984–85	Celtic	11	1
1985–86	....	16	1
1986–87	....	38	15
1987–88	Aston Villa.................	25	4
1988–89	....	33	14
From Bayern Munich			
1993–94	Kilmarnock.................	8	—

McINALLY, Jim
Born Glasgow 19.2.64.   Ht 6 0   Wt 12 00
Midfield. From Celtic BC. Scottish Youth,
Under-21. 10 full caps.

Season	Club	Apps	Goals
1982–83	Celtic.........................	1	—
1983–84	....	—	—
1983–84	*Dundee*	11	2
1984–85	Nottingham F.............	24	—
1985–86	....	12	—
1985–86	Coventry C	5	—
1986–87	Dundee U	32	1
1987–88	....	36	2
1988–89	....	29	1
1989–90	....	35	3

Season	Club	Apps	Goals
1990–91	....	33	1
1991–92	....	32	4
1992–93	....	32	—
1993–94	....	31	—

McINTOSH, Craig
Born Watford 30.6.75   Ht 5 8   Wt 12 04
Defender. From Trainee.

Season	Club	Apps	Goals
1992–93	Watford	—	—
1993–94	....	—	—

McINTYRE, Tom
Born Bellshill 26.12.63.   Ht 6 0   Wt 10 10
Defender. From Fir Park BC.

Season	Club	Apps	Goals
1983–84	Aberdeen.....................	10	—
1984–85	....	—	—
1985–86	....	5	—
1986–87	....	4	—
1986–87	Hibernian....................	15	—
1987–88	....	25	—
1988–89	....	17	2
1989–90	....	—	—
1990–91	....	9	—
1991–92	....	37	6
1992–93	....	12	1
1993–94	....	11	—

McKAY, Andrew
Born Bolton 16.1.75   Ht 5 10   Wt 11 10
Defender. From Trainee.

Season	Club	Apps	Goals
1993–94	Bolton W	—	—

MACKAY, Gary
Born Edinburgh 23.1.64.   Ht 5 9
Wt 10 05
Midfield. From Salvesan BC. Scotland
Schools, Youth, 4 full caps.

Season	Club	Apps	Goals
1980–81	Hearts	12	—
1981–82	....	17	2
1982–83	....	34	6
1983–84	....	31	4
1984–85	....	17	2
1985–86	....	32	4
1986–87	....	37	7
1987–88	....	41	5
1988–89	....	29	2
1989–90	....	33	1
1990–91	....	30	3
1991–92	....	43	1

Season	Club	App	Goals
1992–93		37	2
1993–94		36	1

McKAY, Paul
Born Banbury 28.1.71 Ht 5 8 Wt 10 05
Defender. From Trainee.

Season	Club	App	Goals
1992–93	Burnley	12	—
1993–94		—	—

McKEARNEY, David
Born Crosby 20.6.68. Ht 5 10 Wt 11 02
Forward.

Season	Club	App	Goals
1987–88	Bolton W	—	—
1988–89		—	—
1989–90	Crewe Alex	17	1
1990–91		31	1
1991–92		31	4
1992–93		29	6
1993–94	Wigan Ath	28	4

McKEE, Colin
Born Glasgow 22.8.73 Ht 5 10 Wt 11 00
Forward. From Trainee.

Season	Club	App	Goals
1991–92	Manchester U	—	—
1992–93		—	—
1992–93	*Bury*	2	—
1993–94	Manchester U	1	—

McKEE, Kevin
Born Edinburgh 10.6.66 Ht 5 8
Wt 11 11
Defender. Whitburn BC.

Season	Club	App	Goals
1982–83	Hibernian	4	—
1983–84		16	—
1984–85		17	—
1985–86		2	—
1986–87	Hamilton A	29	4
1987–88		40	—
1988–89		36	—
1989–90		39	1
1990–91		38	—
1991–92		34	1
1992–93		20	1
1993–94	Partick T	23	—

McKENZIE, Paul
Born Aberdeen 4.10.69. Ht 5 9 Wt 11 10
Midfield. From Sunderland Trainee,
Peterhead.

Season	Club	App	Goals
1991–92	Burnley	4	—

McKENZIE, Scott
Born Glasgow 7.7.70. Ht 5 9 Wt 10 05
Forward. From Musselburgh Ath.

Season	Club	App	Goals
1990–91	Falkirk	—	—
1991–92		2	—
1992–93		3	—
1993–94		19	—

MacKENZIE, Steve
Born Romford 23.11.61. Ht 5 11
Wt 12 05
Midfield. From Apprentice. England
Youth, Under-21, B.

Season	Club	App	Goals
1979–80	Crystal Palace	—	—
1979–80	Manchester C	19	2
1980–81		39	6
1981–82	WBA	37	5
1982–83		1	—
1983–84		19	4
1984–85		38	8
1985–86		31	4
1986–87		22	2
1987–88	Charlton Ath	32	2
1988–89		36	3
1989–90		17	1
1990–91		15	1
1990–91	Sheffield W	12	2
1991–92		3	—
1991–92	Shrewsbury T	13	1
1992–93		8	—
1993–94		3	—

McKEOWN, Gary
Born Oxford 19.10.70. Ht 5 10 Wt 11 07
Midfield. From Trainee. FA Schools,
England Youth.

Season	Club	App	Goals
1988–89	Arsenal	—	—
1989–90		—	—
1990–91		—	—
1991–92		—	—
1991–92	*Shrewsbury T*	8	1
1992–93	Dundee	20	1
1993–94		19	2

McKILLIGAN, Neil
Born Falkirk 2.1.74 Ht 5 10 Wt 11 0
Midfield. From Southampton trainee.

Season	Club	App	Goals
1992–93	Partick T	5	—
1993–94		3	—

McKIMMIE, Stuart
Born Aberdeen 27.10.62. Ht 5 8
Wt 10 07
Defender. From Banks o'Dee. Scotland
Under-21, 27 full caps.

Season	Club	App	Goals
1980–81	Dundee	17	—
1981–82		16	—
1982–83		31	—
1983–84		16	—
1983–84	Aberdeen	18	1
1984–85		34	3
1985–86		34	3
1986–87		37	—
1987–88		42	—
1988–89		35	—
1989–90		33	—
1990–91		26	1
1991–92		39	—
1992–93		14	—
1993–94		40	—

McKINLAY, Billy
Born Glasgow 22.4.69. Ht 5 9 Wt 9 13
Midfield. From Hamilton T. Scotland B,
Under-21, 4 full caps.

Season	Club	App	Goals
1986–87	Dundee U	3	—
1988–89		30	1
1989–90		13	—
1990–91		34	2
1991–92		22	1
1992–93		37	1
1993–94		39	9

McKINLAY, David
Born Kinross 20.11.75
Defender. From Trainee.

Season	Club	App	Goals
1993–94	Middlesbrough	—	—

McKINLAY, Tosh
Born Glasgow 3.12.64. Ht 5 7 Wt 10 03
Defender. From Celtic BC. Scotland
Youth, Under-21.

Season	Club	App	Goals
1981–82	Dundee	—	—

Season	Club	App	Goals
1982–83		1	
1983–84		36	3
1984–85		34	3
1985–86		22	—
1986–87		32	2
1987–88		19	—
1988–89		18	—
1988–89	Hearts	17	1
1989–90		29	1
1990–91		33	2
1991–92		39	2
1992–93		34	—
1993–94		43	—

McKINNON, Ray
Born Dundee 5.8.70. Ht 5 8 Wt 9 11
Defender. From S form. Scotland
Under-21.

Season	Club	App	Goals
1987–88	Dundee U	—	—
1988–89		1	—
1989–90		10	—
1990–91		17	2
1991–92		25	4
1992–93	Nottingham F	6	1
1993–94		—	—
1993–94	Aberdeen	5	—

McKINNON, Rob
Born Glasgow 31.7.66. Ht 5 11 Wt 11 01
Defender. From Rutherglen Glencairn.
Scotland 1 full cap.

Season	Club	App	Goals
1984–85	Newcastle U	—	—
1985–86		1	—
1986–87	Hartlepool U	45	—
1987–88		42	2
1988–89		46	2
1989–90		46	1
1990–91		45	1
1990–91	*Manchester U*	—	—
1991–92	Hartlepool U	23	1
1991–92	Motherwell	16	1
1992–93		35	—
1993–94		42	4

McKNIGHT, Allen
Born Antrim 27.1.64 Ht 6 1 Wt 13 07
Goalkeeper. From Distillery. Northern
Ireland Under-23, 10 full caps.

Season	Club	App	Goals
1986–87	Celtic	—	—

Season	Club	League App/Goals	
1986–87	*Albion R*	36	—
1987–88	Celtic	12	—
1988–89	West Ham U	23	—
1989–90		—	—
1990–91		—	—
1991–92	Airdrieonians	2	—
1991–92	Stockport Co	—	—
1991–92	Rotherham U	3	—
1991–92	Walsall	8	—
1992–93		—	—
1993–94	Exeter C	10	—

McKOP, Henry
Born Zimbabwe 8.7.67   Ht 5 11   Wt 12 00
Defender. From Bonner Sport Club.

1993–94	Bristol C	4	—

McLAREN, Alan
Born Edinburgh 4.1.71.   Ht 5 11
Wt 11 06
Defender. From Cavalry Bank. Scotland
Under-21, 12 full caps.

1987–88	Hearts	1	—
1988–89		12	1
1989–90		27	1
1990–91		23	1
1991–92		38	1
1992–93		34	—
1993–94		37	1

McLAREN, Andrew
Born Glasgow 5.6.73.   Ht 5 10   Wt 10 06
Forward. From Rangers Amateur BC.
Scotland Under-21.

1989–90	Dundee U	—	—
1990–91		—	—
1991–92		13	—
1992–93		5	—
1993–94		27	1

McLAREN, Christopher
Born Halifax 6.9.74   Ht 5 10   Wt 10 7
Midfield. Dunipace Juniors.

1993–94	Falkirk	1	—

McLAREN, Paul
Born Wycombe 17.11.76   Ht 6 0
Wt 12 06
Defender. From Trainee.

1993–94	Luton T	1	—

MacLAREN, Ross
Born Edinburgh 14.4.62.   Ht 5 10
Wt 12 12
Midfield. From Glasgow Rangers.

1980–81	Shrewsbury T	4	—
1981–82		35	—
1982–83		40	5
1983–84		40	7
1984–85		42	6
1985–86	Derby Co	46	4
1986–87		42	—
1987–88		34	—
1988–89	Swindon T	37	4
1989–90		46	3
1990–91		45	1
1991–92		32	1
1992–93		22	—
1993–94		12	—

McLAUGHLIN, Brian
Born Bellshill 14.5.74   Ht 5 4   Wt 8 7
Midfield. Giffnock N.

1992–93	Celtic	—	—
1993–94		8	—

McLAUGHLIN, Joe
Born Greenock 2.6.60.   Ht 6 1   Wt 12 00
Defender. From school. Scotland
Under-21.

1977–78	Morton	—	—
1978–79		—	—
1979–80		30	2
1980–81		34	1
1981–82		36	—
1982–83		34	—
1983–84	Chelsea	41	—
1984–85		36	1
1985–86		40	1
1986–87		36	2
1987–88		36	1
1988–89		31	—
1989–90	Charlton Ath	31	—
1990–91	Watford	24	1
1991–92		22	—
1992–93		—	—
1992–93	Falkirk	8	1
1993–94		38	2

McLEAN, Ian
Born Paisley 13.8.66   Ht 6 2   Wt 13 02
Defender. From Metroford.

Season	Club	Apps	Goals
1993–94	Bristol R	27	2

McLEARY, Alan
Born London 6.10.64.   Ht 6 0   Wt 11 11
Defender. From Apprentice. England
Youth, B, Under-21.

Season	Club	Apps	Goals
1981–82	Millwall	—	—
1982–83		3	1
1983–84		30	—
1984–85		21	—
1985–86		35	3
1986–87		42	—
1987–88		31	—
1988–89		38	1
1989–90		31	—
1990–91		42	—
1991–92		28	—
1992–93		6	—
1992–93	*Sheffield U*	3	—
1992–93	*Wimbledon*	4	—
1993–94	Charlton Ath	44	3

McLEISH, Alex
Born Glasgow 21.1.59.   Ht 6 1   Wt 12 04
Defender. From Glasgow United. Scotland
Under-21, 77 full caps.

Season	Club	Apps	Goals
1977–78	Aberdeen	1	—
1978–79		19	1
1979–80		35	2
1980–81		32	3
1981–82		32	5
1982–83		34	2
1983–84		32	2
1984–85		30	1
1985–86		34	3
1986–87		40	3
1987–88		36	1
1988–89		34	—
1989–90		32	2
1990–91		33	—
1991–92		7	—
1992–93		27	—
1993–94		35	—

MacLEOD, Ian
Born Glasgow 19.11.59   Ht 5 11   Wt 11 6
Defender. From Claremont BC.

Season	Club	Apps	Goals
1977–78	Motherwell	5	—
1978–79		25	—
1979–80		24	—
1980–81		25	1
1981–82		37	—
1982–83		30	1
1983–84		29	—
1984–85		38	—
1985–86		29	1
1986–87	Falkirk	35	—
1987–88		33	—
1988–89		—	—
1989–90	Raith R	37	—
1990–91		26	1
1991–92		44	1
1992–93		36	2
1993–94		3	—

McLOUGHLIN, Alan
Born Manchester 20.4.67.   Ht 5 8
Wt 10 00
Midfield. From Local. Eire B, 16 full caps.

Season	Club	Apps	Goals
1984–85	Manchester U	—	—
1985–86		—	—
1986–87	Swindon T	9	—
1986–87	Torquay U	16	1
1987–88		8	3
1987–88	Swindon T	8	—
1988–89		26	3
1989–90		46	12
1990–91		17	4
1990–91	Southampton	22	1
1991–92		2	—
1991–92	*Aston Villa*	—	—
1991–92	Portsmouth	14	2
1992–93		46	9
1993–94		38	6

McLOUGHLIN, Paul
Born Bristol 23.12.63.   Ht 5 10   Wt 11 11
Forward. From Bristol C and Gisborne C.

Season	Club	Apps	Goals
1984–85	Cardiff C	17	—
1985–86		32	4
From Gisborne C			
1987–88	Hereford U	29	1
1988–89		45	13
1989–90	Wolverhampton W	19	4

1990–91		6	—
1991–92		3	—
1991–92	*Walsall*	9	4
1991–92	*York C*	1	—
1991–92	Mansfield T	12	3
1992–93		26	4
1993–94		23	2

McMAHON, Gerard

Born Belfast 29.12.73   Ht 5 11   Wt 11 00
Forward.

1992–93	Tottenham H	—	—
1993–94		—	—

McMAHON, Steve

Born Liverpool 20.8.61.   Ht 5 9   Wt 11 08
Midfield. From Apprentice. England
Under-21, B, 17 full caps.

1979–80	Everton	—	—
1980–81		34	5
1981–82		32	2
1982–83		34	4
1983–84	Aston Villa	37	5
1984–85		35	2
1985–86		3	—
1985–86	Liverpool	23	6
1986–87		37	5
1987–88		40	9
1988–89		29	3
1989–90		38	5
1990–91		22	—
1991–92		15	1
1991–92	Manchester C	18	—
1992–93		27	1
1993–94		35	—

McMAHON, Steven

Born Glasgow 22.4.70   Ht 6 4   Wt 14 03
Defender. From Ferguslie.

1991–92	Swansea C	—	—
1992–93		2	—
1993–94	Carlisle U	2	—

McMANAMAN, Steve

Born Liverpool 11.2.72.   Ht 6 0   Wt 10 06
Forward. From School. England Youth,
Under-21.

1989–90	Liverpool	—	—
1990–91		2	—

1991–92		30	5
1992–93		31	4
1993–94		30	2

McMANUS, Steven

Born Nottingham 8.3.75   Ht 5 11
Wt 11 07
Midfield. From Trainee.

1992–93	Walsall	1	—
1993–94		—	—

McMARTIN, Grant

Born Linlithgow 31.12.70.   Ht 5 10
Wt 10 00
Midfield. From Dunipace J.

1989–90	Dundee	4	—
1990–91		19	1
1991–92		25	1
1992–93		3	—
1993–94		3	—
1993–94	St Johnstone	6	—

McMILLAN, Andy

Born Bloemfontein 22.6.68.   Ht 5 11
Wt 11 04
Defender.

1987–88	York C	22	—
1988–89		2	—
1989–90		25	—
1990–91		45	1
1991–92		41	1
1992–93		42	—
1993–94		46	—

McMILLAN, Stephen

Born Edinburgh 19.1.76   Ht 5 10
Wt 11 0
Midfield. Troon Juniors.

1993–94	Motherwell	1	—

McMINN, Ted

Born Castle Douglas 28.9.62.   Ht 5 11
Wt 11 02
Forward. From Glenafton Athletic.

1982–83	Queen of the S	22	1
1983–84		32	3
1984–85		8	1
1984–85	Rangers	20	1
1985–86		28	2

Season	Club	Apps	Goals
1986–87		15	1
From Seville			
1987–88	Derby Co	7	1
1988–89		32	4
1989–90		15	—
1990–91		13	—
1991–92		37	2
1992–93		19	2
1993–94	Birmingham C	22	—
1993–94	Burnley	14	3

McNAB, Neil

Born Greenock 4.6.57. Ht 5 7 Wt 11 00
Midfield. Scotland Schools. Under-21.

Season	Club	Apps	Goals
1972–73	Morton	3	—
1973–74		11	—
1973–74	Tottenham H	1	—
1974–75		2	—
1975–76		15	—
1976–77		10	—
1977–78		42	3
1978–79		2	—
1978–79	Bolton W	23	3
1979–80		12	1
1979–80	Brighton	16	—
1980–81		33	1
1981–82		40	3
1982–83		14	—
1982–83	*Leeds U*	5	—
1982–83	*Portsmouth*	—	—
1983–84	Manchester C	33	1
1984–85		18	—
1985–86		37	4
1986–87		42	4
1987–88		37	2
1988–89		42	5
1989–90		12	—
1989–90	Tranmere R	22	1
1990–91		40	3
1991–92		12	—
1991–92	*Huddersfield T*	11	—
1992–93	Tranmere R	31	2
1993–94	Darlington	4	—

McNALLY, Bernard

Born Shrewsbury 17.2.63. Ht 5 7
Wt 10 12
Midfield. From Apprentice. Northern
Ireland 5 full caps.

Season	Club	Apps	Goals
1980–81	Shrewsbury T	1	—
1981–82		33	1
1982–83		25	1
1983–84		41	4
1984–85		42	2
1985–86		35	6
1986–87		40	5
1987–88		43	2
1988–89		22	2
1989–90	WBA	41	5
1990–91		25	1
1991–92		21	1
1992–93		40	3
1993–94		8	—

McNALLY, Mark

Born Bellshill 10.3.71. Ht 5 9 Wt 10 07
Defender. From Celtic BC. Scotland
Under-21.

Season	Club	Apps	Goals
1987–88	Celtic	—	—
1988–89		—	—
1989–90		—	—
1990–91		19	—
1991–92		25	1
1992–93		27	—
1993–94		32	2

MacPHAIL, John

Born Dundee 7.12.55. Ht 6 0 Wt 12 03
Defender. From St. Columba's.

Season	Club	Apps	Goals
1975–76	Dundee	6	—
1976–77		25	—
1977–78		34	—
1978–79		3	—
1978–79	Sheffield U	15	1
1979–80		44	5
1980–81		39	—
1981–82		26	1
1982–83		11	—
1982–83	York C	12	2
1983–84		46	10
1984–85		42	5
1985–86		42	7
1986–87	Bristol C	26	1
1987–88	Sunderland	46	16
1988–89		45	4
1989–90		38	2
1990–91		1	—
1990–91	Hartlepool U	42	1
1991–92		41	1
1992–93		42	1

Season	Club	League Appearances/Goals		
1993–94			32	1

MacPHERSON, Angus
Born Glasgow 11.10.68 Ht 5 11 Wt 10 4
Defender. From S Form.

Season	Club		App	Goals
1988–89	Rangers		—	—
1989–90			—	—
1989–90	*Exeter C*		11	1
1990–91	Kilmarnock		11	—
1991–92			43	3
1992–93			40	5
1993–94			43	2

McPHERSON, David
Born Paisley 28.1.64. Ht 6 3 Wt 11 11
Defender. From Gartcosh United.
Scotland Youth, B, Under-21, 27 full caps.

Season	Club		App	Goals
1980–81	Rangers		—	—
1981–82			—	—
1982–83			18	1
1983–84			36	2
1984–85			31	—
1985–86			34	5
1986–87			42	7
1987–88			44	4
1988–89	Hearts		32	4
1989–90			35	4
1990–91			34	2
1991–92			44	2
1992–93	Rangers		34	2
1993–94			28	1

McPHERSON, Keith
Born Greenwich 11.9.63. Ht 5 11
Wt 10 11
Defender. From Apprentice.

Season	Club		App	Goals
1981–82	West Ham U		—	—
1982–83			—	—
1983–84			—	—
1984–85			1	—
1985–86			—	—
1985–86	*Cambridge U*		11	1
1985–86	Northampton T		20	—
1986–87			46	5
1987–88			32	—
1988–89			41	2
1989–90			43	1
1990–91	Reading		46	3
1991–92			44	1

Season	Club		App	Goals
1992–93			44	1
1993–94			20	1

McPHERSON, Malcolm
Born Glasgow 9.12.74
Forward. From Yeovil.

Season	Club		App	Goals
1993–94	West Ham U		—	—

McQUEEN, Tommy
Born Bellshill 1.4.63. Ht 5 11 Wt 11 00
Defender. From Gartcosh United.

Season	Club		App	Goals
1981–82	Clyde		39	—
1982–83			35	—
1983–84			38	1
1984–85	Aberdeen		35	3
1985–86			17	1
1986–87			1	—
1986–87	West Ham U		9	—
1987–88			12	—
1988–89			2	—
1989–90			7	—
1990–91			—	—
1990–91	Falkirk		32	2
1991–92			26	1
1992–93			30	4
1993–94			26	—

McQUILKEN, James
Born Glasgow 3.10.74 Ht 5 9 Wt 10 7
Defender. From Giffnock N BC. Scotland
Under-21.

Season	Club		App	Goals
1992–93	Celtic		1	—
1993–94			—	—

McQUILLAN, John
Born Stranraer 20.7.70. Ht 5 10
Wt 10 07
Defender. From Stranraer Sch.

Season	Club		App	Goals
1986–87	Stranraer		—	—
1987–88	Dundee		—	—
1988–89			—	—
1989–90			2	—
1990–91			14	1
1991–92			40	3
1992–93			29	—
1993–94			34	—

McSKIMMING, Shaun

Born Stranraer 29.5.70   Ht 5 11   Wt 10 8
Defender. From Schools.

Season	Club	App	Goals
1986–87	Stranraer	—	—
1987–88	Dundee	—	—
1988–89		—	—
1989–90		7	—
1990–91		16	3
1991–92	Kilmarnock	30	1
1992–93		35	5
1993–94		40	3

McSTAY, John

Born Larkhall 24.12.65   Ht 5 9   Wt 10 12
Defender. From Gartcosh U.

Season	Club	App	Goals
1982–83	Motherwell	—	—
1983–84		1	—
1984–85		6	1
1985–86		10	—
1986–87		4	—
1987–88	Raith R	39	6
1988–89		37	5
1989–90		38	3
1990–91		36	1
1991–92		34	2
1992–93		41	5
1993–94		37	2

McSTAY, Paul

Born Hamilton 22.10.64.   Ht 5 10
Wt 10 07
Midfield. From Celtic BC. Scotland
Schools, Youth, Under-21, 68 full caps.

Season	Club	App	Goals
1981–82	Celtic	10	1
1982–83		36	6
1983–84		34	3
1984–85		32	4
1985–86		34	8
1986–87		43	3
1987–88		44	5
1988–89		33	5
1989–90		35	3
1990–91		30	2
1991–92		31	7
1992–93		43	4
1993–94		35	2

McSWEGAN, Gary

Born Glasgow 24.9.70.   Ht 5 7   Wt 10 09
Forward. From Rangers Amateur BC.

Season	Club	App	Goals
1986–87	Rangers	—	—
1987–88		1	—
1988–89		1	—
1989–90		—	—
1990–91		3	—
1991–92		4	—
1992–93		9	4
1993–94	Notts Co	37	15

McVEIGH, Michael

Born Rotherham 24.9.74   Ht 5 9
Wt 11 05
Midfield. From Trainee.

Season	Club	App	Goals
1993–94	Sheffield W	—	—

MADDEN, Lawrie

Born London 28.9.55.   Ht 5 11   Wt 13 01
Defender. From Arsenal Amateur.

Season	Club	App	Goals
1974–75	Mansfield T	7	—
1975–76		3	—
From Manchester Univ			
1977–78	Charlton Ath	4	—
1978–79		38	3
1979–80		36	1
1980–81		28	1
1981–82		7	2
1981–82	Millwall	10	—
1982–83		37	2
1983–84	Sheffield W	38	1
1984–85		19	—
1985–86		25	—
1986–87		35	1
1987–88		38	—
1988–89		27	—
1989–90		25	—
1990–91		5	—
1990–91	*Leicester C*	3	—
1991–92	Wolverhampton W	43	1
1992–93		24	—
1993–94	Darlington	5	—
1993–94	Chesterfield	26	—

MADDICK, Kevin

Born Durham 18.9.74   Ht 6 0   Wt 12 04
Forward. From Trainee.

Season	Club	App	Goals
1992–93	Darlington	1	—

1993–94		2 —

MADDISON, Lee
Born Bristol 5.10.72. Ht 5 11 Wt 11 00
Defender. From Trainee.

1991–92	Bristol R	10 —
1992–93		12 —
1993–94		37 —

MADDISON, Neil
Born Darlington 2.10.69. Ht 5 10 Wt 10 07
Midfield. From Trainee.

1987–88	Southampton	— —
1988–89		5 2
1989–90		2 —
1990–91		4 —
1991–92		6 —
1992–93		37 4
1993–94		41 7

MADDIX, Danny
Born Ashford 11.10.67. Ht 5 10 Wt 11 07
Defender. From Apprentice.

1985–86	Tottenham H	— —
1986–87		— —
1986–87	*Southend U*	2 —
1987–88	QPR	9 —
1988–89		33 2
1989–90		32 3
1990–91		32 1
1991–92		19 —
1992–93		14 —
1993–94		— —

MAGEE, Kevin
Born Bangour 10.4.71. Ht 5 10 Wt 11 04
Forward. From Armadale Th.

1991–92	Partick T	6 —
1992–93		5 —
1993–94	Preston NE	7 —

MAGILTON, Jim
Born Belfast 6.5.69. Ht 5 10 Wt 12 07
Midfield. From Apprentice. Northern Ireland Under-23, 22 full caps. Football League.

1986–87	Liverpool	— —
1987–88		— —
1988–89		— —
1989–90		— —

1990–91		— —
1990–91	Oxford U	37 6
1991–92		44 12
1992–93		40 11
1993–94		29 5
1993–94	Southampton	15 —

MAGUIRE, Gavin
Born Hammersmith 24.11.67. Ht 5 10 Wt 11 08
Midfield. From Apprentice. Wales B, 7 full caps.

1985–86	QPR	— —
1986–87		14 —
1987–88		18 —
1988–89		8 —
1988–89	Portsmouth	18 —
1989–90		29 —
1990–91		23 —
1991–92		— —
1991–92	*Newcastle U*	3 —
1992–93	Portsmouth	21 —
1992–93	Millwall	9 —
1993–94		3 —
1993–94	*Scarborough*	2 —

MAHORN, Paul
Born Whipps Cross 13.8.73. Ht 5 8 Wt 11 06
Forward. From Trainee.

1991–92	Tottenham H	— —
1992–93		— —
1993–94		1 —
1993–94	*Fulham*	3 —

MAIL, David
Born Bristol 12.9.62. Ht 5 11 Wt 11 12
Defender. From Apprentice.

1980–81	Aston VIlla	— —
1981–82	Blackburn R	— —
1982–83		34 —
1983–84		11 1
1984–85		4 —
1985–86		18 1
1986–87		38 —
1987–88		36 —
1988–89		40 —
1989–90		25 2
1990–91	Hull C	36 1

1991–92 .... 37 1
1992–93 .... 39 —
1993–94 .... 24 —

MAIN, Alan
Born Elgin 5.12.67.   Ht 5 11   Wt 12 03
Goalkeeper. From Elgin C. Scotland
Under-21.
1986–87 Dundee U .... 2 —
1987–88 .... 8 —
1988–89 .... — —
1988–89 *Cowdenbeath* .... 3 —
1988–89 *East Stirling* .... 2 —
1989–90 Dundee U .... 27 —
1990–91 .... 31 —
1991–92 .... 17 —
1992–93 .... 43 —
1993–94 .... 18 —

MAKEL, Lee
Born Sunderland 11.1.73.   Ht 5 10
Wt 9 10
Midfield. From Trainee.
1990–91 Newcastle U .... 3 —
1991–92 .... 9 1
1992–93 Blackburn R .... 1 —
1993–94 .... 2 —

MAKIN, Chris
Born Manchester 8.5.73   Ht 5 11
Wt 11 00
Defender. From Trainee. England
Under-21.
1991–92 Oldham Ath .... — —
1992–93 .... — —
1992–93 *Wigan Ath* 15 2
1993–94 Oldham Ath 27 1

MALKIN, Chris
Born Bebington 4.6.67.   Ht 6 0   Wt 10 12
Forward. From Stork, Overpool.
1987–88 Tranmere R .... 5 —
1988–89 .... 20 4
1989–90 .... 40 18
1990–91 .... 25 4
1991–92 .... 35 3
1992–93 .... 36 7
1993–94 .... 28 8

MALONE, Chris
Born Drogheda 29.12.75
Forward.
1993–94 Blackburn R .... — —

MALPAS, Maurice
Born Dunfermline 3.8.62.   Ht 5 8
Wt 10 11
Defender. 'S' Form. Scotland Schools,
Youth, Under-21, 55 full caps.
1979–80 Dundee U .... — —
1980–81 .... — —
1981–82 .... 19 —
1982–83 .... 34 1
1983–84 .... 34 2
1984–85 .... 35 2
1985–86 .... 36 2
1986–87 .... 36 —
1987–88 .... 44 —
1988–89 .... 36 1
1989–90 .... 30 2
1990–91 .... 36 1
1991–92 .... 44 3
1992–93 .... 37 —
1993–94 .... 35 —

MANN, Neil
Born Nottingham 9.11.72   Ht 5 10
Wt 12 00
Midfield. From Grimsby T trainee.
1993–94 Hull C .... 5 —

MANNING, Paul
Born Lewisham 21.1.74   Ht 5 10
Wt 11 04
Midfield. From Trainee.
1991–92 Millwall .... — —
1992–93 .... 1 —
1993–94 .... — —

MANUEL, Billy
Born Hackney 28.6.69.   Ht 5 5   Wt 10 00
Defender. From Apprentice.
1987–88 Tottenham H .... — —
1988–89 .... — —
1988–89 Gillingham 17 1
1989–90 .... 32 4

Season	Club	App	Goals
1990–91	....	38	—
1991–92	Brentford	35	—
1992–93	....	41	1
1993–94	....	18	—

MARDENBOROUGH, Steve

Born Birmingham 11.9.64. Ht 5 8
Wt 11 09
Forward. From Apprentice.

Season	Club	App	Goals
1982–83	Coventry C	—	—
1983–84	Wolverhampton W	9	1
1983–84	*Cambridge U*	6	—
1984–85	Swansea C	36	7
1985–86	Newport Co	39	7
1986–87	....	25	4
1986–87	Cardiff C	11	1
1987–88	....	21	—
1988–89	Hereford U	27	—
1989–90	Darlington	*17*	*1*
1990–91	....	35	1
1991–92	....	29	6
1992–93	....	42	11
1993–94	Lincoln C	21	2

MARDON, Paul

Born Bristol 14.9.69. Ht 6 0 Wt 11 10
Defender. From Trainee.

Season	Club	App	Goals
1987–88	Bristol C	8	—
1988–89	....	20	—
1989–90	....	7	—
1990–91	....	7	—
1990–91	*Doncaster R*	3	—
1991–92	Birmingham C	35	—
1992–93	....	21	1
1993–94	....	8	—
1993–94	WBA	22	1

MARGETSON, Martyn

Born West Glamorgan 8.9.71. Ht 6 0
Wt 13 10
Goalkeeper. From Trainee. Wales
Under-21.

Season	Club	App	Goals
1990–91	Manchester C	2	—
1991–92	....	3	—
1992–93	....	1	—
1993–94	....	—	—
1993–94	*Bristol R*	3	—
1993–94	*Bolton W*	—	—

MARGINSON, Karl

Born Manchester 11.11.70 Ht 6 0
Wt 11 00
Midfield.

Season	Club	App	Goals
1992–93	Rotherham U	1	—
1993–94	....	6	—

MARKER, Nick

Born Exeter 3.5.65. Ht 6 1 Wt 13 00
Defender. From Apprentice.

Season	Club	App	Goals
1981–82	Exeter C	14	1
1982–83	....	18	1
1983–84	....	31	—
1984–85	....	45	—
1985–86	....	40	—
1986–87	....	43	1
1987–88	....	11	—
1987–88	Plymouth Arg	26	1
1988–89	....	43	6
1989–90	....	43	1
1990–91	....	39	2
1991–92	....	44	1
1992–93	....	7	2
1992–93	Blackburn R	15	—
1993–94	....	23	—

MARPLES, Chris

Born Chesterfield 3.8.64. Ht 6 0
Wt 13 03
Goalkeeper. From Sutton T and Goole.

Season	Club	App	Goals
1984–85	Chesterfield	38	—
1985–86	....	32	—
1986–87	....	14	—
1986–87	Stockport Co	13	—
1987–88	....	44	—
1988–89	York C	45	—
1989–90	....	46	—
1990–91	....	29	—
1991–92	....	16	—
1991–92	*Scunthorpe U*	1	—
1992–93	York C	2	—
1992–93	Chesterfield	25	—
1993–94	....	11	—

MARQUIS, Paul

Born Enfield 29.8.72. Ht 6 1 Wt 12 00
Defender. From Trainee.

Season	Club	App	Goals
1991–92	West Ham U	—	—
1992–93	....	—	—

1993–94 .... 1 —
1993–94 Doncaster R................ 9 —

MARRIOTT, Andrew
Born Nottingham 11.10.70. Ht 6 0
Wt 12 07
Goalkeeper. From Trainee. FA Schools,
England Youth, Under-21.
1988–89 Arsenal........................ — —
1989–90 Nottingham F............. — —
1989–90 *WBA* .... 3 —
1989–90 *Blackburn R* .... 2 —
1989–90 *Colchester U*.............. 10 —
1990–91 Nottingham F............. — —
1991–92 .... 6 —
1991–92 *Burnley*...................... 15 —
1992–93 Nottingham F............. 5 —
1993–94 .... — —
1993–94 Wrexham .... 36 —

MARSDEN, Chris
Born Sheffield 3.1.69. Ht 5 11 Wt 10 12
Midfield. From Trainee.
1986–87 Sheffield U .... — —
1987–88 .... 16 1
1988–89 Huddersfield T............ 14 1
1989–90 .... 32 2
1990–91 .... 43 5
1991–92 .... 23 1
1992–93 .... 7 —
1993–94 .... 2 —
1993–94 *Coventry C*................ 7 —
1993–94 Wolverhampton W ..... 8 —

MARSH, Chris
Born Dudley 14.1.70. Ht 5 10 Wt 12 11
Midfield. From Trainee.
1987–88 Walsall .... 3 —
1988–89 .... 13 —
1989–90 .... 9 —
1990–91 .... 23 2
1991–92 .... 37 1
1992–93 .... 33 3
1993–94 .... 39 4

MARSH, Mike
Born Liverpool 21.7.69. Ht 5 8 Wt 11 00
Forward. From Kirkby T.
1987–88 Liverpool .... — —

1988–89 .... 1 —
1989–90 .... 2 —
1990–91 .... 2 —
1991–92 .... 34 —
1992–93 .... 28 1
1993–94 .... 2 1
1993–94 West Ham U 33 1

MARSHALL, Andy
Born Bury 14.4.75 Ht 6 2 Wt 13 03
Goalkeeper. From Trainee.
1993–94 Norwich C .... — —

MARSHALL, Dwight
Born Jamaica 3.10.65. Ht 5 7 Wt 10 10
Forward. From Grays Ath.
1991–92 Plymouth Arg............. 44 14
1992–93 .... 24 1
1992–93 *Middlesbrough*........... 3 —
1993–94 Plymouth Arg............. 31 12

MARSHALL, Gordon
Born Edinburgh 19.4.64. Ht 6 2
Wt 12 00
Goalkeeper. From Schools. Scotland 1 full
cap.
1982–83 East Stirling................ 15 —
1982–83 East Fife .... 10 —
1983–84 .... 34 —
1984–85 .... 39 —
1985–86 .... 39 —
1986–87 .... 36 —
1986–87 Falkirk .... 10 —
1987–88 .... 44 —
1988–89 .... 39 —
1989–90 .... 39 —
1990–91 .... — —
1986–87 .... 36 —
1986–87 Falkirk .... 10 —
1987–88 .... 44 —
1988–89 .... 39 —
1989–90 .... 39 —
1990–91 .... 39 —
1991–92 Celtic......................... 25 —
1992–93 .... 11 —
1993–94 .... 1 —
1993–94 *Stoke C* .... 10 —

MARSHALL, Ian

Born Oxford 20.3.66.   Ht 6 1   Wt 12 12
Forward. From Apprentice.

Season	Club	Apps	Goals
1983–84	Everton	—	—
1984–85		—	—
1985–86		9	—
1986–87		2	1
1987–88		4	—
1987–88	Oldham Ath	10	—
1988–89		41	4
1989–90		25	3
1990–91		26	17
1991–92		41	10
1992–93		27	2
1993–94	Ipswich T	29	10

MARSHALL, John

Born Surrey 18.8.64.   Ht 5 10   Wt 12 01
Defender. From Apprentice.

Season	Club	Apps	Goals
1982–83	Fulham	—	—
1983–84		25	—
1984–85		32	1
1985–86		42	3
1986–87		29	4
1987–88		25	2
1988–89		41	7
1989–90		36	4
1990–91		35	2
1991–92		41	—
1992–93		41	2
1993–94		21	1

MARSHALL, Lee

Born Nottingham 1.8.75   Ht 5 9   Wt 9 12
Forward. From Trainee.

Season	Club	Apps	Goals
1992–93	Nottingham F	—	—
1993–94		—	—

MARSHALL, Scott

Born Edinburgh 1.5.73   Ht 6 1   Wt 12 05
Defender. From Trainee.

Season	Club	Apps	Goals
1992–93	Arsenal	2	—
1993–94		—	—
1993–94	*Rotherham U*	10	1
1993–94	*Oxford U*	—	—

MARTIN, Alvin

Born Bootle 29.7.58.   Ht 6 1   Wt 13 07
Defender. From Apprentice. England
Youth, B, 17 full caps.

Season	Club	Apps	Goals
1976–77	West Ham U	—	—
1977–78		7	1
1978–79		22	1
1979–80		40	2
1980–81		41	1
1981–82		28	4
1982–83		38	3
1983–84		29	3
1984–85		40	1
1985–86		40	4
1986–87		16	2
1987–88		15	—
1988–89		27	1
1989–90		31	—
1990–91		20	1
1991–92		7	—
1992–93		23	1
1993–94		7	2

MARTIN, Brian

Born Bellshill 24.2.63.   Ht 6 0   Wt 13 00
Midfield. From Shotts Bon Accord.

Season	Club	Apps	Goals
1985–86	Falkirk	25	1
1986–87		34	1
1986–87	Hamilton A	7	—
1987–88		23	—
1987–88	St Mirren	12	1
1988–89		34	2
1989–90		35	2
1990–91		31	2
1991–92		17	2
1991–92	Motherwell	25	—
1992–93		44	3
1993–94		43	2

MARTIN, David

Born East Ham 25.4.63.   Ht 6 1
Wt 13 01
Midfield. From Apprentice. England
Youth.

Season	Club	Apps	Goals
1979–80	Millwall	3	—
1980–81		33	1
1981–82		38	1
1982–83		33	1
1983–84		31	3

Season	Club	App	Goals
1984–85		2	—
1984–85	Wimbledon	20	2
1985–86		15	1
1986–87	Southend U	32	2
1987–88		41	—
1988–89		37	1
1989–90		39	3
1990–91		41	11
1991–92		5	1
1992–93		26	1
1993–94	Bristol C	34	1

MARTIN, Dean

Born Halifax 9.9.67. Ht 5 11 Wt 11 10
Midfield. From Local.

Season	Club	App	Goals
1984–85	Halifax T	—	—
1985–86		—	—
1986–87		16	1
1987–88		40	3
1988–89		32	2
1989–90		37	—
1990–91		28	1
1991–92	Scunthorpe U	37	2
1992–93		38	3
1993–94		26	2

MARTIN, Eliot

Born Plumstead 27.9.72. Ht 5 6
Wt 10 00
Defender. From Trainee.

Season	Club	App	Goals
1990–91	Gillingham	—	—
1991–92		22	—
1992–93		22	1
1993–94		9	—

MARTIN, Jae

Born London 5.2.76. Ht 5 10 Wt 12 04
Forward. From Trainee.

Season	Club	App	Goals
1992–93	Southend U	—	—
1993–94		4	—

MARTIN, Lee

Born Huddersfield 9.9.68. Ht 6 0
Wt 13 00
Goalkeeper. From Trainee. England
Schools.

Season	Club	App	Goals
1987–88	Huddersfield T	18	—
1988–89		—	—
1989–90		25	—

Season	Club	App	Goals
1990–91		4	—
1991–92		7	—
1992–93	Blackpool	24	—
1993–94		43	—

MARTIN, Lee

Born Hyde 5.2.68. Ht 5 11 Wt 11 05
Defender. England Under-21.

Season	Club	App	Goals
1986–87	Manchester U	—	—
1987–88		1	—
1988–89		24	1
1989–90		32	—
1990–91		14	—
1991–92		1	—
1992–93		—	—
1993–94		1	—
1993–94	Celtic	15	—

MARTINDALE, Dave

Born Liverpool 9.4.64. Ht 5 11 Wt 11 10
Midfield. From Liverpool Apprentice,
Southport, Caernarfon.

Season	Club	App	Goals
1987–88	Tranmere R	34	4
1988–89		32	1
1989–90		19	2
1990–91		11	—
1991–92		31	—
1992–93		26	2
1993–94		13	—

MARTINDALE, Gary

Born Liverpool 24.6.71 Ht 5 11
Wt 11 09
Forward. From Burscough.

Season	Club	App	Goals
1993–94	Bolton W	—	—

MARTYN, Nigel

Born St Austell 11.8.66. Ht 6 2 Wt 14 00
Goalkeeper. From St Blazey. England B,
Under-21, 3 full caps.

Season	Club	App	Goals
1987–88	Bristol R	39	—
1988–89		46	—
1989–90		16	—
1989–90	Crystal Palace	25	—
1990–91		38	—
1991–92		38	—
1992–93		42	—
1993–94		46	—

MARWOOD, Brian

Born Seaham Harbour 5.2.60.   Ht 5 7
Wt 11 06
Midfield. From Apprentice. England 1 full cap.

Season	Club	Apps	Goals
1977–78	Hull C	—	—
1978–79		—	—
1979–80		6	—
1980–81		31	4
1981–82		42	12
1982–83		40	19
1983–84		39	16
1984–85	Sheffield W	41	7
1985–86		37	13
1986–87		32	5
1987–88		18	2
1987–88	Arsenal	4	1
1988–89		31	9
1989–90		17	6
1990–91		—	—
1990–91	Sheffield U	17	2
1991–92		5	1
1991–92	*Middlesbrough*	3	—
1992–93	Sheffield U	—	—
1992–93	Swindon T	11	1
1993–94	Barnet	23	—

MASEFIELD, Paul

Born Birmingham 21.10.70.   Ht 6 1
Wt 12 12
Defender. From Trainee.

Season	Club	Apps	Goals
1989–90	Birmingham C	—	—
1990–91		—	—
1991–92	Preston NE	—	—
1991–92	Exeter C	1	—
1992–93	Stockport Co	7	—
1992–93	Doncaster R	9	—
1993–94	Preston NE	6	—

MASKELL, Craig

Born Aldershot 10.4.68.   Ht 5 10
Wt 11 04
Forward. From Apprentice. Football League.

Season	Club	Apps	Goals
1985–86	Southampton	2	1
1986–87		4	—
1986–87	*Swindon T*	—	—
1987–88	Southampton	—	—
1988–89	Huddersfield T	46	28
1989–90		41	15
1990–91	Reading	38	10
1991–92		34	16
1992–93	Swindon T	33	19
1993–94		14	3
1993–94	Southampton	10	1

MASKREY, Steve

Born Edinburgh 16.8.62.   Ht 5 6
Wt 10 00
Forward. From Strathbrock Jun.

Season	Club	Apps	Goals
1984–85	East Stirling	37	12
1985–86		21	12
1985–86	Queen of the S	12	2
1986–87		31	2
1987–88	St Johnstone	33	5
1988–89		31	12
1989–90		29	11
1990–91		34	7
1991–92		24	2
1992–93		19	2
1993–94		4	—

MASON, Andrew

Born Bolton 22.11.74   Ht 5 11   Wt 11 08
Forward. From Trainee.

Season	Club	Apps	Goals
1993–94	Bolton W	—	—

MASON, Paul

Born Liverpool 3.9.63.   Ht 5 8   Wt 11 09
Midfield. From Groningen.

Season	Club	Apps	Goals
1988–89	Aberdeen	28	4
1989–90		34	9
1990–91		26	3
1991–92		31	7
1992–93		39	4
1993–94	Ipswich T	22	3

MASSEY, Stuart

Born Crawley 17.11.64   Ht 5 10   Wt 10 10
Midfield. From Sutton U.

Season	Club	Apps	Goals
1992–93	Crystal Palace	1	—
1993–94		1	—

MASTERS, Neil

Born Lisburn 25.5.72   Ht 6 1   Wt 13 03
Defender. From Trainee.

Season	Club	Apps	Goals
1992–93	Bournemouth	20	—

Season	Club	Appearances	Goals
1993–94		18	2
1993–94	Wolverhampton W	4	—

MATHERS, Paul
Born Aberdeen 17.1.70.   Ht 5 11
Wt 10 07
Goalkeeper. From Sunnybank A.

Season	Club	Appearances	Goals
1989–90	Dundee	8	—
1990–91		6	—
1991–92		31	—
1992–93		36	—
1993–94		33	—

MATHIE, Alex
Born Bathgate 20.12.68   Ht 5 10
Wt 10 07
Forward. From Celtic BC.

Season	Club	Appearances	Goals
1987–88	Celtic	—	—
1988–89		1	—
1989–90		6	—
1990–91		4	—
1991–92	Morton	42	18
1992–93		32	13
1992–93	*Port Vale*	3	—
1993–94	Newcastle U	16	3

MATTEO, Dominic
Born Dumfries 28.4.74   Ht 6 1   Wt 11 10
Defender. From Trainee. England
Under-21.

Season	Club	Appearances	Goals
1992–93	Liverpool	—	—
1993–94		11	—

MATTHEW, Damian
Born Islington, London 23.9.70.   Ht 5 11
Wt 10 10
Midfield. From Trainee. England
Under-21.

Season	Club	Appearances	Goals
1989–90	Chelsea	2	—
1990–91		8	—
1991–92		7	—
1992–93		4	—
1992–93	*Luton T*	5	—
1993–94	Chelsea	—	—
1993–94	Crystal Palace	12	1

MATTHEWS, Neil
Born Grimsby 19.9.66.   Ht 6 0   Wt 12 12
Forward.

Season	Club	Appearances	Goals
1984–85	Grimsby T	4	1

Season	Club	Appearances	Goals
1985–86		4	—
1985–86	*Scunthorpe U*	1	—
1986–87	Grimsby T	3	—
1986–87	*Halifax T*	9	2
1986–87	*Bolton W*	1	—
1987–88	Halifax T	32	10
1988–89		34	7
1989–90		39	12
1990–91	Stockport Co	29	14
1991–92		9	1
1991–92	*Halifax T*	3	—
1992–93	Stockport Co	5	—
1992–93	Lincoln C	24	11
1993–94		36	7

MATTHEWS, Neil
Born Manchester 3.12.67.   Ht 6 0
Wt 11 07
Defender. From Apprentice.

Season	Club	Appearances	Goals
1985–86	Blackpool	1	—
1986–87		22	—
1987–88		27	—
1988–89		14	1
1989–90		12	—
1990–91	Cardiff C	37	1
1991–92		15	—
1992–93		14	1
1993–94	Rochdale	6	—

MATTHEWS, Rob
Born Slough 14.10.70.   Ht 6 0   Wt 12 05
Forward. From Loughborough Univ.

Season	Club	Appearances	Goals
1991–92	Notts Co	5	3
1992–93		8	2
1993–94		12	3

MATTHEWSON, Trevor
Born Sheffield 12.2.63.   Ht 6 1   Wt 12 05
Defender. From Apprentice.

Season	Club	Appearances	Goals
1980–81	Sheffield W	1	—
1981–82		1	—
1982–83		1	—
1983–84		—	—
1983–84	Newport Co	32	—
1984–85		43	—
1985–86	Stockport Co	35	—
1986–87		45	—
1987–88	Lincoln C	40	6
1988–89		43	2

Season	Club	Apps	Goals
1989–90	Birmingham C	46	1
1990–91		46	3
1991–92		36	6
1992–93		40	2
1993–94	Preston NE	12	1

MAUGE, Ron
Born Islington 10.3.69   Ht 5 10   Wt 10 06
Defender. From Trainee.

Season	Club	Apps	Goals
1987–88	Charlton Ath	—	—
1988–89	Fulham	13	—
1989–90		37	2
1990–91	Bury	29	6
1991–92		22	—
1991–92	*Manchester C*	—	—
1992–93	Bury	13	1
1993–94		26	3

MAXWELL, Ally
Born Hamilton 16.2.65.   Ht 6 1   Wt 12 07
Goalkeeper. From Fir Park BC.

Season	Club	Apps	Goals
1981–82	Motherwell	—	—
1982–83		—	—
1983–84		4	—
1984–85		15	—
1985–86		4	—
1986–87		21	—
1987–88		1	—
1987–88	*Clydebank*	1	—
1988–89	Motherwell	17	—
1989–90		36	—
1990–91		36	—
1991–92		—	—
1991–92	*Liverpool*	—	—
1991–92	*Bolton W*	3	—
1992–93	Rangers	10	—
1993–94		32	—

MAY, Andy
Born Bury 26.2.64.   Ht 5 8   Wt 11 10
Midfield. From Apprentice. England
Under-21.

Season	Club	Apps	Goals
1980–81	Manchester C	1	—
1981–82		6	—
1982–83		8	—
1983–84		42	5
1984–85		39	3
1985–86		37	—
1986–87		17	—

Season	Club	Apps	Goals
1987–88	Huddersfield T	28	3
1987–88	*Bolton W*	10	2
1988–89	Huddersfield T	45	2
1989–90		41	—
1990–91	Bristol C	45	3
1991–92		45	1
1992–93	Millwall	35	1
1993–94		3	—

MAY, David
Born Oldham 24.6.70.   Ht 6 0   Wt 11 07
Defender. From Trainee.

Season	Club	Apps	Goals
1988–89	Blackburn R	1	—
1989–90		17	—
1990–91		19	1
1991–92		12	—
1992–93		34	1
1993–94		40	1

MAY, Edward
Born Edinburgh 30.8.67.   Ht 5 7
Wt 10 03
Forward. From Hutchison Vale BC.
Scotland Youth, Under-21.

Season	Club	Apps	Goals
1983–84	Dundee U	—	—
1984–85		—	—
1984–85	Hibernian	—	—
1985–86		19	1
1986–87		30	5
1987–88		35	2
1988–89		25	2
1989–90	Brentford	30	8
1990–91		17	2
1990–91	Falkirk	13	6
1991–92		36	9
1992–93		42	6
1993–94		38	9

MAY, Leroy
Born Wolverhampton 12.8.69.   Ht 6 1
Wt 11 07
Forward. From Tividale.

Season	Club	Apps	Goals
1991–92	Walsall	4	—
From Tividale			
1992–93	Hereford U	14	2
1993–94		7	1

MEAKER, Michael
Born Greenford 18.8.71.   Ht 5 11
Wt 11 05
Midfield. From Trainee. Wales Under-21.

Season	Club	App	Goals
1989–90	QPR	—	—
1990–91		8	—
1991–92		1	—
1991–92	*Plymouth Arg*	4	—
1992–93	QPR	3	—
1993–94		14	1

MEAN, Scott
Born Crawley 13.12.73   Ht 5 11   Wt 11 11
Midfield. From Trainee.

Season	Club	App	Goals
1992–93	Bournemouth	15	1
1993–94		5	—

MEARA, Jim
Born London 7.10.72   Ht 5 7   Wt 10 06
Midfield. From Trainee.

Season	Club	App	Goals
1991–92	Watford	—	—
1992–93		2	—
1993–94		—	—

MEASHAM, Ian
Born Barnsley 14.12.64.   Ht 5 11
Wt 11 08
Defender. From Apprentice.

Season	Club	App	Goals
1982–83	Huddersfield T	—	—
1983–84		—	—
1984–85		17	—
1985–86		—	—
1985–86	*Lincoln C*	6	—
1985–86	*Rochdale*	12	—
1986–87	Cambridge U	46	—
1987–88		—	—
1988–89		—	—
1988–89	Burnley	30	1
1989–90		35	—
1990–91		45	—

Season	Club	App	Goals
1991–92		27	1
1992–93		39	—
1993–94		6	—
1993–94	Doncaster R	21	—

MEGSON, Gary
Born Manchester 2.5.59.   Ht 5 10
Wt 12 00
Midfield. From Apprentice.

Season	Club	App	Goals
1977–78	Plymouth Arg	24	2
1978–79		42	8
1979–80		12	—
1979–80	Everton	12	1
1980–81		10	1
1981–82	Sheffield W	40	5
1982–83		41	4
1983–84		42	4
1984–85	Nottingham F	—	—
1984–85	Newcastle U	20	1
1985–86		4	—
1985–86	Sheffield W	20	3
1986–87		35	6
1987–88		37	2
1988–89		18	1
1988–89	Manchester C	22	1
1989–90		19	—
1990–91		19	1
1991–92		22	—
1992–93	Norwich C	23	1
1993–94		22	—

MEHEW, David
Born Camberley 29.10.67.   Ht 5 11
Wt 12 06
Forward.

Season	Club	App	Goals
1984–85	Leeds U	—	—
1985–86	Bristol R	4	—
1986–87		21	10
1987–88		18	8
1988–89		31	7

Season	Club	Apps	Goals
1989–90	....	46	18
1990–91	....	41	8
1991–92	....	37	9
1992–93	....	24	3
1993–94	....	—	—
1993–94	*Exeter C*	7	—

MELLON, Michael

Born Paisley 18.3.72.   Ht 5 8   Wt 11 03
Midfield. From Trainee.

Season	Club	Apps	Goals
1989–90	Bristol C	9	—
1990–91	....	—	—
1991–92	....	16	—
1992–93	....	10	1
1992–93	WBA	17	3
1993–94	....	21	2

MELVILLE, Andy

Born Swansea 29.11.68.   Ht 6 0   Wt 12 00
Defender. From school. Wales B, Under-21, 20 full caps.

Season	Club	Apps	Goals
1985–86	Swansea C	5	—
1986–87	....	42	3
1987–88	....	37	4
1988–89	....	45	10
1989–90	....	46	5
1990–91	Oxford U	46	3
1991–92	....	45	4
1992–93	....	44	6
1993–94	Sunderland	44	2

MENDONCA, Clive

Born Tullington 9.9.68.   Ht 5 10   Wt 10 07
Forward. From Apprentice.

Season	Club	Apps	Goals
1986–87	Sheffield U	2	—
1987–88	....	11	4
1987–88	*Doncaster R*	2	—
1987–88	Rotherham U	8	2
1988–89	....	10	1
1989–90	....	32	14
1990–91	....	34	10
1991–92	Sheffield U	10	1
1991–92	*Grimsby T*	10	3
1992–93	Grimsby T	42	10
1993–94	....	39	14

MENDUM, Craig

Born Saltburn 13.4.77.   Ht 5 9   Wt 10 08
Forward. From Trainee.

Season	Club	Apps	Goals
1993–94	Nottingham F	—	—

MERCER, William

Born Liverpool 22.5.69.   Ht 6 1   Wt 13 05
Goalkeeper. From Trainee.

Season	Club	Apps	Goals
1987–88	Liverpool	—	—
1988–89	....	—	—
1988–89	Rotherham U	—	—
1989–90	....	2	—
1990–91	....	13	—
1991–92	....	35	—
1992–93	....	36	—
1993–94	....	17	—

MERSON, Paul

Born London 20.3.68.   Ht 6 0   Wt 13 02
Forward. From Apprentice. England Youth, Under-21 B, 14 full caps.

Season	Club	Apps	Goals
1985–86	Arsenal	—	—
1986–87	....	7	3
1986–87	*Brentford*	7	—
1987–88	Arsenal	15	5
1988–89	....	37	10
1989–90	....	29	7
1990–91	....	37	13
1991–92	....	42	12
1992–93	....	33	6
1993–94	....	33	7

METCALF, Joshua

Born Dublin 8.10.74   Ht 5 8   Wt 11 05
Midfield. From Trainee.

Season	Club	Apps	Goals
1993–94	Blackburn R	—	—

METCALF, Matthew

Born Norwich 28.7.69   Ht 5 10   Wt 12 01
Forward. From Braintree.

Season	Club	Apps	Goals
1993–94	Brentford	7	—

MEYER, Adrian

Born Bristol 22.9.70.   Ht 6 0   Wt 14 00
Defender. From Trainee.

Season	Club	Apps	Goals
1989–90	Scarborough	18	2
1990–91	....	17	1

Season	Club	Apps	Goals
1991–92		30	5
1992–93		—	—
1993–94		36	1

McGARRIGLE, Kevin
Born Newcastle 9.4.77
Midfield. From Trainee.

Season	Club	Apps	Goals
1993–94	Brighton	1	—

MICKLEWHITE, Gary
Born Southwark 21.3.61. Ht 5 7
Wt 10 04
Forward. From Apprentice.

Season	Club	Apps	Goals
1977–78	Manchester U	—	—
1978–79		—	—
1979–80	QPR	—	—
1980–81		1	—
1981–82		26	2
1982–83		34	6
1983–84		30	2
1984–85		15	1
1984–85	Derby Co	19	4
1985–86		46	11
1986–87		42	6
1987–88		16	1
1988–89		26	3
1989–90		18	2
1990–91		35	2
1991–92		32	2
1992–93		6	—
1993–94	Gillingham	29	1

MIDDLETON, Craig
Born Nuneaton 10.9.70. Ht 5 9
Wt 11 00
Forward. From Trainee.

Season	Club	Apps	Goals
1989–90	Coventry C	1	—
1990–91		—	—
1991–92		1	—
1992–93		1	—
1993–94	Cambridge U	19	2

MIDDLETON, Lee
Born Nuneaton 10.9.70 Ht 5 9 Wt 11 09
Defender. From Trainee.

Season	Club	Apps	Goals
1991–92	Coventry C	2	—
1992–93	Swindon T	—	—
1993–94		—	—

MIDDLETON, Matthew
Born Lambeth 22.1.75
Defender. From Trainee.

Season	Club	Apps	Goals
1992–93	Millwall	—	—
1993–94		—	—

MIKE, Adie
Born Manchester 16.11.73. Ht 6 0
Wt 11 06
Forward. From Trainee. England Youth.

Season	Club	Apps	Goals
1991–92	Manchester C	2	1
1992–93		3	—
1992–93	*Bury*	7	1
1993–94	Manchester C	9	1

MIKHAILICHENKO, Alexei
Born Kiev 30.3.63. Ht 6 2 Wt 13 03
Midfield. From Sampdoria. USSR, CIS
full caps.

Season	Club	Apps	Goals
1991–92	Rangers	27	10
1992–93		29	5
1993–94		34	5

MIKLOSKO, Ludek
Born Ostrava 9.12.61. Ht 6 5 Wt 14 00
Goalkeeper. From Banik Ostrava.
Czechoslovakia full caps.

Season	Club	Apps	Goals
1989–90	West Ham U	18	—
1990–91		46	—
1991–92		36	—
1992–93		46	—
1993–94		42	—

MILLAR, John
Born Lanark 8.12.66. Ht 5 10 Wt 10 00
Midfield.

Season	Club	Apps	Goals
1984–85	Chelsea	—	—
1985–86		7	—
1986–87		4	—
1986–87	*Hamilton A*	10	—
1986–87	*Northampton T*	1	—
1987–88	Blackburn R	15	—
1988–89		38	—
1989–90		39	1
1990–91		34	—
1991–92	Hearts	41	7

Season	Club	App	Goals
1992–93	....	24	—
1993–94	....	20	4

MILLAR, Paul

Born Belfast 16.11.66.   Ht 6 2   Wt 12 07
Forward. From Portadown. Northern
Ireland Under-23.

Season	Club	App	Goals
1988–89	Port Vale..................	—	—
1989–90	....	23	4
1990–91	....	17	1
1990–91	*Hereford U*..................	5	2
1991–92	Cardiff C..................	15	—
1992–93	....	33	3
1993–94	....	37	7

MILLAR, Robert

Born Manchester 3.11.72   Ht 6 0
Wt 11 10
Defender. From Trainee.

Season	Club	App	Goals
1991–92	Oldham Ath..............	—	—
1992–93	Hull C..................	25	—
1993–94	....	3	—

MILLEN, Andrew

Born Glasgow 10.6.65   Ht 5 11   Wt 11 4
Defender. Pollok Juniors.

Season	Club	App	Goals
1983–84	St Johnstone		
1984–85	....	4	—
1985–86	....	36	1
1986–87	....	31	1
1987–88	Alloa..................	36	4
1988–89	....	38	3
1989–90	....	37	2
1990–91	Hamilton A..................	39	—
1991–92	....	39	1
1992–93	....	41	3
1993–94	Kilmarnock..................	44	—

MILLEN, Keith

Born Croydon 26.9.66.   Ht 6 2   Wt 12 04
Defender. From Juniors.

Season	Club	App	Goals
1984–85	Brentford	17	—
1985–86	....	32	2
1986–87	....	39	2
1987–88	....	40	3
1988–89	....	36	3
1989–90	....	32	—
1990–91	....	32	2

Season	Club	App	Goals
1991–92	....	34	1
1992–93	....	43	4
1993–94	....	—	—
1993–94	Watford	10	—

MILLER, Allan

Born Epping 29.3.70.   Ht 6 3   Wt 14 07
Goalkeeper. From Trainee. FA Schools,
England Under-21.

Season	Club	App	Goals
1987–88	Arsenal..................	—	—
1988–89	....	—	—
1988–89	*Plymouth Arg*..................	13	—
1989–90	Arsenal..................	—	—
1990–91	....	—	—
1991–92	....	—	—
1991–92	*WBA*	3	—
1991–92	*Birmingham C*..................	15	—
1992–93	Arsenal..................	4	—
1993–94	....	4	—

MILLER, Charles

Born Glasgow 18.3.76   Ht 5 9   Wt 10 8
Forward. Rangers BC.

Season	Club	App	Goals
1992–93	Rangers..................	—	—
1993–94	....	3	—

MILLER, Colin

Born Lanark 4.10.64   Ht 5 8   Wt 11 07
Defender. From Toronto Blizzard. Canada
full caps.

Season	Club	App	Goals
1985–86	Rangers..................	2	—
1986–87	Doncaster R..............	20	2
1987–88	....	41	1
From Hamilton Steelers			
1988–89	Hamilton A..................	21	—
1989–90	....	37	1
1990–91	....	37	—
1991–92	....	43	1
1992–93	....	29	3
1993–94	....	31	—
1993–94	St Johnstone	12	—

MILLER, David

Born Burnley 8.1.64.   Ht 5 11   Wt 11 12
Midfield. From Apprentice.

Season	Club	App	Goals
1981–82	Burnley	—	—
1982–83	....	1	—
1982–83	*Crewe Alex*..................	3	—

Season	Club	League Appearances/Goals	
1983–84	Burnley	17	2
1984–85		14	1
1985–86	Tranmere R	29	1
1986–87	Preston NE	15	—
1987–88		28	2
1988–89		12	—
1988–89	*Burnley*	4	—
1989–90	Preston NE	3	—
1989–90	Carlisle U	42	3
1990–91		41	4
1991–92		26	—
1991–92	Stockport Co	3	—
1992–93		37	1
1993–94		38	—

MILLER, Graeme

Born Glasgow 21.2.73. Ht 5 7 Wt 9 5
Midfield. From Tynecastle BC.

1992–93	Hibernian	1	—
1993–94		1	—

MILLER, Joe

Born Glasgow 8.12.67. Ht 5 8 Wt 9 12
Forward. 'S' Form. Scotland Schools, Youth, Under-21.

1984–85	Aberdeen	1	—
1985–86		18	3
1986–87		27	6
1987–88		14	4
1987–88	Celtic	27	3
1988–89		22	8
1989–90		24	5
1990–91		30	8
1991–92		26	2
1992–93		23	2
1993–94	Aberdeen	27	4

MILLER, Kevin

Born Falmouth 15.3.69. Ht 6 1 Wt 12 10
Goalkeeper. From Newquay.

1988–89	Exeter C	3	—
1989–90		28	—
1990–91		46	—
1991–92		42	—
1992–93		44	—
1993–94	Birmingham C	24	—

MILLER, Paul

Born Bisley 31.1.68. Ht 6 0 Wt 11 00
Forward. From Trainee.

1987–88	Wimbledon	5	—
1987–88	*Newport Co*	6	2
1988–89	Wimbledon	18	5
1989–90		15	2
1989–90	*Bristol C*	3	—
1990–91	Wimbledon	1	—
1991–92		22	2
1992–93		19	1
1993–94		—	—

MILLER, William

Born Edinburgh 1.11.69. Ht 5 8
Wt 10 06
Defender. From Edina Hibs BC. Scotland Under-21.

1989–90	Hibernian	11	—
1990–91		25	1
1991–92		30	—
1992–93		34	—
1993–94		37	—

MILLIGAN, Mike

Born Manchester 20.2.67. Ht 5 8
Wt 11 00
Midfield. Eire Under-21 B, 1 full cap.

1984–85	Oldham Ath	—	—
1985–86		5	1
1986–87		38	2
1987–88		39	1
1988–89		39	6
1989–90		41	7
1990–91	Everton	17	1
1991–92	Oldham Ath	36	3
1992–93		42	3
1993–94		39	—

MILLS, Danny

Born Sidcup 13.2.75. Ht 6 0 Wt 11 05
Midfield. From Trainee.

1993–94	Charlton Ath	—	—

MILLS, Gary
Born Northampton 11.11.61.   Ht 5 9
Wt 11 10
Forward. From Apprentice. England
Schools, Youth, Under-21.

Season	Club	App	Goals
1978–79	Nottingham F	4	1
1979–80		13	1
1980–81		27	5
1981–82		14	1
From Seattle S			
1982–83	Derby Co	18	1
From Seattle S			
1983–84	Nottingham F	7	—
1984–85		26	4
1985–86		14	—
1986–87		32	—
1987–88	Notts Co	46	5
1988–89		29	3
1988–89	Leicester C	13	—
1989–90		29	4
1990–91		45	5
1991–92		46	6
1992–93		43	—
1993–94		23	—

MILLS, Lee
Born Mexborough 10.7.70   Ht 6 1
Wt 12 11
Forward. From Stocksbridge.

Season	Club	App	Goals
1992–93	Wolverhampton W	—	—
1993–94		14	1

MILLS, Simon
Born Sheffield 16.8.64.   Ht 5 8   Wt 11 04
Defender. From Apprentice. England
Youth.

Season	Club	App	Goals
1982–83	Sheffield W	1	—
1983–84		2	—
1984–85		2	—
1985–86	York C	36	2
1986–87		45	1
1987–88		18	2
1987–88	Port Vale	19	5
1988–89		43	—
1989–90		45	1
1990–91		41	—
1991–92		33	2
1992–93		3	—
1993–94		—	—

MILNE, Callum
Born Edinburgh 27.8.65.   Ht 5 8
Wt 10 07
Defender. From Salvesen BC.

Season	Club	App	Goals
1983–84	Hibernian	—	—
1984–85		1	—
1985–86		7	—
1986–87		2	—
1987–88		3	—
1988–89		19	—
1989–90		3	—
1990–91		21	—
1991–92		8	—
1992–93		15	—
1993–94	Partick T	31	1

MILNER, Andy
Born Kendal 10.2.67.   Ht 5 11   Wt 11 07
Forward. From Netherfield.

Season	Club	App	Goals
1988–89	Manchester C	—	—
1989–90		—	—
1989–90	Rochdale	16	4
1990–91		35	5
1991–92		33	10
1992–93		18	4
1993–94		25	2

MILSOM, Paul
Born Bristol 5.10.74   Ht 6 1   Wt 13 03
Forward. From Trainee.

Season	Club	App	Goals
1993–94	Bristol C	3	—

MILTON, Simon
Born London 23.8.63.   Ht 5 10   Wt 11 05
Midfield. From Bury St Edmunds.

Season	Club	App	Goals
1987–88	Ipswich T	8	1
1987–88	*Exeter C*	2	3
1987–88	*Torquay U*	4	1
1988–89	Ipswich T	35	10
1989–90		41	10
1990–91		31	6
1991–92		34	7
1992–93		12	2
1993–94		15	1

MIMMS, Bobby

Born York 12.10.63. Ht 6 2 Wt 12 13
Goalkeeper. From Halifax T Apprentice.
England Under-21.

Season	Club	App	Goals
1981–82	Rotherham U	2	—
1982–83		13	—
1983–84		22	—
1984–85		46	—
1985–86	Everton	10	—
1985–86	*Notts Co*	2	—
1986–87	Everton	11	—
1986–87	*Sunderland*	4	—
1986–87	*Blackburn R*	6	—
1987–88	Everton	8	—
1987–88	*Manchester C*	3	—
1987–88	Tottenham H	13	—
1988–89		20	—
1989–90		4	—
1989–90	*Aberdeen*	6	—
1990–91	Tottenham H	—	—
1990–91	Blackburn R	22	—
1991–92		45	—
1992–93		42	—
1993–94		13	—

MINETT, Jason

Born Peterborough 12.8.71. Ht 5 10
Wt 10 02
Midfield. From Trainee.

Season	Club	App	Goals
1989–90	Norwich C	—	—
1990–91		2	—
1991–92		—	—
1992–93		1	—
1992–93	*Exeter C*	12	—
1993–94	Exeter C	38	1

MINTO, Scott

Born Cheshire 6.8.71. Ht 5 10 Wt 10 00
Defender. From Trainee. England Youth,
Under-21.

Season	Club	App	Goals
1988–89	Charlton Ath	3	—
1989–90		23	2
1990–91		43	1
1991–92		33	1
1992–93		36	1
1993–94		42	2

MINTON, Jeffrey

Born Hackney 28.12.73. Ht 5 5
Wt 11 07
Forward. From Trainee.

Season	Club	App	Goals
1991–92	Tottenham H	2	1
1992–93		—	—
1993–94		—	—

MISON, Michael

Born London 8.11.75 Ht 6 3 Wt 13 02
Midfield. From Trainee.

Season	Club	App	Goals
1993–94	Fulham	4	—

MITCHELL, Alistair

Born Kirkcaldy 3.12.68. Ht 5 7 Wt 11 0
Forward. From Ballingry Rovers.

Season	Club	App	Goals
1988–89	East Fife	18	4
1989–90		35	12
1990–91		34	7
1991–92	Kilmarnock	42	10
1992–93		32	6
1993–94		34	5

MITCHELL, Andrew

Born Rotherham 12.9.76 Ht 5 10
Wt 11 06
Defender. From Trainee.

Season	Club	App	Goals
1993–94	Aston Villa	—	—

MITCHELL, Brian

Born Stonehaven 16.7.63. Ht 6 1
Wt 13 01
Defender. From King St. Scotland
Schools.

Season	Club	App	Goals
1981–82	Aberdeen	1	—
1982–83		1	—
1983–84		9	—
1984–85		14	1
1985–86		23	—
1986–87		17	—
1986–87	Bradford C	16	—
1987–88		42	6
1988–89		45	1
1989–90		35	2
1990–91		20	—
1991–92		20	—
1992–93	Bristol C	16	—
1993–94	Hull C	9	—

MITCHELL, David

Born Glasgow 13.6.62. Ht 6 1 Wt 12 07
Forward. Australia full caps.

Season	Club	App	Goals
1983–84	Rangers	12	2
1984–85		14	4
From Feyenoord			
1988–89	Chelsea	6	—
1989–90		—	—
1990–91		1	—
1990–91	*Newcastle U*	2	1
1991–92	Swindon T	27	5
1992–93		41	11
From Altay Izmir			
1993–94	Millwall	27	9

MITCHELL, Graham

Born Glasgow 2.11.62. Ht 5 10 Wt 11 08
Defender. From Auchengill BC.

Season	Club	App	Goals
1980–81	Hamilton A	4	—
1981–82		37	—
1982–83		32	1
1983–84		21	1
1984–85		30	—
1985–86		32	6
1986–87		23	1
1986–87	Hibernian	17	1
1987–88		41	1
1988–89		20	—
1989–90		31	—
1990–91		28	—
1991–92		27	—
1992–93		41	—
1993–94		36	1

MITCHELL, Graham

Born Shipley 16.2.68. Ht 6 0 Wt 11 05
Defender. From Apprentice.

Season	Club	App	Goals
1986–87	Huddersfield T	17	—
1987–88		29	1
1988–89		34	—
1989–90		37	1
1990–91		46	—
1991–92		43	—
1992–93		4	—
1993–94		22	—

MITCHELL, Neil

Born Lytham 7.11.74.
Midfield. From Trainee.

Season	Club	App	Goals
1991–92	Blackpool	1	—
1992–93		12	1
1993–94		24	3

MITCHELL, Paul

Born Bournemouth 20.10.71. Ht 5 10
Wt 12 00
Defender. From Trainee.

Season	Club	App	Goals
1990–91	Bournemouth	2	—
1991–92		5	—
1992–93		5	—
1993–94		4	—
1993–94	West Ham U	1	—

MOBILIO, Domenic

Born Vancouver 14.1.69 Ht 5 11
Wt 12 3
Midfield. Vancouver 86-ers.

Season	Club	App	Goals
1993–94	Dundee	2	—

MOCKLER, Andrew

Born Stockton 18.11.70. Ht 5 11
Wt 11 13
Midfield. From Trainee.

Season	Club	App	Goals
1988–89	Arsenal	—	—
1989–90		—	—
1990–91	Scarborough	34	5
1991–92		24	4
1992–93		10	1
1993–94		6	—

MOHAN, Nicky

Born Middlesbrough 6.10.70. Ht 6 2
Wt 12 00
Defender. From Trainee.

Season	Club	App	Goals
1987–88	Middlesbrough	—	—
1988–89		6	—
1989–90		22	—
1990–91		—	—
1991–92		27	2
1992–93		18	2
1992–93	*Hull C*	5	1
1993–94	Middlesbrough	26	—

MOLBY, Jan
Born Kolding 4.7.63.   Ht 6 1   Wt 14 07
Midfield. From Kolding, Ajax. Denmark
Youth, Under-21, full caps.

Season	Club	Apps	Goals
1984–85	Liverpool	22	1
1985–86		39	14
1986–87		34	7
1987–88		7	—
1988–89		13	2
1989–90		17	1
1990–91		25	9
1991–92		26	3
1992–93		10	3
1993–94		11	2

MONCUR, John
Born Stepney 22.9.66.   Ht 5 7   Wt 9 10
Midfield. From Apprentice.

Season	Club	Apps	Goals
1984–85	Tottenham H	—	—
1985–86		—	—
1986–87		1	—
1986–87	*Cambridge U*	4	—
1986–87	*Doncaster R*	4	—
1987–88	Tottenham H	5	—
1988–89		1	—
1988–89	*Portsmouth*	7	—
1989–90	Tottenham H	5	1
1989–90	*Brentford*	5	1
1990–91	Tottenham H	9	—
1991–92	*Ipswich T*	6	—
1991–92	*Nottingham F*	—	—
1991–92	Swindon T	3	—
1992–93		14	1
1993–94		41	4

MONINGTON, Mark
Born Bilsthorpe 21.10.70.   Ht 6 1
Wt 13 00
Midfield. From Schoolboy.

Season	Club	Apps	Goals
1988–89	Burnley	8	1
1989–90		13	—
1990–91		—	—
1991–92		12	1
1992–93		31	2
1993–94		20	1

MONKOU, Kenneth
Born Surinam 29.11.64.   Ht 6 3   Wt 14 05
Defender. From Feyenoord. Holland
Under-21.

Season	Club	Apps	Goals
1988–89	Chelsea	2	—
1989–90		34	1
1990–91		27	1
1991–92		31	—
1992–93		—	—
1992–93	Southampton	33	1
1993–94		35	4

MONTGOMERIE, Ray
Born Irvine 17.4.61   Ht 5 8   Wt 11 7
Defender. From Saltcoats Vic.

Season	Club	Apps	Goals
1980–81	Newcastle U	—	—
1981–82	Dumbarton	20	5
1982–83		25	2
1983–84		39	1
1984–85		6	—
1985–86		24	—
1986–87		35	—
1987–88		31	—
1988–89	Kilmarnock	31	2
1989–90		35	3
1990–91		37	—
1991–92		30	1
1992–93		42	—
1993–94		42	—

MOODY, Paul
Born Portsmouth 13.6.67.   Ht 6 3
Wt 14 03
Forward. From Waterlooville.

Season	Club	Apps	Goals
1991–92	Southampton	4	—
1992–93		3	—
1992–93	*Reading*	5	1
1993–94	Southampton	5	—
1993–94	Oxford U	15	8

MOONEY, Tommy
Born Teesside North 11.8.71.   Ht 5 10
Wt 12 05
Forward. From Trainee.

Season	Club	Apps	Goals
1989–90	Aston Villa	—	—
1990–91	Scarborough	27	13
1991–92		40	8
1992–93		40	9

Season	Club	League Appearances/Goals	
1993–94	Southend U	14	5
1993–94	*Watford*	10	2

MOORE, Alan
Born Dublin 25.11.74. Ht 5 10 Wt 11 00
Midfield. From Rivermount.

1991–92	Middlesbrough	—	—
1992–93		2	—
1993–94		42	10

MOORE, Allan
Born Glasgow 23.12.64. Ht 5 6 Wt 9 10
Forward. From Possil YM.

1983–84	Dumbarton	4	—
1984–85		4	—
1985–86		33	4
1986–87		18	3
1986–87	Hearts	10	—
1987–88		7	1
1988–89		12	2
1989–90	St Johnstone	33	13
1990–91		31	5
1991–92		21	1
1992–93		17	3
1993–94		13	1

MOORE, Craig
Born Canterbury, Australia 12.12.75
Ht 6 1 Wt 12 0
Defender. Australian Institute.

1993–94	Rangers	1	—

MOORE, Darren
Born Birmingham 22.4.74. Ht 6 2
Wt 15 00
Defender. From Trainee.

1991–92	Torquay U	5	1
1992–93		31	2
1993–94		37	2

MOORE, Kevin
Born Grimsby 29.4.58. Ht 6 0 Wt 13 00
Defender. From Local. England Schools.

1976–77	Grimsby T	28	—
1977–78		42	—
1978–79		46	6
1979–80		41	4
1980–81		41	1

1981–82		36	4
1982–83		38	—
1983–84		41	1
1984–85		31	4
1985–86		31	2
1986–87		25	5
1986–87	Oldham Ath	13	1
1987–88	Southampton	35	3
1988–89		25	3
1989–90		21	1
1990–91		19	1
1991–92		16	—
1991–92	*Bristol R*	7	—
1992–93	Southampton	18	2
1992–93	*Bristol R*	4	1
1993–94	Southampton	14	—

MOORE, Michael
Born Derby 7.10.73. Ht 5 10 Wt 11 01
Forward. From Derby Co.

1993–94	Swansea C	1	—

MOORE, Neil
Born Liverpool 21.9.72. Ht 6 1 Wt 12 02
Defender. From Trainee.

1991–92	Everton	—	—
1992–93		1	—
1993–94		4	—

MORALEE, Jamie
Born Wandsworth 2.12.71. Ht 5 11
Wt 11 05
Forward. From Trainee.

1989–90	Crystal Palace	—	—
1990–91		—	—
1991–92		6	—
1992–93		—	—
1992–93	Millwall	37	15
1993–94		30	4

MORAN, Kevin
Born Dublin 29.4.56. Ht 5 11 Wt 12 09
Defender. From Pegasus-Eire Gaelic
Football. Eire 70 full caps.

1977–78	Manchester U	—	—
1978–79		1	—
1979–80		9	1
1980–81		32	—

Season	Club	League Appearances/Goals	
1981–82	....	30	7
1982–83	....	29	2
1983–84	....	38	7
1984–85	....	19	4
1985–86	....	19	—
1986–87	....	33	—
1987–88	....	21	—
From Sporting Gijon			
1989–90	Blackburn R	19	2
1990–91	....	32	1
1991–92	....	41	2
1992–93	....	36	4
1993–94	....	19	1

MORAN, Paul
Born Enfield 22.5.68. Ht 5 10 Wt 11 00
Forward. From Trainee.

Season	Club	League Appearances/Goals	
1984–85	Tottenham H	—	—
1985–86	....	—	—
1986–87	....	1	—
1987–88	....	13	1
1988–89	....	8	—
1988–89	*Portsmouth*	3	—
1989–90	Tottenham H	5	1
1989–90	*Leicester C*	10	1
1990–91	Tottenham H	1	—
1990–91	*Newcastle U*	1	—
1990–91	*Southend U*	1	—
1991–92	Tottenham H	—	—
1992–93	....	3	—
1992–93	*Cambridge U*	—	—
1993–94	Tottenham H	5	—

MORAN, Steve
Born Croydon 10.1.61. Ht 5 8 Wt 11 03
Forward. From Amateur. England
Under-21.

Season	Club	League Appearances/Goals	
1979–80	Southampton	1	1
1980–81	....	31	18
1981–82	....	18	9
1982–83	....	36	10
1983–84	....	34	21
1984–85	....	32	11
1985–86	....	28	8
1986–87	....	—	—
1986–87	Leicester C	27	9
1987–88	....	16	5
1987–88	Reading	28	7
1988–89	....	34	4

Season	Club	League Appearances/Goals	
1989–90	....	28	11
1990–91	....	26	8
1991–92	Exeter C	34	19
1992–93	....	23	8
1993–94	Hull C	17	5

MORGAN, Alan
Born Aberystwyth 2.11.73. Ht 5 10
Wt 11 00
Forward. From Trainee.

Season	Club	League Appearances/Goals	
1991–92	Tranmere R	—	—
1992–93	....	—	—
1993–94	....	—	—

MORGAN, Andrew
Born Glasgow 10.12.74 Ht 5 7 Wt 10 9
Midfield. Hutcheson Vale BC.

Season	Club	League Appearances/Goals	
1992–93	St Johnstone	—	—
1993–94	....	3	—

MORGAN, Gregory
Born Batley 12.10.73 Ht 5 7 Wt 10 00
Midfield.

Season	Club	League Appearances/Goals	
1992–93	Barnsley	—	—
1993–94	....	—	—

MORGAN, Jamie
Born Plymouth 1.10.75 Ht 5 11
Wt 11 00
Midfield. From Trainee.

Season	Club	League Appearances/Goals	
1992–93	Plymouth Arg	3	—
1993–94	....	—	—

MORGAN, Nicky
Born East Ham 30.10.59. Ht 5 10
Wt 13 10
Forward. From Apprentice.

Season	Club	League Appearances/Goals	
1977–78	West Ham U	—	—
1978–79	....	2	—
1979–80	....	6	1
1980–81	....	6	1
1981–82	....	—	—
1982–83	....	7	—
1982–83	Portsmouth	6	1
1983–84	....	25	9
1984–85	....	30	8
1985–86	....	30	14
1986–87	....	4	—

Season	Club	Apps	Goals
1986–87	Stoke C	29	10
1987–88		28	5
1988–89		18	5
1989–90		13	1
1989–90	Bristol C	7	4
1990–91		44	13
1991–92		19	3
1992–93		10	3
1992–93	*Bournemouth*	6	1
1993–94	Bristol C	—	—
1993–94	Exeter C	12	4

MORGAN, Philip
Born Stoke 18.12.74 Ht 6 1 Wt 13 00
Goalkeeper. From Trainee.

Season	Club	Apps	Goals
1993–94	Ipswich T	—	—

MORGAN, Scott
Born Colchester 22.3.75 Ht 6 1 Wt 11 06
Defender. From Bournemouth trainee.

Season	Club	Apps	Goals
1993–94	Brentford	1	—

MORGAN, Simon
Born Birmingham 5.9.66. Ht 5 10
Wt 11 07
Defender. From England Under-21.

Season	Club	Apps	Goals
1984–85	Leicester C	—	—
1985–86		30	—
1986–87		41	1
1987–88		40	—
1988–89		32	—
1989–90		17	2
1990–91		—	—
1990–91	Fulham	32	—
1991–92		36	3
1992–93		39	8
1993–94		37	6

MORGAN, Steve
Born Oldham 19.9.68. Ht 5 11 Wt 13 00
Defender. From Apprentice. England
Youth.

Season	Club	Apps	Goals
1985–86	Blackpool	5	—
1986–87		11	—
1987–88		46	6
1988–89		44	3
1989–90		38	1
1990–91	Plymouth Arg	40	3

Season	Club	Apps	Goals
1991–92		45	2
1992–93		36	1
1993–94	Coventry C	40	2

MORGAN, Thomas
Born Dublin 30.3.77
Midfield. From Trainee.

Season	Club	Apps	Goals
1993–94	Blackburn R	—	—

MORGAN, Trevor
Born Forest Gate 30.9.56 Ht 6 2
Wt 13 04
Forward. Leytonstone & Ilford.

Season	Club	Apps	Goals
1980–81	Bournemouth	42	10
1981–82		11	3
1981–82	Mansfield T	12	6
1981–82	Bournemouth	14	4
1982–83		45	16
1983–84		29	13
1983–84	Bristol C	15	5
1984–85		17	3
1984–85	Exeter C	26	9
1985–86		4	—
1985–86	Bristol R	36	16
1986–87		19	8
1986–87	Bristol C	19	8
1987–88	Bolton W	38	7
1988–89		39	10
1989–90		—	—
1989–90	Colchester U	32	12
1990–91	Exeter C	17	3

From Hong Kong

Season	Club	Apps	Goals
1993–94	Birmingham C	1	—

MORLEY, Trevor
Born Nottingham 20.3.61. Ht 5 11
Wt 12 01
Forward. From Derby Co, Corby T,
Nuneaton.

Season	Club	Apps	Goals
1985–86	Northampton T	43	13
1986–87		37	16
1987–88		27	10
1987–88	Manchester C	15	4
1988–89		40	12
1989–90		17	2
1989–90	West Ham U	19	10
1990–91		38	12
1991–92		24	2
1992–93		41	20

1993–94 .... 42 13

MORRELL, Paul
Born Poole 23.3.61.   Ht 5 11   Wt 13 05
Defender. From Poole, Bath &
Weymouth.

1983–84	Bournemouth	22	2
1984–85		44	1
1985–86		38	1
1986–87		45	2
1987–88		42	—
1988–89		44	—
1989–90		21	—
1990–91		42	1
1991–92		24	1
1992–93		21	—
1993–94		—	—

MORRIS, Andy
Born Sheffield 17.11.67.   Ht 6 4   Wt 15 07
Forward.

1984–85	Rotherham U	1	—
1985–86		—	—
1986–87		6	—
1987–88		—	—
1987–88	Chesterfield	10	—
1988–89		42	9
1989–90		43	4
1990–91		15	4
1991–92		8	2
1991–92	*Exeter C*	7	2
1992–93	Chesterfield	40	10
1993–94		34	11

MORRIS, Chris
Born Newquay 24.12.63.   Ht 5 10
Wt 10 08
Defender. From England Schools. Eire 35
full caps.

1982–83	Sheffield W	—	—
1983–84		13	1
1984–85		14	—
1985–86		30	—
1986–87		17	—
1987–88	Celtic	44	3
1988–89		33	3
1989–90		32	1
1990–91		19	—
1991–92		32	1

1992–93		3	—
1992–93	Middlesbrough	25	1
1993–94		15	—

MORRIS, David
Born Plumstead 19.11.71.   Ht 5 11
Wt 12 00
Midfield. From Trainee.

1990–91	Bournemouth	1	—
1991–92		—	—
1992–93	Hereford U	11	—
1993–94		29	1

MORRIS, Mark
Born Morden 26.9.62.   Ht 6 1   Wt 13 08
Defender. From Apprentice.

1980–81	Wimbledon	—	—
1981–82		33	1
1982–83		26	3
1983–84		39	3
1984–85		29	1
1985–86		20	1
1985–86	*Aldershot*	14	—
1986–87	Wimbledon	21	—
1987–88	Watford	39	1
1988–89		2	—
1989–90	Sheffield U	42	3
1990–91		14	—
1991–92	Bournemouth	43	3
1992–93		43	1
1993–94		38	—

MORRIS, Mark
Born Chester 1.8.68.   Ht 6 0   Wt 12 00
Goalkeeper.

1985–86	Wrexham	3	—
1986–87		—	—
1987–88		6	—
1988–89		3	—
1989–90		3	—
1990–91		40	—
1991–92		8	—
1992–93		34	—
1993–94		4	—

MORRIS, Paul
Born Bolton 6.2.75
Defender. From Trainee.

| 1992–93 | Bury | 1 | — |

1993–94 .... — —

MORRISON, Andy

Born Inverness 30.7.70.   Ht 5 11
Wt 12 00
Midfield. From Trainee.

Season	Club	App	Goals
1987–88	Plymouth Arg	1	—
1988–89		2	—
1989–90		19	1
1990–91		32	2
1991–92		30	3
1992–93		29	—
1993–94	Blackburn R	5	—

MORRISON, David

Born Waltham Forest 30.11.74
Midfield. From Chelmsford C.

Season	Club	App	Goals
1993–94	Peterborough U	—	—

MORRISSEY, John

Born Liverpool 8.3.65.   Ht 5 8   Wt 11 09
Midfield. From Apprentice. England
Youth.

Season	Club	App	Goals
1982–83	Everton	—	—
1983–84		—	—
1984–85		1	—
1985–86	Wolverhampton W	10	1
1985–86	Tranmere R	32	5
1986–87		38	7
1987–88		39	4
1988–89		42	4
1989–90		27	4
1990–91		40	9
1991–92		40	5
1992–93		43	5
1993–94		25	1

MORROW, Grant

Born Glasgow 4.10.70.   Ht 5 10   Wt 11 07
Forward. From Rowntree Mackintosh.

Season	Club	App	Goals
1989–90	Doncaster R	7	2
1990–91		14	1
1991–92		20	—
1992–93		23	4
1993–94	Colchester U	1	—

MORROW, John

Born Belfast 20.11.71   Ht 5 7   Wt 10 0
Forward. Linfield.

Season	Club	App	Goals
1988–89	Rangers	—	—
1989–90		—	—
1990–91		—	—
1991–92		3	—
1992–93		—	—
1993–94		2	—

MORROW, Steve

Born Belfast 2.7.70.   Ht 5 11   Wt 12 02
Defender. From Bangor, Arsenal Trainee.
Northern Ireland Youth, Under-23, 13 full
caps.

Season	Club	App	Goals
1987–88	Arsenal	—	—
1988–89		—	—
1989–90		—	—
1990–91	*Reading*	10	—
1991–92	Arsenal	2	—
1991–92	*Watford*	8	—
1991–92	*Reading*	3	—
1991–92	*Barnet*	1	—
1992–93	Arsenal	16	—
1993–94		11	—

MORTIMER, Paul

Born London 8.5.68.   Ht 5 11   Wt 11 03
Midfield. From Fulham Apprentice.
England Under-21.

Season	Club	App	Goals
1987–88	Charlton Ath	12	—
1988–89		33	5
1989–90		36	5
1990–91		32	7
1991–92	Aston Villa	12	1
1991–92	Crystal Palace	21	2
1992–93		1	—
1992–93	*Brentford*	6	—
1993–94	Crystal Palace	—	—

MORTON, Neil

Born Congleton 21.12.68.   Ht 5 9
Wt 10 07
Forward. From Trainee.

Season	Club	App	Goals
1986–87	Crewe Alex	2	—
1987–88		24	1
1988–89		5	—

From Northwich Vic

Season	Club	App	Goals
1990–91	Chester C	34	7

1991–92 .... 34 2
1992–93 .... 27 4
1993–94 Wigan Ath.................. 39 4

MOSES, Adrian
Born Doncaster 4.5.75   Ht 6 1   Wt 12 08
Defender. From school.
1993–94 Barnsley .... — —

MOSS, David
Born Doncaster 15.11.68   Ht 6 0
Wt 13 04
Midfield. From Boston U.
1992–93 Doncaster R................ 9 3
1993–94 .... 9 2
1993–94 Chesterfield................ 26 6

MOSS, Neil
Born New Milton 10.5.75   Ht 6 1
Wt 12 11
Goalkeeper. From Trainee.
1992–93 Bournemouth.............. 1 —
1993–94 .... 6 —

MOULDEN, Paul
Born Farnworth 6.9.67.   Ht 5 8   Wt 11 03
Forward. From Apprentice. England
Youth.
1984–85 Manchester C .... — —
1985–86 .... 2 —
1986–87 .... 20 5
1987–88 .... 6 —
1988–89 .... 36 13
1989–90 Bournemouth.............. 32 13
1989–90 Oldham Ath................ 8 —
1990–91 .... 24 3
1991–92 .... 2 1
1992–93 .... 4 —
1992–93 *Brighton* 11 5
1992–93 Birmingham C............. 13 5
1993–94 .... 7 —

MOUNTFIELD, Derek
Born Liverpool 2.11.62.   Ht 6 1   Wt 12 07
Defender. From Apprentice. England B,
Under-21.
1980–81 Tranmere R .... 5 —
1981–82 .... 21 1

1982–83 Everton .... 1 —
1983–84 .... 31 3
1984–85 .... 37 10
1985–86 .... 15 3
1986–87 .... 13 3
1987–88 .... 9 —
1988–89 Aston Villa.................. 24 1
1989–90 .... 32 4
1990–91 .... 32 4
1991–92 .... 2 —
1991–92 Wolverhampton W 28 1
1992–93 .... 36 2
1993–94 .... 19 1

MOUSSADDIK, Chuck
Born Morocco 23.2.70   Ht 5 11   Wt 12 03
Goalkeeper. From Wimbledon.
1993–94 Wycombe W .... — —

MOWBRAY, Tony
Born Saltburn 22.11.63.   Ht 6 1   Wt 13 00
Defender. From Apprentice. England B.
1981–82 Middlesbrough............ — —
1982–83 .... 26 —
1983–84 .... 35 1
1984–85 .... 40 2
1985–86 .... 35 4
1986–87 .... 46 7
1987–88 .... 44 3
1988–89 .... 37 3
1989–90 .... 28 2
1990–91 .... 40 3
1991–92 .... 17 —
1991–92 Celtic 15 2
1992–93 .... 26 2
1993–94 .... 22 1

MOYES, David
Born Glasgow 25.4.63   Ht 6 1   Wt 12 10
Defender. From Drumchapel A.
1980–81 Celtic .... — —
1981–82 .... 19 —
1982–83 .... 5 —
1983–84 .... — —
1983–84 Cambridge U.............. 30 —
1984–85 .... 40 1
1985–86 .... 9 —
1985–86 Bristol C 27 2
1986–87 .... 41 3

Season	Club	League Appearances/Goals	
1987–88	....	15	1
1987–88	Shrewsbury T	17	2
1988–89	....	33	1
1989–90	....	46	8
1990–91	Dunfermline Ath	35	7
1991–92	....	39	5
1992–93	....	30	1
1993–94	....	1	—
1993–94	Hamilton A	5	—
1993–94	Preston NE	29	4

MUDD, Paul
Born Hull 13.11.70.   Ht 5 8   Wt 11 02
Defender. From Trainee.

Season	Club	League Appearances/Goals	
1988–89	Hull C	1	—
1989–90	....	—	—
1990–91	Scarborough	24	—
1991–92	....	36	1
1992–93	....	38	1
1993–94	Scunthorpe U	33	3

MUGGLETON, Carl
Born Leicester 13.9.68.   Ht 6 2   Wt 13 07
Goalkeeper. From Apprentice. England
Under-21.

Season	Club	League Appearances/Goals	
1986–87	Leicester C	—	—
1987–88	....	—	—
1987–88	Chesterfield	17	—
1987–88	Blackpool	2	—
1988–89	Leicester C	3	—
1988–89	Hartlepool U	8	—
1989–90	Leicester C	—	—
1989–90	Stockport Co	4	—
1990–91	Leicester C	22	—
1990–91	Liverpool	—	—
1991–92	Leicester C	4	—
1992–93	....	17	—
1993–94	....	—	—
1993–94	Stoke C	6	—
1993–94	Sheffield U	—	—
1993–94	Celtic..........................	12	—

MUIR, Ian
Born Coventry 5.5.63.   Ht 5 8   Wt 11 00
Forward. From Apprentice. England
Youth.

Season	Club	League Appearances/Goals	
1980–81	QPR	2	2
1981–82	....	—	—
1982–83	....	—	—
1982–83	*Burnley*	2	1
1983–84	Birmingham C	1	—
1983–84	Brighton......................	2	—
1984–85	....	2	—
1984–85	*Swindon T*	2	—
1985–86	Tranmere R	32	14
1986–87	....	46	20
1987–88	....	43	27
1988–89	....	46	21
1989–90	....	46	23
1990–91	....	35	13
1991–92	....	20	5
1992–93	....	11	2
1993–94	....	16	9

MUIR, John
Born Sedgley 26.4.63.   Ht 6 2   Wt 14 06
Forward. From Dudley T.

Season	Club	League Appearances/Goals	
1989–90	Doncaster R	16	4
1990–91	....	39	13
1991–92	....	20	1
1991–92	Stockport Co	4	—
1992–93	....	9	3
1992–93	*Torquay U*	12	—
1993–94	Preston NE	—	—

MULLIGAN, James
Born Dublin 21.4.74   Ht 5 7   Wt 10 12
Forward. From Trainee.

Season	Club	League Appearances/Goals	
1992–93	Stoke C	—	—
1993–94	....	—	—
1993–94	*Bury*	3	1

MULLIN, John
Born Bury 11.8.75   Ht 6 0   Wt 11 05
Forward. From School.

Season	Club	League Appearances/Goals	
1992–93	Burnley	—	—
1993–94	....	6	1

MULRAIN, Steve
Born Lambeth 23.10.72   Ht 5 10
Wt 11 07
Forward. From Trainee.

Season	Club	League Appearances/Goals	
1991–92	Leeds U	—	—
1992–93	Rochdale.....................	6	2
1993–94	....	2	—

MUNDAY, Stuart
Born London 28.9.72.　Ht 5 11　Wt 11 00
Defender. From Trainee.

Season	Club	Apps	Goals
1990–91	Brighton	—	—
1991–92		14	1
1992–93		7	—
1993–94		34	1

MUNDEE, Denny
Born Swindon 10.10.68.　Ht 5 10 Wt 11 00
Forward. From Apprentice.

Season	Club	Apps	Goals
1986–87	QPR	—	—
1986–87	Swindon T	—	—
1987–88	Bournemouth	—	—
1988–89		2	—
1989–90		10	—
1989–90	*Torquay U*	9	—
1990–91	Bournemouth	21	2
1991–92		41	2
1992–93		26	2
1993–94	Brentford	39	11

MUNGALL, Steve
Born Bellshill 22.5.58.　Ht 5 8　Wt 11 05
Defender.

Season	Club	Apps	Goals
1976–77	Motherwell	3	—
1977–78		13	—
1978–79		4	—
1979–80	Tranmere R	24	—
1980–81		38	3
1981–82		44	1
1982–83		31	1
1983–84		26	—
1984–85		23	—
1985–86		46	1
1986–87		46	—
1987–88		45	—
1988–89		42	1
1989–90		17	1
1990–91		33	1
1991–92		18	—
1992–93		35	3
1993–94		12	—

MUNOZ, Mark
Born Lambeth 16.10.74　Ht 5 11
Midfield. From Trainee.

Season	Club	Apps	Goals
1993–94	Fulham	—	—

MUNRO, Stuart
Born Falkirk 15.9.62.　Ht 5 8　Wt 10 05
Defender. From Bo'ness United. Scotland B.

Season	Club	Apps	Goals
1980–81	St Mirren	1	—
1981–82		—	—
1982–83	Alloa	39	5
1983–84		21	1
1983–84	Rangers	5	—
1984–85		13	—
1985–86		29	—
1986–87		43	—
1987–88		17	—
1988–89		22	2
1989–90		36	1
1990–91		14	—
1991–92	Blackburn R	1	—
1992–93		—	—
1992–93	Bristol C	16	—
1993–94		44	—

MUNSON, Nathan
Born Colchester 10.11.74
Goalkeeper. From Trainee.

Season	Club	Apps	Goals
1992–93	Colchester U	1	—
1993–94		3	—

MURDOCH, Andrew
Born Greenock 20.7.68.　Ht 5 11 Wt 11 00
Goalkeeper. From Johnstone Burgh.

Season	Club	Apps	Goals
1987–88	Celtic	—	—
1988–89		—	—
1988–89	*Partick T*	13	—
1989–90	Celtic	—	—
1989–90	*Partick T*	13	—
1990–91	Celtic	—	—
1990–91	Partick T	18	—
1991–92		32	—
1992–93		17	—
1993–94		6	—

MURDOCK, Colin
Born Ballymena 2.7.75　Ht 6 1　Wt 12 00
Defender. From Trainee.

Season	Club	Apps	Goals
1992–93	Manchester U	—	—
1993–94		—	—

MURPHY, Danny
Born Chester 18.3.77   Ht 5 9   Wt 10 03
Midfield. From Trainee.
1993–94 Crewe Alex   12   2

MURPHY, Jamie
Born Manchester 25.2.73   Ht 6 1
Wt 13 00
Defender. From Trainee.
1991–92 Blackpool....................   —   —
1992–93   33   —
1993–94   16   —

MURPHY, John
Born Cork 9.9.75
Defender.
1993–94 Aston Villa..................   —   —

MURPHY, Matthew
Born Northampton 20.8.71   Ht 5 10
Wt 11 00
Forward. From Corby.
1992–93 Oxford U   2   —
1993–94 ....   —   —

MURPHY, Shaun
Born Sydney 5.11.70   Ht 6 0   Wt 12 00
Defender. From Perth Italia.
1992–93 Notts Co   8   1
1993–94   11   1

MURRAY, Bruce
Born Washington 25.1.66   Ht 6 3
Wt 13 08
Forward. From USSF.
1993–94 Millwall......................   13   2
1993–94 *Stockport Co*   3   —

MURRAY, Edwin
Born Redbridge 31.8.73.   Ht 5 11
Wt 12 00
Defender. From Trainee.
1990–91 Swindon T   1   —
1991–92 ....   —   —
1992–93 ....   —   —
1993–94 ....   —   —

MURRAY, Mark
Born Manchester 13.6.73.   Ht 5 8
Wt 10 12
Defender. From Trainee.
1990–91 Blackpool....................   —   —
1991–92   2   —
1992–93   1   —
1993–94 ....   —   —

MURRAY, Nathan
Born South Shields 10.9.75
Defender. From Trainee.
1992–93 Newcastle U................   —   —
1993–94 ....   —   —

MURRAY, Neil
Born Bellshill 21.2.73   Ht 5 9   Wt 10 10
Midfield. From Rangers Ams. Scotland
Under-21.
1989–90 Rangers.......................   —   —
1990–91 ....   —   —
1991–92 ....   —   —
1992–93   16   —
1993–94   22   —

MURRAY, Paul
Born Carlisle 31.8.76
Defender. From Trainee.
1993–94 Carlisle U....................   8   —

MURRAY, Robert
Born Hammersmith 31.10.74   Ht 5 11
Wt 11 07
Forward. From Trainee. Scotland
Under-21.
1992–93 Bournemouth.................   25   4
1993–94   20   4

MURRAY, Scott
Born Aberdeen 26.5.74   Ht 5 10
Wt 11 00
Forward. From Fraserburgh.
1993–94 Aston Villa..................   —   —

MURRAY, Shaun
Born Newcastle 7.2.70.   Ht 5 8   Wt 11 02
Forward. From Trainee. England Youth.
1987–88 Tottenham H ....   —   —

Season	Club	App	Goals
1988–89	....	—	—
1989–90	Portsmouth	—	—
1990–91	....	25	1
1991–92	....	2	—
1992–93	....	7	—
1993–94	....	—	—
1993–94	*Millwall*	—	—
1993–94	Scarborough	29	5

MURTY, Graeme
Born Middlesbrough 13.11.74   Ht 5 10
Wt 11 05
Midfield. From Trainee.

Season	Club	App	Goals
1992–93	York C	—	—
1993–94	....	1	—

MUSGRAVE, Sean
Born Penshaw 27.10.74   Ht 5 10
Goalkeeper. From Trainee.

Season	Club	App	Goals
1993–94	Sunderland	—	—

MUSSELWHITE, Paul
Born Portsmouth 22.12.68.   Ht 6 2
Wt 12 07
Goalkeeper.

Season	Club	App	Goals
1987–88	Portsmouth	—	—
1988–89	Scunthorpe U	41	—
1989–90	....	29	—
1990–91	....	38	—
1991–92	....	24	—
1992–93	Port Vale	41	—
1993–94	....	46	—

MUSTOE, Robbie
Born Oxford 28.8.68.   Ht 5 10   Wt 10 08
Midfield.

Season	Club	App	Goals
1986–87	Oxford U	3	—
1987–88	....	17	—
1988–89	....	33	3
1989–90	....	38	7
1990–91	Middlesbrough	41	4
1991–92	....	30	2
1992–93	....	23	1
1993–94	....	38	2

MUTCH, Andy
Born Liverpool 28.12.63.   Ht 5 10
Wt 11 00
Forward. From Southport. England B,
Under-21.

Season	Club	App	Goals
1985–86	Wolverhampton W	15	7
1986–87	....	41	12
1987–88	....	46	19
1988–89	....	45	21
1989–90	....	37	11
1990–91	....	29	8
1991–92	....	37	10
1992–93	....	39	9
1993–94	Swindon T	30	6

MUTCHELL, Robert
Born Solihull 2.1.74   Ht 5 10   Wt 11 02
Defender. From Trainee.

Season	Club	App	Goals
1992–93	Oxford U	—	—
1993–94	....	—	—
1993–94	Barnet	14	—

MYALL, Stuart
Born Eastbourne 12.11.74   Ht 5 10
Wt 12 12
Defender. From Trainee.

Season	Club	App	Goals
1992–93	Brighton	7	—
1993–94	....	13	—

MYDDLETON, Phil
Born St Asaph 22.12.72   Ht 5 8   Wt 10 12
Defender. From Trainee.

Season	Club	App	Goals
1992–93	Wrexham	—	—
1993–94	....	—	—

MYERS, Andy
Born Hounslow 3.11.73.   Ht 5 8   Wt 9 10
Midfield. From Trainee. England Youth.

Season	Club	App	Goals
1990–91	Chelsea	3	—
1991–92	....	11	1
1992–93	....	3	—
1993–94	....	6	—

MYERS, Chris
Born Yeovil 1.4.69.   Ht 5 10   Wt 11 10
Midfield. From Apprentice.

Season	Club	App	Goals
1986–87	Torquay U	9	—

From local

Season	Club		
1990–91	Torquay U	29	2
1991–92		39	4
1992–93		28	1
1993–94	Dundee U	5	—
1993–94	*Torquay U*	6	—

NAPIER, Craig

Born East Kilbride 14.11.65   Ht 5 9
Wt 10 10
Midfield. Kirkton Utd.

Season	Club		
1984–85	Clyde	—	—
1985–86		8	—
1986–87		42	—
1987–88		42	1
1988–89		14	—
1988–89	Hamilton A	20	—
1989–90		39	6
1990–91		39	6
1991–92		22	2
1992–93		29	1
1993–94		27	2
1993–94	Kilmarnock	15	—

NARBETT, Jon

Born Birmingham 21.11.68.   Ht 5 10
Wt 10 08
Midfield. From Apprentice.

Season	Club		
1986–87	Shrewsbury T	1	—
1987–88		25	3
1988–89		—	—
1988–89	Hereford U	36	7
1989–90		36	5
1990–91		44	11
1991–92		33	8
1991–92	*Leicester C*	—	—
1992–93	Oxford U	14	—
1993–94		1	—

NAREY, David

Born Dundee 21.6.56.   Ht 6 0   Wt 12 06
Defender. 'S' Form. Scotland Youth,
Under-21, Under-23, 35 full caps.

Season	Club		
1973–74	Dundee U	12	—
1974–75		31	6
1975–76		33	—
1976–77		32	2
1977–78		35	—
1978–79		36	5
1979–80		35	1
1980–81		32	—
1981–82		34	1
1982–83		36	5
1983–84		34	1
1984–85		29	1
1985–86		35	—

1986–87		33	—
1987–88		39	—
1988–89		33	—
1989–90		31	—
1990–91		4	—
1991–92		24	—
1992–93		28	—
1993–94		6	—

Nayim (Mohamed Ali Amar)

Born Morocco 5.11.66.   Ht 5 8   Wt 11 08
Midfield. From Barcelona. Spain Youth, Under-21.

1988–89	Tottenham H	11	2
1989–90		19	—
1990–91		33	5
1991–92		31	1
1992–93		18	3
To Zaragoza			

NAYLOR, Dominic

Born Watford 12.8.70.   Ht 5 9   Wt 11 07
Defender. From Trainee.

1988–89	Watford	—	—
1989–90		—	—
1989–90	Halifax T	6	1
To Barnet			
1991–92	Barnet	26	—
1992–93		25	—
1993–94	Plymouth Arg	43	—

NAYLOR, Glenn

Born York 11.8.72.   Ht 5 11   Wt 11 02
Forward. From Trainee.

1989–90	York C	1	—
1990–91		20	5
1991–92		21	8
1992–93		4	—
1993–94		10	1

NAYLOR, Stuart

Born Wetherby 6.12.62.   Ht 6 4   Wt 12 02
Goalkeeper. From Yorkshire A. England Youth, B.

1980–81	Lincoln C	—	—
1981–82		3	—
1982–83		1	—

1982–83	*Peterborough U*	8	—
1983–84	Lincoln C	—	—
1983–84	*Crewe Alex*	38	—
1984–85	*Crewe Alex*	17	—
1984–85	Lincoln C	25	—
1985–86		20	—
1985–86	WBA	12	—
1986–87		42	—
1987–88		35	—
1988–89		44	—
1989–90		39	—
1990–91		28	—
1991–92		34	—
1992–93		32	—
1993–94		20	—

NAYLOR, Tony

Born Manchester 29.3.67.   Ht 5 8   Wt 10 08
Forward. From Droylsden.

1989–90	Crewe Alex	2	—
1990–91		14	1
1991–92		34	15
1992–93		35	16
1993–94		37	13

NDAH, George

Born Camberwell 23.12.74   Ht 6 1   Wt 10 00
Midfield. From Trainee.

1992–93	Crystal Palace	13	—
1993–94		1	—

NDLOVU, Peter

Born Zimbabwe 25.2.73.   Ht 5 8   Wt 10 02
Forward. From Highlanders.

1991–92	Coventry C	23	2
1992–93		32	7
1993–94		40	11

NEAL, Ashley

Born Liverpool 16.12.74   Ht 6 00   Wt 11 10
Midfield. From Trainee.

1992–93	Liverpool	—	—
1993–94		—	—

NEBBELING, Gavin
Born Johannesburg 15.5.63.   Ht 6 0
Wt 12 10
Defender. From Arcadia Shepherds.

Season	Club	League Appearances	Goals
1981–82	Crystal Palace	1	—
1982–83		28	1
1983–84		16	—
1984–85		16	—
1985–86		14	—
1985–86	*Northampton T*	11	—
1986–87	Crystal Palace	23	—
1987–88		39	6
1988–89		14	1
1989–90	Fulham	36	—
1990–91		6	—
1991–92		16	—
1991–92	*Hereford U*	3	—
1992–93	Fulham	30	2
1993–94	Preston NE	22	4

NEILL, Warren
Born Acton 21.11.62.   Ht 5 9   Wt 11 05
Defender. From Apprentice. England
Schools.

Season	Club	League Appearances	Goals
1980–81	QPR	4	—
1981–82		11	—
1982–83		39	2
1983–84		41	1
1984–85		18	1
1985–86		16	—
1986–87		29	—
1987–88		23	—
1988–89	Portsmouth	43	—
1989–90		37	—
1990–91		30	—
1991–92		38	—
1992–93		28	—
1993–94		35	2

NEILSON, Alan
Born Wegburg 26.9.72.   Ht 5 11
Wt 11 07
Defender. From Trainee. Wales Under-21,
3 full caps.

Season	Club	League Appearances	Goals
1990–91	Newcastle U	3	—
1991–92		16	1
1992–93		3	—
1993–94		14	—

NELSON, Craig
Born Coatbridge 28.5.71.   Ht 6 1
Wt 13 00
Goalkeeper. From Ashfield.

Season	Club	League Appearances	Goals
1990–91	Partick T	1	—
1991–92		11	—
1992–93		27	—
1993–94		39	—

NELSON, Garry
Born Braintree 16.1.61.   Ht 5 10
Wt 11 04
Forward. From Amateur.

Season	Club	League Appearances	Goals
1979–80	Southend U	22	2
1980–81		22	3
1981–82		40	4
1982–83		45	8
1983–84	Swindon T	36	4
1984–85		43	3
1985–86	Plymouth Arg	42	13
1986–87		32	7
1987–88	Brighton	42	22
1988–89		46	15
1989–90		33	4
1990–91		23	5
1990–91	*Notts Co*	2	—
1991–92	Charlton Ath	41	6
1992–93		44	6
1993–94		43	15

NESTOR, Terry
Born Warrington 22.10.74   Ht 5 10
Wt 11 04
Midfield. From Trainee.

Season	Club	League Appearances	Goals
1992–93	Liverpool	—	—
1993–94		—	—

NETHERCOTT, Stuart
Born Chadwell Heath 21.3.73.   Ht 6 0
Wt 12 04
Defender. From Trainee. England
Under-21.

Season	Club	League Appearances	Goals
1991–92	Tottenham H	—	—
1991–92	*Maidstone U*	13	1
1991–92	*Barnet*	3	—
1992–93	Tottenham H	5	—

Season	Club	Apps	Goals
1993–94		10	—

NEVILLE, Gary
Born Bury 18.2.75   Ht 5 10   Wt 11 04
Defender. From Trainee.

Season	Club	Apps	Goals
1992–93	Manchester U	—	—
1993–94		1	—

NEVIN, Pat
Born Glasgow 6.9.63.   Ht 5 6   Wt 11 09
Forward. From Gartcosh U. Scotland,
Youth, Under-21, B, 22 full caps.

Season	Club	Apps	Goals
1981–82	Clyde	34	12
1982–83		39	5
1983–84	Chelsea	38	14
1984–85		41	4
1985–86		40	7
1986–87		37	5
1987–88		37	6
1988–89	Everton	25	2
1989–90		30	4
1990–91		37	8
1991–92		17	2
1991–92	*Tranmere R*	8	—
1992–93	Tranmere R	43	13
1993–94		45	8

NEWELL, Mike
Born Liverpool 27.1.65.   Ht 6 1   Wt 11 00
Forward. From Liverpool Amateur.
England, B, Under-21.

Season	Club	Apps	Goals
1983–84	Crewe Alex	3	—
1983–84	Wigan Ath	9	—
1984–85		39	9
1985–86		24	16
1985–86	Luton T	16	6
1986–87		42	12
1987–88		5	—
1987–88	Leicester C	36	8
1988–89		45	13
1989–90	Everton	26	7
1990–91		29	7
1991–92		13	1
1991–92	Blackburn R	20	6
1992–93		40	13
1993–94		28	6

NEWELL, Paul
Born Greenwich 23.2.69.   Ht 6 1
Wt 11 05
Goalkeeper. From Trainee.

Season	Club	Apps	Goals
1987–88	Southend U	13	—
1988–89		2	—
1989–90		—	—
1990–91	Leyton Orient	8	—
1991–92		10	—
1992–93		3	—
1992–93	*Colchester U*	14	—
1993–94	Leyton Orient	40	—

NEWHOUSE, Aidan
Born Wallasey 23.5.72.   Ht 6 2   Wt 13 05
Midfield. From Schoolboy, Trainee.
England Youth.

Season	Club	Apps	Goals
1987–88	Chester C	1	—
1988–89		25	2
1989–90		18	4
1989–90	Wimbledon	2	—
1990–91		8	1
1991–92		12	1
1992–93		1	—
1993–94		—	—
1993–94	*Tranmere R*	—	—
1993–94	*Port Vale*	2	—

NEWLAND, Ray
Born Liverpool 19.7.71   Ht 6 1   Wt 12 01
Goalkeeper. From Everton trainee.

Season	Club	Apps	Goals
1992–93	Plymouth Arg	21	—
1993–94		5	—

NEWMAN, Ricky
Born Guildford 5.8.70.   Ht 5 10
Wt 11 00
Midfield.

Season	Club	Apps	Goals
1987–88	Crystal Palace	—	—
1998–89		—	—
1989–90		—	—
1990–91		—	—
1991–92		—	—
1991–92	*Maidstone U*	10	1
1992–93	Crystal Palace	2	—
1993–94		11	—

NEWMAN, Rob
Born Bradford-on-Avon 13.12.63. Ht 6 0 Wt 13 00
Defender. From Apprentice.

Season	Club	App	Goals
1981–82	Bristol C	21	3
1982–83		43	3
1983–84		30	1
1984–85		34	3
1985–86		39	3
1986–87		45	6
1987–88		44	11
1988–89		46	6
1989–90		46	8
1990–91		46	8
1991–92	Norwich C	41	7
1992–93		18	2
1993–94		32	2

NEWSOME, Jon
Born Sheffield 6.9.70. Ht 6 2 Wt 13 11
Defender. From Trainee.

Season	Club	App	Goals
1989–90	Sheffield W	6	—
1990–91		1	—
1991–92	Leeds U	10	2
1992–93		37	—
1993–94		29	1

NEWSON, Mark
Born Stepney 7.12.60. Ht 5 10 Wt 12 06
Defender. From Apprentice.

Season	Club	App	Goals
1979–80	Charlton Ath	—	—
From Maidstone U			
1985–86	Bournemouth	46	5
1986–87		46	7
1987–88		29	3
1988–89		40	7
1989–90		16	1
1989–90	Fulham	16	—
1990–91		31	1
1991–92		26	3
1992–93		29	—
1993–94	Barnet	29	2

NEWTON, Eddie
Born Hammersmith 13.12.71. Ht 5 11 Wt 11 02
Forward. From Trainee. England Under-21.

Season	Club	App	Goals
1990–91	Chelsea	—	—
1991–92		1	1
1991–92	*Cardiff C*	18	4
1992–93	Chelsea	34	5
1993–94		36	—

NEWTON, Shaun
Born Camberwell 20.8.75 Ht 5 8 Wt 10 04
Midfield. From Trainee.

Season	Club	App	Goals
1992–93	Charlton Ath	2	—
1993–94		19	2

NICHOLAS, Charlie
Born Glasgow 30.12.61. Ht 5 10 Wt 11 00
Forward. From Celtic BC. Scotland Youth. Under-21, 20 full caps.

Season	Club	App	Goals
1980–81	Celtic	29	16
1981–82		10	3
1982–83		35	29
1983–84	Arsenal	41	11
1984–85		38	9
1985–86		41	10
1986–87		28	4
1987–88		3	—
1987–88	Aberdeen	16	3
1988–89		29	16
1989–90		33	11
1990–91	Celtic	14	6
1991–92		37	21
1992–93		16	2
1993–94		35	8

NICHOLL, Jimmy
Born Hamilton,Canada 20.12.56 Ht 5 10 Wt 11 10
Defender. From Apprentice. Northern Ireland U-21, 73 full caps.

Season	Club	App	Goals
1973–74	Manchester U	—	—
1974–75		1	—
1975–76		20	—
1976–77		30	—
1977–78		37	2
1978–79		21	—
1979–80		42	—
1980–81		36	1
1981–82		1	—
1981–82	Sunderland	3	—

From Toronto B.

Season	Club	App	Goals
1982–83	Sunderland	29	—

From Toronto B.

Season	Club	App	Goals
1983–84	Rangers	17	—
1984–85	WBA	27	—
1985–86		29	—
1986–87	Rangers	42	—
1987–88		22	—
1988–89		1	—
1989–90	Dunfermline Ath	17	—
1990–91		7	—
1990–91	Raith R	10	—
1991–92		32	1
1992–93		38	5
1993–94		34	1

NICHOLLS, Alan
Born Birmingham 28.8.73   Ht 6 0
Goalkeeper. From Cheltenham T.

Season	Club	App	Goals
1993–94	Plymouth Arg	38	—

NICHOLSON, Max
Born Leeds 3.10.71.   Ht 5 10   Wt 12 03
Forward. From Trainee.

Season	Club	App	Goals
1989–90	Doncaster R	2	—
1990–91		1	—
1991–92		24	2
1992–93	Hereford U	36	3
1993–94		27	4

NICHOLSON, Shane
Born Newark 3.6.70.   Ht 5 10   Wt 11 00
Defender. From Trainee.

Season	Club	App	Goals
1986–87	Lincoln C	7	—
1987–88		*33*	*1*
1988–89		34	1
1989–90		23	—
1990–91		40	4
1991–92		29	1
1991–92	Derby Co	—	—
1992–93		17	—
1993–94		22	1

NICOL, Steve
Born Irvine 11.12.61.   Ht 5 10   Wt 12 00
Midfield. From Ayr U. BC. Scotland
Under-21, 27 full caps.

Season	Club	App	Goals
1979–80	Ayr U	20	2

Season	Club	App	Goals
1980–81		39	3
1981–82		11	2
1981–82	Liverpool	—	—
1982–83		4	—
1983–84		23	5
1984–85		31	5
1985–86		34	4
1986–87		14	3
1987–88		40	6
1988–89		38	2
1989–90		23	6
1990–91		35	3
1991–92		34	1
1992–93		32	—
1993–94		31	1

NIJHOLT, Luc
Born Zaandam 29.7.61   Ht 5 11
Wt 12 01
Defender. From BSC Old Boys Basel.

Season	Club	App	Goals
1990–91	Motherwell	23	—
1991–92		39	5
1992–93		34	—
1993–94	Swindon T	32	1

NILSEN, Roger
Born Norway 8.8.69   Ht 5 9   Wt 11 08
Defender. From Viking Stavanger.
Norway full caps.

Season	Club	App	Goals
1993–94	Sheffield U	22	—

NILSSON, Roland
Born Helsingborg 27.11.63.   Ht 5 10
Wt 12 00
Defender. From IFK Gothenburg. Sweden
full caps.

Season	Club	App	Goals
1989–90	Sheffield W	20	—
1990–91		22	—
1991–92		39	1
1992–93		32	1
1993–94		38	—

NIXON, Eric
Born Manchester 4.10.62.   Ht 6 2
Wt 14 03
Goalkeeper. From Curzon Ashton.

Season	Club	App	Goals
1983–84	Manchester C	—	—
1984–85		—	—

Season	Club	Apps	Goals
1985–86	....	28	—
1986–87	....	5	—
1986–87	*Wolverhampton W*	16	—
1986–87	*Bradford C*	3	—
1986–87	*Southampton*	4	—
1986–87	*Carlisle U*	16	—
1987–88	Manchester C	25	—
1987–88	*Tranmere R*	8	—
1988–89	Tranmere R	45	—
1989–90	....	46	—
1990–91	....	43	—
1991–92	....	46	—
1992–93	....	45	—
1993–94	....	42	—

NIXON, Jerry
Born Trinidad 25.6.73   Ht 6 0   Wt 11 11
Forward. ECM Motown.

Season	Club	Apps	Goals
1993–94	Dundee U	15	1

NOGAN, Kurt
Born Cardiff 9.9.70.   Ht 5 11   Wt 12 07
Forward. From Trainee. Wales Under-21.

Season	Club	Apps	Goals
1989–90	Luton T	10	2
1990–91	....	9	—
1991–92	....	14	1
1992–93	Peterborough U	—	—
1992–93	Brighton	30	20
1993–94	....	41	22

NOGAN, Lee
Born Cardiff 21.5.69.   Ht 5 10   Wt 11 00
Forward. From Apprentice. Wales B,
Under-21, 1 full cap.

Season	Club	Apps	Goals
1986–87	Oxford U	—	—
1986–87	*Brentford*	11	2
1987–88	Oxford U	3	—
1987–88	*Southend U*	6	1
1988–89	Oxford U	3	—
1989–90	....	4	—
1990–91	....	32	5
1991–92	....	22	5
1991–92	Watford	23	5
1992–93	....	42	11
1993–94	....	26	3
1993–94	*Southend U*	5	—

NOLAN, Ian
Born Liverpool 9.7.70.   Ht 6 0   Wt 11 10
Defender. From Preston NE Trainee,
Northwich V, Marine.

Season	Club	Apps	Goals
1991–92	Tranmere R	34	1
1992–93	....	14	—
1993–94	....	40	—

NORBURY, Mike
Born Hemsworth 22.1.69.   Ht 6 1
Wt 11 10
Forward. From Ossett, Scarborough,
Bridlington.

Season	Club	Apps	Goals
1991–92	Cambridge U	14	2
1992–93	....	12	1
1992–93	Preston NE	21	8
1993–94	....	21	5

NORMAN, Alec
Born Reading 14.2.75   Ht 6 1   Wt 13 00
Forward.

Season	Club	Apps	Goals
1993–94	Wycombe W	—	—

NORMAN, Craig
Born Perivale 21.3.75   Ht 5 10   Wt 11 09
Defender. From Trainee.

Season	Club	Apps	Goals
1993–94	Chelsea	—	—

NORMAN, Tony
Born Mancot 24.2.58.   Ht 6 2   Wt 13 10
Goalkeeper. From Amateur. Wales B, 5
full caps.

Season	Club	Apps	Goals
1976–77	Burnley	—	—
1977–78	....	—	—
1978–79	....	—	—
1979–80	....	—	—
1979–80	Hull C	17	—
1980–81	....	42	—
1981–82	....	36	—
1982–83	....	36	—
1983–84	....	46	—
1984–85	....	46	—
1985–86	....	42	—
1986–87	....	42	—
1987–88	....	44	—
1988–89	....	21	—
1988–89	Sunderland	24	—
1989–90	....	28	—

Season Club League Appearances/Goals

1990–91		37	—
1991–92		44	—
1992–93		33	—
1993–94		3	—

NORRIS, Steve

Born Coventry 22.9.61 Ht 5 10 Wt 10 10
Forward. From Telford.

1988–89	Scarborough	31	9
1989–90		14	4
1989–90	*Notts Co.*	1	—
1989–90	Carlisle U	24	3
1990–91		5	2
1990–91	Halifax T	39	30
1991–92		17	5
1991–92	Chesterfield	21	10
1992–93		30	11
1993–94		39	19

NORTON, David

Born Cannock 3.3.65. Ht 5 7 Wt 11 03
Midfield. From Apprentice. England Youth.

1982–83	Aston Villa	—	—
1983–84		—	—
1984–85		2	—
1985–86		20	2
1986–87		20	—
1987–88		2	—
1988–89	Notts Co	8	—
1989–90		15	1
1990–91		4	—
1990–91	*Rochdale*	9	—
1990–91	*Hull C*	15	—
1991–92	Hull C	45	2
1992–93		45	1
1993–94		44	2

NOTEMAN, Kevin

Born Preston 15.10.69. Ht 5 10 Wt 11 12
Forward. From Trainee.

1987–88	Leeds U	1	—
1988–89		—	—
1989–90		—	—
1989–90	Doncaster R	30	3
1990–91		42	7
1991–92		34	10
1991–92	Mansfield T	6	—
1992–93		24	4
1993–94		33	5

NTAMARK, Charlie

Born Paddington 22.7.64. Ht 5 8 Wt 11 12
Midfield. Cameroon full caps.

1990–91	Walsall	42	3
1991–92		41	3
1992–93		41	4
1993–94		37	—

NUGENT, Kevin

Born Edmonton 10.4.69. Ht 6 1 Wt 12 04
Forward. From Trainee. Eire Youth.

1987–88	Leyton Orient	11	3
1988–89		3	—
1988–89	*Cork C*	—	—
1989–90	Leyton Orient	11	—
1990–91		33	5
1991–92		36	12
1991–92	Plymouth Arg	4	—
1992–93		45	11
1993–94		39	14

NWAOKOLO, Danny

Born London 11.10.73. Ht 5 11 Wt 11 10
Defender. From Trainee.

1991–92	Watford	—	—
1992–93		—	—
1993–94		—	—

NYAMAH, Kofi

Born Islington 20.6.75 Ht 5 8 Wt 10 07
Forward. From Trainee.

1993–94	Cambridge U	14	2

OAKES, Michael
Born Northwich 30.10.73. Ht 6 1
Wt 12 07
Goalkeeper. From Trainee. England
Under-21.

Season	Club	App	Goals
1991–92	Aston Villa	—	—
1992–93		—	—
1993–94		—	—
1993–94	*Scarborough*	1	—
1993–94	*Tranmere R*	—	—

OAKES, Scott
Born Leicester 5.8.72. Ht 5 11   Wt 11 04
Forward. From Trainee.

Season	Club	App	Goals
1989–90	Leicester C	2	—
1990–91		—	—
1991–92		1	—
1991–92	Luton T	21	2
1992–93		44	5
1993–94		36	8

O'BRIEN, Liam
Born Dublin 5.9.64. Ht 6 1   Wt 13 03
Midfield. From Shamrock R. Eire Youth,
11 full caps.

Season	Club	App	Goals
1986–87	Manchester U	11	—
1987–88		17	2
1988–89		3	—
1988–89	Newcastle U	20	4
1989–90		19	2
1990–91		33	3
1991–92		40	4
1992–93		33	6
1993–94		6	—
1993–94	Tranmere R	17	1

O'BRIEN, Roy
Born Cork 27.11.74. Ht 6 1   Wt 12 00
Defender. From Trainee.

Season	Club	App	Goals
1993–94	Arsenal	—	—

O'CONNELL, Brendan
Born London 12.11.66. Ht 5 10
Wt 10 09
Forward.

Season	Club	App	Goals
1984–85	Portsmouth	—	—
1985–86		—	—
1986–87	Exeter C	42	8

Season	Club	App	Goals
1987–88		39	11
1988–89	Burnley	43	13
1989–90		21	4
1989–90	*Huddersfield T*	11	1
1989–90	Barnsley	11	2
1990–91		45	9
1991–92		36	4
1992–93		40	6
1993–94		38	6

O'CONNOR, Jonathan
Born Darlington 29.10.76 Ht 5 10
Wt 11 03
Midfield. From Trainee.

Season	Club	App	Goals
1993–94	Everton	—	—

O'CONNOR, Mark
Born Rochdale 10.3.63. Ht 5 7   Wt 10 02
Midfield. From Apprentice. Eire Under-21.

Season	Club	App	Goals
1980–81	QPR	—	—
1981–82		1	—
1982–83		2	—
1983–84		—	—
1983–84	*Exeter C*	38	1
1984–85	Bristol R	46	8
1985–86		34	2
1985–86	Bournemouth	9	1
1986–87		43	7
1987–88		37	2
1988–89		33	2
1989–90		6	—
1989–90	Gillingham	15	1
1990–91		41	3
1991–92		39	3
1992–93		21	1
1993–94	Bournemouth	45	3

O'CONNOR, Martyn
Born Walsall 10.12.67 Ht 5 8   Wt 10 08
Midfield. From Bromsgrove R.

Season	Club	App	Goals
1992–93	Crystal Palace	—	—
1992–93	*Walsall*	10	1
1993–94	Crystal Palace	2	—
1993–94	*Walsall*	14	2

O'DONNELL, Paul
Born Limerick 6.10.75. Ht 5 10   Wt 11 03
Midfield. From Trainee.

Season	Club	App	Goals
1992–93	Liverpool	—	—

Season	Club	Apps	Goals
1993–94		—	—

O'DONNELL, Phillip

Born Bellshill 25.3.72   Ht 5 10   Wt 10 05
Midfield. From X Form. Scotland Under-21, 1 full cap.

Season	Club	Apps	Goals
1990–91	Motherwell	12	—
1991–92		42	4
1992–93		32	4
1993–94		35	7

O'DRISCOLL, Sean

Born Wolverhampton 1.7.57.   Ht 5 8   Wt 11 03
Midfield. From Alvechurch. Eire Under-21, 3 full caps.

Season	Club	Apps	Goals
1979–80	Fulham	10	1
1980–81		42	2
1981–82		42	7
1982–83		42	3
1983–84		12	—
1983–84	*Bournemouth*	19	1
1984–85	Bournemouth	44	1
1985–86		46	5
1986–87		46	5
1987–88		39	4
1988–89		41	—
1989–90		39	—
1990–91		45	2
1991–92		44	1
1992–93		42	—
1993–94		8	—

OGDEN, Neil

Born Billinge 29.11.75   Ht 5 10   Wt 10 04
Defender. From Trainee.

Season	Club	Apps	Goals
1992–93	Wigan Ath	2	—
1993–94		2	—

OGHANI, George

Born Manchester 2.9.60   Ht 5 11   Wt 12 01
Forward. From Hyde.

Season	Club	Apps	Goals
1983–84	Bolton W	3	—
1984–85		41	16
1985–86		36	7
1986–87		19	4
1986–87	*Wrexham*	7	—

Season	Club	Apps	Goals
1987–88	Burnley	37	14
1988–89		37	7
1989–90	Stockport Co	8	2
1989–90	Hereford U	8	2
1989–90	Scarborough	14	4
1990–91		36	14
From Evagoras			
1992–93	Carlisle U	39	15
1993–94		14	—

OGRIZOVIC, Steve

Born Mansfield 12.9.57.   Ht 6 5   Wt 15 00
Goalkeeper. From ONRYC.

Season	Club	Apps	Goals
1977–78	Chesterfield	16	—
1977–78	Liverpool	2	—
1978–79		—	—
1979–80		1	—
1980–81		1	—
1981–82		—	—
1982–83	Shrewsbury T	42	—
1983–84		42	—
1984–85	Coventry C	42	—
1985–86		42	—
1986–87		42	1
1987–88		40	—
1988–89		38	—
1989–90		37	—
1990–91		37	—
1991–92		38	—
1992–93		33	—
1993–94		33	—

O'HANLON, Kelham

Born Saltburn 16.5.62.   Ht 6 1   Wt 13 01
Goalkeeper. From Apprentice. Eire Under-21, 1 full cap.

Season	Club	Apps	Goals
1980–81	Middlesbrough	—	—
1981–82		—	—
1982–83		19	—
1983–84		30	—
1984–85		38	—
1985–86	Rotherham U	46	—
1986–87		40	—
1987–88		40	—
1988–89		46	—
1989–90		43	—
1990–91		33	—
1991–92	Carlisle U	42	—
1992–93		41	—

Season	Club	League Appearances/Goals
1993–94	Preston NE	23 —

O'HARA, Gary
Born Belfast 13.12.73
Defender. From Trainee.

| 1992–93 | Leeds U | — — |
| 1993–94 | | — — |

O'HARA, Steve
Born Lanark 21.2.71. Ht 6 1 Wt 12 02
Defender. From Trainee.

1989–90	Walsall	18 —
1990–91		20 —
1991–92		37 3
1992–93		26 1
1993–94		21 —

OKAI, Stephen
Born Ghana 3.12.73. Ht 5 8 Wt 10 12
Midfield. From Schoolboy.

1991–92	Leyton Orient	1 1
1992–93		13 1
1993–94		11 2

O'KANE, John
Born Nottingham 15.11.74 Ht 5 10
Wt 11 04
Defender. From Trainee.

| 1992–93 | Manchester U | — — |
| 1993–94 | | — — |

OKORIE, Chima
Born Izomber 8.10.68 Ht 5 10 Wt 12 08
Forward.

1993–94	Peterborough U	— —
1993–94	Grimsby T	5 —
1993–94	Torquay U	9 1

OLDFIELD, David
Born Perth, Australia 30.5.68. Ht 5 11
Wt 13 02
Midfield. From Apprentice. England
Under-21.

1986–87	Luton T	— —
1987–88		8 3
1988–89		21 1
1988–89	Manchester C	11 3

1989–90		15 3
1989–90	Leicester C	20 5
1990–91		42 7
1991–92		41 4
1992–93		44 5
1993–94		27 4

O'LEARY, David
Born London 2.5.58. Ht 6 1 Wt 13 09
Defender. From Apprentice. Eire Youth,
67 full caps.

1975–76	Arsenal	27 —
1976–77		33 2
1977–78		41 1
1978–79		37 2
1979–80		34 1
1980–81		24 1
1981–82		40 1
1982–83		36 1
1983–84		36 —
1984–85		36 —
1985–86		35 —
1986–87		39 —
1987–88		23 —
1988–89		26 —
1989–90		34 —
1990–91		21 1
1991–92		25 —
1992–93		11 —
1993–94	Leeds U	10 —

OLIVER, Darren
Born Liverpool 1.11.71 Ht 5 8 Wt 10 05
Defender.

1991–92	Bolton W	— —
1992–93		3 —
1993–94		— —
1993–94	*Peterborough U*	— —
1993–94	Rochdale	19 —

OLIVER, Gavin
Born Felling 6.9.62. Ht 6 0 Wt 12 10
Defender. From Apprentice.

1980–81	Sheffield W	2 —
1981–82		— —
1982–83		2 —
1982–83	*Tranmere R*	17 1
1983–84	Sheffield W	6 —
1984–85		10 —

Season	Club	App	Goals
1985–86	....	—	—
1985–86	*Brighton*	16	—
1985–86	Bradford C	27	1
1986–87	....	40	—
1987–88	....	43	—
1988–89	....	39	1
1989–90	....	22	—
1990–91	....	46	5
1991–92	....	10	—
1992–93	....	40	2
1993–94	....	35	—

OLIVER, Keith

Born South Shields 15.1.76   Ht 5 8
Wt 10 03
Midfield. From Trainee.

| 1993–94 | Hartlepool U .... | 1 | — |

OLIVER, Michael

Born Cleveland 2.8.75   Ht 5 10   Wt 12 04
Midfield. From Trainee.

| 1992–93 | Middlesbrough............. | — | — |
| 1993–94 | .... | — | — |

OLIVER, Neil

Born Berwick 11.4.67.   Ht 5 11   Wt 11 10
Defender. From Coldstream.

1985–86	Berwick R	5	—
1986–87	....	37	—
1987–88	....	12	—
1988–89	....	39	—
1989–90	Blackburn R	3	—
1990–91	....	3	—
1991–92	Falkirk	35	—
1992–93	....	25	—
1993–94	....	32	2

OLNEY, Ian

Born Luton 17.12.69.   Ht 6 1   Wt 11 00
Forward. From Trainee. England
Under-21.

1988–89	Aston Villa.................	15	2
1989–90	....	35	9
1990–91	....	18	3
1991–92	....	20	2
1992–93	Oldham Ath...............	34	12
1993–94	....	10	1

OLSSON, Paul

Born Hull 24.12.65.   Ht 5 8   Wt 10 11
Midfield. From Apprentice.

1983–84	Hull C	—	—
1984–85	....	—	—
1985–86	....	—	—
1986–87	....	—	—
1986–87	*Exeter C*......................	8	—
1987–88	Exeter C....................	35	2
1988–89	Scarborough................	32	4
1989–90	....	16	1
1989–90	Hartlepool U	23	2
1990–91	....	31	1
1991–92	....	46	6
1992–93	....	39	2
1993–94	....	32	2

OMOGBEHIN, Colin

Born Croydon 10.9.74   Ht 6 0
Defender. From Trainee.

| 1993–94 | Fulham .... | — | — |

O'NEIL, Brian

Born Paisley 6.9.72.   Ht 6 1   Wt 12 04
Midfield. From X form. Scotland
Under-21.

1991–92	Celtic......................	28	1
1992–93	....	17	3
1993–94	....	28	2

O'NEIL, John

Born Bellshill 6.7.71.   Ht 5 7   Wt 10 02
Midfield. From Fir Park BC. Scotland
Under-21.

1988–89	Dundee U	1	—
1989–90	....	10	—
1990–91	....	15	—
1991–92	....	12	—
1992–93	....	28	3
1993–94	....	12	1

O'NEILL, Michael

Born Portadown 5.7.69.   Ht 5 11
Wt 10 10
Forward. From Coleraine. Northern
Ireland 23 full caps.

| 1987–88 | Newcastle U................ | 21 | 12 |
| 1988–89 | .... | 27 | 3 |

Season	Club	League Appearances/Goals	
1989–90	Dundee U	18	5
1990–91		13	—
1991–92		8	4
1992–93		25	2
1993–94	Hibernian	36	3

ONUORA, Iffy
Born Glasgow 28.7.67.   Ht 5 10   Wt 11 10
Forward. From British Universities.

1989–90	Huddersfield T	20	3
1990–91		43	7
1991–92		41	8
1992–93		39	6
1993–94		22	6

ONWERE, Udo
Born Hammersmith 9.11.71.   Ht 6 0
Wt 11 07
Midfield. From Trainee.

1990–91	Fulham	7	1
1991–92		27	3
1992–93		29	3
1993–94		22	—

ORD, Richard
Born Easington 3.3.70.   Ht 6 2   Wt 12 08
Defender. From Trainee. England
Under-21.

1987–88	Sunderland	8	—
1988–89		34	1
1989–90		7	1
1989–90	*York C*	3	—
1990–91	Sunderland	14	—
1991–92		6	—
1992–93		24	—
1993–94		28	2

O'REGAN, Kieran
Born Cork 9.11.63.   Ht 5 8   Wt 10 12
Midfield. From Tramore Ath. Eire Youth,
Under-21, 4 full caps.

1982–83	Brighton	1	—
1983–84		31	1
1984–85		15	—
1985–86		15	1
1986–87		24	—
1987–88	Swindon T	26	1
1988–89	Huddersfield T	36	2

1989–90		37	3
1990–91		46	11
1991–92		39	4
1992–93		41	5
1993–94	WBA	25	2

O'RIORDAN, Don
Born Dublin 14.5.57.   Ht 6 0   Wt 12 08
Midfield. From Apprentice. Eire Youth,
Under-21.

1975–76	Derby Co	—	—
1976–77		1	—
1977–78		5	1
1977–78	*Doncaster R*	2	—
From Tulsa			
1978–79	Preston NE	32	—
1979–80		18	—
1980–81		21	—
1981–82		46	4
1982–83		41	4
1983–84	Carlisle U	42	8
1984–85		42	10
1985–86	Middlesbrough	41	2
1986–87	Grimsby T	40	6
1987–88		46	8
1988–89	Notts Co	43	3
1989–90		17	—
1989–90	*Mansfield T*	6	—
1990–91	Notts Co	31	1
1991–92		1	—
1992–93		17	1
1992–93	Torquay U	16	—
1993–94		31	2

ORLYGSSON, Thorvaldur
Born Odense 2.8.66.   Ht 5 11   Wt 10 08
Midfield. From FC Akureyri. Iceland full
caps.

1989–90	Nottingham F	12	1
1990–91		—	—
1991–92		5	—
1992–93		20	1
1993–94	Stoke C	45	9

ORMONDROYD, Ian
Born Bradford 22.9.64.   Ht 6 4   Wt 13 05
Forward. From Thackley.

1985–86	Bradford C	12	3
1986–87		13	4

Season	Club	Apps	Goals
1986–87	*Oldham Ath*	10	1
1987–88	Bradford C	37	9
1988–89		25	4
1988–89	Aston Villa	12	1
1989–90		25	4
1990–91		18	1
1991–92		1	—
1991–92	Derby Co	25	8
1991–92	Leicester C	14	1
1992–93		26	2
1993–94		31	4

OSBORN, Simon

Born New Addington 19.1.72.   Ht 5 10
Wt 11 04
Midfield. From Apprentice.

Season	Club	Apps	Goals
1989–90	Crystal Palace	—	—
1990–91		4	—
1991–92		14	2
1992–93		31	2
1993–94		6	1

O'SHAUGHNESSY, Steve

Born Wrexham 13.10.67.   Ht 6 2
Wt 13 01
Defender. Wales Youth.

Season	Club	Apps	Goals
1984–85	Leeds U	—	—
1985–86		—	—
1985–86	Bradford C	—	—
1986–87		—	—
1987–88		1	—
1988–89	Rochdale	41	6
1989–90		30	8
1990–91		38	2
1991–92	Exeter C	3	—
1991–92	Darlington	15	1
1992–93		41	1
1993–94		32	—

O'SHEA, Danny

Born Kennington 26.3.63.   Ht 6 0
Wt 12 08
Defender. From Apprentice.

Season	Club	Apps	Goals
1980–81	Arsenal	—	—
1981–82		—	—
1982–83		6	—
1983–84		—	—
1983–84	*Charlton Ath*	9	—
1984–85	Exeter C	45	2

Season	Club	Apps	Goals
1985–86	Southend U	35	9
1986–87		41	2
1987–88		22	—
1988–89		20	1
1989–90	Cambridge U	26	—
1990–91		40	—
1991–92		31	1
1992–93		37	—
1993–94		38	—

OSMAN, Russell

Born Repton 14.2.59.   Ht 5 11   Wt 12 01
Defender. From Apprentice. England
Under-21, B, 11 full caps.

Season	Club	Apps	Goals
1975–76	Ipswich	—	—
1976–77		—	—
1977–78		28	—
1978–79		39	2
1979–80		42	2
1980–81		42	1
1981–82		39	2
1982–83		38	4
1983–84		37	3
1984–85		29	3
1985–86	Leicester C	40	—
1986–87		31	3
1987–88		37	5
1988–89	Southampton	36	—
1989–90		35	5
1990–91		20	1
1991–92		5	—
1991–92	Bristol C	31	2
1992–93		34	—
1993–94		5	1

O'SULLIVAN, Wayne

Born Akrotiri 25.2.74.   Ht 5 8   Wt 10 06
Defender. From Trainee.

Season	Club	Apps	Goals
1992–93	Swindon T	—	—
1993–94		—	—

O'TOOLE, Gavin

Born Dublin 19.9.75   Ht 5 9   Wt 11 01
Midfield. From Trainee.

Season	Club	Apps	Goals
1993–94	Coventry C	—	—

O'TOOLE, Pat
Born Dublin 2.1.65.   Ht 5 7   Wt 11 00
Midfield. From Shelbourne.

Season	Club	App	Goals
1989–90	Leicester C	—	—
1990–91		—	—
1990–91	Exeter C	6	—
1990–91	Shrewsbury T	11	—
1991–92		27	—
1992–93		8	1
1993–94	Torquay U	3	—

OTTO, Ricky
Born London 9.11.67.   Ht 5 10   Wt 11 00
Midfield. From Dartford.

Season	Club	App	Goals
1990–91	Leyton Orient	1	—
1991–92		32	5
1992–93		23	8
1993–94	Southend U	45	13

OVERSON, Vince
Born Kettering 15.5.62.   Ht 6 0   Wt 14 10
Defender. From Apprentice.

Season	Club	App	Goals
1979–80	Burnley	22	—
1980–81		39	1
1981–82		36	4
1982–83		6	—
1983–84		38	—
1984–85		42	1
1985–86		28	—
1986–87	Birmingham C	34	1
1987–88		37	—
1988–89		41	—
1989–90		30	—
1990–91		40	2
1991–92	Stoke C	35	3
1992–93		43	1
1993–94		39	2

OWEN, Gareth
Born Chester 21.10.71.   Ht 5 7   Wt 11 10
Midfield. From Trainee. Wales Under-21.

Season	Club	App	Goals
1989–90	Wrexham	13	—
1990–91		27	2
1991–92		36	7
1992–93		41	3
1993–94		27	3

OWEN, Phil
Born Bangor 11.1.75.
Midfield. From Trainee.

Season	Club	App	Goals
1991–92	Manchester C	—	—
1992–93		—	—
1993–94	Stockport C	—	—

OWERS, Gary
Born Newcastle 3.10.68.   Ht 5 10
Wt 11 10
Midfield. From Apprentice.

Season	Club	App	Goals
1986–87	Sunderland	—	—
1987–88		37	4
1988–89		38	3
1989–90		43	9
1990–91		38	1
1991–92		30	4
1992–93		33	1
1993–94		30	2

PAATELAINEN, Mixu
Born Helsinki 3.2.67. Ht 6 0 Wt 13 11
Forward. From Valkeakosken Haka.
Finland full caps.

Season	Club	App	Goals
1987–88	Dundee U	19	9
1988–89		33	10
1989–90		31	7
1990–91		20	1
1991–92		30	6
1991–92	Aberdeen	6	1
1992–93		33	16
1993–94		36	6

PAGE, Don
Born Manchester 18.1.64   Ht 5 10
Wt 11 03
Forward. From Runcorn.

Season	Club	App	Goals
1988–89	Wigan Ath	15	2
1989–90		25	—
1990–91		34	13
1991–92	Rotherham U	31	11
1992–93		24	2
1992–93	*Rochdale*	4	1
1993–94	Rotherham U	—	—
1993–94	Doncaster R	22	4

PAGE, Robert
Born Llwyn 3.9.74 Ht 6 0 Wt 11 08
Defender. From Trainee.

Season	Club	App	Goals
1992–93	Watford	—	—
1993–94		4	—

PAGEAUD, Michel
Born Paris 30.8.66 Ht 6 0 Wt 12 9
Goalkeeper. Valenciennes.

Season	Club	App	Goals
1993–94	Dundee	11	—

PAINTER, Robert
Born Ince 26.1.71. Ht 5 11 Wt 11 00
Midfield. From Trainee.

Season	Club	App	Goals
1987–88	Chester C	2	—
1988–89		8	1
1989–90		32	4
1990–91		42	3
1991–92	Maidstone U	30	5
1991–92	Burnley	9	2
1992–93		17	—
1993–94		—	—

Season	Club	App	Goals
1993–94	Darlington	36	11

PALLISTER, Gary
Born Ramsgate 30.6.65. Ht 6 4 Wt 13 04
Defender. England B, 13 full caps.

Season	Club	App	Goals
1984–85	Middlesbrough	—	—
1985–86		28	—
1985–86	*Darlington*	7	—
1986–87	Middlesbrough	44	1
1987–88		44	3
1988–89		37	1
1989–90		3	—
1989–90	Manchester U	35	3
1990–91		36	—
1991–92		40	1
1992–93		42	1
1993–94		41	1

PALMER, Carlton
Born West Bromwich 5.12.65. Ht 6 2
Wt 12 04
Defender. From Trainee. England B,
Under-21, 18 full caps.

Season	Club	App	Goals
1984–85	WBA	—	—
1985–86		20	—
1986–87		37	1
1987–88		38	3
1988–89		26	—
1988–89	Sheffield W	13	1
1989–90		34	—
1990–91		45	2
1991–92		42	5
1992–93		34	1
1993–94		37	5

PALMER, Charlie
Born Aylesbury 10.7.63. Ht 6 0
Wt 12 03
Defender. From Apprentice.

Season	Club	App	Goals
1981–82	Watford	—	—
1982–83		—	—
1983–84		10	1
1984–85	Derby Co	33	2
1985–86		18	—
1986–87		—	—
1986–87	Hull C	17	—
1987–88		35	—
1988–89		18	1
1988–89	Notts Co	11	—

Season	Club	App	Goals
1989–90		37	5
1990–91		40	1
1991–92		41	—
1992–93		31	—
1993–94		22	1

PALMER, Lee
Born Gillingham 19.9.70 Ht 5 11
Wt 13 00
Defender. From Trainee.

Season	Club	App	Goals
1987–88	Gillingham	1	—
1988–89		—	—
1989–90		39	3
1990–91		21	1
1991–92		11	—
1992–93		10	—
1993–94		28	—

PALMER, Roger
Born Manchester 30.1.59. Ht 5 10
Wt 11 00
Forward. From Apprentice.

Season	Club	App	Goals
1976–77	Manchester C	—	—
1977–78		5	3
1978–79		14	4
1979–80		7	1
1980–81		5	1
1980–81	Oldham Ath	21	6
1981–82		37	7
1982–83		42	15
1983–84		42	13
1984–85		36	9
1985–86		41	15
1986–87		42	16
1987–88		42	17
1988–89		46	15
1989–90		42	16
1990–91		29	9
1991–92		21	3
1992–93		17	—
1993–94		8	—

PALMER, Steve
Born Brighton 31.3.68. Ht 6 1 Wt 12 13
Midfield. From Cambridge University.

Season	Club	App	Goals
1989–90	Ipswich T	5	—
1990–91		23	1
1991–92		23	—
1992–93		7	—

Season	Club	App	Goals
1993–94		36	1

PAPAVASILIOU, Nicos
Born Limassol 31.8.70   Ht 5 8   Wt 10 02
Midfield. From Ofi Crete.

Season	Club	App	Goals
1993–94	Newcastle U	7	—

PAPE, Andy
Born London 22.3.62.   Ht 6 0   Wt 12 00
Goalkeeper. From QPR, Charlton Ath, Enfield.

Season	Club	App	Goals
1991–92	Barnet	36	—
1992–93		—	—
1993–94		4	—

PARDEW, Alan
Born Wimbledon 18.7.61.   Ht 5 10
Wt 11 00
Midfield. From Yeovil.

Season	Club	App	Goals
1986–87	Crystal Palace	—	—
1987–88		20	—
1988–89		45	1
1989–90		36	6
1990–91		19	1
1991–92		8	—
1991–92	Charlton Ath	24	2
1992–93		30	9
1993–94		26	10

PARKER, Garry
Born Oxford 7.9.65.   Ht 5 11   Wt 12 05
Midfield. From Apprentice. England Youth, B, Under-21.

Season	Club	App	Goals
1982–83	Luton T	1	—
1983–84		13	2
1984–85		20	1
1985–86		8	—
1985–86	Hull C	12	—
1986–87		38	—
1987–88		34	8
1987–88	Nottingham F	2	—
1988–89		22	7
1989–90		37	6
1990–91		36	3
1991–92		6	1
1991–92	Aston Villa	25	1
1992–93		37	9
1993–94		19	2

PARKER, Paul

Born Essex 4.4.64.   Ht 5 7   Wt 10 13
Defender. From Apprentice. England
Youth, B, Under-21, 19 full caps.

Season	Club	Apps	Goals
1980–81	Fulham	1	—
1981–82		5	—
1982–83		16	—
1983–84		34	—
1984–85		36	—
1985–86		30	—
1986–87		31	2
1987–88	QPR	40	—
1988–89		36	—
1989–90		32	—
1990–91		17	1
1991–92	Manchester U	26	—
1992–93		31	1
1993–94		40	—

PARKIN, Brian

Born Birkenhead 12.10.65.   Ht 6 1
Wt 12 00
Goalkeeper. From Local.

Season	Club	Apps	Goals
1982–83	Oldham Ath	—	—
1983–84		5	—
1984–85		1	—
1984–85	*Crewe Alex*	12	—
1985–86	Crewe Alex	39	—
1986–87		44	—
1987–88		3	—
1987–88	*Crystal Palace*	—	—
1988–89	Crystal Palace	19	—
1989–90		1	—
1989–90	Bristol R	30	—
1990–91		39	—
1991–92		43	—
1992–93		26	—
1993–94		43	—

PARKIN, Steve

Born Mansfield 7.11.65.   Ht 5 6   Wt 11 07
Defender. From Apprentice. England
Schools, Youth, Under-21.

Season	Club	Apps	Goals
1982–83	Stoke C	2	—
1983–84		1	—
1984–85		13	1
1985–86		12	1
1986–87		38	—
1987–88		43	3
1988–89		4	—
1989–90	WBA	14	1
1990–91		25	1
1991–92		9	—
1992–93	Mansfield T	16	—
1993–94		23	1

PARKINSON, Gary

Born Middlesbrough 10.1.68.   Ht 5 10
Wt 11 06
Defender. From Everton Amateur.

Season	Club	Apps	Goals
1985–86	Middlesbrough	—	—
1986–87		46	—
1987–88		38	—
1988–89		36	2
1989–90		41	2
1990–91		10	1
1991–92		27	—
1992–93		4	—
1992–93	*Southend U*	6	—
1992–93	Bolton W	2	—
1993–94		1	—
1993–94	Burnley	20	1

PARKINSON, Joe

Born Eccles 11.6.71.   Ht 5 11   Wt 12 02
Defender. From Trainee.

Season	Club	Apps	Goals
1988–89	Wigan Ath	12	1
1989–90		33	2
1990–91		25	—
1991–92		36	3
1992–93		13	—
1993–94	Bournemouth	30	1
1993–94	Everton	—	—

PARKINSON, Philip

Born Chorley 1.12.67.   Ht 6 0   Wt 11 06
Midfield. From Apprentice.

Season	Club	Apps	Goals
1985–86	Southampton	—	—
1986–87		—	—
1987–88		—	—
1987–88	Bury	8	1
1988–89		39	—
1989–90		22	2
1990–91		44	2
1991–92		32	—
1992–93	Reading	39	4
1993–94		42	3

PARKINSON, Steve
Born Lincoln 27.8.74   Ht 5 11   Wt 11 11
Midfield. From Trainee.

Season	Club	Apps	Goals
1992–93	Lincoln C	2	—
1993–94		3	—

PARKS, Tony
Born Hackney 26.1.63.   Ht 5 11
Wt 10 08
Goalkeeper. From Apprentice.

Season	Club	Apps	Goals
1980–81	Tottenham H	—	—
1981–82		2	—
1982–83		1	—
1983–84		16	—
1984–85		—	—
1985–86		—	—
1986–87		2	—
1986–87	*Oxford U*	5	—
1987–88	Tottenham H	16	—
1987–88	*Gillingham*	2	—
1988–89	Brentford	33	—
1989–90		37	—
1990–91		1	—
1990–91	*QPR*	—	—
1990–91	Fulham	2	—
1991–92	West Ham U	6	—
1992–93	Stoke C	2	—
1992–93	Falkirk	15	—
1993–94		41	—

PARLOUR, Ray
Born Romford 7.3.73.   Ht 5 10   Wt 11 12
Midfield. From Trainee. England
Under-21.

Season	Club	Apps	Goals
1990–91	Arsenal	—	—
1991–92		6	1
1992–93		21	1
1993–94		27	2

PARRIS, George
Born Ilford 11.9.64.   Ht 5 9   Wt 13 00
Defender. From Apprentice. England
Schools.

Season	Club	Apps	Goals
1982–83	West Ham U	—	—
1983–84		—	—
1984–85		1	—
1985–86		26	1
1986–87		36	2

Season	Club	Apps	Goals
1987–88		30	1
1988–89		27	1
1989–90		38	2
1990–91		44	5
1991–92		21	—
1992–93		16	—
1992–93	Birmingham C	13	—
1993–94		24	—

PARSLEY, Neil
Born Liverpool 25.4.66.   Ht 5 10
Wt 10 11
Defender. From Witton Alb.

Season	Club	Apps	Goals
1988–89	Leeds U	—	—
1989–90		—	—
1989–90	*Chester C*	6	—
1990–91	Huddersfield T	8	—
1990–91	*Doncaster R*	3	—
1991–92	Huddersfield T	5	—
1992–93		44	—
1993–94		—	—
1993–94	WBA	20	—

PARSONS, Mark
Born Luton 24.2.75.
Defender.

Season	Club	Apps	Goals
1991–92	Northampton T	13	—
1992–93		19	—
1993–94		19	—

PARTNER, Andy
Born Colchester 21.10.74   Ht 6 1
Wt 12 10
Defender. From Trainee.

Season	Club	Apps	Goals
1992–93	Colchester U	1	—
1993–94		—	—

PARTRIDGE, Scott
Born Leicester 13.10.74   Ht 5 9   Wt 10 09
Forward. From Trainee.

Season	Club	Apps	Goals
1992–93	Bradford C	4	—
1993–94		1	—
1993–94	Bristol C	9	4

PASCOE, Colin

Born Port Talbot 9.4.65. Ht 5 9
Wt 10 00
Forward. From Apprentice. Wales Youth,
Under-21, 10 full caps.

Season	Club	App	Goals
1982–83	Swansea C	7	1
1983–84		32	2
1984–85		41	9
1985–86		19	3
1986–87		41	11
1987–88		34	13
1987–88	Sunderland	9	4
1988–89		39	10
1989–90		33	1
1990–91		25	5
1991–92		20	2
1992–93		—	—
1992–93	*Swansea C*	15	4
1993–94		33	5

PASKIN, John

Born Capetown 1.2.62. Ht 6 2   Wt 12 05
Forward. From Seiko.

Season	Club	App	Goals
1988–89	WBA	25	5
1989–90	Wolverhampton W	17	2
1990–91		15	1
1991–92		2	—
1991–92	*Stockport Co*	5	1
1991–92	*Birmingham C*	10	3
1991–92	*Shrewsbury T*	1	—
1991–92	Wrexham	17	3
1992–93		19	8
1993–94		15	—

PATERSON, Craig

Born South Queensferry 2.10.59   Ht 6 2
Wt 12 12
Defender. From Bonnyrigg Rose. Scotland
U-21.

Season	Club	App	Goals
1978–79	Hibernian	—	—
1979–80		30	—
1980–81		38	3
1981–82		36	1
1982–83	Rangers	20	—
1983–84		21	1
1984–85		22	2
1985–86		18	1
1986–87		2	—
1986–87	Motherwell	16	—

Season	Club	App	Goals
1987–88		44	2
1988–89		33	1
1989–90		33	3
1990–91		32	2
1991–92	Kilmarnock	28	—
1992–93		21	1
1993–94		6	—

PATERSON, Garry

Born Dunfermline 10.11.69   Ht 6 4
Wt 13 10
Midfield. From Lochore Welfare.

Season	Club	App	Goals
1992–93	Dundee	20	2
1993–94		20	2

PATERSON, Scott

Born Aberdeen 13.5.72   Ht 5 11
Wt 12 00
Midfield. From Cove Rangers.

Season	Club	App	Goals
1991–92	Liverpool	—	—
1992–93		—	—
1993–94		—	—

PATES, Colin

Born Mitcham 10.8.61.   Ht 6 0   Wt 13 00
Defender. From Apprentice. England
Youth.

Season	Club	App	Goals
1979–80	Chelsea	16	—
1980–81		15	—
1981–82		42	1
1982–83		35	4
1983–84		42	—
1984–85		36	1
1985–86		35	1
1986–87		33	2
1987–88		17	—
1988–89		10	1
1988–89	Charlton Ath	21	—
1989–90		17	—
1989–90	Arsenal	2	—
1990–91		1	—
1990–91	*Brighton*	17	—
1991–92	Arsenal	11	—
1992–93		7	—
1993–94	Brighton	34	—

PATMORE, Warren
Born Kingsbury 14.8.71
Midfield.

1992–93	Cambridge U	1	—
1993–94	Millwall	1	—
1993–94	Northampton T	17	2

PATTERSON, Darren
Born Belfast 15.10.69. Ht 6 2 Wt 11 10
Defender. From Trainee. Northern Ireland
2 full caps.

1988–89	WBA	—	—
1989–90	Wigan Ath	29	1
1990–91		28	4
1991–92		40	1
1992–93	Crystal Palace		
1993–94		—	—

PATTERSON, Gary
Born Newcastle 27.11.72. Ht 5 11
Wt 11 05
Midfield. From Trainee.

1991–92	Notts Co	—	—
1992–93		—	—
1993–94	Shrewsbury T	39	1

PATTERSON, Ian
Born Chatham 4.4.73. Ht 6 2 Wt 13 00
Defender. From Trainee.

1991–92	Sunderland	—	—
1992–93		—	—
1993–94	Burnley	1	—
1993–94	Wigan Ath	4	—

PATTERSON, Mark
Born Darwen 24.5.65. Ht 5 6 Wt 10 10
Forward. From Apprentice.

1983–84	Blackburn R	29	7
1984–85		9	—
1985–86		26	10
1986–87		24	1
1987–88		13	2
1988–89	Preston NE	42	15
1989–90		13	4
1989–90	Bury	20	4
1990–91		22	6
1990–91	Bolton W	19	2
1991–92		36	2

| 1992–93 | | 37 | 2 |
| 1993–94 | | 35 | 1 |

PATTERSON, Mark
Born Leeds 13.9.68. Ht 5 10 Wt 11 05
Defender. From Trainee.

1986–87	Carlisle U	6	—
1987–88		16	—
1987–88	Derby Co	—	—
1988–89		1	—
1989–90		9	—
1990–91		11	1
1991–92		12	2
1992–93		18	—
1993–94	Plymouth Arg	41	—

PAUL, Martin
Born Whalley 2.2.75. Ht 5 8 Wt 9 07
Forward. From Trainee.

| 1993–94 | Bristol R | 4 | — |

PAYNE, Derek
Born Edgware 26.4.67. Ht 5 7 Wt 10 01
Midfield. From Kingsbury T, Burnham,
Hayes.

1991–92	Barnet	14	1
1992–93		37	5
1993–94	Southend U	35	—

PAYNE, Grant
Born Woking 25.12.75 Ht 5 9 Wt 11 04
Forward. From Trainee.

| 1992–93 | Wimbledon | — | — |
| 1993–94 | | — | — |

PAYNE, Stephen
Born Pontefract 1.8.75 Ht 5 11 Wt 12 00
Defender. From Trainee.

| 1993–94 | Huddersfield T | — | — |

PAYTON, Andy
Born Burnley 23.10.66. Ht 5 9 Wt 10 06
Midfield. From Apprentice.

1985–86	Hull C	—	—
1986–87		2	—
1987–88		22	2
1988–89		28	4
1989–90		39	17

Season	Club	App	Goals
1990–91	....	43	25
1991–92	....	10	7
1991–92	Middlesbrough............	19	3
1992–93	Celtic..........................	29	13
1993–94	....	7	2
1993–94	Barnsley	25	12

PEACOCK, Darren
Born Bristol 3.2.68.   Ht 6 2   Wt 12 06
Defender. From Apprentice.

Season	Club	App	Goals
1984–85	Newport Co...............	—	—
1985–86	....	18	—
1986–87	....	5	—
1987–88	....	5	—
1988–89	Hereford U	8	—
1989–90	....	36	3
1990–91	....	15	1
1990–91	QPR............................	19	—
1991–92	....	39	1
1992–93	....	38	2
1993–94	....	30	3
1993–94	Newcastle U................	9	—

PEACOCK, Gavin
Born Kent 18.11.67.   Ht 5 8   Wt 11 08
Midfield. England School, Youth. Football
League.

Season	Club	App	Goals
1984–85	QPR............................	—	—
1985–86	....	—	—
1986–87	....	12	1
1987–88	....	5	—
1987–88	Gillingham	26	2
1988–89	....	44	9
1989–90	Bournemouth.............	41	4
1990–91	....	15	4
1990–91	Newcastle U................	27	7
1991–92	....	46	16
1992–93	....	32	12
1993–94	Chelsea.......................	37	8

PEACOCK, Lee
Born Paisley 9.10.76
Forward. From Trainee.

Season	Club	App	Goals
1993–94	Carlisle U...................	1	—

PEACOCK, Richard
Born Sheffield 29.10.72   Ht 5 11
Wt 11 00
Midfield. From Sheffield FC.

Season	Club	App	Goals
1993–94	Hull C.........................	11	1

PEAKE, Andy
Born Market Harborough 1.11.61.
Ht 5 10   Wt 12 00
Midfield. From Apprentice. England
Youth, Under-21.

Season	Club	App	Goals
1978–79	Leicester C.................	18	2
1979–80	....	25	3
1980–81	....	24	1
1981–82	....	31	2
1982–83	....	4	—
1983–84	....	24	4
1984–85	....	21	1
1985–86	Grimsby T	36	4
1986–87	....	3	—
1986–87	Charlton Ath	29	—
1987–88	....	16	—
1988–89	....	31	1
1989–90	....	36	—
1990–91	....	45	4
1991–92	....	20	—
1991–92	Middlesbrough............	23	—
1992–93	....	33	—
1993–94	....	30	1

PEAKE, Jason
Born Leicester 29.9.71.   Ht 5 9   Wt 11 05
Midfield. From Trainee. England Youth.

Season	Club	App	Goals
1989–90	Leicester C.................	—	—
1990–91	....	8	1
1991–92	....	—	—
1991–92	*Hartlepool U*	6	1
1992–93	Halifax T	33	1
1993–94	Rochdale.....................	10	—

PEAKE, Trevor
Born Nuneaton 10.2.57.   Ht 6 0
Wt 12 10
Defender. From Nuneaton Bor.

Season	Club	App	Goals
1979–80	Lincoln C....................	45	1
1980–81	....	43	1
1981–82	....	37	4
1982–83	....	46	1

Season	Club	League Appearances/Goals
1983–84	Coventry C	33 3
1984–85		35 1
1985–86		37 1
1986–87		39 —
1987–88		31 —
1988–89		32 —
1989–90		33 —
1990–91		36 1
1991–92		2 —
1991–92	Luton T	38 —
1992–93		40 —
1993–94		36 —

PEARCE, Andy
Born Bradford 20.4.66. Ht 6 4   Wt 13 00
Defender. From Halesowen.

1990–91	Coventry C	11 1
1991–92		36 2
1992–93		24 1
1993–94	Sheffield W	32 3

PEARCE, Dennis
Born Wolverhampton 10.9.74   Ht 5 9
Wt 11 00
Forward. From Trainee.

1993–94	Aston Villa	— —

PEARCE, Ian
Born Bury St Edmunds 7.5.74.   Ht 6 1
Wt 12 04
Defender. From Schoolboy. England Youth.

1990–91	Chelsea	1 —
1991–92		2 —
1992–93		1 —
1993–94		— —
1993–94	Blackburn R	5 1

PEARCE, Stuart
Born London 24.4.62.   Ht 5 10   Wt 12 09
Defender. From Wealdstone. England Under-21, 56 full caps.

1983–84	Coventry C	23 —
1984–85		28 4
1985–86	Nottingham F	30 1
1986–87		39 6
1987–88		34 5
1988–89		36 6

1989–90		34 5
1990–91		33 11
1991–92		30 5
1992–93		23 2
1993–94		42 6

PEARCEY, Jason
Born Leamington Spa 2.7.71.   Ht 6 1
Wt 13 06
Goalkeeper. From Trainee.

1988–89	Mansfield T	1 —
1989–90		5 —
1990–91		4 —
1991–92		22 —
1992–93		33 —
1993–94		9 —

PEARS, Richard
Born Exeter 16.7.76
Forward. From Trainee.

1993–94	Exeter C	11 1

PEARS, Steve
Born Brandon 22.1.62.   Ht 6 0   Wt 12 11
Goalkeeper. From Apprentice.

1978–79	Manchester U	— —
1979–80		— —
1980–81		— —
1981–82		— —
1982–83		— —
1983–84		— —
1983–84	*Middlesbrough*	12 —
1984–85	Manchester U	4 —
1985–86	Middlesbrough	38 —
1986–87		46 —
1987–88		43 —
1988–89		26 —
1989–90		25 —
1990–91		27 —
1991–92		45 —
1992–93		26 —
1993–94		46 —

PEARSON, John
Born Sheffield 1.9.63.   Ht 6 3   Wt 13 00
Forward. From Apprentice. England Youth.

1980–81	Sheffield W	15 4

Season	Club			
1981–82	....	24	7	
1982–83	....	30	7	
1983–84	....	27	4	
1984–85	....	9	2	
1985–86	Charlton Ath	42	14	
1986–87	....	19	1	
1986–87	Leeds U	18	4	
1987–88	....	28	6	
1988–89	....	33	1	
1989–90	....	7	—	
1990–91	....	13	1	
1990–91	*Rotherham U*...............	11	5	
1991–92	Barnsley	10	1	
1991–92	*Hull C*........................	15	—	
1992–93	Barnsley	22	3	
1993–94	Carlisle U...................	7	—	

PEARSON, Laurie
Born Newcastle 2.7.65   Ht 6 0   Wt 13 00
Midfield. From Gateshead.

Season	Club		
1984–85	Hull C........................	31	—
1985–86	....	20	—
1986–87	....	8	—
1987–88	Bristol C	—	—
1987–88	Port Vale....................	3	—
To Scotland			
1993–94	Darlington	28	4
1993–94	Chesterfield................	1	—

PEARSON, Nigel
Born Nottingham 21.8.63.   Ht 6 1
Wt 14 11
Defender. From Heanor T.

Season	Club		
1981–82	Shrewsbury T..............	—	—
1982–83	....	39	1
1983–84	....	26	—
1984–85	....	—	—
1985–86	....	35	1
1986–87	....	42	3
1987–88	....	11	—
1987–88	Sheffield W.................	19	2
1988–89	....	37	2
1989–90	....	33	1
1990–91	....	39	6
1991–92	....	31	2
1992–93	....	16	1
1993–94	....	5	—

PEDERSEN, Tore
Born Norway 29.9.69
Defender. From Brann. Norway full caps.

Season	Club		
1993–94	Oldham Ath................	10	—

PEEL, Nathan
Born Blackburn 17.5.72.   Ht 6 1
Wt 12 07
Forward. From Trainee.

Season	Club		
1990–91	Preston NE.................	10	1
1991–92	Sheffield U	1	—
1992–93	....	—	—
1992–93	*Halifax T*	3	—
1993–94	Sheffield U	—	—
1993–94	Burnley	13	2

PEER, Dean
Born Dudley 8.8.69.   Ht 6 2   Wt 12 00
Midfield. From Trainee.

Season	Club		
1986–87	Birmingham C	2	—
1987–88	....	—	—
1988–89	....	17	1
1989–90	....	27	3
1990–91	....	40	2
1991–92	....	21	1
1992–93	....	13	1
1992–93	*Mansfield T*.................	10	—
1993–94	Birmingham C	—	—
1993–94	Walsall	33	8

PEJIC, Mel
Born Chesterton 27.4.59.   Ht 5 9
Wt 10 13
Defender. From Local.

Season	Club		
1977–78	Stoke C.......................	—	—
1978–79	....	—	—
1979–80	....	1	—
1980–81	Hereford U	13	—
1981–82	....	27	—
1982–83	....	45	1
1983–84	....	44	—
1984–85	....	46	1
1985–86	....	45	1
1986–87	....	31	—
1987–88	....	44	1
1988–89	....	18	3
1989–90	....	38	5
1990–91	....	46	1

Season	Club		
1991–92	....	15	1
1991–92	Wrexham	7	—
1992–93	....	39	2
1993–94	....	40	—

PEMBERTON, John

Born Oldham 18.11.64. Ht 5 11
Wt 12 03
Defender. From Chadderton.

Season	Club		
1984–85	Rochdale	1	—
1984–85	Crewe Alex	6	—
1985–86	....	41	—
1986–87	....	43	—
1987–88	....	31	1
1987–88	Crystal Palace	2	—
1988–89	....	42	1
1989–90	....	34	1
1990–91	Sheffield U	21	—
1991–92	....	20	—
1992–93	....	19	—
1993–94	....	8	—
1993–94	Leeds U	9	—

PEMBRIDGE, Mark

Born Methyr Tydfil 29.11.70. Ht 5 7
Wt 11 01
Midfield. From Trainee. Wales B, Under-21, 8 full caps.

Season	Club		
1989–90	Luton T	—	—
1990–91	....	18	1
1991–92	....	42	5
1992–93	Derby Co	42	8
1993–94	....	41	11

PENDER, John

Born Luton 19.11.63. Ht 6 0 Wt 12 03
Defender. From Apprentice. Eire Youth, Under-21.

Season	Club		
1981–82	Wolverhampton W	8	—
1982–83	....	39	1
1983–84	....	34	1
1984–85	....	36	1
1985–86	Charlton Ath	38	—
1986–87	....	1	—
1987–88	....	2	—
1987–88	Bristol C	28	2
1988–89	....	45	1
1989–90	....	10	—
1990–91	....	—	—

Season	Club		
1990–91	Burnley	40	—
1991–92	....	39	3
1992–93	....	44	4
1993–94	....	42	1

PENNEY, David

Born Wakefield 17.8.64. Ht 5 8
Wt 10 07
Forward. From Pontefract.

Season	Club		
1985–86	Derby Co	—	—
1986–87	....	1	—
1987–88	....	9	—
1988–89	....	9	—
1989–90	Oxford U	29	2
1990–91	....	9	1
1990–91	*Swansea C*	12	3
1991–92	Oxford U	23	4
1992–93	....	33	6
1993–94	....	16	2
1993–94	*Swansea C*	11	2

PENNOCK, Adrian

Born Ipswich 27.3.71. Ht 5 11 Wt 12 01
Defender. From Trainee.

Season	Club		
1989–90	Norwich C	1	—
1990–91	....	—	—
1991–92	....	—	—
1992–93	Bournemouth	43	1
1993–94	....	40	3

PENNOCK, Tony

Born Swansea 10.4.71. Ht 5 11 Wt 10 09
Goalkeeper. From School.

Season	Club		
1990–91	Stockport Co	—	—
1990–91	*Wigan Ath*	2	—
1991–92	Wigan Ath	—	—
1992–93	....	8	—
1993–94	....	—	—

PENNYFATHER, Glenn

Born Billericay 11.2.63. Ht 5 8 Wt 11 05
Midfield. From Apprentice.

Season	Club		
1980–81	Southend U	1	—
1981–82	....	33	4
1982–83	....	34	1
1983–84	....	33	4
1984–85	....	41	7
1985–86	....	41	7

1986–87	....	38	10
1987–88	....	17	3
1987–88	Crystal Palace.............	19	1
1988–89	....	15	—
1989–90	....	—	—
1989–90	Ipswich T....................	8	1
1990–91	....	—	—
1991–92	....	3	—
1992–93	....	4	—
1992–93	Bristol C	14	1
1993–94	....	12	—

PENRICE, Gary
Born Bristol 23.3.64. Ht 5 8 Wt 10 06
Forward. From Bristol C. Apprentice.

1984–85	Bristol R.....................	5	1
1985–86	....	39	5
1986–87	....	43	7
1987–88	....	46	18
1988–89	....	43	20
1989–90	....	12	3
1989–90	Watford.....................	29	13
1990–91	....	14	5
1990–91	Aston Villa..................	12	—
1991–92	....	8	1
1991–92	QPR.........................	19	3
1992–93	....	15	6
1993–94	....	26	8

PEPPER, Nigel
Born Rotherham 25.4.68. Ht 5 10
Wt 11 05
Midfield. From Apprentice.

1985–86	Rotherham U	7	—
1986–87	....	2	—
1987–88	....	15	—
1988–89	....	2	—
1989–90	....	19	1
1990–91	York C......................	39	3
1991–92	....	35	4
1992–93	....	34	8
1993–94	....	23	—

PERCIVAL, Jason
Born Nuneaton 20.9.73. Ht 5 7
Wt 10 11
Midfield. From Trainee.

| 1991–92 | Stoke C...................... | — | — |
| 1992–93 | .... | — | — |

| 1993–94 | Exeter C...................... | 4 | — |

PERKINS, Chris
Born Nottingham 9.1.74. Ht 5 11
Wt 10 09
Defender. From Trainee.

| 1992–93 | Mansfield T................. | 5 | — |
| 1993–94 | .... | 3 | — |

PERRETT, Darren
Born Cardiff 29.12.69. Ht 5 9 Wt 11 06
Forward. From Cheltenham T.

| 1992–93 | Swansea C.................. | — | — |
| 1993–94 | .... | 11 | 1 |

PERRY, Chris
Born London 26.4.73. Ht 5 9 Wt 11 01
Defender. From Trainee.

1991–92	Wimbledon	—	—
1992–93	....	—	—
1993–94	....	2	—

PERRY, Jason
Born Newport 2.4.70. Ht 5 11 Wt 10 04
Defender. Wales B, Under-21, 1 full cap.

1986–87	Cardiff C....................	1	—
1987–88	....	3	—
1988–89	....	—	—
1989–90	....	36	—
1990–91	....	43	—
1991–92	....	36	—
1992–93	....	39	3
1993–94	....	40	1

PERRY, Mark
Born Aberdeen 7.2.71. Ht 6 1 Wt 11 0
Defender. From Cove R.

1988–89	Dundee U	—	—
1989–90	....	—	—
1990–91	....	—	—
1991–92	....	—	—
1992–93	....	18	1
1993–94	....	9	—

PESCHISOLIDO, Paul
Born Canada 25.5.71. Ht 5 4 Wt 10 05
Forward. From Toronto Blizzard. Canada
full caps.

| 1992–93 | Birmingham C............ | 19 | 7 |

1993–94 .... 24 9

PETERS, Mark
Born St Asaph 6.7.72 Ht 6 0 Wt 11 03
Defender. From Trainee. Wales Under-21.
1991–92	Manchester C	— —
1992–93	Norwich C	— —
1993–94	Peterborough U	19 —

PETERS, Rob
Born Kensington 18.5.71. Ht 5 8
Wt 11 02
Defender. From Trainee.
1989–90	Brentford	2 —
1990–91		6 1
1991–92		9 —
1992–93		1 —
1993–94		12 —

PETHICK, Robbie
Born Tavistock 8.9.70 Ht 5 10 Wt 11 07
Defender. From Weymouth.
| 1993–94 | Portsmouth | 18 — |

PETRIC, Gordan
Born Belgrade 30.7.69 Ht 6 2 Wt 13 9
Defender. Partizan Belgrade. Yugoslavia
full caps.
| 1993–94 | Dundee U | 27 1 |

PETTERSON, Andrew
Born Fremantle 26.9.69 Ht 6 1 Wt 14 10
Goalkeeper.
1988–89	Luton T	— —
1988–89	*Swindon T*	— —
1989–90	Luton T	— —
1990–91		— —
1991–92		— —
1991–92	*Ipswich T*	— —
1992–93	Luton T	14 —
1992–93	*Ipswich T*	1 —
1993–94	Luton T	5 —

PETTINGER, Paul
Born Sheffield 1.10.75
Goalkeeper. From Barnsley.
| 1992–93 | Leeds U | — — |

1993–94 .... — —

PEVERELL, Nick
Born Middlesbrough 28.4.73 Ht 5 11
Wt 11 10
Forward. From Trainee.
1991–92	Middlesbrough	— —
1992–93	Hartlepool U	19 1
1993–94		16 2

PEYTON, Gerry
Born Birmingham 20.5.56. Ht 6 2
Wt 13 09
Goalkeeper. From Atherstone T. Eire
Under-21, 33 full caps.
1975–76	Burnley	20 —
1976–77		10 —
1976–77	Fulham	23 —
1977–78		42 —
1978–79		40 —
1979–80		31 —
1980–81		28 —
1981–82		44 —
1982–83		42 —
1983–84		27 —
1983–84	*Southend U*	10 —
1984–85	Fulham	32 —
1985–86		36 —
1986–87	Bournemouth	46 —
1987–88		42 —
1988–89		39 —
1989–90		39 —
1990–91		36 —
1991–92	Everton	— —
1991–92	*Bolton W*	1 —
1991–92	*Norwich C*	— —
1992–93	Everton	— —
1992–93	*Chelsea*	1 —
1992–93	Brentford	19 —
1993–94	West Ham U	— —

PHELAN, Mike
Born Nelson 24.9.62. Ht 5 11 Wt 11 01
Defender. From Apprentice. England
Youth, 1 full cap.
1980–81	Burnley	16 2
1981–82		23 1
1982–83		42 3
1983–84		44 2

Season	Club	App	Goals
1984–85		43	1
1985–86	Norwich C	42	3
1986–87		40	4
1987–88		37	—
1988–89		37	2
1989–90	Manchester U	38	1
1990–91		33	1
1991–92		18	—
1992–93		11	—
1993–94		2	—

PHELAN, Terry

Born Manchester 16.3.67. Ht 5 8
Wt 10 00
Defender. Eire Youth, B, Under-21,
Under-23, 22 full caps.

Season	Club	App	Goals
1984–85	Leeds U	—	—
1985–86		14	—
1986–87	Swansea C	45	—
1987–88	Wimbledon	30	—
1988–89		29	—
1989–90		34	—
1990–91		29	—
1991–92		37	1
1992–93		—	—
1992–93	Manchester C	37	—
1993–94		30	1

PHILIP, Richard

Born Surrey 20.10.74. Ht 5 11 Wt 11 07
Defender. From Trainee.

Season	Club	App	Goals
1993–94	Luton T	—	—

PHILLIBEN, John

Born Stirling 14.3.64. Ht 5 10 Wt 11 00
Defender. From Gairdoch U. Scotland
Youth.

Season	Club	App	Goals
1980–81	Stirling A	15	—
1981–82		37	1
1982–83		34	—
1983–84		23	—
1983–84	Doncaster R	12	—
1984–85		36	1
1985–86		22	—
1985–86	*Cambridge U*	6	—
1986–87	Doncaster R	1	—
1986–87	Motherwell	37	—
1987–88		35	2
1988–89		19	—

Season	Club	App	Goals
1989–90		24	—
1990–91		11	1
1991–92		32	1
1992–93		31	—
1993–94		28	2

PHILLIPS, David

Born Wegberg 29.7.63. Ht 5 10
Wt 11 02
Midfield. From Apprentice. Wales Under-
21, 52 full caps.

Season	Club	App	Goals
1981–82	Plymouth Arg	8	1
1982–83		23	8
1983–84		42	6
1984–85	Manchester C	42	12
1985–86		39	1
1986–87	Coventry C	39	4
1987–88		35	2
1988–89		26	2
1989–90	Norwich C	38	4
1990–91		38	4
1991–92		34	1
1992–93		42	9
1993–94	Nottingham F	43	4

PHILLIPS, Gary

Born St Albans 20.9.61. Ht 6 0 Wt 14 00
Goalkeeper. England Schools.

Season	Club	App	Goals
1979–80	WBA	—	—
1980–81		—	—
From Barnet			
1884–85	Brentford	21	—
1985–86		43	—
1986–87		44	—
1987–88		35	—
1988–89		—	—
1988–89	Reading	24	—
1989–90		—	—
1989–90	Hereford U	6	—
1990–91	Barnet	—	—
1991–92		6	—
1992–93		42	—
1993–94		42	—

PHILLIPS, Jimmy

Born Bolton 8.2.66. Ht 6 0 Wt 12 00
Defender. From Apprentice.

Season	Club	App	Goals
1983–84	Bolton W	1	—
1984–85		40	1

Season	Club	Apps	Goals
1985–86	....	33	1
1986–87	....	34	—
1986–87	Rangers........................	6	—
1987–88	....	19	—
1988–89	Oxford U	45	5
1989–90	....	34	3
1989–90	Middlesbrough.............	12	—
1990–91	....	44	2
1991–92	....	43	2
1992–93	....	40	2
1993–94	Bolton W	42	—

PHILLIPS, Justin
Born Derby 17.12.71. Ht 6 3 Wt 14 07
Defender. From Trainee. England Youth.

Season	Club	Apps	Goals
1990–91	Derby Co	3	—
1991–92	....	—	—
1992–93	....	—	—
1993–94	....	—	—

PHILLIPS, Les
Born Lambeth 7.1.63. Ht 5 8 Wt 10 06
Midfield. From Apprentice.

Season	Club	Apps	Goals
1980–81	Birmingham C	—	—
1981–82	....	11	1
1982–83	....	13	2
1983–84	....	20	—
1983–84	Oxford U	6	—
1984–85	....	3	—
1985–86	....	28	2
1986–87	....	35	—
1987–88	....	30	4
1988–89	....	26	2
1989–90	....	8	—
1990–91	....	25	1
1991–92	....	7	—
1992–93	....	11	—
1993–94	Northampton T	26	—

PHILLIPS, Marcus
Born Bradford on Avon 17.10.73
Ht 5 11 Wt 11 07
Midfield. From Trainee.

Season	Club	Apps	Goals
1992–93	Swindon T	—	—
1993–94	....	—	—

PHILLIPS, Martin
Born Exeter 13.3.76
Forward. From Trainee.

Season	Club	Apps	Goals
1992–93	Exeter C......................	6	—
1993–94	....	9	—

PHILLIPS, Wayne
Born Bangor 15.12.70. Ht 5 10 Wt 11 00
Midfield. From Trainee.

Season	Club	Apps	Goals
1989–90	Wrexham	5	—
1990–91	....	28	—
1991–92	....	30	3
1992–93	....	15	—
1993–94	....	21	1

PHILLISKIRK, Tony
Born Sunderland 10.2.65. Ht 6 1
Wt 12 02
Forward. From Amateur. England
Schools.

Season	Club	Apps	Goals
1983–84	Sheffield U	21	8
1984–85	....	23	2
1985–86	....	4	—
1986–87	....	6	1
1986–87	*Rotherham U*..............	6	1
1987–88	Sheffield U	26	9
1988–89	Oldham Ath.................	10	1
1988–89	Preston NE	14	6
1989–90	Bolton W	45	18
1990–91	....	43	19
1991–92	....	43	12
1992–93	....	10	2
1992–93	Peterborough U	32	11
1993–94	....	11	4
1993–94	Burnley	19	7

PHILPOTT, Lee
Born Barnet 21.2.70. Ht 5 9 Wt 12 00
Forward. From Trainee.

Season	Club	Apps	Goals
1987–88	Peterborough U	1	—
1988–89	....	3	—
1989–90	Cambridge U	42	5
1990–91	....	45	5
1991–92	....	31	2
1992–93	....	16	2
1992–93	Leicester C.................	27	3
1993–94	....	19	—

PICK, Gary

Born Leicester 9.7.71 Ht 5 8 Wt 11 08
Midfield. From Leicester U.

Season	Club	App	Goals
1992–93	Stoke C	—	—
1993–94		—	—

PICKARD, Owen

Born Barnstaple 18.11.69. Ht 5 10
Wt 11 03
Forward. From Trainee.

Season	Club	App	Goals
1988–89	Plymouth Arg	2	—
1989–90		5	—
1990–91		7	1
1991–92		2	—
1992–93	Hereford U	37	9
1993–94		36	5

PICKERING, Ally

Born Manchester 22.6.67. Ht 5 11
Wt 11 01
Defender. From Buxton.

Season	Club	App	Goals
1989–90	Rotherham U	10	—
1990–91		1	—
1991–92		27	—
1992–93		38	1
1993–94		12	1
1993–94	Coventry C	4	—

PICKERING, Chris

Born Stockport 18.12.74 Ht 5 11
Wt 11 08
Defender. From Trainee.

Season	Club	App	Goals
1993–94	Southampton	—	—

PICKERING, Nick

Born Newcastle 4.8.63. Ht 6 0 Wt 11 10
Midfield. From Apprentice. England
Youth, Under-21, 1 full cap.

Season	Club	App	Goals
1981–82	Sunderland	37	3
1982–83		39	7
1983–84		42	1
1984–85		37	2
1985–86		24	5
1985–86	Coventry C	15	4
1986–87		36	5
1987–88		27	—
1988–89	Derby Co	8	—
1989–90		23	3

Season	Club	App	Goals
1990–91		13	—
1991–92		1	—
1991–92	Darlington	29	5
1992–93		28	2
1992–93	Burnley	4	—
1993–94		—	—

PIEARCE, Stephen

Born Sutton Coldfield 29.9.74 Ht 5 11
Wt 10 10
Forward. From Trainee.

Season	Club	App	Goals
1993–94	Wolverhampton W	—	—

PIECHNIK, Torben

Born Copenhagen 21.5.63 Ht 6 0
Wt 12 04
Defender. From Copenhagen. Denmark
full caps.

Season	Club	App	Goals
1992–93	Liverpool	16	—
1993–94		1	—

PIKE, Chris

Born Cardiff 19.10.61. Ht 6 2 Wt 13 07
Forward. From Barry T.

Season	Club	App	Goals
1984–85	Fulham	—	—
1985–86		26	4
1986–87		13	—
1986–87	*Cardiff C*	6	2
1987–88	Fulham	3	—
1988–89		—	—
1989–90	Cardiff C	41	18
1990–91		39	14
1991–92		40	21
1992–93		28	12
1993–94	Hereford U	34	18

PIKE, Martin

Born South Shields 21.10.64. Ht 5 11
Wt 11 07
Defender. From Apprentice.

Season	Club	App	Goals
1982–83	WBA	—	—
1983–84	Peterborough U	35	2
1984–85		45	4
1985–86		46	2
1986–87	Sheffield U	42	—
1987–88		39	—
1988–89		45	5
1989–90		3	—

Season	Club	App	Goals
1989–90	*Tranmere R*	2	—
1989–90	*Bolton W*	5	1
1989–90	Fulham	20	2
1990–91		46	3
1991–92		45	2
1992–93		46	6
1993–94		33	1

PILKINGTON, Kevin

Born Hitchin 5.3.74. Ht 6 0 Wt 12 00
Goalkeeper. From Trainee.

Season	Club	App	Goals
1992–93	Manchester U	—	—
1993–94		—	—

PIRIE, David

Born Glasgow 15.4.75. Ht 5 9 Wt 11 05
Forward. From Trainee.

Season	Club	App	Goals
1993–94	Ipswich T	—	—

PITCHER, Darren

Born London 12.10.69. Ht 5 9 Wt 12 02
Defender. From Trainee.

Season	Club	App	Goals
1987–88	Charlton Ath	—	—
1988–89		—	—
1988–89	*Galway*	—	—
1989–90	Charlton Ath	—	—
1990–91		44	3
1991–92		46	2
1992–93		41	2
1993–94		42	1

PITCHER, Geoffrey

Born Sutton 15.8.75
Midfield. From Trainee.

Season	Club	App	Goals
1992–93	Millwall	—	—
1993–94		—	—

PITTMAN, Stephen

Born N Carolina 18.7.67 Ht 5 10 Wt 12 5
Defender. From Broxburn J.

Season	Club	App	Goals
1986–87	East Fife	11	—
1987–88		31	2
1988–89		25	8
1988–89	Shrewsbury T	12	—
1989–90		20	2
1990–91		—	
1991–92		—	

Season	Club	App	Goals
1992–93	Dundee	20	1
1993–94		36	3

PLATNAUER, Nicky

Born Leicester 10.6.61. Ht 5 11 Wt 12 10
Defender. From Northampton T Amateur and Bedford T.

Season	Club	App	Goals
1982–83	Bristol R	24	7
1983–84	Coventry C	34	6
1984–85		10	—
1984–85	Birmingham C	11	1
1985–86		17	1
1985–86	*Reading*	7	—
1986–87	Cardiff C	38	3
1987–88		38	1
1988–89		39	2
1989–90	Notts Co	44	—
1990–91		13	1
1990–91	*Port Vale*	14	—
1991–92	Leicester C	29	—
1992–93		6	—
1992–93	Scunthorpe U	14	2
1993–94	Mansfield T	25	—
1993–94	Lincoln C	13	—

PLATT, David

Born Chadderton 10.6.66. Ht 5 10 Wt 11 12
Forward. From Chadderton. England B, Under-21, 48 full caps.

Season	Club	App	Goals
1984–85	Manchester U	—	—
1984–85	Crewe Alex	22	5
1985–86		43	8
1986–87		43	23
1987–88		26	19
1987–88	Aston Villa	11	5
1988–89		38	7
1989–90		37	19
1990–91		35	19
1991–92	Bari	29	11
1992–93	Juventus	16	3
1993–94	Sampdoria	29	9

POINTON, Neil

Born Church Warsop 28.11.64. Ht 5 10 Wt 11 00
Defender. From Apprentice.

Season	Club	App	Goals
1981–82	Scunthorpe U	5	—

280

Season	Club	League Appearances/Goals	
1982–83	....	46	1
1983–84	....	45	1
1984–85	....	46	—
1985–86	....	17	—
1985–86	Everton	15	—
1986–87	....	12	1
1987–88	....	33	3
1988–89	....	23	—
1989–90	....	19	1
1990–91	Manchester C	35	1
1991–92	....	39	1
1992–93	Oldham Ath	34	3
1993–94	....	24	—

POLLITT, Michael
Born Bolton 29.2.72. Ht 6 4 Wt 14 00
Goalkeeper. From Trainee.

Season	Club		
1990–91	Manchester U	—	—
1990–91	*Oldham Ath*	—	—
1991–92	Bury	—	—
1992–93	Lincoln C	27	—
1993–94	....	30	—

POLLOCK, Jamie
Born Stockton 16.2.74. Ht 6 0 Wt 11 12
Midfield. From Trainee. England Youth.

Season	Club		
1990–91	Middlesbrough	1	—
1991–92	....	26	1
1992–93	....	22	1
1993–94	....	34	9

POLSTON, John
Born London 10.6.68. Ht 5 11 Wt 11 03
Defender. From Apprentice. England Youth.

Season	Club		
1985–86	Tottenham H	—	—
1986–87	....	6	—
1987–88	....	2	—
1988–89	....	3	—
1989–90	....	13	1
1990–91	Norwich C	27	4
1991–92	....	19	1
1992–93	....	34	1
1993–94	....	24	—

POOLE, Gary
Born Stratford 11.9.67. Ht 6 0 Wt 11 00
Defender. From Arsenal Schoolboys.

Season	Club		
1984–85	Tottenham H	—	—

Season	Club		
1985–86	....	—	—
1986–87	....	—	—
1987–88	Cambridge U	42	—
1988–89	....	1	—
Barnet			
1991–92	Barnet	40	2
1992–93	Plymouth Arg	39	5
1993–94	Southend U	38	2

POOLE, Kevin
Born Bromsgrove 21.7.63. Ht 5 10 Wt 12 06
Goalkeeper. From Apprentice.

Season	Club		
1981–82	Aston Villa	—	—
1982–83	....	—	—
1983–84	....	—	—
1984–85	....	7	—
1984–85	*Northampton T*	3	—
1985–86	Aston Villa	11	—
1986–87	....	10	—
1987–88	Middlesbrough	1	—
1988–89	....	12	—
1989–90	....	21	—
1990–91	....	—	—
1990–91	*Hartlepool U*	12	—
1991–92	Leicester C	42	—
1992–93	....	19	—
1993–94	....	14	—

PORIC, Adem
Born London 22.4.73. Ht 5 9 Wt 11 13
Midfield. From St George's Budapest.

Season	Club		
1993–94	Sheffield W	6	—

PORTEOUS, Ian
Born Glasgow 21.11.64. Ht 5 7 Wt 10 6
Midfield. From Eastercraigs. Scotland Youth.

Season	Club		
1981–82	Aberdeen	—	—
1982–83	....	1	—
1983–84	....	14	3
1984–85	....	13	1
1985–86	....	6	—
1986–87	....	9	2
1987–88	....	3	1
1988–89	....	—	—
1988–89	*Swansea C*	—	—
From Herfolge FC, Denmark			
1990–91	Kilmarnock	—	—

Season	Club	App	Goals
1991–92		24	1
1992–93		20	6
1993–94		13	1

PORTER, Andy

Born Manchester 17.9.68.   Ht 5 9
Wt 11 02
Midfield. From Trainee.

Season	Club	App	Goals
1986–87	Port Vale	1	—
1987–88		6	—
1988–89		14	1
1989–90		36	1
1990–91		40	—
1991–92		32	1
1992–93		17	1
1993–94		37	—

PORTER, Gary

Born Sunderland 6.3.66.   Ht 5 6
Wt 10 06
Midfield. From Apprentice. England
Youth, Under-21.

Season	Club	App	Goals
1983–84	Watford	2	—
1984–85		9	—
1985–86		8	1
1986–87		26	4
1987–88		40	3
1988–89		42	10
1989–90		32	4
1990–91		45	4
1991–92		44	8
1992–93		33	—
1993–94		43	9

POTTER, Brian

Born Dunfermline 26.1.77   Ht 5 10
Wt 11 4
Goalkeeper. Rosyth Recreation.

Season	Club	App	Goals
1993–94	Raith R	1	—

POTTER, Graham

Born Solihull 20.5.75
Defender. From Trainee.

Season	Club	App	Goals
1992–93	Birmingham C	18	2
1993–94		7	—
1993–94	*Wycombe W*	3	—
1993–94	Stoke C	3	—

POTTS, Steven

Born Hartford (USA) 7.5.67.   Ht 5 7
Wt 10 11
Defender. From Apprentice. England
Youth.

Season	Club	App	Goals
1984–85	West Ham U	1	—
1985–86		1	—
1986–87		8	—
1987–88		8	—
1988–89		28	—
1989–90		32	—
1990–91		37	1
1991–92		34	—
1992–93		46	—
1993–94		41	—

POUNDER, Tony

Born Yeovil 11.3.66.   Ht 5 8   Wt 11 00
Forward. From Westland Sports and
Weymouth.

Season	Club	App	Goals
1990–91	Bristol R	45	3
1991–92		40	4
1992–93		18	1
1993–94		10	2

POWELL, Chris

Born Lambeth 8.9.69.   Ht 5 8   Wt 11 03
Defender.

Season	Club	App	Goals
1987–88	Crystal Palace	—	—
1988–89		3	—
1989–90		—	—
1989–90	*Aldershot*	11	—
1990–91	Southend U	45	1
1991–92		44	—
1992–93		42	2
1993–94		46	—

POWELL, Darryl

Born Lambeth 15.1.71.   Ht 6 0   Wt 12 03
Forward. From Trainee.

Season	Club	App	Goals
1988–89	Portsmouth	3	—
1989–90		—	—
1990–91		8	—
1991–92		36	6
1992–93		23	—
1993–94		28	5

POWELL, Gary
Born Holylake 2.4.69. Ht 5 10   Wt 10 02
Forward. From Trainee.

Season	Club	Apps	Goals
1987–88	Everton	—	—
1988–89		—	—
1989–90		—	—
1990–91		—	—
1990–91	*Lincoln C*	11	—
1990–91	*Scunthorpe U*	4	1
1990–91	*Wigan Ath*	14	4
1991–92	Wigan Ath	34	7
1992–93		36	6
1993–94	Bury	5	—

POWELL, Lee
Born Newport 2.6.73. Ht 5 5   Wt 9 00
Forward. From Trainee. Wales Under-21.

Season	Club	Apps	Goals
1990–91	Southampton	—	—
1991–92		4	—
1992–93		2	—
1993–94		1	—

POWELL, Mark
Born Ellesmere Port 8.5.75   Ht 5 9
Wt 10 08
Defender. From Trainee.

Season	Club	Apps	Goals
1993–94	Everton	—	—

POWELL, Stephen
Born Derby 14.12.76
Midfield. From Trainee.

Season	Club	Apps	Goals
1993–94	Derby Co	—	—

POWER, Lee
Born Lewisham 30.6.72. Ht 5 11
Wt 11 02
Forward. From Trainee. Eire Youth,
Under-21, B.

Season	Club	Apps	Goals
1989–90	Norwich C	1	—
1990–91		16	3
1991–92		4	1
1992–93		18	6
1992–93	*Charlton Ath*	5	—
1993–94	Norwich C	5	—
1993–94	*Sunderland*	3	—
1993–94	*Portsmouth*	2	—
1993–94	Bradford C	3	2

PRATT, David
Born London 17.12.74   Ht 5 8   Wt 11 00
Forward.

Season	Club	Apps	Goals
1993–94	West Ham U	—	—

PREDDY, Phil
Born Hereford 20.11.75
Defender. From Trainee.

Season	Club	Apps	Goals
1993–94	Hereford U	13	—

PREECE, Andy
Born Evesham 27.3.67. Ht 6 1   Wt 12 00
Midfield.

Season	Club	Apps	Goals
1988–89	Northampton T	1	—
From Worcester C.			
1989–90	Wrexham	7	1
1990–91		34	4
1991–92		10	2
1991–92	Stockport Co	25	13
1992–93		29	8
1993–94		43	21

PREECE, David
Born Bridgnorth 28.5.63. Ht 5 6
Wt 11 05
Midfield. From Apprentice. England B.

Season	Club	Apps	Goals
1980–81	Walsall	8	—
1981–82		8	—
1982–83		42	2
1983–84		41	3
1984–85		12	—
1984–85	Luton T	21	2
1985–86		41	2
1986–87		14	—
1987–88		13	—
1988–89		26	—
1989–90		32	1
1990–91		37	1
1991–92		38	3
1992–93		43	3
1993–94		29	5

PREECE, Roger
Born Much Wenlock 9.6.69. Ht 5 9
Wt 10 12
Midfield. From Coventry C Apprentice.

Season	Club	Apps	Goals
1986–87	Wrexham	7	2
1987–88		40	4

1988–89		31	5
1989–90		32	1
1990–91	Chester C	35	—
1991–92		29	—
1992–93		23	—
1993–94		39	2

PRESSLEY, Steven

Born Elgin 11.10.73.   Ht 6 0   Wt 11 00
Defender. From Inverkeithling BC.
Scotland Under-21.

1991–92	Rangers	1	—
1992–93		8	—
1993–94		23	1

PRESSMAN, Kevin

Born Fareham 6.11.67.   Ht 6 1   Wt 14 02
Goalkeeper. From Apprentice. England
Schools, Youth, Under-21.

1985–86	Sheffield W	—	—
1986–87		—	—
1987–88		11	—
1988–89		9	—
1989–90		15	—
1990–91		23	—
1991–92		1	—
1991–92	Stoke C	4	—
1992–93	Sheffield W	3	—
1993–94		32	—

PRESTON, Allan

Born Edinburgh 16.8.68.   Ht 5 10
Wt 10 01
Midfield. From Hutchison Vale BC.

1985–86	Dundee U	—	—
1986–87		—	—
1987–88		2	—
1988–89		9	1
1989–90		8	—
1990–91		3	—
1991–92		2	—
1991–92		2	—
1992–93	Hearts	21	2
1993–94	St Johnstone	9	—

PRESTON, Richard

Born Basildon 7.5.76   Ht 5 11   Wt 11 02
Defender. From Trainee.

1993–94	Northampton T	1	—

PRICE, Chris

Born Hereford 30.3.60.   Ht 5 7   Wt 10 02
Defender. From Apprentice. England
Youth.

1976–77	Hereford U	2	—
1977–78		13	—
1978–79		29	—
1979–80		42	—
1980–81		42	2
1981–82		41	10
1982–83		42	5
1983–84		37	1
1984–85		41	5
1985–86		41	4
1986–87	Blackburn R	40	1
1987–88		43	10
1988–89	Aston Villa	36	—
1989–90		34	1
1990–91		38	1
1991–92		2	—
1991–92	Blackburn R	13	3
1992–93		6	—
1992–93	Portsmouth	13	—
1993–94		5	—

PRIEST, Chris

Born Leigh 18.10.73   Ht 5 9   Wt 10 10
Midfield. From Trainee.

1992–93	Everton	—	—
1993–94		—	—

PRIMUS, Linvoy

Born Stratford 14.9.73   Ht 5 10   Wt 12 04
Defender. From Trainee.

1992–93	Charlton Ath	4	—
1993–94		—	—

PRINDIVILLE, Steve

Born Harlow 26.12.68.   Ht 5 9   Wt 11 07
Defender. From Apprentice.

1986–87	Leicester C	—	—
1987–88		1	—
1988–89	Chesterfield	43	1
1989–90	Mansfield T	22	—
1990–91		6	—
1991–92	Doncaster R	16	—
1992–93		42	2
1993–94		1	—

1993–94 Wycombe W .... — —

PRINS, Jason
Born Wisbech 1.11.74.
Midfield.

1991–92	Carlisle U..................	4 —
1992–93	....	9 —
1993–94	....	5 —

PRIOR, Spencer
Born Rochford 22.4.71. Ht 6 1 Wt 12 09
Defender. From Trainee.

1988–89	Southend U................	14	1
1989–90	....	15	1
1990–91	....	19	—
1991–92	....	42	1
1992–93	....	45	—
1993–94	Norwich C	13	—

PRITCHARD, David
Born Wolverhampton 27.5.72 Ht 5 7
Wt 11 04
Defender. From Telford.

1993–94	Bristol R	11	—

PROCTOR, Mark
Born Middlesbrough 30.1.61. Ht 5 10
Wt 11 13
Midfield. From Apprentice. England
Youth, Under-21.

1978–79	Middlesbrough............	33	9
1979–80	....	38	2
1980–81	....	38	1
1981–82	Nottingham F.............	37	1
1982–83	....	27	4
1982–83	*Sunderland*..................	5	—
1983–84	Sunderland.................	41	2
1984–85	....	17	2
1985–86	....	19	7
1986–87	....	31	8
1987–88	....	4	—
1987–88	Sheffield W.................	35	2
1988–89	....	24	2
1988–89	Middlesbrough............	10	—
1989–90	....	45	4
1990–91	....	18	—
1991–92	....	36	2
1992–93	....	11	—

1992–93	*Tranmere R*..................	13	1
1993–94	Tranmere R	18	—

PRUDHOE, Mark
Born Washington 8.11.63. Ht 6 0
Wt 13 00
Goalkeeper. From Apprentice.

1981–82	Sunderland.................	—	—
1982–83	....	7	—
1983–84	....	—	—
1983–84	*Hartlepool U*	3	—
1984–85	Sunderland	—	—
1984–85	Birmingham C	1	—
1985–86	Walsall	16	—
1986–87	....	10	—
1986–87	*Doncaster R*	5	—
1986–87	*Sheffield W*	—	—
1986–87	*Grimsby T*...................	8	—
1987–88	Walsall	—	—
1987–88	*Hartlepool U*	13	—
1987–88	*Bristol C*.....................	3	—
1987–88	Carlisle U....................	22	—
1988–89	....	12	—
1988–89	Darlington	12	—
1989–90	....	*34*	—
1990–91	....	46	—
1991–92	....	46	—
1992–93	....	42	—
1993–94	Stoke C.......................	30	—

PUGH, David
Born Liverpool 19.9.64. Ht 5 10
Wt 11 02
Midfield. From Runcorn.

1989–90	Chester C....................	35	3
1990–91	....	37	3
1991–92	....	35	—
1992–93	....	35	5
1993–94	....	37	12

PUGH, Stephen
Born Bangor 27.11.73 Ht 5 10 Wt 11 00
Forward. From Trainee. Wales Under-21.

1992–93	Wrexham	3	—
1993–94	....	7	—

PURSE, Darren
Born London 14.2.77
Defender. From Trainee.

Season	Club		
1993–94	Leyton Orient	5	—

PUTNEY, Trevor
Born Harold Hill 11.2.61.   Ht 5 9
Wt 11 08
Midfield. From Brentwood & W.

Season	Club		
1980–81	Ipswich T	—	—
1981–82		—	—
1982–83		20	3
1983–84		35	2
1984–85		27	2
1985–86		21	1
1986–87	Norwich C	23	4
1987–88		26	1
1988–89		33	4
1989–90	Middlesbrough	25	—
1990–91		23	1
1991–92	Watford	28	2
1992–93		24	—
1993–94	Leyton Orient	22	2

PUTTNAM, David
Born Leicester 3.2.67.   Ht 5 10   Wt 11 09
Midfield. From Leicester U.

Season	Club		
1988–89	Leicester C	3	—
1989–90		4	—
1989–90	Lincoln C	23	1
1990–91		43	6
1991–92		39	6
1992–93		37	2
1993–94		13	1

QUIGLEY, Jim
Born Derry 21.9.76   Ht 5 8   Wt 11 02
Midfield. From Trainee.

Season	Club		
1993–94	Everton	—	—

QUIGLEY, Mike
Born Manchester 2.10.70.   Ht 5 6
Wt 9 04
Midfield. From Trainee.

Season	Club		
1990–91	Manchester C	—	—
1991–92		5	—
1992–93		5	—
1993–94		2	—

QUINN, James
Born Coventry 15.12.74
Forward. From Trainee.

Season	Club		
1992–93	Birmingham C	4	—
1993–94	Blackpool	14	2
1993–94	*Stockport Co*	1	—

QUINN, Jimmy
Born Belfast 18.11.59.   Ht 6 0   Wt 12 07
Forward. From Oswestry T. Northern
Ireland 41 full caps.

Season	Club		
1981–82	Swindon T	4	—
1982–83		13	3
1983–84		32	7
1984–85	Blackburn R	25	10
1985–86		31	4
1986–87		15	3
1986–87	Swindon T	22	9
1987–88		42	21
1988–89	Leicester C	31	6
1988–89	Bradford C	12	8
1989–90		23	6
1989–90	West Ham U	21	12
1990–91		26	6
1991–92	Bournemouth	43	19
1992–93	Reading	42	17
1993–94		46	35

QUINN, Mick
Born Liverpool 2.5.62.   Ht 5 9   Wt 13 00
Forward. From Derby Co Apprentice.

Season	Club		
1979–80	Wigan Ath	4	1
1980–81		36	14
1981–82		29	4

Season	Club	Apps	Goals
1982–83	Stockport Co	39	24
1983–84		24	15
1983–84	Oldham Ath	14	5
1984–85		40	18
1985–86		26	11
1985–86	Portsmouth	11	6
1986–87		39	22
1987–88		32	8
1988–89		39	18
1989–90	Newcastle U	45	32
1990–91		43	18
1991–92		22	7
1992–93		5	2
1992–93	Coventry C	26	17
1993–94		32	8

QUINN, Niall

Born Dublin 6.10.66.   Ht 6 3   Wt 13 10
Forward. From Eire Youth, B, Under-21,
Under-23, 42 full caps.

Season	Club	Apps	Goals
1983–84	Arsenal	—	—
1984–85		—	—
1985–86		12	1
1986–87		35	8
1987–88		11	2
1988–89		3	1
1989–90		6	2
1989–90	Manchester C	9	4
1990–91		38	20
1991–92		35	12
1992–93		39	9
1993–94		15	5

RADOSAVLJEVIC, Predrag

Born Belgrade 24.6.63   Ht 5 11   Wt 12 10
Forward. From St Louis Storms.

Season	Club	Apps	Goals
1992–93	Everton	23	3
1993–94		23	1

RAE, Alex

Born Glasgow 30.9.69.   Ht 5 9   Wt 11 05
Midfield. From Bishopbriggs. Scotland
Under-21.

Season	Club	Apps	Goals
1987–88	Falkirk	12	—
1988–89		37	12
1989–90		34	8
1990–91	Millwall	39	10
1991–92		38	11
1992–93		30	6
1993–94		36	13

RAMAGE, Andrew

Born Hornchurch 3.10.74   Ht 5 11
Wt 12 02
Midfield. From Millwall, Dagenham &
Redbridge.

Season	Club	Apps	Goals
1993–94	Gillingham	—	—

RAMAGE, Craig

Born Derby 30.3.70.   Ht 5 9   Wt 11 08
Forward. From Trainee. England
Under-21.

Season	Club	Apps	Goals
1988–89	Derby Co	—	—
1988–89	*Wigan Ath*	10	2
1989–90	Derby Co	12	1
1990–91		17	1
1991–92		7	2
1992–93		1	—
1993–94		5	—
1993–94	Watford	13	—

RAMMELL, Andy

Born Nuneaton 10.2.67.   Ht 5 10
Wt 11 07
Forward. From Atherstone U.

Season	Club	Apps	Goals
1989–90	Manchester U	—	—
1990–91	Barnsley	40	12
1991–92		37	8
1992–93		30	7

Season	Club	Appearances	Goals
1993–94	....	34	6

RAMSEY, Paul

Born Londonderry 3.9.62. Ht 5 11
Wt 13 00
Defender. From Apprentice. Northern
Ireland 14 full caps.

Season	Club	Appearances	Goals
1979–80	Leicester C..................	—	—
1980–81	....	3	—
1981–82	....	10	—
1982–83	....	40	1
1983–84	....	33	1
1984–85	....	39	—
1985–86	....	13	1
1986–87	....	29	6
1987–88	....	42	1
1988–89	....	22	—
1989–90	....	35	3
1990–91	....	24	—
1991–92	Cardiff C....................	39	3
1992–93	....	30	4
1993–94	St Johnstone..............	22	—

RANDALL, Adrian

Born Amesbury 10.11.68. Ht 5 11
Wt 10 11
Forward. From Apprentice. England
Youth.

Season	Club	Appearances	Goals
1985–86	Bournemouth..............	2	—
1986–87	....	—	—
1987–88	....	1	—
1988–89	....	—	—
1988–89	Aldershot	37	2
1989–90	....	34	2
1990–91	....	36	8
1991–92	....	9	—
1991–92	Burnley	18	2
1992–93	....	23	1
1993–94	....	37	4

RANKINE, Mark

Born Doncaster 30.9.69. Ht 5 10
Wt 11 01
Midfield. From Trainee.

Season	Club	Appearances	Goals
1987–88	Doncaster R................	18	2
1988–89	....	46	11
1989–90	....	36	2
1990–91	....	40	2
1991–92	....	24	3

Season	Club	Appearances	Goals
1991–92	Wolverhampton W.....	15	1
1992–93	....	27	—
1993–94	....	31	—

RANSON, Ray

Born St. Helens 12.6.60. Ht 5 9
Wt 11 12
Defender. From Apprentice. England
Schools, Youth, Under-21.

Season	Club	Appearances	Goals
1978–79	Manchester C.............	8	—
1979–80	....	40	—
1980–81	....	33	1
1981–82	....	36	—
1982–83	....	40	—
1983–84	....	26	—
1984–85	....	—	—
1984–85	Birmingham C.............	28	—
1985–86	....	37	—
1986–87	....	17	—
1987–88	....	38	—
1988–89	....	17	—
1988–89	Newcastle U................	14	1
1989–90	....	33	—
1990–91	....	27	—
1991–92	....	6	—
1992–93	....	3	—
1992–93	Manchester C.............	17	—
1993–94	Reading......................	24	—

RATCLIFFE, Kevin

Born Mancot 12.11.60. Ht 5 11
Wt 12 07
Defender. From Apprentice. Wales
Schools, Youth, Under-21, 59 caps.

Season	Club	Appearances	Goals
1978–79	Everton	—	—
1979–80	....	2	—
1980–81	....	21	—
1981–82	....	25	—
1982–83	....	29	1
1983–84	....	38	—
1984–85	....	40	—
1985–86	....	39	1
1986–87	....	42	—
1987–88	....	24	—
1988–89	....	30	—
1989–90	....	24	—
1990–91	....	36	—
1991–92	....	9	—
1992–93	Dundee........................	4	—

1992–93	Everton	—	—
1992–93	Cardiff C	19	1
1993–94		6	—
1993–94	Nottingham F	—	—
1993–94	Derby Co	6	—

RATCLIFFE, Simon

Born Davyhulme 8.2.67. Ht 5 11
Wt 11 09
Defender. From Apprentice. England
Schools, Youth.

1984–85	Manchester U	—	—
1985–86		—	—
1986–87		—	—
1987–88	Norwich C	9	—
1988–89		—	—
1988–89	Brentford	9	1
1989–90		35	2
1990–91		38	2
1991–92		34	2
1992–93		30	2
1993–94		43	4

RAVEN, Paul

Born Salisbury 28.7.70. Ht 6 0 Wt 12 03
Defender. From School. England Schools,
Youth.

1987–88	Doncaster R	17	3
1988–89		35	1
1988–89	WBA	3	—
1989–90		7	—
1990–91		13	—
1991–92		7	1
1991–92	Doncaster R	7	—
1992–93	WBA	44	7
1993–94		34	1

RAVENSCROFT, Craig

Born London 20.12.74 Ht 5 6 Wt 9 07
Forward. From Trainee.

| 1993–94 | Brentford | 7 | 1 |

RAWLINSON, Mark

Born Bolton 9.6.75 Ht 5 8 Wt 11 11
Midfield. From Trainee.

| 1993–94 | Manchester U | — | — |

RAYNOR, Paul

Born Nottingham 29.4.66. Ht 6 0
Wt 11 04
Forward. From Apprentice.

1983–84	Nottingham F	—	—
1984–85		3	—
1984–85	Bristol R	8	—
1985–86	Huddersfield T	30	5
1986–87		20	4
1986–87	Swansea C	12	1
1987–88		44	8
1988–89		26	5
1988–89	Wrexham	6	—
1989–90	Swansea C	40	6
1990–91		43	5
1991–92		26	2
1991–92	Cambridge U	8	—
1992–93		41	2
1993–94	Preston NE	39	6

READ, Paul

Born Harlow 25.9.73. Ht 5 11 Wt 12 06
Forward. From Trainee.

1991–92	Arsenal	—	—
1992–93		—	—
1993–94		—	—

READY, Karl

Born Neath 14.8.72. Ht 6 1 Wt 12 00
Defender. Wales Under-21.

1990–91	QPR	—	—
1991–92		1	—
1992–93		3	—
1993–94		22	1

REDDISH, Shane

Born Bolsover 5.5.71. Ht 5 10 Wt 11 10
Midfield. From Mansfield T Trainee and
Doncaster R Trainee.

1989–90	Doncaster R	1	—
1990–91		11	—
1991–92		17	2
1992–93		31	1
1993–94	Carlisle U	35	1

REDFEARN, Neil

Born Dewsbury 20.6.65.   Ht 5 10
Wt 12 09
Midfield. From Nottingham F Apprentice.

Season	Club	Apps	Goals
1982–83	Bolton W	10	—
1983–84		25	1
1983–84	*Lincoln C*	10	1
1984–85	Lincoln C	45	4
1985–86		45	8
1986–87	Doncaster R	46	14
1987–88	Crystal Palace	42	8
1988–89		15	2
1988–89	Watford	12	2
1989–90		12	1
1989–90	Oldham Ath	17	2
1990–91		45	14
1991–92	Barnsley	36	4
1992–93		46	3
1993–94		46	12

REDKNAPP, Jamie

Born Barton on Sea 25.6.73.   Ht 6 0
Wt 12 00
Midfield. From Tottenham H Schoolboy,
Bournemouth Trainee. England Youth,
Under-21.

Season	Club	Apps	Goals
1989–90	Bournemouth	4	—
1990–91		9	—
1990–91	Liverpool	—	—
1991–92		6	1
1992–93		29	2
1993–94		35	4

REDMOND, Steven

Born Liverpool 2.11.67.   Ht 5 11
Wt 12 13
Defender. From Apprentice. England
Youth, Under-21.

Season	Club	Apps	Goals
1984–85	Manchester C	—	—
1985–86		9	—
1986–87		30	2
1987–88		44	—
1988–89		46	1
1989–90		38	—
1990–91		37	3
1991–92		31	1
1992–93	Oldham Ath	31	—
1993–94		33	1

REDWOOD, Toby

Born Newton Abbot 7.10.73.   Ht 5 11
Wt 11 08
Defender. From Trainee.

Season	Club	Apps	Goals
1991–92	Exeter C	1	—
1992–93		6	—
1993–94		13	—

REECE, Andy

Born Shrewsbury 5.9.62.   Ht 5 11
Wt 12 04
Midfield. From Walsall, Worcester C,
Willenhall.

Season	Club	Apps	Goals
1987–88	Bristol R	40	1
1988–89		42	7
1989–90		43	2
1990–91		46	1
1991–92		42	4
1992–93		26	2
1992–93	*Walsall*	9	1
1993–94	Bristol R	—	—
1993–94	*Walsall*	6	—
1993–94	Hereford U	28	1

REECE, Paul

Born Nottingham 16.7.68.   Ht 5 11
Wt 12 07
Goalkeeper. From Kettering T.

Season	Club	Apps	Goals
1988–89	Grimsby T	14	—
1989–90		15	—
1990–91		—	—
1991–92		25	—
1992–93	Doncaster R	1	—
1992–93	Oxford U	35	—
1993–94		4	—

REED, Adam

Born Bishop Auckland 18.2.75.   Ht 6 0
Wt 12 00
Defender. From Trainee.

Season	Club	Apps	Goals
1991–92	Darlington	1	—
1992–93		—	—
1993–94		13	—

REED, John

Born Rotherham 27.8.72.   Ht 5 10
Wt 10 11
Forward. From Trainee.

Season	Club	Apps	Goals
1990–91	Sheffield U	—	—

Season	Club	League Appearances/Goals	
1990–91	*Scarborough*	14	6
1991–92	Sheffield U	1	—
1991–92	*Scarborough*	6	—
1992–93	Sheffield U	—	—
1992–93	*Darlington*	10	2
1993–94	Sheffield U	—	—
1993–94	*Mansfield T*	13	2

REES, Jason

Born Pontypridd 22.12.69. Ht 5 5
Wt 9 10
Midfield. From Trainee. Wales Schools,
Youth, B, Under-21, 1 full cap.

Season	Club	League Appearances/Goals	
1988–89	Luton T	—	—
1989–90		14	—
1990–91		21	—
1991–92		5	—
1992–93		32	—
1993–94		10	—
1993–94	*Mansfield T*	15	1

REES, Tony

Born Merthyr Tydfil 1.8.64. Ht 5 9
Wt 11 13
Forward. From Apprentice. Wales Youth,
Under-21, 1 full cap.

Season	Club	League Appearances/Goals	
1982–83	Aston Villa	—	—
1983–84	Birmingham C	25	2
1984–85		9	2
1985–86		8	—
1985–86	*Peterborough U*	5	2
1985–86	*Shrewsbury T*	2	—
1986–87	Birmingham C	30	4
1987–88		23	4
1987–88	Barnsley	14	2
1988–89		17	1
1989–90	Grimsby T	35	13
1990–91		36	10
1991–92		23	5
1992–93		31	5
1993–94		16	—

REEVES, Alan

Born Birkenhead 19.11.67. Ht 6 0
Wt 12 00
Defender.

Season	Club	League Appearances/Goals	
1988–89	Norwich C	—	—
1988–89	*Gillingham*	18	—
1989–90	Chester C	30	2
1990–91		10	—
1991–92	Rochdale	34	3
1992–93		41	3
1993–94		41	3

REEVES, David

Born Birkenhead 19.11.67. Ht 6 0
Wt 11 05
Forward. From Heswall.

Season	Club	League Appearances/Goals	
1986–87	Sheffield W	—	—
1986–87	*Scunthorpe U*	4	2
1987–88	Sheffield W	—	—
1987–88	*Scunthorpe U*	6	4
1987–88	*Burnley*	16	8
1988–89	Sheffield W	17	2
1989–90	Bolton W	41	10
1990–91		44	10
1991–92		35	8
1992–93		14	1
1992–93	Notts Co	9	2
1993–94		4	—
1993–94	Carlisle U	34	11

REEVES, Steve

Born Dagenham 24.9.74 Ht 6 0
Wt 11 09
Goalkeeper. From Trainee.

Season	Club	League Appearances/Goals	
1993–94	Everton	—	—

REGIS, Cyrille

Born French Guyana 9.2.58. Ht 6 0
Wt 13 04
Forward. From Moseley, Hayes. England
Under-21, B, 5 full caps.

Season	Club	League Appearances/Goals	
1977–78	WBA	34	10
1978–79		39	13
1979–80		26	8
1980–81		38	14
1981–82		37	17
1982–83		26	9
1983–84		30	10
1984–85		7	1
1984–85	Coventry C	31	5
1985–86		34	5
1986–87		40	12
1987–88		31	10
1988–89		34	7
1989–90		34	4
1990–91		34	4

Season	Club	App	Goals
1991–92	Aston Villa	39	11
1992–93		13	1
1993–94	Wolverhampton W	19	2

REGIS, Dave
Born Paddington 3.3.64. Ht 6 1
Wt 13 08
Forward. From Barnet.

Season	Club	App	Goals
1990–91	Notts Co	37	15
1991–92		9	—
1991–92	Plymouth Arg	24	2
1992–93		7	2
1992–93	*Bournemouth*	6	2
1992–93	Stoke C	25	5
1993–94		38	10

REID, Andrew
Born Manchester 4.7.62. Ht 6 0 Wt 13 01
Midfield. From Altrincham.

Season	Club	App	Goals
1992–93	Bury	29	—
1993–94		4	1

REID, Nicky
Born Ormston 30.10.60. Ht 5 10
Wt 12 00
Defender. From Apprentice. England
Under-21.

Season	Club	App	Goals
1978–79	Manchester C	8	—
1979–80		23	—
1980–81		37	—
1981–82		36	—
1982–83		25	—
1983–84		19	2
1984–85		32	—
1985–86		30	—
1986–87		7	—
1987–88	Blackburn R	44	1
1988–89		37	1
1989–90		42	4
1990–91		30	2
1991–92		21	1
1992–93		—	—
1992–93	*Bristol C*	4	—
1992–93	WBA	15	—
1993–94		5	—
1993–94	Wycombe W	5	—

REID, Paul
Born Warley 19.1.68. Ht 5 8 Wt 10 08
Forward. From Apprentice.

Season	Club	App	Goals
1985–86	Leicester C	—	—
1986–87		6	—
1987–88		26	5
1988–89		45	6
1989–90		40	8
1990–91		33	2
1991–92		12	—
1991–92	*Bradford C*	7	—
1992–93	Bradford C	44	6
1993–94		38	9

REID, Peter
Born Huyton 20.6.56. Ht 5 8 Wt 10 07
Midfield. From Apprentice. England
Under-21, 13 full caps.

Season	Club	App	Goals
1974–75	Bolton W	27	—
1975–76		42	2
1976–77		42	5
1977–78		38	9
1978–79		14	—
1979–80		17	3
1980–81		18	2
1981–82		12	1
1982–83		15	1
1982–83	Everton	7	—
1983–84		35	2
1984–85		36	2
1985–86		15	1
1986–87		16	1
1987–88		32	1
1988–89		18	1
1988–89	QPR	14	1
1989–90		15	—
1989–90	Manchester C	18	1
1990–91		30	—
1991–92		31	—
1992–93		20	—
1993–94		4	—
1993–94	Southampton	7	—
1993–94	Notts Co	5	—

REID, Shaun
Born Huyton 13.10.65. Ht 5 8 Wt 11 10
Midfield. From Local.

Season	Club	App	Goals
1983–84	Rochdale	17	—
1984–85		21	1

1985–86	....	8	—
1985–86	*Preston NE*	3	—
1986–87	Rochdale.....................	41	1
1987–88	....	28	—
1988–89	....	18	2
1988–89	York C........................	24	2
1989–90	....	25	4
1990–91	....	29	—
1991–92	....	28	1
1992–93	Rochdale.....................	40	4
1993–94	....	39	3

REILLY, Mark

Born Bellshill 30.3.69   Ht 5 8   Wt 10 0
Defender. From Wishaw J.

1988–89	Motherwell.................	—	—
1989–90	....	4	—
1990–91	....	—	—
1991–92	Kilmarnock.................	19	—
1992–93	....	19	3
1993–94	....	38	—

REINELT, Robert

Born Epping 11.3.74.   Ht 5 10   Wt 11 13
Forward. From Trainee.

1990–91	Aldershot	5	—
1991–92	....	*11*	—
1992–93	Gillingham..................	—	—
1993–94	....	25	1

RENNIE, David

Born Edinburgh 29.8.64.   Ht 6 0
Wt 12 00
Defender. From Apprentice. Scotland Youth.

1982–83	Leicester C.................	—	—
1983–84	....	15	—
1984–85	....	3	1
1985–86	....	3	—
1985–86	Leeds U	16	2
1986–87	....	24	—
1987–88	....	28	2
1988–89	....	33	1
1989–90	Bristol C.....................	45	4
1990–91	....	32	2
1991–92	....	27	2
1991–92	Birmingham C.............	17	2
1992–93	....	18	2
1992–93	Coventry C..................	9	—

1993–94	....	34	1

RENNIE, Paul

Born Nantwich 26.10.71.   Ht 5 9
Wt 11 04
Defender. From Trainee.

1989–90	Crewe Alex	2	—
1990–91	Stoke C.......................	3	—
1991–92	....	1	—
1992–93	....	—	—
1993–94	Wigan Ath..................	26	2

RETALLICK, Graham

Born Cambridge 8.2.70   Ht 5 10
Wt 11 13
Midfield. From Histon.

1992–93	Peterborough U..........	5	—
1993–94	....	—	—

RHODES, Andy

Born Doncaster 23.8.64.   Ht 6 1
Wt 13 06
Goalkeeper. From Apprentice.

1982–83	Barnsley	—	—
1983–84	....	31	—
1984–85	....	5	—
1985–86	....	—	—
1985–86	Doncaster R................	30	—
1986–87	....	41	—
1987–88	....	35	—
1987–88	Oldham Ath................	11	—
1988–89	....	27	—
1989–90	....	31	—
1990–91	Dunfermline Ath	35	—
1991–92	....	44	—
1992–93	St Johnstone	44	—
1993–94	....	44	—

RICE, Brian

Born Glasgow 11.10.63.   Ht 6 0   Wt 12 04
Midfield. From Whitburn Central.
Scotland Youth, Under-21.

1980–81	Hibernian...................	1	—
1981–82	....	1	—
1982–83	....	22	2
1983–84	....	25	5
1984–85	....	35	4
1985–86	Nottingham F.............	19	3

Season	Club	Apps	Goals
1986–87		3	1
1986–87	*Grimsby T*	4	—
1987–88		30	2
1988–89		20	1
1988–89	*WBA*	3	—
1989–90	Nottingham F	18	2
1990–91		1	
1990–91	*Stoke C*	18	—
1991–92	Falkirk	16	1
1992–93		17	2
1993–94		37	3

RICHARDS, Dean

Born Bradford 9.6.74. Ht 6 0 Wt 12 00
Defender. From Trainee.

Season	Club	Apps	Goals
1991–92	Bradford C	7	1
1992–93		3	—
1993–94		46	2

RICHARDS, Jonathan

Born Southend 3.10.74
Forward. From Trainee.

Season	Club	Apps	Goals
1993–94	Fulham	—	—

RICHARDSON, Barry

Born Willington Key 5.8.69. Ht 6 0
Wt 12 00
Goalkeeper. From Trainee.

Season	Club	Apps	Goals
1987–88	Sunderland	—	—
1988–89	Scunthorpe U	—	—
1989–90	Scarborough	24	—
1990–91		6	—
1991–92	Northampton T	27	—
1992–93		42	—
1993–94		27	—

RICHARDSON, John

Born Durham 28.7.66
Forward. From Chesham U.

Season	Club	Apps	Goals
1993–94	Colchester U	8	—

RICHARDSON, Jon

Born Nottingham 29.8.75
Midfield.

Season	Club	Apps	Goals
1993–94	Exeter C	7	—

RICHARDSON, Kevin

Born Newcastle 4.12.62. Ht 5 7
Wt 11 07
Midfield. From Apprentice. England 1 full
cap.

Season	Club	Apps	Goals
1980–81	Everton	—	—
1981–82		18	2
1982–83		29	3
1983–84		28	4
1984–85		15	4
1985–86		18	3
1986–87		1	—
1986–87	Watford	39	2
1987–88	Arsenal	29	4
1988–89		34	1
1989–90		33	—
From Real Sociedad			
1991–92	Aston Villa	42	6
1992–93		42	2
1993–94		40	5

RICHARDSON, Lee

Born Halifax 12.3.69. Ht 5 11 Wt 11 00
Midfield.

Season	Club	Apps	Goals
1986–87	Halifax T	1	—
1987–88		30	1
1988–89		25	1
1988–89	Watford	9	—
1989–90		32	1
1990–91	Blackburn R	38	2
1991–92		24	1
1992–93		—	—
1992–93	Aberdeen	29	2
1993–94		35	4

RICHARDSON, Neil

Born Sunderland 3.3.68. Ht 5 11
Wt 13 02
Defender. From Brandon U.

Season	Club	Apps	Goals
1989–90	Rotherham U	2	—
1990–91		16	2
1991–92		18	2
1992–93		14	—
1993–94		27	—

RICHARDSON, Nick

Born Halifax 11.4.67. Ht 6 0 Wt 12 07
Midfield. From Local.

Season	Club	Apps	Goals
1988–89	Halifax T	7	—

Season	Club	League Appearances/Goals	

1989–90		27	6
1990–91		26	3
1991–92		41	8
1992–93	Cardiff C	39	4
1993–94		39	5

RIDEOUT, Paul

Born Bournemouth 14.8.64.   Ht 5 11
Wt 12 01
Forward. From Apprentice. England
Schools, Youth, Under-21.

1980–81	Swindon T	16	4
1981–82		35	14
1982–83		44	20
1983–84	Aston Villa	25	5
1984–85		29	14
1985–86	Bari	28	6
1986–87		34	10
1987–88		37	7
1988–89	Southampton	24	6
1989–90		31	7
1990–91		16	6
1990–91	*Swindon T*	9	1
1991–92	Southampton	4	—
1991–92	Notts Co	11	3
1991–92	Rangers	11	1
1992–93		1	—
1992–93	Everton	24	3
1993–94		24	6

RIDGERS, Scott

Born Colchester 9.9.74
Midfield. From Trainee.

| 1993–94 | Colchester U | — | — |

RIDINGS, David

Born Farnworth 27.2.70   Ht 6 0
Wt 12 00
Midfield. From Cutzon Ashton.

| 1992–93 | Halifax T | 21 | 4 |
| 1993–94 | Lincoln C | 10 | — |

RIGBY, Tony

Born Ormskirk 10.8.72   Ht 5 10
Wt 12 01
Midfield. From Barrow.

| 1992–93 | Bury | 21 | 2 |

| 1993–94 | | 33 | 7 |

RILEY, Steven

Born Manchester 6.2.75   Ht 5 9   Wt 10 09
Defender. From Trainee.

| 1993–94 | Manchester U | — | — |

RIMMER, Neill

Born Liverpool 13.11.67.   Ht 5 6
Wt 10 03
Midfield. From Apprentice. England
Schools, Youth.

1984–85	Everton	1	—
1985–86	Ipswich T	2	—
1986–87		1	—
1987–88		19	3
1988–89	Wigan Ath	25	3
1989–90		38	1
1990–91		34	2
1991–92		9	—
1992–93		1	—
1993–94		20	—

RIMMER, Stuart

Born Southport 12.10.64.   Ht 5 8
Wt 11 00
Forward. From Apprentice. England
Youth.

1981–82	Everton	2	—
1982–83		—	—
1983–84		1	—
1984–85		—	—
1984–85	Chester C	24	14
1985–86		18	16
1986–87		38	13
1987–88		34	24
1987–88	Watford	9	1
1988–89		1	—
1988–89	Notts Co	4	2
1988–89	Walsall	20	8
1989–90		41	10
1990–91		27	13
1990–91	Barnsley	15	1
1991–92	Chester C	44	13
1992–93		43	20
1993–94		35	8

RIOCH, Greg
Born Sutton Coldfield 24.6.75   Ht 5 11
Wt 10 09
Defender. From Trainee.

Season	Club		
1993–94	Luton T	—	—
1993–94	*Barnet*	3	—

RIPLEY, Andrew
Born Middlesbrough 10.12.75   Ht 5 8
Wt 11 10
Midfield. From Trainee.

Season	Club		
1993–94	Darlington	2	—

RIPLEY, Stuart
Born Middlesbrough 20.11.67.   Ht 5 11
Wt 12 06
Forward. From Apprentice. England
Youth, Under-21, 1 full cap.

Season	Club		
1984–85	Middlesbrough	1	—
1985–86		8	—
1985–86	*Bolton W*	5	1
1986–87	Middlesbrough	44	4
1987–88		43	8
1988–89		36	4
1989–90		39	1
1990–91		39	6
1991–92		39	3
1992–93	Blackburn R	40	7
1993–94		40	4

RISTIC, Dragutin
Born Pula, Yugoslavia 5.8.64   Ht 6 0
Wt 12 7
Forward. Benevento Sporting.

Season	Club		
1993–94	Dundee	18	6
1993–94	Falkirk	12	4

RITCHIE, Andy
Born Manchester 28.11.60.   Ht 5 10
Wt 11 11
Forward. From Apprentice. England
Schools, Youth, Under-21.

Season	Club		
1977–78	Manchester U	4	—
1978–79		17	10
1979–80		8	3
1980–81		4	—
1980–81	Brighton	26	5
1981–82		39	13

Season	Club		
1982–83		24	5
1982–83	Leeds U	10	3
1983–84		38	7
1984–85		28	12
1985–86		29	11
1986–87		31	7
1987–88	Oldham Ath	36	19
1988–89		31	14
1989–90		38	15
1990–91		31	15
1991–92		14	3
1992–93		12	3
1993–94		22	1

RITCHIE, Paul
Born St Andrews 25.1.69.   Ht 5 11
Wt 12 00
Forward. From Kirkcaldy YMCA.

Season	Club		
1986–87	Dundee	—	—
1987–88		—	—
1987–88	*Brechin C*	8	3
1988–89	Dundee	—	—
1988–89	*Brechin C*	18	7
1989–90	Brechin C	38	9
1990–91		38	14
1991–92		24	12
1991–92	Dundee	6	1
1992–93		19	3
1992–93	*Gillingham*	6	3
1993–94	Dundee	17	2

ROBERTS, Andy
Born Dartford 20.3.74.   Ht 5 10
Wt 13 00
Midfield. From Trainee.

Season	Club		
1991–92	Millwall	7	—
1992–93		45	—
1993–94		42	2

ROBERTS, Ben
Born Bishop Auckland 22.6.75   Ht 6 0
Wt 12 06
Goalkeeper.

Season	Club		
1992–93	Middlesbrough	—	—
1993–94		—	—

ROBERTS, Darren

Born Birmingham 12.10.69 Ht 6 0
Wt 12 10
Forward. From Burton Alb.

Season	Club	App	Goals
1991–92	Wolverhampton W	—	—
1992–93		21	5
1993–94		—	—
1993–94	*Hereford U*	6	5

ROBERTS, Glyn

Born Ipswich 19.10.74 Ht 5 11 Wt 12 02
Midfield. From Norwich C trainee.

Season	Club	App	Goals
1993–94	Rotherham U	14	1

ROBERTS, Iwan

Born Bangor 26.6.68. Ht 6 3 Wt 12 06
Forward. Wales Youth, 5 full caps.

Season	Club	App	Goals
1985–86	Watford	4	—
1986–87		3	1
1987–88		25	2
1988–89		22	6
1989–90		9	—
1990–91	Huddersfield T	44	13
1991–92		46	24
1992–93		37	9
1993–94		15	4
1993–94	Leicester C	26	13

ROBERTS, Joe

Born Crewe 12.9.74 Ht 5 8 Wt 10 10
Forward. From Trainee.

Season	Club	App	Goals
1993–94	Manchester U	—	—

ROBERTS, Mark

Born Irvine 29.10.75 Ht 5 9 Wt 9 10
Forward. From Bellfield BC.

Season	Club	App	Goals
1991–92	Kilmarnock	1	—
1992–93		5	—
1993–94		13	2

ROBERTS, Paul

Born London 27.4.62 Ht 5 9 Wt 11 13
Defender. From Apprentice.

Season	Club	App	Goals
1978–79	Millwall	2	—
1979–80		27	—
1980–81		45	—
1981–82		41	—
1982–83		31	—
1983–84		—	—
1983–84	Brentford	34	—
1984–85		28	—
1985–86	Swindon T	27	—
1986–87	Southend U	38	—
1987–88	Aldershot	39	—
1988–89	Exeter C	3	—
1988–89	Southend U	23	—
1989–90		31	—

From Fisher Ath

Season	Club	App	Goals
1991–92	Colchester U	*31*	*1*
1992–93		42	1
1993–94		21	—

ROBERTS, Tony

Born Bangor 4.8.69. Ht 6 0 Wt 12 00
Goalkeeper. From Trainee. Wales Under-21, 1 full cap.

Season	Club	App	Goals
1987–88	QPR	1	—
1988–89		—	—
1989–90		5	—
1990–91		12	—
1991–92		1	—
1992–93		28	—
1993–94		16	—

ROBERTSON, David

Born Aberdeen 17.10.68. Ht 5 11
Wt 11 00
Defender. From Deeside BC. Scotland
Under-21, 3 full caps.

Season	Club	App	Goals
1986–87	Aberdeen	34	—
1987–88		23	—
1988–89		23	—
1989–90		20	1
1990–91		35	1
1991–92	Rangers	42	1
1992–93		39	3
1993–94		32	1

ROBERTSON, Hugh

Born Aberdeen 19.3.75 Ht 5 9 Wt 12 7
Defender. Lewis United. Scotland
Under-21.

Season	Club	App	Goals
1993–94	Aberdeen	8	—

ROBERTSON, John

Born Edinburgh 2.10.64.   Ht 5 7
Wt 11 06
Forward. From Edina Hibs. Scotland B,
Under-21, 11 full caps.

Season	Club	App	Goals
1980–81	Hearts	—	—
1981–82		1	—
1982–83		23	19
1983–84		35	15
1984–85		33	8
1985–86		35	20
1986–87		37	16
1987–88		39	26
1987–88	Newcastle U	—	—
1988–89		12	—
1988–89	Hearts	15	4
1989–90		32	17
1990–91		31	12
1991–92		42	14
1992–93		42	11
1993–94		36	10

ROBERTSON, John

Born Liverpool 8.1.74.   Ht 6 2   Wt 13 02
Defender. From Trainee.

Season	Club	App	Goals
1992–93	Wigan Ath	24	1
1993–94		34	1

ROBERTSON, Sandy

Born Edinburgh 26.4.71.   Ht 5 9
Wt 10 07
Midfield. From S Form. Scotland
Under-21.

Season	Club	App	Goals
1987–88	Rangers	—	—
1988–89		2	—
1989–90		1	—
1990–91		15	1
1991–92		6	—
1992–93		2	—
1993–94		—	—
1993–94	Coventry C	3	—

ROBINS, Mark

Born Ashton-under-Lyme. 22.12.69.
Ht 5 7   Wt 10 04
Forward. From Apprentice. England
Under-21.

Season	Club	App	Goals
1986–87	Manchester U	—	—
1987–88		—	—
1988–89		10	—
1989–90		17	7
1990–91		19	4
1991–92		2	—
1992–93	Norwich C	37	15
1993–94		13	1

ROBINSON, Anthony

Born Sunderland 5.10.73
Defender. From Trainee.

Season	Club	App	Goals
1992–93	Sunderland	—	—
1993–94		—	—

ROBINSON, David

Born Newcastle 27.11.69.   Ht 6 0
Wt 13 02
Forward. From Trainee.

Season	Club	App	Goals
1988–89	Newcastle U	1	—
1989–90		1	—
1990–91		3	—
1990–91	*Peterborough U*	7	3
1991–92	Newcastle U	3	—
1991–92	Reading	8	—
1992–93	Blackpool	14	2
1993–94		12	2

ROBINSON, David

Born Cleveland 14.1.65.   Ht 6 0   Wt 13 00
Defender.

Season	Club	App	Goals
1983–84	Hartlepool U	7	—
1984–85		38	—
1985–86		21	1
1986–87	Halifax T	10	—
1987–88		32	—
1988–89		30	1
1989–90	Peterborough U	45	4
1990–91		6	2
1991–92		43	3
1992–93		1	—
1992–93	Notts Co	1	—
1993–94		2	1

ROBINSON, Jamie

Born Liverpool 26.2.72   Ht 6 0   Wt 12 03
Defender. From Trainee.

Season	Club	App	Goals
1991–92	Liverpool	—	—
1992–93	Barnsley	8	—

| 1993–94 | .... | 1 | — |
| 1993–94 | Carlisle U.................. | 16 | 1 |

ROBINSON, John

Born Bulawayo, Rhodesia 29.8.71.
Ht 5 10 Wt 11 05
Midfield. From Apprentice. Wales
Under-21.

1989–90	Brighton....................	5	—
1990–91	....	15	—
1991–92	....	36	6
1992–93	....	6	—
1992–93	Charlton Ath	15	2
1993–94	....	27	1

ROBINSON, Les

Born Mansfield 1.3.67. Ht 5 8 Wt 11 01
Defender. From Local.

1984–85	Mansfield T................	6	—
1985–86	....	7	—
1986–87	....	2	—
1986–87	Stockport Co	30	1
1987–88	....	37	2
1987–88	Doncaster R................	7	1
1988–89	....	43	3
1989–90	....	32	8
1989–90	Oxford U	1	—
1990–91	....	43	—
1991–92	....	27	—
1992–93	....	16	—
1993–94	....	36	2

ROBINSON, Liam

Born Bradford 29.12.65. Ht 5 7
Wt 11 05
Forward. From Nottingham F Schoolboy.

1983–84	Huddersfield T............	5	1
1984–85	....	15	1
1985–86	....	1	—
1985–86	*Tranmere R*................	4	3
1986–87	Bury........................	33	13
1987–88	....	43	19
1988–89	....	43	20
1989–90	....	45	17
1990–91	....	43	4
1991–92	....	41	10
1992–93	....	14	6
1993–94	Bristol C	41	4

ROBINSON, Mark

Born Manchester 21.11.68. Ht 5 9
Wt 11 08
Midfield. From Trainee.

1985–86	WBA	1	—
1986–87	....	1	—
1987–88	Barnsley	3	—
1988–89	....	18	2
1989–90	....	24	—
1990–91	....	22	1
1991–92	....	41	2
1992–93	....	29	1
1992–93	Newcastle U................	9	—
1993–94	....	16	—

ROBINSON, Matthew

Born Exeter 23.12.74 Ht 5 11 Wt 10 07
Midfield. From Trainee.

| 1993–94 | Southampton .... | — | — |

ROBINSON, Paul

Born Scarborough 2.1.74
Goalkeeper. From Trainee.

| 1992–93 | Sheffield W................ | — | — |
| 1993–94 | Scarborough................ | 4 | — |

ROBINSON, Phil

Born Stafford 6.1.67. Ht 5 10 Wt 10 10
Midfield. From Apprentice.

1984–85	Aston Villa................	—	—
1985–86	....	—	—
1986–87	....	3	1
1987–88	Wolverhampton W	41	5
1988–89	....	30	3
1989–90	Notts Co	46	2
1990–91	....	19	3
1990–91	*Birmingham C*............	9	—
1991–92	Notts Co	1	—
1992–93	....	—	—
1992–93	Huddersfield T	36	4
1993–94	....	39	1

ROBINSON, Ronnie

Born Sunderland 22.10.66. Ht 5 9
Wt 11 05
Defender.

1984–85	Ipswich T	—	—
From Vaux Breweries			
1985–86	Leeds U	16	—

Season	Club	Apps	Goals
1986–87		11	—
1986–87	Doncaster R	12	—
1987–88		37	1
1988–89		29	4
1988–89	WBA	1	—
1989–90	Rotherham U	43	1
1990–91		38	—
1991–92		5	1
1991–92	Peterborough U	27	—
1992–93		20	—
1993–94	Exeter C	22	1
1993–94	*Huddersfield T*	2	—

ROBINSON, Stephen

Born Lisburn 10.12.74 Ht 5 9 Wt 11 00
Forward. From Trainee.

Season	Club	Apps	Goals
1992–93	Tottenham H	—	—
1993–94		2	—

ROBINSON, Steven

Born Nottingham 17.1.75 Ht 5 4
Wt 10 11
Midfield. From Trainee.

Season	Club	Apps	Goals
1993–94	Birmingham C	—	—

ROBSON, Bryan

Born Chester-le-Street 11.1.57. Ht 5 10
Wt 11 11
Midfield. From Apprentice. England
Schools, Youth, Under-21, B, 90 full caps.

Season	Club	Apps	Goals
1974–75	WBA	3	2
1975–76		16	1
1976–77		23	8
1977–78		35	3
1978–79		41	7
1979–80		34	8
1980–81		40	10
1981–82		5	—
1981–82	Manchester U	32	5
1982–83		33	10
1983–84		33	12
1984–85		33	9
1985–86		21	7
1986–87		30	7
1987–88		36	11
1988–89		34	4
1989–90		20	2
1990–91		17	1
1991–92		27	4
1992–93		14	1
1993–94		15	1

ROBSON, Gary

Born Durham 6.7.65. Ht 5 7 Wt 10 12
Midfield. From Apprentice.

Season	Club	Apps	Goals
1982–83	WBA	2	—
1983–84		7	—
1984–85		11	—
1985–86		14	—
1986–87		5	1
1987–88		31	1
1988–89		38	8
1989–90		25	5
1990–91		31	2
1991–92		32	9
1992–93		22	2
1993–94	Bradford C	46	2

ROBSON, Mark

Born Newham 22.5.69. Ht 5 7 Wt 10 05
Forward. From Trainee.

Season	Club	Apps	Goals
1986–87	Exeter C	26	7
1987–88	Tottenham H	—	—
1987–88	*Reading*	7	—
1988–89	Tottenham H	5	—
1989–90		3	—
1989–90	*Watford*	1	—
1989–90	*Plymouth Arg*	7	—
1990–91	Tottenham H	—	—
1991–92		—	—
1991–92	*Exeter C*	8	1
1992–93	West Ham U	44	8
1993–94		3	—
1993–94	Charlton Ath	23	2

ROBSON, Stewart

Born Billericay 6.11.64. Ht 5 11
Wt 12 04
Midfield. From Apprentice. England
Youth, Under-21.

Season	Club	Apps	Goals
1981–82	Arsenal	20	2
1982–83		31	2
1983–84		28	6
1984–85		40	2
1985–86		27	4
1986–87		5	—
1986–87	West Ham U	18	1
1987–88		37	2

Season	Club	Apps	Goals
1988–89	....	6	—
1989–90	....	7	1
1990–91	....	1	—
1990–91	*Coventry C*	4	—
1991–92	Coventry C	37	3
1992–93	....	15	—
1993–94	....	1	—

ROCASTLE, David
Born Lewisham 2.5.67.   Ht 5 9   Wt 11 12
Forward. From Apprentice. England
Under-21, B, 14 full caps.

Season	Club	Apps	Goals
1984–85	Arsenal	—	—
1985–86	....	16	1
1986–87	....	36	2
1987–88	....	40	7
1988–89	....	38	6
1989–90	....	33	2
1990–91	....	16	2
1991–92	....	39	4
1992–93	Leeds U	18	1
1993–94	....	7	1
1993–94	Manchester C	21	2

ROCHE, David
Born Newcastle 13.12.70.   Ht 5 11
Wt 12 01
Defender. From Trainee.

Season	Club	Apps	Goals
1988–89	Newcastle U	2	—
1989–90	....	—	—
1990–91	....	8	—
1991–92	....	26	—
1992–93	....	—	—
1992–93	*Peterborough U*	4	—
1993–94	Newcastle U	—	—
1993–94	Doncaster R	30	5

ROCKETT, Jason
Born London 26.9.69.   Ht 5 11   Wt 12 00
Midfield.

Season	Club	Apps	Goals
1991–92	Rotherham U	—	—
1992–93	....	—	—
1993–94	Scarborough	34	—

RODDIE, Andrew
Born Glasgow 4.11.71.   Ht 5 9   Wt 11 00
Midfield. S Form. Scotland Under-21.

Season	Club	Apps	Goals
1988–89	Aberdeen	—	—

Season	Club	Apps	Goals
1989–90	....	—	—
1990–91	....	—	—
1991–92	....	10	2
1992–93	....	11	2
1993–94	....	6	1

RODEN, Damien
Born Wrexham 17.9.74   Ht 5 10
Wt 11 02
Defender. From Trainee.

Season	Club	Apps	Goals
1993–94	Wrexham	—	—

RODGER, Graham
Born Glasgow 1.4.67.   Ht 6 2   Wt 11 13
Defender. From Apprentice. England
Under-21.

Season	Club	Apps	Goals
1983–84	Wolverhampton W	1	—
1984–85	Coventry C	—	—
1985–86	....	10	—
1986–87	....	6	—
1987–88	....	12	1
1988–89	....	8	1
1989–90	Luton T	2	—
1990–91	....	14	2
1991–92	....	12	—
1991–92	Grimsby T	16	—
1992–93	....	30	7
1993–94	....	24	1

RODGER, Simon
Born Shoreham 3.10.71.   Ht 5 9
Wt 11 07
Defender. From Trainee.

Season	Club	Apps	Goals
1989–90	Crystal Palace	—	—
1990–91	....	—	—
1991–92	....	22	—
1992–93	....	23	2
1993–94	....	42	3

RODGERSON, Ian
Born Hereford 9.4.66.   Ht 5 10   Wt 10 07
Midfield. From Pegasus Juniors.

Season	Club	Apps	Goals
1984–85	Hereford U	—	—
1985–86	....	19	2
1986–87	....	44	1
1987–88	....	37	3
1988–89	Cardiff C	40	—
1989–90	....	45	4

Season	Club	App	Goals
1990–91	....	14	—
1990–91	Birmingham C	25	2
1991–92	....	39	9
1992–93	....	31	2
1993–94	Sunderland	4	—

RODWELL, Tony

Born Southport 26.8.62. Ht 5 11
Wt 11 02
Forward. From Colne Dynamoes.

Season	Club	App	Goals
1990–91	Blackpool	45	7
1991–92	....	40	8
1992–93	....	20	1
1993–94	....	28	1

ROGAN, Anton

Born Belfast 25.3.66.   Ht 5 11   Wt 12 06
Defender. From Distillery. Northern
Ireland, 17 full caps.

Season	Club	App	Goals
1986–87	Celtic	10	1
1987–88	....	33	1
1988–89	....	34	1
1989–90	....	18	—
1990–91	....	27	1
1991–92	....	5	—
1991–92	Sunderland	33	1
1992–93	....	13	—
1993–94	Oxford U	29	2

ROGERS, Darren

Born Birmingham 9.4.71.   Ht 5 10
Wt 11 02
Defender. From Trainee.

Season	Club	App	Goals
1988–89	WBA	—	—
1989–90	....	—	—
1990–91	....	4	—
1991–92	....	10	1
1992–93	Birmingham C	17	—
1993–94	....	1	—
1993–94	*Wycombe W*	1	—

ROGERS, Lee

Born Doncaster 21.10.66.   Ht 5 11
Wt 12 01
Defender. From Doncaster R.

Season	Club	App	Goals
1986–87	Chesterfield	36	—
1987–88	....	43	—
1988–89	....	24	—

Season	Club	App	Goals
1989–90	....	32	—
1990–91	....	34	—
1991–92	....	18	—
1992–93	....	35	1
1993–94	....	32	—

ROGERS, Paul

Born Portsmouth 21.3.65.   Ht 6 0
Wt 12 05
Midfield. From Sutton U.

Season	Club	App	Goals
1991–92	Sheffield U	13	—
1992–93	....	27	3
1993–94	....	25	3

ROOKYARD, Carl

Born Burton on Trent 3.9.75   Ht 5 9
Wt 10 05
Forward. From Trainee.

Season	Club	App	Goals
1992–93	Nottingham F.............	—	—
1993–94	....	—	—

ROSARIO, Robert

Born Hammersmith 4.3.66.   Ht 6 3
Wt 12 01
Forward. From Hillingdon Bor. England
Youth.

Season	Club	App	Goals
1983–84	Norwich C	8	1
1984–85	....	4	1
1985–86	....	8	2
1985–86	*Wolverhampton W*	2	1
1986–87	Norwich C	25	3
1987–88	....	14	2
1988–89	....	27	4
1989–90	....	31	5
1990–91	....	9	—
1990–91	Coventry C	2	—
1991–92	....	29	4
1992–93	....	28	4
1992–93	Nottingham F.............	10	1
1993–94	....	16	2

ROSCOE, Andrew

Born Liverpool 4.6.73   Ht 5 11   Wt 12 00
Midfield. From Trainee.

Season	Club	App	Goals
1991–92	Liverpool	—	—
1992–93	Bolton W	—	—
1993–94	....	3	—

ROSENIOR, Leroy

Born London 24.3.64. Ht 6 1 Wt 11 10
Forward. From School. England Schools.

Season	Club	App	Goals
1982–83	Fulham	1	—
1983–84		23	8
1984–85		30	8
1985–86	QPR	18	3
1986–87		20	4
1987–88	Fulham	34	20
1987–88	West Ham U	9	5
1988–89		28	7
1989–90		5	2
1990–91		2	—
1990–91	*Fulham*	11	3
1991–92	West Ham U	9	1
1991–92	*Charlton Ath*	3	—
1991–92	Bristol C	8	5
1992–93		38	7
1993–94		5	—

ROSENTHAL, Ronny

Born Haifa 11.10.63. Ht 5 11 Wt 12 00
Forward. From Maccabi Haifa, FC
Brugge, Standard Liege. Israel full caps.

Season	Club	App	Goals
1989–90	*Luton T*	—	—
1989–90	*Liverpool*	8	7
1990–91	Liverpool	16	5
1991–92		20	3
1992–93		27	6
1993–94		3	—
1993–94	Tottenham H	15	2

ROSLER, Uwe

Born Attenburg 15.11.68 Ht 6 0
Wt 12 04
Forward. From Dynamo Dresden,
Nuremberg.

Season	Club	App	Goals
1993–94	Manchester C	12	5

ROSS, Mike

Born Southampton 2.9.71. Ht 5 6
Wt 9 13
Forward.

Season	Club	App	Goals
1988–89	Portsmouth	1	—
1989–90		—	—
1990–91		—	—
1991–92		3	—
1992–93		—	—

Season	Club	App	Goals
1993–94	Exeter C	27	9

ROUND, Steve

Born Buxton 9.11.70. Ht 5 10 Wt 11 00
Defender. From Trainee.

Season	Club	App	Goals
1990–91	Derby Co	—	—
1991–92		3	—
1992–93		6	—
1993–94		—	—

ROUSE, Shaun

Born Gt Yarmouth 28.2.72 Ht 5 9
Wt 11 02
Midfield. From Rangers.

Season	Club	App	Goals
1992–93	Bristol C	—	—
1993–94	Carlisle U	5	—

ROWBOTHAM, Darren

Born Cardiff 22.10.66. Ht 5 10 Wt 11 05
Midfield. From Trainee.

Season	Club	App	Goals
1984–85	Plymouth Arg	7	—
1985–86		14	1
1986–87		16	1
1987–88		9	—
1987–88	Exeter C	23	2
1988–89		45	20
1989–90		32	21
1990–91		13	3
1991–92		5	1
1991–92	Torquay U	14	3
1991–92	Birmingham C	22	4
1992–93		14	2
1992–93	*Hereford U*	8	2
1992–93	*Mansfield T*	4	—
1993–94	Crewe Alex	40	15

ROWBURY, Neil

Born Barking 27.12.74. Ht 5 11 Wt 11 04
Midfield. From Trainee.

Season	Club	App	Goals
1993–94	Southend U	—	—

ROWE, Rodney

Born Huddersfield 30.7.75 Ht 5 8
Wt 12 08
Forward. From Trainee.

Season	Club	App	Goals
1993–94	Huddersfield T	13	1

ROWE, Zeke
Born Stoke Newington 30.10.73 Ht 5 6
Wt 9 08
Midfield. From Trainee.

Season	Club		
1992–93	Chelsea	—	—
1993–94		—	—
1993–94	*Barnet*	10	2

ROWETT, Gary
Born Bromsgrove 6.3.74. Ht 6 0
Wt 12 10
Forward. From Trainee.

1991–92	Cambridge U	13	2
1992–93		21	2
1993–94		29	5
1993–94	Everton	2	—

ROWLAND, Keith
Born Portadown 1.9.71. Ht 5 10
Wt 10 00
Midfield. From Trainee.

1990–91	Bournemouth	—	—
1991–92		37	—
1992–93		35	2
1992–93	*Coventry C*	2	—
1993–94	West Ham U	23	—

ROYCE, Simon
Born Forest Gate 9.9.71. Ht 6 2
Wt 11 07
Goalkeeper. From Heybridge Swifts.

1991–92	Southend U	1	—
1992–93		3	—
1993–94		6	—

RUDDOCK, Neil
Born London 9.5.68. Ht 6 2 Wt 12 06
Defender. From Apprentice. England
Youth, Under-21.

1985–86	Millwall	—	—
1985–86	Tottenham H	—	—
1986–87		4	—
1987–88		5	—
1988–89	Millwall	2	1
1988–89	Southampton	13	3
1989–90		29	3
1990–91		35	3
1991–92		30	—

1992–93	Tottenham H	38	3
1993–94	Liverpool	39	3

RUDGLEY, Simon
Born London 25.9.73 Ht 5 11 Wt 11 10
Goalkeeper. From Fulham.

1993–94	Bristol C	—	—

RUFFER, Carl
Born Chester 20.12.74 Ht 5 8 Wt 10 04
Midfield. From Trainee.

1993–94	Everton	—	—

RUFUS, Richard
Born Lewisham 12.1.75 Ht 6 1 Wt 11 02
Defender. From Trainee.

1993–94	Charlton Ath	—	—

RUSH, David
Born Sunderland 15.5.71. Ht 5 11
Wt 10 10
Forward. From Trainee.

1989–90	Sunderland	—	—
1990–91		11	2
1991–92		25	4
1991–92	*Hartlepool U*	8	2
1992–93	Sunderland	18	6
1993–94		5	—
1993–94	*Peterborough U*	4	1

RUSH, Ian
Born St. Asaph 20.10.61. Ht 6 0
Wt 12 06
Forward. From Apprentice. Wales
Schools, Under-21, 66 full caps.

1978–79	Chester	1	—
1979–80		33	14
1979–80	Liverpool	—	—
1980–81		7	—
1981–82		32	17
1982–83		34	24
1983–84		41	32
1984–85		28	14
1985–86		40	22
1986–87		42	30
1987–88	Juventus	29	7
1988–89	Liverpool	24	7
1989–90		36	18

1990–91		37	16
1991–92		18	4
1992–93		32	14
1993–94		42	14

RUSH, Matthew

Born Dalston 6.8.71.   Ht 5 11   Wt 12 10
Midfield. From Trainee. Eire Under-21.

1990–91	West Ham U	5	—
1991–92		10	2
1992–93		—	—
1992–93	*Cambridge U*	10	—
1993–94		10	1
1993–94	*Swansea C*	13	—

RUSHTON, Paul

Born Buckley 25.1.74.   Ht 5 10   Wt 11 10
Defender. From Trainee.

| 1992–93 | Crewe Alex | — | — |
| 1993–94 | | — | — |

RUSSELL, Craig

Born South Shields 4.2.74.
Forward. From Trainee.

1991–92	Sunderland	4	—
1992–93		—	—
1993–94		35	9

RUSSELL, Kevin

Born Portsmouth 6.12.66.   Ht 5 8
Wt 10 12
Forward. From Brighton Apprentice.
England Youth.

1984–85	Portsmouth	—	—
1985–86		1	—
1986–87		3	1
1987–88	Wrexham	38	21
1988–89		46	22
1989–90	Leicester C	10	—
1990–91		13	5
1990–91	*Peterborough U*	7	3
1990–91	*Cardiff C*	3	—
1991–92	Leicester C	20	5
1991–92	*Hereford U*	3	1
1991–92	*Stoke C*	5	1
1992–93	Stoke C	40	5
1993–94	Burnley	28	6
1993–94	Bournemouth	17	1

RUSSELL, Lee

Born Southampton 3.9.69.   Ht 5 11
Wt 11 04
Defender. From Trainee.

1988–89	Portsmouth	2	—
1989–90		3	—
1990–91		19	1
1991–92		9	—
1992–93		14	—
1993–94		10	—

RUSSELL, Wayne

Born Cardiff 29.11.67   Ht 6 2   Wt 13 07
Goalkeeper. From Ebbw Vale.

| 1993–94 | Burnley | — | — |

RUST, Nicky

Born Cambridge 25.9.74.   Ht 6 0
Wt 13 01
Goalkeeper. From Arsenal trainee.

| 1993–94 | Brighton | 46 | — |

RUTHERFORD, Mark

Born Birmingham 25.3.72.   Ht 5 11
Wt 11 00
Forward. From Trainee.

1989–90	Birmingham C	2	—
1990–91		3	—
1991–92		—	—

From Shelbourne

| 1993–94 | *Shrewsbury T* | 14 | — |

RYAN, Darren

Born Oswestry 3.7.72.   Ht 5 10   Wt 11 00
Midfield. From Trainee.

1990–91	Shrewsbury T	2	—
1991–92		2	—
1992–93	Chester C	17	2
1992–93	Stockport Co	4	—
1993–94		32	6

RYAN, John

Born Ashton 18.2.62.   Ht 5 10   Wt 11 07
Defender. From Apprentice. England
Under-21.

| 1979–80 | Oldham Ath | — | — |
| 1980–81 | | — | — |

Season	Club	App	Goals
1981–82	....	37	—
1982–83	....	40	8
1983–84	Newcastle U.................	22	1
1984–85	....	6	—
1984–85	Sheffield W..................	8	1
1985–86	Oldham Ath.................	22	—
1986–87	....	1	—
1987–88	....	—	—
1987–88	Mansfield T..................	32	1
1988–89	....	30	—
1989–90	Chesterfield	43	4
1990–91	....	39	2
1991–92	Rochdale......................	32	2
1992–93	....	26	—
1993–94	....	12	—
1993–94	Bury	9	—

RYAN, Keith
Born Northampton 25.6.70   Ht 5 11
Wt 12 07
Midfield. From Berkhamsted T.

Season	Club	App	Goals
1993–94	Wycombe W	42	1

RYAN, Neil
Born Luton 27.1.75   Ht 5 10   Wt 11 08
Midfield. From Trainee.

Season	Club	App	Goals
1993–94	Luton T	—	—

RYAN, Tim
Born Stockport 10.12.74
Defender. From Trainee.

Season	Club	App	Goals
1992–93	Scunthorpe U	1	—
1993–94	....	1	—

RYAN, Vaughan
Born Westminster 2.9.68.   Ht 5 8
Wt 10 12
Midfield.

Season	Club	App	Goals
1986–87	Wimbledon	1	—
1987–88	....	22	1
1988–89	....	5	—
1988–89	*Sheffield U*....................	3	—
1989–90	Wimbledon	31	—
1990–91	....	2	—
1991–92	....	21	2
1992–93	Leyton Orient	20	—
1993–94	....	17	—

RYDER, Stuart
Born Sutton Coldfield 6.11.73   Ht 6 0
Wt 12 01
Defender. From Trainee.

Season	Club	App	Goals
1992–93	Walsall	22	—
1993–94	....	26	—

ROWBOTHAM, Jason
Born Cardiff 3.1.69   Ht 5 9   Wt 11 00
Midfield. From Trainee.

Season	Club	App	Goals
1987–88	Plymouth Arg.............	4	—
1988–89	....	5	—
1989–90	....	—	—
1990–91	....	—	—
1991–92	Shrewsbury T..............	—	—
1992–93	Hereford U	5	1
1993–94	Raith R........................	36	1

SADDINGTON, James
Born Cambridge 12.9.72   Ht 6 0
Wt 11 13
Defender. From Cambridge C.

Season	Club	App	Goals
1993–94	Millwall	—	—

SAGE, Mel
Born Gillingham 24.3.64.   Ht 5 8
Wt 10 04
Defender. From Apprentice.

Season	Club	App	Goals
1981–82	Gillingham	1	—
1982–83		9	—
1983–84		40	2
1984–85		36	1
1985–86		46	2
1986–87	Derby Co	26	2
1987–88		13	—
1988–89		16	1
1989–90		34	—
1990–91		34	1
1991–92		17	—
1992–93		—	—
1993–94		—	—

SALAKO, John
Born Nigeria, 11.2.69.   Ht 5 9   Wt 11 00
Forward. From Trainee. England 5 full
caps.

Season	Club	App	Goals
1986–87	Crystal Palace	4	—
1987–88		31	—
1988–89		28	—
1989–90		17	2
1989–90	*Swansea C*	13	3
1990–91	Crystal Palace	35	6
1991–92		10	2
1992–93		13	—
1993–94		38	8

SALE, Mark
Born Burton-on-Trent 27.2.72.   Ht 6 5
Wt 13 08
Forward. From Trainee.

Season	Club	App	Goals
1989–90	Stoke C	2	—
1990–91		—	—
1991–92	Cambridge U	—	—
1991–92	Birmingham C	6	—
1992–93		15	—
1992–93	Torquay U	11	2

Season	Club	App	Goals
1993–94		33	6

SALMON, Mike
Born Leyland 14.7.64.   Ht 6 2   Wt 13 00
Goalkeeper. From Local.

Season	Club	App	Goals
1981–82	Blackburn R	1	—
1982–83		—	—
1982–83	*Chester C*	16	—
1983–84	Stockport Co	46	—
1984–85		46	—
1985–86		26	—
1986–87	Bolton W	26	—
1986–87	*Wrexham*	17	—
1987–88	Wrexham	40	—
1988–89		43	—
1989–90	Charlton Ath	—	—
1990–91		7	—
1991–92		—	—
1992–93		19	—
1993–94		41	—

SALTON, Darren
Born Edinburgh 16.3.72.   Ht 6 2
Wt 13 00
Forward. From Trainee. Scotland Schools,
Youth, Under-21.

Season	Club	App	Goals
1988–89	Luton T	—	—
1989–90		—	—
1990–91		—	—
1991–92		3	—
1992–93		15	—
1993–94		—	—

SAMPSON, Ian
Born Wakefield 14.11.68.   Ht 6 2
Wt 12 08
Defender. From Goole T.

Season	Club	App	Goals
1990–91	Sunderland	—	—
1991–92		8	—
1992–93		5	1
1993–94		4	—
1993–94	*Northampton T*	8	—

SAMWAYS, Mark
Born Doncaster 11.11.68.   Ht 6 2
Wt 13 10
Goalkeeper. From Trainee.

Season	Club	App	Goals
1987–88	Doncaster R	11	—

Season	Club	Apps	Goals
1988–89	....	12	—
1989–90	....	46	—
1990–91	....	26	—
1991–92	....	26	—
1991–92	*Scunthorpe U*	8	—
1992–93	Scunthorpe U	31	—
1993–94	....	41	—

SAMWAYS, Vinny

Born Bethnal Green 27.10.68. Ht 5 8
Wt 11 00
Midfield. From Apprentice. England
Youth, Under-21.

Season	Club	Apps	Goals
1985–86	Tottenham H	—	—
1986–87	....	2	—
1987–88	....	26	—
1988–89	....	19	3
1989–90	....	23	3
1990–91	....	23	1
1991–92	....	27	1
1992–93	....	34	—
1993–94	....	39	3

SANCHEZ, Lawrie

Born Lambeth 22.10.59. Ht 5 11
Wt 12 00
Midfield. From Thatcham. Northern
Ireland 3 caps.

Season	Club	Apps	Goals
1977–78	Reading	8	1
1978–79	....	39	4
1979–80	....	46	5
1980–81	....	37	2
1981–82	....	35	3
1982–83	....	37	1
1983–84	....	45	10
1984–85	....	15	2
1984–85	Wimbledon	20	5
1985–86	....	42	9
1986–87	....	29	—
1987–88	....	38	4
1988–89	....	36	5
1989–90	....	18	1
1990–91	....	29	—
1991–92	....	16	3
1992–93	....	27	4
1993–94	....	15	2
1993–94	Swindon T	8	—

SANDEMAN, Bradley

Born Northampton 24.2.70. Ht 5 10
Wt 10 08
Midfield. From Trainee.

Season	Club	Apps	Goals
1987–88	Northampton T	2 ·	—
1988–89	....	22	2
1989–90	....	29	1
1990–91	....	5	—
1990–91	Maidstone U	20	1
1991–92	....	37	7
1992–93	Port Vale	22	1
1993–94	....	9	—

SANDFORD, Lee

Born Basingstoke 22.4.68. Ht 6 1
Wt 12 02
Defender. From Apprentice. England
Youth.

Season	Club	Apps	Goals
1985–86	Portsmouth	7	—
1986–87	....	—	—
1987–88	....	21	1
1988–89	....	31	—
1989–90	....	13	—
1989–90	Stoke C	23	2
1990–91	....	32	2
1991–92	....	38	—
1992–93	....	42	2
1993–94	....	42	1

SANSAM, Christian

Born Hull 26.12.75
Midfield. From Trainee.

Season	Club	Apps	Goals
1993–94	Scunthorpe U	10	—

SANSOME, Paul

Born N. Addington 6.10.61. Ht 6 0
Wt 13 07
Goalkeeper. From Crystal Palace
Apprentice.

Season	Club	Apps	Goals
1979–80	Millwall	—	—
1980–81	....	—	—
1981–82	....	8	—
1982–83	....	24	—
1983–84	....	31	—
1984–85	....	46	—
1985–86	....	36	—
1986–87	....	10	—
1987–88	....	1	—

1987–88	Southend U	6 —
1988–89		44 —
1989–90		46 —
1990–91		46 —
1991–92		45 —
1992–93		43 —
1993–94		42 —

SAUNDERS, Carl
Born Marston Green 26.11.64. Ht 5 8
Wt 11 02
Forward. From Local.

1982–83	Stoke C	1 —
1983–84		— —
1984–85		23 2
1985–86		37 2
1986–87		31 13
1987–88		17 3
1988–89		33 2
1989–90		22 1
1989–90	Bristol R	20 5
1990–91		38 16
1991–92		36 10
1992–93		41 11
1993–94		7 —
1993–94	Oxford U	5 —
1993–94	Walsall	2 —
1993–94	Middlesbrough	— —

SAUNDERS, Dean
Born Swansea 21.6.64. Ht 5 8 Wt 10 06
Forward. From Apprentice. Wales 44 full
caps.

1982–83	Swansea C	— —
1983–84		19 3
1984–85		30 9
1984–85	*Cardiff C*	4 —
1985–86	Brighton	42 15
1986–87		30 6
1986–87	Oxford U	12 6
1987–88		37 12
1988–89		10 4
1988–89	Derby Co	30 14
1989–90		38 11
1990–91		38 17
1991–92	Liverpool	36 10
1992–93		6 1
1992–93	Aston Villa	35 12
1993–94		38 10

SAVAGE, Robert
Born Wrexham 18.10.74. Ht 5 11
Wt 10 01
Forward. From Trainee.

1993–94	Manchester U	— —

SAVILLE, Andrew
Born Hull 12.12.64. Ht 6 0 Wt 12 06
Forward. From local.

1983–84	Hull C	1 —
1984–85		4 1
1985–86		9 1
1986–87		35 9
1987–88		31 6
1988–89		20 1
1988–89	Walsall	12 4
1989–90		26 1
1989–90	Barnsley	15 3
1990–91		45 12
1991–92		22 6
1991–92	Hartlepool U	1 —
1992–93		36 13
1992–93	Birmingham C	10 7
1993–94		39 10

SCALES, John
Born Harrogate 4.7.66. Ht 6 2 Wt 12 07
Defender.

1984–85	Leeds U	— —
1985–86	Bristol R	29 1
1986–87		43 1
1987–88	Wimbledon	25 1
1988–89		38 5
1989–90		28 2
1990–91		36 2
1991–92		41 —
1992–93		32 1
1993–94		37 —

SCARGILL, Wayne
Born Barnsley 30.4.68. Ht 5 10 Wt 11 09
Defender. From Frickley Ath.

1993–94	Bradford C	— —

SCHMEICHEL, Peter

Born Glodsone 18.11.68.   Ht 6 4
Wt 13 06
Goalkeeper. From Hvidovre, Brondby.
Denmark full caps.

Season	Club	App	Goals
1991–92	Manchester U	40	—
1992–93		42	—
1993–94		40	—

SCHOFIELD, Jon

Born Barnsley 16.5.65.   Ht 5 11   Wt 11 03
Midfield. From Gainsborough T.

Season	Club	App	Goals
1988–89	Lincoln C	29	2
1989–90		29	2
1990–91		42	3
1991–92		39	1
1992–93		40	—
1993–94		40	2

SCHOLES, Paul

Born Salford 16.11.74.   Ht 5 8   Wt 10 07
Forward. From Trainee.

Season	Club	App	Goals
1992–93	Manchester U	—	—
1993–94		—	—

SCIMECA, Riccardo

Born Leamington Spa 13.6.75   Ht 6 1
Wt 12 09
Defender. From Trainee.

Season	Club	App	Goals
1993–94	Aston Villa	—	—

SCOTT, Andrew

Born Manchester 27.6.75
Defender.

Season	Club	App	Goals
1992–93	Blackburn R	—	—
1993–94		—	—

SCOTT, Andy

Born Epsom 2.8.72   Ht 6 1   Wt 11 05
Midfield. From Sutton U.

Season	Club	App	Goals
1992–93	Sheffield U	2	1
1993–94		15	—

SCOTT, Colin

Born Glasgow 19.5.70   Ht 6 1   Wt 12 4
Goalkeeper. Dalry Thistle.

Season	Club	App	Goals
1987–88	Rangers	—	—

Season	Club	App	Goals
1988–89		—	—
1989–90		—	—
1990–91		—	—
1990–91	*Airdrieonians*	1	—
1991–92	Rangers	—	—
1992–93		—	—
1993–94		6	—

SCOTT, John

Born Aberdeen 9.3.75   Ht 5 8   Wt 10 09
Defender. From Trainee.

Season	Club	App	Goals
1992–93	Liverpool	—	—
1993–94		—	—

SCOTT, Keith

Born London 9.6.67   Ht 6 3   Wt 14 03
Forward. From Leicester U.

Season	Club	App	Goals
1989–90	Lincoln C	10	2
1990–91		6	—
To Wycombe W			
1993–94	Wycombe W	15	10
1993–94	Swindon T	27	4

SCOTT, Kevin

Born Easington 17.12.66.   Ht 6 2
Wt 11 06
Defender.

Season	Club	App	Goals
1984–85	Newcastle U	—	—
1985–86		—	—
1986–87		3	1
1987–88		4	1
1988–89		29	—
1989–90		42	3
1990–91		42	—
1991–92		44	1
1992–93		45	2
1993–94		18	—
1993–94	Tottenham H	12	1

SCOTT, Martin

Born Sheffield 7.1.68.   Ht 5 8   Wt 10 10
Midfield. From Apprentice.

Season	Club	App	Goals
1984–85	Rotherham U	3	—
1985–86		—	—
1986–87		12	—
1987–88		19	—
1987–88	*Nottingham F*	—	—
1988–89	Rotherham U	19	1

1989–90	....	28	1
1990–91	....	13	1
1990–91	Bristol C	27	1
1991–92	....	46	3
1992–93	....	35	3
1993–94	....	45	5

SCOTT, Peter

Born London 1.10.63. Ht 5 9   Wt 11 12
Midfield. From Apprentice.

1981–82	Fulham	1	—
1982–83	....	—	—
1983–84	....	32	4
1984–85	....	19	1
1985–86	....	32	5
1986–87	....	30	6
1987–88	....	23	2
1988–89	....	37	3
1989–90	....	41	3
1990–91	....	23	2
1991–92	....	39	1
1992–93	Bournemouth	10	—
1993–94	Barnet	30	2

SCOTT, Philip

Born Perth 14.11.74   Ht 5 8   Wt 10 2
Midfield. From Scone Thistle. Scotland
Under-21.

1992–92	St Johnstone	—	—
1992–93	....	3	—
1993–94	....	24	3

SCOTT, Richard

Born Dudley 29.9.74   Ht 5 9   Wt 10 10
Defender. From Trainee.

1992–93	Birmingham C	1	—
1993–94	....	6	—

SCOTT, Rob

Born Epsom 15.8.73   Ht 6 1   Wt 11 08
Forward. From Sutton U.

1993–94	Sheffield U	—	—

SCOTT, Ryan

Born Saltburn 20.3.76
Defender. From Trainee.

1993–94	Darlington	1	—

SCULLY, Anthony

Born Dublin 12.6.76   Ht 5 7   Wt 11 12
Forward. From Trainee.

1993–94	Crystal Palace	—	—

SCULLY, Pat

Born Dublin 23.6.70.   Ht 6 1   Wt 13 02
Defender. Eire Schools, Youth, B, Under-
21, Under-23, 1 full cap.

1987–88	Arsenal	—	—
1988–89	....	—	—
1989–90	....	—	—
1989–90	Preston NE	13	1
1990–91	Arsenal	—	—
1990–91	Northampton T	15	—
1990–91	Southend U	21	—
1991–92	....	44	3
1992–93	....	42	3
1993–94	....	8	—
1993–94	Huddersfield T	11	—

SEABURY, Kevin

Born Shrewsbury 24.11.73   Ht 5 9
Wt 11 06
Midfield. From Trainee.

1992–93	Shrewsbury T	1	—
1993–94	....	—	—

SEAGRAVES, Mark

Born Bootle 22.10.66.   Ht 6 1   Wt 12 10
Defender. England Schools, Youth.

1983–84	Liverpool	—	—
1984–85	....	—	—
1985–86	....	—	—
1986–87	....	—	—
1986–87	Norwich C	3	—
1987–88	Liverpool	—	—
1987–88	Manchester C	17	—
1988–89	....	23	—
1989–90	....	2	—
1990–91	Bolton W	32	—
1991–92	....	40	1
1992–93	....	37	5
1993–94	....	35	1

SEALEY, Les
Born Bethnal Green 29.9.57. Ht 6 1
Wt 13 06
Goalkeeper. From Apprentice.

Season	Club	Apps	Goals
1975–76	Coventry C	—	—
1976–77		11	—
1977–78		2	—
1978–79		36	—
1979–80		20	—
1980–81		35	—
1981–82		15	—
1982–83		39	—
1983–84	Luton T	42	—
1984–85		26	—
1984–85	*Plymouth Arg*	6	—
1985–86	Luton T	35	—
1986–87		41	—
1987–88		31	—
1988–89		32	—
1989–90		—	—
1989–90	*Manchester U*	2	—
1990–91	Manchester U	31	—
1991–92	Aston Villa	18	—
1991–92	*Coventry C*	2	—
1992–93	Aston Villa	—	—
1992–93	*Birmingham C*	12	—
1992–93	Manchester U	—	—
1993–94		—	—

SEAMAN, David
Born Rotherham 19.9.63. Ht 6 4
Wt 14 10
Goalkeeper. From Apprentice. England B,
Under-21, 14 full caps.

Season	Club	Apps	Goals
1981–82	Leeds U	—	—
1982–83	Peterborough U	38	—
1983–84		45	—
1984–85		8	—
1984–85	Birmingham C	33	—
1985–86		42	—
1986–87	QPR	41	—
1987–88		32	—
1988–89		35	—
1989–90		33	—
1990–91	Arsenal	38	—
1991–92		42	—
1992–93		39	—
1993–94		39	—

SEARLE, Damon
Born Cardiff 26.10.71. Ht 5 11 Wt 10 04
Defender. From Trainee. Wales Youth,
Under-21.

Season	Club	Apps	Goals
1990–91	Cardiff C	35	—
1991–92		42	1
1992–93		42	1
1993–94		42	—

SEDGEMORE, Ben
Born Wolverhampton 5.8.75 Ht 5 10
Wt 13 11
Midfield. From Trainee.

Season	Club	Apps	Goals
1993–94	Birmingham C	—	—

SEDGLEY, Steve
Born Enfield 26.5.68. Ht 6 1 Wt 13 03
Midfield. From Apprentice. England
Under-21.

Season	Club	Apps	Goals
1986–87	Coventry C	26	—
1987–88		27	2
1988–89		31	1
1989–90	Tottenham H	32	—
1990–91		34	—
1991–92		34	—
1992–93		22	3
1993–94		42	5

SEGERS, Hans
Born Eindhoven 30.10.61. Ht 5 11
Wt 12 12
Goalkeeper. From PSV Eindhoven.

Season	Club	Apps	Goals
1984–85	Nottingham F	28	—
1985–86		11	—
1986–87		14	—
1986–87	*Stoke C*	1	—
1987–88	Nottingham F	5	—
1987–88	*Sheffield U*	10	—
1987–88	*Dunfermline Ath*	4	—
1988–89	Nottingham F	—	—
1988–89	Wimbledon	33	—
1989–90		38	—
1990–91		37	—
1991–92		41	—
1992–93		41	—
1993–94		41	—

SELLARS, Scott

Born Sheffield 27.11.65.   Ht 5 7   Wt 9 10
Midfield. From Apprentice. England
Under-21.

Season	Club	Apps	Goals
1982–83	Leeds U	1	—
1983–84		19	3
1984–85		39	7
1985–86		17	2
1986–87	Blackburn R	32	4
1987–88		42	7
1988–89		46	2
1989–90		43	14
1990–91		9	1
1991–92		30	7
1992–93	Leeds U	7	—
1992–93	Newcastle U	13	2
1993–94		30	3

SELLEY, Ian

Born Chertsey 14.6.74.   Ht 5 9   Wt 10 01
Midfield. From Trainee. England Youth,
Under-21.

Season	Club	Apps	Goals
1992–93	Arsenal	9	—
1993–94		18	—

SERTORI, Mark

Born Manchester 1.9.67.   Ht 6 1
Wt 13 00
Defender.

Season	Club	Apps	Goals
1986–87	Stockport Co	3	—
1987–88		1	—
1987–88	Lincoln C	28	6
1988–89		26	4
1989–90		24	5
1989–90	Wrexham	18	2
1990–91		29	—
1991–92		36	—
1992–93		12	—
1993–94		15	1

SHAIL, Mark

Born Sweden 15.10.63.   Ht 6 1   Wt 13 03
Defender. From Yeovil.

Season	Club	Apps	Goals
1992–93	Bristol C	4	—
1993–94		36	2

SHAKESPEARE, Craig

Born Birmingham 26.10.63.   Ht 5 10
Wt 12 05
Midfield. From Apprentice.

Season	Club	Apps	Goals
1981–82	Walsall	—	—
1982–83		31	4
1983–84		46	6
1984–85		41	9
1985–86		32	4
1986–87		44	11
1987–88		45	8
1988–89		45	3
1989–90	Sheffield W	17	—
1989–90	WBA	18	1
1990–91		36	1
1991–92		44	8
1992–93		14	2
1993–94	Grimsby T	33	3

SHANNON, Rab

Born Bellshill 20.4.66   Ht 5 11   Wt 11 8
Defender. St Columba's BC. Scotland
Youth, Under-21.

Season	Club	Apps	Goals
1982–83	Dundee	—	—
1983–84		6	—
1984–85		3	—
1985–86		33	—
1986–87		39	5
1987–88		41	—
1988–89		29	1
1989–90		36	1
1990–91		37	2
1991–92	*Middlesbrough*	1	—
1991–92	Dundee	3	—
1991–92	Dunfermline Ath	27	—
1992–93		42	—
1993–94	Motherwell	43	—

SHARP, Graeme

Born Glasgow 16.10.60.   Ht 6 1   Wt 11 09
Forward. From Eastercraigs. Scotland
Under-21, 12 full caps.

Season	Club	Apps	Goals
1978–79	Dumbarton	6	1
1979–80		34	16
1979–80	Everton	2	—
1980–81		4	—
1981–82		29	15
1982–83		41	15
1983–84		28	7

Season	Club		App	Goals
1984–85	....		36	21
1985–86	....		37	19
1986–87	....		27	5
1987–88	....		32	13
1988–89	....		26	7
1989–90	....		33	6
1990–91	....		27	3
1991–92	Oldham Ath...............		42	12
1992–93	....		21	7
1993–94	....		34	9

SHARP, Kevin
Born Ontario 19.9.74. Ht 5 9 Wt 10 07
Midfield. From Auxerre. England Youth.

Season	Club	App	Goals
1992–93	Leeds U	4	—
1993–94	....	10	—

SHARPE, John
Born Birmingham 9.8.75 Ht 5 11
Wt 11 06
Midfield. From Trainee.

Season	Club	App	Goals
1993–94	Manchester C	—	—

SHARPE, Lee
Born Halesowen 25.7.71. Ht 5 11
Wt 11 04
Midfield. From Trainee. England Under-
21, B, 8 full caps.

Season	Club	App	Goals
1987–88	Torquay U	14	3
1988–89	Manchester U	22	—
1989–90	....	18	1
1990–91	....	23	2
1991–92	....	14	1
1992–93	....	27	1
1993–94	....	30	9

SHAW, Darren
Born Telford 20.12.74. Ht 6 0 Wt 12 02
Defender. From Trainee.

Season	Club	App	Goals
1993–94	Wolverhampton W	—	—

SHAW, George
Born Glasgow 10.2.69. Ht 5 7 Wt 9 02
Forward. From Ayresome N.

Season	Club	App	Goals
1987–88	St Mirren	2	—
1988–89	....	10	1
1989–90	....	23	2
1990–91	....	33	1

Season	Club	App	Goals
1991–92	Partick T.....................	43	9
1992–93	....	31	10
1993–94	....	17	2
1993–94	Dundee........................	17	6

SHAW, Graham
Born Stoke 7.6.67. Ht 5 8 Wt 10 05
Forward. From Apprentice.

Season	Club	App	Goals
1985–86	Stoke C......................	20	5
1986–87	....	18	2
1987–88	....	33	6
1988–89	....	28	5
1989–90	Preston NE................	31	5
1990–91	....	44	10
1991–92	....	46	14
1992–93	Stoke C......................	29	5
1993–94	....	4	—

SHAW, Greg
Born Dumfries 15.2.70. Ht 6 0 Wt 10 12
Forward. From Dalbeattie Star.

Season	Club	App	Goals
1988–89	Ayr U	2	—
1989–90	....	3	—
1990–91	....	9	—
1991–92	....	39	10
1992–93	....	5	—
1992–93	Falkirk	6	2
1993–94	....	28	10

SHAW, Paul
Born Burnham 4.9.73. Ht 5 11 Wt 12 02
Forward. From Trainee.

Season	Club	App	Goals
1991–92	Arsenal........................	—	—
1992–93	....	—	—
1993–94	....	—	—

SHAW, Richard
Born Brentford 11.9.68. Ht 5 9 Wt 11 08
Defender. From Apprentice.

Season	Club	App	Goals
1986–87	Crystal Palace.............	—	—
1987–88	....	3	—
1988–89	....	14	—
1989–90	....	21	—
1989–90	*Hull C*	4	—
1990–91	Crystal Palace.............	36	1
1991–92	....	10	—
1992–93	....	33	—
1993–94	....	34	2

SHAW, Simon
Born Teeside 21.9.73. Ht 6 0   Wt 12 00
Midfield. From Trainee.

Season	Club	App	Goals
1991–92	Darlington	1	—
1992–93		23	4
1993–94		30	1

SHEARER, Alan
Born Newcastle 13.8.70. Ht 5 11
Wt 11 03
Forward. From Trainee. England Youth,
Under-21 B, 10 full caps.

Season	Club	App	Goals
1987–88	Southampton	5	3
1988–89		10	—
1989–90		26	3
1990–91		36	4
1991–92		41	13
1992–93	Blackburn R	21	16
1993–94		40	31

SHEARER, Duncan
Born Fort William 28.8.62. Ht 5 10
Wt 10 09
Forward. From Inverness Clach. Scotland
2 full caps.

Season	Club	App	Goals
1983–84	Chelsea	—	—
1984–85		—	—
1985–86		2	1
1985–86	Huddersfield T	8	7
1986–87		42	21
1987–88		33	10
1988–89	Swindon T	36	14
1989–90		42	20
1990–91		44	22
1991–92		37	22
1991–92	Blackburn R	6	1
1992–93	Aberdeen	34	22
1993–94		43	17

SHEARER, Peter
Born Birmingham 4.2.67. Ht 6 0
Wt 11 06
Forward. From Apprentice.

Season	Club	App	Goals
1984–85	Birmingham C	4	—
1985–86		—	—
1986–87	Rochdale	1	—
From Cheltenham T			
1988–89	Bournemouth	4	1

Season	Club	App	Goals
1989–90		34	4
1990–91		5	—
1991–92		8	1
1992–93		34	4
1993–94		—	—
1993–94	Birmingham C	2	—

SHEEDY, Kevin
Born Builth Wells 21.10.59. Ht 5 9
Wt 10 11
Midfield. From Apprentice. Eire Youth,
Under-21, 45 full caps.

Season	Club	App	Goals
1975–76	Hereford U	1	—
1976–77		16	1
1977–78		34	3
1978–79	Liverpool	—	—
1979–80		—	—
1980–81		1	—
1981–82		2	—
1982–83	Everton	40	11
1983–84		28	4
1984–85		29	11
1985–86		31	5
1986–87		28	13
1987–88		17	1
1988–89		26	8
1989–90		37	9
1990–91		22	4
1991–92		16	1
1991–92	Newcastle U	13	1
1992–93		24	3
1993–94	Blackpool	26	1

SHEERIN, Paul
Born Edinburgh 28.8.74 Ht 5 10
Wt 10 13
Midfield. From Whitehill Welfare.

Season	Club	App	Goals
1992–93	Alloa	9	—
1992–93	Southampton	—	—
1993–94		—	—

SHEFFIELD, Jon
Born Bedworth 1.2.69. Ht 5 11 Wt 11 07
Goalkeeper.

Season	Club	App	Goals
1986–87	Norwich C	—	—
1987–88		—	—
1988–89		1	—
1989–90		—	—
1989–90	*Aldershot*	11	—

Season	Club	App	Goals
1989–90	*Ipswich T*	—	—
1990–91	Norwich C	—	—
1990–91	*Aldershot*	15	—
1990–91	*Cambridge U*	2	—
1991–92	Cambridge U	13	—
1992–93		13	—
1993–94		—	—
1993–94	*Colchester U*	6	—
1993–94	*Swindon T*	2	—

SHELTON, Gary
Born Nottingham 21.3.58.   Ht 5 7
Wt 10 12
Midfield. From Apprentice. England
Under-21.

Season	Club	App	Goals
1975–76	Walsall	2	—
1976–77		10	—
1977–78		12	—
1977–78	Aston Villa	—	—
1978–79		19	7
1979–80		4	—
1979–80	*Notts Co*	8	—
1980–81	Aston Villa	—	—
1981–82		1	—
1981–82	Sheffield W	9	1
1982–83		40	4
1983–84		40	5
1984–85		41	4
1985–86		31	1
1986–87		37	3
1987–88	Oxford U	32	—
1988–89		33	1
1989–90	Bristol C	43	9
1990–91		43	8
1991–92		19	3
1992–93		42	4
1993–94		3	—
1993–94	*Rochdale*	3	—

SHEPPARD, Simon
Born Clevedon 7.8.73   Ht 6 4   Wt 14 03
Goalkeeper. From Trainee. England
Youth.

Season	Club	App	Goals
1991–92	Watford	—	—
1992–93		5	—
1993–94		18	—
1993–94	*Scarborough*	9	—

SHEPSTONE, Paul
Born Coventry 8.11.70.   Ht 5 8   Wt 10 06
Midfield. From FA Schools.

Season	Club	App	Goals
1987–88	Coventry C	—	—
1988–89		—	—
1989–90	Birmingham C	—	—
1989–90	Blackburn R	—	—
From Atherstone U			
1990–91		25	1
1991–92		1	—
1991–92	*York C*	2	—
1992–93	Motherwell	1	—
1993–94	Wycombe W	—	—

SHERIDAN, Darren
Born Manchester 8.12.67   Ht 5 6
Wt 10 12
Midfield. From Winsford.

Season	Club	App	Goals
1993–94	Barnsley	3	—

SHERIDAN, John
Born Manchester 1.10.64.   Ht 5 9
Wt 12 00
Midfield. From Local. Eire Youth, Under-
21, Under-23, B, 20 full caps.

Season	Club	App	Goals
1981–82	Leeds U	—	—
1982–83		27	2
1983–84		11	1
1984–85		42	6
1985–86		32	4
1986–87		40	15
1987–88		38	12
1988–89		40	7
1989–90	Nottingham F	—	—
1989–90	Sheffield W	27	2
1990–91		46	10
1991–92		24	6
1992–93		25	3
1993–94		20	3

SHERIDAN, Tony
Born Dublin 21.10.74   Ht 6 0   Wt 11 08
Forward.

Season	Club	App	Goals
1991–92	Coventry C	—	—
1992–93		1	—
1993–94		8	—

SHERINGHAM, Teddy

Born Highams Park 2.4.66.   Ht 6 0
Wt 12 05
Forward. From Apprentice. England
Youth, 2 full caps.

Season	Club	App	Goals
1983–84	Millwall	7	1
1984–85		—	—
1984–85	*Aldershot*	5	—
1985–86	Millwall	18	4
1986–87		42	13
1987–88		43	22
1988–89		33	11
1989–90		31	9
1990–91		46	33
1991–92	Nottingham F	39	13
1992–93		3	1
1992–93	Tottenham H	38	21
1993–94		19	14

SHERLOCK, Paul

Born Wigan 17.11.73   Ht 5 11   Wt 11 05
Defender. From Trainee.

Season	Club	App	Goals
1992–93	Notts Co	—	—
1993–94		7	—

SHERON, Mike

Born Liverpool 11.1.72.   Ht 5 9   Wt 11 03
Midfield. From Trainee. England
Under-21.

Season	Club	App	Goals
1990–91	Manchester C	—	—
1990–91	*Bury*	5	1
1991–92	Manchester C	29	7
1992–93		38	11
1993–94		33	6

SHERWOOD, Steve

Born Selby 10.12.53.   Ht 6 4   Wt 14 07
Goalkeeper. From Apprentice.

Season	Club	App	Goals
1970–71	Chelsea	—	—
1971–72		1	—
1972–73		3	—
1973–74		—	—
1973–74	*Brighton*	—	—
1973–74	*Millwall*	1	—
1973–74	*Brentford*	16	—
1974–75	Chelsea	—	—
1974–75	*Brentford*	46	—
1975–76	Chelsea	12	—
1976–77		—	—
1976–77	Watford	8	—
1977–78		16	—
1978–79		16	—
1979–80		4	—
1980–81		22	—
1981–82		41	—
1982–83		42	—
1983–84		40	1
1984–85		9	—
1985–86		2	—
1986–87		11	—
1987–88	Grimsby T	46	—
1988–89		32	—
1989–90		31	—
1990–91		46	—
1991–92		21	—
1992–93		7	—
1993–94	Northampton T	16	—

SHERWOOD, Tim

Born St Albans 6.2.69.   Ht 6 1   Wt 11 04
Midfield. From Trainee. England
Under-21.

Season	Club	App	Goals
1986–87	Watford	—	—
1987–88		13	—
1988–89		19	2
1989–90	Norwich C	27	3
1990–91		37	7
1991–92		7	—
1991–92	Blackburn R	11	—
1992–93		39	3
1993–94		38	2

SHILTON, Peter

Born Leicester 18.9.49.   Ht 6 0   Wt 14 00
Goalkeeper. From Apprentice. England
Schools, Youth, Under-23, 125 full caps.
Football League.

Season	Club	App	Goals
1965–66	Leicester C	1	—
1966–67		4	—
1967–68		35	1
1968–69		42	—
1969–70		39	—
1970–71		40	—
1971–72		37	—
1972–73		41	—
1973–74		42	—
1974–75		5	—

Season	Club	Appearances	Goals
1974–75	Stoke C	25	—
1975–76		42	—
1976–77		40	—
1977–78		3	—
1977–78	Nottingham F	37	—
1978–79		42	—
1979–80		42	—
1980–81		40	—
1981–82		41	—
1982–83	Southampton	39	—
1983–84		42	—
1984–85		41	—
1985–86		37	—
1986–87		29	—
1987–88	Derby Co	40	—
1988–89		38	—
1989–90		35	—
1990–91		31	—
1991–92		31	—
1991–92	Plymouth Arg	7	—
1992–93		23	—
1993–94		4	—

SHIPPERLEY, Neil
Born Chatham 30.10.74. Ht 6 1 Wt 13 12
Forward. From Trainee. England
Under-21.

Season	Club	Appearances	Goals
1992–93	Chelsea	3	1
1993–94		24	4

SHIRTLIFF, Peter
Born Barnsley 6.4.61. Ht 6 0 Wt 13 03
Defender. From Apprentice.

Season	Club	Appearances	Goals
1978–79	Sheffield W	26	1
1979–80		3	—
1980–81		28	—
1981–82		31	2
1982–83		8	—
1983–84		36	1
1984–85		35	—
1985–86		21	—
1986–87	Charlton Ath	33	3
1987–88		36	2
1988–89		34	2
1989–90	Sheffield W	33	2
1990–91		39	2
1991–92		12	—
1992–93		20	—
1993–94	Wolverhampton W	39	—

SHORT, Chris
Born Munster 9.5.70. Ht 5 10 Wt 12 02
Defender.

Season	Club	Appearances	Goals
1988–89	Scarborough	2	—
1989–90		41	1
1990–91		—	—
1990–91	Manchester U	—	—
1990–91	Notts Co	15	1
1991–92		27	—
1992–93		31	1
1993–94		6	—

SHORT, Craig
Born Bridlington 25.6.68. Ht 6 2
Wt 12 03
Defender. From Pickering T. England
Schools.

Season	Club	Appearances	Goals
1987–88	Scarborough	21	2
1988–89		42	5
1989–90	Notts Co	44	2
1990–91		—	—
1990–91		43	—
1991–92		38	3
1992–93		3	1
1992–93	Derby Co	38	3
1993–94		43	3

SHOWLER, Paul
Born Doncaster 10.10.66. Ht 5 10
Wt 11 06
Forward. From Sheffield W, Sunderland,
Colne D, Altrincham.

Season	Club	Appearances	Goals
1991–92	Barnet	39	7
1992–93		32	5
1993–94	Bradford C	32	5

SHUTT, Carl
Born Sheffield 10.10.61. Ht 5 10
Wt 11 13
Forward. From Spalding U.

Season	Club	Appearances	Goals
1984–85	Sheffield W	—	—
1985–86		19	9
1986–87		20	7
1987–88		1	—
1987–88	Bristol C	22	9
1988–89		24	1
1988–89	Leeds U	3	4
1989–90		20	2

1990–91	....	28	10
1991–92	....	14	1
1992–93	....	14	—
1993–94	....	—	—
1993–94	Birmingham C	26	4
1993–94	*Manchester C*...............	6	—

SIDDALL, Barry
Born Ellesmere Port 12.9.54.   Ht 6 1
Wt 14 02
Goalkeeper. From Apprentice. England
Youth.

1971–72	Bolton W	—	—
1972–73	....	4	—
1973–74	....	42	—
1974–75	....	42	—
1975–76	....	42	—
1976–77	....	7	—
1976–77	Sunderland......................	34	—
1977–78	....	42	—
1978–79	....	41	—
1979–80	....	12	—
1980–81	....	15	—
1980–81	*Darlington*	8	—
1981–82	Sunderland......................	23	—
1982–83	Port Vale........................	33	—
1983–84	....	39	—
1983–84	*Blackpool*	7	—
1984–85	Port Vale........................	9	—
1984–85	Stoke C	15	—
1985–86	....	5	—
1985–86	*Tranmere R*......................	12	—
1985–86	*Manchester C*	6	—
1986–87	Blackpool......................	37	—
1987–88	....	38	—
1988–89	....	35	—
1989–90	Stockport Co	21	—
1989–90	Hartlepool U	11	—
1990–91	WBA	—	—
1990–91	Carlisle U	24	—
1991–92	Chester C	9	—
1992–93	Preston NE	1	—
1993–94	Bury	—	—

SIMKIN, Darren
Born Walsall 24.3.70   Ht 6 0   Wt 12 00
Defender. From Blakenhall.

| 1991–92 | Wolverhampton W ..... | — | — |
| 1992–93 | .... | 7 | — |

| 1993–94 | .... | 8 | — |

SIMMONDS, Danny
Born Eastbourne 17.12.74   Ht 5 11
Wt 11 05
Defender. From Trainee.

| 1993–94 | Brighton...................... | 14 | — |

SIMPSON, Fitzroy
Born Trowbridge 26.2.70.   Ht 5 8
Wt 10 07
Midfield. From Trainee.

1988–89	Swindon T	7	—
1989–90	....	30	2
1990–91	....	38	3
1991–92	....	30	4
1991–92	Manchester C	11	1
1992–93	....	29	1
1993–94	....	15	—

SIMPSON, Michael
Born Nottingham 28.2.74   Ht 5 9
Wt 10 08
Midfield. From Trainee.

| 1992–93 | Notts Co........................ | — | — |
| 1993–94 | .... | 6 | 1 |

SIMPSON, Paul
Born Carlisle 26.7.66.   Ht 5 7   Wt 11 04
Forward. From Apprentice. England
Youth, Under-21.

1982–83	Manchester C	3	—
1983–84	....	—	—
1984–85	....	10	6
1985–86	....	37	8
1986–87	....	32	3
1987–88	....	38	1
1988–89	....	1	—
1988–89	Oxford U	25	8
1989–90	....	42	9
1990–91	....	46	17
1991–92	....	31	9
1991–92	Derby Co......................	16	7
1992–93	....	35	12
1993–94	....	34	9

SIMPSON, Robert
Born Luton 3.3.76 Ht 5 10
Forward. From Trainee.

Season	Club	App	Goals
1993–94	Tottenham H	—	—

SINCLAIR, David
Born Dunfermline 6.10.69 Ht 5 11
Wt 12 10
Midfield. From Kelty U21.

Season	Club	App	Goals
1990–91	Raith R	23	1
1991–92		22	1
1992–93	*Portadown*	—	—
1992–93	Raith R	32	—
1993–94		36	2

SINCLAIR, Frank
Born Lambeth 3.12.71. Ht 5 8 Wt 11 02
Defender. From Trainee.

Season	Club	App	Goals
1989–90	Chelsea	—	—
1990–91		4	—
1991–92		8	1
1991–92	*WBA*	6	1
1992–93	Chelsea	32	—
1993–94		35	—

SINCLAIR, Ron
Born Stirling 19.11.64. Ht 5 10 Wt 11 13
Goalkeeper. From Apprentice. Scotland
Schools, Youth.

Season	Club	App	Goals
1982–83	Nottingham F	—	—
1983–84		—	—
1983–84	*Wrexham*	11	—
1984–85	Nottingham F	—	—
1984–85	*Derby Co*	—	—
1985–86	Nottingham F	—	—
1985–86	*Sheffield U*	—	—
1985–86	*Leeds U*	—	—
1986–87	Leeds U	8	—
1986–87	*Halifax T*	4	—
1987–88	Leeds U	—	—
1988–89		—	—
1988–89	*Halifax T*	10	—
1989–90	Leeds U	—	—
1989–90	Bristol C	27	—
1990–91		17	—
1991–92		—	—
1991–92	*Walsall*	10	—
1991–92	Stoke C	26	—

Season	Club	App	Goals
1992–93		29	—
1993–94		—	—

SINCLAIR, Trevor
Born Dulwich 2.3.73. Ht 5 10 Wt 11 02
Midfield. From Trainee. England
Under-21.

Season	Club	App	Goals
1989–90	Blackpool	9	—
1990–91		31	1
1991–92		27	3
1992–93		45	11
1993–94	QPR	32	4

SINNOTT, Lee
Born Pelsall 12.7.65. Ht 6 1 Wt 12 07
Defender. From Apprentice. England
Youth, Under-21.

Season	Club	App	Goals
1981–82	Walsall	4	—
1982–83		32	2
1983–84		4	—
1983–84	Watford	20	—
1984–85		30	—
1985–86		18	2
1986–87		10	—
1987–88	Bradford C	42	1
1988–89		42	2
1989–90		45	2
1990–91		44	1
1991–92	Crystal Palace	36	—
1992–93		19	—
1993–94		—	—
1993–94	Bradford C	18	—

SINTON, Andy
Born Newcastle. 19.3.66. Ht 5 8
Wt 10 10
Midfield. From Apprentice. England
Schools, B, 12 full caps.

Season	Club	App	Goals
1982–83	Cambridge U	13	5
1983–84		34	6
1984–85		26	2
1985–86		20	—
1985–86	Brentford	26	3
1986–87		46	5
1987–88		46	11
1988–89		31	9
1988–89	QPR	10	3
1989–90		38	6
1990–91		38	3

1991–92	....	38	3
1992–93	....	36	7
1993–94	Sheffield W.................	25	3

SKEDD, Tony

Born North Cleveland 19.5.75 Ht 5 5
Wt 10 00
Midfield. From Trainee.

1992–93	Hartlepool U	1	—
1993–94	....	22	—

SKELLY, Richard

Born Norwich 24.3.72
Midfield.

1993–94	Cambridge U	2	—

SKELTON, Aaron

Born Welwyn Garden 22.11.74 Ht 5 10
Wt 11 05
Midfield. From Trainee.

1992–93	Luton T	—	—
1993–94	....	—	—

SKIDMORE, Robert

Born Bristol 22.8.74 Ht 6 0 Wt 12 09
Defender. From Trainee.

1993–94	Bristol C	—	—

SKILLING, Mark

Born Irvine 6.10.72 Ht 5 9 Wt 10 13
Midfield. From Saltcoats Victoria.
Scotland Under-21.

1992–93	Kilmarnock.................	40	4
1993–94	....	23	3

SKINNER, Craig

Born Bury 21.10.70. Ht 5 8 Wt 11 00
Forward. From Trainee.

1989–90	Blackburn R	—	—
1990–91	....	7	—
1991–92	....	9	—
1992–93	Plymouth Arg.............	13	1
1993–94	....	16	—

SKINNER, Justin

Born London 30.1.69. Ht 6 0 Wt 11 03
Midfield. From Apprentice.

1986–87	Fulham	3	—

1987–88	....	32	6
1988–89	....	38	8
1989–90	....	30	4
1990–91	....	32	5
1991–92	Bristol R	42	3
1992–93	....	12	—
1993–94	....	29	5

SKINNER, Justin

Born London 17.9.72 Ht 5 7 Wt 11 00
Defender. From Trainee.

1991–92	Wimbledon	—	—
1992–93	....	1	—
1993–94	....	—	—
1993–94	*Bournemouth*	16	—

SKIPPER, Peter

Born Hull 11.4.58. Ht 6 0 Wt 13 08
Defender. From Local.

1978–79	Hull C........................	17	2
1979–80	....	6	—
1979–80	*Scunthorpe U*	1	—
1980–81	Darlington	46	2
1981–82	....	45	2
1982–83	Hull C........................	46	4
1983–84	....	46	1
1984–85	....	46	5
1985–86	....	40	1
1986–87	....	41	4
1987–88	....	43	2
1988–89	....	3	—
1988–89	Oldham Ath................	27	1
1989–90	Walsall	40	1
1990–91	....	41	1
1991–92	Wrexham	2	—
1991–92	Wigan Ath..................	18	—
From Stafford R			
1992–93	Wigan Ath..................	32	1
1993–94	....	41	3

SKIVERTON, Terry

Born Mile End 20.6.75 Ht 6 0 Wt 12 04
Defender. From Trainee.

1993–94	Chelsea........................	—	—

SLATER, Stuart

Born Sudbury 27.3.69.   Ht 5 9   Wt 10 04
Forward. From Apprentice. England B,
Under-21.

Season	Club	App	Goals
1986–87	West Ham U	—	—
1987–88		2	—
1988–89		18	1
1989–90		40	7
1990–91		40	3
1991–92		41	—
1992–93	Celtic	39	2
1993–94		4	1
1993–94	Ipswich T	28	1

SLAVEN, Bernie

Born Paisley 13.11.60.   Ht 5 11   Wt 12 00
Forward. Eire 7 full caps.

Season	Club	App	Goals
1981–82	Morton	13	1
1982–83		9	—
1983–84	Airdrie	2	—
1983–84	Queen of the South	2	—
1983–84	Albion R	3	—
1984–85		39	27
1985–86	Middlesbrough	32	8
1986–87		46	17
1987–88		44	21
1988–89		37	15
1989–90		46	21
1990–91		46	16
1991–92		38	16
1992–93		18	4
1992–93	Port Vale	10	2
1993–94		23	7
1993–94	Darlington	11	2

SLAWSON, Stephen

Born Nottingham 13.11.72.   Ht 6 0
Wt 12 06
Forward. From Trainee.

Season	Club	App	Goals
1991–92	Notts Co	13	1
1992–93		20	3
1992–93	*Burnley*	5	2
1993–94		4	—

SLINN, Kevin

Born Northampton 2.9.74   Ht 5 11
Wt 11 00
Forward. From Trainee.

Season	Club	App	Goals
1992–93	Watford	—	—

Season	Club	App	Goals
1993–94		—	—

SLOAN, Scott

Born Wallsend 14.12.67.   Ht 5 10
Wt 11 06
Forward. From Ponteland.

Season	Club	App	Goals
1988–89	Berwick R	26	4
1989–90		35	16
1990–91	Newcastle U	16	1
1991–92		—	—
1991–92	Falkirk	23	4
1992–93		29	6
1993–94		12	1
1993–94	*Cambridge U*	4	1

SMALL, Bryan

Born Birmingham 15.11.71.   Ht 5 9
Wt 11 09
Defender. From Trainee. England
Under-21.

Season	Club	App	Goals
1989–90	Aston Villa	—	—
1990–91		—	—
1991–92		8	—
1992–93		14	—
1993–94		9	—

SMALL, Mike

Born Birmingham 2.3.62.   Ht 6 1
Wt 13 05
Forward.

Season	Club	App	Goals
1980–81	Luton T	—	—
1981–82		3	—
1982–83		—	—

Twente, Standard Liege

Season	Club	App	Goals
1982–83	Peterborough U	4	1

From Go Ahead Eagles/PAOK Salonika

Season	Club	App	Goals
1990–91	Brighton	39	15
1991–92	West Ham U	40	13
1992–93		9	—
1993–94		—	—
1993–94	*Wolverhampton W*	3	1
1993–94	*Charlton Ath*	2	—

SMART, Gary

Born Totnes 29.4.64.   Ht 5 9   Wt 11 03
Defender. From Wokingham.

Season	Club	App	Goals
1988–89	Oxford U	17	—
1989–90		40	—

Season	Club	Appearances	Goals
1990–91	....	15	—
1991–92	....	39	—
1992–93	....	41	—
1993–94	....	23	—

SMART, Jason
Born Rochdale 15.2.69 Ht 6 0 Wt 12 10
Defender. From Trainee.

Season	Club	Appearances	Goals
1985–86	Rochdale.....................	1	—
1986–87	....	38	1
1987–88	....	36	3
1988–89	....	42	—
1989–90	Crewe Alex	41	2
1990–91	....	37	—
1991–92	....	11	—
1992–93	Rochdale.....................	—	—
1993–94	....	—	—

SMILLIE, Neil
Born Barnsley 19.7.58. Ht 5 6 Wt 10 07
Forward. From Apprentice.

Season	Club	Appearances	Goals
1975–76	Crystal Palace	—	—
1976–77	....	1	—
1976–77	*Brentford*.....................	3	—
1977–78	Crystal Palace	1	—
1978–79	....	8	1
1979–80	....	8	1
1980–81	....	24	2
1981–82	....	41	3
1982–83	Brighton	25	—
1983–84	....	26	2
1984–85	....	24	—
1985–86	Watford	16	3
1986–87	....	—	—
1986–87	Reading.....................	16	—
1987–88	....	23	—
1988–89	Brentford	28	2
1989–90	....	43	5
1990–91	....	36	3
1991–92	....	44	7
1992–93	....	21	1
1993–94	Gillingham	38	2

SMITH, Alan
Born Birmingham 21.11.62. Ht 6 3
Wt 12 13
Forward. From Alvechurch. England B,
13 full caps. Football League.

Season	Club	Appearances	Goals
1982–83	Leicester C	39	13

Season	Club	Appearances	Goals
1983–84	....	40	15
1984–85	....	39	12
1985–86	....	40	19
1986–87	....	33	14
1986–87	*Leicester C*.....................	9	3
1987–88	Arsenal.....................	39	11
1988–89	....	36	23
1989–90	....	38	10
1990–91	....	37	22
1991–92	....	39	12
1992–93	....	31	3
1993–94	....	25	3

SMITH, Barry
Born Paisley 19.2.74. Ht 5 10 Wt 12 00
Defender. From Giffnock N. Scotland
Under-21.

Season	Club	Appearances	Goals
1991–92	Celtic.....................	3	—
1992–93	....	6	—
1993–94	....	7	—

SMITH, Danny
Born Sheffield 8.1.75 Ht 5 9
Midfield. From Manchester C trainee.

Season	Club	Appearances	Goals
1993–94	Sheffield U	—	—

SMITH, David
Born Liverpool 26.12.70. Ht 5 9
Wt 11 12
Midfield. From Trainee.

Season	Club	Appearances	Goals
1989–90	Norwich C	1	—
1990–91	....	3	—
1991–92	....	1	—
1992–93	....	6	—
1993–94	....	7	—

SMITH, David
Born Sidcup 25.6.61. Ht 5 11 Wt 12 00
Forward. From Welling U.

Season	Club	Appearances	Goals
1986–87	Gillingham	27	1
1987–88	....	35	7
1988–89	....	42	2
1989–90	Bristol C	45	4
1990–91	....	34	5
1991–92	....	18	1
1991–92	Plymouth Arg	18	2
1992–93	Notts Co	37	8
1993–94	....	—	—

SMITH, David

Born Gloucester 29.3.68.   Ht 5 8
Wt 10 02
Midfield. England Under-21.

Season	Club	App	Goals
1986–87	Coventry C	—	—
1987–88		16	4
1988–89		35	3
1989–90		37	6
1990–91		36	1
1991–92		24	4
1992–93		6	1
1992–93	*Bournemouth*	1	—
1992–93	Birmingham C	13	1
1993–94		25	2
1993–94	WBA	18	—

SMITH, Dean

Born West Bromwich 19.3.71.   Ht 6 0
Wt 12 01
Defender. From Trainee.

Season	Club	App	Goals
1988–89	Walsall	15	—
1989–90		7	—
1990–91		33	—
1991–92		9	—
1992–93		42	1
1993–94		36	1

SMITH, Eric

Born Dublin 20.10.75   Ht 6 2   Wt 12 08
Defender. From Trainee.

Season	Club	App	Goals
1992–93	Crystal Palace	—	—
1993–94		—	—

SMITH, Gary

Born Glasgow 25.3.71   Ht 6 0   Wt 10 04
Defender. From Duntocher BC.

Season	Club	App	Goals
1988–89	Falkirk	3	—
1989–90		36	—
1990–91		31	—
1991–92	Aberdeen	16	1
1992–93		40	—
1993–94		21	—

SMITH, Gary

Born Harlow 3.12.68   Ht 5 10   Wt 12 09
Midfield. From Apprentice.

Season	Club	App	Goals
1985–86	Fulham	1	—
1986–87		—	—

Season	Club	App	Goals
1987–88	Colchester U	11	—

From Enfield, Wycombe W, Welling U

Season	Club	App	Goals
1993–94	Barnet	9	—

SMITH, Henry

Born Lanark 10.3.56.   Ht 6 2   Wt 12 00
Goalkeeper. From school. Scotland
Under-21, 3 full caps.

Season	Club	App	Goals
1978–79	Leeds U	—	—
1979–80		—	—
1980–81		—	—
1981–82	Hearts	33	—
1982–83		39	—
1983–84		36	—
1984–85		36	—
1985–86		36	—
1986–87		43	—
1987–88		44	—
1988–89		36	—
1989–90		36	—
1990–91		23	—
1991–92		44	—
1992–93		25	—
1993–94		27	—

SMITH, Ian

Born Bury 28.11.76
Defender. From Trainee.

Season	Club	App	Goals
1993–94	Manchester C	—	—

SMITH, James

Born Birmingham 17.9.74   Ht 5 6
Wt 10 08
Forward. From Trainee.

Season	Club	App	Goals
1993–94	Wolverhampton W	—	—

SMITH, Jason

Born Bromsgrove 6.9.74   Ht 6 2
Wt 12 04
Defender. From Tiverton.

Season	Club	App	Goals
1993–94	Coventry C	—	—

SMITH, Jason

Born Birmingham 21.12.75   Ht 5 4
Wt 10 02
Midfield. From Trainee.

Season	Club	App	Goals
1993–94	Wolverhampton W	—	—

SMITH, Kevan

Born Eaglescliffe 13.12.59. Ht 6 3
Wt 12 07
Defender. From Stockton.

Season	Club	App	Goals
1979–80	Darlington	35	1
1980–81		39	2
1981–82		45	1
1982–83		46	3
1983–84		44	2
1984–85		36	2
1985–86	Rotherham U	43	3
1986–87		16	1
1986–87	Coventry C	—	—
1987–88		6	—
1987–88	York C	—	—
1988–89		31	5
1989–90	Darlington	*39*	*3*
1990–91		46	4
1991–92		39	1
1992–93		13	—
1992–93	*Hereford U*	6	—
1993–94	Hereford U	18	—

SMITH, Mark

Born Sheffield 21.3.60. Ht 6 2 Wt 13 11
Defender. From Apprentice. England
Under-21.

Season	Club	App	Goals
1977–78	Sheffield W	2	—
1978–79		21	—
1979–80		44	9
1980–81		41	1
1981–82		41	—
1982–83		41	2
1983–84		27	2
1984–85		36	2
1985–86		13	—
1986–87		16	—
1987–88	Plymouth Arg	41	6
1988–89		35	—
1989–90		6	—
1989–90	Barnsley	25	3
1990–91		37	6
1991–92		38	1
1992–93		4	—
1992–93	Notts Co	5	—
1992–93	*Chesterfield*	6	1
1992–93	*Huddersfield T*	5	—
1992–93	*Port Vale*	6	—
1993–94	Lincoln C	20	1

SMITH, Mark

Born Sheffield 19.12.61. Ht 5 9 Wt 12 02
Forward.

Season	Club	App	Goals
1979–80	Sheffield U	—	—
1980–81		—	—
1981–82		—	—
From Worksop, Gainsborough T			
1985–86	Scunthorpe U	1	—
From Kettering			
1988–89	Rochdale	27	7
1988–89	Huddersfield T	20	2
1989–90		44	7
1990–91		32	2
1990–91	Grimsby T	11	—
1991–92		40	4
1992–93		26	—
1993–94	Scunthorpe U	30	6

SMITH, Mark

Born Bellshill 16.12.64. Ht 5 9 Wt 10 04
Midfield. From St Mirren BC.

Season	Club	App	Goals
1983–84	Queen's Park	15	2
1984–85		36	2
1985–86		31	3
1986–87	Celtic	6	—
1987–88	Dunfermline Ath	30	5
1988–89		23	1
1989–90	*Stoke C*	2	—
1989–90	Nottingham F	—	—
1990–91		—	—
1990–91	*Reading*	3	—
1991–92	Nottingham F	—	—
1992–93	Shrewsbury T	31	1
1993–94		8	—

SMITH, Mark

Born Birmingham 2.1.73 Ht 6 1
Wt 13 09
Goalkeeper. From Trainee.

Season	Club	App	Goals
1991–92	Nottingham F	—	—
1992–93		—	—
1992–93	Crewe Alex	7	—
1993–94		32	—

SMITH, Martin

Born Sunderland 13.11.74.
Forward. From Trainee.

Season	Club	App	Goals
1992–93	Sunderland	—	—

| 1993–94 | .... | 29 | 8 |

SMITH, Matthew
Born Derby 28.8.73 Ht 5 11
Defender. From Derby Co.

| 1993–94 | Plymouth Arg............. | — | — |

SMITH, Neil
Born London 30.9.71. Ht 5 9 Wt 12 00
Midfield. From Trainee.

1990–91	Tottenham H	—	—
1991–92	....	—	—
1991–92	Gillingham	26	2
1992–93	....	39	3
1993–94	....	35	2

SMITH, Nicky
Born Berkley 28.1.69 Ht 5 7 Wt 10 00
Midfield.

1986–87	Southend U...................	1	—
1987–88	....	34	5
1988–89	....	11	—
1989–90	....	14	1
1990–91	Colchester U.................	34	—
1991–92	....	42	8
1992–93	....	42	4
1993–94	....	39	—

SMITH, Paul
Born Rotherham 9.11.64. Ht 5 10
Wt 10 09
Forward. From Apprentice.

1982–83	Sheffield U	7	—
1983–84	....	3	—
1984–85	....	8	1
1985–86	....	18	—
1985–86	Stockport Co	7	5
1986–87	Port Vale......................	42	7
1987–88	....	2	—
1987–88	Lincoln C......................	33	8
1988–89	....	28	10
1989–90	....	33	5
1990–91	....	46	6
1991–92	....	39	3
1992–93	....	33	3
1993–94	....	36	—

SMITH, Paul
Born Lenham 18.9.71. Ht 5 11 Wt 14 00
Midfield. From Trainee.

1989–90	Southend U.................	10	1
1990–91	....	2	—
1991–92	....	—	—
1992–93	....	8	—
1993–94	Brentford	32	3

SMITH, Paul
Born Burnley 22.1.76
Forward. From Trainee.

| 1993–94 | Burnley .... | 1 | — |

SMITH, Richard
Born Leicester 3.10.70. Ht 5 11
Wt 12 10
Defender. From Trainee.

1988–89	Leicester C...................	—	—
1989–90	....	4	—
1989–90	Cambridge U	4	—
1990–91	Leicester C...................	4	—
1991–92	....	25	1
1992–93	....	44	—
1993–94	....	8	—

SMITH, Richard
Born Lichfield 24.1.74 Ht 5 11 Wt 11 10
Defender. From Trainee.

| 1992–93 | Nottingham F............. | — | — |
| 1993–94 | .... | — | — |

SMITH, Scott
Born Christchurch 6.3.75 Ht 5 8
Wt 11 06
Defender. From Trainee.

| 1993–94 | Rotherham U .... | 7 | — |

SMITH, Shaun
Born Leeds 9.4.71. Ht 5 10 Wt 11 00
Defender. From Trainee.

1988–89	Halifax T	1	—
1989–90	....	6	—
1990–91	....	—	—
1991–92	Crewe Alex	10	—
1992–93	....	36	4
1993–94	....	37	7

SMITH, Thomas

Born Glasgow 12.10.73 Ht 5 8 Wt 11 7
Midfield. S Form.

Season	Club	App	Goals
1990–91	Partick T	1	—
1991–92		—	—
1992–93		2	—
1993–94		8	1

SMITH, Tony

Born Sunderland 21.9.71. Ht 5 10
Wt 11 04
Defender. From Trainee. England Youth.

Season	Club	App	Goals
1990–91	Sunderland	9	—
1991–92		2	—
1991–92	*Hartlepool U*	5	—
1992–93	Sunderland	7	—
1993–94		1	—

SMITHARD, Matthew

Born Leeds 13.6.76
Midfield. From Trainee.

Season	Club	App	Goals
1992–93	Leeds U	—	—
1993–94		—	—

SNELDERS, Theo

Born Westervoort 7.12.63 Ht 6 2
Wt 14 02
Goalkeeper. From Twente. Holland full caps.

Season	Club	App	Goals
1988–89	Aberdeen	36	—
1989–90		23	—
1990–91		21	—
1991–92		42	—
1992–93		41	—
1993–94		33	—

SNODIN, Glynn

Born Rotherham 14.2.60. Ht 5 6
Wt 9 05
Midfield. From Apprentice.

Season	Club	App	Goals
1976–77	Doncaster R	4	—
1977–78		22	2
1978–79		34	3
1979–80		41	1
1980–81		44	3
1981–82		40	7
1982–83		38	14
1983–84		43	13
1984–85		43	18
1985–86	Sheffield W	28	1
1986–87		31	—
1987–88	Leeds U	35	7
1988–89		35	3
1989–90		4	—
1990–91		20	—
1991–92		—	—
1991–92	*Oldham Ath*	8	1
1991–92	Rotherham U	3	—
1991–92	Hearts	7	—
1992–93		27	—
1993–94	Barnsley	11	—

SNODIN, Ian

Born Rotherham 15.8.63. Ht 5 7
Wt 9 01
Midfield. From Apprentice. England Youth, Under-21.

Season	Club	App	Goals
1979–80	Doncaster R	9	1
1980–81		32	2
1981–82		33	2
1982–83		34	3
1983–84		39	9
1984–85		41	8
1985–86	Leeds U	37	5
1986–87		14	1
1986–87	Everton	16	—
1987–88		31	2
1988–89		23	—
1989–90		25	—
1990–91		1	—
1991–92		—	—
1992–93		20	1
1993–94		29	—

SNOOK, Eddie

Born Washington 18.10.68. Ht 5 7
Wt 10 01
Midfield. From Apprentice.

Season	Club	App	Goals
1991–92	Notts Co	—	—
1992–93		—	—
1993–94		—	—

SNOWDEN, Trevor

Born Sunderland 4.10.73 Ht 5 8
Wt 11 00
Midfield. From Seaham Red Star.

Season	Club	App	Goals
1992–93	Rochdale	13	—

327

Season	Club	Apps	Goals
1993–94		1	—

SOLOMAN, Jason

Born Welwyn 6.10.70. Ht 6 0 Wt 11 10
Defender. From Trainee. England Youth.

Season	Club	Apps	Goals
1988–89	Watford	—	—
1989–90		—	—
1990–91		8	—
1991–92		29	—
1992–93		36	2
1993–94		25	3

SOMMER, Jurgen

Born New York 27.2.64. Ht 6 4
Wt 15 12
Goalkeeper.

Season	Club	Apps	Goals
1991–92	Luton T	—	—
1991–92	*Brighton*	1	—
1992–93	Luton T	—	—
1992–93	*Torquay U*	10	—
1993–94	Luton T	43	—

SORRELL, Tony

Born London 17.10.66. Ht 5 11
Wt 12 04
Midfield. From Barking and Bishop's
Stortford (1988).

Season	Club	Apps	Goals
1989–90	Maidstone U	28	3
1990–91		27	5
1991–92		—	—
1992–93	Peterborough U	—	—
1992–93	Colchester U	5	1
1992–93	Barnet	8	2
1993–94	Brentford	—	—

SOUTHALL, Neville

Born Llandudno 16.9.58. Ht 6 1
Wt 12 01
Goalkeeper. From Winsford. Wales
Under-21, 74 full caps.

Season	Club	Apps	Goals
1980–81	Bury	39	—
1981–82	Everton	26	—
1982–83		17	—
1982–83	*Port Vale*	9	—
1983–84	Everton	35	—
1984–85		42	—
1985–86		32	—
1986–87		31	—
1987–88		32	—
1988–89		38	—
1989–90		38	—
1990–91		38	—
1991–92		42	—
1992–93		40	—
1993–94		42	—

SOUTHALL, Nicky

Born Teeside 28.1.72. Ht 5 10 Wt 11 02
Forward. From Trainee.

Season	Club	Apps	Goals
1990–91	Hartlepool U	—	—
1991–92		22	3
1992–93		39	6
1993–94		40	9

SOUTHGATE, Gareth

Born Watford 3.9.70. Ht 5 10 Wt 11 12
Defender. From Trainee.

Season	Club	Apps	Goals
1988–89	Crystal Palace	—	—
1989–90		—	—
1990–91		1	—
1991–92		30	—
1992–93		33	3
1993–94		46	9

SOUTHON, Jamie

Born Hornchurch 13.10.74. Ht 5 9
Wt 11 09
Midfield. From Trainee.

Season	Club	Apps	Goals
1992–93	Southend U	1	—
1993–94		—	—

SPACKMAN, Nigel

Born Romsey 2.12.60. Ht 6 1 Wt 13 02
Midfield. From Andover.

Season	Club	Apps	Goals
1980–81	Bournemouth	44	3
1981–82		35	3
1982–83		40	4
1983–84	Chelsea	40	3
1984–85		42	1
1985–86		39	7
1986–87		20	1
1986–87	Liverpool	12	—
1987–88		27	—
1988–89		12	—
1988–89	QPR	16	1
1989–90		13	—

Season	Club	App	Goals
1989–90	Rangers	21	1
1990–91		35	—
1991–92		42	—
1992–93		2	—
1992–93	Chelsea	6	—
1993–94		9	—

SPARROW, Paul

Born London 24.3.75   Ht 6 0   Wt 11 04
Defender. From Trainee.

Season	Club	App	Goals
1993–94	Crystal Palace	—	—

SPEAK, Chris

Born Preston 20.8.73   Ht 6 0   Wt 12 04
Forward. From Trainee.

Season	Club	App	Goals
1992–93	Blackpool	1	—
1993–94		—	—

SPEARING, Tony

Born Romford 7.10.64.   Ht 5 9   Wt 10 12
Defender. From Apprentice. England Youth.

Season	Club	App	Goals
1982–83	Norwich C	—	—
1983–84		4	—
1984–85		—	—
1984–85	*Stoke C*	9	—
1984–85	*Oxford U*	5	—
1985–86	Norwich C	8	—
1986–87		39	—
1987–88		18	—
1988–89	Leicester C	36	—
1989–90		20	1
1990–91		17	—
1991–92	Plymouth Arg	30	—
1992–93		5	—
1992–93	Peterborough U	22	—
1993–94		34	1

SPEED, Gary

Born Hawarden 8.9.69.   Ht 5 9   Wt 10 06
Midfield. From Trainee. Wales Under-21, 25 full caps.

Season	Club	App	Goals
1988–89	Leeds U	1	—
1989–90		25	3
1990–91		38	7
1991–92		41	7
1992–93		39	7
1993–94		36	10

SPEEDIE, David

Born Glenrothes 20.2.60.   Ht 5 7   Wt 11 01
Forward. From Amateur. Scotland Under-21, 10 full caps.

Season	Club	App	Goals
1978–79	Barnsley	10	—
1979–80		13	—
1980–81	Darlington	44	4
1981–82		44	17
1982–83	Chelsea	34	7
1983–84		37	13
1984–85		35	10
1985–86		34	14
1986–87		22	3
1987–88	Coventry C	36	6
1988–89		36	14
1989–90		32	8
1990–91		18	3
1990–91	Liverpool	12	6
1991–92	Blackburn R	36	23
1992–93	Southampton	11	—
1992–93	*Birmingham C*	10	2
1992–93	*WBA*	7	2
1992–93	*West Ham U*	11	4
1993–94	Leicester C	37	12

SPENCER, John

Born Glasgow 11.9.70.   Ht 5 6   Wt 10 00
Forward. From Rangers Am BC. Scotland Under-21.

Season	Club	App	Goals
1986–87	Rangers	—	—
1987–88		—	—
1988–89		—	—
1988–89	*Morton*	4	1
From Lisbung, HK			
1990–91	Rangers	5	1
1991–92		8	1
1992–93	Chelsea	23	7
1993–94		19	5

SPINK, Dean

Born Birmingham 22.1.67.   Ht 5 11   Wt 13 08
Forward. From Halesowen.

Season	Club	App	Goals
1989–90	Aston Villa	—	—
1989–90	*Scarborough*	3	2
1989–90	*Bury*	6	1
1989–90	Shrewsbury T	13	5
1990–91		43	6

Season	Club	Apps	Goals
1991–92		40	1
1992–93		23	1
1993–94		40	18

SPINK, Nigel

Born Chelmsford 8.8.58. Ht 6 2
Wt 14 08
Goalkeeper. From Chelmsford C. England
B, 1 full cap.

Season	Club	Apps	Goals
1976–77	Aston Villa	—	—
1977–78		—	—
1978–79		—	—
1979–80		1	—
1980–81		—	—
1981–82		—	—
1982–83		22	—
1983–84		28	—
1984–85		19	—
1985–86		31	—
1986–87		32	—
1987–88		44	—
1988–89		34	—
1989–90		38	—
1990–91		34	—
1991–92		23	—
1992–93		25	—
1993–94		15	—

SPOONER, Nicky

Born Manchester 5.6.71. Ht 5 8
Wt 11 00
Defender. From Trainee.

Season	Club	Apps	Goals
1990–91	Bolton W	—	—
1991–92		15	1
1992–93		6	1
1993–94		1	—

SPOONER, Steve

Born London 25.1.61. Ht 5 10 Wt 12 00
Midfield. From Apprentice.

Season	Club	Apps	Goals
1978–79	Derby Co	1	—
1979–80		1	—
1980–81		2	—
1981–82		4	—
1981–82	Halifax T	29	2
1982–83		43	11
1983–84	Chesterfield	20	3
1984–85		41	6
1985–86		32	5

Season	Club	Apps	Goals
1986–87	Hereford U	42	11
1987–88		42	8
1988–89	York C	31	5
1989–90		41	6
1990–91	Rotherham U	19	1
1990–91	Mansfield T	12	—
1991–92		31	2
1992–93		15	1
1992–93	Blackpool	2	—
1993–94		—	—
1993–94	Chesterfield	5	—

SQUIRES, Jamie

Born Preston 15.11.75. Ht 6 1 Wt 12 00
Defender. From Trainee.

Season	Club	Apps	Goals
1993–94	Preston NE	4	—

SRNICEK, Pavel

Born Ostrava 10.3.68. Ht 6 2 Wt 14 09
Goalkeeper. From Banik Ostrava.
Czechoslovakia full caps.

Season	Club	Apps	Goals
1990–91	Newcastle U	7	—
1991–92		13	—
1992–93		32	—
1993–94		21	—

STACEY, Steven

Born Bristol 9.6.75
Defender. From Trainee.

Season	Club	Apps	Goals
1993–94	Torquay U	1	—

STACKMAN, Harry

Born Arizona 16.11.75 Ht 5 11 Wt 12 06
Defender. From Trainee.

Season	Club	Apps	Goals
1993–94	Northampton T	1	—

STAINROD, Simon

Born Sheffield 1.2.59. Ht 5 10 Wt 12 09
Forward. From Apprentice. England
Youth.

Season	Club	Apps	Goals
1975–76	Sheffield U	7	2
1976–77		21	3
1977–78		25	6
1978–79		14	3
1978–79	Oldham Ath	14	5
1979–80		37	11
1980–81		18	5
1980–81	QPR	15	4

Season	Club	App	Goals
1981–82		39	17
1982–83		31	9
1983–84		41	13
1984–85		19	5
1984–85	Sheffield W	9	1
1985–86		6	1
1985–86	Aston Villa	30	10
1986–87		29	6
1987–88		4	—
1987–88	Stoke C	12	2
1988–89		16	4
From Strasbourg			
1990–91	Falkirk	37	16
1991–92		23	5
1991–92	Dundee	13	2
1992–93		20	7
1993–94		1	—

STALKER, Mark
Born Liverpool 24.9.74   Ht 5 10
Wt 11 05
Midfield.

Season	Club	App	Goals
1992–93	Liverpool	—	—
1993–94		—	—

STALLARD, Mark
Born Derby 24.10.74.   Ht 6 0   Wt 12 06
Forward. From Trainee.

Season	Club	App	Goals
1991–92	Derby Co	3	—
1992–93		5	—
1993–94		—	—

STAMP, Philip
Born Middlesbrough 12.12.75   Ht 5 9
Wt 11 09
Midfield. From Trainee.

Season	Club	App	Goals
1992–93	Middlesbrough	—	—
1993–94		10	—

STAMPS, Scott
Born Edgbaston 20.3.75   Ht 5 11
Wt 11 00
Defender. From Trainee.

Season	Club	App	Goals
1992–93	Torquay U	2	—
1993–94		6	—

STANCLIFFE, Paul
Born Sheffield 5.5.58.   Ht 6 2   Wt 13 05
Defender. From Apprentice.

Season	Club	App	Goals
1975–76	Rotherham U	42	2
1976–77		46	—
1977–78		32	3
1978–79		33	—
1979–80		33	1
1980–81		44	—
1981–82		42	2
1982–83		13	—
1983–84	Sheffield U	43	1
1984–85		33	1
1985–86		40	1
1986–87		36	2
1987–88		41	3
1988–89		42	3
1989–90		40	1
1990–91		3	—
1990–91	*Rotherham U*	5	—
1990–91	Wolverhampton W	17	—
1991–92	York C	18	1
1992–93		41	1
1993–94		28	1

STANISLAUS, Roger
Born Hammersmith 2.11.68.   Ht 5 9
Wt 12 06
Defender. From Trainee.

Season	Club	App	Goals
1986–87	Arsenal	—	—
1987–88	Brentford	37	2
1988–89		43	1
1989–90		31	1
1990–91	Bury	44	2
1991–92		40	3
1992–93		24	—
1993–94		35	—

STANNARD, Jim
Born London 6.10.62.   Ht 6 2   Wt 14 12
Goalkeeper. From Local.

Season	Club	App	Goals
1980–81	Fulham	17	—
1981–82		2	—
1982–83		—	—
1983–84		15	—
1984–85		7	—
1984–85	*Charlton Ath*	1	—
1984–85	*Southend U*	17	—
1985–86	Southend U	46	—

Season	Club	Apps	Goals
1986–87	....	46	—
1987–88	Fulham	46	—
1988–89	....	45	—
1989–90	....	44	1
1990–91	....	42	—
1991–92	....	46	—
1992–93	....	43	—
1993–94	....	46	—

STANT, Phil

Born Bolton 13.10.62.   Ht 6 1   Wt 12 07
Forward. From Camberley.

Season	Club	Apps	Goals
1982–83	Reading......................	4	2
From Army			
1986–87	Hereford U	9	1
1987–88	....	39	9
1988–89	....	41	28
1989–90	Notts Co	22	6
1990–91	....	—	—
1990–91	*Blackpool*	12	5
1990–91	*Lincoln C*	4	—
1990–91	*Huddersfield T*............	5	1
1990–91	Fulham	19	5
1991–92	Mansfield T.................	40	26
1992–93	....	17	6
1992–93	Cardiff C.....................	24	11
1993–94	....	36	10
1993–94	*Mansfield T*	4	1

STAPLETON, Frank

Born Dublin 10.7.56.   Ht 6 0   Wt 13 01
Forward. From Apprentice. Eire Youth,
70 full caps.

Season	Club	Apps	Goals
1973–74	Arsenal......................	—	—
1974–75	....	1	—
1975–76	....	25	4
1976–77	....	40	13
1977–78	....	39	13
1978–79	....	41	17
1979–80	....	39	14
1980–81	....	40	14
1981–82	Manchester U	41	13
1982–83	....	41	14
1983–84	....	42	13
1984–85	....	24	6
1985–86	....	41	7
1986–87	....	34	7
1987–88	Ajax	4	—
1987–88	Derby Co	10	1

Season	Club	Apps	Goals
From Le Havre			
1989–90	Blackburn R	43	3
1990–91	....	38	10
1991–92	Aldershot	1	—
1991–92	Huddersfield T............	5	—
1991–92	Bradford C	27	—
1992–93	....	13	2
1993–94	....	28	—

STAPLETON, Simon

Born Oxford 10.12.68.   Ht 6 0   Wt 13 00
Midfield. Portsmouth trainee.

Season	Club	Apps	Goals
1988–89	Bristol R	5	—
1989–90	....	—	—
To Wycombe W			
1993–94	Wycombe W	22	1

STARBUCK, Philip

Born Nottingham 24.11.68.   Ht 5 10
Wt 10 13
Forward. From Apprentice.

Season	Club	Apps	Goals
1986–87	Nottingham F.............	5	2
1987–88	....	10	—
1987–88	*Birmingham C*.............	3	—
1988–89	Nottingham F..............	7	—
1989–90	....	2	—
1989–90	*Hereford U*	6	—
1990–91	Nottingham F..............	12	—
1990–91	*Blackburn R*	6	1
1991–92	Huddersfield T............	44	14
1992–93	....	38	9
1993–94	....	46	12

STARK, Billy

Born Glasgow 1.12.56   Ht 6 1   Wt 11 11
Midfield. From Anniesland W. Scotland
U-21.

Season	Club	Apps	Goals
1975–76	St Mirren	21	6
1976–77	....	35	11
1977–78	....	33	7
1978–79	....	32	9
1979–80	....	36	8
1980–81	....	34	5
1981–82	....	33	10
1982–83	....	31	4
1983–84	Aberdeen....................	14	6
1984–85	....	32	15
1985–86	....	30	8
1986–87	....	35	12

Season	Club	App	Goals
1987–88	Celtic	37	8
1988–89		25	9
1989–90		2	—
1990–91	Kilmarnock	21	6
1991–92		1	—
1991–92	Hamilton A	14	—
1992–93	Kilmarnock	28	3
1993–94		8	—

STARK, Wayne
Born Derby 14.10.76
Midfield. From Trainee.

Season	Club	App	Goals
1993–94	Mansfield T	1	—

STATHAM, Brian
Born Zimbabwe 21.5.69.   Ht 5 11
Wt 11 00
Defender. From Apprentice. England
Youth, Under-21.

Season	Club	App	Goals
1987–88	Tottenham H	18	—
1988–89		6	—
1989–90		—	—
1990–91		—	—
1990–91	*Reading*	8	—
1991–92	Tottenham H	—	—
1991–92	*Bournemouth*	2	—
1991–92	*Brentford*	18	—
1992–93	Brentford	45	—
1993–94		31	1

STATHAM, Mark
Born Barnsley 11.11.75   Ht 6 2   Wt 12 02
Goalkeeper. From Trainee.

Season	Club	App	Goals
1992–93	Nottingham F	—	—
1993–94		—	—

STAUNTON, Steve
Born Drogheda 19.1.69.   Ht 6 0
Wt 12 04
Defender. From Dundalk. Eire Under-21,
47 full caps.

Season	Club	App	Goals
1986–87	Liverpool	—	—
1987–88		—	—
1987–88	*Bradford C*	8	—
1988–89	Liverpool	21	—
1989–90		20	—
1990–91		24	—
1991–92	Aston Villa	37	4
1992–93		42	2
1993–94		24	2

STEELE, Tim
Born Coventry 1.2.67.   Ht 5 9   Wt 11 00
Forward. From Apprentice.

Season	Club	App	Goals
1985–86	Shrewsbury T	2	—
1986–87		11	1
1987–88		33	3
1988–89		15	1
1988–89	Wolverhampton W	11	1
1989–90		15	1
1990–91		28	2
1991–92		17	3
1991–92	*Stoke C*	7	1
1992–93	Wolverhampton W	4	—
1993–94	Bradford C	11	—
1993–94	Hereford U	20	2

STEIN, Mark
Born S. Africa 28.1.66.   Ht 5 6   Wt 11 02
Forward. England Youth.

Season	Club	App	Goals
1983–84	Luton T	1	—
1984–85		1	—
1985–86		6	—
1985–86	*Aldershot*	2	1
1986–87	Luton T	21	8
1987–88		25	11
1988–89	QPR	31	4
1989–90		2	—
1989–90	Oxford U	41	9
1990–91		34	8
1991–92		7	1
1991–92	Stoke C	36	16
1992–93		46	26
1993–94		12	8
1993–94	Chelsea	18	13

STEJSKAL, Jan
Born Czechoslovakia 15.1.62.   Ht 6 3
Wt 12 00
Goalkeeper. From Sparta Prague.
Czechoslovakia full caps.

Season	Club	App	Goals
1990–91	QPR	26	—
1991–92		41	—
1992–93		15	—
1993–94		26	—

STEPHENSON, Michael

Born Coventry 6.10.73 Ht 5 9 Wt 12 00
Forward. From Trainee.

Season	Club	App	Goals
1992–93	Coventry C	—	—
1993–94		—	—

STEPHENSON, Paul

Born Wallsend 2.1.68. Ht 5 10 Wt 12 02
Forward. From Apprentice. England
Youth.

Season	Club	App	Goals
1985–86	Newcastle U	22	1
1986–87		24	—
1987–88		7	—
1988–89		8	—
1989–90	Millwall	12	1
1989–90		23	2
1990–91		30	1
1991–92		28	2
1992–93		5	—
1992–93	*Gillingham*	12	2
1992–93	Brentford	11	—
1993–94		25	—

STERLING, Worrell

Born Bethnal Green 8.6.65. Ht 5 7
Wt 10 11
Midfield. From Apprentice.

Season	Club	App	Goals
1982–83	Watford	3	—
1983–84		10	1
1984–85		15	4
1985–86		24	3
1986–87		18	4
1987–88		21	2
1988–89		3	—
1988–89	Peterborough U	12	3
1989–90		46	5
1990–91		46	9
1991–92		45	4
1992–93		44	8
1993–94	Bristol R	43	5

STEVEN, Trevor

Born Berwick 21.9.63. Ht 5 8 Wt 10 09
Midfield. From Apprentice. England
Under-21, 36 full caps.

Season	Club	App	Goals
1980–81	Burnley	1	—
1981–82		36	3
1982–83		39	8
1983–84	Everton	27	1
1984–85		40	12
1985–86		41	9
1986–87		41	14
1987–88		36	6
1988–89		29	6
1989–90	Rangers	34	3
1990–91		19	2
1991–92		2	1
1991–92	Marseille	27	3
1992–93	Rangers	24	5
1993–94		32	4

STEVENS, Gary

Born Barrow 27.3.63. Ht 5 11 Wt 10 11
Defender. From Apprentice. England 46
full caps.

Season	Club	App	Goals
1980–81	Everton	—	—
1981–82		19	1
1982–83		28	—
1983–84		27	1
1984–85		37	3
1985–86		41	1
1986–87		25	2
1987–88		31	—
1988–89	Rangers	35	1
1989–90		35	1
1990–91		36	4
1991–92		43	2
1992–93		9	—
1993–94		29	—

STEVENS, Ian

Born Malta 21.10.66. Ht 5 9 Wt 12 00
Forward. From Trainee.

Season	Club	App	Goals
1984–85	Preston NE	4	1
1985–86		7	1
1986–87	Stockport Co	2	—
From Lancaster C			
1986–87	Bolton W	8	2
1987–88		9	—
1988–89		21	5
1989–90		4	—
1990–91		5	—
1991–92	Bury	45	17
1992–93		32	14
1993–94		33	7

STEVENS, Keith

Born Merton 21.6.64. Ht 6 0   Wt 12 10
Defender. From Apprentice.

Season	Club	App	Goals
1980–81	Millwall	1	—
1981–82		7	—
1982–83		26	—
1983–84		17	—
1984–85		41	—
1985–86		33	1
1986–87		35	1
1987–88		35	1
1988–89		23	—
1989–90		28	—
1990–91		42	1
1991–92		27	—
1992–93		31	2
1993–94		44	1

STEWART, Billy

Born Liverpool 1.1.65. Ht 5 11   Wt 11 07
Goalkeeper. From Apprentice.

Season	Club	App	Goals
1982–83	Liverpool	—	—
1983–84		—	—
1984–85	Wigan Ath	6	—
1985–86		8	—
1986–87	Chester C	29	—
1987–88		27	—
1988–89		46	—
1989–90		46	—
1990–91		38	—
1991–92		37	—
1992–93		42	—
1993–94		7	—

STEWART, Marcus

Born Bristol 7.11.72. Ht 5 10   Wt 10 03
Forward. From Trainee. Football League.

Season	Club	App	Goals
1991–92	Bristol R	33	5
1992–93		38	11
1993–94		29	5

STEWART, Paul

Born Manchester 7.10.64. Ht 5 11
Wt 11 03
Forward. From Apprentice. England
Youth, B, Under-21, 3 full caps.

Season	Club	App	Goals
1981–82	Blackpool	14	3
1982–83		38	7
1983–84		44	10
1984–85		31	7
1985–86		42	8
1986–87		32	21
1986–87	Manchester C	11	2
1987–88		40	24
1988–89	Tottenham H	30	12
1989–90		28	8
1990–91		35	3
1991–92		38	5
1992–93	Liverpool	24	1
1993–94		8	—
1993–94	*Crystal Palace*	18	3

STEWART, Simon

Born Leeds 1.11.73 Ht 6 1 Wt 12 00
Defender. From Trainee.

Season	Club	App	Goals
1992–93	Sheffield W	6	—
1993–94		—	—

STILLIE, Derek

Born Irvine 3.12.73. Ht 6 0   Wt 11 10
Goalkeeper. S form. Scotland Under-21.

Season	Club	App	Goals
1991–92	Aberdeen	—	—
1992–93		—	—
1993–94		5	—

STIMSON, Mark

Born Plaistow 27.12.67. Ht 5 11
Wt 11 00
Defender. From Trainee.

Season	Club	App	Goals
1984–85	Tottenham H	—	—
1985–86		—	—
1986–87		1	—
1987–88		—	—
1987–88	*Leyton Orient*	10	—
1988–89	Tottenham H	1	—
1988–89	*Gillingham*	18	—
1989–90	Newcastle U	37	1
1990–91		23	1
1991–92		24	—
1992–93		2	—
1992–93	*Portsmouth*	4	—
1993–94	Portsmouth	29	1

STOCKWELL, Mick

Born Chelmsford 14.2.65. Ht 5 9
Wt 11 04
Midfield. From Apprentice.

Season	Club	App	Goals
1982–83	Ipswich T	—	—
1983–84		—	—
1984–85		—	—
1985–86		8	—
1986–87		21	1
1987–88		43	1
1988–89		23	2
1989–90		34	3
1990–91		44	6
1991–92		46	2
1992–93		39	4
1993–94		42	1

STOKES, Dean

Born Birmingham 23.5.70
Defender. From Halesowen.

Season	Club	App	Goals
1992–93	Port Vale	—	—
1993–94		21	—

STOKOE, Paul

Born Sidcup 19.7.75
Midfield. From Trainee.

Season	Club	App	Goals
1993–94	Crystal Palace	—	—

STONE, Steven

Born Gateshead 20.8.71. Ht 5 9
Wt 11 03
Midfield. From Trainee.

Season	Club	App	Goals
1989–90	Nottingham F	—	—
1990–91		—	—
1991–92		1	—
1992–93		12	1
1993–94		45	5

STONEMAN, Paul

Born Whitley Bay 26.2.73. Ht 6 1
Wt 13 06
Defender. From Trainee.

Season	Club	App	Goals
1991–92	Blackpool	19	—
1992–93		10	—
1993–94		10	—

STORER, Stuart

Born Harborough 16.1.67. Ht 5 11
Wt 11 08
Forward. From Local.

Season	Club	App	Goals
1983–84	Mansfield T	1	—
1984–85	Birmingham C	—	—
1985–86		2	—
1986–87		6	—
1986–87	Everton	—	—
1987–88		—	—
1987–88	*Wigan Ath*	12	—
1987–88	Bolton W	15	1
1988–89		23	2
1989–90		38	4
1990–91		35	5
1991–92		9	—
1992–93		3	—
1992–93	Exeter C	10	4
1993–94		44	2

STOWE, Dean

Born Burnley 27.3.75 Ht 5 9 Wt 11 02
Midfield. From Trainee.

Season	Club	App	Goals
1992–93	Hull C	1	—
1993–94		—	—

STOWELL, Mike

Born Preston 19.4.65. Ht 6 2 Wt 11 10
Goalkeeper. From Leyland Motors.

Season	Club	App	Goals
1984–85	Preston NE	—	—
1985–86		—	—
1985–86	Everton	—	—
1986–87		—	—
1987–88	*Chester C*	14	—
1987–88	*York C*	6	—
1987–88	*Manchester C*	14	—
1988–89	Everton	—	—
1988–89	*Port Vale*	7	—
1988–89	*Wolverhampton W*	7	—
1989–90	Everton	—	—
1989–90	*Preston NE*	2	—
1990–91	Wolverhampton W	39	—
1991–92		46	—
1992–93		26	—
1993–94		46	—

STRACHAN, Gordon
Born Edinburgh 9.2.57.   Ht 5 6   Wt 10 06
Midfield. Scotland Youth, Under-21, 50
full caps.

1974–75	Dundee	1	—
1975–76		23	6
1976–77		36	7
1977–78	Aberdeen	12	2
1978–79		31	5
1979–80		33	10
1980–81		20	6
1981–82		30	7
1982–83		32	12
1983–84		25	13
1984–85	Manchester U	41	15
1985–86		28	5
1986–87		34	4
1987–88		36	8
1988–89		21	1
1988–89	Leeds U	11	3
1989–90		46	16
1990–91		34	7
1991–92		36	4
1992–93		31	4
1993–94		33	3

STRANDLI, Frank
Born Norway 16.5.72   Ht 5 10   Wt 12 07
Forward. From IK Start. Norway full
caps.

1992–93	Leeds U	10	2
1993–94		4	—

STRANEY, Paul
Born Downpatrick 7.10.75   Ht 5 11
Wt 12 04
Goalkeeper. From Trainee.

1993–94	Stoke C	—	—

STRATFORD, Lee
Born Barnsley 11.11.75   Ht 5 10
Wt 10 08
Midfield. From Trainee.

1992–93	Nottingham F	—	—
1993–94		—	—

STRINGFELLOW, Ian
Born Nottingham 8.5.69.   Ht 5 9
Wt 11 04
Forward. From Apprentice.

1985–86	Mansfield T	3	—
1986–87		22	4
1987–88		30	8
1988–89		8	1
1989–90		19	3
1990–91		24	2
1991–92		17	2
1992–93		30	5
1992–93	*Blackpool*	3	1
1993–94	Mansfield T	14	3
1993–94	*Chesterfield*	1	—

STRODDER, Gary
Born Leeds 1.4.65.   Ht 6 1   Wt 12 06
Defender. From Apprentice.

1982–83	Lincoln C	8	—
1983–84		22	1
1984–85		26	2
1985–86		43	1
1986–87		33	2
1986–87	West Ham U	12	—
1987–88		30	1
1988–89		7	—
1989–90		16	1
1990–91	WBA	34	1
1991–92		37	3
1992–93		29	1
1993–94		21	2

STRONG, Greg
Born Bolton 5.9.75   Ht 6 2   Wt 11 12
Defender. From Trainee.

1992–93	Wigan Ath	—	—
1993–94		18	1

STUART, Graham
Born Tooting, London 24.10.70.   Ht 5 8
Wt 11 06
Forward. From Trainee. FA Schools.
England Under-21.

1989–90	Chelsea	2	1
1990–91		19	4
1991–92		27	—
1992–93		39	9

1993–94	Everton	30	3

STUART, Mark

Born Hammersmith 15.12.66.   Ht 5 10
Wt 11 03
Forward. From QPR Schoolboy.

1984–85	Charlton Ath	6	1
1985–86		30	12
1986–87		36	9
1987–88		31	6
1988–89		4	—
1988–89	Plymouth Arg	32	5
1989–90		25	6
1989–90	*Ipswich T*	5	2
1990–91	Bradford C	13	2
1991–92		16	3
1992–93		—	—
1992–93	Huddersfield T	15	3
1993–94	Rochdale	42	13

STUBBS, Alan

Born Kirkby 6.10.71.   Ht 6 2   Wt 12 12
Defender. From Trainee.

1990–91	Bolton W	23	—
1991–92		32	1
1992–93		42	2
1993–94		41	1

STURGESS, Paul

Born Dartford 4.8.75   Ht 5 11   Wt 12 05
Midfield. From Trainee.

1992–93	Charlton Ath	4	—
1993–94		8	—

STURRIDGE, Dean

Born Birmingham 26.7.73.   Ht 5 7
Wt 10 10
Forward. From Trainee.

1991–92	Derby Co	1	—
1992–93		10	—
1993–94		—	—

STURRIDGE, Simon

Born Birmingham 9.12.69.   Ht 5 5
Wt 10 07
Forward. From Trainee.

1988–89	Birmingham C	21	3
1989–90		31	10

1990–91		38	6
1991–92		40	10
1992–93		20	1
1993–94		—	—
1993–94	Stoke C	13	—

SUCKLING, Perry

Born Leyton 12.10.65.   Ht 6 2   Wt 13 02
Goalkeeper. From Apprentice. England
Youth, Under-21.

1982–83	Coventry C	3	—
1983–84		24	—
1984–85		—	—
1985–86		—	—
1986–87	Manchester C	37	—
1987–88		2	—
1987–88	Crystal Palace	17	—
1988–89		27	—
1989–90		12	—
1989–90	*West Ham U*	6	—
1990–91	Crystal Palace	—	—
1991–92		3	—
1991–92	*Brentford*	8	—
1992–93	Watford	37	—
1993–94		2	—

SULLEY, Chris

Born Camberwell 3.12.59.   Ht 5 8
Wt 10 00
Defender. From Apprentice.

1978–79	Chelsea	—	—
1979–80		—	—
1980–81		—	—
1980–81	Bournemouth	8	—
1981–82		46	—
1982–83		46	1
1983–84		46	2
1984–85		23	—
1985–86		37	—
1986–87	Dundee U	7	—
1986–87	Blackburn R	13	—
1987–88		34	—
1988–89		19	—
1989–90		36	—
1990–91		25	3
1991–92		7	—
1992–93	Port Vale	40	1
1993–94	Preston NE	21	1

SULLIVAN, Neil

Born Sutton 24.2.70. Ht 6 0 Wt 12 01
Goalkeeper. From Trainee.

Season	Club	Apps	Goals
1988–89	Wimbledon	—	—
1989–90		—	—
1990–91		1	—
1991–92		1	—
1991–92	*Crystal Palace*	1	—
1992–93	Wimbledon	1	—
1993–94		2	—

SUMMERBEE, Nicky

Born Altrincham 26.8.71. Ht 5 11
Wt 11 08
Forward. From Trainee. England
Under-21.

Season	Club	Apps	Goals
1989–90	Swindon T	1	—
1990–91		7	—
1991–92		27	—
1992–93		39	3
1993–94		38	3

SUMMERFIELD, Kevin

Born Walsall 7.1.59. Ht 5 11 Wt 11 00
Midfield. From Apprentice.

Season	Club	Apps	Goals
1976–77	WBA	—	—
1977–78		—	—
1978–79		2	1
1979–80		3	1
1980–81		—	—
1981–82		4	2
1982–83	Birmingham C	5	1
1982–83	Walsall	21	9
1983–84		33	8
1984–85	Cardiff C	10	1
1984–85	Plymouth Arg	17	2
1985–86		26	7
1986–87		28	9
1987–88		37	5
1988–89		20	2
1989–90		10	1
1989–90	*Exeter C*	4	—
1990–91	Plymouth Arg	1	—
1990–91	Shrewsbury T	32	5
1991–92		44	7
1992–93		35	7
1993–94		33	3

SUNLEY, Mark

Born Stockton 13.10.71. Ht 6 1
Wt 12 07
Defender.

Season	Club	Apps	Goals
1990–91	Middlesbrough	—	—
1991–92	Darlington	15	—
1992–93		2	—
1993–94		18	—

SUSSEX, Andy

Born Enfield 23.11.64. Ht 6 0 Wt 13 11
Forward. From Apprentice.

Season	Club	Apps	Goals
1981–82	Orient	8	1
1982–83		24	2
1983–84		29	6
1984–85		19	2
1985–86		36	4
1986–87		20	1
1987–88		8	1
1988–89	Crewe Alex	25	4
1989–90		33	9
1990–91		44	11
1991–92	Southend U	15	3
1992–93		23	4
1993–94		21	6

SUTCH, Daryl

Born Lowestoft 11.9.71. Ht 6 0
Wt 12 00
Midfield. From Trainee. England Youth,
Under-21.

Season	Club	Apps	Goals
1989–90	Norwich C	—	—
1990–91		4	—
1991–92		9	—
1992–93		22	2
1993–94		3	—

SUTTON, Chris

Born Nottingham 10.3.73. Ht 6 3
Wt 12 01
Forward. From Trainee. England
Under-21.

Season	Club	Apps	Goals
1990–91	Norwich C	2	—
1991–92		21	2
1992–93		38	8
1993–94		41	25

SUTTON, Steve

Born Hartington 16.4.61. Ht 6 1
Wt 13 07
Goalkeeper. From Apprentice.

Season	Club	App	Goals
1980–81	Nottingham F	1	—
1980–81	*Mansfield T*	8	—
1981–82	Nottingham F	1	—
1982–83		17	—
1983–84		6	—
1984–85		14	—
1984–85	*Derby Co*	14	—
1985–86	Nottingham F	31	—
1986–87		28	—
1987–88		35	—
1988–89		36	—
1989–90		30	—
1990–91		—	—
1990–91	*Coventry C*	1	—
1991–92	Nottingham F	—	—
1991–92	*Luton T*	14	—
1991–92	Derby Co	10	—
1992–93		25	—
1993–94		—	—

SUTTON, Wayne

Born Derby 1.10.75
Defender. From Trainee.

Season	Club	App	Goals
1992–93	Derby Co	—	—
1993–94		—	—

SWAILES, Chris

Born Gateshead 19.10.70 Ht 6 2
Wt 12 07
Defender. From Bridlington T.

Season	Club	App	Goals
1993–94	Doncaster R	17	—

SWALES, Steve

Born Whitby 26.12.73. Ht 5 8 Wt 10 00
Defender. From Trainee.

Season	Club	App	Goals
1991–92	Scarborough	4	—
1992–93		3	—
1993–94		26	—

SWAN, Adrian

Born Middlesbrough 31.7.73.
Goalkeeper.

Season	Club	App	Goals
1991–92	Darlington	—	—
1991–92	*Leicester C*	—	—
1992–93		—	—
1993–94		—	—

SWAN, Peter

Born Leeds 29.9.66. Ht 6 0 Wt 12 00
Forward. From Local.

Season	Club	App	Goals
1984–85	Leeds U	—	—
1985–86		16	3
1986–87		7	—
1987–88		25	8
1988–89		1	—
1988–89	Hull C	11	1
1989–90		31	11
1990–91		38	12
1991–92	Port Vale	33	3
1992–93		38	2
1993–94		40	—

SWANN, Gary

Born York 11.4.62. Ht 5 11 Wt 11 13
Midfield. From Apprentice.

Season	Club	App	Goals
1980–81	Hull C	20	2
1981–82		20	—
1982–83		25	—
1983–84		41	2
1984–85		32	3
1985–86		39	2
1986–87		9	—
1986–87	Preston NE	30	5
1987–88		46	12
1988–89		18	2
1989–90		46	8
1990–91		30	5
1991–92		29	5
1992–93	York C	38	—
1993–94		44	4

SWEETMAN, Nicky

Born Herts 21.10.74. Ht 5 8 Wt 11 00
Forward. From Trainee.

Season	Club	App	Goals
1993–94	Leyton Orient	—	—

SWITZER, George

Born Salford 13.10.73. Ht 5 6 Wt 9 10
Defender. From Trainee.

Season	Club	App	Goals
1992–93	Manchester U	—	—
1993–94	Darlington	14	—

SYKES, Alex
Born Mansfield 2.4.74 Ht 5 4 Wt 11 07
Forward. From School.

Season	Club	Apps	Goals
1992–93	Mansfield T	—	—
1993–94		2	1

SYMONS, Kit
Born Basingstoke 8.3.71. Ht 6 1
Wt 10 10
Defender. From Trainee. Wales Under-21,
13 full caps.

Season	Club	Apps	Goals
1988–89	Portsmouth	2	—
1989–90		1	—
1990–91		1	—
1991–92		46	1
1992–93		41	2
1993–94		29	3

SYMONS, Paul
Born North Shields 20.4.76
Forward.

Season	Club	Apps	Goals
1993–94	Blackpool	1	—

TAGGART, Craig
Born Glasgow 17.1.73. Ht 5 10 Wt 11 00
Midfield.

Season	Club	Apps	Goals
1991–92	Falkirk	8	—
1992–93		5	—
1993–94		13	1

TAGGART, Gerry
Born Belfast 18.10.70. Ht 6 1 Wt 12 03
Defender. From Trainee. Northern Ireland
Under-23, 28 full caps.

Season	Club	Apps	Goals
1988–89	Manchester C	11	1
1989–90		1	—
1989–90	Barnsley	21	2
1990–91		30	2
1991–92		38	3
1992–93		44	4
1993–94		38	2

TAIT, Mick
Born Wallsend 30.9.56. Ht 5 11
Wt 12 05
Midfield. From Apprentice.

Season	Club	Apps	Goals
1974–75	Oxford U	4	—
1975–76		37	12
1976–77		23	11
1976–77	Carlisle U	13	3
1977–78		43	10
1978–79		46	7
1979–80		4	—
1979–80	Hull C	33	3
1980–81	Portsmouth	38	8
1981–82		35	9
1982–83		44	6
1983–84		36	3
1984–85		33	1
1985–86		26	2
1986–87		28	1
1987–88		—	—
1987–88	Reading	35	2
1988–89		36	4
1989–90		28	3
1990–91	Darlington	45	2
1991–92		34	—
1992–93	Hartlepool U	35	1
1993–94		26	—

341

TAIT, Paul
Born Sutton Coldfield 31.1.71.   Ht 6 1
Wt 10 00
Midfield. From Trainee.

Season	Club	App	Goals
1987–88	Birmingham C	1	—
1988–89		10	—
1989–90		14	2
1990–91		17	3
1991–92		12	—
1992–93		28	2
1993–94		10	—
1993–94	*Millwall*	—	—

TAIT, Paul
Born Newcastle 24.10.74   Ht 5 8
Wt 10 10
Forward. From Trainee.

Season	Club	App	Goals
1993–94	Everton	—	—

TALBOYS, Steve
Born Bristol 18.9.66   Ht 5 11   Wt 11 10
Midfield. From Gloucester C.

Season	Club	App	Goals
1991–92	Wimbledon	—	—
1992–93		7	—
1993–94		7	—

TALIA, Frank
Born Melbourne 20.7.72
Goalkeeper. From Sunshine George Cross.

Season	Club	App	Goals
1992–93	Blackburn R	—	—
1992–93	*Hartlepool U*	14	—
1993–94	Blackburn R	—	—

TALLON, Gary
Born Drogheda 5.9.73.   Ht 5 10
Wt 11 02
Forward. From Trainee.

Season	Club	App	Goals
1991–92	Blackburn R	—	—
1992–93		—	—
1993–94		—	—

TANKARD, Allen
Born Fleet 21.5.69.   Ht 5 10   Wt 11 07
Defender. From Trainee. England Youth.

Season	Club	App	Goals
1985–86	Southampton	3	—
1986–87		2	—
1987–88		—	—
1988–89	Wigan Ath	33	1
1989–90		45	1
1990–91		46	1
1991–92		44	—
1992–93		41	1
1993–94	Port Vale	26	—

TANNER, Adam
Born Maldon 25.10.73   Ht 6 0   Wt 12 01
Midfield. From Trainee.

Season	Club	App	Goals
1992–93	Ipswich T	—	—
1993–94		—	—

TAVINOR, Steve
Born Oxford 28.1.74   Ht 5 10   Wt 11 06
Defender. From Trainee.

Season	Club	App	Goals
1992–93	Oxford U	—	—
1993–94		—	—

TAYLOR, Alex
Born Baillieston 13.6.62.   Ht 5 7
Wt 10 11
Midfield. From Blantyre St J.

Season	Club	App	Goals
1982–83	Dundee U	3	—
1983–84		9	1
1984–85		21	5
1985–86		—	—
1986–87	Hamilton A	25	1
1987–88		41	4
1988–89	Walsall	13	3
1989–90		32	3
1990–91		—	—
1990–91	Falkirk	29	2
1991–92		22	1
1992–93		8	1
1992–93	Partick T	8	1
1993–94		32	4

TAYLOR, Bob
Born Horden 3.2.67.   Ht 5 10   Wt 11 09
Forward. From Horden CW.

Season	Club	App	Goals
1985–86	Leeds U	2	—
1986–87		2	—
1987–88		32	9
1988–89		6	—
1988–89	Bristol C	12	8
1989–90		37	27
1990–91		39	11

Season	Club	App	Goals
1991–92		18	4
1991–92	WBA	19	8
1992–93		46	30
1993–94		42	18

TAYLOR, Gareth
Born Weston-Super-Mare 25.2.73.
Ht 6 2 Wt 12 05
Defender. From Southampton Trainee.

Season	Club	App	Goals
1991–92	Bristol R	1	—
1992–93		—	—
1993–94		—	—

TAYLOR, Ian
Born Birmingham 4.6.68 Ht 6 1
Wt 12 00
Midfield. From Moor Green.

Season	Club	App	Goals
1992–93	Port Vale	41	15
1993–94		42	13

TAYLOR, Jamie
Born Bury 11.1.77 Ht 5 6 Wt 9 12
Forward. From Trainee.

Season	Club	App	Goals
1993–94	Rochdale	10	1

TAYLOR, John
Born Norwich 24.10.64. Ht 6 2 Wt 11 12
Forward. From Local.

Season	Club	App	Goals
1982–83	Colchester U	—	—
1983–84		—	—
1984–85		—	—
From Sudbury			
1988–89	Cambridge U	40	12
1989–90		45	15
1990–91		40	14
1991–92		35	5
1991–92	Bristol R	8	7
1992–93		42	14
1993–94		45	23

TAYLOR, Mark
Born Hartlepool 20.11.64. Ht 5 7
Wt 11 00
Midfield. From Local.

Season	Club	App	Goals
1982–83	Hartlepool U	—	—
1983–84		6	—
1984–85		36	4
1985–86		5	—

Season	Club	App	Goals
1985–86	*Crewe Alex*	3	—
1986–87	Blackpool	40	14
1987–88		41	21
1988–89		9	3
1989–90		—	—
1990–91		—	—
1990–91	*Cardiff C*	6	3
1991–92	Blackpool	10	2
1991–92	Wrexham	9	—
1992–93		19	2
1993–94		30	7

TAYLOR, Mark
Born Walsall 22.2.66. Ht 5 8 Wt 11 08
Midfield. From Local.

Season	Club	App	Goals
1984–85	Walsall	4	—
1985–86		18	2
1986–87		17	—
1987–88		40	1
1988–89		34	1
1989–90	Sheffield W	9	—
1990–91	*Shrewsbury T*	19	2
1991–92	Shrewsbury T	29	2
1992–93		42	5
1993–94		41	2

TAYLOR, Mark
Born Saltburn 8.11.74 Ht 6 2 Wt 13 03
Forward. From Trainee.

Season	Club	App	Goals
1992–93	Middlesbrough	—	—
1993–94		—	—

TAYLOR, Martin
Born Tamworth 9.12.66. Ht 5 11
Wt 12 04
Goalkeeper. From Mile Oak R.

Season	Club	App	Goals
1986–87	Derby Co	—	—
1987–88		—	—
1987–88	*Carlisle U*	10	—
1987–88	*Scunthorpe U*	8	—
1988–89	Derby Co	—	—
1989–90		3	—
1990–91		7	—
1991–92		5	—
1992–93		21	—
1993–94		46	—

TAYLOR, Robert

Born Norwich 30.4.71. Ht 6 0   Wt 11 07
Forward. From Trainee.

Season	Club	Apps	Goals
1989–90	Norwich C	—	—
1990–91		—	—
1990–91	*Leyton Orient*	3	1
1991–92	Birmingham C	—	—
1991–92	Leyton Orient	11	1
1992–93		39	18
1993–94		23	1
1993–94	Brentford	5	2

TAYLOR, Scott

Born Portsmouth 23.11.70. Ht 5 9
Wt 11 00
Midfield. From Trainee.

Season	Club	Apps	Goals
1988–89	Reading	3	—
1989–90		29	2
1990–91		32	1
1991–92		29	2
1992–93		32	5
1993–94		38	6

TAYLOR, Shaun

Born Plymouth 26.3.63. Ht 6 1   Wt 13 00
Defender. From Bideford.

Season	Club	Apps	Goals
1986–87	Exeter C	23	—
1987–88		41	1
1988–89		46	6
1989–90		45	5
1990–91		45	4
1991–92	Swindon T	42	4
1992–93		46	11
1993–94		42	4

TAYLOR, Steve

Born Chesterfield 18.12.73
Forward.

Season	Club	Apps	Goals
1993–94	Chesterfield	1	—

TEALE, Shaun

Born Southport 10.3.64. Ht 6 0
Wt 13 10
Defender. From Southport, Northwich
Vics, Weymouth.

Season	Club	Apps	Goals
1988–89	Bournemouth	20	—
1989–90		34	—
1990–91		46	4
1991–92	Aston Villa	42	—
1992–93		39	1
1993–94		38	1

TEASDALE, Michael

Born Elgin 28.7.69 Ht 6 0   Wt 13 0
Defender. Elgin City.

Season	Club	Apps	Goals
1993–94	Dundee	5	—

TELFER, Paul

Born Edinburgh 21.10.71. Ht 5 9
Wt 11 06
Midfield. From Trainee. Scotland
Under-21.

Season	Club	Apps	Goals
1988–89	Luton T	—	—
1989–90		—	—
1990–91		1	—
1991–92		20	1
1992–93		32	2
1993–94		45	7

TEN CAAT, Theo

Born Scheveld 8.12.64. Ht 5 11   Wt 11 00
Midfield. From Groningen.

Season	Club	Apps	Goals
1991–92	Aberdeen	30	5
1992–93		15	—
1993–94		3	—

TERRY, Steve

Born Clapton 14.6.62. Ht 6 1   Wt 13 05
Defender. From Apprentice.

Season	Club	Apps	Goals
1979–80	Watford	2	—
1980–81		5	—
1981–82		26	2
1982–83		7	1
1983–84		17	1
1984–85		38	4
1985–86		41	4
1986–87		18	2
1987–88		6	—
1988–89	Hull C	33	1
1989–90		29	3
1989–90	Northampton T	17	2
1990–91		46	6
1991–92		37	3
1992–93		42	5
1993–94		39	1

THACKERAY, Andy

Born Huddersfield 13.2.68. Ht 5 9
Wt 11 00
Midfield.

Season	Club		
1985–86	Manchester C	—	—
1986–87	Huddersfield T	2	—
1986–87	Newport Co	11	3
1987–88		43	1
1988–89	Wrexham	35	2
1989–90		34	7
1990–91		41	2
1991–92		42	3
1992–93	Rochdale	41	6
1993–94		37	4

THATCHER, Ben

Born Swindon 30.11.75. Ht 5 10
Wt 11 10
Defender.

Season	Club		
1992–93	Millwall	—	—
1993–94		8	—

THEW, Lee

Born Sunderland 23.10.74. Ht 5 10
Wt 11 05
Midfield. From Trainee.

Season	Club		
1993–94	Doncaster R	11	1

THIRLBY, Anthony

Born Germany 4.3.76
Midfield. From Trainee.

Season	Club		
1993–94	Exeter C	10	—

THOM, Stuart

Born Dewsbury 27.12.76. Ht 6 2
Wt 11 08
Defender. From Trainee.

Season	Club		
1993–94	Nottingham F	—	—

THOMAS, Brian

Born Neath 7.6.76
Goalkeeper. From Trainee.

Season	Club		
1993–94	Hereford U	3	—

THOMAS, Dean

Born Bedworth 19.12.61. Ht 5 10
Wt 11 08
Defender. From Nuneaton Borough.

Season	Club		
1981–82	Wimbledon	18	—

1982–83		24	5
1983–84		15	3
From Fortuna Dusseldorf			
1988–89	Northampton T	43	9
1989–90		31	2
1989–90	Notts Co	10	1
1990–91		44	3
1991–92		36	1
1992–93		37	3
1993–94		7	—

THOMAS, Geoff

Born Manchester 5.8.64. Ht 5 10
Wt 10 07
Midfield. From Local. England B, 9 full caps.

Season	Club		
1981–82	Rochdale	—	—
1982–83		1	—
1983–84		10	1
1983–84	Crewe Alex	8	1
1984–85		40	4
1985–86		37	6
1986–87		40	9
1987–88	Crystal Palace	41	6
1988–89		22	5
1989–90		35	1
1990–91		38	6
1991–92		30	6
1992–93		29	2
1993–94	Wolverhampton W	8	4

THOMAS, Glen

Born Hackney 6.10.67. Ht 6 1 Wt 12 07
Defender. From Apprentice.

Season	Club		
1985–86	Fulham	—	—
1986–87		1	—
1987–88		27	—
1988–89		40	1
1989–90		17	1
1990–91		34	1
1991–92		45	3
1992–93		43	—
1993–94		37	—

THOMAS, Kevin

Born Edinburgh 25.4.75. Ht 5 8 Wt 12 0
Forward. From Links U. Scotland Under-21.

Season	Club		
1992–93	Hearts	4	2

1993–94 .... 12 —

THOMAS, Mark
Born Tooting 22.11.74. Ht 5 9   Wt 10 10
Midfield. From Trainee.
1993–94 Wimbledon .... — —

THOMAS, Martin
Born Lyndhurst 12.9.73   Ht 5 8   Wt 10 08
Midfield. From Trainee.
1992–93 Southampton .... — —
1993–94 .... — —
1993–94 Leyton Orient 5   2

THOMAS, Michael
Born Lambeth 24.8.67.   Ht 5 9   Wt 12 06
Midfield. From Apprentice. England
Schools, Youth, B, Under-21, 2 full caps.

Season	Club	App	Goals
1985–86	Arsenal	—	—
1986–87		12	—
1986–87	Portsmouth	3	—
1987–88	Arsenal	37	9
1988–89		37	7
1989–90		36	5
1990–91		31	2
1991–92		10	1
1991–92	Liverpool	17	3
1992–93		8	1
1993–94		7	—

THOMAS, Mitchell
Born Luton 2.10.64.   Ht 6 2   Wt 12 00
Defender. From Apprentice. England
Youth, B, Under-21.

Season	Club	App	Goals
1982–83	Luton T	4	—
1983–84		26	—
1984–85		36	—
1985–86		41	1
1986–87	Tottenham H	39	4
1987–88		36	—
1988–89		25	1
1989–90		26	1
1990–91		31	—
1991–92	West Ham U	35	3
1992–93		3	—
1993–94		—	—
1993–94	Luton T	20	1

THOMAS, Rod
Born London 10.10.70.   Ht 5 6   Wt 10 10
Forward. From Trainee. England Youth,
Under-21.

Season	Club	App	Goals
1987–88	Watford	4	—
1988–89		18	2
1989–90		32	6
1990–91		24	1
1991–92		5	—
1991–92	Gillingham	8	1
1992–93	Watford	1	—
1993–94	Carlisle U	38	9

THOMAS, Scott
Born Bury 30.10.74.   Ht 5 9   Wt 10 08
Midfield. From Trainee.

Season	Club	App	Goals
1991–92	Manchester C	—	—
1992–93		—	—
1993–94		—	—

THOMAS, Tony
Born Liverpool 12.7.71.   Ht 5 11
Wt 12 05
Defender. From Trainee.

Season	Club	App	Goals
1988–89	Tranmere R	9	2
1989–90		42	2
1990–91		33	3
1991–92		30	3
1992–93		16	—
1993–94		40	2

THOMPSON, Alan
Born Newcastle 22.12.73.   Ht 6 0
Wt 12 05
Midfield. From Trainee. England Youth.

Season	Club	App	Goals
1990–91	Newcastle U	—	—
1991–92		14	—
1992–93		2	—
1993–94	Bolton W	27	6

THOMPSON, Andy
Born Carnock 9.11.67.   Ht 5 4   Wt 10 06
Midfield. From Apprentice.

Season	Club	App	Goals
1985–86	WBA	15	1
1986–87		9	—
1986–87	Wolverhampton W	29	8
1987–88		42	2
1988–89		46	6

Season	Club	App	Goals
1989–90		33	4
1990–91		44	3
1991–92		17	—
1992–93		20	—
1993–94		37	3

THOMPSON, David

Born Manchester 27.5.62. Ht 5 11
Wt 12 10
Forward. From Local.

Season	Club	App	Goals
1981–82	Rochdale	2	—
1982–83		46	5
1983–84		40	4
1984–85		40	2
1985–86		27	2
1985–86	*Manchester U*	—	—
1986–87	Notts Co	46	7
1987–88		9	1
1987–88	Wigan Ath	27	2
1988–89		42	7
1989–90		39	5
1990–91	Preston NE	21	2
1991–92		25	2
1992–93	Chester C	39	3
1993–94		41	6

THOMPSON, David

Born Ashington 20.11.68. Ht 6 3
Wt 12 07
Defender. From Trainee.

Season	Club	App	Goals
1986–87	Millwall	—	—
1987–88		—	—
1988–89		15	1
1989–90		27	2
1990–91		17	3
1991–92		33	—
1992–93	Bristol C	17	—
1993–94		—	—
1993–94	Brentford	10	1

THOMPSON, Garry

Born Birmingham 7.10.59. Ht 6 1
Wt 14 00
Forward. From Apprentice. England
Under-21.

Season	Club	App	Goals
1977–78	Coventry C	6	2
1978–79		20	8
1979–80		17	6
1980–81		35	8

Season	Club	App	Goals
1981–82		36	10
1982–83		20	4
1982–83	WBA	12	7
1983–84		37	13
1984–85		42	19
1985–86	Sheffield W	36	7
1986–87	Aston Villa	31	6
1987–88		24	11
1988–89		5	—
1988–89	Watford	21	7
1989–90		13	1
1989–90	Crystal Palace	9	2
1990–91		11	1
1991–92	QPR	15	1
1992–93		4	—
1993–94	Cardiff C	30	5

THOMPSON, Gary

Born Ipswich 7.9.72. Ht 6 0   Wt 11 04
Forward.

Season	Club	App	Goals
1991–92	Ipswich T	—	—
1992–93		—	—
1993–94		—	—

THOMPSON, Ian

Born Leicester 17.2.75.
Midfield. From Trainee.

Season	Club	App	Goals
1992–93	Leicester C	—	—
1993–94		—	—

THOMPSON, Les

Born Cleethorpes 23.9.68. Ht 5 10
Wt 11 00
Defender.

Season	Club	App	Goals
1986–87	Hull C	—	—
1987–88		7	2
1988–89		7	—
1988–89	*Scarborough*	3	1
1989–90	Hull C	1	—
1990–91		20	2
1991–92	Maidstone U	38	—
1992–93	Burnley	3	—
1993–94		36	—

THOMPSON, Neil

Born Beverley 2.10.63. Ht 5 11 Wt 13 08
Defender. From Nottingham F
Apprentice.

Season	Club	App	Goals
1981–82	Hull C	23	—

1982–83		8	—
To Scarborough			
1987–88	Scarborough	41	6
1988–89		46	9
1989–90	Ipswich T	45	3
1990–91		38	6
1991–92		45	6
1992–93		31	3
1993–94		32	—

THOMPSON, Paul
Born Newcastle 17.4.73   Ht 5 11
Wt 11 10
Forward. From Trainee.

1991–92	Hartlepool U	—	—
1992–93		2	1
1993–94		26	4

THOMPSON, Simon
Born Sheffield 27.2.70.   Ht 5 9   Wt 10 06
Defender. From Trainee.

1988–89	Rotherham U	1	—
1989–90		11	—
1990–91		16	—
1991–92		—	—
1991–92	Scarborough	23	3
1992–93		37	—
1993–94		32	2

THOMPSON, Steve
Born Oldham 2.11.64.   Ht 5 10   Wt 12 00
Midfield. From Apprentice.

1982–83	Bolton W	3	—
1983–84		40	3
1984–85		34	4
1985–86		35	8
1986–87		44	7
1987–88		44	7
1988–89		43	9
1989–90		45	6
1990–91		45	5
1991–92		2	—
1991–92	Luton T	5	—
1991–92	Leicester C	34	3
1992–93		44	8
1993–94		30	7

THOMPSON, Steve
Born Plymouth 12.1.63   Ht 5 7   Wt 11 09
Midfield. From Slough T.

1993–94	Wycombe W	27	1

THOMPSTONE, Ian
Born Manchester 17.1.71.   Ht 6 1
Wt 13 02
Midfield. From Trainee.

1987–88	Manchester C	1	1
1988–89		—	—
1989–90		—	—
1990–91	Oldham Ath	—	—
1991–92		—	—
1991–92	Exeter C	15	3
1992–93	Halifax T	31	9
1992–93	Scunthorpe U	11	2
1993–94		30	5

THOMSON, Andrew
Born Swindon 28.3.74   Ht 6 3   Wt 13 08
Defender. From Trainee.

1992–93	Swindon T	—	—
1993–94		1	—

THOMSON, Greg
Born Edinburgh 13.9.75   Ht 5 10
Wt 10 10
Midfield. From Trainee.

1992–93	Manchester C	—	—
1993–94		—	—

THOMSON, Jon
Born Newcastle 23.12.73   Ht 5 10
Wt 12 00
Goalkeeper. From Trainee.

1992–93	Derby Co	—	—
1993–94	Chesterfield	—	—

THOMSON, Martin
Born Bradford 3.10.74   Ht 5 10   Wt 11 08
Defender. From Trainee.

1993–94	Sheffield U	—	—

THOMSON, Scott M
Born Aberdeen 29.1.72   Ht 5 10
Wt 11 10
Midfield. Shrewsbury T trainee.

1990–91	Brechin C	30	3

Season	Club	League Appearances/Goals
1991–92	....	11 3
1991–92	Aberdeen......................	— —
1992–93	....	2 —
1993–94	....	3 —

THOMSON, Scott Y
Born Edinburgh 8.11.66 Ht 6 0 Wt 11 9
Goalkeeper. Hutcheson Vale BC.

Season	Club	League Appearances/Goals
1986–87	Dundee U....................	3 —
1987–88	....	— —
1988–89	....	1 —
1989–90	....	2 —
1990–91	....	— —
1991–92	Forfar Ath....................	44 —
1992–93	....	39 —
1993–94	....	5 —
1993–94	Raith R......................	34 —

THORN, Andy
Born Carshalton 12.11.66. Ht 6 0
Wt 11 05
Defender. From Apprentice. England
Under-21.

Season	Club	League Appearances/Goals
1984–85	Wimbledon	10 —
1985–86	....	28 —
1986–87	....	34 2
1987–88	....	35 —
1988–89	Newcastle U................	26 1
1989–90	....	10 1
1989–90	Crystal Palace.............	17 1
1990–91	....	34 1
1991–92	....	33 —
1992–93	....	34 1
1993–94	....	10 —

THORNBER, Stephen
Born Dewsbury 11.10.65. Ht 5 10
Wt 11 02
Midfield. From Local.

Season	Club	League Appearances/Goals
1983–84	Halifax T	4 1
1984–85	....	31 3
1985–86	....	18 —
1986–87	....	16 —
1987–88	....	35 —
1988–89	Swansea C...................	31 —
1989–90	....	34 1
1990–91	....	19 1
1991–92	....	33 4
1992–93	Blackpool....................	24 —

Season	Club	League Appearances/Goals
1993–94	Scunthorpe U	24 2

THORNE, Peter
Born Manchester 21.6.73. Ht 6 0
Wt 12 10
Forward. From Trainee.

Season	Club	League Appearances/Goals
1991–92	Blackburn R	— —
1992–93	....	— —
1993–94	....	— —
1993–94	*Wigan Ath*..................	11 —

THORNLEY, Ben
Born Bury 21.4.75 Ht 5 8 Wt 10 07
Forward. From Trainee.

Season	Club	League Appearances/Goals
1992–93	Manchester U.............	— —
1993–94	....	1 —

THORPE, Jeff
Born Whitehaven 17.11.72. Ht 5 10
Wt 12 06
Midfield. From Trainee.

Season	Club	League Appearances/Goals
1990–91	Carlisle U...................	13 —
1991–92	....	28 1
1992–93	....	28 —
1993–94	....	— —

THORPE, Lee
Born Wolverhampton 14.12.75
Forward.

Season	Club	League Appearances/Goals
1993–94	Blackpool....................	1 —

THORPE, Tony
Born Leicester 10.4.74 Ht 5 9 Wt 12 00
Forward.

Season	Club	League Appearances/Goals
1992–93	Luton T	— —
1993–94	....	14 1

THORSTVEDT, Erik
Born Stavanger 28.10.62 Ht 6 4
Wt 14 03
Goalkeeper. From IFK Gothenburg.
Norway full caps.

Season	Club	League Appearances/Goals
1988–89	Tottenham H..............	18 —
1989–90	....	34 —
1990–91	....	37 —
1991–92	....	24 —
1992–93	....	27 —

Season	Club	App	Goals
1993–94		32	—

TIERLING, Lee
Born Wegberg 25.10.72 Ht 5 7 Wt 11 08
Forward. From Trainee.

Season	Club	App	Goals
1991–92	Portsmouth	—	—
1992–93	Fulham	5	—
1993–94		14	—

TIERNEY, Francis
Born Liverpool 10.9.75 Ht 5 10
Wt 10 12
Midfield. From Trainee.

Season	Club	App	Goals
1992–93	Crewe Alex	1	—
1993–94		8	1

TIERNEY, Grant
Born Falkirk 11.10.61. Ht 6 0 Wt 11 06
Defender. From Bainsford F.

Season	Club	App	Goals
1978–79	Hearts	—	—
1979–80		—	—
1980–81	Cowdenbeath	32	1
1981–82		32	2
1982–83		32	2
1983–84		35	1
1984–85		25	3
1984–85	Meadowbank T	8	—
1985–86		35	4
1986–87		36	4
1987–88		36	2
1988–89		18	—
1988–89	Dunfermline Ath	18	1
1989–90		33	2
1990–91	Partick T	28	1
1991–92		13	1
1992–93		16	2
1993–94		22	1

TILER, Carl
Born Sheffield 11.2.70. Ht 6 2 Wt 13 00
Defender. From Trainee. England
Under-21.

Season	Club	App	Goals
1987–88	Barnsley	1	—
1988–89		4	—
1989–90		21	1
1990–91		45	2
1991–92	Nottingham F	26	1
1992–93		37	—

Season	Club	App	Goals
1993–94		3	—

TILLSON, Andy
Born Huntingdon 30.6.66. Ht 6 2
Wt 12 07
Defender. From Kettering T.

Season	Club	App	Goals
1988–89	Grimsby T	45	2
1989–90		42	3
1990–91		18	—
1990–91	QPR	19	2
1991–92		10	—
1992–93		—	—
1992–93	*Grimsby T*	4	—
1992–93	Bristol R	29	—
1993–94		13	—

TILSON, Steve
Born Essex 27.7.66. Ht 5 11 Wt 12 05
Forward. From Burnham.

Season	Club	App	Goals
1988–89	Southend U	16	2
1989–90		16	—
1990–91		38	8
1991–92		46	7
1992–93		31	3
1993–94		10	—
1993–94	*Brentford*	2	—

TIMONS, Chris
Born Nottingham 8.12.74.
Defender. From Clipstone Welfare.

Season	Club	App	Goals
1993–94	Mansfield T	16	1

TINKLER, John
Born Trimdon 24.8.68. Ht 5 8 Wt 11 07
Midfield.

Season	Club	App	Goals
1986–87	Hartlepool U	2	—
1987–88		20	—
1988–89		38	3
1989–90		45	2
1990–91		26	2
1991–92		39	—
1992–93	Preston NE	24	2
1993–94	Walsall	6	—

TINKLER, Mark
Born Bishop Auckland 24.10.74. Ht 5 10
Wt 10 02
Midfield. From Trainee. England Youth.

Season	Club	App	Goals
1991–92	Leeds U	—	—

1992–93 .... 7 —
1993–94 .... 3 —

TINNION, Brian
Born Stanley 23.2.68. Ht 5 11 Wt 11 05
Defender. From Apprentice.
1985–86 Newcastle U............... — —
1986–87 .... 3 —
1987–88 .... 16 1
1988–89 .... 13 1
1988–89 Bradford C 14 1
1989–90 .... 37 5
1990–91 .... 41 5
1991–92 .... 26 8
1992–93 .... 27 3
1992–93 Bristol C 11 2
1993–94 .... 41 5

TISDALE, Paul
Born Malta 14.1.73 Ht 5 9 Wt 10 08
Midfield. From School.
1991–92 Southampton .... — —
1992–93 .... — —
1992–93 *Northampton T*........... 5 —
1993–94 Southampton .... — —

TITTERTON, David
Born Hatton 25.9.71. Ht 5 11 Wt 10 09
Defender. From Trainee. England Youth.
1989–90 Coventry C .... 1 —
1990–91 .... 1 —
1991–92 .... — —
1991–92 Hereford U 25 1
1992–93 .... 26 —
1993–94 Wycombe W 18 1

TOAL, Kieran
Born Manchester 14.12.71. Ht 5 8
Wt 11 01
Midfield. From Trainee.
1991–92 Manchester U .... — —
1992–93 .... — —
1993–94 Stockport Co .... — —

TOBIN, Steven
Born Manchester 24.3.75
Forward. From Trainee.
1993–94 Leeds U .... — —

TODD, Andrew
Born Derby 21.9.74. Ht 5 10 Wt 10 11
Defender. From Trainee.
1991–92 Middlesbrough............ — —
1992–93 .... — —
1993–94 .... 3 —

TODD, Lee
Born Hartlepool 7.3.72. Ht 5 5 Wt 10 03
Defender. From Hartlepool U Trainee.
1990–91 Stockport Co .... 14 —
1991–92 .... 19 —
1992–93 .... 39 —
1993–94 .... 33 —

TODD, Mark
Born Belfast 4.12.67. Ht 5 8 Wt 10 04
Midfield. From Trainee. Northern Ireland
Under-23.
1985–86 Manchester U .... — —
1986–87 .... — —
1987–88 Sheffield U .... 12 —
1988–89 .... 39 4
1989–90 .... 16 1
1990–91 .... 3 —
1990–91 *Wolverhampton W*....... 7 —
1991–92 Sheffield U .... — —
1991–92 Rotherham U 23 2
1992–93 .... 16 4
1993–94 .... 11 1

TOLSON, Neil
Born Wordley 25.10.73. Ht 6 1 Wt 10 07
Forward. From Trainee.
1991–92 Walsall 9 1
1991–92 Oldham Ath............... — —
1992–93 .... 3 —
1993–94 .... — —
1993–94 Bradford C 22 2

TOMAN, Andy
Born Northallerton 7.3.62. Ht 5 10
Wt 11 07
Midfield. From Bishop Auckland.
1985–86 Lincoln C................... 24 4
1986–87 Hartlepool U 21 5
1987–88 .... 46 17
1988–89 .... 45 6

1989–90	Darlington	*40*	7
1990–91		43	5
1991–92		43	4
1992–93		29	1
1992–93	*Scarborough*	6	—
1993–94	Scunthorpe U	15	5
1993–94	Scarborough	13	1

TOMLINSON, Graeme
Born Keighley 10.12.75   Ht 5 9   Wt 11 07
Forward. From Trainee.

| 1993–94 | Bradford C | 17 | 6 |

TOMLINSON, Michael
Born Lambeth 15.9.72.   Ht 5 9   Wt 11 00
Midfield. From Trainee.

1990–91	Leyton Orient	1	1
1991–92		1	—
1992–93		8	—
1993–94		4	—
1993–94	Barnet	11	—

TOMLINSON, Paul
Born Brierley Hill 22.2.64.   Ht 6 2
Wt 13 12
Goalkeeper. From Middlewood R.

1983–84	Sheffield U	30	—
1984–85		2	—
1985–86		—	—
1986–87		5	—
1986–87	*Birmingham C*	11	—
1987–88	Bradford C	42	—
1988–89		38	—
1989–90		41	—
1990–91		43	—
1991–92		45	—
1992–93		24	—
1993–94		23	—

TONGE, Alan
Born Bury 25.2.72.   Ht 5 8   Wt 11 11
Defender. From Trainee.

1990–91	Manchester U	—	—
1991–92	Exeter C	3	—
1992–93		15	1
1993–94		1	—

TORFASON, Gudmundor
Born Westann Isles 13.12.61.   Ht 6 1
Wt 13 02
Forward. From RSC Genk. Iceland full
caps.

1989–90	St Mirren	29	12
1990–91		18	4
1991–92		29	8
1992–93	St Johnstone	10	4
1993–94		29	5

TORPEY, Stephen
Born Islington 8.12.70.   Ht 6 2   Wt 12 11
Forward. From Trainee.

1988–89	Millwall	—	—
1989–90		7	—
1990–91		—	—
1990–91	Bradford C	29	7
1991–92		43	10
1992–93		24	5
1993–94	Swansea C	40	9

TORTOLANO, Joe
Born Stirling 6.4.66.   Ht 5 8   Wt 11 02
Forward. From Apprentice. Scotland
Under-21.

1983–84	WBA	—	—
1984–85		—	—
1985–86	Hibernian	20	3
1986–87		33	—
1987–88		21	4
1988–89		25	—
1989–90		7	—
1990–91		18	1
1991–92		25	1
1992–93		21	3
1993–94		18	1

TOSH, Paul
Born Arbroath 18.10.73   Ht 5 10   Wt 11 4
Forward. Arbroath Lads.

1991–92	Arbroath	8	1
1992–93		34	12
1993–94	Dundee	26	1

TOVEY, Paul
Born Wokingham 5.12.73   Ht 5 8
Wt 11 07
Midfield. From Trainee.

Season	Club	Apps	Goals
1992–93	Bristol R	—	—
1993–94		1	—

TOWN, David
Born Bournemouth 9.12.76
Forward. From Trainee.

Season	Club	Apps	Goals
1993–94	Bournemouth	1	—

TOWNSEND, Andy
Born Maidstone 23.7.63.   Ht 5 11
Wt 12 13
Midfield. From Welling and Weymouth.
Eire 45 full caps.

Season	Club	Apps	Goals
1984–85	Southampton	5	—
1985–86		27	1
1986–87		14	1
1987–88		37	3
1988–89	Norwich C	36	5
1989–90		35	3
1990–91	Chelsea	34	2
1991–92		35	6
1992–93		41	4
1993–94	Aston Villa	32	3

TRACEY, Simon
Born Woolwich 9.12.67.   Ht 6 0
Wt 12 00
Goalkeeper. From Apprentice.

Season	Club	Apps	Goals
1985–86	Wimbledon	—	—
1986–87		—	—
1987–88		—	—
1988–89		1	—
1988–89	Sheffield U	7	—
1989–90		46	—
1990–91		31	—
1991–92		29	—
1992–93		10	—
1993–94		15	—

TREBBLE, Neil
Born Hitchin 16.2.69
Forward. From Stevenage Borough.

Season	Club	Apps	Goals
1993–94	Scunthorpe U	14	2

TRETTON, Andrew
Born Derby 9.10.76
Defender. From Trainee.

Season	Club	Apps	Goals
1993–94	Derby Co	—	—

TREVITT, Simon
Born Dewsbury 20.12.67.   Ht 5 11
Wt 11 02
Defender. From Apprentice.

Season	Club	Apps	Goals
1986–87	Huddersfield T	11	—
1987–88		37	1
1988–89		39	—
1989–90		7	—
1990–91		38	—
1991–92		41	1
1992–93		—	—
1993–94		31	1

TRICKETT, Andrew
Born Burnley 24.1.75   Ht 5 10   Wt 11 07
Midfield. From Trainee.

Season	Club	Apps	Goals
1993–94	Blackpool	—	—

TROLLOPE, Paul
Born Swindon 3.6.72.   Ht 6 0   Wt 12 02
Midfield. From Trainee.

Season	Club	Apps	Goals
1989–90	Swindon T	—	—
1990–91		—	—
1991–92		—	—
1991–92	*Torquay U*	10	—
1992–93	Torquay U	36	2
1993–94		42	10

TROTT, Robin
Born Orpington 17.8.74   Ht 6 1   Wt 13 04
Defender. From Trainee.

Season	Club	Apps	Goals
1993–94	Gillingham	1	—

TROTTER, Michael
Born Hartlepool 27.10.69.   Ht 6 0
Wt 12 12
Midfield. From Trainee.

Season	Club	Apps	Goals
1987–88	Middlesbrough	—	—
1988–89		—	—
1988–89	*Doncaster R*	3	—
1989–90	Middlesbrough	—	—
1990–91	Darlington	24	2

1991–92	....	5	—
1991–92	Leicester C	2	—
1992–93	....	1	—
1993–94	....	—	—
1993–94	*Chesterfield*	15	1

TUCK, Stuart

Born Brighton 1.10.74 Ht 5 11 Wt 11 02
Defender. From Trainee.

| 1993–94 | Brighton .... | 11 | — |

TULLY, Craig

Born Stirling 7.1.76
Defender. Victoria Juveniles.

| 1993–94 | Dundee .... | 1 | — |

TURNBULL, Lee

Born Teesside 27.9.67. Ht 6 0 Wt 11 09
Midfield. From Local.

1985–86	Middlesbrough	2	—
1986–87	....	14	4
1987–88	....	—	—
1987–88	Aston Villa	—	—
1987–88	Doncaster R	30	1
1988–89	....	32	4
1989–90	....	42	10
1990–91	....	19	6
1990–91	Chesterfield	19	9
1991–92	....	27	7
1992–93	....	33	8
1993–94	....	8	2
1993–94	Doncaster R	11	1
1993–94	Wycombe W	6	—

TURNER, Andy

Born Woolwich 23.3.75 Ht 5 9 Wt 11 00
Forward. From Trainee.

1991–92	Tottenham H	—	—
1992–93	....	18	3
1993–94	....	1	—

TURNER, Chris

Born Sheffield 15.9.58. Ht 5 11 Wt 11 12
Goalkeeper. From Apprentice. England Youth.

1976–77	Sheffield W	45	—
1977–78	....	23	—
1978–79	....	23	—
1978–79	*Lincoln C*	5	—
1979–80	Sunderland	30	—
1980–81	....	27	—
1981–82	....	19	—
1982–83	....	35	—
1983–84	....	42	—
1984–85	....	42	—
1985–86	Manchester U	17	—
1986–87	....	23	—
1987–88	....	24	—
1988–89	....	—	—
1988–89	Sheffield W	29	—
1989–90	....	23	—
1989–90	*Leeds U*	2	—
1990–91	Sheffield W	23	—
1991–92	....	—	—
1991–92	Leyton Orient	34	—
1992–93	....	17	—
1993–94	....	6	—

TURNER, Mark

Born Bebbington 4.10.72 Ht 6 0 Wt 11 01
Midfield. From Trainee.

1991–92	Wolverhampton W	—	—
1992–93	....	1	—
1993–94	....	—	—

TURNER, Phil

Born Sheffield 12.2.62. Ht 5 9 Wt 10 13
Midfield. From Apprentice.

1979–80	Lincoln C	14	1
1980–81	....	38	4
1981–82	....	28	1
1982–83	....	40	3
1983–84	....	42	3
1984–85	....	36	3
1985–86	....	43	4
1986–87	Grimsby T	34	3
1987–88	....	28	5
1987–88	Leicester C	8	—
1988–89	....	16	2
1988–89	Notts Co	16	2
1989–90	....	44	6
1990–91	....	38	1
1991–92	....	29	1
1992–93	....	20	1
1993–94	....	40	3

TURNER, Robert

Born Durham 18.9.66.   Ht 6 3   Wt 14 01
Midfield. From Apprentice.

Season	Club	App	Goals
1984–85	Huddersfield T	1	—
1985–86	Cardiff C	34	7
1986–87		5	1
1986–87	*Hartlepool U*	7	1
1986–87	Bristol R	17	1
1987–88		9	1
1987–88	Wimbledon	4	—
1988–89		6	—
1988–89	Bristol C	19	6
1989–90		33	6
1990–91	Plymouth Arg	39	14
1991–92		25	3
1992–93		2	—
1992–93	Notts Co	8	1
1992–93	*Shrewsbury T*	9	—
1993–94	Notts Co	—	—
1993–94	Exeter C	22	3

TURNER, Tommy

Born Johnstone 11.10.63.   Ht 5 9
Wt 10 07
Midfield. From Glentyan Thistle.

Season	Club	App	Goals
1983–84	Morton	—	—
1984–85		13	1
1985–86		34	7
1986–87		38	4
1987–88		29	1
1988–89		31	10
1989–90		30	6
1990–91	St Johnstone	28	3
1991–92		33	3
1992–93		28	1
1993–94		39	—

TUTILL, Steve

Born Derwent 1.10.69.   Ht 6 0   Wt 12 02
Defender. From Trainee. England Schools.

Season	Club	App	Goals
1987–88	York C	21	—
1988–89		22	1
1989–90		42	—
1990–91		42	—
1991–92		39	1
1992–93		8	—
1993–94		46	4

TUTTLE, David

Born Reading 6.2.72.   Ht 5 9   Wt 12 10
Defender. From Trainee. England Youth.

Season	Club	App	Goals
1989–90	Tottenham H	—	—
1990–91		6	—
1991–92		2	—
1992–93		5	—
1992–93	*Peterborough U*	7	—
1993–94	Sheffield U	31	—

TWEED, Steven

Born Edinburgh 8.8.72.   Ht 6 3   Wt 13 02
Defender. From Hutcheson Vale. Scotland
Under-21.

Season	Club	App	Goals
1991–92	Hibernian	1	—
1992–93		14	—
1993–94		29	3

ULLATHORNE, Robert
Born Wakefield 11.10.71.   Ht 5 8
Wt 10 00
Defender. From Trainee.

Season	Club	App	Goals
1989–90	Norwich C	—	—
1990–91		2	—
1991–92		20	3
1992–93		—	—
1993–94		16	2

UNSWORTH, David
Born Preston 16.10.73.   Ht 5 11   Wt 12 02
Forward. From Trainee. England Youth.

Season	Club	App	Goals
1991–92	Everton	2	1
1992–93		3	—
1993–94		8	—

VALENTINE, Peter
Born Huddersfield 16.6.63.   Ht 5 10
Wt 12 00
Defender. From Apprentice.

Season	Club	App	Goals
1980–81	Huddersfield T	—	—
1981–82		14	1
1982–83		5	—
1983–84	Bolton W	42	1
1984–85		26	—
1985–86	Bury	46	3
1986–87		46	2
1987–88		42	2
1988–89		30	1
1989–90		38	—
1990–91		42	2
1991–92		39	3
1992–93		36	3
1993–94	Carlisle U	20	2

VAN DE KAMP, Guido
Born Den Bosch 8.2.64.   Ht 6 2   Wt 13 01
Goalkeeper. From Den Bosch.

Season	Club	App	Goals
1991–92	Dundee U	27	—
1992–93		1	—
1993–94		25	—

VAN DE VEN, Peter
Born Hunsel 8.1.61   Ht 6 1   Wt 13 05
Defender. From Willem II.

Season	Club	App	Goals
1990–91	Aberdeen	—	—
1991–92		23	2
1992–93	Hearts	37	—
1993–94		2	—

VAN DEN HAUWE, Pat
Born Dendermonde 16.12.60.   Ht 5 11
Wt 11 10
Defender. From Apprentice. Wales 13 full
caps.

Season	Club	App	Goals
1978–79	Birmingham C	8	—
1979–80		1	—
1980–81		4	—
1981–82		31	—
1982–83		31	1
1983–84		42	—
1984–85		6	—
1984–85	Everton	31	—
1985–86		40	1

Season	Club	League Appearances/Goals
1986–87		11 1
1987–88		28 —
1988–89		25 —
1989–90		— —
1989–90	Tottenham H	31 —
1990–91		32 —
1991–92		35 —
1992–93		18 —
1993–94		— —
1993–94	Millwall	23 —

VAN DER HOORN, Freddy

Born Den Bosch 12.10.63.   Ht 6 0 Wt 12 06
Defender. From Den Bosch.

Season	Club	League Appearances/Goals
1989–90	Dundee U	31 2
1990–91		32 1
1991–92		41 1
1992–93		32 —
1993–94		28 —

VAN DER LAAN, Robin

Born Schiedam 5.9.68.   Ht 5 11   Wt 12 05
Forward. From Wageningen.

Season	Club	League Appearances/Goals
1990–91	Port Vale	18 4
1991–92		43 5
1992–93		38 6
1993–94		33 4

VARADI, Imre

Born Paddington 8.7.59.   Ht 5 10 Wt 12 00
Forward. From Letchworth GC.

Season	Club	League Appearances/Goals
1977–78	Sheffield U	— —
1978–79		10 4
1978–79	Everton	— —
1979–80		4 —
1980–81		22 6
1981–82	Newcastle U	42 18
1982–83		39 21
1983–84	Sheffield W	38 17
1984–85		38 16
1985–86	WBA	32 9
1986–87		— —
1986–87	Manchester C	30 9
1987–88		32 17
1988–89		3 —

Season	Club	League Appearances/Goals
1988–89	Sheffield W	20 3
1989–90		2 —
1989–90	Leeds U	13 2
1990–91		6 2
1991–92		3 —
1991–92	*Luton T*	6 1
1992–93	Leeds U	4 1
1992–93	*Oxford U*	5 —
1992–93	Rotherham U	11 4
1993–94		39 19

VATA, Rudi

Born Shkoder,Albania. 13.2.69   Ht 6 1 Wt 12 5
Midfield. From Dinamo Tirana.

Season	Club	League Appearances/Goals
1992–93	Celtic	22 2
1993–94		10 1

VAUGHAN, Danny

Born Liverpool 18.2.72   Ht 5 8   Wt 10 00
Defender.

Season	Club	League Appearances/Goals
1992–93	Crewe Alex	7 —
1993–94	Wigan Ath	4 —

VAUGHAN, John

Born Isleworth 26.6.64.   Ht 5 10 Wt 13 01
Goalkeeper. From Apprentice.

Season	Club	League Appearances/Goals
1981–82	West Ham U	— —
1982–83		— —
1983–84		— —
1984–85		— —
1984–85	*Charlton Ath*	6 —
1985–86		— —
1985–86	*Bristol R.*	6 —
1985–86	*Wrexham*	4 —
1985–86	*Bristol C.*	2 —
1986–87	Fulham	44 —
1987–88		— —
1987–88	*Bristol C.*	3 —
1988–89	Cambridge U	29 —
1989–90		46 —
1990–91		43 —
1991–92		33 —
1992–93		27 —
1993–94	Charlton Ath	6 —

VENISON, Barry

Born Consett 16.8.64.   Ht 5 10   Wt 11 09
Defender. From Apprentice. England
Youth, Under-21.

Season	Club	App	Goals
1981–82	Sunderland	20	1
1982–83		37	—
1983–84		41	—
1984–85		39	1
1985–86		36	—
1986–87	Liverpool	33	—
1987–88		18	—
1988–89		15	—
1989–90		25	—
1990–91		6	—
1991–92		13	1
1992–93	Newcastle U	44	—
1993–94		37	—

VENUS, Mark

Born Hartlepool 6.4.67.   Ht 6 0   Wt 11 08
Defender.

Season	Club	App	Goals
1984–85	Hartlepool U	4	—
1985–86	Leicester C	1	—
1986–87		39	—
1987–88		21	1
1987–88	Wolverhampton W	4	—
1988–89		35	—
1989–90		44	2
1990–91		6	—
1991–92		46	1
1992–93		12	—
1993–94		39	1

VERVEER, Etienne

Born Surinam 22.9.67.   Ht 5 11   Wt 11 12
Midfield. From Chur.

Season	Club	App	Goals
1991–92	Millwall	25	2
1992–93		1	—
1993–94		30	5

VEYSEY, Ken

Born Hackney 8.6.67.   Ht 5 11   Wt 11 08
Goalkeeper. From Arsenal Apprentice.

Season	Club	App	Goals
1987–88	Torquay U	—	—
1988–89		25	—
1989–90		46	—
1990–91		1	—
1990–91	Oxford U	25	—

Season	Club	App	Goals
1991–92		32	—
1992–93		—	—
1992–93	*Sheffield U*	—	—
1993–94	Exeter C	12	—

VICKERS, Steve

Born Bishop Auckland 13.10.67.   Ht 6 2
Wt 12 00
Defender. From Spennymoor U.

Season	Club	App	Goals
1985–86	Tranmere R	3	—
1986–87		36	2
1987–88		46	1
1988–89		46	3
1989–90		42	3
1990–91		42	1
1991–92		43	1
1992–93		42	—
1993–94		11	—
1993–94	Middlesbrough	26	3

VINCENT, Jamie

Born London 18.6.75   Ht 5 10   Wt 11 09
Defender. From Trainee.

Season	Club	App	Goals
1993–94	Crystal Palace	—	—

VINNICOMBE, Chris

Born Exeter 20.10.70   Ht 5 9   Wt 10 04
Midfield. England Under-21.

Season	Club	App	Goals
1988–89	Exeter C	25	—
1989–90		14	1
1989–90	Rangers	7	—
1990–91		10	1
1991–92		2	—
1992–93		—	—
1993–94		4	—

VIVEASH, Adrian

Born Swindon 30.9.69.   Ht 6 1   Wt 11 12
Forward. From Trainee.

Season	Club	App	Goals
1988–89	Swindon T	—	—
1989–90		—	—
1990–91		25	1
1991–92		10	—
1992–93		5	—
1992–93	*Reading*	5	—
1993–94	Swindon T	—	—

VOICE, Scott
Born Wolverhampton 12.8.74 Ht 6 0
Wt 11 10
Forward. From Trainee.
1993–94 Wolverhampton W .....

VONK, Michael
Born Holland 28.10.68. Ht 6 3 Wt 13 03
Defender. From SVV/Dordrecht.

Season	Club	A	G
1991–92	Manchester C	9	—
1992–93		26	2
1993–94		35	1

VRTO, Dusan
Born Banksa Stiavnica 29.10.65 Ht 6 0
Wt 11 12
Midfield. From Banik Ostrava.

Season	Club	A	G
1992–93	Dundee	32	1
1993–94		38	—

WADDLE, Chris
Born Hepworth 14.12.60. Ht 6 2
Wt 12 13
Forward. From Tow Law T. England
Under-21, 62 full caps. Football League.

Season	Club	A	G
1980–81	Newcastle U	13	1
1981–82		42	7
1982–83		37	7
1983–84		42	18
1984–85		36	13
1985–86	Tottenham H	39	11
1986–87		39	6
1987–88		22	2
1988–89		38	14
1989–90	Marseille	37	9
1990–91		35	6
1991–92		35	7
1992–93	Sheffield W	33	1
1993–94		19	3

WADDOCK, Gary
Born Alperton 17.3.62. Ht 5 10
Wt 11 12
Midfield. From Apprentice. Eire Youth B,
Under-21, Under-23, 20 full caps.

Season	Club	A	G
1979–80	QPR	16	1
1980–81		33	3
1981–82		35	—
1982–83		33	—
1983–84		36	3
1984–85		31	1
1985–86		15	—
1986–87		4	—
1987–88		—	—
From Charleroi			
1989–90	Millwall	18	—
1990–91		40	2
1991–92	QPR	—	—
1991–92	*Swindon T*	6	—
1992–93	QPR	—	—
1992–93	Bristol R	31	—
1993–94		39	1

WAINWRIGHT, Lee
Born Sheffield 9.1.75 Ht 5 11
Defender. From Trainee.
1993–94 Sheffield U .... — —

WALKER, Alan

Born Mossley 17.12.59.   Ht 6 2   Wt 12 11
Defender. From Stockport Co and Telford U.

Season	Club	App	Goals
1983–84	Lincoln C	33	2
1984–85		42	2
1985–86	Millwall	26	3
1986–87		40	1
1987–88		26	4
1987–88	Gillingham	7	—
1988–89		22	1
1989–90		38	1
1990–91		44	4
1991–92		40	1
1992–93	Plymouth Arg	2	1
1992–93	Mansfield T	22	1
1993–94	Barnet	38	1

WALKER, Andy

Born Glasgow 6.4.65.   Ht 5 8   Wt 10 07
Forward. From Baillieston Juniors.
Scotland, Under-21, 1 full cap.

Season	Club	App	Goals
1984–85	Motherwell	11	3
1985–86		22	4
1986–87		43	10
1987–88	Celtic	42	16
1988–89		22	8
1989–90		32	6
1990–91		11	—
1991–92		1	—
1991–92	*Newcastle U*	2	—
1991–92	Bolton W	24	15
1992–93		32	26
1993–94		11	3

WALKER, Des

Born Hackney 26.11.65.   Ht 5 10   Wt 11 05
Defender. From Apprentice. England Under-21, 59 full caps.

Season	Club	App	Goals
1983–84	Nottingham F	4	—
1984–85		3	—
1985–86		39	—
1986–87		41	—
1987–88		35	—
1988–89		34	—
1989–90		38	—
1990–91		37	—
1991–92		33	1

Season	Club	App	Goals
1992–93	Sampdoria	30	—
1993–94	Sheffield W	42	—

WALKER, Ian

Born Watford 31.10.71.   Ht 6 1   Wt 11 09
Goalkeeper. From Trainee. England Youth, Under-21.

Season	Club	App	Goals
1989–90	Tottenham H	—	—
1990–91		1	—
1990–91	*Oxford U*	2	—
1990–91	*Ipswich T*	—	—
1991–92	Tottenham H	18	—
1992–93		17	—
1993–94		11	—

WALKER, James

Born Mansfield 9.7.73.   Ht 5 11   Wt 11 00
Goalkeeper. From Trainee.

Season	Club	App	Goals
1991–92	Notts Co	—	—
1992–93		—	—
1993–94	Walsall	31	—

WALKER, Justin

Born Nottingham 6.9.75   Ht 5 10   Wt 11 08
Midfield. From Trainee.

Season	Club	App	Goals
1992–93	Nottingham F	—	—
1993–94		—	—

WALKER, Keith

Born Edinburgh 17.4.66.   Ht 6 0   Wt 11 09
Midfield. From ICI Juveniles.

Season	Club	App	Goals
1984–85	Stirling Albion	38	6
1985–86		32	5
1986–87		21	6
1987–88	St Mirren	19	3
1988–89		14	1
1989–90		10	2
1989–90	Swansea C	13	—
1990–91		24	—
1991–92		32	1
1992–93		42	2
1993–94		27	2

WALKER, Lee

Born Pontypool 27.6.76
Midfield. From Trainee.

Season	Club	App	Goals
1993–94	Cardiff C	1	—

WALKER, Nicky

Born Aberdeen 29.9.62. Ht 6 2 Wt 11 12
Goalkeeper. From Elgin C. Scotland
Youth, 1 full cap.

Season	Club		
1980–81	Leicester C	—	—
1981–82		6	—
1982–83	Motherwell	16	—
1983–84		15	—
1983–84	Rangers	8	—
1984–85		14	—
1985–86		34	—
1986–87		2	—
1987–88		5	—
1987–88	*Dunfermline Ath*	1	—
1988–89	Rangers	12	—
1989–90	Hearts	—	—
1990–91		13	—
1991–92		—	—
1991–92	*Burnley*	6	—
1992–93	Hearts	18	—
1993–94		17	—

WALKER, Ray

Born North Shields 28.9.63. Ht 5 10
Wt 11 12
Midfield. From Apprentice. England
Youth.

Season	Club		
1981–82	Aston Villa	—	—
1982–83		1	—
1983–84		8	—
1984–85		7	—
1984–85	*Port Vale*	15	1
1985–86	Aston Villa	7	—
1986–87	Port Vale	45	4
1987–88		42	6
1988–89		43	5
1989–90		40	—
1990–91		45	6
1991–92		26	2
1992–93		35	9
1993–94		—	—

WALKER, Richard

Born Derby 9.11.71 Ht 6 0 Wt 12 00
Defender. From Trainee.

Season	Club		
1991–92	Notts Co	—	—
1992–93		12	3
1993–94		21	1

WALKER, Steve

Born Worcester 7.10.74 Ht 5 7 Wt 11 02
Midfield. From Wolverhampton W
trainee.

Season	Club		
1993–94	Hereford U	—	—

WALLACE, Danny

Born London 21.1.64. Ht 5 4 Wt 10 04
Forward. From Apprentice. England
Youth, Under-21, 1 full cap.

Season	Club		
1980–81	Southampton	2	—
1981–82		7	—
1982–83		35	12
1983–84		41	11
1984–85		35	7
1985–86		35	8
1986–87		31	8
1987–88		33	11
1988–89		31	5
1989–90		5	2
1989–90	Manchester U	26	3
1990–91		19	3
1991–92		—	—
1992–93		2	—
1992–93	*Millwall*	3	—
1993–94	Manchester U	—	—
1993–94	Birmingham C	10	1

WALLACE, Michael

Born Farnworth 5.10.70 Ht 5 8
Wt 10 02
Midfield. From Trainee.

Season	Club		
1991–92	Manchester C	—	—
1992–93	Stockport Co	8	—
1993–94		37	3

WALLACE, Ray

Born Lewisham 2.10.69. Ht 5 6
Wt 10 02
Defender. From Trainee, England
Under-21.

Season	Club		
1987–88	Southampton	—	—
1988–89		26	—
1989–90		9	—
1990–91		—	—
1991–92	Leeds U	—	—
1991–92	*Swansea C*	2	—
1992–93	Leeds U	6	—

| 1993–94 | .... | 1 | — |
| 1993–94 | *Reading* .... | 3 | — |

WALLACE, Rodney

Born Lewisham 2.10.69. Ht 5 7
Wt 10 01
Forward. From Trainee. England B,
Under-21.

1987–88	Southampton	15	1
1988–89	....	38	12
1989–90	....	38	18
1990–91	....	37	14
1991–92	Leeds U	34	11
1992–93	....	32	7
1993–94	....	37	17

WALLEY, Mark

Born Barnsley 17.9.76 Ht 5 10 Wt 10 06
Forward. From Trainee.

| 1993–94 | Nottingham F............. | — | — |

WALLING, Dean

Born Leeds 17.4.69. Ht 6 0 Wt 12 00
Defender.

1986–87	Leeds U	—	—
1987–88	Rochdale.....................	12	2
1988–89	....	34	3
1989–90	....	19	3
From Guiseley			
1991–92	Carlisle U...................	37	5
1992–93	....	23	—
1993–94	....	40	5

WALSH, Colin

Born Hamilton 22.7.62. Ht 5 9 Wt 10 11
Midfield. From Apprentice. Scotland
Youth, Under-21.

1979–80	Nottingham F.............	—	—
1980–81	....	16	4
1981–82	....	15	3
1982–83	....	37	5
1983–84	....	38	13
1984–85	....	13	1
1985–86	....	20	6
1986–87	....	—	—
1986–87	Charlton Ath	33	6
1987–88	....	11	3
1988–89	....	5	—
1988–89	*Peterborough U*...........	5	1

1989–90	Charlton Ath	27	2
1990–91	....	13	—
1990–91	*Middlesbrough*.............	13	1
1991–92	Charlton Ath	42	4
1992–93	....	42	1
1993–94	....	35	4

WALSH, Derek

Born Hamilton 24.10.67. Ht 5 7
Wt 11 05
Midfield. From Apprentice.

1984–85	Everton	1	—
1985–86	....	—	—
1986–87	....	—	—
1987–88	Hamilton A.................	2	—
1988–89	Carlisle U...................	35	3
1989–90	....	28	3
1990–91	....	19	—
1991–92	....	15	—
1992–93	....	24	1
1993–94	....	—	—

WALSH, Gary

Born Wigan 21.3.68. Ht 6 1 Wt 13 01
Goalkeeper. England Under-21.

1984–85	Manchester U..............	—	—
1985–86	....	—	—
1986–87	....	14	—
1987–88	....	16	—
1988–89	....	—	—
1988–89	*Airdrie*.......................	3	—
1989–90	Manchester U..............	—	—
1990–91	....	5	—
1991–92	....	2	—
1992–93	....	—	—
1993–94	....	3	—
1993–94	*Oldham Ath*.................	6	—

WALSH, Paul

Born Plumstead 1.10.62. Ht 5 7
Wt 10 08
Forward. From Apprentice. England
Youth, Under-21, 3 full caps.

1979–80	Charlton Ath	9	—
1980–81	....	40	11
1981–82	....	38	13
1982–83	Luton T	41	13
1983–84	....	39	11
1984–85	Liverpool	26	8

Season	Club	App	Goals
1985–86	....	20	11
1986–87	....	23	6
1987–88	....	8	—
1987–88	Tottenham H	11	1
1988–89	....	33	6
1989–90	....	26	2
1990–91	....	29	7
1991–92	....	29	3
1991–92	QPR	2	—
1992–93	Portsmouth	43	9
1993–94	....	30	5
1993–94	Manchester C	11	4

WALSH, Steve
Born Fulwood 3.11.64. Ht 6 2 Wt 13 13
Defender. From Local.

Season	Club	App	Goals
1982–83	Wigan Ath	31	—
1983–84	....	42	1
1984–85	....	40	2
1985–86	....	13	1
1986–87	Leicester C	21	—
1987–88	....	32	7
1988–89	....	30	2
1989–90	....	34	3
1990–91	....	35	3
1991–92	....	43	7
1992–93	....	40	15
1993–94	....	10	4

WALTERS, Mark
Born Birmingham 12.1.64. Ht 5 9
Wt 11 08
Forward. From Apprentice. England
Youth, B, Under-21, 1 full cap.

Season	Club	App	Goals
1981–82	Aston Villa	1	—
1982–83	....	22	1
1983–84	....	37	8
1984–85	....	36	10
1985–86	....	40	10
1986–87	....	21	3
1987–88	....	24	7
1987–88	Rangers	18	7
1988–89	....	31	8
1989–90	....	27	5
1990–91	....	30	12
1991–92	Liverpool	25	3
1992–93	....	34	11
1993–94	....	17	—
1993–94	Stoke C	9	2

WALTERS, Scott
Born Hemel Hempstead 23.9.75
Forward. From Watford trainee.

Season	Club	App	Goals
1993–94	Colchester U	—	—

WALTERS, Steve
Born Plymouth 9.1.72. Ht 5 10 Wt 11 08
Forward. From Schoolboy, Trainee. FA
Schools.

Season	Club	App	Goals
1987–88	Crewe Alex	1	—
1988–89	....	22	1
1989–90	....	30	1
1990–91	....	4	—
1991–92	....	35	3
1992–93	....	23	3
1993–94	....	20	1

WALTON, David
Born Bedlingham 10.4.73. Ht 6 2
Wt 13 04
Defender. From Trainee.

Season	Club	App	Goals
1991–92	Sheffield U	—	—
1992–93	....	—	—
1993–94	....	—	—
1993–94	Shrewsbury T	27	5

WALTON, Mark
Born Merthyr 1.6.69. Ht 6 2 Wt 13 13
Goalkeeper. From Swansea C. Wales
Under-21.

Season	Club	App	Goals
1986–87	Luton T	—	—
1987–88	....	—	—
1987–88	Colchester U	17	—
1988–89	....	23	—
1989–90	Norwich C	1	—
1990–91	....	4	—
1991–92	....	17	—
1992–93	....	—	—
1993–94	....	—	—
1993–94	Wrexham	6	—
1993–94	Dundee	—	—
1993–94	Bolton W	3	—

WANLESS, Paul
Born Banbury 14.12.73. Ht 6 1 Wt 13 04
Midfield. From Trainee.

Season	Club	App	Goals
1991–92	Oxford U	6	—
1992–93	....	7	—

1993–94	....	9	—

WARBURTON, Ray

Born Rotherham 7.10.67.   Ht 6 0
Wt 12 09
Defender. From Apprentice.

1984–85	Rotherham U	1	—
1985–86	....	—	—
1986–87	....	3	—
1987–88	....	—	—
1988–89	....	—	—
1989–90	York C....................	43	2
1990–91	....	22	4
1991–92	....	9	—
1992–93	....	10	3
1993–94	....	6	—
1993–94	*Northampton T*...........	17	1

WARD, Ashley

Born Manchester 24.11.70.   Ht 6 1
Wt 11 07
Forward. From Trainee.

1989–90	Manchester C	1	—
1990–91	....	—	—
1990–91	*Wrexham*....................	4	2
1991–92	Leicester C	10	—
1992–93	....	—	—
1992–93	*Blackpool*	2	1
1992–93	Crewe Alex	20	4
1993–94	....	25	13

WARD, Darren

Born Worksop 11.5.74   Ht 5 11   Wt 12 09
Goalkeeper. From Trainee.

1992–93	Mansfield T.................	13	—
1993–94	....	33	—

WARD, Derek

Born Birkenhead 17.5.72   Ht 5 10
Wt 11 03
Midfield.

1992–93	Bury	25	—
1993–94	....	3	—

WARD, Gavin

Born Sutton Coldfield 30.6.70.   Ht 6 2
Wt 12 12
Goalkeeper. From Aston Villa Trainee.

1988–89	Shrewsbury T.............	—	—

1989–90	WBA........................	—	—
1989–90	Cardiff C...................	2	—
1990–91	....	1	—
1991–92	....	24	—
1992–93	....	32	—
1993–94	Leicester C	32	—

WARD, Mark

Born Prescot 10.10.62.   Ht 5 6   Wt 9 12
Midfield. From Everton Apprentice and
Northwich Vic.

1983–84	Oldham Ath................	42	6
1984–85	....	42	6
1985–86	West Ham U	42	3
1986–87	....	37	1
1987–88	....	37	1
1988–89	....	30	2
1989–90	....	19	5
1989–90	Manchester C	19	3
1990–91	....	36	11
1991–92	Everton	37	4
1992–93	....	19	1
1993–94	....	27	1
1993–94	*Birmingham C*	9	1

WARD, Mitch

Born Sheffield 18.6.71.   Ht 5 8   Wt 10 12
Defender. From Trainee.

1989–90	Sheffield U	—	—
1990–91	....	4	—
1990–91	*Crewe Alex*................	4	1
1991–92	Sheffield U	6	2
1992–93	....	26	—
1993–94	....	22	1

WARD, Paul

Born Sedgefield 15.9.63.   Ht 5 11
Wt 12 05
Midfield. From Apprentice.

1981–82	Chelsea......................	—	—
1982–83	Middlesbrough............	15	—
1983–84	....	28	1
1984–85	....	30	—
1985–86	....	3	—
1985–86	Darlington	35	2
1986–87	....	44	1
1987–88	....	45	6
1988–89	Leyton Orient	28	1
1989–90	....	3	—

Season	Club		Appearances	Goals
1989–90	Scunthorpe U		25	4
1990–91			30	2
1990–91	Lincoln C		9	—
1991–92			29	—
1992–93			1	—
1993–94			—	—

WARD, Peter

Born Durham 15.10.64. Ht 6 0 Wt 11 10
Forward. From Chester-le-Street.

Season	Club		Appearances	Goals
1986–87	Huddersfield T		7	—
1987–88			26	2
1988–89			4	—
1989–90	Rochdale		40	5
1990–91			44	5
1991–92	Stockport Co		44	1
1992–93			35	3
1993–94			35	3

WARD, Richard

Born Scarborough 17.11.73 Ht 5 8
Wt 11 00
Midfield. From Trainee.

Season	Club		Appearances	Goals
1992–93	Notts Co		—	—
1993–94	Huddersfield T		—	—
1993–94	Scarborough		—	—

WARD, Richard

Born Middlesbrough 6.1.77
Defender. From Trainee.

Season	Club		Appearances	Goals
1993–94	Middlesbrough		—	—

WARE, Paul

Born Congleton 7.11.70. Ht 5 9
Wt 11 05
Midfield. From Trainee.

Season	Club		Appearances	Goals
1987–88	Stoke C		1	—
1988–89			11	1
1989–90			16	—
1990–91			34	2
1991–92			24	3
1992–93			28	4
1993–94			1	—

WARHURST, Paul

Born Stockport 26.9.69. Ht 6 1 Wt 12 07
Defender. From Trainee. England
Under-21.

Season	Club		Appearances	Goals
1987–88	Manchester C		—	—

Season	Club		Appearances	Goals
1988–89	Oldham Ath		4	—
1989–90			30	1
1990–91			33	1
1991–92	Sheffield W		33	—
1992–93			29	6
1993–94			4	—
1993–94	Blackburn R		9	—

WARK, John

Born Glasgow 4.8.57. Ht 5 11 Wt 12 12
Defender. From Apprentice. Scotland
Under-21, 29 full caps.

Season	Club		Appearances	Goals
1974–75	Ipswich T		3	—
1975–76			3	—
1976–77			33	10
1977–78			18	5
1978–79			42	6
1979–80			41	12
1980–81			40	18
1981–82			42	18
1982–83			42	20
1983–84			32	5
1983–84	Liverpool		9	2
1984–85			40	18
1985–86			9	3
1986–87			11	5
1987–88			1	—
1987–88	Ipswich T		7	—
1988–89			41	13
1989–90			41	10
1990–91	Middlesbrough		32	2
1991–92	Ipswich T		37	3
1992–93			37	6
1993–94			38	3

WARNER, Anthony

Born Liverpool 11.5.74 Ht 6 4 Wt 13 09
Goalkeeper. From School.

Season	Club		Appearances	Goals
1993–94	Liverpool		—	—

WARNER, Vance

Born Leeds 3.9.74 Ht 5 11 Wt 11 05
Defender.

Season	Club		Appearances	Goals
1991–92	Nottingham F		—	—
1992–93			—	—
1993–94			1	—

WARREN, Lee

Born Manchester 28.2.69.   Ht 6 0
Wt 11 13
Midfield. From Trainee.

Season	Club	Apps	Goals
1987–88	Leeds U	—	—
1987–88	Rochdale	31	1
1988–89	Hull C	28	—
1989–90		10	—
1990–91		15	—
1990–91	*Lincoln C*	3	1
1991–92	Hull C	31	1
1992–93		36	—
1993–94		33	—

WARREN, Mark

Born Clapton 12.11.74.   Ht 5 9   Wt 10 05
Midfield. From Trainee.

Season	Club	Apps	Goals
1991–92	Leyton Orient	1	—
1992–93		14	—
1993–94		6	—
1993–94	*West Ham U*	—	—

WARZYCHA, Robert

Born Poland 20.6.63.   Ht 5 8   Wt 11 10
Forward. From Gornik Zabrze. Poland
full caps.

Season	Club	Apps	Goals
1990–91	Everton	8	2
1991–92		37	3
1992–93		20	1
1993–94		7	—

WASSALL, Darren

Born Edgbaston 27.6.68.   Ht 5 11
Wt 11 09
Defender.

Season	Club	Apps	Goals
1987–88	Nottingham F	3	—
1987–88	*Hereford U*	5	—
1988–89	Nottingham F	—	—
1988–89	*Bury*	7	1
1989–90	Nottingham F	3	—
1990–91		7	—
1991–92		14	—
1992–93	Derby Co	24	—
1993–94		25	—

WATKIN, Steve

Born Wrexham 16.6.71.   Ht 5 10
Wt 10 05
Forward. From School.

Season	Club	Apps	Goals
1989–90	Wrexham	—	—
1990–91		9	1
1991–92		28	8
1992–93		33	18
1993–94		40	9

WATKINS, Darren

Born Middlesbrough 17.3.77   Ht 5 11
Wt 11 02
Defender. From Trainee.

Season	Club	Apps	Goals
1993–94	Nottingham F	—	—

WATKISS, Stuart

Born Wolverhampton 8.5.66   Ht 6 2
Wt 13 08
Defender. From Apprentice.

Season	Club	Apps	Goals
1983–84	Wolverhampton W	2	—
From Rushall Olympic			
1993–94	Walsall	39	2

WATSON, Alex

Born Liverpool 5.4.68.   Ht 6 0   Wt 11 09
Defender. From Apprentice. England
Youth.

Season	Club	Apps	Goals
1984–85	Liverpool	—	—
1985–86		—	—
1986–87		—	—
1987–88		2	—
1988–89		2	—
1989–90		—	—
1990–91		—	—
1990–91	*Derby Co*	5	—
1990–91	Bournemouth	23	3
1991–92		15	—
1992–93		46	1
1993–94		45	1

WATSON, Andy

Born Huddersfield 1.4.67.   Ht 5 9
Wt 11 02
Defender. From Harrogate T.

Season	Club	Apps	Goals
1988–89	Halifax T	45	5
1989–90		38	10
1990–91	Swansea C	14	1

Season	Club		
1991–92	....	—	—
1991–92	Carlisle U	35	14
1992–93	....	21	8
1992–93	Blackpool	15	2
1993–94	....	40	20

WATSON, Dave

Born Liverpool 20.11.61.   Ht 6 0
Wt 11 12
Defender. From Amateur. England Under-21, 12 full caps.

Season	Club		
1979–80	Liverpool	—	—
1980–81	....	—	—
1980–81	Norwich C	18	3
1981–82	....	38	3
1982–83	....	35	1
1983–84	....	40	1
1984–85	....	39	—
1985–86	....	42	3
1986–87	Everton	35	4
1987–88	....	37	4
1988–89	....	32	3
1989–90	....	29	1
1990–91	....	32	2
1991–92	....	35	3
1992–93	....	40	1
1993–94	....	28	1

WATSON, David

Born Barnsley 10.11.73   Ht 5 11
Wt 12 00
Goalkeeper. From Trainee. England Youth, Under-21.

Season	Club		
1992–93	Barnsley	5	—
1993–94	....	9	—

WATSON, Gordon

Born Kent 20.3.71.   Ht 5 7   Wt 13 03
Forward. From Trainee. England Under-21.

Season	Club		
1988–89	Charlton Ath	—	—
1989–90	....	9	—
1990–91	....	22	7
1990–91	Sheffield W	5	—
1991–92	....	4	—
1992–93	....	11	1
1993–94	....	23	12

WATSON, Gregg

Born Glasgow 21.9.70   Ht 5 9   Wt 10 9
Defender. Aberdeen Lads. Scotland Youth.

Season	Club		
1987–88	Aberdeen	—	—
1988–89	....	4	—
1989–90	....	4	—
1990–91	....	7	—
1991–92	....	8	—
1992–93	....	—	—
1993–94	Partick T	37	—

WATSON, John

Born South Shields 14.4.74.   Ht 5 9
Wt 10 10
Midfield. From Trainee.

Season	Club		
1990–91	Newcastle U	1	—
1991–92	....	—	—
1992–93	....	—	—
1993–94	Scunthorpe U	5	—

WATSON, Kevin

Born Hackney 3.1.74   Ht 5 9   Wt 12 06
Midfield. From Trainee.

Season	Club		
1991–92	Tottenham H	—	—
1992–93	....	5	—
1993–94	....	—	—
1993–94	*Brentford*	3	—

WATSON, Liam

Born Liverpool 21.5.70   Ht 5 11
Wt 11 10
Forward. From Warrington T.

Season	Club		
1992–93	Preston NE	8	3
1993–94	....	1	—

WATSON, Mark

Born Vancouver 8.9.70   Ht 6 0   Wt 12 06
Defender.

Season	Club		
1993–94	Watford	17	—

WATSON, Paul

Born Hastings 4.1.75   Ht 5 8   Wt 10 10
Defender. From Trainee.

Season	Club		
1992–93	Gillingham	1	—
1993–94	....	14	—

WATSON, Steve

Born North Shields 1.4.74. Ht 6 0
Wt 12 07
Defender. From Trainee. England Youth,
Under-21.

1990–91	Newcastle U	24	—
1991–92		28	1
1992–93		2	—
1993–94		32	2

WATSON, Tommy

Born Liverpool 29.9.69. Ht 5 8 Wt 10 10
Midfield. From Trainee.

1987–88	Grimsby T	19	—
1988–89		21	4
1989–90		16	1
1990–91		41	9
1991–92		17	2
1992–93		24	4
1993–94		11	1

WATT, Michael

Born Aberdeen 27.11.70. Ht 6 1
Wt 11 10
Goalkeeper. From Cove R. Scotland
Under-21.

1989–90	Aberdeen	7	—
1990–91		10	—
1991–92		2	—
1992–93		3	—
1993–94		4	—

WATTS, Grant

Born Croydon 5.11.73 Ht 6 0 Wt 11 02
Forward. From Trainee.

1992–93	Crystal Palace	4	—
1993–94		—	—
1993–94	*Colchester U*	12	2

WATTS, Julian

Born Sheffield 17.3.71. Ht 6 3 Wt 12 01
Defender.

1990–91	Rotherham U	10	—
1991–92		10	1
1991–92	Sheffield W	—	—
1992–93		4	—
1992–93	*Shrewsbury T*	9	—
1993–94	Sheffield W	1	—

WDOWCZYK, Dariusz

Born Warsaw 21.9.62. Ht 5 11 Wt 11 11
Defender. From Legia Warsaw. Poland
full caps.

1989–90	Celtic	23	1
1990–91		24	—
1991–92		19	—
1992–93		25	3
1993–94		25	—

WEBB, Neil

Born Reading 30.7.63. Ht 6 0 Wt 13 07
Midfield. From Apprentice. England
Youth, B, Under-21, 26 full caps. Football
League.

1979–80	Reading	5	—
1980–81		27	7
1981–82		40	15
1982–83	Portsmouth	42	8
1983–84		40	10
1984–85		41	16
1985–86	Nottingham F	38	14
1986–87		32	14
1987–88		40	13
1988–89		36	6
1989–90	Manchester U	11	2
1990–91		32	3
1991–92		31	3
1992–93		1	—
1992–93	Nottingham F	9	—
1993–94		21	3

WEBSTER, Ken

Born Hammersmith 2.3.73. Ht 5 8
Wt 13 02
Defender. From Trainee.

1991–92	Arsenal	—	—
1992–93		—	—
1993–94		—	—

WEBSTER, Simon

Born Earl Shilton 20.1.64. Ht 6 0
Wt 11 07
Defender. From Apprentice.

1981–82	Tottenham H	—	—
1982–83		2	—
1983–84		1	—
1983–84	*Exeter C*	26	—

Season	Club	App	Goals
1984–85	Tottenham H	—	—
1984–85	*Norwich C*	—	—
1984–85	Huddersfield T	16	1
1985–86		41	2
1986–87		39	1
1987–88		22	—
1987–88	Sheffield U	5	1
1988–89		12	2
1989–90		20	—
1990–91	Charlton Ath	40	—
1991–92		44	5
1992–93		43	2
1993–94	West Ham U	—	—

WEGERLE, Roy

Born South Africa 19.3.64.   Ht 5 11
Wt 11 00
Forward. From Tampa Bay R. USA full caps.

Season	Club	App	Goals
1986–87	Chelsea	12	2
1987–88		11	1
1987–88	*Swindon T*	7	1
1988–89	Luton T	30	8
1989–90		15	2
1989–90	QPR	19	6
1990–91		35	18
1991–92		21	5
1991–92	Blackburn R	12	1
1992–93		22	4
1992–93	Coventry C	6	—
1993–94		21	6

WEIR, David

Born Falkirk 10.5.70   Ht 6 2   Wt 13 7
Defender. From Celtic BC.

Season	Club	App	Goals
1992–93	Falkirk	30	1
1993–94		37	3

WEIR, Jim

Born Motherwell 15.6.69   Ht 6 1   Wt 12 2
Defender. Motherwell Orbiston BC.

Season	Club	App	Goals
1987–88	Hamilton A	6	—
1988–89		29	—
1989–90		30	1
1990–91		39	2
1991–92		40	1
1992–93		37	1
1993–94		2	—
1993–94	Hearts	26	—

WELCH, Brian

Born South Shields 17.7.73.   Ht 5 08
Wt 11 11
Midfield. From Hebburn.

Season	Club	App	Goals
1991–92	Burnley	—	—
1992–93		—	—
1993–94		—	—

WELCH, Keith

Born Bolton 3.10.68.   Ht 6 0   Wt 12 0
Goalkeeper. From Trainee.

Season	Club	App	Goals
1986–87	Bolton W	—	—
1986–87	Rochdale	24	—
1987–88		46	—
1988–89		46	—
1989–90		46	—
1990–91		43	—
1991–92	Bristol C	26	—
1992–93		45	—
1993–94		45	—

WELLER, Paul

Born Brighton 6.3.75   Ht 5 8   Wt 10 10
Midfield. From Trainee.

Season	Club	App	Goals
1993–94	Burnley	—	—

WELLS, Mark

Born Leicester 15.10.71.   Ht 5 9
Wt 10 10
Midfield. From Trainee.

Season	Club	App	Goals
1990–91	Notts Co	—	—
1991–92		1	—
1992–93		1	—
1993–94	Huddersfield T	23	4

WELSH, Brian

Born Edinburgh 23.2.69.   Ht 6 2
Wt 12 01
Defender. From Tynecastle BC.

Season	Club	App	Goals
1986–87	Dundee U	1	—
1987–88		1	1
1988–89		1	—
1989–90		5	—
1990–91		17	—
1991–92		11	1
1992–93		15	1
1993–94		37	1

WELSH, Steve
Born Glasgow 19.4.68.   Ht 6 0   Wt 12 03
Defender. From Army.

Season	Club	App	Goals
1989–90	Cambridge U	—	—
1990–91		1	—
1991–92	Peterborough U	42	—
1992–93		45	1
1993–94		45	1

WEST, Colin
Born Wallsend 13.11.62.   Ht 6 0
Wt 13 11
Forward. From Apprentice.

Season	Club	App	Goals
1980–81	Sunderland	—	—
1981–82		18	6
1982–83		23	3
1983–84		38	9
1984–85		23	3
1984–85	Watford	12	7
1985–86		33	13
1986–87	Rangers	9	2
1987–88		1	—
1987–88	Sheffield W	25	7
1988–89		20	1
1988–89	WBA	17	8
1989–90		21	4
1990–91		28	8
1991–92		7	2
1991–92	*Port Vale*	5	1
1992–93	Swansea C	33	12
1993–94	Leyton Orient	43	14

WEST, Colin
Born Middlesbrough 19.9.67.   Ht 5 8
Wt 11 10
Forward. From Apprentice.

Season	Club	App	Goals
1985–86	Chelsea	—	—
1986–87		7	1
1986–87	*Partick T*	24	10
1987–88	Chelsea	9	3
1988–89		—	—
1988–89	*Swansea C*	14	3
1989–90	Chelsea	—	—
1990–91	Dundee	19	3
1991–92		9	3
1992–93		7	—
1993–94	Hartlepool U	36	5

WEST, Daniel
Born Poole 17.4.75
Defender.

Season	Club	App	Goals
1993–94	Aston Villa	—	—

WEST, Dean
Born Wakefield 5.12.72.   Ht 5 10
Wt 11 07
Defender. From Leeds U Schoolboy.

Season	Club	App	Goals
1990–91	Lincoln C	1	1
1991–92		32	3
1992–93		19	3
1993–94		18	6

WEST, Paul
Born 22.6.70   Ht 5 11   Wt 11 00
Defender. From Alcester T.

Season	Club	App	Goals
1991–92	Port Vale	—	—
1992–93	Bradford C	—	—
1993–94	Wigan Ath	2	—

WESTLEY, Shane
Born Canterbury 16.6.65.   Ht 6 2
Wt 13 08
Defender. From Apprentice.

Season	Club	App	Goals
1983–84	Charlton Ath	8	—
1984–85		—	—
1984–85	Southend U	12	—
1985–86		36	5
1986–87		32	—
1986–87	*Norwich C*	—	—
1987–88	Southend U	36	5
1988–89		28	—
1989–90	Wolverhampton W	37	—
1990–91		5	1
1991–92		—	—
1992–93		8	1
1992–93	Brentford	17	1
1993–94		31	—

WESTWATER, Ian
Born Loughborough 8.11.63.   Ht 6 0
Wt 13 00
Goalkeeper. From Salvesen BC.

Season	Club	App	Goals
1980–81	Hearts	2	—
1981–82		—	—
1982–83		—	—
1983–84		—	—

Season	Club	App	Goals
1984–85	....	—	—
1984–85	Dunfermline Ath	8	—
1985–86	....	38	—
1986–87	....	42	—
1987–88	....	28	—
1988–89	....	39	—
1989–90	....	36	—
1990–91	....	1	—
1991–92	Falkirk	40	—
1992–93	....	24	—
1993–94	....	3	—

WETHERALL, David
Born Sheffield 14.3.71. Ht 6 3 Wt 12 00
Defender. From School.

Season	Club	App	Goals
1989–90	Sheffield W	—	—
1990–91	....	—	—
1991–92	Leeds U	1	—
1992–93	....	13	1
1993–94	....	32	1

WHALLEY, Gareth
Born Manchester 19.12.73 Ht 5 10
Wt 11 00
Midfield. From Trainee.

Season	Club	App	Goals
1992–93	Crewe Alex	25	1
1993–94	....	15	1

WHALLEY, Neil
Born Liverpool 29.10.65 Ht 6 0
Wt 12 09
Midfield. From Warrington T.

Season	Club	App	Goals
1992–93	Preston NE	14	—
1993–94	....	21	—

WHEELER, Paul
Born Caerphilly 3.1.65. Ht 5 9 Wt 11 00
Forward. From Apprentice.

Season	Club	App	Goals
1982–83	Bristol R	—	—
1983–84	....	—	—
From Aberaman			
1985–86	Cardiff C	21	2
1986–87	....	37	7
1987–88	....	16	—
1988–89	....	27	1
1989–90	....	—	—
1989–90	Hull C	5	—
1989–90	Hereford U	21	8

Season	Club	App	Goals
1990–91	....	33	4
1991–92	Stockport Co	22	5
1992–93	....	1	—
1992–93	*Scarborough*	7	1
1992–93	Chester C	14	—
1993–94	....	25	7

WHELAN, Noel
Born Leeds 30.12.74 Ht 5 11 Wt 10 07
Forward. From Trainee.

Season	Club	App	Goals
1992–93	Leeds U	1	—
1993–94	....	16	—

WHELAN, Phil
Born Stockport 7.8.72. Ht 6 4 Wt 14 01
Defender. England Under-21.

Season	Club	App	Goals
1989–90	Ipswich T	—	—
1990–91	....	—	—
1991–92	....	8	2
1992–93	....	32	—
1993–94	....	29	—

WHELAN, Ronnie
Born Dublin 25.9.61. Ht 5 9 Wt 10 13
Midfield. From Home Farm. Eire Schools,
Youth, Under-21, 50 full caps.

Season	Club	App	Goals
1979–80	Liverpool	—	—
1980–81	....	1	1
1981–82	....	32	10
1982–83	....	28	2
1983–84	....	23	4
1984–85	....	37	7
1985–86	....	39	10
1986–87	....	39	3
1987–88	....	28	1
1988–89	....	37	4
1989–90	....	34	1
1990–91	....	14	1
1991–92	....	10	—
1992–93	....	17	1
1993–94	....	23	1

WHELAN, Spencer
Born Liverpool 17.9.71. Ht 6 1 Wt 11 13
Defender. From Liverpool.

Season	Club	App	Goals
1990–91	Chester C	11	—
1991–92	....	32	—
1992–93	....	28	—

1993–94 .... 22 —

WHISTON, Peter
Born Widnes 4.1.68. Ht 6 0 Wt 11 06
Forward.

Season	Club	App	Goals
1987–88	Plymouth Arg	—	—
1988–89		2	—
1989–90		8	—
1989–90	*Torquay U*	8	1
1990–91	Torquay U	28	—
1991–92		4	—
1991–92	Exeter C	36	3
1992–93		27	3
1993–94		22	1

WHITBREAD, Adrian
Born Epping 22.10.71. Ht 6 2 Wt 11 13
Defender. From Trainee.

Season	Club	App	Goals
1989–90	Leyton Orient	8	—
1990–91		38	—
1991–92		43	1
1992–93		36	1
1993–94	Swindon T	35	1

WHITE, Chris
Born Chatham 11.12.70. Ht 5 11 Wt 11 10
Defender. From Trainee.

Season	Club	App	Goals
1988–89	Portsmouth	—	—
1989–90		—	—
1990–91		—	—
1991–92	Peterborough U	8	—
1992–93		5	—
1992–93	*Doncaster R*	6	—
1992–93	Exeter C	11	—
1993–94		8	—

WHITE, David
Born Manchester 30.10.67. Ht 6 1 Wt 12 09
Forward. England Youth, B, Under-21, 1 full cap.

Season	Club	App	Goals
1985–86	Manchester C	—	—
1986–87		24	1
1987–88		44	13
1988–89		45	6
1989–90		37	8
1990–91		38	16
1991–92		39	18
1992–93		42	16
1993–94		16	1
1993–94	Leeds U	15	5

WHITE, Devon
Born Nottingham 2.3.64. Ht 6 3 Wt 14 00
Forward. From Arnold T.

Season	Club	App	Goals
1984–85	Lincoln C	7	1
1985–86		22	3
1986–87		—	—
From Boston U			
1987–88	Bristol R	39	15
1988–89		40	5
1989–90		43	12
1990–91		45	11
1991–92		35	10
1991–92	Cambridge U	2	—
1992–93		20	4
1992–93	QPR	7	2
1993–94		18	7

WHITE, Jason
Born Meriden 19.10.71. Ht 6 0 Wt 12 10
Forward. From Derby Co Trainee.

Season	Club	App	Goals
1991–92	Scunthorpe U	22	11
1992–93		37	5
1993–94		9	—
1993–94	*Darlington*	4	1
1993–94	Scarborough	24	9

WHITE, John
Born Honiton 9.9.74. Ht 5 8 Wt 11 03
Midfield. From Trainee.

Season	Club	App	Goals
1992–93	Watford	—	—
1993–94		—	—

WHITE, Steve
Born Chipping Sodbury 2.1.59. Ht 5 10 Wt 11 04
Forward. From Mangotsfield U.

Season	Club	App	Goals
1977–78	Bristol R	8	4
1978–79		27	10
1979–80		15	6
1979–80	Luton T	9	—
1980–81		21	7
1981–82		42	18

Season	Club	App	Goals
1982–83	Charlton Ath	29	12
1982–83	*Lincoln C*	3	—
1982–83	*Luton T*	4	—
1983–84	Bristol R	43	9
1984–85		18	3
1985–86		40	12
1986–87	Swindon T	35	15
1987–88		25	11
1988–89		43	13
1989–90		43	18
1990–91		35	9
1991–92		23	10
1992–93		34	7
1993–94		6	—

WHITEHALL, Steve
Born Bromborough 8.12.66. Ht 5 9
Wt 10 11
Forward. From Southport.

Season	Club	App	Goals
1991–92	Rochdale	34	8
1992–93		42	14
1993–94		39	14

WHITEHEAD, Philip
Born Halifax 17.12.69. Ht 6 3 Wt 13 07
Goalkeeper. From Trainee.

Season	Club	App	Goals
1986–87	Halifax T	12	—
1987–88		—	—
1988–89		11	—
1989–90		19	—
1989–90	Barnsley	—	—
1990–91		—	—
1990–91	*Halifax T*	9	—
1991–92	Barnsley	3	—
1991–92	*Scunthorpe U*	8	—
1992–93	Barnsley	13	—
1992–93	*Scunthorpe U*	8	—
1992–93	*Bradford C*	6	—
1993–94	Barnsley	—	—
1993–94	Oxford U	39	—

WHITEHEAD, Scot
Born Doncaster 13.8.75. Ht 5 8 Wt 11 09
Defender. From Trainee.

Season	Club	App	Goals
1993–94	Huddersfield T	—	—

WHITEHEAD, Scott
Born Doncaster 20.4.74. Ht 5 9
Wt 11 10
Midfield. From Trainee.

Season	Club	App	Goals
1991–92	Chesterfield	5	—
1992–93		4	—
1993–94		—	—

WHITEHOUSE, Dane
Born Sheffield 14.10.70. Ht 5 9 Wt 10 13
Midfield. From Trainee.

Season	Club	App	Goals
1988–89	Sheffield U	5	—
1989–90		12	1
1990–91		4	—
1991–92		34	7
1992–93		14	5
1993–94		38	5

WHITINGTON, Craig
Born Brighton 3.9.70. Ht 5 11 Wt 12 04
Forward. From Crawley T.

Season	Club	App	Goals
1993–94	Scarborough	27	10

WHITLEY, Jim
Born Zambia 14.4.75. Ht 5 9 Wt 11 00
Midfield. From Trainee.

Season	Club	App	Goals
1993–94	Manchester C	—	—

WHITLOW, Mike
Born Northwich 13.1.68. Ht 5 11
Wt 12 03
Defender. From Witton Alb.

Season	Club	App	Goals
1988–89	Leeds U	20	1
1989–90		29	1
1990–91		18	1
1991–92		10	1
1991–92	Leicester C	5	—
1992–93		24	1
1993–94		31	2

WHITMARSH, Paul
Born London 18.9.73. Ht 5 8 Wt 10 12
Forward. From Trainee.

Season	Club	App	Goals
1992–93	West Ham U	—	—
1993–94		—	—
1993–94	Doncaster R	6	1

WHITNEY, Jonathan

Born Nantwich 23.12.70   Ht 5 10
Defender. From Winsford.

Season	Club	Apps	Goals
1993–94	Huddersfield T	14	—

WHITTAKER, Stuart

Born Liverpool 2.1.75   Ht 5 7   Wt 9 03
Forward. From Liverpool trainee.

Season	Club	Apps	Goals
1993–94	Bolton W	2	—

WHITTINGHAM, Guy

Born Evesham 10.11.64.   Ht 5 10
Wt 11 12
Forward. From Yeovil and Army.

Season	Club	Apps	Goals
1989–90	Portsmouth	42	23
1990–91		37	12
1991–92		35	11
1992–93		46	42
1993–94	Aston Villa	18	3
1993–94	*Wolverhampton W*	13	8

WHITTON, Steve

Born East Ham 4.12.60.   Ht 6 1
Wt 13 06
Forward. From Apprentice.

Season	Club	Apps	Goals
1978–79	Coventry C	—	—
1979–80		7	—
1980–81		1	—
1981–82		28	9
1982–83		38	12
1983–84	West Ham U	22	5
1984–85		17	1
1985–86		—	—
1985–86	*Birmingham C*	8	2
1986–87	Birmingham C	39	9
1987–88		33	14
1988–89		23	5
1988–89	Sheffield W	12	3
1989–90		19	1
1990–91		1	—
1990–91	Ipswich T	10	2
1991–92		43	9
1992–93		24	3
1993–94		11	1

Season	Club	Apps	Goals
1993–94	Colchester U	8	2

WHITWORTH, Neil

Born Ince 12.4.72.   Ht 6 2   Wt 12 06
Defender. From Trainee. England Youth.

Season	Club	Apps	Goals
1989–90	Wigan Ath	2	—
1990–91	Manchester U	1	—
1991–92		—	—
1991–92	*Preston NE*	6	—
1991–92	*Barnsley*	11	—
1992–93	Manchester U	—	—
1993–94		—	—
1993–94	*Rotherham U*	8	1
1993–94	*Blackpool*	3	—

WHYTE, Chris

Born London 2.9.61.   Ht 6 1   Wt 11 10
Defender. From Amateur. England
Under-21.

Season	Club	Apps	Goals
1979–80	Arsenal	—	—
1980–81		—	—
1981–82		32	2
1982–83		36	3
1983–84		15	2
1984–85		—	—
1984–85	*Crystal Palace*	13	—
1985–86	Arsenal	7	1
From Los Angeles R			
1988–89	WBA	40	3
1989–90		44	4
1990–91	Leeds U	38	3
1991–92		41	1
1992–93		34	1
1993–94	Birmingham C	33	—

WHYTE, David

Born Greenwich 20.4.71.   Ht 5 9
Wt 10 06
Forward.

Season	Club	Apps	Goals
1988–89	Crystal Palace	—	—
1989–90		—	—
1990–91		—	—
1991–92		11	1
1991–92	*Charlton Ath*	8	2
1992–93		—	—
1993–94	Crystal Palace	16	3

WHYTE, Derek

Born Glasgow 31.8.68.   Ht 5 11   Wt 11 05
Defender. From Celtic BC. Scotland
Schools, Youth, B, Under-21, 6 full caps.

Season	Club	App	Goals
1985–86	Celtic	11	—
1986–87		42	—
1987–88		41	3
1988–89		22	—
1989–90		35	1
1990–91		24	2
1991–92		40	1
1992–93		1	—
1992–93	Middlesbrough	35	—
1993–94		42	1

WIDDRINGTON, Tommy

Born Newcastle 21.11.71.   Ht 5 10
Wt 11 07
Midfield. From Trainee.

Season	Club	App	Goals
1989–90	Southampton	—	—
1990–91		—	—
1991–92		3	—
1991–92	*Wigan Ath*	6	—
1992–93	Southampton	12	—
1993–94		11	1

WIEGHORST, Morten

Born Glostrup, Denmark 25.2.71   Ht 6 3
Wt 14 0
Midfield. From Lyngby.

Season	Club	App	Goals
1992–93	Dundee	23	2
1993–94		24	2

WIETECHA, David

Born Colchester 1.11.74   Ht 6 4
Goalkeeper.

Season	Club	App	Goals
1993–94	Millwall	—	—
1993–94	*Crewe Alex*	—	—
1993–94	*Rotherham U*	—	—

WIGG, Nathan

Born Cardiff 27.9.74   Ht 5 9   Wt 10 05
Midfield. From Trainee.

Season	Club	App	Goals
1993–94	Cardiff C	19	—

WIGLEY, Steve

Born Ashton 15.10.61.   Ht 5 9   Wt 10 05
Forward. From Curzon Ashton.

Season	Club	App	Goals
1980–81	Nottingham F	—	—

Season	Club	App	Goals
1981–82		—	—
1982–83		4	—
1983–84		35	1
1984–85		35	1
1985–86		8	—
1985–86	Sheffield U	10	1
1986–87		18	—
1986–87	Birmingham C	11	1
1987–88		43	2
1988–89		33	1
1988–89	Portsmouth	11	—
1989–90		45	4
1990–91		41	5
1991–92		23	3
1992–93		—	—
1993–94	Exeter C	23	1

WILCOX, Jason

Born Bolton 15.7.71.   Ht 5 10   Wt 11 06
Forward. From Trainee.

Season	Club	App	Goals
1989–90	Blackburn R	1	—
1990–91		18	—
1991–92		38	4
1992–93		33	4
1993–94		33	6

WILCOX, Russell

Born Hemsworth 25.3.64.   Ht 6 0
Wt 11 10
Defender. From Apprentice.

Season	Club	App	Goals
1980–81	Doncaster R	1	—

From Cambridge U, Frickley Ath.

Season	Club	App	Goals
1986–87	Northampton T	35	1
1987–88		46	4
1988–89		11	1
1989–90		46	3
1990–91	Hull C	31	1
1991–92		40	4
1992–93		29	2
1993–94	Doncaster R	40	2

WILDER, Chris

Born Wortley 23.9.67.   Ht 5 11   Wt 11 02
Defender. From Apprentice.

Season	Club	App	Goals
1985–86	Southampton	—	—
1986–87	Sheffield U	11	—
1987–88		25	—
1988–89		29	1
1989–90		8	—

Season	Club	League Appearances/Goals	
1989–90	*Walsall*	4	—
1990–91	Sheffield U	16	—
1990–91	*Charlton Ath*	1	—
1991–92	Sheffield U	4	—
1991–92	*Charlton Ath*	2	—
1991–92	*Leyton Orient*	16	1
1992–93	Rotherham U	32	8
1993–94		37	2

WILKERSON, Paul
Born Hertford 11.12.74 Ht 6 3 Wt 13 11
Goalkeeper.

1993–94	Watford	—	—

WILKIN, Kevin
Born Cambridge 1.10.67
Forward. From Cambridge C.

1990–91	Northampton T	9	2
1991–92		—	—
1992–93		41	4
1993–94		24	5

WILKINS, Dean
Born Hillingdon 12.7.62. Ht 5 10
Wt 12 04
Midfield. From Apprentice.

1980–81	QPR	2	—
1981–82		1	—
1982–83		3	—
1983–84	Brighton	2	—
1983–84	*Orient*	10	—

From PEC Zwolle

1987–88	Brighton	44	3
1988–89		43	1
1989–90		46	6
1990–91		46	7
1991–92		26	—
1992–93		35	3
1993–94		21	2

WILKINS, Ray
Born Hillingdon 14.9.56. Ht 5 8
Wt 11 02
Midfield. From Apprentice. England
Under-21, Under-23, 84 full caps. Football
League.

1973–74	Chelsea	6	—
1974–75		21	2
1975–76		42	11
1976–77		42	7
1977–78		33	7
1978–79		35	3
1979–80	Manchester U	37	2
1980–81		13	—
1981–82		42	1
1982–83		26	1
1983–84		42	3
1984–85	AC Milan	28	—
1985–86		29	2
1986–87		16	—

From Paris St Germain

1987–88	Rangers	24	1
1988–89		31	1
1989–90		15	—
1989–90	QPR	23	1
1990–91		38	2
1991–92		27	1
1992–93		27	2
1993–94		39	1

WILKINS, Richard
Born London 28.5.65. Ht 6 0 Wt 12 00
Midfield. From Haverhill R.

1986–87	Colchester U	23	2
1987–88		46	9
1988–89		40	7
1989–90		43	4
1990–91	Cambridge U	41	3
1991–92		32	4
1992–93		1	—
1993–94		7	—

WILKINSON, Darron
Born Reading 24.11.69 Ht 5 11
Wt 12 08
Midfield. From Wokingham.

1992–93	Brighton	27	3
1993–94		11	—

WILKINSON, Ian
Born Warrington 2.7.73. Ht 5 11
Wt 12 00
Goalkeeper. From Trainee.

1991–92	Manchester U	—	—
1992–93		—	—
1993–94	Stockport Co	—	—
1993–94	Crewe Alex	3	—

WILKINSON, Paul

Born Louth 30.10.64.   Ht 6 0   Wt 11 09
Forward. From Apprentice. England
Under-21.

Season	Club	App	Goals
1982–83	Grimsby T	4	1
1983–84		37	12
1984–85		30	14
1984–85	Everton	5	2
1985–86		4	1
1986–87		22	4
1986–87	Nottingham F	8	—
1987–88		26	5
1988–89	Watford	45	19
1989–90		43	15
1990–91		46	18
1991–92	Middlesbrough	46	15
1992–93		41	13
1993–94		45	15

WILKINSON, Steve

Born Lincoln 1.9.68.   Ht 6 0   Wt 11 02
Forward. From Apprentice.

Season	Club	App	Goals
1986–87	Leicester C	1	—
1987–88		5	1
1988–89		1	—
1988–89	Rochdale	—	—
1988–89	Crewe Alex	5	2
1989–90	Leicester C	2	—
1989–90	Mansfield T	37	15
1990–91		39	11
1991–92		30	14
1992–93		43	11
1993–94		42	10

WILL, James

Born Turiff 7.10.72.   Ht 6 2   Wt 13 13
Goalkeeper. From Trainee. Scotland
Under-21.

Season	Club	App	Goals
1991–92	Arsenal	—	—
1991–92	Sheffield U	—	—
1992–93	Arsenal	—	—
1993–94		—	—

WILLIAMS, Adrian

Born Reading 16.8.71.   Ht 5 10   Wt 11 00
Defender. From Trainee. Wales 1 full cap.

Season	Club	App	Goals
1988–89	Reading	8	—
1989–90		16	2

Season	Club	App	Goals
1990–91		7	—
1991–92		40	4
1992–93		31	4
1993–94		41	—

WILLIAMS, Andy

Born Birmingham 29.7.62.   Ht 6 0
Wt 11 09
Midfield. From Dudley and Solihull B.

Season	Club	App	Goals
1985–86	Coventry C	8	—
1986–87		1	—
1986–87	Rotherham U	36	4
1987–88		36	6
1988–89		15	3
1988–89	Leeds U	18	1
1989–90		16	2
1990–91		12	—
1991–92		—	—
1991–92	Port Vale	5	—
1991–92	Notts Co	15	1
1992–93		22	1
1993–94		2	—
1993–94	Huddersfield T	6	—
1993–94	Rotherham U	34	2

WILLIAMS, Bill

Born Rochdale 7.10.60.   Ht 5 10
Wt 12 11
Defender. From Local.

Season	Club	App	Goals
1981–82	Rochdale	6	—
1982–83		37	—
1983–84		27	2
1984–85		25	—
1985–86	Stockport Co	22	—
1986–87		30	—
1987–88		45	1
1988–89		7	—
1988–89	Manchester C	1	—
1988–89	Stockport Co	28	2
1989–90		37	—
1990–91		18	1
1991–92		35	2
1992–93		22	1
1993–94		16	1

WILLIAMS, Brett

Born Dudley 19.3.68.   Ht 5 10   Wt 11 12
Defender. From Apprentice.

Season	Club	App	Goals
1985–86	Nottingham F	11	—

Season	Club	Apps	Goals
1986–87	....	3	—
1986–87	*Stockport Co*	2	—
1987–88	Nottingham F	4	—
1987–88	*Northampton T*	4	—
1988–89	Nottingham F	2	—
1989–90	....	1	—
1989–90	*Hereford U*	14	—
1990–91	Nottingham F	4	—
1991–92	....	9	—
1991–92	*Oxford U*	7	—
1992–93	Nottingham F	9	—
1993–94	....	—	—
1993–94	*Stoke C*	2	—

WILLIAMS, Carwyn
Born Pwllheli 21.10.74
Forward. From Trainee.

Season	Club	Apps	Goals
1993–94	Crewe Alex	—	—

WILLIAMS, Chris
Born Neath 21.9.76
Forward. From Trainee.

Season	Club	Apps	Goals
1993–94	Hereford U	2	—

WILLIAMS, David
Born Liverpool 18.9.68.   Ht 6 0   Wt 12 00
Goalkeeper. From Trainee.

Season	Club	Apps	Goals
1987–88	Oldham Ath	—	—
1987–88	Burnley	—	—
1988–89	....	7	—
1989–90	....	7	—
1990–91	....	3	—
1991–92	....	5	—
1991–92	*Rochdale*	6	—
1992–93	Burnley	2	—
1992–93	*Crewe Alex*	—	—
1993–94	Burnley	—	—

WILLIAMS, Dean A
Born Hampstead 14.11.70   Ht 6 1
Wt 13 00
Forward. From St Albans.

Season	Club	Apps	Goals
1993–94	Brentford	3	1

WILLIAMS, Dean P
Born Lichfield 5.1.72   Ht 6 1   Wt 12 08
Goalkeeper. From Tamworth.

Season	Club	Apps	Goals
1993–94	Brentford	7	—

WILLIAMS, Gareth
Born Isle of Wight 12.3.67.   Ht 5 10
Wt 11 08
Forward. From Gosport Borough.

Season	Club	Apps	Goals
1987–88	Aston Villa	1	—
1988–89	....	1	—
1989–90	....	10	—
1990–91	....	—	—
1991–92	Barnsley	17	—
1992–93	....	8	5
1992–93	*Hull C*	4	—
1993–94	Barnsley	9	1
1993–94	*Hull C*	16	2

WILLIAMS, Gary
Born Wolverhampton 17.6.60.   Ht 5 9
Wt 11 12
Defender. From Apprentice.

Season	Club	Apps	Goals
1978–79	Aston Villa	23	—
1979–80	....	2	—
1979–80	*Walsall*	9	—
1980–81	Aston Villa	22	—
1981–82	....	28	—
1982–83	....	36	—
1983–84	....	40	—
1984–85	....	38	—
1985–86	....	25	—
1986–87	....	26	—
1987–88	Leeds U	31	3
1988–89	....	8	—
1989–90	....	—	—
1989–90	Watford	18	—
1990–91	....	24	—
1991–92	....	—	—
1991–92	Bradford C	22	—
1992–93	....	31	3
1993–94	....	32	2

WILLIAMS, Geraint
Born Treorchy 5.1.62.   Ht 5 7   Wt 10 06
Midfield. From Apprentice. Wales Youth,
Under-21, 12 full caps.

Season	Club	Apps	Goals
1979–80	Bristol R	—	—
1980–81	....	28	1
1981–82	....	16	—
1982–83	....	35	3
1983–84	....	34	4
1984–85	....	28	—
1984–85	Derby Co	12	—

Season	Club	App	Goals
1985–86	....	40	4
1986–87	....	40	1
1987–88	....	40	1
1988–89	....	37	1
1989–90	....	38	—
1990–91	....	31	—
1991–92	....	39	2
1992–93	Ipswich T	37	—
1993–94	....	34	—

WILLIAMS, John

Born Birmingham 11.5.68. Ht 6 2
Wt 12 04
Midfield. From Cradley T.

Season	Club	App	Goals
1991–92	Swansea C..................	39	11
1992–93	Coventry C	41	8
1993–94	....	32	3

WILLIAMS, Lee

Born Birmingham 3.2.73 Ht 5 7
Wt 11 00
Midfield. From Trainee.

Season	Club	App	Goals
1991–92	Aston Villa.................	—	—
1992–93	....	—	—
1992–93	Shrewsbury T	3	—
1993–94	Aston Villa.................	—	—
1993–94	Peterborough U	18	—

WILLIAMS, Mark S

Born Cheshire 28.9.70. Ht 6 0 Wt 13 00
Defender. From Newtown.

Season	Club	App	Goals
1991–92	Shrewsbury T	3	—
1992–93	....	28	1
1993–94	....	36	1

WILLIAMS, Martin

Born Luton 12.7.73. Ht 5 9 Wt 11 12
Forward. From Leicester C Trainee.

Season	Club	App	Goals
1991–92	Luton T	1	—
1992–93	....	22	1
1993–94	....	15	1

WILLIAMS, Mike

Born Bradford 21.11.69 Ht 5 10
Wt 11 02
Midfield. From Maltby.

Season	Club	App	Goals
1991–92	Sheffield W..................	—	—
1992–93	....	3	—

Season	Club	App	Goals
1992–93	Halifax T	9	1
1993–94	Sheffield W..................	4	—

WILLIAMS, Paul

Born Liverpool 25.9.70. Ht 6 0 Wt 12 02
Midfield. From Trainee.

Season	Club	App	Goals
1988–89	Sunderland..................	1	—
1989–90	....	1	—
1990–91	Swansea C	12	1—
1991–92	Sunderland..................	7	—
1992–93	....	—	—
1993–94	Doncaster R................	1	—

WILLIAMS, Paul

Born Leicester 11.9.69. Ht 5 7 Wt 10 00
Forward. From Trainee.

Season	Club	App	Goals
1988–89	Leicester C	—	—
1989–90	Stockport Co	7	—
1990–91	....	24	2
1991–92	....	13	1
1992–93	....	26	1
1993–94	Coventry C	9	—
1993–94	WBA	5	—

WILLIAMS, Paul

Born Burton 26.3.71. Ht 5 11 Wt 12 00
Midfield. From Trainee. England
Under-21.

Season	Club	App	Goals
1989–90	Derby Co.....................	10	1
1989–90	Lincoln C	3	—
1990–91	Derby Co.....................	19	4
1991–92	....	41	13
1992–93	....	19	4
1993–94	....	34	1

WILLIAMS, Paul

Born London 16.8.65. Ht 5 7 Wt 10 03
Forward. From Woodford T. England B,
Under-21.

Season	Club	App	Goals
1986–87	Charlton Ath	—	—
1987–88	....	12	—
1987–88	Brentford	7	3
1988–89	Charlton Ath	32	13
1989–90	....	38	10
1990–91	Sheffield W..................	46	15
1991–92	....	40	9
1992–93	....	7	1
1992–93	Crystal Palace.............	18	—

1993–94 .... 24 7

WILLIAMS, Paul A
Born Sheffield 8.9.63. Ht 6 3 Wt 14 06
Forward. From Distillery, Leeds U,
Grenaker R, Nuneaton. Northern Ireland
1 full cap.

Season	Club	App	Goals
1986–87	Preston NE	1	—
1987–88	Newport Co	26	3
1987–88	Sheffield U	6	—
1988–89		2	—
1989–90	Hartlepool U	8	—
1990–91	Stockport Co	24	14
1990–91	WBA	10	—
1991–92		34	5
1992–93		—	—
1992–93	*Coventry C*	2	—
1992–93	Stockport Co	16	3
1993–94		—	—
1993–94	Rochdale	11	2

WILLIAMS, Scott
Born Bangor 7.8.74 Ht 6 0 Wt 11 00
Defender. From Trainee.

Season	Club	App	Goals
1992–93	Wrexham	1	—
1993–94		14	—

WILLIAMS, Steven
Born Mansfield 18.7.70. Ht 5 11
Wt 10 06
Midfield. From Trainee.

Season	Club	App	Goals
1986–87	Mansfield T	4	—
1987–88		4	—
1988–89		3	—
1989–90	Chesterfield	11	1
1990–91		25	4
1991–92		31	2
1992–93		31	5
1993–94		—	—

WILLIAMS, Steven
Born Aberystwyth 16.10.74 Ht 6 3
Wt 12 12
Goalkeeper. From Coventry C.

Season	Club	App	Goals
1993–94	Cardiff C	18	—

WILLIAMS, Steven
Born Sheffield 3.11.75
Forward. From Trainee.

Season	Club	App	Goals
1993–94	Lincoln C	8	1

WILLIAMSON, Bobby
Born Glasgow 13.8.61 Ht 5 8 Wt 12 9
Forward. From Auchengill BC.

Season	Club	App	Goals
1980–81	Clydebank	2	—
1981–82		12	1
1982–83		39	23
1983–84		17	4
1983–84	Rangers	17	6
1984–85		1	—
1985–86		23	6
1986–87	WBA	31	8
1987–88		22	3
1988–89	Rotherham U	42	27
1989–90		42	19
1990–91		9	3
1990–91	Kilmarnock	23	14
1991–92		36	9
1992–93		33	6
1993–94		38	7

WILLIAMSON, Danny
Born London 5.12.73 Ht 5 10 Wt 11 06
Midfield. From Trainee.

Season	Club	App	Goals
1992–93	West Ham U	—	—
1993–94		3	1
1993–94	*Doncaster R*	13	1

WILLIS, Jimmy
Born Liverpool 12.7.68. Ht 6 0 Wt 12 02
Defender. From Blackburn R.

Season	Club	App	Goals
1986–87	Halifax T	—	—
1987–88	Stockport Co	10	—
1987–88	Darlington	9	—
1988–89		41	2
1989–90		*38*	*2*
1990–91		28	2
1991–92		12	2
1991–92	Leicester C	10	—
1991–92	*Bradford C*	9	1
1992–93	Leicester C	—	—
1993–94		9	1

WILLIS, Roger

Born Sheffield 17.6.67. Ht 6 1 Wt 11 06
Defender.

Season	Club	Apps	Goals
1989–90	Grimsby T	9	—
To Barnet			
1991–92	Barnet	38	12
1992–93		6	1
1992–93	Watford	32	2
1993–94		4	—
1993–94	Birmingham C	16	5

WILMOT, Rhys

Born Newport 21.2.62. Ht 6 1 Wt 12 00
Goalkeeper. From Apprentice. Wales
Youth, Under-21.

Season	Club	Apps	Goals
1979–80	Arsenal	—	—
1980–81		—	—
1981–82		—	—
1982–83		—	—
1982–83	*Hereford U*	9	—
1983–84	Arsenal	—	—
1984–85	*Orient*	46	—
1985–86	Arsenal	2	—
1986–87		6	—
1987–88			
1988–89			
1988–89	*Swansea C*	16	—
1988–89	*Plymouth Arg*	17	—
1989–90	Plymouth Arg	46	—
1990–91		36	—
1991–92		34	—
1992–93	Grimsby T	33	—
1993–94			

WILSON, Clive

Born Manchester 13.11.61. Ht 5 7
Wt 10 00
Midfield. From Local.

Season	Club	Apps	Goals
1979–80	Manchester C	—	—
1980–81		—	—
1981–82		4	—
1982–83		—	—
1982–83	*Chester*	21	2
1983–84	Manchester C	11	—
1984–85		27	4
1985–86		25	5
1986–87		31	—
1986–87	Chelsea	—	—
1986–87	*Manchester C*	11	—

Season	Club	Apps	Goals
1987–88	Chelsea	31	2
1988–89		32	3
1989–90		18	—
1990–91	QPR	13	1
1991–92		40	3
1992–93		41	3
1993–94		42	3

WILSON, Danny

Born Wigan 1.1.60. Ht 5 6 Wt 11 00
Midfield. From Wigan Ath. Northern
Ireland 24 full caps.

Season	Club	Apps	Goals
1977–78	Bury	12	1
1978–79		46	7
1979–80		32	—
1980–81	Chesterfield	33	3
1981–82		43	3
1982–83		24	7
1982–83	Nottingham F	10	1
1983–84	*Scunthorpe U*	6	3
1983–84	Brighton	26	10
1984–85		38	5
1985–86		33	11
1986–87		38	7
1987–88	Luton T	38	8
1988–89		37	9
1989–90		35	7
1990–91	Sheffield W	36	6
1991–92		36	3
1992–93		26	2
1993–94	Barnsley	43	—

WILSON, Gus

Born Manchester 11.4.63. Ht 5 11
Wt 12 00
Defender. From Runcorn.

Season	Club	Apps	Goals
1991–92	Crewe Alex	41	—
1992–93		35	—
1993–94		18	—

WILSON, Kevin

Born Banbury 18.4.61. Ht 5 7 Wt 10 10
Forward. From Banbury U. Northern
Ireland 40 full caps.

Season	Club	Apps	Goals
1979–80	Derby Co	4	—
1980–81		27	7
1981–82		24	9
1982–83		22	4
1983–84		32	2

Season	Club	Apps	Goals
1984–85		13	8
1984–85	Ipswich T	17	7
1985–86		39	7
1986–87		42	20
1987–88	Chelsea	25	5
1988–89		46	13
1989–90		37	14
1990–91		22	7
1991–92		22	3
1991–92	Notts Co	8	1
1992–93		32	1
1993–94		29	1
1993–94	*Bradford C*	5	—

WILSON, Lee
Born Mansfield 23.5.72 Ht 5 10
Wt 11 03
Forward. From Clipstone Welfare.

Season	Club	Apps	Goals
1992–93	Mansfield T	4	—
1993–94		14	1

WILSON, Paul
Born Bradford 2.8.68. Ht 5 10 Wt 13 00
Defender. From Trainee.

Season	Club	Apps	Goals
1985–86	Huddersfield T	7	—
1986–87		8	—
1987–88	Norwich C	—	—
1987–88	Northampton T	15	1
1988–89		39	1
1989–90		27	—
1990–91		44	3
1991–92		16	1
1991–92	Halifax T	23	5
1992–93		22	2
1992–93	Burnley	20	—
1993–94		11	—

WILSON, Paul
Born London 26.9.64. Ht 5 9 Wt 11 04
Defender. From West Ham U, Billericay, Barking.

Season	Club	Apps	Goals
1991–92	Barnet	25	1
1992–93		9	—
1993–94		34	3

WILSON, Richard
Born Bradford 12.3.75
Defender. From Trainee.

Season	Club	Apps	Goals
1993–94	Bradford C	—	—

WILSON, Ross
Born Chatham 29.9.76 Ht 5 8 Wt 10 00
Midfield. From Trainee.

Season	Club	Apps	Goals
1993–94	Nottingham F	—	—

WILSON, Steve
Born Hull 24.4.74. Ht 5 11 Wt 11 00
Goalkeeper. From Trainee.

Season	Club	Apps	Goals
1990–91	Hull C	2	—
1991–92		3	—
1992–93		26	—
1993–94		9	—

WINDASS, Dean
Born Hull 1.4.69. Ht 5 9 Wt 12 03
Midfield.

Season	Club	Apps	Goals
1991–92	Hull C	32	6
1992–93		41	7
1993–94		43	23

WINNIE, David
Born Glasgow 26.10.66. Ht 5 1 Wt 10 07
Defender. S Form. Scotland Schools, Youth, Under-21.

Season	Club	Apps	Goals
1983–84	St Mirren	8	—
1984–85		30	3
1985–86		20	1
1986–87		14	—
1987–88		26	2
1988–89		30	—
1989–90		17	—
1990–91		1	—
1991–92	Aberdeen	28	1
1992–93		21	—
1993–94		6	—
1993–94	*Middlesbrough*	1	—

WINSTANLEY, Mark
Born St. Helens 22.1.68. Ht 6 1
Wt 12 04
Defender. From Trainee.

Season	Club	Apps	Goals
1984–85	Bolton W	—	—
1985–86		3	—
1986–87		13	—
1987–88		8	1
1988–89		44	—
1989–90		43	1
1990–91		32	—

1991–92		27	—
1992–93		29	1
1993–94		21	—

WINSTONE, Simon
Born Bristol 4.10.74   Ht 5 7
Defender. From Trainee.

1993–94	Stoke C	—	—

WINTER, Steven
Born Bristol 26.10.73.   Ht 5 7   Wt 10 03
Midfield. From Trainee.

1991–92	Walsall	16	—
1992–93		2	—
1993–94		—	—

WINTERBURN, Nigel
Born Coventry 11.12.63.   Ht 5 8
Wt 11 04
Defender. From Local. England Youth, B,
Under-21, 2 full caps.

1981–82	Birmingham C	—	—
1982–83		—	—
1983–84	Oxford U	—	—
1983–84	Wimbledon	43	1
1984–85		41	4
1985–86		39	1
1986–87		42	2
1987–88	Arsenal	17	—
1988–89		38	3
1989–90		36	—
1990–91		38	—
1991–92		41	1
1992–93		29	1
1993–94		34	—

WIRMOLA, Jonas
Born Sweden 17.7.69
Defender. From Sparvagens.

1993–94	Sheffield U	8	—

WISE, Dennis
Born Kensington 15.12.66.   Ht 5 6
Wt 9 05
Forward. From Southampton Apprentice.
England B, Under-21, 6 full caps.

1984–85	Wimbledon	1	—
1985–86		4	—

1986–87		28	4
1987–88		30	10
1988–89		37	5
1989–90		35	8
1990–91	Chelsea	33	10
1991–92		38	10
1992–93		27	3
1993–94		35	4

WISHART, Fraser
Born Johnstone 1.3.65.   Ht 5 8   Wt 10 00
Defender. From Pollok.

1983–84	Motherwell	6	—
1984–85		—	—
1985–86		26	—
1986–87		44	3
1987–88		43	1
1988–89		35	1
1989–90	St Mirren	20	—
1990–91		22	—
1991–92		9	—
1992–93	Falkirk	24	2
1993–94	Rangers	5	—

WITHE, Chris
Born Liverpool 25.9.62.   Ht 5 10
Wt 11 12
Defender. From Apprentice.

1980–81	Newcastle U	2	—
1981–82		—	—
1982–83		—	—
1983–84	Bradford C	45	1
1984–85		45	—
1985–86		33	—
1986–87		18	1
1987–88		2	—
1987–88	Notts Co	35	2
1988–89		45	1
1989–90	Bury	31	1
1990–91		—	—
1990–91	*Chester C*	2	—
1990–91	*Mansfield T*	11	—
1990–91	Mansfield T	10	—
1991–92		10	1
1992–93		45	4
1993–94	Shrewsbury T	26	—

WITTER, Tony

Born London 12.8.65.   Ht 6 1   Wt 12 07
Defender. From Grays Ath.

Season	Club	App	Goals
1990–91	Crystal Palace	—	—
1991–92	QPR	—	—
1991–92	*Millwall*	—	—
1991–92	*Plymouth Arg*	3	1
1992–93	QPR	—	—
1993–94		1	—
1993–94	*Reading*	4	—

WOAN, Ian

Born Wirrall 14.12.67.   Ht 5 10   Wt 11 09
Midfield. From Runcorn.

Season	Club	App	Goals
1989–90	Nottingham F	—	—
1990–91		12	3
1991–92		21	5
1992–93		28	3
1993–94		24	5

WOOD, Darren

Born Derby 22.10.68.   Ht 6 1   Wt 12 08
Defender. From Trainee.

Season	Club	App	Goals
1986–87	Chesterfield	10	1
1987–88		35	1
1988–89		22	1
1989–90	Reading	32	2
1990–91	Northampton T	2	1
1991–92		1	—
1992–93		—	—
1993–94		1	—

WOOD, Paul

Born Middlesbrough 1.11.64.   Ht 5 9
Wt 10 01
Forward. From Apprentice.

Season	Club	App	Goals
1982–83	Portsmouth	—	—
1983–84		8	1
1984–85		6	1
1985–86		25	4
1986–87		8	—
1987–88		—	—
1987–88	Brighton	31	4
1988–89		35	1
1989–90		26	3
1989–90	Sheffield U	17	3
1990–91		7	—
1990–91	*Bournemouth*	21	—

Season	Club	App	Goals
1991–92	Sheffield U	4	—
1991–92	Bournemouth	35	9
1992–93		27	4
1993–94		16	5
1993–94	Portsmouth	12	1

WOOD, Simon

Born Hull 24.9.76   Ht 5 9   Wt 11 08
Midfield. From Trainee.

Season	Club	App	Goals
1993–94	Coventry C	—	—

WOOD, Steve

Born Bracknell 2.2.63.   Ht 6 1   Wt 12 04
Defender. From Apprentice.

Season	Club	App	Goals
1979–80	Reading	2	—
1980–81		6	—
1981–82		32	—
1982–83		18	—
1983–84		37	3
1984–85		46	1
1985–86		46	4
1986–87		32	1
1987–88	Millwall	22	—
1988–89		35	—
1989–90		21	—
1990–91		25	—
1991–92		7	—
1991–92	Southampton	15	—
1992–93		4	—
1993–94		27	—

WOOD, Trevor

Born Jersey 3.11.68.   Ht 5 11   Wt 13 00
Goalkeeper. From Apprentice.

Season	Club	App	Goals
1986–87	Brighton	—	—
1987–88		—	—
1988–89	Port Vale	2	—
1989–90		3	—
1990–91		32	—
1991–92		—	—
1992–93		5	—
1993–94		—	—

WOODING, Tim

Born Wellingborough 5.7.73.   Ht 6 00
Wt 12 00
Defender. From Trainee.

Season	Club	App	Goals
1991–92	Norwich C	—	—

Season	Club	App	Goals
1992–93		—	—
1993–94	Bournemouth	—	—

WOODMAN, Andy

Born Denmark Hill 11.8.71. Ht 6 1
Wt 12 04
Goalkeeper. From Apprentice.

Season	Club	App	Goals
1989–90	Crystal Palace	—	—
1990–91		—	—
1991–92		—	—
1992–93		—	—
1993–94		—	—

WOODS, Chris

Born Boston 14.11.59. Ht 6 2 Wt 14 05
Goalkeeper. From Apprentice. England B, Under-21, 43 full caps.

Season	Club	App	Goals
1976–77	Nottingham F	—	—
1977–78		—	—
1978–79		—	—
1979–80	QPR	41	—
1980–81		22	—
1980–81	Norwich C	10	—
1981–82	Norwich C	42	—
1982–83		42	—
1983–84		42	—
1984–85		38	—
1985–86		42	—
1986–87	Rangers	42	—
1987–88		39	—
1988–89		24	—
1989–90		32	—
1990–91		36	—
1991–92	Sheffield W	41	—
1992–93		39	—
1993–94		10	—

WOODS, Kenny

Born Liverpool 15.4.74 Ht 5 10
Wt 11 07
Forward. From Trainee.

Season	Club	App	Goals
1992–93	Everton	—	—
1993–94	Bury	2	—

WOODS, Neil

Born York 30.7.66. Ht 6 0 Wt 12 11
Forward. From Apprentice.

Season	Club	App	Goals
1982–83	Doncaster R	4	—
1983–84		7	1
1984–85		6	2
1985–86		30	7
1986–87		18	6
1986–87	Rangers	3	—
1987–88	Ipswich T	19	4
1988–89		1	—
1989–90		7	1
1989–90	Bradford C	14	2
1990–91		—	—
1990–91	Grimsby T	44	12
1991–92		37	8
1992–93		30	4
1993–94		11	—

WOODS, Ray

Born Birkenhead 7.6.65. Ht 5 11
Wt 10 00
Forward. From Apprentice.

Season	Club	App	Goals
1982–83	Tranmere R	1	—
1983–84		6	2

From Colne D.

Season	Club	App	Goals
1988–89	Wigan Ath	8	—
1989–90		—	—
1990–91		20	3
1990–91	Coventry C	12	1
1991–92		9	—
1992–93		—	—
1992–93	Wigan Ath	13	—
1993–94	Coventry C	—	—
1993–94	Shrewsbury T	9	1

WOODS, Steve

Born Glasgow 23.2.70 Ht 6 1 Wt 13 00
Goalkeeper. From Kilpatrick BC.

Season	Club	App	Goals
1989–90	Hibernian	—	—
1990–91		—	—
1991–92		—	—
1991–92	Clydebank	5	—
1992–93		42	—
1993–94	Preston NE	20	—

WOODTHORPE, Colin

Born Ellesmere Pt 13.1.69. Ht 5 11
Wt 11 08
Defender. From Apprentice.

Season	Club	App	Goals
1986–87	Chester C	30	2
1987–88		35	—
1988–89		44	3

Season	Club		Apps	Goals
1989–90	....		46	1
1990–91	Norwich C	....	1	—
1991–92	....		15	1
1992–93	....		7	—
1993–94	....		20	—

WOODWARD, Andy

Born Stockport 23.9.73 Ht 5 10
Wt 10 12
Defender. From Trainee.

Season	Club		Apps	Goals
1992–93	Crewe Alex	....	6	—
1993–94	....		12	—

WOOLFORD, Stephen

Born Leeds 24.11.76 Ht 5 10 Wt 11 00
Forward. From Trainee.

Season	Club		Apps	Goals
1993–94	Nottingham F	....	—	—

WORBOYS, Gavin

Born Doncaster 14.7.74. Ht 6 0
Wt 11 00
Forward. From Trainee.

Season	Club		Apps	Goals
1991–92	Doncaster R	....	7	2
1992–93	Notts Co	....	—	—
1993–94	....		—	—
1993–94	*Exeter C*	....	4	1

WORSLEY, Graeme

Born Liverpool 4.1.69. Ht 5 10 Wt 11 02
Defender. From Bootle.

Season	Club		Apps	Goals
1988–89	Shrewsbury T	....	6	—
1989–90	....		15	—
1990–91	....		31	1
1991–92	....		25	1
1992–93	....		28	2
1993–94	Bury	....	1	—
1993–94	Doncaster R	....	—	—

WORTHINGTON, Gary

Born Cleethorpes 10.11.66. Ht 5 10
Wt 10 05
Forward. From Apprentice. England Youth.

Season	Club		Apps	Goals
1984–85	Manchester U	....	—	—
1985–86	....		—	—
1986–87	Huddersfield T	....	—	—
1987–88	Darlington	....	9	3
1988–89	....		31	12

Season	Club		Apps	Goals
1989–90	Wrexham	....	42	12
1990–91	....		30	6
1990–91	Wigan Ath	....	12	5
1991–92	....		41	15
1992–93	....		10	—
1993–94	Exeter C	....	15	1
1993–94	*Doncaster R*	....	8	2

WORTHINGTON, Nigel

Born Ballymena 4.11.61. Ht 5 11
Wt 12 05
Defender. From Ballymena U. Northern Ireland Youth, 50 full caps.

Season	Club		Apps	Goals
1981–82	Notts Co	....	2	—
1982–83	....		41	3
1983–84	....		24	1
1983–84	Sheffield W	....	14	1
1984–85	....		38	1
1985–86	....		15	—
1986–87	....		35	—
1987–88	....		38	—
1988–89	....		28	—
1989–90	....		32	2
1990–91	....		33	1
1991–92	....		34	5
1992–93	....		40	1
1993–94	....		31	1

WOSAHLO, Bradley

Born Ipswich 14.2.75 Ht 5 10 Wt 10 06
Midfield. From Trainee.

Season	Club		Apps	Goals
1993–94	Brighton	....	1	—

WRATTEN, Adam

Born Coventry 30.11.74 Ht 6 0
Defender. From Trainee.

Season	Club		Apps	Goals
1993–94	Birmingham C	....	—	—

WRATTEN, Paul

Born Middlesbrough 29.11.70 Ht 5 7
Wt 10 00
Midfield. From Trainee. England Youth.

Season	Club		Apps	Goals
1988–89	Manchester U	....	—	—
1989–90	....		—	—
1990–91	....		2	—
1991–92	....		—	—
1992–93	Hartlepool U	....	15	1
1993–94	....		42	—

WRIGHT, Alan

Born Ashton-under-Lyme 28.9.71.
Ht 5 4   Wt 9 04
Midfield. From Schoolboy, Trainee.
England Schools, Youth, Under-21.

Season	Club	Apps	Goals
1987–88	Blackpool	1	—
1988–89		16	—
1989–90		24	—
1990–91		45	—
1991–92		12	—
1991–92	Blackburn R	33	1
1992–93		24	—
1993–94		12	—

WRIGHT, Dale

Born Middlesbrough 21.12.74.   Ht 6 00
Wt 12 05
Defender. From Trainee.

Season	Club	Apps	Goals
1991–92	Nottingham F	—	—
1992–93		—	—
1993–94		—	—

WRIGHT, Evran

Born Wolverhampton 17.1.64   Ht 5 9
Wt 11 00
Forward. From Halesowen.

Season	Club	Apps	Goals
1993–94	Walsall	29	5

WRIGHT, George

Born South Africa 22.12.69.   Ht 5 7
Wt 10 02
Defender. From Hutcheson Vale BC.

Season	Club	Apps	Goals
1987–88	Hearts	—	—
1988–89		—	—
1989–90		1	—
1990–91		17	2
1991–92		24	1
1992–93		12	—
1993–94		12	—

WRIGHT, Ian

Born Lichfield 10.3.72.   Ht 6 1   Wt 12 08
Defender. From Trainee.

Season	Club	Apps	Goals
1989–90	Stoke C	1	—
1990–91		1	—
1991–92		3	—
1992–93		1	—
1993–94		—	—

Season	Club	Apps	Goals
1993–94	Bristol R	29	—

WRIGHT, Ian

Born Woolwich 3.11.63.   Ht 5 9
Wt 11 08
Forward. From Greenwich Borough.
England B, 18 full caps.

Season	Club	Apps	Goals
1985–86	Crystal Palace	32	9
1986–87		38	8
1987–88		41	20
1988–89		42	24
1989–90		26	8
1990–91		38	15
1991–92		8	5
1991–92	Arsenal	30	24
1992–93		31	15
1993–94		39	23

WRIGHT, Jermaine

Born Greenwich 21.10.75
Forward. From Trainee.

Season	Club	Apps	Goals
1992–93	Millwall	—	—
1993–94		—	—

WRIGHT, Keith

Born Edinburgh 17.5.65.   Ht 5 11
Wt 11 00
Forward. From Melbourne Th. Scotland 1
full cap.

Season	Club	Apps	Goals
1983–84	Raith R	37	5
1884–85		38	22
1985–86		39	21
1986–87		17	13
1986–87	Dundee	20	10
1987–88		42	15
1988–89		35	8
1989–90		34	11
1990–91		36	18
1991–92	Hibernian	40	9
1992–93		42	11
1993–94		42	16

WRIGHT, Mark

Born Manchester 29.1.70.   Ht 5 11
Wt 10 12
Defender. From Trainee.

Season	Club	Apps	Goals
1988–89	Everton	—	—
1989–90		1	—

Season	Club	Apps	Goals
1990–91	.....	—	—
1990–91	*Blackpool*	3	—
1990–91	*Huddersfield T*	10	1
1991–92	Huddersfield T	8	—
1992–93	.....	14	—
1993–94	.....	—	—
1993–94	Wigan Ath	14	1

WRIGHT, Mark

Born Dorchester 1.8.63. Ht 6 2 Wt 13 03
Defender. From Amateur. England Under-21, 43 full caps.

Season	Club	Apps	Goals
1980–81	Oxford U	—	—
1981–82		10	—
1981–82	Southampton	3	—
1982–83		39	2
1983–84		29	1
1984–85		36	—
1985–86		33	3
1986–87		30	1
1987–88		—	—
1987–88	Derby Co	38	3
1988–89		33	1
1989–90		36	6
1990–91		37	—
1991–92	Liverpool	21	—
1992–93		33	2
1993–94		31	1

WRIGHT, Paul

Born East Kilbride 17.8.67. Ht 5 8 Wt 10 08
Forward. S Form. Scotland Youth, Under-21.

Season	Club	Apps	Goals
1983–84	Aberdeen	1	—
1984–85		—	—
1985–86		10	2
1986–87		25	4
1987–88		9	4
1988–89		23	6
1989–90	QPR	15	5
1989–90	Hibernian	3	1
1990–91		33	6
1991–92	St Johnstone	41	18
1992–93		42	14
1993–94		17	7

WRIGHT, Stephen

Born Bellshill 27.8.71. Ht 5 10 Wt 10 10
Defender. From Aberdeen Lads. Scotland Under-21, 2 full caps.

Season	Club	Apps	Goals
1987–88	Aberdeen	—	—
1988–89		—	—
1989–90		1	—
1990–91		17	1
1991–92		23	—
1992–93		36	—
1993–94		36	—

WRIGHT, Tommy

Born Belfast 29.8.63. Ht 6 1 Wt 13 05
Goalkeeper. From Linfield. Northern Ireland 22 full caps. Football League.

Season	Club	Apps	Goals
1987–88	Newcastle U	—	—
1988–89		9	—
1989–90		14	—
1990–91		—	—
1990–91	*Hull C*	6	—
1991–92	Newcastle U	33	—
1992–93		14	—
1993–94		3	—
1993–94	Nottingham F	10	—

WRIGHT, Tommy

Born Dunfermline 10.1.66. Ht 5 7 Wt 9 10
Forward. From Apprentice. Scotland Under-21.

Season	Club	Apps	Goals
1982–83	Leeds U	4	1
1983–84		25	8
1984–85		42	14
1985–86		10	1
1986–87		—	—
1986–87	Oldham Ath	28	7
1987–88		41	9
1988–89		43	7
1989–90	Leicester C	41	3
1990–91		44	7
1991–92		44	12
1992–93	Middlesbrough	36	5
1993–94		16	—

WYATT, Michael

Born Bristol 12.9.74. Ht 5 11 Wt 11 03
Forward. From Trainee.

Season	Club	Apps	Goals
1993–94	Bristol C	10	—

YALLOP, Frank
Born Watford 4.4.64.　Ht 5 11　Wt 12 00
Defender. From Apprentice. England
Youth, Canada full caps.

Season	Club	App	Goals
1981–82	Ipswich T	—	—
1982–83		—	—
1983–84		6	—
1984–85		10	—
1985–86		34	—
1986–87		31	—
1987–88		41	2
1988–89		40	2
1989–90		31	—
1990–91		45	—
1991–92		17	—
1992–93		6	2
1993–94		7	—

YATES, Dean
Born Leicester 26.10.67.　Ht 6 1
Wt 12 00
Defender. From Apprentice. England
Under-21.

Season	Club	App	Goals
1984–85	Notts Co	8	—
1985–86		44	4
1986–87		42	9
1987–88		46	2
1988–89		41	6
1989–90		45	6
1990–91		41	4
1991–92		25	2
1992–93		—	—
1993–94		1	—

YATES, Jason
Born Walsall 10.12.74　Ht 5 11　Wt 12 11
Forward. From Trainee.

Season	Club	App	Goals
1993–94	Scunthorpe U	—	—

YATES, Mark
Born Birmingham 24.1.70.　Ht 5 11
Wt 11 09
Midfield. From Trainee.

Season	Club	App	Goals
1987–88	Birmingham C	3	—
1988–89		20	3
1989–90		20	2
1990–91		9	1
1991–92		2	—

Season	Club	App	Goals
1991–92	Burnley	17	1
1992–93		1	—
1992–93	Lincoln C	14	—
1993–94	Doncaster R	34	4

YATES, Steve
Born Bristol 29.1.70.　Ht 5 11　Wt 11 00
Defender. From Trainee.

Season	Club	App	Goals
1986–87	Bristol R	2	—
1987–88		—	—
1988–89		35	—
1989–90		42	—
1990–91		34	—
1991–92		39	—
1992–93		44	—
1993–94		1	—
1993–94	QPR	29	—

YORKE, Dwight
Born Tobago 3.12.71.　Ht 5 11　Wt 11 13
Forward. From St Clair's Coaching
School, Tobago.

Season	Club	App	Goals
1989–90	Aston Villa	2	—
1990–91		18	2
1991–92		32	11
1992–93		27	6
1993–94		12	2

YOUDS, Edward
Born Liverpool 3.5.70.　Ht 6 1　Wt 13 03
Defender. From Trainee.

Season	Club	App	Goals
1988–89	Everton	—	—
1989–90		—	—
1989–90	Cardiff C	1	—
1989–90	Wrexham	20	2
1990–91	Everton	8	—
1991–92		—	—
1991–92	Ipswich T	1	—
1992–93		16	—
1993–94		23	1

YOUNG, Eric
Born Singapore 25.3.60.　Ht 6 2
Wt 13 00
Defender. From Slough Town. Wales 20
full caps.

Season	Club	App	Goals
1982–83	Brighton	—	—
1983–84		30	4

Season	Club	Apps	Goals
1984–85	....	35	3
1985–86	....	32	2
1986–87	....	29	1
1987–88	Wimbledon	29	3
1988–89	....	35	1
1989–90	....	35	5
1990–91	Crystal Palace	34	3
1991–92	....	30	1
1992–93	....	38	6
1993–94	....	46	5

YOUNG, Kenneth
Born Edinburgh 6.5.74.   Ht 5 6   Wt 10 7
Forward. From Links U.

Season	Club	Apps	Goals
1992–93	Falkirk	1	—
1993–94	....	1	—

YOUNG, Neil
Born Harlow 31.8.73.   Ht 5 8   Wt 11 03
Defender. From Trainee.

Season	Club	Apps	Goals
1991–92	Tottenham H	—	—
1992–93	....	—	—
1993–94	....	—	—

YOUNG, Nicky
Born Liverpool 24.4.73   Ht 5 7   Wt 10 01
Forward. From Trainee.

Season	Club	Apps	Goals
1993–94	Everton	—	—

YOUNG, Roy
Born Romsey 28.10.73   Ht 5 9   Wt 11 00
Forward.

Season	Club	Apps	Goals
1992–93	Portsmouth	—	—
1993–94	....	—	—

YOUNG, Scott
Born Pontypridd 14.1.76
Forward. From Trainee.

Season	Club	Apps	Goals
1993–94	Cardiff C	6	—

YOUNG, Stuart
Born Hull 16.12.72.   Ht 5 11   Wt 12 00
Forward. From Arsenal Trainee.

Season	Club	Apps	Goals
1991–92	Hull C	15	2
1992–93	....	4	—
1992–93	Northampton T	8	2
1993–94	Scarborough	28	9

ZORICICH, Chris
Born New Zealand 3.5.69.   Ht 5 11
Wt 11 10
Defender.

Season	Club	Apps	Goals
1989–90	Leyton Orient	—	—
1990–91	....	28	—
1991–92	....	22	—
1992–93	....	12	1
1993–94	....	—	—

ZUMRUTEL, Soner
Born Islington 6.10.74   Ht 5 6   Wt 11 00
Forward. From Trainee.

Season	Club	Apps	Goals
1993–94	Arsenal	—	—